THE LANTERN IN THE SKULL

MYSTICAL ENCOUNTERS IN
AOTEAROA NEW ZEALAND

Prophecy on the River
Judith Hoch

The Luminous Nun
Kerryn Levy

People of the Earth
Peter Calvert, Richard Bentley
Carolyn Longden, Trisha Wren

The Lantern in the Skull
Hugh Major

RELATED PUBLICATIONS
FROM ATTAR BOOKS

The New Mysticism
Keith Hill

The Matapaua Conversations
Peter Calvert and Keith Hill

The Lantern In The Skull

Consciousness and marginal zones of the extraordinary

Hugh Major

attar books

First edition published in 2019 by Attar Books
Auckland, New Zealand.

Casebook ISBN 978-0-9951203-0-3
Paperback ISBN 978-0-9951203-1-0
Ebook ISBN 978-0-9951203-2-7

Copyright © Hugh Major 2019
Introduction © Keith Hill 2019

The right of Hugh Major to be identified as the author of this work in terms of Section 96 of the Copyright Act 1996 is hereby asserted.

All rights reserved. Copying and distributing passages excerpted from this book for the purpose of sharing and debating is permitted on the condition that (1) excerpts are brief, (2) the source of each excerpt is fully acknowledged, and (3) such excerpts are not onsold. Otherwise, except for fair dealing or brief passages quoted in a newspaper, magazine, radio, television or internet review, no part of this book may be reproduced in any form or by any means, or in any form of binding or cover other than that in which it is published, without permission in writing from the Publisher. This same condition is imposed on any subsequent purchaser.

Cover image by Frankie/Shutterstock

Attar Books is a New Zealand company that focuses on work which explores today's spiritual and mystical experiences, culture, concepts and practices. For more information on our publications visit the website:

www.attarbooks.com

HUGH MAJOR studied English and Philosophy at Auckland University and has taught these subjects at secondary schools, as well as English and Drama in both Scotland and Japan. He has also taught mask-making and the culture and history of masks at Auckland College of Education.

Hugh studied painting at La Bottega d'arte Fiorentina, the studio of Gabrielle Panerai in Florence, and with Dr David Cranswick at the Great Western Studio in London. He has exhibited in Yokohama and Auckland. Between 2002 and 2008 he was a finalist in four of the Adam Portraiture Awards, administered by the National Portrait Gallery in Wellington. In 2011, he was a finalist in Sydney's Gallipoli Art Prize.

In his writing, Hugh explores new thinking in the fields of consciousness, science, spirituality and culture. Five times he has been a finalist in New Zealand's premiere Ashton Wylie Award for writing in the mind, body, spirit genre. His published books include *Notes on the Mysterium Tremendum* (2010) and *From Monkey to Moth* (2015).

Hugh lives in Matakana, New Zealand, with his partner Kirsty.

Contents

The Consciousness Dilemma 9

THE LANTERN IN THE SKULL

Prologue: A House of Loyal Fetishes 21

MARGINAL ZONES

1. Driving a Forked Stick 31
2. Mind Excursions 43
3. Peak Experiences 54

THE SEVERED STATE

4. An Ever-Widening Rift 67
5. Running Like Clockwork 76
6. The Ultimate Scintilla 91

VISIONS OF THE APEX DWELLERS

7. Sovereign Mentality 101
8. Esalen's Luminaries 110
9. The World Behind the World 119

References 129
Author's Acknowledgements 131

The Consciousness Dilemma

CONSCIOUSNESS IS AN INSIDE JOB. Scientists can measure rapid eye movement, the twitch of facial muscles, the sparking of neurons in the brain, even identify which part of the brain is being lit up, and from the data conclude a subject is dreaming. But they cannot access the dream's content. They have no way of knowing that the subject was dreaming of his deceased father, woke remembering an idea they once shared, and had decided it was now time to put that idea into action. For the subject, the dream was filled with heartfelt meaning and led to a change in life purpose. Yet the observing scientists saw none of it, perceiving only twitching facial muscles and afterwards having only an instrument read-out denoting the sleeping brain's electrochemical surges.

Hugh Major's *The Lantern in the Skull* explores the disparity between objectively observing the world around us and our subjective experience of living in the world. Conforming to the focus of this series, he gives special attention to experiences that involve mystical, psychic and mystical perceptions, which occur outside—usually well outside—the parameters of our normal, physically-oriented everyday life. Yet, as Hugh Major intriguingly argues, perhaps such experiences are more natural, and therefore more normal, than we acknowledge.

Today, occupied as we so much are with gadgets and machines, our attention is continually dragged away from the centre of ourselves. Social media channels our attention into exchanges that fit within protocols defined by machine algorithms. Yet there are alternative modes for interacting with other people, subtler, more fragile modes, such as empathy, intuition and telepathy, which enable us to connect very differently with those around us.

The other three books in this series, *The Luminous Nun*, *People of the Earth* and *Prophecy on the River*, explore these different modes of connection in a wide variety of contexts. *The Lantern in the Skull* offers a way of appreciating the full range of these modalities and of considering where they fit into contemporary human experience. However, extraordinary modalities, particularly those that are mystical and paranormal, do not easily fit our modern materialist outlook. The widespread cultural unease with them goes back to the origins of modernity itself.

During the pre-modern Renaissance, the awareness that resides within our body, which we experience as the seat of our sense of being alive, was called the soul. The soul was discussed within the frame of Christian theology, and those who considered it were prohibited from stepping outside their religious obligations. In 1641, René Descartes changed this situation radically. Seeking to examine the physical world without religion imposing theological limitations, he proposed the soul be given the philosophic name of "mind" and be separated from matter. He acknowledged the mind's significance, then put it to one side so scientists could freely investigate the material world.

Machines were much admired by Descartes and his fellow Enlightenment thinkers. Accordingly, the material universe, and all bodies moving in it, came to be thought of as machines. When Isaac Newton discovered the laws of motion, light and gravity that governed the "world machine", scientists excitedly focused their efforts on using the new scientific disciplines of physics, chemistry, biology and geology to investigate the natural world. In the process, the machine metaphor became a truism, to the extent that for us today machine comparisons are automatic, with our bodies often being treated as biological machines, and our brains viewed as computers. However, in their enthusiastic exploration of the physical world, scientists neglected mind and consciousness. It wasn't until two hundred years after Descartes that researchers, working in the new field of psychology, turned their attention to our mind's internal processing.

William James, a leading founder of modern psychology, identified two forms of research. The first he called brass instrument psychology. This involved seeking hard data, such as that obtained by measuring the impact of light on the retina, or dissecting a brain to see what that might disclose about mental processing. The second approach examined mental processing itself, particularly the vast range of subjective experiences involved in humanity's sensation of being conscious. While James carried out instrument-based laboratory work in his early years, he soon decided that because the mind is grounded in subjective experiencing, examining consciousness from the inside was ultimately the most informative approach.

Among the categories of consciousness that most interested James were the religious, mystical and paranormal. Not given to prejudging what people said they had perceived, he gathered numerous personal testimonies of non-everyday perceptions, which provided the data for his still unrivalled *The Varieties of Religious Experience* (1894). However, as Western culture entered the twentieth century, leading scientists, academics and educationalists agreed that truth statements are best based exclusively on descriptions of physical processes. As a result, James' focus on interior experiences was rejected in favour of a more narrowly conceived external physicalist approach.

The initial phase of this rejection occurred during the first decades of the twentieth century, when Sigmund Freud developed psychoanalysis to examine the mechanism of the human mind. Freud rejected James' interest in spiritual and psychic perceptions. James had argued that our normal waking consciousness "is but one special type of consciousness, whilst all about it, parted from it by the filmiest of screens, there lie potential forms of consciousness entirely different. ... No account of the universe in its totality can be final which leaves these other forms of consciousness quite disregarded." (*Varieties*, pg 388.) As already noted, James was drawn to what he termed extra-normal cognitions, including deep intuitions, ecstasies, transporting insights, and mystic feelings of oneness.

In contrast, Freud emphasised normal waking consciousness and dismissed other forms of consciousness, including the extra-normal, as abnormal. Freud regarded all non-everyday aspects of the human psyche as deviations from normal rational consciousness. To explain why these deviations occurred, he proposed that the human mind was animated by deeply buried sexual and asocial impulses, such as penis envy among woman and an Oedipus complex among men, which are rooted in childhood experiences. Adopting a scientific reductionist approach (reducing complex behaviours to simple causes), he proposed that these asocial impulses may be attributed to the deeply buried id. Only the ego, formed as a result of socialisation during childhood, and the superego, consisting of wider social mores projected onto the growing child, kept the asocial, and therefore potentially dangerous, id in check. When French author Romain Rolland suggested that the oceanic feelings of oneness with the eternal, of which James recorded many instances, provided the transcendent basis for all religious feelings, Freud dismissed the notion of transcendence and alternatively argued that oceanic feelings were rooted in the infant's unformed ego, which hadn't yet developed socialised feelings of individuality and so felt one with all around it.

For a time Freud's ideas were highly regarded, their influence reaching beyond the therapeutic and being adopted by mainstream intellectual culture. But by the 1960s Freud's analysis had begun falling out of favour. Objectors maintained there was no scientific evidence that Freud's id, ego and superego existed, and no statistical evidence to support the manifestation of his famed complexes. As Freud's view of the mind was increasingly found wanting, behaviorism, founded by John Watson early in the twentieth century, rose in popularity, eventually supplanting it. Nonetheless, Freud's emphasis on waking consciousness, his drive to explain all human experience in reductive, rational terms, and his denigration of extra-normal states, remain pillars of today's Western intellectual outlook.

John Watson's behaviourism succeeded because he gave psychology the scientific basis Freud was unable to provide. Watson argued that for psychology to align with the sciences, its field of study should be limited to external behaviour. This meant that only hard data, captured via measurements, was scientifically valid—ironically, a return to James' brass instrument psychology. Watson's advocacy of observable behaviour swept away Freud's notion of deep drives. Deep drives couldn't be observed, let alone measured, so became irrelevant, while the varieties of depth experiences that had fascinated William James were simply out of the frame. Behaviourism instead focused on what was clear and obvious: stimulus and response, perceptual input and behavioural output. What occurred inside the psyche, between input and output, couldn't be measured so was ignored.

The result was that during the second half of the twentieth century depth psychology was widely discarded in favour of surface behaviourism and its companion, functionalism. Not only was Freud, the first significant (though clearly flawed) theoretician of the mind's depths cast out as a fantasist, his ideas deemed to have more in common with literary fiction than science, the very idea that we have a mind was jettisoned. Three hundred years earlier, when Descartes laid the foundations for the modern world view by separating matter from mind, he considered the mind fundamental to human existence: *I think, therefore I am*. By the mid-twentieth century this had been declared a colossal mistake. Philosopher Gilbert Ryle summed up the situation when he decreed Descrates' mind to be "the ghost in the machine"—and, as all rational people know, ghosts do not exist.

By the 1970s, denial of the existence of consciousness and mind had become the default position for Western scientific and intellectual culture. The notion of consciousness was so thoroughly debunked that it became professional suicide to seek to study consciousness either in the medical professions or in the educational academies. After all, you can't study what doesn't exist. As a result, the academy and professional psychologists discarded the initial fruitful modern start to studying the mind made by James and the introspective psychologists who followed him, particularly Freud and his colleagues Alfred Adler and Carl Jung. While James remains tolerated, largely because he is considered a philosopher and not a psychologist, today Freud is rejected as unscientific, Adler's work is pilfered but remains unacknowledged, and Jung is derided for being a mystic.

Jung is an important figure in psychology because he was, like James, open to extra-normal perceptions, including paranormal, supernatural and mystical encounters. Jung spent many years studying their historical expressions in myths and religious histories, and in esoteric practices such as alchemy and Gnosticism. This interest led to Jung's break with Freud, who privately admitted to having had his own extra-normal experiences, but who, in order to maintain his professional credibility, publicly denied their existence and derided Jung for being a mystic. As a result, Jung spent much of his career fighting the label of mystic, because to be called a mystic was to be written off as at best deluded, at worst mad, and certainly not worthy of a place in the academy. This situation remains the case today, with academics who study extra-normal perceptions being careful to position their studies within the norms of academic study, which in turn are dictated by the principles of scientific materialism. Hugh Major discusses how this situation is maintained in a fascinating section included here, *The Institution*.

Yet where has this anathema towards the depths of the human mind left us? With a huge hole in our intellectual culture, which instructs us to only pay attention to everyday, physically measurable phenomena, and as a result of which our own consciousness, which pulses at the centre of our lives, is ignored. The Western mind, which materialists assert is not a mind but ephemeral neural static, has been left skating away from itself on the thin ice of its own surface engagement with reality. Clearly, this is inadequate, especially when extra-normal perceptions and altered states of consciousness continue to be widely experienced, recorded and discussed—outside mainstream media and intellectual culture, of course.

Hugh Major calls the cultural crossroads to which the modern materialist outlook has brought us the Severed State. It is a state of disjunction, in which our normal waking awareness is disconnected from our own depth perceptions. Not only does this mean that culturally we lack the willingness to make deep connections to reality, it means that when others make their own deep connections and seek to share what they have experienced emotionally, aesthetically and spiritually, we are unable to process their accounts and respond intelligibly.

Now, in the second decade of the twenty-first century, when faced with extraordinary perceptions far outside the norm, the default position of those who support the consensus of surface-only reality is to loudly pronounce, "No such thing!", and attack those who report having them. This extends to censuring researchers who explore extra-normal consciousness events and labelling their work pseudoscience.

Nonetheless, people keep having extra-normal experiences. And while their numbers have never been large, researchers remain motivated by the same curiosity that drove William James to investigate what is involved. It was in the countercultural sphere, founded in the U.S. during the 1950s, that the foundations for today's studies of the human mind's non-ordinary capabilities were laid.

The countercultural movement included many who were, or later became, leading scientists and academics. Their investigations began far outside the academy's walls, in anthropological field studies, among shamans in traditional tribal cultures, or in commercial laboratories where transformative psychedelics were concocted, at rock concerts where they were tested, and thereafter in military psychic research facilities, in artists' studios, in nature retreats, in meditation sittings, and during the creation of experimental literature, music, theatre and art. In these experiential contexts, bold self-experimenters not only found vivid depths in the human mind that science had ignored for three hundred years, they waded into those depths, swam in them, and were sometimes swept away by the strange, beautiful and challenging currents they found. Intriguingly, many of these experiences involved intensities of consciousness that extended far beyond anything James or Jung observed.

From the 1970s, the educational academies were too engrossed in ever-germinating *isms*—structualism, contructivism, deconstructionism, essentialism, colonialism, postcolonialism, postmodernism—to notice what their counter-culture colleagues were investigating, let alone pay attention to what they were bringing back for consideration. Instead, places like Esalen, founded in 1962, ran exploratory workshops where extra-normal perceptions were reported on and their significance debated. It was followed, in the early 1970s, by Stanford Research Institute and the Institute of Noetic Sciences, which were established as scientific research facilities, in part, to study human consciousness and its perceptual possibilities. Their experiments, backed by data produced by many other researchers, has extended our appreciation of what human consciousness is capable of perceiving and, concomitantly, of the multilayered nature of the reality in which we collectively participate. All this research directly challenges the assumptions behind the materialistic mindset, that humanity exists exclusively within purely physical processes. It has also laid the foundations for what has recently come to be identified as the post-materialist perspective.

Among the researchers referenced by Hugh Major are academics and scientists whose work is seminal to the development of the post-materialist outlook. They include Rupert Sheldrake and Thomas Nagel, who reveal the limitations of an exclusively materialist interpretation of reality, Stanislav Grof and Abraham Maslow, whose work with heightened states and peak experiences has added to our understanding of the transpersonal roots of human consciousness, Iain McGilchrist, who speculates on the modern emphasis on the brain's narrowly focused left hemisphere at the expense of the wholistic right hemisphere, and Dale E. Graff and Lawrence LeShan, who have experimentally explored the psychic possibilities of the human mind. To brief summaries of their research, Hugh has added his own experiences. Acknowledging the personal nature of extra-normal perceptions is significant, because ultimately it is only via direct perception that we gain empirical knowledge of what our own mind is capable of doing. As was stated at the start of this introduction: consciousness is an inside job.

The value of *The Lantern in the Skull* is that it is a report on what researchers into the mind's depths have found over the last seventy years. Naturally, it is not definitive. Such a short book can only survey a few key concepts. But what Hugh Major does do very successfully is indicate the nature of the territory being explored, and outline major lines of enquiry. These lines involve concepts that are likely, over the next few decades, to significantly advance our understanding of what human consciousness is, and what it is capable of experiencing and doing.

—Keith Hill, series editor

The Lantern In The Skull

Still life, they call it—like a bursting bomb
That keeps bursting, one burst, on and on:
A new existence, continually being born,
Emerging out of white into the sombre
Garishness of the spectrum, refusing the easy,
Clenching its strength on nothing but how to be.

— From *Still Life* by Norman MacCaig

Prologue: A House of Loyal Fetishes

THE WAY DIALLO GRIPPED the steering wheel I could tell something wasn't right. His tension spread through the car. It was 1997. I was in Burkina Faso with my partner, Kirsty, touring the southwest of the country with two Malians: Diallo, the driver, and Sori, an English-speaking guide. Our objective that day was the settlement of Gaoua, located one hundred kilometres from the mining town of Banfora, down a long, dusty red road. As we neared Gaoua, Diallo made his misgivings clear, suggesting we turn back. But Sori was sanguine, saying he didn't want a wasted trip.

Our first stop was an empty, rather sinister hotel on the outskirts of town. Locals watched us suspiciously as we parked; we weren't welcome. The hotel owner was a portly, dishevelled Lebanese man. He had a bored, young wife who spent the entire evening grazing between three television channels—the first with wailing music and sensuously-dancing Middle-Eastern women, then CNN, then a local station showing a steamy soap opera in French featuring a submissive female and a serious-looking macho man with bulging pectorals and a grunty voice.

Was it this strange town, so far off the beaten track, that was making Diallo nervous? Or had he sensed the power of spirits peculiar to the area? Whichever, Diallo's unease was contagious. Sori had planned our route, and Kirsty and I had only the vaguest idea of where we were. We didn't know if Sori was following the tour company's directions in bringing us here, or if this detour resulted from him acting on a whim.

The next day Sori guided us to the outskirts of town. Clouds of dust billowed through the car, coating seats, bags, clothes and hair. We arrived at a large mud building standing in fields of tall and dying sorghum. Rounded, sculpted of the same earth it rose from, this was the home of Lobi chief Daprrr and his three wives. The living quarters were above ground. We were taken underneath, into a smoke-blackened basement with low beams, an oven, and a goat lurking in the gloom. The only illumination came from the far corner of a long gallery, a powerful cone of sunlight that poured through a hole cut in the ceiling, its edges defined by tumbling dust motes. Adding to the eerie setting, bats occasionally flitted through the light, then disappeared into holes hidden in the walls.

There was just enough light to view the fetishes. Composed of wood, iron, stones and cowrie shells, there was something humble and unpretentious about them. Shouldn't a fetish be an imposing sculptural creation with the power to impress and intimidate? These were only unobtrusive little mounds, like something that hadn't been tidied away, barely visible in the gloom.

As was later explained to us, fetishes were traditionally assembled by a girl's father before she was married to guard her against evil. Other fetishes were comprised of objects mutually significant to the chief and his wives. A protector or overseer, a fetish could be used when a wife wanted to go out—before leaving she would pour water into the bowls incorporated into the assemblage and wash herself.

Kirsty started taking photos of the basement and fetishes with her SLR camera, but to her frustration the flash wouldn't work. She went outside to see what was wrong. The camera now worked perfectly, the flash popping up and firing as it was meant to. But back in the basement, as she attempted to continue photographing, it again shut down. To get any shots at all, Kirsty had to set the camera on long exposure. Weeks later, when the negatives were developed, we discovered all her photos of the fetishes were blank. This was despite the camera and flash working perfectly during the previous four months of travel, and for the three months after.

What might account for the camera's mechanism failing in the dim basement? Could it somehow have been interfered with? A Malian friend who helped organise our trip gave another instance of a European tourist visiting Mali and taking photos of a ritual procession. An elderly onlooker told the tourist it was no use taking pictures of the procession because none would come out. This blanking of the film indeed happened. So our experience wasn't unique.

It was through this and other similarly strange experiences, some stretching back to childhood, that I encountered an alternative facet of reality—what we call the otherworldly, the mystical. Most people can likely recount their own strange psychic experiences or paranormal phenomena. My next example involves an unexpectedly predictive experience.

One summer, before heading to Piha Beach to spend the day at a friend's house, I felt an intuitive impulse that I should take a name card with my phone number on it. Not possessing one, and despite having no idea why I would need it, I cut a piece of veneer to business card size and wrote my ID details in ballpoint.

That day in Piha was when I first met Kirsty, my partner-to-be. She was part of a large party of Palm Society members who traipsed in to inspect my friend's garden. She had an unmistakable effect on me, making the chattering crowd and the sound of the waves recede into the background. After the group had emptied their cups of tea they prepared to move on. Not so fast! Out came my card and, as the cliché goes, the rest is history. How did I know I was about to meet my future partner? An interesting question, but it hardly mattered to me. The important thing was that somehow I *did* know.

It makes sense that such psychic experiences occur in the context of close relationships, because these relationships form over long periods, building a strong binding power. The difference in this case was that a psychic bond occurred in a close relationship that was yet to be.

Another example of this type involved my father. His house had recently been burgled. A few days afterwards I needed to visit him, and as I drove into his street I had a flash that the burglar was back. Rationality immediately stepped in, dismissing the idea. As I drew up to the house, I noticed my father was out. I retrieved the key from its usual hiding place and opened the back door. I then heard a clatter at the far end of the house. It was the sound of the burglar as he made his escape through a window close to the road. I knew this because, when I went to check, the window was wide open. In my father's study computer discs were strewn over the floor and various items missing. Intuition involves understanding immediately, without needing any proof from observation. In this case I had a strong connection with the family home.

The following example involves a special kind of dramatist, a "projector" of deep personal imagery. In 1991 I was in Tokyo where I saw a solo performance by Kazuo Ohno, nonagenarian and co-founder of butoh dance in post-war Japan. It was a short but highly focused performance, set to evocative ambient music. As the dance proceeded a tension developed, a feeling faraway and immediate, epic and sad—though words fall short of capturing the intensity of what I felt. I wondered if I was the only one caught in a rising well of emotion, and glanced down my row of the audience. Everyone was transfixed by the performer, holding their breath, some already in tears.

What was this collective emotion if not a subtle force field transmitted via the body and mind of the performer, in collaboration with the music, which held us all in one shared psychic space? It is in times of togetherness, when we share laughter or intense empathic contact, that we bridge the gap between self and other. So why couldn't psychic connection also be stimulated by powerful aesthetic experiences?

My last example is exceptional in that it concerns human-animal interaction. Millicent, one of our four chickens, was ten years old and dying. We brought her inside, to a confined area in the garage, where we set up straw and water. The day came when it was clear she would last no longer than a few hours. We made regular checks on her condition. At some stage in the afternoon, about ten minutes after visiting her, I had a subtle, naturally-fragrant olfactory sensation, lasting no longer than one in-breath. I went straight to the garage. Millicent had died. Were my perceptions an illusion? Or merely a coincidence? Yet why shouldn't there be such an indicator of her departure, after having spent a decade with her? She was far more than anonymous poultry. We had a special connection.

Telepathic connection is common in the animal world. Large schools of sardines or murmurations of starlings move in coordinated waves, the changes too fast for any individual fish or bird to be able to follow. The simplest, sensible explanation is that they are connected via a collective, psychic link. What the examples recounted here suggest to me is that psychic connections are far more common in both the human and animal worlds than we ordinarily think.

I don't claim any special capability. Rather, I consider our psychic faculties to be natural, but underrated and underdeveloped. Some readers might suspect an unreasonable credulity on my part in ascribing the above incidents to psychic and paranormal phenomena—although paranormal is misleading; a better label would be "normal but rare". In fact, I consider scepticism valuable when reviewing or judging these types of experiences. Yet there is healthy scepticism and unhealthy scepticism. Healthy scepticism keeps us questioning and helps prevent self-delusion. Unhealthy scepticism takes the form of a blanket dismissal of any and all such cases, viewing them as irrational superstition, dishonesty, occult nonsense, or self-deception that discloses some psychological problem such as suggestibility or the need for security.

Unhealthy scepticism is the attitude that currently prevails in the secular West. Through the Western education system we are taught that the world works within the senses' geography of truth. Whether we are conscious of it or not, the Western world is dominated by a materialist world view, the tenets of which are rarely spelled out. Materialism is defined by the Oxford English Dictionary as a doctrine maintaining that nothing exists except matter and its movements and modifications. Matter being unconscious, the implication is that we live in an unconscious, purposeless universe, our sense of self is an illusion, and our mind is nothing more than activity of the brain, the result of neurones firing in concert.

The problem is that non-ordinary experiences, such as those that involve ESP, telepathy and intuition, are the imps nibbling at materialism's fringes. Because they contradict materialism's conclusions, a common reaction is to simply ignore the intruders, or deny their existence. Yet the question remains: psychic and paranormal experiences occur, so what are we to make of them? How can an event, such as the one my partner and I experienced in Burkina Faso, dovetail with our secular, "enlightened" viewpoint—the prevailing philosophy of a mechanical, completely desanctified world? It can't. Consequently, sceptics dismiss psychic perceptions as mere anecdotes about vague coincidences or as supernatural mumbo-jumbo. This refusal persists despite a widening of perspective among researchers working in a number of scientific fields who question the nature and extent of human perception. The result is a growing rift in science.

On the one hand is the power of scientific and educational institutions, which teach and defend the materialist paradigm. Advocates of materialism demonise as pseudoscience any theories or practices unfaithful to its guiding assumptions. On the other are scientists who are applying the scientific method to investigate areas such as non-ordinary perceptions, while continuing to study the natural world through observation and to experiment and apply the scientific tradition of free enquiry.

In *Manifesto for a Post-Materialist Science*,[1] published in 2014, eminent scientists in the fields of psychology, neuroscience, medicine, biology and psychiatry have made a direct challenge to materialism, claiming it is now an outmoded ideology. They do so while acknowledging scientific accomplishments and grounding their investigations in empirical observations. Their concern is to make use of recent discoveries to broaden knowledge of fringe experiences and the contribution our own minds make to them. One item in their manifesto states: *Mind (will/intention) can influence the state of the physical world and operate in a non-local (or extended) fashion, i.e., it is not confined to specific points in time, such as the present. Also, events may be meaningfully, rather than causally, connected.*

This points in the direction this book travels. In the following pages I will use my experiences as springboards to explore a range of trans-conscious, non-local and extended perceptions. I suggest these are as essential to our experience as any "rational" forms. Furthermore, they point to a new paradigm of reality.

Consider this last example. At the start of our trip to West Africa, Kirsty and I had flown into Bamako in Mali. We were supposed to meet the tour guide of a local company but had no information about where to find him. Our Malian friend in New Zealand said we should just ask someone in the street, saying that Big John had sent us—a highly tentative arrangement, to say the least.

Bamako is a big city; at that time it had a million residents. As the sun rose on our first day there, the temperature climbed quickly. Streets filled up fast. Produce was being laid out. Women swathed in beautifully-coloured fabrics, and others in rags, were feeding their babies. Men were fixing mopeds, carrying loads, sawing wood or sitting around fires. Behind them all was a jumble of tin shacks, rubbish piled beside open sewers, and close, congested traffic edging its way through the throng of merchants, mothers, barrow-boys and infants. We desperately needed to sort out our onward travel, but by mid-morning had got nowhere, just becoming hot, bewildered and lost.

Our only recourse was to try the far-fetched method suggested to us. I approached a group of teenage boys and in incompetent French said that Big John had sent us. The one I spoke to seemed to instantly comprehend. A battered taxi was summoned, instructions given to the driver, and we were taken on a labyrinthine journey down roads, where no traffic rules applied, to a hotel where the shoe-shiners had a throne for their customers and two men could be seen lounging in the sun. They were Sori and Diallo, waiting to drive us to Mopti, Bandiagara and Burkina Faso.

How did that work? Could it have been pure serendipity that those boys knew Big John and where we needed to go? There may have been only one hotel in town organising tours for foreign travellers. Or perhaps fortune favoured the questing traveller?

But there was also something about this old and entirely different culture. It was a place where the limits of the possible are established, and breached, by the ideas, beliefs and traditions of the people. Deep down, these regions of West Africa have their own anima loci, their own regard for the spirits that animate their world, and their own long-accumulated, collectively-determined perception of reality. That difference—from the secular, rational Western world view—could somehow authorise what had happened to us in Gaoua: sacrosanct fetishes that were part of a long-established animist culture, that were assembled and consecrated to protect others, also had a means for protecting themselves.

No, declaim the rationalists among us. Yet Western culture has its own marginal zones of the extraordinary. They are grounded in the sentient glow we wake to every morning. What is this lantern in our skull? What is the wider context that enables marginal experiences to occur? And what are their implications for our picture of reality?

Marginal Zones

CHAPTER 1

Driving a Forked Stick

MY FATHER PRESENTED a forked stick to me and my three brothers, saying we were going to try water divining. I don't know whether he had set out to try this experiment and looked for the stick, or whether he had found the Y-shaped instrument and decided to put it to the test. Moving from the oldest to the youngest, we each looked slightly idiotic as we walked around holding the tiny handlebars in expectation the stem would suddenly dip when it detected water underground.

My father's efforts got nowhere. He even resorted to standing beside the toilet where water was clearly in evidence—but the dowsing rod remained inert and unconcerned. We all failed until Tony, my youngest brother, gripped the stick. He had barely walked three metres before the stem twisted downwards, indicating the exact position of a buried drainage pipe. It happened again when he approached it from another angle.

In the 1990s, the German government funded a well-documented project to find ground water. For over a decade, at 2,000 sites in Kenya, Namibia, Zaire, Yemen and Sri Lanka, geologists worked with dowsers to find water for well-drilling. With a scientific group monitoring the results, 691 wells were drilled. The dowsers found water in 96% of the cases. In Sri Lanka it was noted the chances of finding water were very low, because the springs were up to one hundred feet deep and there was no evidence of moisture on the surface land.

Is it possible there is a connection between the energy field of water and receptors in the unconscious, such that the dowsing rod can respond as a kind of mediator? Orthodox science answers unequivocally, declaring water divining no more effective than random chance.

In the 1940s the term *psi*, which is the twenty third letter of the Greek alphabet, became a convenient tag to denote all unexplained psychic phenomena, including ESP and other similar mind-based powers. Practitioners in psi, or researchers who seek evidence first-hand, need determination and a thick skin to pursue what can be helpful to others in the face of criticism and ridicule. Physicist and researcher Dale E. Graff presents a good example.[2]

In 1975 Graff was working in the aerospace industry in Ohio, USA. He wrote papers on emerging technologies, his interest centring more on psychological than economic and political factors. He decided that if psychic phenomena are real, why shouldn't they be explored and put to use? Citing extensive study of telepathy in the Soviet Union, Graff's suggestions were taken seriously by elements of the US government, who teamed him with physicists from the Stanford Research Institute. Their focus: remote viewing. The programme eventually came to be called Project Stargate, a name inspired by the vision of pushing the margins of science in a quest to maximise human potential. In practical terms, Stargate was designed to identify and train natural psychics, who could use their abilities to discover otherwise inaccessible intelligence. Project Stargate was given a total budget of $20,000,000 over a decade, and its services were used by branches of the US military, customs, intelligence organisations and the Drug Enforcement Agency.

Working with those talented in remote viewing, Graff found that, as the term "remote viewing" suggests, distance was no barrier to obtaining useful information. The project was grounded in learning by trial and error, with mistakes made by the psi sensitives being mitigated by experience.

On one occasion, Graff's team was enlisted in the search for a missing aircraft. The only indication of its crash site was an area of 40,000 to 50,000 square miles—about the same size as England—except it was somewhere in the continent of Africa. Graff's gifted remote viewer, Diane, was tasked with looking for any correspondence between the plane and landscape features in the broad zone of possibility. Diane prepared herself by clearing her mind and relaxing, then Graff showed her the photo of a Soviet plane, telling her that one of the same make was missing. Could she describe its location?

A quarter of an hour later Diane began sketching, making a generalised reference to a wide terrain of mountains and lakes. Graff handed the sketch to the search team, who consulted topographical maps, then allowed Diane to view the likely sites they had selected. From them she selected one, marking the map with X. Just days later the aircraft was found within three miles of her X. As a partial explanation for how this was possible, Graff suggested visual impressions in Diane's mind, correlated with recognisable features on the supplied maps, had led to her correctly identifying the plane's crash site. He ruled out any telepathic communication with the search team, because they were not in the correct vicinity. He concluded she had somehow grasped a truth of what and where: the aircraft is *there*.

The value of Project Stargate for the various high-level US organisations that used its psychics was entirely focused on *that* it worked. *How* it worked was of no concern. Yet it is the *how* that is most intriguing. Over a century of research has established the existence of psychic powers beyond doubt, yet psychic powers continue to defy definitive, repeatable testing. The psychics used in Project Stargate had their own views on what occurred to them during their remote viewing sessions. The irregular and transitory nature of psychic perceptions is seized on as proof of delusion and falsity by sceptics, who are not prepared to accept that complex psychodynamics are undoubtedly involved, that psychic abilities might function in different ways for different people, or that performance could be highly sensitive to the relationship between subject and researcher. Research also suggests that since psi involves consciously directing mental power, experiments can be skewed due to the unconscious interference of others who are present.

Given these factors, plus the difficulty of isolating a phenomenon and controlling all variables, experimenters in psi have been careful to apply stringent measures in order to establish psi's credibility and respectability. Double-blind testing (in which the tester doesn't know the result, so can't unconsciously transfer knowledge to the psychic), extensive statistical analysis, including meta-data analysis that correlates large numbers of studies, and the randomising of targets for psychic's identification, have been extensively employed. While most of Project Stargate's data remains classified, enough has been declassified to allow Graff to draw some conclusions. The first conclusion is that sensitives need a suitably adapted neurophysiology, established from childhood or from years of fostering intuitive ability. Then there is linkage to a distant locality, the wavelike qualities of consciousness enabling contact with that locale. Given the field of consciousness has unbounded extension, it could hold the accruing knowledge of manifold minds in what Graff calls "psi space".

People in all societies across the world have recorded their own experiences of deep connection with others, with animals, and with the natural world—experiences in the domain of psi. Yet when scientists seek to investigate what is involved, they find their reputations under attack. Biologist Rupert Sheldrake has dedicated a considerable part of his professional life to investigating psi phenomena.

In one notable series of experiments, Sheldrake showed that, on a statistical average, dogs can know when their owners are coming home.[3] He set up continuously running cameras in dog owners' houses. When an owner was on the way home, videos recorded the pet's anticipation prior to the owner's arrival, observing if the dog moved to a door or window, or adopted a mode of waiting. Sometimes a dog's preparation was made half an hour before the owner's arrival time. It also occurred when the arrival time was unexpected, and when the arrival was by taxi instead of the usual family car.

In the face of considerable accumulated video evidence and statistical data, should Sheldrake's experimental results be doubted? Sheldrake is a reputable scientist, and it was in his own interest to ensure his experiments were rigorously controlled. Yet a sceptic might reject the data because it violates an assumed tenet of physical law: that psi effects don't exist. In fact, Sheldrake was charged with heresy by the senior editor of the reputable *Nature* magazine. In a review of Sheldrake's first book, *A New Science of Life*, headlined *A Book for Burning?*, he was actually accused of propounding magic instead of science.

Among the other perceptions Sheldrake has dared to explore is that people can get the feeling someone is watching them from behind, then turn around to find that this is the case. This "sense of being stared at" was made the subject of an issue of *Journal of Consciousness Studies*.[4] One of the contributors, David Fontana, gave his own account of unthinkingly staring through a window at someone, who then looked over her shoulder at him with a startled expression. Before turning around she had been walking away from him, having no cause to think she was being observed.

Fontana favours Sheldrake's explanatory view that in the staring effect both observer and observed are tied together as a unit. The mind of the observer is extended to encompass the observed. There is a consequent interplay or intrusion in the perceptual field of the person being observed, causing their reaction of turning back to identify the source of the disturbance. It is also significant that Fontana describes his act of staring as heedless or unthinking, because psi researchers refer to their subjects' quietening of the mind, suggesting a calmness or openness permitting the frictionless reception or transmission of thoughts and intentions.

It would be in this state of consciousness—a kind of fluid neutrality—that a friend or acquaintance will pop into our mind unbidden, just moments before the phone rings and we discover that person is in fact at the other end of the line. Over the years I have heard a number of people report this coincidence. Although it is only anecdotal, it is interesting to consider its statistical likelihood, given the closeness in time between spontaneous thought and phone call, and the number of other friends, acquaintances or unknowns who could also have called.

All this reinforces my view that the conditions for telepathy are both normal and universal. Two people think, feel or sense something at the same time—for which we use words like rapport, empathy, agreement, mutuality and fellow-feeling. Long-term partners have this connection through wordless understanding, occasionally finishing the other's sentence, or sensing a shadow of tension falling between them. It is so normal we take it for granted.

It is only when we use the word *telepathy* that it seems we are referring to a special category of perception, and placing a particular focus on this common faculty. It is only when we refer to psychic powers, or to the unexplained, that the faculty and its purported consequences become spooky or enter a forbidden zone.

Given the widespread scepticism that psi abilities exist, there's a strong suggestion that over time our ability has become stunted—especially in Western countries where structured, rational thinking is the norm. Establishing closer bonds between people is better for families and communities. As we gradually jettison the materialist mindset, reclaiming our innate powers, psi will lose its outsider status and become more integrated—a part of evolutionary change.

When I was seven or eight years old, our family visited the thermal baths in Matamata. I had been swimming and saw my parents walking down the hill towards me. I climbed out, ran up, said 'Watch me jump in!', then ran back. I made the mistake of jumping into the big pool, way over my head; they made the mistake of not watching me.

For a while I kept going down. My breath ran out and I started gulping water involuntarily, a kind of panic mechanism. In suspension, all I could hear was a pressured ringing sound as I took in more and more water. Then there was a change. It could have risen slowly from my toes, or inwards from the perimeter of the tiles—the turmoil and terror faded away, and I felt myself submitting to a warmth and serenity, something that was absolutely known and inevitable. Then I started feeling its attractive power. It drew me in, and it was all I wanted.

Suddenly, there was a violent interruption. I felt my hair being seized. I was lifted out, into the open, steamy air above the pool. I became aware of the voices of bathers and spectators, my parents homing in, the man who saved me glistening like a seal, his suit saturated. I coughed up a pint of the pool onto the coping stones.

A 1975 study of one hundred and fifty near-death experiences (NDEs) established several recurring experiences, such as passing through a tunnel, encountering discarnate beings, leaving one's body, and experiencing a life review. None of these happened to me in the pool, but two other commonly recorded experiences did: a feeling of peace, and a reluctance to return to my body. It's hard to know whether the dissolving of terror into calmness could be accounted for by leaving the body—a cosy and inviolable core starting to drift off, abandoning the body of a boy in togs gulping and flailing slowly in a haze of warm water, until drowned.

Decades later, it is easy to be dispassionate about what happened to me, but there is an interesting relationship between two fields of love, both apparently exclusive. There was my family and life in New Zealand on one hand, and the great Other to which I was being drawn. Initially, I was in panicked rejection of death; then it became so powerfully seductive that I felt thwarted or robbed of the coming transition. One consistent theme in NDEs is the feeling of returning home, and of the dying feeling a deep, natural connection with the other place. That is our real home. It is associated with certainty about our true identity, with the drawing towards the brink being so overwhelming it seems impossible to "look back over the shoulder" at what is being left behind.

According to the hundreds of accounts reported in the many separate studies of NDEs, the features are consistent. Though no two experiences are exactly the same, they will always have at least one of the eight or nine features in common. Perhaps the most universal of these is the connection between the light one feels drawn to (to which one's own lantern corresponds), and feelings of warm reception, of love and bliss. Many reports confirm that for people returning from NDEs to their usual lives, what lingers is that vision of love, acceptance and tranquillity. Their normal lives have been given this new context, and many go on with a deeper sense of the importance of human relationships.

In a 1979 study, 37% of people who had experienced a NDE reported having a concomitant out-of-body experience. Many have reported the astounding ability to look down on their body as it was being tended to by surgeons in an operating theatre, and afterwards being able to correctly identify the means of resuscitation used. To 'see' without eyeballs implies that the mind can behave in a ridiculously unfettered manner. This shows, yet again, how much such powers are still far beyond our understanding.

Lawrence LeShan is a significant figure in the history of psi. In an interview recorded for the sixty-fifth year of the US-based Parapsychology Foundation, he spoke of an important change in his career as a psychologist. While working with terminal cancer patients, he came across people he referred to as charlatans who were going around speaking 'obvious nonsense' about the apparent reality of the paranormal. Resolving to dispose of them for good, he made an application for research funding, which was granted. This led to his meeting an Irish medium, Eileen Garrett.[5] She was seeking a researcher from mainstream science who could make a serious evaluation of her abilities, while LeShan had found an apparently perfect subject to debunk the nonsense of the paranormal. However, after rigorously testing her, LeShan came to the conclusion that Eileen Garrett was completely genuine. He then secured further funds to continue his research, believing it would be highly valuable to understanding human psychology.

His work with Garrett led him to identify a 'clairvoyant reality'. This is the mental state in which extra-sensory psi abilities operate. It is a state of consciousness, often reached when meditating, in which there is a sense of presence and oneness. In LeShan's view, the clairvoyant reality involves a state of profound union, as opposed to our familiar sensory state in which we feel separate from everything around us. Each allows certain actions or occurrences to take place when we are in that state. These actions and occurrences are normal in each. The opposite is also true: for our commonplace sensory reality ESP is paranormal, while in the clairvoyant reality ESP is normal.

To investigate the relationship between these two realities, LeShan decided on psychic healing. The procedure began with the healer entering a connected, unified state of consciousness, then using that state to coalesce with the patient. Beyond this there was no prescribed work to do, no method at all, other than this conjoining and the healer maintaining a disposition of loving kindness. Due to this connection, the patient's natural capacity for self-cure was stimulated, which proved conducive to positive organic change. Although, on principle, many objectors dismiss this type of procedure as pseudoscience, double-blind testing proved significant success. Furthermore, as I will explore later, the procedure is related scientifically to quantum interconnection.

What is clear about this method, and is stressed by LeShan, is the attitude of the healer as the necessary agent. Emotional factors are the key; empathy, sympathy and telepathy—in-feeling, with-feeling, feeling-at-a-distance. This is unquestionably in right-brain territory: depth, wholeness, spirit. (I will consider the right brain's contribution to psi abilities later.)

Focusing on the restorative and therapeutic, LeShan also investigated the relationship between emotional states and malignant disease. Data analysis showed a connection between the loss of intimate relationships and the first-noted symptoms of a tumour. Such connections, given little or no credence by orthodox medicine, support a three-way principle in treating illness: the physical, mental and spiritual.

Researchers like LeShan and Sheldrake have used different approaches to identify and access the same phenomena: a field of energy that apparently extends beyond the body, which is the first thing encountered when we enter an expanded state of consciousness. Meditation can shift the mind into this potentially clairvoyant state where, in its most integrated, fluid form, there is no discrete separation from anything.

One of the more remarkable documented cases of developing psi perceptions during concerted meditation comes from *People of the Earth*, by Peter Calvert and his fellow Agapeschoolinz meditators of Hamilton, New Zealand.[6] The book records dialogues with discarnate beings, particularly nature spirits related to habitats of the natural world. Through deep concentration, the meditators roused beings who occupy the localities of rocks, rivers, trees and mountains; to use less poetic terminology, they made contact with invisible occupants in the field.

Because human consciousness accesses the field at its own frequency, it makes sense to conclude that consciousness itself is its vital energy. It is represented by the quantum wave from which particles materialise in the familiar sensory realm. Being fully integrated, there is no such thing as a special coincidence in the field. The field explains my spontaneous thought of person X and their phoning just seconds afterwards. That the field is unified explains why sympathy, friendship and compassion are intensified in association with it—and, conversely, why work stress, ugly architecture, consumerism and pervasive advertising, which draw our attention away from the field, become the means for separating us from one another.

As language users, we are senders and receivers; as a consciously-linked society, we are also senders and receivers. Anyone who has grown up in a family knows how the bad mood of one family member can be sensed as soon as you enter the house, before you've even seen the one who is frustrated or angry. Negative vibes can be taken on, the same way you're lifted and lightened by laughter. A student at school dies and the whole class that lost her takes on not just sadness but a feeling more complex than that—the peculiar, suspended intensity of melancholy. Quietly, they all share this feeling, as though partially pulled out of their workaday reality and half dreaming the disembodied one. Panic, too, broadcasts itself before you are aware of its cause, the whole house on edge when a thrush falls down the flue and is trapped behind the mesh of the fireguard, fluttering in the ashes, then bangs against the glass when released, flying desperately for the light. Only when it is through the door and free does the air lose its agitation.

A similar disturbance can be transmitted instantly across the globe when the news media seize on a crisis and it hits our homes simultaneously. Millions of viewers focus on exactly the same edited presentation, while what is invisible—the emotional wave that comes with it—floods the mass mind. Even those who missed the news item can sense its electrical charge, the tension jostling the collective unconscious with the latest emergency. The German word zeitgeist (spirit of the times) alludes to this, but in the sense of a more protracted state or attitude that colonises consciousness, an unprecedented mixture of cultural and intellectual qualities shared but never specified until a historical perspective can be applied.

The parameters of these shared experiences can shift from culture to culture. Writing in 1977, Stuart Holroyd referred to the Freudian concept of different reality principles, especially in relation to long-established indigenous cultures in Africa, India and Brazil, where paranormal events were common.[7] He cites anthropological studies where beliefs comprising the reality principles of a society will determine to a large extent the boundaries of the possible. In other words, what is jointly accepted, shared and practised can become the reality. This may be a clue to the selectively blanked-out film taken in Burkina Faso I referred to earlier. Holroyd mentions these arcane events and practices of indigenous societies because, in the spirit of the seventies counterculture, many people were looking beyond the constraints of their materialist Western inheritance to sources of knowledge from other countries—Sufism, the Qabala, Tantra, I-Ching and Zen Buddhism. At that time a fascination with separate realities and new vistas of thought prevailed.

Today materialism provides the reality principle that dominates our culture. Yet there are many other reality principles available to us. As this brief exploration of psi shows, giving credence to psychic phenomena, and assimilating it into our world view, provides us with another kind of reality principle.

The countercultural researchers of the 1960s and 70s sustain their appeal to us today because of the exciting possibilities they opened up. They also challenged the orthodox materialist view that defined a human being mechanically—as a creature who is self-contained, one hundred percent physical, driven by blind chance, and ultimately doomed to oblivion. Today psi makes the same challenge, promising to replace the isolating materialist outlook with the view that all life is linked via the unified field.

Another equally fascinating approach to this field, which also dates back to the 1960s counterculture, is offered by psychedelics. This is my next topic.

CHAPTER 2

Mind Excursions

WAVES CRASHED AROUND the base of the lighthouse. From an aerial vantage point the waves were surging rhythmically against the rocks, wind-whipped lines of foam coming off their crests, below them the blue depths of the sea. A ship rode the turbulence and danger, wind tearing at its sails, waves washing across its decks. It looked so delicate, vulnerable, fighting against the strong onshore current, the conditions threatening to wreck the vessel on rocks at the base of the very lighthouse that could have saved it.

I looked up from this maritime drama to find the dimly-lit room pulsing, swirling particles like magnetised iron-filings clustering at the corners. It made sense, later, that the coastal drama I witnessed was set in motion by a cloth of brushed blue velvet covering a small side table, the lighthouse a lamp-base standing on it. Somewhere in the delirious night of the soul, a fluorescent power-pole was sizzling in the darkness, neurones crackling at its charged cross-trees.

Dawn finally came, replacing the heaving night visions with a gorgeous amber glow—a divine presence pervading the verandah outside. First rays made enlivened eyes of an Austin A30's headlights, hit the pursed chrome lips of its radiator, its plump little body breathing regularly. The beleaguered visual field was pulling itself together, a broken grid of red and green pixels stringing themselves across the morning scene of Williamson Avenue.

There's an interesting truism that visions in an LSD trip don't come from the drug, but from the transmogrified mind, its intensified imagination. Acid is only the agent, the facilitator, the concierge.

LSD-25 was originally synthesised by Albert Hofmann in a laboratory in Switzerland in 1938. It was shelved until 1943, when his skin accidentally absorbed a tiny dosage, and he experienced a rush of imagery and colours as he cycled home. The ordinary street furniture of Hofmann's Basel was magically and alarmingly transformed. It is from this date that brain science swerved into a new avenue of possibilities. The discovery changed minds in postwar Western societies, especially in the United States, through advocates like Timothy Leary and Aldous Huxley. But how can as little as one hundred micrograms (less than half what Hofmann absorbed) have such an intense effect?

Here's what a friend, Raymond, said of one LSD experience:

> We were in a big, communal environment, which was lucky. We had a music room, lined with pegboard. I remembered, well nothing's happening, and I was compelled to go to the pegboard. I looked into one of the holes and could see right through it. I could see a whole group of people on the other side, standing there. They were in the peg-board. And ... oh dear, there were a lot of people behind the wall. Other people were dealing with their own imaginings ... I looked again and there they all were, and I thought, I'm looking back through the peg-board at us, in this room, and ... this is staggering. This is something I'd never experienced.

According to his account, Raymond didn't prompt the through-the-hole apparition himself. His mind had a mind of its own. 'I was compelled ...' seems to suggest the mind was independently, of its own volition, doing the entertainingly big reveal. He continues:

> I did a lot of portal work, finding frames I could look into. Looking into a mirror, at first it's yourself. But then it becomes not you. ... Someone else in the mirror, looking at you, but then—

who's that? Then it would be: who's looking at who? ... And you'd go off down into the mirror. I'd spend hours in a cupboard, with a couple of mirrors. It was an old battered dressing thing, just in this room, but it became a world. And I became aware that [what I was seeing] could be whatever I imagined ... terrible, or inspiring.

Raymond's mental forays can be seen to be a mixture of the recreational and the seriously exploratory. However, the initial research into the effects of LSD involved its use for therapy. In controlled conditions, with precise dosages, it is possible for the mentally ill to be awakened to their creative potential, or re-oriented to their spiritual foundation. In traditional societies, shamans had the specialised knowledge and experience to administer psychedelics. Shamans underwent specialised training, learning to collaborate with cactus or fungus to enter levels of interconnected reality, and as a result becoming able to heal the sick or assist spirits of the deceased cross over.

Michael Pollan, while researching his book, *How to Change your Mind, the New Science of Psychedelics*,[8] was careful before taking the drug. He located experienced guides, discussed the known effects, and clarified what might occur. Stressing that there should be protocols governing the use of psychoactive drugs, Pollan was a responsible psychonaut. He was also making himself both subject and researcher, knowing his study needed to be as a participant, from the inside. His descriptions and insights showed that manageable doses make the trip navigable while providing a wealth of detail in the pictures, perceptions and unfolding narratives of his mind. Raymond was similarly careful when planning further psychedelic excursions:

> We processed what happened, then made a plan of how to do it again, how we could better set it up. Knowing that, it became ... how can you be sure of what you're taking? It was remarkably good, we knew it was, so let's buy enough of it. And it was about the environment. Where would we like to be? Go to the bush,

pack a box of food, music ... We took care of our travellers. Quite a bit of effort was needed in setting up the whole weekend—like a mountaineering expedition.

During the sixties the Beatles admitted taking LSD. The public had a substance-free taste of their trips in the lysergic-soaked *Sgt. Pepper's Lonely Hearts Club Band* album. Then, in the seventies, psychedelics were criminalised, LSD sinking firmly into the black market. The issue arising from this political move was one of personal freedom. Transcendence had become outlawed. Users could be jailed for a victimless crime. Others asked: Who controls my cortex? Who has jurisdiction over the content and scope of my consciousness?

It is interesting to consider the underlying reasons for prohibition. Youth's slogans, like Front Up, Freak Out and Freight Off, were a challenge to the older generation, both to their authority and to the rational order they promoted. The reality principle in which society was invested, which assumed the secure materiality of the world, was threatened by altered states and mystical experience—this is one obvious explanation for the prohibition of psychedelics. It also explains LSD's prevalence among the young during the 1960s and 70s. They had been born into an industrialised postwar society, which was uniform, consumerist and spiritually barren. Chemically-induced reconnection was available. Just turn on.

Yet the remedy brought ambiguous gifts. Not only was lysergic acid diethylamide formidably powerful, its effects depended on the mind it was modifying. The outcomes were as varied as LSD's acronyms: from Love, Sex and Dreams, to Light Show Dynamics, to Limited Slip Differential, to Leafy Sea Dragon.

With a range of factors determining whether a trip would involve venturing into Brahmic Bliss, or dropping into a quagmire in Hell, lysergic acid carried its own negative advertising. Especially for first-time users, it was unpredictable, offering a roller-coaster ride—and you couldn't get off once it was in motion. Flashbacks and lasting psychosis were possible. There were many suicides. LSD could not be classed alongside pharmaceutical drugs, which have a specific focus and predictable effects, so there was every reason for both the maladjusted and the level-headed to leave it alone. Back to Raymond:

> I remember looking at my eye, and blood welled up in it, ran along my eyelid, then down my cheek. I thought, I'm bleeding from inside. Then I remember wiping my cheek in a ... sweaty panic. ... I looked at my finger and there was no blood on it. I asked someone else, am I bleeding? They said no.
>
> And someone else would say, I can't get up. And you'd say, why can't you get up? And they'd say, I'm way too big for the room. I just can't get up, my head will hit the ceiling. So then you'd think, there's someone here who needs help. And you'd say, you can get up, you're just lying down. Look at me, I'm standing up, and I wouldn't be standing up if my head was hitting the ceiling. I'm as tall as you are. This person, lying down, had decided they were way too big for the room.

The drug's endowment to the experiencer of free association, *of anything you can imagine* is a two-edged sword. It may usher in the magically creative or the utterly terrifying. This is especially true because of the wide-awake clarity of the experience. What does it signify that by chemically-induced means you are able to imagine anything into existence? It's important to remember that this is not the colourings and potentialities of the molecule itself, rather it is the augmented waveband of the mind. A vitalised, almost restless imagination seizes an initiative and starts to have fun. Moreover, it is nonchalant about natural laws, and keen to reveal the enchanting equally with the macabre. Is the almost tangible, multifarious display simply the otherwise untapped power of the imagination? Is it the degree of strangeness that seriously tests the onlooker, a kind of incredulity not just about the fertility of one's mind, but its being so opaque to normal introspection?

Consider these actual occurrences people reported having:

- Sheryl watched her partner slowly and deliberately lift his arm to his mouth and start to eat it.
- Robin saw the face of a fellow tripper sliced into horizontal strata that slid off sideways in both directions.
- Leon found himself poised over the bottomless crevasse of his own subconscious, crossing the void on the most tenuous tightrope, the odds slim he wouldn't topple into insanity.
- Stefan had taken one too many tablets of California Sunshine and gone to the beach. Right in front of him, out of a dune, rose a huge fist, sand pouring off its knuckles as it forced itself skyward. Immediately under the clenched fist was a plaque, its message in full view: You're insane.

Was each horrifying vision just an indicator of the duality of existence—that there's no gentleness without brutality, no angels without demons, no idyllic landscapes without voracious predators? Is it an indicator of imagination's Janus head—a playmate sometimes enchanting, sometimes rogue? Are such extreme scenarios presented to test the maturity of the essentially imperturbable self?

In the latter case, perhaps the size and seismic force of the signposting fist was the persuasion Stefan needed to move towards moderation or abstinence. But who sent the message? It wasn't the shocked recipient, because he had been taken completely by surprise. Was it his turbocharged conscience, coming to the rescue of a wayward self temporarily lost in hedonistic experimentation? Or was it another, discarnate overseer who thought some shock therapy wouldn't go amiss? If we are to remain open-minded about what happens during these mental excursions, these are all possibilities.

What is facilitated by the drug may include scenarios that test mental resilience. This is quite possible, given the successes of LSD and psilocybin in therapy. Yet the dangers can't be ignored. Psychiatrists appreciate the consequences of treating mentally-precarious patients with these substances, so they're unlikely to risk using them unless part of an officially-approved study. Part of this dilemma is that in favourable conditions psychedelics can be immediately effective, unearthing deep memories and unresolved ordeals, as well as dissolving the ego and dissipating anxieties.

Author Michael Pollan refers to a trial conducted concurrently by researchers in the US at Johns Hopkins, UCLA and New York University. Generous quantities of psilocybin (magic mushrooms) were given to patients with terminal cancer, and the transcendent, ego-dissolving experiences that followed were shown to dispel trauma about the prospect of approaching death. More than this, one in three of patients reported the experience being the most important or meaningful of their whole lives, while 80% reported or demonstrated a marked change from distress and depression to calm resignation and serenity. This transformation persisted for months.

My own experience with psilocybin dominated a day, but reverberated across decades. A veil fell away, the natural world revealing itself in full, sap-rising translucency, in radiant greens rich enough to taste, and in plants' growing tips pushing up in mutual glory to the sun from infused, tightly-packed centres. Hyperbole? Language that waxes lyrically is required when you try to describe the subjective and objective merging into one, into a kind of effervescent living energy. A common reaction might be: that's just a drug experience, i.e. it's only chemicals. Yet to dismiss such an experience from the outside, without having joined the trip, is like devaluing the experience of eating sticky date pudding without having tasted it. To the subject, chemicals become irrelevant as the state of mind begins to alter. After all, who is having the mystical experience: the chemicals, or me? This is from another occasion, when I was on Mindoro Island in the Philippines:

> After the mushrooms were rustled up for breakfast, the already beautiful beach became something even more. It was idyllic in the virgin, pre-cliché sense of the word. I felt overwhelmed by a feeling of intense privilege just to exist there. The easy wash of waves onto sand was the even, regular breathing of me and

the whole island. The sea stretched out into a haze of cobalt blue without horizon. Peals of laughter from the local kids—the childlike joy of the beach itself—echoed round the dome of sky. Time slowed to a simple, beatific presence. I merged with the whole scene: experience and experiencer became one. This was the experiential reality behind the stereotypical sun-bronzed hedonist idling on a tropical shore under lightly-swaying palms and a cerulean sky.

To a sceptical outsider, the tripper's claim to have experienced real spiritual insight might be dismissed as just part of a roller-coaster ride—no more than a hallucination. This ignores the consistency of similar reports made by numerous psychedelic adventurers, and so many of the experiencers ranking their experiences as the most memorable and significant of all their altered states, if not their whole lives. While it is easy to see why the challenge psychedelics posed to mainstream beliefs would be discredited as delusion, researchers in the 1960s showed otherwise. They drew together what could be called the defining features of psychedelic experience, categorising them in terms of the sensory, the recollective-analytic, the symbolic and, most elevated of all, the integral or mystical. The second of these categories, the recollective-analytic, includes not only the ability to access one's own deep memory, which is extremely useful in psychiatry, but to plumb what Carl Jung called the collective memory as well. Judy's account is firmly in this territory:

> There were four of us. We went on the ferry over to Rangitoto Island. We must have taken it once we got off, then we went up to the top. There was just this ... primordial, volcanic landscape, denuded, nothing there, like the beginning of time. We went into this whole evolutionary thing. We got down to the other side and there was a great swimming beach, with no-one there, we had it to ourselves. We went into the water and pretended we were evolving—we were swimming, then walking up on land

like the first creatures coming out of the sea, discovering land for the first time. Something was unlocked and we reverted to the primitive brain. We all went deep into that thinking. It was a collective experience.

All four had taken the same dosage of LSD. As they walked up the hillside of scoria a mutually-realised situation took hold—something shared, atavistic. It was a descent into the collective unconscious, to a distant time in terrestrial chronology. Their 'pretending', their acting out, was like a celebration of the creatures from which we all evolved.

In *The End of Stupor?*[9] Ronald Conway traces a similar evolutionary succession while under the influence of LSD. He progressed from unicellular life, through the reptilian and mammalian, to our current homo sapiens, then to a more enlarged, unified vision of cosmic consciousness. He also regressed to suspension in amniotic fluid before re-living his birth with all its attendant sensations. The experience is all about context: these grand sequences of personal and planetary life shift one's awareness, normally caught up in the plodding course of daily existence, and elevates it into a sweeping overview, into full universal relation.

Judy's story suggests a special mutuality of consciousness in those who have taken the same drug. Stuart Holroyd relates a remarkable case of this mutuality, concerning a young Peruvian who was abducted by Amazonian Indians. He subsequently participated in a communal imbibing of ayahuasca. Taking the drug was accompanied by rituals intended to establish the group's close bonding; the boy reported that the hallucinations were all shared. A jaguar, conjured collectively, found its way into the group. The boy was initially awed by its power, then the cat's sudden change to a fierce posture caused a responding shudder from all present. The experience then became even more remarkable. The boy remembered an incident from earlier in his life, when he confronted a black jaguar while walking on a track through the forest. As soon as the memory was recalled, a mutual tremor ran through the group—all had picked up on his past scare. At the end of the session, and because of this contribution, the boy was dubbed Ino Moxo (black panther).

Neurological studies have attempted to explain "the science of ascension"—how one can achieve the expansive mystical experience. Canadian sociologist Mike Sosteric[10] points out that the sectors of the brain affected by psychedelics are all part of the Default Mode Network (DMN). During purposeful activity such as study, playing tennis or teaching a class, the DMN is in a dormant state, but when one is relaxed and aimless it is activated. Neurologists consider the DMN has the highest number of interbrain connections, and as a result it is the seat of self-identity. When nothing active is otherwise occupying the brain the DMN becomes active, retracing memories, contemplating future courses of action, and engaging in self-reflection. This makes the DMN essentially ego-focused and ego-driven.

Sosteric notes that psychedelics like psilocybin repress the ego, which fits with the most common feature of mystical states induced by psychedelics—the replacement of self-centredness by wholeness, and mergence with the All. Sosteric calls these mystical states connection experiences. He then goes on to consider the nature and intensity of connection experiences, giving them a consciousness quotient (QC). If normal consciousness hovers around the 40% mark, then a view of the celestial splendour of the Milky Way might lift one's CQ to 60%. A strong connection experience, such as that generated by psilocybin, might push it up to 80% or 90%—into the blissful, unforgettable zone.

This makes psychedelics, which are known in scholarly circles as entheogens, part of what Sosteric terms connection technologies. Entheogen is an impartial term for psychoactive substances that induce mystical experiences. The term hallucinogen has been dropped from current academic usage due to their suggesting psychedelic explorers are suffering from the perception of something not present.

As generators of divinity, entheogens present a particular problem for the advocates of conventional neurology. That a material molecule can awaken a transcendent state casts doubt on materialist belief. Accumulated anecdotal evidence supporting the existence of connection experiences is one thing, but there can be no substitute for the actual experience. What magical spell does the entheogen perform in that elusive interface between brain and mind? Grand associations of a connection event may link synaptic sparks to the heliosphere, the bloodstream to the sap of surrounding plants, and the present self to its whole cavalcade of history.

Recent research into entheogens is being undertaken in the context of a new science whose boundaries have been pushed outwards due to the inexplicable power and ubiquity of consciousness. A raised CQ is a catalyst for creativity; perceivers transcend their immediate surroundings and are opened to broader pictures and vaster ranges of energy. New science is, axiomatically, a search for something new— for new orders of relationship, and for an innovative, more inclusive paradigm of reality. There is an increasingly widespread recognition, directly confirmed by personal experiences, of altered, transcendent states of consciousness, suggesting we have only begun to tap the latent powers of the mind.

CHAPTER 3

Peak Experiences

A KIND OF VALVE OPENED at the top of my head to allow a brief inflow from the vertical axis—a single inhalation of rarified air. Recapturing the experience requires pitting its intense, revelatory power against the fact that it was no more than three seconds in duration, and it occurred forty years ago. It was such a memorable experience because it was unprecedented. To say what it was is next to impossible. Words try to gain purchase at the edges, then slide off, carried away by the strength and nature of flooding experience. Like an elusive dream, trying to scoop up its essence in the net of memory was futile because the gleaming fish faded fast as it returned to the depths.

Now all I can salvage is the sense of levels—of a realm or realms beyond our own. That these realms are intelligible, but indescribable, goes without saying. We belong there as much as here. But we are not there now—or, perhaps, we are partially there. I also felt a sense of *why not?* about that realm, or realms, as though they were, like one's creative imagination, authentic, and open to all possibilities.

If this could be seen as an encounter with the Other, then there is another demonstration of it—closer to home, so to speak, but likewise numinous. This is the Other as Thou. I-Thou involves an intense, meaningful relationship that is explored in the philosophy of Martin Buber. This relationship is not at all the sole preserve of scholars or mystics. It belongs to lovers. Lovers gaze into each other's eyes and something is activated—what could be called pure relationship, or an intercourse between both identities, as if the wattage in their two concordant lanterns has been turned up. There is a reciprocity of feeling—but again, it can't be put into words. In general terms, this love is the confirmation of a transcendent principle, something exalted and intrinsically good.

A peak experience is an altered state, ecstatic and blissful, that stands out in sharp relief over the chronology of one's life. Despite being ephemeral, it is concentrated, and heavily freighted, because it is full of meaning—even though that meaning can't be communicated.

Twentieth century psychology was initially influenced by Freud's plumbing of the unconscious. Freud's approach was subsequently rejected by behaviourists such as Watson, Pavlov and Skinner, who recoiled from any consideration of the depths, preferring to focus on surface behaviours. In the 1950s Abraham Maslow sought a radical change of perspective.[11] He wanted to integrate peak experiences into a view of the developed, self-actualised human being. This heightened consciousness, with its suggestion of a mystical dimension to the psyche, was vehemently opposed by both Freudians and behaviourists, who refused to acknowledge the existence of heightened states, labelling them a derangement or affliction.

Maslow is best known for his hierarchy of needs, expressed diagrammatically as a triangle or pyramid. The base is constituted of bodily needs such as food and shelter. Above this is security—of health, employment and family. The next level above them is the need for friendship and sexual intimacy. Further up is the higher, more abstract stratum of confidence, self-esteem and mutual respect. The apex of the pyramid includes qualities required for self-actualisation: creativity, spontaneity, morality, equanimity, an acceptance of facts, lack of prejudice and a capacity for problem solving. Peak experiences belong at, or spring from, the pinnacle of the pyramid.

Maslow identified the character traits and positive qualities that define the self-actualised human being. Honesty and high ethical standards were important, as were people having intimate relationships with others, but being self-sufficient on their own. An aesthetic sense was indispensable, and a propensity for spontaneity and play. The self-actualised were unique, integrated individuals, rich with ideas and experience, in many cases leading simple lives, and not valued according to material gain.

Maslow saw the peak experience as intensified consciousness—involving feelings of elation and delight, of mutuality, sincerity and of being deeply in love. The experiencer is vitalised and feels intimately linked to the natural order. It is rare, exciting, oceanic, deeply moving, exhilarating and elevating. He regarded it as an advanced form of perceiving reality. As a psychiatrist, he was more interested in studying those whose self-directed, thriving lifestyles were more naturally conducive to the transcendent. In this way Maslow put the famous religious revelation of a prophet or seer into a broader, less esoteric, psychological context. He showed that peak experiences could be activated by music, fine art, making love, interactions with the natural world, and from deep introspection. To this could be added extreme sports, the experiences of astronauts and special moments for those involved in creative work. Peak experiences are always private and personal, the degree of their intensity and significance reduced to a shadow by crude translation into language.

Maslow's pyramid is planted in the same metaphorical landscape as Aristotle's oak—the mighty tree that sprouts from the acorn of human potential. Self-actualisation incorporates the same guiding principles: the ideal society governed by fairness, which values knowledge and appreciates the inherent worth of everyone.

In the latter stage of his life, Maslow began to focus on a new vista in psychology, the transhuman. This is not to be confused with the more contemporary reference of transhumanism—uploading one's mind to a computer, shedding the physical body to become an immortal, machine-based entity. Rather, Maslow's transhumanism involved the harmonising of the refined, actualised individual with his or her universal, cosmic counterpart.

Maslow saw various modes of life as being conducive to peak experiences. Yet it is also important to note that the truest and most significant peak experiences are those that come unbidden, that are ephemeral, but carry enough concentrated power to change a life. Peak experiences could bear the grand title of Mystical Revelation, yet small, more specific peak experiences, still give a sense that authentic action can bring the reimbursement of heightened awareness or delight. For athletes, long periods of training and self-sacrifice are instrumental in bringing about this experience. The footballer, fencer or tennis player set themselves against others just as highly-trained, just as motivated. The fencer's reflexes, long-honed technique, physical fitness, and intuitive reading of her opponent overcome those same opposing forces, leading to a lift, a feeling of mastery at having won —something far above pride and swagger. It is a triumph of the body and mind, linked with a feeling of capability and having achieved when put to the test. The striker who scores against a skilled and assertive opposing football team has the same euphoria, reinforced by half a stadium of triumphant fans.

For my fiftieth birthday, my brother gave me a ticket for a tandem parachute jump. As the plane gained altitude, a tension rose due to the fact that this aircraft was to have no part in bringing me back down to the ground. It had effectively become just a platform for launching two pairs of bodies into space. This eventuality became all too evident when, at 12,000 feet, the whole side of the plane was opened up. We were going over the brink, my survival of the long fall dependent on straps, buckles and a fully-aerated canopy.

Another pair were the first to jump. It took just a second for them to diminish to a dot. Then it was our turn. After the rush of free-fall and confused tumbling into a fuzz of cloud, the canopy opened. I looked down at my feet dangling over an agrarian picture. The descent was nowhere near long enough; we swooped into the landing area, skimmed the ground, and touched down. But meeting the earth didn't stop the feeling of racing headlong—the sheer exhilaration of it. All that incident, danger, anticipation and surrender was compressed into just a few minutes of falling. Doing a tandem jump is not something I would have chosen. When the ticket arrived out of the blue it was a case of seeking payback for taking on a dangerous activity: Do you want an adrenalin high, or not?

Peak experiences couldn't be more appropriate when associated with mountaineering. Climbers, almost without fail, report an enraptured, ecstatic feeling on reaching the summit, the short rush of happiness and fulfilment resulting from a year of hard training and possibly a week of ascent to the final camp. It is about the moment of breasting the rise and standing on top—this is why the trials of preparation and perils of crevasse, blizzard or avalanche are endured. Perhaps the mountaineer considers the scaling of a Himalayan peak will bring a mental or spiritual elevation commensurate with the physical elevation.

Cellphones have made it possible for climbers to speak to loved ones from high altitudes, their words of exultation, and messages of love, relayed from base camp to another part of the world. For sixty-one year old French amateur mountaineer, Hugues Gaspard, the day before he died on K2 in 2008, his final communication by cellphone was inspired and mournful: *I would like everybody to contemplate the ocean of mountains and glaciers. I am suffering for it, but it is too beautiful. The night will be long, but beautiful.*

Musicians speak of times when, during a concert, a special synergy occurs between them such that they're acting as one and have a perfect accommodation with what is being played. It might be short-lived, but the feeling is intoxicating, imparting a strong sense of privilege and common purpose. Steven Berkoff, the veteran actor, writer and theatre director, expressed a similar kind of payback through dedication to his craft:

> At times you're on stage, or off stage directing, and something happens, and you know that you're getting a beam, almost like a laser beam, from another place. And something in you just stops. You are surfing on this wave and it's fantastic.

In the high art of theatre, the goal is to make a performance unforgettable. The creative vision that can take a performance to alpine heights has to be through some combination of script, set, costume, music and movement; then, sometimes, perhaps for just moments, the audience can be lifted into the clear air of enchantment and grace. It is a state so perfect and integrated that thoughts transcend the onstage spectacle, triggering other associations, possibilities or models of excellence. In this sense the practitioner, as Berkoff suggests, can function like a guide, beguiler or shaman of the dramatic, ushering the audience into a higher or refined vision of reality.

Byakko-Sha were among the first wave of large butoh ensembles in Japan, drawing inspiration from butoh's founders, Ohno and Hijikata. Director Isamu Ohsuka admitted it was hard to define what his twenty-eight member performance group actually did. He suggested the audience keep an open mind and reach their own conclusions, without preconceptions. Their production *Deja-vu and Watermelons* was a means of bringing unconscious archetypes to life onstage, images at once primitive and beautiful, incongruous and fantastic.

The opening sequence was a spotlight on some kind of disc in a void, horizontal and spinning. As the light widened and intensified, it became clear that the disc was a wide oriental hat sheltering three figures wrapped together in a cylinder of linen and shuffling in a clockwise direction. At some point this material unravelled and two chickens were freed, fluttering out to spend the rest of the performance pecking at their own little mound of seed downstage. An evolutionary theme developed, with human lizards crawling across a shaded stage under dappled patches of green light.

Sequences of bizarre images followed, a human/animal ascendency through time, elevated into ritualistic and sometimes savage dances as they lived their lives and passed away. This was our early close-to-the-land existence in desert, taiga or tundra, close to fish, foetus or flower, beings slithering, crying and ecstatic, their antennae tingling.

This full immersion in such strange, energetic and stylised images was deeply affecting, and at the same time provided a privileged overview of a species' whole trajectory, progressing through millennia. Described as 'volatile as a volcano', Byakko-Sha's grand vision of evolution was crammed into just two hours—a peak experience of theatre.

Another innovative, confronting performance group is Punchdrunk. Their scheme is to remove the auditorium and involve the audience directly in the action. In effect, and assuming the productions are well conceived and executed, the directors become engineers of peak experiences. They have used warehouses, gardens and empty schools, exploiting spaces that don't look like a stage, with unexpected performers meticulously choreographed and precisely fitted into the sound design.

One of their early shows, *The Moonslave*, ran for four nights to only four people. The audience member expects the performance will take place at a village hall. When she turns up, she finds the place deserted but full of two hundred chairs, a programme placed on each one. A phone rings. Hoping to find the reason for being abandoned, she picks it up. She is told her car is waiting outside. It is driven by a chauffeur behind a mask who takes her down country lanes to the sweeping music of Shostakovich. The driver pulls up at a large country estate. It is in darkness, except for a light at one upstairs window. The nocturnal journey continues, dream-like, past rows of still-steaming coffee cups and still-lit cigarettes. She arrives at a forest. The incidental music starts to assert itself, then she's confronted by two hundred smiling scarecrows lit in red by a marine flare.

The macabre element prompts a quiver of fear for the subject of this night journey: the mute and masked chauffeur suggests the horror of abduction, the empty but prepared village hall creates an unexpected bewilderment, and the phone call conveys a feeling of importance or immediacy to the vulnerable subject caught up in this adventure. The usually passive role of the seated audience, a crowd with safety in numbers, is removed. The subject is put on a stage with no borders. The event is lived, not just observed. The director needs to have the audience exposed, but also wants to enchant and thrill with incident and strange images, with something that feels dangerous. In this way the director choreographs and delivers his or her concept of a peak experience.

For some of the highs just described, neurologists might account for them through the commonly-known neurotransmitters, dopamine and adrenaline, the former supporting actions resulting from a reward, the latter increasing heart-rate and heightening alertness in response to risk.

For anything 'higher' than these addictive thrills, the consensus of orthodox science is that all is reducible to brain activity. Peak experiences can be fully explained by areas such as the pre-frontal cortex, parietal lobe and limbic system, which become active or close off, stimulation or cessation altering the way one apprehends reality. Since MRI scans can now pinpoint the activated or dormant areas, it is concluded they must be malfunctioning sites causing hallucinations. Neurologists have also examined patterns of blood flow in parts of the brain while the subject is meditating, concluding that reduced circulation in these areas must signal a stoppage of sensory input. The subject then interprets this as a dissolving of the margins of the physical. Scans providing these 'map references' for altered states of consciousness have led neurologists to infer that religious figures such as Jesus and the prophet Muhammad suffered from hyperactive limbic systems, or epilepsy.

For orthodox science peak experiences are anomalies. As the cranial sector is observed to be activated or in abeyance during the experience, that part of the brain becomes the locus of breakdown or electrochemical fault. What is experienced as blissful, elevated and inexpressible is interpreted as merely an illusion, in which the brain's critical faculties are temporarily idle.

These observations are all from the outside. The neural scintillation denoting the 'illusion,' clearly visible in the MRI scan, is not the experience. Thus it seems misleading, if not mistaken, to allow an objective assessment to be the determinant of a subjective experience. When a peak experience radically changes a life, to the extent that feelings of love and empathy begin to dominate one's outlook and behaviour, this is quite an achievement for a brain malfunction.

Peak experiences relating to psi have a different character, duration and significance to those induced by psychedelic drugs. Yet they share the common elements of altered perception, and the arrival of a state of oneness charged with meaning. Both are a temporary cresting of the normal flow of events, thus prominent and usually unforgettable.

I was once flying out of Auckland when the message was delivered—instantly. It was a hollow marble plinth opening onstage in the city below, revealing a young dancer. Having directed a group of young performers, this flight meant missing the show, the finale, after six weeks of rehearsals. The time was 12.10 pm, the synchronisation perfect for the denouement of their ten minute presentation that started at noon. During the aircraft's ascent this climactic, theatrical moment arrived—a body, hidden in the pillar, pushed four hinged sides to the floor, just as the prop was designed to do, and made a little magic onstage. The disclosure flashed a straight laser from the hall of young dancers, going straight through the plane like it didn't exist, and capturing my thoughts.

People have a deep interior that is intertwined with the fabric of the universe. A telepathic experience breaks into this usually unrevealed realm of linkages and meaning by instant, frictionless access. Psychedelics offer a means of entering that realm by widening the normal vibrational bandwidth. It should be fitting that a peak experience on LSD occurs at high altitude: the summit of Mount Eden, Auckland stretching away in all directions, the Southern Motorway running through Newmarket and further south like an artery carrying its corpuscles of cars, the urban organism curving into branches and tributaries, drawing in or distributing thousands of different drivers and their different agendas, and giving off a low roar like the rush of cells and platelets in plasma.

Such experiences seem to feed the mind's need for transcendence, as if the mind is instinctively aware of its own shortcomings and, restless for insight and knowledge, it tries to perceive reality from an elevated, non-human perspective.

Psi, and the effects of psychedelics and of all altered and peak perceptions, together constitute something so widespread and pervasive in human experience, it is necessary to investigate why they remain hidden in the shadows. To account for this situation, we need to investigate the Severed State.

The Severed State

CHAPTER 4

An Ever-Widening Rift

I HAVE ONLY BEEN TO PRISON ONCE. This was with a debating team from Northcote College, a mix of teachers and students preparing to face a talented group from Paremoremo Prison who, unsurprisingly, always hosted opposition teams on home ground. We probably lost the contest, but this wasn't the memorable part of the evening. What stayed in my mind was the directness and passion of this group of inmates—no social niceties, just an instant engagement with what mattered socially, politically and spiritually. Perhaps they saw the rare occasions of conversation with those outside as special opportunities, their removal from 'normal' society bringing *what really mattered* into sharp focus.

After that encounter, normal society seemed to me complacent, passionless and adrift. The common concern for the prisoners seemed to be: *What's the problem?* or perhaps: *How did I get here? What's the root of my offending and incarceration?* For them, their problem was more basic, more profound, than questions around socio-economic disadvantage, misdeeds from the wildness of youth, or even meditations on the nature of "evil". Without trying to account for the behaviour of every offender, I would contend that their problem reflects our long-standing, deeply-conditioned separation from the natural world—and each other.

This separation has its roots in the seventeenth century Enlightenment, also known as the Age of Reason, when religious beliefs were cast off in favour of rationality, and mechanistic science laid claim to the generative centre of the human mind, which was deemed to be the brain and its neurological network. Thinkers from the Age of Reason introduced the idea that human beings are no more than biochemical mechanisms. They saw the world as being governed by predictable laws, the operations of which are entirely external to us and blind to human concerns. On the other hand, it was a world that man (and they meant *man*) could measure, administer and control, creating machines to encourage nature to more efficiently surrender its resources.

The emphasis in all of this was on the material. Over generations of being conditioned to the materialist outlook, it has weighed down the modern mass mind, which in response has focused on the literal, mechanical, predictable, and at the same time moved away from what is inward and intuitive, from the aesthetic, imaginative and emotional. Distrust of the depth dimension of human experience, and a downgrading of its significance, is a malaise that I consider is best expressed by the term the Severed State.

This condition doesn't apply to all aspects of life. It is important to acknowledge the material comforts of our age, the widescreen televisions, electric toothbrushes, Google maps, heated car seats and remote garage door openers. There have also been improvements in basic hygiene, literacy, transportation systems, and in many areas of life. I am not referring here to the improvements to the quality of our lives. The Severed State has a different focus. It concerns deeper issues of personal and collective identity, how our collective psyche has been altered by degrading work, by an education system that has adopted a "learn to earn" approach, and by inequality, mental illness and other manifestations of social division.

How a mechanistic mindset began to dominate science is an interesting story and will be unpacked shortly. For now it is helpful to ask: what are the aspects of the modern world exemplifying the Severed State, and how do they compare to traditional societies where there was no such division? Could they be reversed if we could remedy this rift in our thinking?

During a visit to Siena I was drawn to enter one of those long-established boutique shops in the *centro storico* (historical centre). This had a varnished wooden door and elegant brass handle, with *Profumeria* painted in graceful gold lettering on the window. Inside, rows of bottles gave the impression of an old apothecary's store, the sort of place you expect to see an elderly gent in charge. But Paolo, the profumiere, was young. He spoke with authority about the traditional methods used to produce natural perfumes without a hint of the stink exuded by commercial varieties.

Sensitively-formulated scents were just the starting point for a conversation that drifted naturally into traditional societies of the past, where apprentices would serve their masters, learning a craft that took a lifetime to refine skills directly benefitting the community. This was good work. In Paolo's native Italy some shoemakers could still demonstrate the comfort and durability of their product by folding a shoe in half, but cheap imports were putting these craftspeople out of business, nepotism was reducing opportunity, and competition favoured only the big players.

Traditional societies pooled resources. They were supportive and close-knit, having what Paolo's countryman Julius Evola describes as two connected and complementary natures: a physical order and a metaphysical order, a mortal nature and an immortal nature, a higher realm of being and a lower realm of becoming. Traditional societies cultivated a constant awareness of the life-power flowing through both the human organism and the natural world. Human beings exist in the visible, material world; beyond it is an invisible, transcendent world that is the great Other, the Source. Simple physical existence is empty unless it resembles the superior realm, and an individual's highest aspiration is eventual liberation from the limitations of material existence.

Like my conversations with the inmates of Paremoremo prison, this exchange had far surpassed mere pleasantries. It seemed significant that the subtle whiffs of sandalwood and patchouli were part of the art form Paolo had chosen as a means of connection with the higher reality. The structure and ideals of traditional societies suggest that it is in our nature to do good for a community, that this is a necessary and fulfilling social role, but we have lost the sense of being part of an interconnected and caring human community. In traditional societies people participated in nature, had reverence for the land, and sought to harmonise with its inherent order—life was cyclic, self-sustaining. They had minimal material possessions but were rich in spirit, while our consumerist culture is the opposite.

Paolo referred to another aspect of the traditional world as described by Evola: space was considered to be vitalised, aether being the enigmatic, psychic force that infused it. Pleasant whiffs pervading the profumeria created the brief illusion that the aether had a fragrance, but Evola was alluding to a quality of light that varied in intensity from place to place. It followed that rites should be enacted in hallowed locales to enhance their power. By contrast, secular rationalism adopted a complete disregard for the qualitative and symbolic, because they could be neither observed nor measured. Being so installed in materiality, modern man has become incompetent at recognising or working with anything outside it. Higher faculties of intuition, figurative thinking, knowledge of archetypes and of nature's vital soul have withered, being largely irrelevant to modern urban life. Evola and his contemporary Rene Guénon lamented what had occurred, that traditional, esoteric knowledge had been overtaken by mechanism. Once the sacred had been expelled, profane science concerned itself with brute matter—the lowest, densest level of reality.

Our condition is now one of exile from the sacred, the Severed State expressing a kind of melancholy or not-at-homeness, arising from our intimation of a spiritual closeness not just lost but receding further each passing day. It persists as the smallest tincture in the bloodstream—the knowledge that we were part of this holistic order. Dislocation has taken its toll on our spiritual health. Mechanistic materialism has reduced people to mere existences with no sense of the beyond, lacking divine sustenance.

Fifty kilometres to the north of Siena was another indicator of the divide between the traditional and the industrial, the profound and the superficial.

I can guarantee, for myself at least, that there is a peak experience lying in wait in a room of the Uffizi Gallery in Florence. Booking is always necessary to avoid waiting in a long queue before shuffling shoulder to shoulder down the halls. On my last visit I was one of the first to get through the baggage searchers at opening time. From there I climbed post-haste to chamber 10 14, where I had an uninterrupted ten minutes with the Botticelli tondos, two portals through which spiritualised beings gaze mysteriously across a span of five hundred years. Once again the eyeballs drank in those images—meditative, beautiful, the soft-skinned figures composed in circles captured in the midst of a ritualistic choreography, each scene washed with rays of golden sunlight. Best experienced in complete silence, there was only the low rumble of air conditioners before the horde's advance.

An observer is necessary to complete a picture. For me, these paintings transcend the physical—they are informed by numinous reality, by the Other, each tondo supplying its own character in this genus of peak experience. Of course, many people are transported by these artworks, otherwise there would be no queue outside the gallery. But in the postmodern context of the Severed State, it is irrelevant, even embarrassing, to speak of beauty. Beauty is old hat for the contemporary art scene, being superseded by intellectual enquiry, the self-referential, the ironic. Exquisitely-rendered garments, lush detail and finely-honed technique belong to an older world of painters fulfilling commissions for wealthy patrons, their work dedicated to the spiritually inspiring. In today's consumerist techno-culture, artworks tend instead towards the novel, the analytic, the confrontational. Shock tactics have become a common response to the superficiality and boredom generated by our monetarised, spiritually barren Western lifestyle. The best of these works are powerful, brilliantly-conceived statements about society and the human condition and in my view they're high points in a huge field of expression that is otherwise dominated by the sensationalist, the ugly and the nihilistic. The best of modern artworks necessarily reflect where we are and what we've become. Where we are is in a spiritual void filled with shopping, social media, video games, celebrity gossip, and desire for wealth and status. What we've become is reflected in the rising rates of depression and suicide in Western countries. All point to one overriding problem in our culture and society: the absence of meaning or purpose. This absence has led to the existential crisis I am calling the Severed State.

It might seem that I am making a case to deal with the crisis denoted by the Severed State by returning to more genuine and uncomplicated past times, such as the spiritually rich, integrated traditional societies of the Renaissance, which created so many masterpieces. This is not what I am proposing, as it would fail to come to grips with the Severed State in the here and now.

Peak experiences are more relevant, as they feature an inrush of meaning, plenitude and unity. The aspirant is not simply looking for an adrenalin fix, but for expanded perception and a deep sense of relatedness. A peak experience may involve an epiphany, a meditative state, or a transcendent religious belief that gives us a sense of significance and wonder regarding our place in the grand scheme. Having such experiences is statistically proven to be conducive to a happier, more fulfilling life.

So far I have been considering cases of personal, individual experience. But let's imagine the effect on Western societies if, for example, near death experiences (NDEs) were generally accepted as fact. Materialist belief is that the death of the body is the death of the whole person—this is a mainstay of the Severed State. Alternatively, NDEs suggest that the death of the body does not mean the eradication of the person but their return to the spirit realm. This means that death is not extinction, but instead migration to another realm. Appreciating what is involved could come about by reputable scientists and the media acknowledging the significant number of NDE cases, publicising the features that are common and consistent to them, and giving credibility to experiencers' statements. What would this mean for the phantom in the skull, hovering in the brain's various neuronal precincts, condemned to eventual annihilation? What would it mean for the materialists' view that actions reduce to brain states, and personal extinction means nothing else follows?

It would be an understatement to say that this change in outlook would radically alter the mass mind. It would be tantamount to a public declaration of something that transcends the material world, that human consciousness possesses reality and permanence. We would then suppose our present embodied existence to be ordained, to have a purpose.

Let's also imagine what it would mean if paranormal abilities were considered normal. What if it became commonly accepted that the mind was not an illusion generated by neural coruscation, but a transpersonal facility operating outside the constraints of space and time? This revolutionary change would result from scientists' admission that sufficient rigorously-obtained experimental data has been assembled, and that it has provided irrefutable evidence of extrasensory powers. How would this change the picture materialism would sell us, of the tenuous human spook existing in isolation among the whirling atoms of an unconscious, purposeless, meaningless, insignificant universe?

Such an admission would show that there's no such divide, that actually people are intimately linked to others. Acknowledgement of psi as a normal human capacity capable of further development and control would affirm the primacy of consciousness, the ability for instant rather than processed knowledge, and the possibility of achieving greater empathy between people. In short, it would be a revolutionary change. Collective identity would be established through recognition of the field that seamlessly connects all minds. At the same time it would abolish the notion of an illusory, brain-based self severed from the outer world of real physical events.

Maslow's self-actualised human being would, in the above scenario, become the ideal to which people could aspire. Intuitive, self-assured, appreciative of beauty, morally principled and considerate of others, these apex dwellers on Maslow's pyramid would also aim towards an intensity of consciousness conducive to peak experiences. The self-actualised human being would replace the one the Severed State has instead allowed to thrive—the executive of external power who is associated with political, financial or social status, authorised by the evolutionary maxim that only the strong survive.

It was frivolously suggested by early advocates of LSD that the psychedelic be added to the city water supply. Irresponsible and impractical though the suggestion might have been (and the consequences unpredictably dangerous), the motive was public-spirited. They at least meant well.

In this narrative, assuming the dosage was perfect and all went smoothly, the veil of normality would have been lifted from the eyes of the populace, revealing the richer, all-abiding and ever-vitalising substrate on which everyday existence had been superimposed. Though many thousands of innocent drinkers would never have anticipated this alteration of their perception, would they go through it again, reproducing the trip by filling from the faucet the following day?

If the story did play out according to this mischievous fantasy, would the citizenry's collective consciousness truly set a precedent, the mass mind modified forever in a new and inward direction? Not only would there be a chemically-induced change, but also a mutually-experienced shift in perspective, a juicing of the perceived world and a refertilisation of the subconscious, everyone sensing and tasting its fresh fruits.

The rogue homeopaths' objective in making this admixture of acidified water would show the errors of the Severed State, instantly, from within, rather than by statistics, anecdotal evidence or persuasive words. How can the subject-object divide be instantaneously bridged, they may have asked, and how can the noetic quality of experience be swiftly and widely communicated, if not by going straight to the neuroreceptors?

Increasingly, modern secular society has left people stressed, confused and adrift, because they are separated from their spiritual roots. The plea from those who have paused long enough in their busy lives to realise it is that there is something of crucial significance in subjective existence, something our contemporary culture wants to deny or avoid. Evolving consciousness implies minds in sympathy, no matter the physical degree of separation.

What has been suggested regarding a widespread acceptance of the validity of NDEs and extrasensory power presents just two ways that a fresh and unrestrained growth in human psychic potential could be set in motion—and also potentially lead to a demolition of the Severed State.

It is helpful now to survey the rise of mechanistic materialism since the Enlightenment, to understand how this came about.

CHAPTER 5

Running Like Clockwork

AT UNIVERSITY I ENROLLED in a paper called Contemporary Analytic Philosophy. It was a bad idea. The approach was entirely logical and reductive, with a narrow focus on empirical, scientifically-confirmed facts, offering no open vistas of the speculative. I had been under the impression that philosophy is a search for the essence of life, a study or game where questions are more intriguing than neat answers. Analytic philosophers resolutely stayed away from any of that, fixing instead on language and logic that reinforced the empirically verifiable. But the world was already mechanistic and over-rationalised. Why make it more so? Shouldn't the best philosophy, the best science, question what we know and challenge what has become a standardised, scientifically-grounded view of the world?

Science has a long and illustrious history that dates back two thousand years, to the Greek philosophers, and beyond. But it was only during the Enlightenment that the scientific outlook, and its emphasis on the mechanical, came to the fore. This developmental path has been well-trodden by historians, but one less examined aspect concerns the desire to cleanse science of the irrational, removing all traces of instinct, conjecture, inscape, psyche, soul, élan vital, and other similar vestiges of the immaterial. The end point reached by this intellectual quest, which is much more widely known due to the writings of atheists like Richard Dawkins, is a godless universe.

I first noticed this in General Science classes at school, where study of photosynthesis and magnetic fields focused entirely on the proficiency of method and the reliability of observation. The conclusion we were supposed to reach was: there's the mechanism that dispels the mystery. Yet after class was over, I remember thinking the mystery had not been dispelled. Instead I was left wondering: *Where was the awe and reverence that such organisms and forces could exist at all?*

From our vantage point, four centuries after the Enlightenment, we can see it as a period that liberated us from superstition, from the dogma of institutionalised religion and unquestioning faith. Nature was desanctified, and the focus shifted from human beings being guided by divine forces to becoming arbiters of their own beliefs, conduct and advancement.

Sir Francis Bacon is known as the father of empiricism. *The Advancement of Learning* (1605) revealed him as the surfer who spotted the wave of reason just before it crested; he rode it into the seventeenth century. Baconian empiricism involved investigating the natural world using observation and experiment in order to produce reasoned conclusions. It subsequently provided the basis of the hugely successful scientific method.

Bacon accepted two sources of knowledge: divine knowledge acquired by revelation, and scientific knowledge acquired by disciplined empirical observation. For Bacon these two sources were distinct and yielded very different kinds of knowledge. Revelation provided insights into God's mind, while the empirical method provided specific observations from which general principles could be reached. Bacon proposed inductive reasoning be used to extract general laws from collections of observations. It was a pared down, practical alternative to then prevailing Aristotelian scholasticism, which relied on logic and ultimately sought to defend dogmatic positions derived from Biblical texts.

As the modern world shows us, Bacon's method was hugely successful. But it came at a cost, because it initiated a shift from the aesthetic strand of thought that also prevailed at the time, a strand that revelled in nature and the arts. Bacon's pragmatism proved to be hard-hearted: he decreed that instead of revelling in nature, humanity should fulfil what he interpreted as a directive from God and seek the means to control nature.

Bacon's approach signalled an epistemological change in how knowledge should be obtained. The legacy of the past was mostly discarded in favour of forward thinking, which promised advancement through reason. It moved from generalised deduction, which relied on uncertain introspection, to focused induction built on the certainty of observation. Nonetheless, while Bacon's building blocks of rationality were firmly in place, his position was still firmly theistic. More work had yet to be done to lock the nascent scientific outlook into its dominant position.

On the chilly night of 10th November 1619, the French mathematician, philosopher and scientist René Descartes shut himself in an oven-heated chamber to escape the cold. Lulled to sleep by the enveloping warmth, he eventually awoke and recorded three visions disclosed to him by a higher being. One provided a way to formulate analytical geometry. Another provided what became his most famous axiom: *Cogito ergo sum*—I think, therefore I am—consciousness being the one thing that cannot be doubted in experience.

This last led to his most significant contribution to the Enlightenment's new world view: Cartesian dualism, or the separation of mind and body into two distinct but mysteriously interacting entities. Since, in Descartes' view, the body and nature work as mechanisms, we need to think like machines to gain a dependable knowledge of the world. The best language for this approach was mathematics. *Rules for the Direction of the Mind* (1629) established a philosophical basis for the development of the physical sciences. Descartes considered matter to be the primary reality, with the body. The mind, capable of thought, had an independent existence without the body, but not vice-versa.

Descartes' cogitations, oven-heated into a newly solidified form, laid the groundwork for the Severed State, providing the philosophic engine that drove continental Enlightenment rationalism into the second half of the seventeenth century.

Sir Isaac Newton, the English mathematician, theologian and physicist, is widely acknowledged as the greatest scientist of all time. His laws of motion and gravitation, his development of calculus, and his work on the science of light and sound, generated unprecedented advances in knowledge. The precision and uniformity of his mechanical laws were welcomed as a practical alternative to Christian dogma.

The philosophers Thomas Hobbes, David Hume and John Locke, all empiricists, were contemporaries of Newton. Hobbes had a materialist approach to mental phenomena, Hume considered the self to be no more than a collection of sensations, and Locke rejected the notion of innate ideas. In line with these thinkers, and true to the spirit of the Enlightenment, Newton believed that knowledge of the universe could be gained by reason, in particular via the predictability and surety offered by the scientific method.

Newton's mathematics provided such clear, certifiable evidence that patterns in nature result from predictable natural laws that those who wished to maintain their religious views were required to assimilate their theological positions to Newton's discoveries. Yet, at the same time, Newton himself believed the cosmos had been set in motion by, and continued to be sustained through, a divine source. For this reason Newton could not accept the universal model of a predictable machine running like clockwork—a view adopted by many among the Enlightenment thinkers who embraced Newton's discoveries. They ignored the problem of origins, considering divine intervention unnecessary once the heavenly bodies had found their fixed patterns. For them, only present physical reality was under scrutiny, and it was possible to be as certain about it as about the gears, balance wheel and mainspring that determine the action of a timepiece.

These acolytes ignored the master's convictions regarding primary causes and contexts, favouring only his empirical findings. This is one instance in which the scientific community were selective in what they gleaned from the master. There are others.

For example, Newton refused to accept that the power of gravity was intrinsic to matter. However, his collaborator Roger Cotes contradicted this assertion, even managing to publish his denial in the preface to one of Newton's works, the interpretation then gaining general acceptance. Similarly, in 1675 Newton proposed that aether, a medium that transmitted energy between corpuscles of matter, must exist to explain action over a distance. There was a hostile response to this claim, for aether suggested the supernatural, and Newton's followers decreed "occult forces" were to play no part in scientific investigation—even though they had no alternative explanation.

As the scientist who formulated the laws of motion, it is significant that Newton held God to be the prime mover. This cornerstone of his famous and enduring canon is conspicuously absent from physics textbooks. He held a teleological view of the universe (this proved by what follows), believing that adjustments would be required by the creator to keep the cosmos on an even keel. On the other hand, Newton was no religious conformist. After studying the scriptures closely, he adopted a position at odds with an important part of the Christian creed, believing the worship of Christ as equivalent to the deity was false. This was a heresy he judiciously kept hidden.

An inventory of books from Newton's library showed that only about 20 of the 1750 volumes he had collected were concerned with his most important discoveries. More than a quarter of the library comprised books on theology, while another ten per cent were alchemical texts. He had an association with the Rosicrucians. This related to his extensive work on alchemy and his fascination with ancient wisdom, which offered knowledge of both the natural and spiritual realms. Newton's notes on alchemy corroborate his view about divine immanence, that the natural world is governed from within. These writings remained unacknowledged, like those critical of Christian scripture, until long after his death. Authorities of the time had severe punishments for those engaged in alchemy in case the philosopher's stone was found (it changes base metal into gold), resulting in the devaluation of gold's price.

Newton was also well-versed in architecture. He made studies of the Temple of Solomon, finding a building not only internally consistent and beautiful, but discerning in it a mathematical model of the relative dimensions of man and earth, set in a temporal framework. This shows Newton was as much a holistic thinker as he was a mechanist or reductionist.

While Newton made a huge contribution to science's machine model of reality, it does no justice to the man that his other interests have never been given equal weight. His acolytes gleaned only what they needed to feed the new machine paradigm. In this sense, their motivation was political, but probably the real driver was psychological. In a world of danger and uncertainty, reasoned reductive clockwork laws created the picture of a concrete and dependable world. Newton's belief in a mysterious, God-imbued universe, driven by alchemical as well as physical processes, removed these safe supports. Excluding the mysterious and intangible from science kept uncertainty away from individual minds.

From Newton's time, knowledge accumulated with remarkable speed—a testament to the success of science. The Industrial Revolution, which followed in the nineteenth century, cannot be separated from the Scientific Revolution, because it was in technological developments that scientific advances took physical form.

One important driver of the Industrial Revolution was Newtonian physics, as his natural laws were not just abstract theory but provided a fully comprehensible and practical system for designing and making machines. What used to be produced by hand was now given over to the looms, pumps and engines that are synonymous with the Industrial Revolution. With the arrival of locomotives, steel ships powered by steam, the electrical telegraph, and new weaponry (in England, in particular), no part of society could escape the influence of mechanised industry.

Each train that stops at a platform is an affirmation of scientific prowess. It is in the speed, the roar, the motive power, the weight of iron. Travellers hit by the wind of the arriving juggernaut feel part of the boldness and engineering skill that man could conceive and build such a thing. Thus we all became the wide-eyed children of technology.

Charles Darwin was the most prominent scientist of the nineteenth century. His version of evolution driven by natural selection consolidated a theory proposed by several predecessors (including Greek philosophers), supplying a mechanism for progressive physical mutation. "Survival of the fittest" is a four word summary of that mechanism, becoming a maxim for business, politics and society as the twentieth century advanced.

Evolution by natural selection explained gradual changes in organisms over time as an adaptation to their environment, which in turn could ensure the successful continuation of species. The theory dealt a body blow to the Christian religion, which claimed everything was created by God, the age of terrestrial life forms being no more than several thousand years. Science offered the alternative time frame of hundreds of millions of years. Evolution also removed the need for a creator, since life forms' advancement and survival was only dependent on successful adaptation.

Darwin's theory of evolution clearly still provides the best overall picture for biological evolution. However, it does not yet provide a complete explanation. The Neo-Darwinian synthesis, agreed after genes were discovered (Darwin suspected something like genes existed, but died before they were found), has had to fight for survival in the face of subsequent discoveries and changed perspectives. Problems that remain include:

- The tendency towards greater complexity and intricacy, as well as how matter became intelligent, remains unexplained.
- Survival in nature is not only dependent on competition, as Darwinians suppose, but also on cooperation, as evidenced by clownfish and anemone's mutual arrangement, and many other collaborating life forms.
- Evolution is a given, but according to some scientists natural selection is an inadequate explanation for how species evolve because it doesn't impose sufficient structure to give

rise to the complex organisms, and the communities of co-operating organisms, that exist on Earth.
- The human mind has far surpassed what is biologically necessary. We are driven to ask how and why this has happened to a degree far beyond what is needed to survive.
- The Darwinian scheme offers no explanation of what drives the evolutionary process, of what motivates everything to survive. Ecological systems have an inherent creative capacity, fitting with a more holistic view of nature.

The theory of evolution has itself evolved into a much wider picture than the strictly biological. Teilhard de Chardin, a paleontologist and Jesuit priest, considered that the universe is evolving towards an ultimate spiritual state, called the Omega Point. Drawing on de Chardin's ideas, author Carter Phipps[12] makes the case that culture, consciousness and the cosmos are all evolving. A new generation of thinkers from science, psychology, theology, philosophy and other disciplines, who he calls evolutionaries, have effectively joined forces to develop a much more comprehensive evolutionary vision.

Biological evolution is a given, but needs to accommodate new ground discovered across a variety of fields. Evolution is best understood as a concept, not a mechanism. It is a holistic system giving rise to progressive development and change, and thus meaningful and purposeful. We see the outworking of evolution in the Earth's ecosystems, but there is also an "involution", or deepening of consciousness as new ideas alter human thought.

Science has, and deserves, undoubted intellectual authority. It has improved our way of life in health, education, technology, recreation and other areas. As such, science itself is beyond criticism or disproof. Individual findings of the sciences may be challenged, but the scientific method itself remains unquestionably valid because of the practical results it has achieved—the proof is in the pudding. This is why it has enjoyed phenomenal success, and continues to work so successfully to broaden our understanding of the natural world. Yet it is important to separate the scientific method from beliefs that lie behind the sciences.

It is necessary to separate the process of enquiry from the institution. This is because the application of the scientific method reveals a fundamental problem. The problem is with the prevailing ideology behind science, mechanistic materialism. The success of the sciences has resulted in this ideology becoming a rigid model that excludes anything outside its borders.

The human-machine paradigm established by Descartes and his Enlightenment followers has become a concrete certainty. In the twenty-first century, its most refined physical expression is the smartphone. People configure their minds to its electronic pathways and liquid crystal displays as they sit in trains, on park benches, at the dining table, intimately stroking their screens. The idea has taken hold that the brain is like a computer, engaged in analysis and categorisation, using logic and making calculations. Yet if this is what thinking reduces to, then computers are already far outstripping us in performance.

That the brain is like a computer implies that the non-logical, intuitive and reflective mind can be dispensed with. From flywheels, intake valves, output frequencies, waste-gate actuators and inductively-coupled charge ports, to the realm of wireheads, aggregators, sync-ups, hyperlinks and clicktivism, we advance further into the machine. In the process we lose both our biological context and our spiritual inheritance: the sacred is supplanted by the profane.

Those people Carter Phipps identified as evolutionaries are questioning the dogmas of scientific materialism and its faith in natural law. They see those dogmas have created an Institution, whose tenets the Institution's defenders never want to be tested. They foresee the need for a radical renovation of the old edifice—and are ready to supply the scaffolding. Since our world is evolving, evolution must include ideas. The best ideas survive because they are practical, fitted to our current purposes and outlook, possess relevant intellectual rigour, and liberate us from the limiting ideas of the past. Alternatively, ideas fail because they aren't relevant, the tide of opinion turns against them, or because they are superseded by ideas that are better, fitter, more focused, and tell us more about the world.

Today the Institution of science is being seriously questioned for the first time in its four hundred year history. New ideas are being canvassed. New approaches to reality, that include both the rational material and the mysterious immaterial, are being explored. It is not that anyone intends to overthrow the scientific method. Far from it. Adventurous researchers are not adding new cogs to the old, tiring mechanism, but seeking an entirely new means of understanding it— by including the inner as well as the outer. It is this addition that the defenders of the seventeenth century mechanical, clockwork view of the world wish to halt. What are the politics of our time that keep those old cogs turning? They are the politics of the Institution.

THE INSTITUTION

In early 2018, an International Holistic Cancer Symposium was to take place at Auckland University of Technology (AUT). However, at the eleventh hour AUT withdrew its hosting of the event. The organisers had to locate a new venue at very short notice, being lucky to find a hotel conference room near the city centre. All the speakers at the symposium were trained scientists. But because of their alternative, innovative approaches they were also considered heretics by the supporters of mainstream medical science. According to one organiser I spoke to, AUT's withdrawal as a host venue was due to "vested industry competitors".

Several questions are raised by this. Why should an association with alternative modes of cancer treatment and research be so targeted? What are the powers who are afraid of such research? Are they only afraid of a loss of profits? Or of a loss of credibility? After all, when it comes down to seeking the best health outcomes, shouldn't all those who are trying to cure diseases and save lives be working together?

The answer involves telling a story of power and money. It is a story grounded in the Institution.

Numerous researchers, including those I have already discussed—Rupert Sheldrake, Dale Graff, Lawrence LeShan, Michael Pollan, Martin Buber, Abraham Maslow, Julius Evola, Mike Sosteric—are adding to our knowledge of the marginal zones of consciousness. Yet just as the Enlightenment thinkers had to defend themselves against the attacks of religious apologists, so those researching non-ordinary states of consciousness are being attacked by the defenders of scientific materialism.

Change is always slow. The gears of the old clockwork model haven't jammed just yet. The Institution of science has defenders who tenaciously resist any research that questions the exclusivity of materialist explanations. In part, they are protecting themselves, their work, their status, their funding and income. The Institution's key players are our modern-day sages; some work inside the circles of government and corporate power. This elite is primarily Occidental and patriarchal, the male sex who are associated with good sense and possess an incisive, analytical approach to problems. Their language is salted with the argot of high science—domain-specific asymmetry, the phospholipid bilayer and graded incoherence, in a world of cardiac perfusionists, phlebotomists and zymologists—which is only for the initiated.

The Institution does have its interrogators and correctors. There are those who challenge the standard paradigms. Yet challenges must be made within strict protocols. Any who step outside these protocols are censored. If they persist, they are discredited, then relieved of their positions.

Those who defend the Institution do so in many contexts, often without being aware this is what they are doing. These are the self-made men who, according to the Darwinian spirit, are the fittest leaders and decision-makers. If they have material wealth, then they deserve it. All this fits a neo-liberal culture of self-interest and greed, selfish genes providing a biological basis for the mercenary, amoral individual. Altruism and idealism have little traction in a neo-liberal culture.

The New Atheists are rabid defenders, attack dogs even, of the Institution. They dismiss religion as superstitious, that it advocates having blind irrational faith in crude pre-Enlightenment metaphysics, and, in psychiatric terms, religious believers have some kind of wish-fulfilment syndrome. Those who pursue more sophisticated enquiries, investigating depth perceptions and feelings with empirical rigour, are dismissed as practising pseudoscience, and as being deluded or irrelevant. The irony is that belief in the general scientific consensus has itself taken on the appearance of a religion, as they preach their materialist creed and singe those who disagree with rhetorical fire and brimstone.

Religion derives from the Latin word, *religare*, meaning to bind together. This is the basic understanding of the word: religion incorporates thoughts and beliefs that hold a society together, to which everyone conforms. Science has colonised the outer domain of life, but not our inner life of spirituality and perennial philosophy. Einstein understood this distinction when he observed that science without religion is lame, religion without science is blind.

Aside from its ideology, the Institution has a commercial and economic function, promoting consumer spending in a competitive environment, and providing profits for industry. I interviewed a doctor about this. He said:

> We have been influenced by pharmaceutical companies through inducements. They pay for us to go to these nice locations, feed us and pamper us, then expect some dividend by our being so impressed that we happily prescribe their product.
>
> We were purchased by a pharmaceutical company, a corporation. ... They were looking at us to apply pharmacy-type rules of business to our medical practice, but it doesn't work like that. Medical practices aren't a retail outlet. ... Basically, all the targeting is that you need to make a profit, whereas we had a different philosophy in medicine. We said, if you provide a good service you will always get clients.

> Medicine has gone from being an art form, where we were so dependent on our skills, listening, then what we heard and saw and felt played a very big part in how we would determine a patient's well-being. Now we depend so much on technology, on CT scans, and very elaborate blood tests. ... You gain experience from multiple contexts you've had with all sorts of people, and for me it's thirty-six years, you get a feel for what's happening, and no amount of tests are going to determine that. The younger doctors I work with order every test known to man on a lot of patients, when that's totally unnecessary. It's gaining nothing in terms of information. But you feel obligated to do it in case of potential litigation.

Pseudoscience is one of the convenient labels for scientists who think outside the designated square. It has also become an umbrella term for all the amateurs and charlatans: herbalists, homeopathists, dowsers, astrologers, shamans, acupuncturists, clairvoyants, naturopaths, faith-healers and various practitioners of dubious Eastern methods and medicines. Many of these apostates are involved in the health sector, their natural remedies and alternative therapies threatening the pharmaceutical industry and other business interests. Part of this is about profits, but more important is the doubt cast on the efficacy of allopathic medicine, that applied science might not be infallible in treating illness.

Demonising "false science" is equally matched with the promotion of positive stereotypes. For decades we've witnessed everything from pills and detergent to motor oil and toothpaste being developed or endorsed by an earnest, white-coated scientist wearing studious spectacles, surrounded by the clear authority of laboratory glassware. The writer Barbara Ehrenreich, who trained as a chemist, maintained that one of the purposes assumed by scientists (herself included) was to eliminate any non-human authority figures—spooks, ghouls, ghosts.[13] Anything supernatural was to be pursued and expelled from the clinical sanctum of the laboratory. The fear-inducing presence of the uncanny, what can't be controlled and doesn't belong in the ordered left-brain world, must be denied or annihilated.

This attitude also works against the prospect that religion and science could amalgamate to obtain a synthesis of outer and inner reality. Having no truck with the immaterial and transcendent, orthodox science refuses to acknowledge the numinous inner realm.

Writers have been prominent in the campaign for the promotion of science and the attendant debunking of religion. Perhaps the most notable of these is Richard Dawkins, the eminent biologist and former professor of the public understanding of science. A consistent but unstated subtext in his books is that science is synonymous with atheism, a view which, according to Einstein, already quoted, is both lame and blind. His book *Unweaving the Rainbow* was partly an exercise in damage control against critics who saw his Darwinian world view as sterile and dispiriting.

Unweaving the Rainbow is a quote from the poem *Lamia*, in which John Keats takes a light-hearted swipe at Isaac Newton for analysing a rainbow and robbing it of poetry. Dawkins claims that science finds poetry in the natural world, and proceeds to "unweave" other aspects of nature, looking for their statistical significance. Though trying to bridge the gap between science and the arts, he misses the point of Keats's dig at Newton. The response to nature through poetry is subjective and emotional, and this would explain why (in Dawkins' words) such high-flown language might risk "the postulating of faulty theories".

If poetry aims at anything it is emotional truth, not facts or hypotheses about the empirical world. By looking for the statistical and exacting, scientists are unversed (pun intended) in figurative language and the noumenal feelings that drive it. According to W.B. Yeats, poetry and religion are the same thing, a sentiment with which Dawkins is sure to disagree. He appears to live with a strange disjunction. On one hand his mechanistic belief proclaims a joyless universe of no design, no purpose and pointless indifference. He then characterises his atheism as a source of pleasure at the beauty of nature as revealed by science. Other thinkers maintain that when the "rainbow is unwoven" it reveals not just beauty but signifies a higher power. For Dawkins it signifies nothing.

The secular rationalism of scientists such as Richard Dawkins and Steven Pinker, and philosophers such as Daniel Dennett and AC Grayling, applies its own constraints. These are all reputable writers with broad thematic concerns, but some areas remain out of bounds. The astonishing implications of psychic research, the altered states of consciousness provided by psychedelics, and the widened perspective offered by Eastern mysticism, are noticeably absent from their agendas.

Another area where the implications for human consciousness are often conveniently bypassed is quantum theory. This is a subject we need to look at more closely.

CHAPTER 6

The Ultimate Scintilla

CLIVE PEARSON, ONE OF THE MORE inspired and alternative lecturers at the time I was studying philosophy at university, wanted to make a point about the limits of rationality. He wrote a large "S" on the whiteboard, then said: "Analyse that." The mind grappled for a starting point, then gave up, because "S" was clearly unanalysable. His point was that there were only certain things to which we could apply our rational faculties.

In practice, we learn about most things through experience, not via reasoning. Knowing that something exists, such as "that cumulus cloud", can only be ascertained by sense perception—we can't know about clouds by reasoning, independent of perceiving them. All kinds of statements and observations have meaning for us, yet are irrational. These include abstract ideas, like Joan Miró's brand of surrealism, metaphors, humour, and applying qualities—"she's in love", "that music is sublime".

This puts the Age of Reason into context: reason is just one aspect of an extensive range of human capabilities. Nonetheless, by the dawning of the twentieth century the Age of Reason had virtually become the Age of Certainty—yet all its assumptions were about to be challenged. The next great revolution in science, quantum mechanics, presented phenomena that tested reason to its limits.

In the 1890s scientists were seeking to understand the fundamental properties possessed by matter at the sub-atomic level. In particular, physicists sought to identity the micro-granule, the ultimate scintilla.

I am far from possessing any expertise in nuclear physics. My mathematical ability is rudimentary. But any enthusiastic amateur who is fascinated by its discoveries can learn about it through books that circumvent the forest of equations. One explanation that piqued my interest was a physics major interviewed on a student radio station. He said that if a baseball were blown up to the size of the earth, its atoms would be about the size of cherries. But in order to see the nucleus of one of those atoms, it would need to be blown up again to the size of the dome in St Pauls Cathedral in London, and in that space the nucleus, powerfully claiming the exact centre, would be no bigger than a grain of salt. There was a pause, then the DJ responded, "We know nothing."

With quantum physics, the certainties of Newton's classical physics were replaced with probability and indeterminacy. Potential realities were seen to exist as a kind of vacillating vapour that instantly coheres or consolidates when observed—that is, they are seen to have definite form by the conscious observer. The indeterminate nature of reality can be seen in relation to light, which has dual aspects: it can be observed either as particle or wave.

According to Newtonian physics, light is a stream of particles, or quanta. But an experiment by Thomas Young in 1801 instead proved the wave nature of light. Decades later it was found that both conclusions were correct. In Young's double-slit experiment, light was projected through two slits in a plate, producing patterns on a far wall. These patterns were considered to confirm the then current theory (contra Newton) that light is a wave. But in later decades subsequent experiments showed that when light is projected through a double slit, it can be observed to be acting as either a wave or a particle. By the end of the nineteenth century measurements were precise and able to be replicated, but classical physics was unable to explain light's contradictory behaviour. The solution was only achieved after Albert Einstein, Max Planck, Niels Bohr and others created the entirely new field of quantum physics.

A close look at the Canadian flag shows either a maple leaf in red, or two angry faces in white, glaring at each other. The white alternative was probably not foreseen in the design, but the leaf and faces are mutually constitutive—the botanical and anthropomorphic co-exist in this national emblem.

The same principle applies to complementarity as outlined by Niels Bohr. Objects have correlated properties, one of which is the wave-particle duality, but there are also such counterparts as position and momentum, energy and duration. These can't be measured or observed simultaneously. Like the Canadian flag, each side awaits an act of observation. Focusing on one of the pairs collapses the wave function into a definite observation. Before that moment, what has yet to be observed is only a cloud of probability.

The underlying condition for this choice of A or B is that we can't focus on both at once. Perceiving the maple leaf cancels the angry faces. Similarly, wave characteristics can't be observed at the same time as particle characteristics. Bohr's principle of complementarity says that together they present a complete picture: mutually exclusive, but jointly indispensable. And behind all this is the necessary presence of the conscious observer.

Quantum theory also introduced the concept of entanglement. The interrelationship of particle and wave indicates a unified state. This linkage can also apply between two objects, irrespective of distance. That one object can exert an influence over another at a remove suggests some mysterious conduit of communication, since there is no intervention by a third party. Entanglement implies non-local correlations between widely-separated systems. That this occurs was proven experimentally by John Bell in 1964; it is known today as action at a distance. There is locality for us as existents in space and time, but not in the substructure. Action at a distance points to a transcendent realm where place is meaningless and communication instantaneous.

Complementarity provides the theoretical basis for conscious choice—realising what is latent in perception. Far from being the isolated bystander observing from a distance, which classical physics proposes, the implication of quantum physics is that we are invested with full participation in electrified, interconnected reality.

Quantum theory was nothing short of a revolution in science. Yet the theory's startlingly paradoxical implications for our view of the world have been largely over-ridden by its practical applications—lasers, television, computers, and more besides. Why should anyone tie their brains in knots over the philosophy behind quantum physics when there is money to be made improving cellphones and building better, thinner, higher-resolution television screens?

Quantum mechanics is the science that connects the subjective and objective worlds. It suited orthodox science to keep subjective experiencing, fundamental to quantum physics, downgraded on the grounds it was at best unreliable, and at worst deceptive or unreal. Quantum theory reminds us that our view of reality has been so strongly weighted in favour of an objective world, leading scientists forget the living beings in the midst of it.

THE DIVIDED BRAIN

Who lit the lantern and what is its fuel source? How the brain can create or mediate consciousness is the crux of what has become known as the Hard Problem—how the brain's soft matter can create the immaterial mind. Another perspective doesn't rescue us from this central predicament, but it does offer a partial explanation of how we have fallen into it. This is the theory of the bicameral brain, which proposes that the brain divides into two hemispheres, each with its own kinds of specialisation.

In *The Master and his Emissary*[14] Iain McGilchrist delves deeply into these two mental rooms and their relationship to each other. His ultimate conclusion about them is incendiary. Identifying the main characteristics of each hemisphere reveals two sides of our nature: one possessing a disposition towards the objective and determined, the other towards the subjective and numinous.

The right brain has a global or holistic kind of consciousness which gives us the experiential overview we need to interact with the world around us. Research shows greater interconnectivity and more neural proliferation in this hemisphere. It is highly attentive, especially to what is new. It is also intuitive, perceptive of greater depth than the left, and specialises in those qualities distinguishing human beings from animals—music, art, humour, poetry, philosophy, spirituality and emotional understanding. Symbolism and metaphor are located in the right hemisphere, along with the facility for extracting implicit meaning and context from sense data, and for assimilating a range of input instantly and synthetically. It also houses the inner, ever-accumulating sense of self.

Language is primarily located in the left hemisphere, which facilitates organisation and categorisation. This is the everyday language of naming, describing, explaining. The left is administrative, arranging the world in a way it can understand. So it is also practical, purposeful and sequential. Reason belongs here, along with our proclivity for control. The brain's left hemisphere naturally prefers the mechanistic and uniform, so it is at home with electronic devices and the modern ordered, time-driven urban life.

Location of intellectual categories in the right or left hemisphere tells us not only how they are grouped into broadly similar characteristics, but perhaps why they are divided. Intuition is differentiated from rationality—forever, as far as the brain is concerned, with hard data forever separated from poetry.

Using McGilchrist's two-hemisphere theory, the Severed State can be understood as resulting from the split of the intuitive and holistic right brain from the rational, sequentially-oriented left brain, and the latter's dominance. This explains our progression away from a balanced, organic and connected world-view to an indifferent, artificial and fixed reality.

McGilchrist also makes clear with his model of the bicameral brain that we need both halves. The left hemisphere opens out, or extracts, unmediated experience from the right, making it distinct and unambiguous. But in the process, the left brain doesn't know what it is losing when adapting and ordering the right's rich rush of ideas. The left is only concerned with manufacturing a systematic and manageable interpretation of reality. In this way, the left brain's functioning is mechanistic, meaning it is appropriate to account for it by emphasising its neural functioning.

By contrast, the right brain's appreciation of symphonies and absurd humour seems as far from axon bundles and chemoreceptors as it is possible to get. McGilchrist notes that strangeness is anathema to the left, as it represents what cannot be controlled. Any greater or unknown power is better denied, given the difficulties that arise when trying to fit it into the already-established, prescribed system. For the right brain, however, the Other, the Origin, the Outside, is simply part of the whole.

With reference to neuroscience, psychology, philosophy, art, history and literature, McGilchrist's thesis is that not only is there an imbalance in favour of the left brain, but the left brain is *deliberately suppressing* the qualities and status of the right. This has become a collective psychological problem for Western society—it means we are unbalanced.

Because the right brain manages the world before partition and interpretation into particulars, it is the "master". The left is the "emissary", being the agent or messenger that structures our mentality so that we can organise our lives. The problem is that the emissary has taken its mode of reception and classification to be the only acceptable perspective. This is in line with government and corporate control, bureaucracy, technology, exploitation, productivity, specialisation and predictability.

It isn't difficult to discern the persistence and promotion of mechanistic thinking in the emissary's campaign. The systematising and control of the right's holistic conscious stream is reduced by the left's propensity for social governance and ordering of diversity into narrow conformity. The best advertisement for this standardising of behaviour is the techno-toy, particularly the smartphone and its algorithmic imitation of intelligence. Its convenience is obvious, but its familiar pathways and apps channel all users into the linear and sequential rather than into creative, integrated, holistic thinking.

The left brain has an urge to categorise. In social interactions, "What do you do?" is a convention of phatic communion, but it shows the need for pigeon-holing and assessment of status in someone's mind. International travellers often encounter "occupation" in the arrival card questionnaire. My father and his brother, on a flight to Sydney, decided to subvert this official craving for data by entering the entirely fictitious "Reverend" and "Tinker". Precise record-keeping has little appreciation of levity.

A picture can be painted of what our society would look like if the left brain continues its colonisation of our experience. The urban worker, ensconced in her high-rise, under artificial light, has her attention projected into the virtual computer world for eight hours a day. She deals with schemes, programmes, statistics and administration, with optimised reciprocal interavailability, integrated operational pluralisation, and concretised value-added configurations. Her work is invariable, and she is largely anonymous, a cipher identified on the corporation's database. The corporation's sole purpose is to increase the number of units throughput and maintain control of the process.

Through his focus on the bicameral brain, McGilchrist's version of the Severed State is one of disequilibrium, because both sides are necessary to function as a fully-rounded individual.

The right is the receiver of consciousness, the left the necessary converter. Right hemisphere consciousness is fundamental and unadulterated. It comes straight from the source, hence the right's strong affinity for what is Other. It possesses instant acceptance and has a natural openness to the extraordinary. It is interesting to speculate whether the right harbours answers to its secrets that our culture's increasing orientation to the left has made more difficult to access. Those secrets concern the right's mode of reception to consciousness before it is converted and specialised by the left. If Francis Bacon's *Advancement of Learning*, with its emphasis on material observation and rational thought processes, signalled the beginning of the Severed State, then we have had four hundred years of conditioning away from the right's amorphous, creative, unbiased, go-as-you-please domain. With the glow of awareness being more drawn to the organised complex of the left, the lights on the byways of the right are switched off and so that region becomes even darker.

Another outcome of increased left brain dominance is the externalising of thought into speech, a tendency that draws us away from the inner voice that assimilates our experience, and into publicly expressing our thoughts and feelings. The psychoanalyst presents a good example of this process, excavating the deepest motives and secrets from unconscious strata of the right brain then rationalising them in the harsh light of day using the left.

Wooed by the same rationalist orthodoxy as science, philosophy packed up and moved to the left brain, limiting its comprehension to the logical. It then laboured under the error that metaphysics (accessed from the hemisphere it had abandoned) could be submitted to reason. Through the passage of time it has forgotten that metaphysics is a set of eternal principles governed by the pure intellect, centred in the right brain, that benefits from wide context.

It is clear that a rebalancing of the two hemispheres requires a reclaiming of the free, which in turn requires recognising when the left brain is becoming a control freak, and making it learn to live with the attributes of its twin: the vast, the figurative, the wondrous and the strange.

Visions of the Apex Dwellers

CHAPTER 7

Sovereign Mentality

IN THE TELEVISION PROGRAMME *Outnumbered*, a father is shown educating his daughter about a basic principle of science: everything is made of atoms. With the insight typical of some child philosophers, his daughter responds:

"What about shadows, are they made of atoms?"

"Well ... "

"What about dreams, are they made of atoms?"

In the diversity of conscious life, we have faculties, feelings and propensities which seem to bear no relationship to matter as such. In one respect the daughter was (unconsciously) taking a swipe at reductionism, our tendency to reduce complex processes to simpler, often simplistic, material causes. But her questions also show how unpindownable consciousness is. While aspects of consciousness like imagination, emotion and willpower can be described, consciousness itself eludes both description and explanation. No scientific instrument can monitor or measure it. These facts notwithstanding, here is a rough sketch:

Consciousness is the flow and feeling of existence. It is our window onto everything. Both a source of knowledge and a reality composer with the self at the centre, consciousness has "reach" physically and mentally, locally and globally. It is a means of self-illumination from an unknown source, where subjective and objective reality are brought together, the whole condition of awareness pointing to higher states of awareness.

One time, when I was living in Tauranga, I was walking home from school and saw a vista towards Mount Maunganui that lodged in my six or seven year old mind. It was only a view of trees, sky and estuary, but some impulse made it move from the ordinary to extraordinary. Perhaps it was just a small push towards a widening of my mind, but the picture shifted away from physicality, taking on a feeling of mystery and promise that whispered something like: *This is what the road home has conjured. This is where you are. This is what you're in.*

As a child you know that everything is infused with mind and magic. It is only subsequent education that systematically sucks it dry. This process is explained by McGilchrist's model of the bicameral brain: the right brain's imagination, creativity and idealism are disregarded in favour of the left brain's certainty and pragmatic realism. Visions, dreams and play are supplanted by directed attention and practicality.

Consciousness is the lantern in the skull. It is the illuminist and orchestrator of experience. Not only is everything mediated through the psyche (mind or spirit), it is also neither finite nor still: it is always potentially on the verge of greater intensity or altered perception.

On the other hand, there's a tendency to constrict consciousness to routine, practical concerns. This is what the left brain does to the right brain's processing of perceptions. It is the standard procedure for an organ that receives and specialises consciousness that there should be an end in view for a measure of control over the world; but our minds are also hugely adaptable to fulfil new functions and adopt new perspectives.

Another angle on consciousness is suggested by *ignis sentio—I feel the fire.* The blaze of present experience is primarily visual, but it is not involved in perception alone. We are charged with life-power, which we experience as a constant current of sentience. This power is depicted on the Tarot card of *The Fool*, where the sleeves of a figure walking on a mountaintop in bright sunshine resemble flames. To some readers I need to say: don't panic. This reference to the Tarot is not to introduce fortune-telling or arcane divination by swirly-skirted gypsy women in dimly-lit fun-fair tents. Rather, I refer to the Tarot because it uses symbols and figurative imagery in an attempt to understand our sentient experience and the faculties with which we have been gifted. Kerryn Levy's book, *The Luminous Nun*,[15] provides an innovative application of this fascinating system.

The Fool is the first symbolic image in a map of consciousness that runs from 0 to 21, illustrating a pure, accomplished aspect of the self. Flames that break from the sleeves symbolise existence in the Now, feeling the fire of a higher consciousness. Schopenhauer's philosophy allowed the same recognition—that life is known to be a process of combustion, and intellect is the light produced by it.

Allied to ignis sentio is vitalism, the idea that organisms have an animating, vitalising energy or spirit, as distinct from purely physical or chemical energy. The physical body alone has no real congruence. Its essential element is life—an invisible dynamism. Without it the body collapses and decomposes. Vitalism is significant in evolution because somehow this élan vital entered the world when living beings first appeared, yet it can't be explained solely in physicochemical terms. Vitalism doesn't deny that organisms have a mechanistic aspect; it suggests there is something else acting in us as well, of a different order or dimensionality. Biology studies the observable variety of life, but it can't pinpoint the vital spark that animates life. In this sense, it could be said the answer to what conscious life is, and how it has arisen, lies outside empirical science.

The term *qualia* describes the features of conscious experience. In the constant, abundant flow of mentality, qualia are the particular attributes of every perception, emotion or imagining we register in that flow. It could be experienced in the way a planned action coheres in the mind, the faint scent of frangipani released into the night air, or the prickled numbness of dental anaesthetic.

When I was young I had an occasional "seeing stars" hallucination. Perhaps it was caused by my suddenly standing, and a rush of blood to the head resulting in several small moving meteors being etched into my visual field. Other times I "saw stars" they recurred in the same form—it was as if the same qualia were imposed from inside, onto the fabric of the outside world. I could never focus attention on one of them; they were sharp, but somehow out of range. As a child I read it as a special display; now it might feel ominous.

Everyone constantly shifts from one quale of consciousness into another, each intimately and confidentially occurring in a lifelong sequential ribbon, from the barely remembered to the deeply meaningful. I need just a few seconds listening to the Stone Poney's *Different Drum* to establish the song as a quale freighted with associations. All return in the replay as they were before, wrapped around Linda Ronstadt's vocals—some summer long passed away, some association with old friends, the singer caught in love the same way I was because it is in the lyrics, the same amalgam of happy and sad, a bounty of correlations carried in the sound. Words can't easily describe the quale of each one, because every experience is pure, personalised and particular.

To know, or to be sure of, qualia only requires attention or introspection—and as Descartes observed, the one thing we can be certain of is our subjective experience. So it should follow that the existence of qualia is undeniable. Despite this, the reductionist materialist view is that qualia are inseparable from the neurophysiology of the brain. However, this presents a special difficulty. If my brain is being monitored by an MRI scan while I am thinking of early Polynesian explorers in the Pacific, the MRI records my brain waves but not my conjured image of the canoes. If brain function and qualia were identical, wouldn't the scanner record the mental image of canoes among the little thundercloud of sparking synapses? Shouldn't they be inseparable? Wouldn't the mental image of canoes be superimposed over or pixellated among the axons and dendrites? Of course, this is a preposterous suggestion.

Anthropologist Richard Grossinger takes it as a given that an objective, scientific study of consciousness, focused on the physical brain, will get nowhere. In *Dark Pool of Light*[16] he sets the ground rules by saying that the process creating reality is invisible to its actors. He rejects the notion that by means unknown, the quality of consciousness miraculously emerged and transformed matter into a private interior theatre for its participants. Instead, this may only be explained by consciousness already being present in organisms. It is too much of a stretch to expect matter to transmute its molecules into states of awareness, when it had never possessed this quality before.

Moreover, there is a necessity in consciousness. The quality of being alive and conscious is what makes and completes us, just as the subjectivity inherent to it is what makes it so resistant (if not opaque) to study. Subconsciousness multiplies the problem of explanation a hundredfold, because its unrepresented components are so deep, and it is constantly performing operations below the level of awareness. The stream of consciousness of which we are cognisant is just part of a deeper flow that personifies us more comprehensively. Grossinger is convinced we are spiritual beings, but that this aspect of our being is maintained under the restrictions imposed by the much denser physical dimension we inhabit. He concludes that together these two aspects make us "physical-etheric".

The realisation that consciousness is integral to our nature is at the centre of the shift away from a purely materialist view of reality. In *Mind and Cosmos*,[17] Thomas Nagel shows that our accounts of the development of life, especially through standard evolution, are incomplete—because consciousness is left out of the picture. The natural world is organised in such a way as to produce beings able to understand it. We are rational and can be certain that the world has produced us, so it must have the propensity to produce rational beings. That this is latent in the nature of things is the most likely explanation for our existence. This suggests a teleological principle is inherent in nature, a principle that is also linked to our ethical awareness and our need for values: we possess them because the cosmos has produced them. Nagel sees this process—the unfolding of consciousness—as evidence that the universe is progressively waking up.

Consequently, a strong case can be made that the constituents of the physical world are also mental. This brings us to the concept of panpsychism.

One of the biggest problems for a materialist interpretation of reality is explaining how subjective consciousness, and its qualia that manifest in our moment-by-moment experience of being alive, came out of unconscious, purposeless, randomly-connected matter. Materialist theories that seek to explain this essentially offer variations on emergentism, the idea that in the beginning there were only physical processes and no mental processing. Not only does emergentism propose that hugely complex, interlocked chemical and biological systems "magically" came into existence entirely as a result of chance combinations, it has to do so within a time frame far shorter than what mathematicians have calculated it would take, and in at least one life form consciousness was "magically" instilled into biological material that was utterly devoid of it. This is the Hard Problem that all emergenist theories remain unable to explain.

Panpsychism offers the alternative view that mind is here because it was always here. Mind is ubiquitous, which resolves all difficulties. It has already been noted that everything perceived, formulated, felt or imagined, occurs in the psyche. From this perspective physical existence is secondary, reducing information experienced mentally to sensory phenomena.

The prefix *pan* of the word panpsychism denotes "all inclusive". The theory is that psyche, or mind, is universal. This makes panpsychism a holistic philosophy, in contrast to the reductionist approach of materialist science. Consciousness is a unity for the stag beetle, the octopus and ourselves as individuals, and each is a nested whole in the oneness of cosmic consciousness. Both stag beetle mind and all-encompassing mind are aspects of each other—the specialised with the general, the finite with the infinite.

Panpsychism interlocks with quantum theory. It proposes that there is just one kind of substance constituting everything, animate and inanimate. This means that at least some proportion of matter is living consciousness, and that there is therefore a close, creative relationship between the physical and mental, such that they resemble two sides of the same coin. Changes of state can be communicated from one part of the system to another, according to quantum theory. These are informational relations. With monitoring of information being an omnipresent feature of the microstructure of matter, consciousness should also be present at those levels.

Nature resembles an organism, and in its most complex, organised form, culminating in human beings, mind assumes ever-greater coherence.

I once found a book of IQ tests and tried three or four of them to see if there was a consistent score. The results did show a consistency, the disappointment being that my score was uniformly low.

> Which of the following geometrical solids is ... ?
> 46 people work in 4 shops, half of the people work ... ?
> What is the fifth number in the following series ... ?
> Which of these pictures is most like ... ?
> Which number logically follows ... ?
> Tom has a new set of golf clubs ...
> Fill in the missing sequence ...

In all cases, deductive reasoning was the keynote. It was a test of reasoning. Can an assessment of intelligence be made purely in terms of reasoning ability? The concept of intelligence is radically narrowed in the above IQ tests. They are actually only assessing left brain skills.

Last century it became a fixation among schools of mechanistic left-brain thinkers that a person's intelligence could and should be assessed. Typically, these left brain thinkers concocted assessment criteria that centred exclusively in their favoured domain.

In 1923 Edwin Boring famously defined intelligence as whatever the test measures. Since no two tests are exactly the same, any score produced is far from definitive. Also, the assessment criteria used by intelligence tests principally relate to our ability to conceptually order things. Social skills are bypassed because there are no rigid guidelines to measure them, while imaginative intelligence cannot be quantified or categorised.

One fundamental problem with intelligence is that no-one really knows what it is. One interpretation is: the ability to acquire and apply knowledge and skills. Behind this is the idea that it is advantageous for us to adapt to the changing conditions of life and environment. So in what way do matched symbols, completed numerical lists, and correctly-ordered pyramids indicate my ability to acquire and apply skills? For that matter, how can they assist me in forming relationships with people, telling whether a child is lying, recognising irony, understanding a painting, coming up with a business strategy, or resolving a dispute with a neighbour?

A rounded, comprehensive view of intelligence needs to take every aspect of human experience into account. The ability to acquire and apply knowledge must relate to our cultural, social, verbal and emotional faculties as well as the capacity to be logical and pragmatic. What this leads to is understanding.

A comparison between understanding—a quality central to intelligence—and abilities possessed by a computer such as language translation, decision-making and speech recognition would suggest that artificial intelligence (AI) is a convenient but misleading name. Despite the refinement of computer technology, none of its abilities imply any understanding whatsoever. The cyberfoe chess whizz only follows a programme and has no underlying desire to beat its opponent. Similarly, a computer doesn't know what irony is, just as a Geiger counter doesn't know what radiation is. Computers do not comprehend things or appreciate their significance. Rather, they process data according to an algorithm in such a way as to give a semblance of intelligence. Even a cyborg, the fictional human of books and movies physically enhanced by machine components, is built to look like a human being but has no knowledge, only data. Its façade of sentient mind really consists just of circuit boards and activated silicon slivers of memory put together by computer engineers. What's missing is a wet organ, evolved over countless millennia into ten billion cells and furnished with the power to derive and translate a non-local domain of consciousness for a fully-functioning human being. In all cases, to portray a cyborg onscreen, a person pretending to be one is required. The machine is not endowed with prudence or perspicacity, diligence or discernment.

Our consciousness is relational when interacting with others, empathy being the act of harmonising, of being "of one mind". For self-aware human beings, our individual consciousness can be seen in relation to the all-inclusive One in which we partake—an invisible, spiritual dimension beyond the five senses. I can describe what can be seen outside—the wind, the sounds of birds and a breeze through the flax bushes—but find it harder to describe the feelings they conjure up. Going even deeper, words can't be found for mental states, where the line between subjective and objective blurs, then disappears. Ultimately, there is just a state of being, with its endless possibilities.

The spiritual world view concerns a wholeness and permanence underlying everything. We are conscious beings in a collectively-sentient world, which itself is part of a mindful cosmos. As Rupert Sheldrake observes, spirituality and empirical scientific investigation can sit together, increasing our depth perceptions and the meaning we extract from our daily experiences.[18]

Given that scientific evidence and our personal experience of being alive affirm that mind is an integral part of the natural world, I propose it is time to reclaim it in the same way the Romantics did two hundred years ago (even if their attempt was short-lived), using art, literature, music and spiritual practices to restore our spiritual depths. Today, in the twenty-first century, part of this salvage operation concerns recompensing for the widespread cultural shift that has occurred into left brain thinking. A re-orientation is required, back into the demoted right hemisphere.

Important groundwork for that shift has already been laid, during the 1960s and 1970s, by a group of researchers and theoreticians who were drawn to Big Sur in California, bringing with them big new ideas regarding human consciousness and its extraordinary possibilities.

CHAPTER 8

Esalen's Luminaries

THE MOVERS AND SHAKERS in seventeenth century science were Bacon, Descartes and Newton. In the expansion of consciousness that took place during the 1960s and 1970s, many of that era's movers and shakers found themselves at Esalen, where they synthesised wonder and rational enquiry, and in the process created today's widely dispersed meme, "spiritual but not religious".

Established in California in 1962, an early mission statement read: *Esalen Institute is a center to explore those trends in the behavioral sciences, religion and philosophy which emphasize the potentialities and values of human existence.* This openness enabled Esalen to quickly become a place that equally welcomed psychiatrists and creative writers, scientists and mystics, encouraging them to expound and test ground-breaking theories that drew on diverse fields: the spiritual traditions of East and West, the implications of quantum physics, religious and mythological studies, and experiments with consciousness, sexuality, and the human body.

The reason Esalen is relevant here is that it was centrally concerned with consciousness and its exploration and development. Jeffrey J. Kripal's intriguing, comprehensive book, *Esalen, America and the Religion of No Religion*[19] explores the history of this remarkable centre of experimentation and learning. He considers reducing Esalen's ideas and activities to definitive statements impossible, but offers some partial interpretations: a Utopian experiment, therapeutic refuge, a place of mystical realism. It was a place at once sacred, sexy and slightly disreputable.

Kripal cautions that there is no specific Esalen philosophy on consciousness and energy. An equivocal stance is also suggested by Kripal's subtitle: "The religion of no religion". Esalen has been a religious group in the sense that a policy of free enquiry gave a common binding purpose and identity (the binding factor which is the original meaning of religion), but it was never a traditional religious group because no creed was ever specified. Freedom of thought was the keynote, Esalen's teachers, students and experimenters always having access to a smorgasbord of philosophies and techniques to satisfy their hunger for deeper knowledge.

Esalen was (and still is) a place where consciousness in particular was examined by eminent researchers. Yet the consciousness of those who participated in Esalen was equally significant—the community pioneered a broadened and deepened consciousness beyond the political, religious and cultural mindset of 1960s America. It has also been sufficiently fluid to survive more than half a century of cultural changes. Today Esalen hosts over seventeen thousand visitors per annum, and offers almost six hundred seminars.

Esalen was founded by Michael Murphy and Dick Price, and was physically established on one hundred and twenty-seven acres of land owned by Murphy's family at Big Sur. Esalen took its name from a tribe of Indians inhabiting the area. Murphy and Price first met in 1960, at the Sri Aurobindo Ashram Cultural Integration Fellowship in San Francisco. It could be said that, through this meeting, Aurobindo became the spiritual father of Esalen. Whether this is a fair claim or not, Aurobindo's spiritual legacy became hugely important, much of it adopted and adapted by Michael Murphy in his thinking and writing, and so incorporated into Esalen's credo.

An Indian philosopher, Aurobindo studied at Kings College, Cambridge, before returning to India and becoming embroiled in the politics of independence. He was imprisoned (though acquitted of any crime) and during his incarceration had mystical experiences that shaped and inspired the rest of his life. In 1926, with Mirra Alfassa, he founded an ashram in Pondicherry.

Aurobindo was deeply influenced by Shankara's Vedanta, which holds that Brahman (the Absolute) is the ultimate reality, outside space and time. Brahman is experienced as being, consciousness and bliss. What we perceive in the world is real, being generated by Brahman for all to benefit from and enjoy. Aurobindo considered the natural world has been imbued by Brahman with evolutionary purpose. In the distant past, life evolved from matter, then consciousness from life. Where Darwinism describes the evolution of life by natural selection but offers no explanation, according to the Vedanta evolution is the means by which the One Ultimate Being liberates itself. Man, a combination of matter, vital power, intellect, feeling and soul, has a purpose—to discover Brahman through self-knowledge. We are not alone in this quest. All existence is urged upwards to the heights of the Supermind, towards attainment of the *corps glorieux*. This "supramental" state will bring to humanity a complete self-discovery, a full manifestation of divine love, knowledge and power. This will be the future "life divine".

Aurobindo is emphatic that homo sapiens is at just one stage in a progression towards far greater transformation—a coming to life out of matter and into mind, with the potential to ascend into even higher spiritual planes of consciousness. Part of Aurobindo's uniqueness as a theorist is his historical overview, re-working the early outlook of Hinduism into a vision of the future.

Michael Murphy studied at Sri Aurobindo's ashram in Pondicherry from 1956 to 1957. He was especially inspired by Aurobindo's perspective on human evolution—an alchemical transmuting of the body from a finite, fleshly state to an enlightened, immortal one. Put in more general, pragmatic terms, he co-established Esalen to investigate and realise our hidden depths.

Murphy's co-founder, Dick Price, arrived at the same philosophy by a different route, after having heard a lecture delivered by Aldous Huxley in 1960 on the huge and underutilised fund of human consciousness and vitality held in check by the strictures of Western culture. Wishing to challenge this constricting Western view, Murphy and Price's collaboration focused on the unfolding of man's essence, in heart, mind, body and soul.

For Aurobindo, human society was about an incessant intercourse of ideas and energies, mostly subliminal or telepathic, but muzzled by old forms of thinking. It needed to be found and freed. This psychic potential was embraced by Murphy and Price, then elaborated through the academy and in their individual work.

Murphy has a passion for sport. At first sight this may appear out of keeping with the intellectual and mystical focus of Esalen, but that would underrate the capacity of sport to develop body and mind, as well as its ability to excite. For Murphy, golf is both invigorating and meditative. Something far more than simple recreation, it contributes to a person becoming a fully-rounded human being. The more time Murphy spent on the fairways, the more he gleaned.

In 1992 Michael Murphy's seminal *The Future of the Body* was published. In it, Murphy contends that human beings have already far outrun evolution as stipulated by the incremental change of natural selection. Such disciplines as meditation, martial arts, sport and spiritual practice are forms of self-discovery that move their practitioners closer to the Supermind.

Esalen's luminaries came to their own understanding of Aurobindo's Supermind by different routes. For some, the road to discovery was LSD, the trips bringing the realisation that our spatio-temporal system is an illusion and the world of spirit, boundless.

Stanislav Grof is a Czech psychiatrist who lived at Esalen with his wife Christina for fourteen years. When the Soviet Union invaded Prague in 1968, Grof, who was then researching in the U.S.A., was ordered back to his home country. He chose instead to remain in the U.S., where he worked as a professor of psychiatry. In 1973 he met Michael Murphy, who offered him a position at Esalen to continue his research and writing. This would prove advantageous to both the institute and the scholar. Grof found an environment highly conducive to his investigations, which eventually explored psi, perinatal experience, transpersonal psychology and psychedelic research. Over the years, Grof made an invaluable contribution to the development of Esalen's understanding of human potential.

It was research into LSD during the 1950s that established Grof's standing in science and medicine.[20] He oversaw hundreds of experiments with LSD while a young doctor and psychoanalyst in Prague. The deep experiences his patients reported having intrigued him, and when he had the opportunity to experiment with LSD himself, the result was a life-changing experience that proved to him the psyche is deeper and more fundamental to existence than his Freudian training had indicated. He continued clinical research into entheogens (psychoactive substances that open the mind), discovering that LSD in particular gave unprecedented opportunities for therapists through its ability to amplify mental processes. When LSD was banned, he developed the techniques of holotropic breathing to induce similar states of heightened awareness.

As a result of his experimental research, Grof became convinced the brain is a mediator of consciousness, and not its source. Nonordinary consciousness, whether induced by psychedelics, holotropic breathing, or by stirring music or meditation practice, can permanently change the experiencer, fostering deep healing and rebalancing. In Grof's psychology, the unconscious stretches back beyond one's birth to past life experiences, and it includes archetypal and mythological figures—a vast symbolic realm deeper than the deepest soundings made by explorers of the psyche. The experiences of numerous workshop subjects suggest proto-consciousness goes as far back as the Big Bang.

Among Grof's most significant contributions is a mapping of psychic spaces that he has identified through his fostering of healing and mystical experiences. As he explains in the introduction to his website: *We need a much larger cartography of the psyche ... the trans-personal overlaps with the idea of the collective unconscious. Until these changes are introduced into psychology and psychiatry we will have a very superficial understanding of emotional and psychosomatic problems.*

As noted earlier in relation to psychedelics, Grof insists that the insights and transformation they offer are experiential. They cannot be known or encountered secondhand. He relates his work to the mystical Indian view that life is a play of consciousness. Extra-ordinary or intensified consciousness floats us out of our individual bay of awareness and into an ocean of possibility and difference.

Another of Esalen's eminent personalities helped to bring Aurobindo's evolutionary mysticism to a new generation. The English philosopher Alan Watts moved to America in 1938. Working on links between Christian scripture and Eastern traditions gained him a university degree of Master in Theology, but he soon turned away from organised religion, disliking its formality, inflexibility and evangelising. Subsequently, it was for his teaching of Eastern wisdom that he became most renowned.

Eloquent, informed, confident and entertaining, Watts's unpaid work as a broadcaster and lecturer placed the man in his element. He synthesised many areas of study, including Zen, western philosophy, natural history, Vedanta, Jungian psychology and quantum physics, presenting them with clarity and humour. He was acutely aware of the average American's estrangement from the natural world and advocated the cultivation of an aesthetic sensibility as one remedy, among others. Though a self-confessed hedonist, he was sceptical at first about the alleged power of psychedelic drugs (especially as reported by Huxley). On the other hand, he was always open to new experiences. He tried LSD, mescaline and psilocybin, was won over by the insights and creative stimulus they engendered, but refused to over-indulge: "If you get the message, hang up the phone."

From the clean-cut priest with his suit and tie in 1945, Watts progressed to a looser, Bohemian persona of his later life: long hair and a beard, strings of beads around his neck, and a curved pipe held to his mouth—the perfect costume for a sage of the sixties counterculture.

He would see this later version of "Alan Watts" as the embodiment of one game the cosmos was playing, one of the more unusual definitions of a human being. His pantheism describes the One Self hiding from itself by becoming a myriad of creatures—a deliberate forgetting of its true or original nature. At the same time it is implied that every sycamore, blenny, swallow, wombat, king and pauper is the Cosmic Self. If this is one answer to the perennial Why? question, Watts's second answer would be that life is an exuberant dance, and our spatio-temporal reality the playground.

In his very explicitly titled *The Book on the Taboo Against Knowing Who You Are*,[21] Watts makes the case that it is human beings who have forgotten who or what they really are, and that our ego-driven, materialist, technological society will eventually destroy our living environment. The cure for this ignorance is to realise our true, interconnected identity: "You are that vast thing that you see far, far off with great telescopes."

Watts was acutely aware of mankind's predicament, that we see ourselves as the accidental spawn of a cooling rock, so we have every right not to feel at home. He counters this wrong-headedness by the simple observation that, on the contrary, we must be absolutely of the Earth, the fact of it being best expressed verbally: Just as the Earth apples, it also peoples.

Watts made poetic interpretations of the quantum revolution, describing the energy of matter in terms of mobile patterns—intelligence in operation. He was very taken by the patterns in nature, sometimes using natural forms like seashells in his lectures to display the beauty inherent in the world. The shell as artefact, illustration, geometrical model and one-time living thing, ties in with Aurobindo's philosophy that all these natural things are imbued with consciousness. It follows that nature is essentially divine, and that realising this in both the inner self and outer world constitutes our highest purpose.

This holistic view of nature is common to all of Esalen's luminaries, even though their intellectual frameworks were at variance. For one of them, Gregory Bateson, these patterns and systems applying across the natural world were arrived at by "a vague mystical feeling". A British anthropologist, social scientist and linguist, Bateson married the eminent American anthropologist Margaret Mead in 1936. They subsequently undertook fieldwork in the South Pacific. In 1956 Bateson became an American citizen, remarried, and spent the rest of his life in the United States, spending his final two years at Esalen.

Bateson came to see that processes applying to natural phenomena in one area could apply across the board, the same principles bearing on the structure of a crystal as they do to a society, or the divisions of the earthworm applying also to the incremental growth of basalt pillars. This holistic view could also pertain to fields of study—that modes of thought from physics and chemistry could usefully be employed in other avenues of enquiry.

In *Steps to an Ecology of Mind*[22] Bateson identified three distinct but interdependent systems: the individual, societies, and ecosystems, competition and dependency being common to each. Holistically, these systems all belong to a paramount, overarching system (in terms of communication and control) which Bateson calls Mind. Consciousness is the link between all systems, and it was in relation to consciousness that Bateson considered the Western model of reality to be dysfunctional. He identified scientific arrogance as the core of the problem, with its linear, sequential left-brain thinking, the standard reductionist approach following rigid rules and wilfully ignoring wider contexts.

This Occidental attitude puts man outside Mind, where he has an authoritarian reign over nature, taming it to suit his own ends. Although Bateson didn't state his case in terms of the bicameral mind, his advocacy of art, emotion and a spiritual perspective as a means of rebalancing our narrowed perception affirmed the significance of right-brain qualities. His underlying view was of complementarity—promoting an understanding of all environments as involving holistic processes, and that they should not to be reduced to linear constructs.

Aurobindo's writing inspired Esalen's luminaries not just through his passionate search for the depths of human identity, but through the empowerment to do something with this self-knowledge—to make it manifest in an evolving world.

Fritjof Capra understood the scale of this evolutionary movement, and expressed it through the complementary opposites of yin and yang. He viewed the required shift in thinking as being from yang's masculine values of control, competition and rationality to yin's feminine qualities of synthesis, intuition and cooperation.

Capra was born in Austria where he completed a PhD in theoretical physics, then moved to the University of Paris in 1966 to conduct research in particle physics and systems theory. He later moved to the United States, arriving at Esalen in 1976. He acknowledged a debt to Stanislaw Grof and Gregory Bateson in his book *The Turning Point*.[23] Following the holistic approach that characterised Bateson's work, Capra's book presented perspectives on psychology, economics, ecology, feminism, medicine and technology to illustrate the crisis in society and outline a paradigm for change.

Capra was among the scientists who reasoned that consciousness is inherent to the universe and necessary for understanding natural phenomena. The systems view of mind he presents accepts the standard neurological perspective that consciousness is an expression of complex material patterns. Yet further to this, the biological structures involved are part of the system's organisation and therefore part of its mind. This makes the biological structures secondary to a wider, governing mentality. Capra holds this to be equally true of the macrocosm—whether we view the minutiae of the atomic world or whole galaxies, amoebae or a herd of wildebeest, all equally evince the "self-organising dynamics" of the cosmos, behind which is Mind.

An interesting observation for the post-materialist age is Capra's view that a science of consciousness would need to dispense with observation and measurement. It would need to focus on quality rather than quantity, and only be found and described in terms of mutual experience.

The "rising culture" of the seventies held the prospect of change to a more integrated, civilised, caring and peaceful society. If only.

CHAPTER 9

The World Behind the World

THIS BOOK BEGAN WITH AN ACCOUNT of fetishes in West Africa, demonstrating their protective power. I also described how the phrase "Big John has sent us" became almost a magical incantation that took us deep into the byways of African culture. My friend Seydou, a Malian trader who sold African artefacts in a shop in Auckland, is "Big John". True to his word, just uttering his name in the seething crowds of Bamako guaranteed a connection for onward travel.

Seydou gave me another insight into the forces operating in this time-honoured land, where everyone lives much closer to the marginal zones of the extraordinary, and where people willingly accept that different principles of reality apply. Here is his account of a marginal incident that involved his brother:

> A farmer was digging by the Niger River and found some ancient pottery underneath, buried. When they broke one pot they found eight statues inside, bronze figurines of animals—buffalo—that existed in Mali a long time ago.
>
> Later my brother, Abdoulaya, helped the villagers shift the statues to Bamako. It was between Segou and Bamako, evening, around 4.00 to 4.30 pm. My uncle Madou was driving, and Abdoulaya was with him in the minivan with two other passengers, hitch hikers they had picked up.
>
> Suddenly, this black cat or leopard—my brother said a black

cat—was following the car. It jumped over the roof and broke the driver's window, trying to get in. Madou tried to grab the cat by the neck, and because he was driving he lost control of the van. It rolled over and the cat disappeared. No-one saw any trace of it.

Madou broke his arm and was badly injured. And they didn't find any trace of the statues. Straight after the accident everything just disappeared—eight heavy statues. So the mystery was, according to villagers in that area, that the black cat was a guardian of the statues. That was their version.

Over the last century, sightings of black leopards have been reported throughout Africa, but they are very infrequent. This rarity adds to its mystique, making it a cat steeped in legend. The incident that Seydou reports happening to his uncle and brother reinforces the mystery. When I first heard the story, I was struck by how perfectly it hovers at the intersection between two worlds, an intersection that manifests in different ways: as present and past, as human and animal, as everyday and supernatural, as profane and sacrosanct, as explicable and unexplained. It is a story that illustrates what happens when the marginal edges into the centre of our consciousness. It is a story that prompts us to ask where the centre and the margins of our perception really are.

Are the centre and margin separate, as we normally conceive of them? Or do they change places? Incidents like a negative turning out blank when photographing fetishes, or having a psychic insight that tells us a thief is about, or feeling that a loved pet has died, or being overwhelmed by the unlikely arrival of a black leopard, immediately followed by the disappearance of ancient statues—to what extent are these events not marginal at all, but really just the inside and outside of a single event that mysteriously fold into each other, giving us a tantalisingly brief insight into the ways that what we think of as alternative aspects of reality actually reflect the way reality is constructed?

According to quantum theory, there is a hidden coherence to the universe, which exists beyond objective reality. How much more than just the physical basis of our existence is hidden from us? It is undeniable that a broader, changeless realm of meaning contains cultural influences different from our own. For example, Abdoulaya's account, as relayed through his brother Seydou, concerns loyalties expressed through animal spirits, belonging to a distinct geographical locality and its people. The Source, the Akashic field, the implicate order, the non-local domain—however we refer to it, this is the invisible yet elephantine presence in the room. For those open to its existence, it can't be ignored any longer. Quantum theory is centred around practical applications, while philosophical and conceptual implications are usually relegated to the too-hard basket. But scientists advocating the shift to a post-materialist paradigm have drawn the elephant from the margins and situated it in the centre of their intellectual outlook.

In February 2014, an international summit conference in Arizona, USA, brought together scientists from different fields—medicine, psychology, neuroscience, biology and psychiatry. Their intention was to examine the influence of materialism on science and society, and to offer an entirely new paradigm. The reason they saw this as necessary was because their own research had produced too much data that did not fit within the strict parameters of scientific materialism. They had witnessed too many anomalous psychological and physical events that, in common parlance, are described as "weird". It had become clear to them that reductive, analytic science was not able to explain what was occurring—which meant its four hundred year reign was coming to a close. Yet they didn't want to overthrow the sciences. They are seeking to establish a new holistic paradigm for the sciences, that acknowledges the observational, empirical basis of the scientific method, but that uses it open-mindedly in conjunction with a composite, seamless, unified model of reality.

Those who proposed this new paradigm are Mario Beauregard, Gary E. Schwartz and Lisa Miller (all psychologists), Charles Tart (parapsychologist), Larry Dossey (medical doctor), Alexander Moreira-Almeida (psychiatrist), Marilyn Schlitz (social anthropologist), and Rupert Sheldrake (biologist). Each has a PhD, has held professional roles within the institutions of the academy and the sciences, and each has become dissatisfied with the limitations of a purely materialist approach to reality. It is a dissatisfaction shared by many other scientists, most notably as expounded by Thomas Nagel in *Mind and Cosmos*.

These scientists' *Manifesto on Post-Materialism* states that the "nearly absolute dominance of materialism in the academic world" has not only impeded scientific progress, but has placed restrictions on the study of consciousness and spirituality. It also states that mind is unbounded, and that it works through the brain, but is not produced by it, and that mental events can affect the physical world. The post-materialist position accepts the findings and achievements of empirical science, but is committed to a broadening of outlook that allows the study of mind and spirit, since it is part of "the core fabric of the universe". The initiative also affirms the interconnectedness of all life, and the evolution of humanity into a new condition of social cooperation, of environmental awareness, and of stewardship of the planet.

The change they advocate will be from a narrowly-focused stagnating science to an open-minded, revolutionary science, a shift that will lead to a radical altering of our entire world view. If the new paradigm takes hold, that is, if it can unseat the high priests of institutionalised science, the change in thinking will be commensurate with the shift from thinking the Earth is flat to appreciating our planet is a globe. As the authors of the *Manifesto* assert: "The shift from materialist science to post-materialist science may be of vital importance to the evolution of the human civilisation. It may be even more pivotal than the transition ... from a geocentric cosmos to a heliocentric one."

Conventional psychology has to expand into the post-materialist paradigm, given its reductive, mechanistic principles are of little use in the study of subjectivity, psi, psychedelics, meditation and peak experiences. In the shift from normal to supernormal, time, space and causality are transcended. The new approach needs to look into the world with open wonder. Ultimately, a mystical viewpoint is essential to this re-orientation.

Another way of describing the required re-orientation is to appreciate that everybody exists in the middle of an infinite sphere of space. No conscious being experiences from the periphery—he or she, prince or pauper, oryx, dotterel or weta, is a centre of awareness that possesses a unique perspective. The centre is the same in every case: the one and only personal, intimate life-power.

Sometimes I think of this while looking at our guinea-fowl, trying to imagine the weirdly-energised mind behind that small head cased in stretched white rubber, with its orange wattle scoops and bony crest. It's the One Mind drilling through the eye of that strange, strutting African-avian portal. Surely there is an exuberant sense of humour behind this?

Human beings learn to negotiate the inner and outer domains of experience, sometimes reaching a balance of subjective and objective. Science has extended our reach into the outer world, which comprises the very large and very small. We can see images of the tracks left by sub-atomic particles in the CERN accelerator, and images of galaxies thousands of light years away. But, at the same time, we float on a vast subconscious ocean where the personal turns into the universal—a fluid realm, dynamic and unbounded, that altered perceptions, and intensified or peak experiences, can render frightening or fascinating.

Non-ordinary experiences challenge our commonly-accepted basis of knowledge. People find it hard to accommodate what is contrary to their acquired beliefs. The effect brings strangeness, disorientation and insecurity, so this mental territory is garrisoned and guarded. Few people are willing to turn their receiving dishes into the cerebral gulfs for impulses from its nether regions. They're uncomfortable with the idea that mind extends beyond the brain, that it escapes containment. For materialists, the brain is the fulcrum, the physical ground from which the phantasm of mind leaps. Without the brain there can be, there never is, any mind. In contrast, many of those who consider mind to be irreducible have begun viewing the brain as a reducing valve, constricting the incoming flow of information. In this sense, the brain can be seen as a reality composer, which receives and processes consciousness. The reality composer reduces the wider stream of consciousness, providing the stability necessary for us to function in the world.

But our reality composer isn't fixed. It is open to alteration. As Sheldrake and his fellow post-materialist scientists have observed, by the facility of the will alone neural changes can be brought about in the brain. Studies of the hypothalami of a group of London taxi drivers showed enlargement consistent with their encyclopaedic knowledge of the city's streets. Similarly, the left brain hemisphere in songbirds is known to expand during the mating season; it returns to normal size when mating season is over. Intention calls the tune, and the reality composer adapts.

Our personal mind also closes down or opens up according to our intention. In *Prophecy on the River*,[24] Judith Hoch offers personal testimony to her gradually expanding view of the Nelson landscape as she and her husband sought to replace dairy pasture with native trees. Over the years, she became aware that other, non-embodied presences were also concerned about the poor state of the land, that the environment possessed a spiritual dimension, and that a deep energy flowed through it all. She uses the concept of veriditas to suggest the all-abiding principle or force that infuses the cosmos and that manifests in the landscape. It takes an expansion of mind to allow such perceptions to become possible.

As discussed earlier, the mind-augmenting powers of psychedelic drugs have drastically altered psychology and psychiatry, providing insights into the creative processes of thought and carrying the promise of previously undreamt therapeutic potential. *Handle with care* has been the unwritten rule for these substances. Not everyone is going to opt for a descent into their own subconscious catacombs; for some trippers there is definitely neither joy nor light in the experience. Yet researchers have found that psychedelics can induce long-lasting changes in the user's state of mind.

Paranormal experiences have also forced a significant shift in thinking. Telepathy and NDEs imply both altered perceptions and the accessing of a normally inaccessible metaphysical system. The former corresponds with the latter. For those with the ability and conviction to operate in marginal zones, the results have compelled the establishing of a new model of reality, as proposed in the *Manifesto on Post-Materialism*.

Post-materialist thinkers affirm interconnection. They share a shift in thinking away from societal regimentation and control towards a deeper, empathic relationship with the natural world. This is helpful, given the change of attitude advocated by Iain McGilchrist, of releasing the creative, empathetic right brain from the culturally approved dominance of the administrating, serially-minded left brain, is precisely in this direction.

For both LSD psychonauts and the psychologists who have studied their experiences, psychedelics provide our reality composer with more real estate in which to expand. The challenge is to broaden the narrow paradigm of biological evolution by natural selection into an all-embracing process of movement *towards*. Intellectually, culturally, socially and spiritually, mankind can consciously choose whether or not to evolve. We are already entering a broader, global consciousness through the world-wide web. Paradoxically, while computer-based interactions keep us locked into superficial modes of interaction, they are also breaking down our physical separation: when we interact via the world wide web, we are part of one vast flow of information.

Evolution offers a continual opportunity for learning, implying that the post-materialist age will be one of rediscovery—that we are part of something greater, that we are co-creators in a grand and ever-developing cosmos. Evolution is about unfolding as well as adapting. It involves a constant process of change and liberation, the goal of which, according to Aurobindo, is supramentalisation. The splendour of this word *supramentalisation* could not be more appropriate. It is not an endpoint, but a process in itself. It involves growing into our true identity and building a new physical nature to accommodate our intensified consciousness.

Human beings understand the concept of perfection because we know we are imperfect. We appreciate that change can only come about through a deliberate effort of heart and mind to break constricting habits we recognise in ourselves. The nature of that perfected being is something that, according to Aurobindo, we cannot envisage in our present state. It will be something more than an advance into knowledge, power, genius, saintliness and love. Whatever the direction and outcome of that expanded potential, we are on that journey. We are part of the evolutionary unfolding, the ultimate products of which are beyond our imaginations.

What am I? Bound and Unbounded,
A pattern among the stars, a point in motion
Tracing my way. I am the way: it is I.
I travel among the wonders.
Held in that gaze and known
In the eye of the abyss,
'Let it be so', I said,
And my heart laughed with joy
To know the death I must die.

—From *Night Sky* by Kathleen Raine

References

INTRODUCTION: A HOUSE OF LOYAL FESTISHES
1. *Manifesto for a Post-Materialist Science*, Explore, September/October 2014, Vol 10, No 5.

CHAPTER 1: DRIVING A FORKED STICK
2. *River Dreams: The Case of the Missing General and other Adventures in Psychic Research*, Dale E. Graff, Element Books, USA, 2000.
3. *Dogs that know when their owners are coming home, and other unexplained powers of animals*, Rupert Sheldrake, Three Rivers Press, New York, 2011.
4. *Journal of Consciousness Studies*, Vol 12, No.6, 2005, Imprint Academic, Exeter, UK.
5. *The Medium, the Mystic and the Physicist: Toward a General Theory of the Paranormal*, Lawrence LeShan, Helios Press, New York, 2003.
6. *People of the Earth*, Peter Calvert, Richard Bentley, Carolyn Longden, Trisha Wren, Attar Books, 2019.
7. *PSI and the Consciousness Explosion*, Stuart Holroyd, Taplinger Publishing Co, New York, 1977.

CHAPTER 2: MIND EXCURSIONS
8. *How to Change Your Mind, The New Science of Psychedelics*, Michael Pollan, Penguin Random House, Great Britain, 2018.
9. *The End of Stupor?* Ronald Conway, Macmillan Co, Melbourne, 1984.
10. *The Science of Ascension: Bodily Ego, Consciousness, Connection*, Mike Sosteric, www.academia.eduhttps//athabascau.academia.edu/DrS.

CHAPTER 3: PEAK EXPERIENCES
11. *Toward a Psychology of Being*, Abraham H. Maslow, D. Van Nostrand Company, Princeton, 1968 (second edition).

CHAPTER 5: RUNNING LIKE CLOCKWORK

12. *Evolutionaries: Unlocking the Spiritual and Cultural Potential of Science's Greatest Idea*, Carter Phipps, Harper Perennial, New York, 2012.
13. *Living with a Wild God*, Barbara Ehrenreich, Twelve, New York, 2015.

CHAPTER 6: THE ULTIMATE SCINTILLA

14. *The Master and his Emissary: The Divided Brain and the Western World*, Iain McGilchrist, Yale University Press, Great Britain, 2012.

CHAPTER 7: SOVEREIGN MENTALITY

15. *The Luminous Nun*, Kerryn Levy, Attar Books, 2019.
16. *Dark Pool of Light*, Richard Grossinger, North Atlantic Books, California, 2012.
17. *Mind and Cosmos*, Thomas Nagel, Oxford University Press, Oxford, 2012.
18. *Science and Spiritual Practice*, Rupert Sheldrake, Coronet, London, 2017.

CHAPTER 8: ESALEN'S LUMINARIES

19. *Esalen: America and the Religion of No Religion*, Jeffrey J. Kripal, The University of Chicago Press, USA, 2007.
20. *Realms of the Human Unconscious, Observations from LSD Research*, Stanislav Grof, Souvenir Press, London, 2018 (first pub: 1975).
21. *The Book on the Taboo Against Knowing Who You Are*, Alan Watts, Jonathan Cape, Great Britain, 1973.
22. *Steps to an Ecology of Mind*, Gregory Bateson, University of Chicago Press, USA, 2000.
23. *The Turning Point: Science, Society and the Rising Culture*, Fritjof Capra, Flamingo, London, 1983.

CHAPTER 9: THE WORLD BEHIND THE WORLD

24. *My Journey to Waitaha*, Judith Hoch, Attar Books, 2019.

Author's Acknowledgements

Thanks to Judy, Steve, Raymond and Seydou.

A special thanks to Keith Hill for his vision, which has made this book part of a unique New Zealand-based series on body, mind and spirit. I am much indebted to him for the clarity of his editorial oversight, his recommendations for support material, and advice that I should engage in some personal archaeology to corroborate the ideas in these pages. He has also saved me from a number of errors—any that remain are entirely my own.

Lastly, to my partner Kirsty, for her love, open mind and unfailing support.

www.ingramcontent.com/pod-product-compliance
Lightning Source LLC
Chambersburg PA
CBHW030448010526
44118CB00011B/854

Chinese Thirdspace

THE PARADOX OF MODERATE
POLITICS, 1946–2020

Jianmei Liu

Columbia University Press
New York

Columbia University Press wishes to express its appreciation for assistance given
by the Chiang Ching-kuo Foundation for International Scholarly Exchange and
the Council for Cultural Affairs in the publication of this series.

Columbia University Press
Publishers Since 1893
New York   Chichester, West Sussex

Copyright © 2025 Columbia University Press
All rights reserved

Library of Congress Cataloging-in-Publication Data
Names: Liu, Jianmei, 1967– author.
Title: Chinese thirdspace : the paradox of moderate politics, 1946–2020 / Jianmei Liu.
Description: New York : Columbia University Press, [2025] | Series: Global Chinese culture |
Includes bibliographical references and index.
Identifiers: LCCN 2024034330 (print) | LCCN 2024034331 (ebook) |
ISBN 9780231214209 (hardback) | ISBN 9780231214216 (trade paperback) |
ISBN 9780231560245 (ebook)
Subjects: LCSH: China—Intellectual life—1949– | Intellectuals—China—Biography. |
Philosophy, Chinese—History. | Philosophy—China—History. |
China—Politics and government—Philosophy.
Classification: LCC DS777.6 .L574 2025 (print) | LCC DS777.6 (ebook) |
DDC 951.05092/2—dc23/eng/20241024

Cover design: Chang Jae Lee
Cover image: *The Eye 2007*, by Gao Xingjian. Reprinted by permission of Gao Xingjian.

GPSR Authorized Representative: Easy Access System Europe,
Mustamäe tee 50, 10621 Tallinn, Estonia, gpsr.requests@easproject.com

Contents

Acknowledgments vii

Introduction 1

I Zhang Dongsun: The Predicament of Thirdspace 37

II Yin Haiguang: Colorless Thought as Thirdspace 79

III Jin Yong: Thirdspace as a Political Stance and Fictional Transgression 110

IV Liu Zaifu: Envisioning Variations of Thirdspace 147

V Gao Xingjian: Transmedia Aesthetics of Thirdspace 181

VI Chinese Female Writers' Construction of Thirdspace 221

Epilogue 245
Notes 265
Bibliography 315
Index 343

Acknowledgments

I was born during the Cultural Revolution when the majority of people were tightly gripped by the binary mentality. Divided into camps of friends or foes, we seldom found any room to breathe or turn around. Although many Chinese intellectuals made a great effort to cast off the spell of "either you die or I live," it constantly crept back to haunt us. After the 2019 Hong Kong protests and the COVID-19 pandemic emerged in the early 2020s, the world became increasingly polarized, not only in China but also in the United States. As I tried hard to remain neutral when caught in the conflicts between two extreme sides, I found it was more difficult than I imagined. From that time, I felt there was an urgency to examine how previous Chinese intellectuals dealt with similar situations of heightened social and political divisions. To my surprise, maintaining the middle way and embracing moderate politics could arouse great controversies, because these positions were inevitably criticized as signs of weakness or as catering to authoritarian rule. Hijacked by the demand for moral responsibilities, the moderate Chinese intellectuals were often accused of not resisting strongly enough and instead hiding in the ivory tower. My inquiry into the cohort of Chinese intellectuals who carried out the mission of exploring moderate politics and establishing Thirdspace from which to avoid the pitfall of the either/or mentality is relevant to our current political landscapes. Their ambitions and dilemmas were undoubtedly reflected in many of my critical concerns.

My greatest intellectual debt is owed to my father, Liu Zaifu, who not only brought up the concept of Thirdspace that is different from that of Homi K. Bhabha but also persistently settled in such a space politically and culturally during his exile years. His personal choice that aligns with his intention to expand the surviving space of Chinese intellectuals sparked my interest to probe this project in both depth and breadth. I am fortunate to benefit from David Der-wei Wang, my longtime mentor, whose broad scope of knowledge and brilliant insights have been invaluable in shaping this book. His analytical acuity and theoretical vision have significantly stimulated me to refine my ideas and push the boundaries of Chinese Thirdspace. He read my original book manuscript with care and strongly advised me to add a chapter about Yin Haiguang, who represents the Taiwanese intellectuals' expedition on Thirdspace. While I was working on the chapter about female writers' constructions of Thirdspace, he generously provided constructive comments and advice.

In the revision stage, Ma Xiaolu and Carlos Rojas played a crucial role in offering their honest critiques on my original book manuscript. I cherished our vigorous intellectual dialogues and have learned enormously from them. Wu Shengqing and Jin Huan responded to my urgent call for help and assisted with the translation of the classical Chinese poetry. I am truly grateful for their generosity and friendship. In addition, Leo Ou-fan Lee, Sebastian Veg, Michel Hockx, Song Mingwei, Song Weijie, Wang Xiaojue, Robin Visser, Li Jie, Tu Hang, and Mabel Lee read either the entirety or potions of my manuscript and offered me incisive and insightful comments instrumental in sharpening my arguments. I am extremely grateful to Qiao Min and Xue Yuyuan for being excellent research assistants who enabled me to bring the project to fruition. Their meticulous and assiduous efforts enriched my research and writing. I also want to thank Guo Yijiao and Zou Sirong for their great efforts in helping me collect a variety of research materials. My research has also benefited from conversations I had with Li Zehou, Gao Xingjian, Yan Lianke, Chan Koonchung, Chi Zijian, Wei Shyy, Li Yijian, Lin Gang, Liu Xiaogan, Nicholas A. Kaldis, Wang Ban, Lee Haiyan, Michelle Yeh, Ji Jin, Christopher Lupke, and David Cheng Chang.

A Prestigious Fellowship of Humanities and Social Science from the Hong Kong University Grants Committee funded the initial book project of *Chinese Thirdspace*. I am grateful to Cameron Campbell, Joshua Derman, and Steven Miles for their strong support for sponsoring the subsidy for the publication of the book via the research funds of the Hong Kong University of Science and Technology. An earlier version of chapter 1 was published by *Prism: Theory and Modern Chinese Literature* 19, no. 1 (2022) under the title "Zhang Dongsun: The Predicament of Thirdspace." In addition, a shorter version of chapter 5 was published by *HKU Journal of Chinese Studies* 1, no. 2 (2023) under the title "The Thirdspace in Gao Xingjian's Cinepoems." I want to thank the editors, Cai Zongqi and Lin Pei-yin, for permitting me to revise them for inclusion in this book. I am deeply indebted to Gao Xingjian, who kindly gave me permission to use his paintings, photos, poetry in my book. In addition, I appreciate Ara Cho, who helped me gain permission from ADAGP, Paris - SACK, Seoul, to use René Magritte's *The Castle of the Pyrenees* in my book.

I want to express my appreciation to the manuscript's anonymous reviewers, whose thought-provoking comments and suggestions have substantially helped to improve the final version. My very special thanks go to my editor at Columbia University Press, Christine Dunbar, whose support and faith in the project gave me enormous confidence and strength. Many thanks go to Leslie Kriesel for giving me vital help throughout the copyediting process. I also want to thank Alexandra Gupta, Ben Kolstad, and Will Oemler for their wonderful jobs in assisting the publication of the book.

My deepest gratitude goes to my parents, Liu Zaifu and Chen Feiya, for cultivating me with strong love. My husband, Kenneth G. Huang, has provided a caring and affectionate home in which I can fully devote time to my academic writing. My daughter, Grace Huang, has been a constant source of delight, and my sister, Liu Lian, has given me unconditional support. My son, Alan Z. Huang, who has become a promising young scholar, inspires me with his creative spirit, intellectual curiosity, and impressive knowledge of world literature. Our numerous talks and insightful discussions were indispensable to the completion of the book.

CHINESE THIRDSPACE

Figure 0.1 The *Castle of the Pyrenees*, 1959 by René Magritte.© René Magritte / ADAGP, Paris—SACK, Seoul, 2024.

Introduction

In Xi Xi's 西西 (1937–2022) short story "Marvels of a Floating City" ("Fucheng zhiyi" 浮城誌異), she intertwines thirteen paintings by René Magritte in an image-text tale of Hong Kong prior to the 1997 handover. It encapsulates the disquieting anxieties held by many Hong Kongers about the future of their city's sovereignty in the 1980s. Magritte's painting *The Castle of the Pyrenees* (figure 0.1) can aptly serve as a core metaphoric image for the perplexing situation of the Chinese Thirdspace discussed in this book. The painting depicts a castle atop a massive rock suspended in midair between the ocean's waves and the sky's clouds. The monolithic magnitude of the rock is contrasted with its weightlessness. This suspension epitomizes the situation of the Chinese Thirdspace: one way signifying the freedom of boundless space with endless possibilities to maneuver in any orientation or trajectory; the other alluding to a sense of rootlessness and loneliness stemming from its very existence, which denotes how politically independent Chinese intellectuals are consistently without support, standing outside the dominant conventions and rules. Caught between the antagonistic forces of the Left and the Right, among other dichotomies, Chinese intellectuals sought alternative pathways to transcend the polarization. However, their efforts met insurmountable challenges posed by prevailing political realities. Chinese Thirdspace is—paradoxically—a struggle for the promise of inclusiveness that always encounters an unsolvable predicament.

The term *Thirdspace* originated in the postcolonial theorist Homi K. Bhabha's *The Location of Culture*, which delineates the titular zone as arising from interactions among different cultures. Among the postcolonial theories that emerged in the 1990s, Bhabha's notion of the "third space" resulted from his intention to dodge a politics of polarity; it is simultaneously differentiated from the universal framework of liberal democracy and from the absolutist position of fundamentalism. As a discursive strategy, his concept effectively questions the idea of a fixed, homogenous culture by revealing the endless malleability within cultural interactions.[1] He discusses how Thirdspace emerges from cultural hybridity within the in-between space, which "gives rise to something different, something new and unrecognisable, a new area of negotiation of meaning and representation."[2] It is apparent that Bhabha wants to challenge the liberal relativist perspective on "cultural diversity," which firmly categorizes diverse cultures within a hegemonic worldview. He criticizes cultural essentialism within a postcolonial context, as this perspective tends to homogenize cultures, thereby diminishing their distinctive characteristics and potential for interactive engagement.

As early as the 1970s, the Marxist theorist and sociologist Henri Lefebvre innovatively established "a triple dialectic" to link historicality, sociality, and spatiality.[3] One of his most important contributions is a significant criticism of the binary logic seen in the philosophies of Georg Wilhelm Friedrich Hegel's absolute idealism and Karl Marx's historical materialism.[4] He also challenges the Western philosophical paradigm from the ancient to the modern era, constituted by numerous oppositions such as subject/object, signifier/signified, center/periphery, continuity/discontinuity, open/closed, etc. Instead, Lefebvre wonders whether there is a "Three," as the "Other," existing beyond the binary.[5] Taking a transdisciplinary perspective, Lefebvre's strategic "trialectics of spatiality" presents a kaleidoscopic display or "a polyphonic fugue" that encourages difference and harmony at the same time.[6]

Building upon Lefebvre's conceptual framework, the postmodern political geographer and urban theorist Edward Soja asserts the critical importance of surpassing all forms of binary logic and moving toward the "both/and also." With the goal to dismantle the discursive closures embedded in the "either/or," Soja's concept of Thirdspace opens up limitless dimensions, accentuating the essence of "all-inclusive simultaneity."[7] His construction has a tendency toward "othering" by synthesizing Michel Foucault's concept of "heterotopology" with theories from Gayatri Chakravorty Spivak, bell hooks, Edward Said, and Homi Bhabha. Compared to the postcolonial context of Bhabha and the Marxist-oriented philosophy of Lefebvre, Soja's theory focuses more on criticizing reductionist positions within modernism and postmodernism. Instead of being fixed in either the postmodern or the modern position, he prefers a "both/and also" logic, exploring a more open and multiple perspective and flexible strategy in dealing with contemporary politics.

Similarly, the ecological feminist Val Plumwood critically reveals that dualism has played a significant role in shaping both ancient and modern Western political landscapes. Plumwood provides compelling examples, such as Plato's emphasis on reason/body, reason/emotion, and universal/particular; René Descartes's focus on mind/body, subject/object, and human/nature; Hegel's and Jean-Jacques Rousseau's exploration of public/private, male/female, and reason/nature; and Marx's contemplation of freedom/necessity, culture/nature, and civilized/primitive, among others. The logic structure of dualism has effectively consolidated and naturalized hierarchical relationships of domination and subordination through radical exclusion, instrumentalism, and homogenization. The most important strategy she proposes to break through a network of dualism is to reconstruct "a relationship and identity in terms of a nonhierarchical concept of difference." Plumwood's antidualist framework, referred to as "the third position" of ecofeminist theory between deep ecologists and social ecologists, akin to the concept of Thirdspace, offers women a valuable alternative to the male-centered dualistic construction of culture and nature.[8]

Thirdspace, in the modern Chinese context, stems from the same purpose of going beyond the epistemological conundrum of the oppositional dichotomy of power. However, it has always been a complex discourse that has different cultural meanings from the Western sense, imbued with its own particularities and universal values. Unnecessarily confined to the postmodern or postcolonial background, it is closely associated with distinct political purposes, challenging the prevailing revolutionary ideologies that are intricately bound up with the either/or mentality. From different historical contingencies, there emerged a multifaceted and profound philosophical, political, and artistic pursuit distinct from the mainstream tendency toward dualism, extending to an infinite realm of possibilities. Nevertheless, this pursuit encountered innumerable impediments, as it was unavoidably constrained by internecine politics and authoritarian ideologies.

The Chinese intellectuals with whom I am concerned are not a united group. Instead, they are independent individualists—philosophers, political commentators, journalists, literary writers, theorists, and artists—based in mainland China, Hong Kong, Taiwan, Europe, and North America. Although living in different historical times—the Republican period, the Cold War era, the Mao years, the postsocialist period—they each played a crucial role in developing the concept of Thirdspace as a discursive strategy to resist dogmatic dichotomous thinking. While Soja amalgamates the theories of multiple postcolonial theorists, such as Michel Foucault, Henri Lefebvre, Gayatri Spivak, Edward Said, and bell hooks, he especially cautions against "the uncritical adaptation of any single conceptualization of Thirdspace."[9] One of the most compelling aspects of modern Chinese intellectuals' creations and appropriations of Thirdspace is their diversified approaches to combat diamantine dualism in different historical contexts. For them, Thirdspace in the Sinophone world could be understood as a survival space for an individual; a public sphere harboring heterogeneous ideas; a life philosophy that embraces tolerance and harmony; a third political route that balances freedom and equality; a pragmatic method mediating human disputes; a moderate heterotopia that is neither utopia nor dystopia; a unique location where linear progress and causality are replaced by a pervasive interrelatedness; or an aesthetic site resisting political controls and generating transmedia explorations. Without fixed boundaries, Chinese Thirdspace refers to not only a critical, idealized, or even imaginative space but also a virtual space with multiple and fluid forms that exists in palpable history and reality, brimming with complementary paradoxes. In essence, these intellectuals have adopted various approaches to broaden and enrich the foundations and ramifications of the notion of Thirdspace, portraying it as a kaleidoscope that refracts myriad dimensions and showcases mobility.

This book contributes to the study of the cultural politics of Thirdspace in modern and contemporary China, which exerted a far-reaching influence on Chinese intellectual history. I intend to provide a critical reflection on a cohort of Chinese intellectuals' choices of Thirdspace, which took on multifarious forms and connotations during different historical conjunctions, as an alternative response to Chinese modernity. I inquire why Thirdspace, directly pertaining to a perceptible lacuna in modern Chinese politics, has had difficulty finding a foothold of existence. How is Thirdspace central to the understanding of "the public sphere" in which individuals from different schools of thought are encouraged to express their opinions, as Jürgen Habermas conceptualized?[10] What are the cultural resources that have fueled Thirdspace across disparate philosophical, political, and literary pathways, which shed light on the dynamics of Chinese intellectuals facing a cluster of problems amid national crises? How has Thirdspace become a solid ground for literature and art to thrive on and even propel pioneering forms of expression? By evoking Chinese Thirdspace as a strategic disruption of conventional conceptual binaries, I aim to illuminate and redeem diverse narratives and representations that have been buried under the tides of history.

In the fluctuating movement of modern Chinese history, Thirdspace has been described as an evasive location for intellectuals to escape political conflicts. However, my principal argument is that the lack of Thirdspace under totalitarian political rule in different historical contexts has become a salient problem. Bringing to the fore many of the tensions implicit in Chinese Thirdspace, the intellectuals covered in this book attempted to create an open and liberal space of existence that would ensure freedom of individual speech and literary creation. Intriguingly, these individuals cannot be unequivocally classified as either strictly revolutionary or conservative, leftists or rightists. None of them fervently supported violent revolution; rather, they espoused moderate politics and gradual reform. They made a great effort to achieve this by creating an environment conducive to the inclusion of diverse and pluralistic ideas.

The concept of Chinese Thirdspace involves three corresponding sets of critical interventions. Primarily, these thinkers and artists adapted traditional Chinese philosophies such as Buddhism, Daoism, and Confucianism to critique the dualism and the rationalization process in modern Western civilization. The pluralistic quality inherent in Chinese philosophies finds new expressions in Zhang Dongsun's 張東蓀 (1886–1973) "correlation logic," Li Zehou's 李澤厚 (1930–2021) "proper measure" (*du* 度), and Liu Zaifu's 劉再復 (1941–) "aesthetic transcendence," which target the criticism of Western modernity that had engendered ceaseless political rivalries. To challenge doctrinaire dualism, they contended that an all-encompassing and heterogenous space was more fertile for instilling tolerance than an exclusionist mentality. Second, these intellectuals are not only deeply indebted to traditional Chinese philosophy that problematizes binary thinking but also well informed by Western liberal theories that highlight individualistic values. The Thirdspace thinkers possess two pivotal characteristics that define their intellectual framework: recognition of the essentiality of the public sphere and reverence for negative freedom, which guarantees a noncoercive personal space and pluralism of inviolable human values.[11] They stood out among their contemporaries by emphasizing individual rights, in contrast to many others who significantly prioritized nationhood and class struggle. Their syncretic theories and practices ultimately indicate the possibility that traditional Chinese philosophical wisdom such as the yin-yang dialectics, Zhuangzi's and Laozi's spirit, the doctrine of nonduality and the middle way of Chan Buddhism, and the golden mean in Confucianism can forge an interesting dialogue with the Euro-American liberal tradition. Third, they carve out an intermediary zone that bridges two nominally antithetical positions, fostering a polyphonic strait imbued with spiritual freedom that exists apart from the oppositional axis. The distinctive features of the transdisciplinary or transmedia approach crystallized in this intermediary zone have generated manifold and innovative creations in the fields of Chinese literature and film.

The hallmark characteristic of Thirdspace lies in its all-encompassing essence. As Soja states, "Everything comes together in Thirdspace: subjectivity and objectivity, the abstract and the concrete, the real and the imagined, the knowable and the unimaginable, the repetitive and the differential, structure and agency, mind and body, consciousness and the unconscious, the disciplined and the transdisciplinary, everyday life and unending history."[12] By employing the analogy of "the Aleph" from Jorge Luis Borges's eponymous short story—"the space where all places are"—as an allegory to conceptualize Thirdspace, Soja underscores its "radical openness" and "infinite complexities of space and time."[13] This all-inclusive nature is evident in Laozi's concept of "one giving birth to two, two to three, three to ten thousand things" in the *Tao Te Ching* 道德經. However, although infinite inclusiveness has greatly challenged the dogmatic either/or mindset, it nevertheless "invokes an immediate sense of impossibility" of comprehensively displaying or exploring Thirdspace.[14]

In the specific modern Chinese context, I intend to add another important dimension—the idea of "tolerating contradiction"—to the undertaking of Thirdspace, which thrives in the endless state of "radical openness." This particular dimension, burdened by the intricacies embedded within its history, has accurately captured the philosophical struggle to present Chinese Thirdspace. Its acuity lies in its revelation of the supplementary nature of all discords and conflicting currents rather than the extremes of a one-and-only disposition. In this sense, "The Zahir," another short story by Jorge Luis Borges, named for a spherical form where one can see two sides of a coin at the same time, adequately emblematizes Chinese Thirdspace that shores up paradoxes as complementary: "First I could see the face of it, then the reverse; now

I can see both sides at once. It is not as though the Zahir were made of glass, since one side is not superimposed upon the other—rather, it is as though the vision were itself spherical, with the Zahir rampant in the center."[15]

The perception of the Zahir is akin to the yin-yang relation that "recognizes and appreciates the coexistence of true opposite elements in the same place at the same time."[16] Paradoxical elements are seen not as irreconcilable but as complementary and interdependent. The spherical vision displays how the coin face is merely an attribute of a three-dimensional object, like the ancient Chinese notion of harmony in one universe. The holistic view of oneness encompassing multiplicity has an innate dynamic and paradoxical nature that regards infinite things in the universe as interrelated and independent. Therefore, the symbol of the Zahir can be regarded as the epitome of Chinese Thirdspace, which mainly draws from philosophical sources such as the "ancient notions of harmony in the One Universe," yin-yang metaphysics, the doctrine of the mean in Confucianism, Laozi's *Tao Te Ching*, and the concepts of nonduality and the middle way in Chan Buddhism.

However, the promising features and the dark side of Thirdspace go hand in hand—its implication of complementary paradoxes parallels its epistemological aporia and intellectual deliberation. There are many predicaments discernible in the approaches of Chinese Thirdspace that await more scrutiny: While Chinese Daoist and Buddhist discourses advocate for nothingness or emptiness as the seemingly unlikely basis for Thirdspace, which implies interrelatedness without substance, how can it shed light on an alternative model to dismantle the philosophy of struggle ingrained in the revolutionary mentality? If what lies behind the attributes of Thirdspace is the pursuit of balance and tolerance, is harmony more important than justice? Why are moderate political tactics—the doctrine of accommodation (*tiaohelun* 調和論), the principle of value neutrality, an independently individual stance, and aesthetic transcendence, which immeasurably enrich and broaden one's horizons—criticized as lacking principles by radical revolutionaries? Why is the freedom of silence, which is protected by the Thirdspace intellectuals, also perceived as inaction and even a cause of further injustice? The various historical expressions related to Thirdspace have advantages and disadvantages underpinning one another, pointing out that there are numerous heterotopic existences between utopian and dystopian solutions. In other words, although complementary paradoxes have greatly contended with the dogmatic either/or mindset as well as notions of linear progress and causality, Thirdspace nevertheless encountered enormous obstacles from the twentieth-century political realities that almost left no quarter for its survival.

The representative cases discussed in this book are far from exhausting the versatile characteristics of Thirdspace that have existed in modern Chinese history. Through an examination of selective individuals who have played an important role in shaping Thirdspace, I aim to shift our scholarly focus away from the mainstreams of modern Chinese literature and culture. Instead, I seek to explore the intricacies of the in-between space, employing syncretic and transdisciplinary approaches that explicitly draw upon diverse historical contexts within Sinophone culture. Those Chinese intellectuals' great efforts to assert the multifarious values of Thirdspace have manifested alternative and heterogeneous routes to replace the totalistic mode of cultural criticism. This reminds us that besides the variety of binary oppositions, there always exist three or more possibilities. These possibilities not only intrepidly grapple with the existing paradigm and offer a critical lens for reevaluating the modern Chinese experience but also hold insightful relevance to our current era, which is once again entangled in the global phenomenon of polarization. Alluding to multiple spaces, which include intangible imaginary space, cultural discursive space, and virtual political space, Thirdspace inevitably has its boons and drawbacks. Because of the term's complex and diverse connotations, it provides thought-provoking and rigorous prospects, venturing indiscriminately rather than serving as a simplistic utopian panacea.

The discourse of Thirdspace has become increasingly imperative as we are once again haunted by the ghost of the either/or mindset under the Xi Jinping 习近平 (1953-) regime. Radicalization seems prevalent, as seen in U.S.-China relations with a parallel to the Cold War mentality. Even in the 2019–2020 Hong Kong protests, moderate voices were largely superseded by radical progovernment and prodemocracy factions. Under such circumstances, it is crucial to examine the successes and pitfalls of previous endeavors of Thirdspace and continue to explore its untapped potential. A more open-minded mode of thinking that enables constructive dialogue about competing ideas and values has become more urgent.

The Shriveling of Thirdspace

Modern China was constantly bifurcated between two rapaciously opposed political forces with starkly contrasting ideologies, both of which claimed to uphold the one and only truth. The tension precipitated, with many Chinese intellectuals eagerly taking sides and others striving to dwell in Thirdspace. However, those who advocated Thirdspace were usually seen as escapists or fence-sitters, obscured and denigrated. This pattern not only is historical but also involves a burden of moral responsibility imposed upon modern Chinese intellectuals, often with a devastating outcome: the fatal shrinkage of Thirdspace.

This predicament has a lot to do with what the historian Yü Ying-shih 余英時 (1930–2021) delineated as "a process of rapid radicalization" in Chinese thought in the twentieth century that eventually culminated in the Cultural Revolution.[17] Although there existed a gamut of various political and cultural positions from the late Qing to the Republican period, the turbulent Chinese societal milieu inhibited the development of the inseparable triad of conservatism/liberalism/radicalism that originally emerged in the Enlightenment of the West in the eighteenth century. Due to the unavoidable national crisis, progress and revolution were gradually elevated as the highest cultural values, and consequently, the conservatives could hardly develop a basis for dialogue with the radicals. Yü Ying-shih especially pointed out that in the United States, the liberals served as mediators between radicals and conservatives, whereas in China, this common ground was virtually feckless, leaving only bitter fractiousness between radicals and conservatives.[18]

Indeed, the Chinese mentality in the twentieth century was tightly gripped by the radical mode of thinking, which revolved around the revolutionary worldview, intensifying the ossified dichotomy between Left and Right, new and old, Western and Chinese, modernity and tradition, revolution and antirevolution. Before the Communist victory in 1949, there was still an active, albeit gradually diminishing, public sphere, which allowed Chinese intellectuals from different political and cultural positions to freely discuss their political ideas, comprising the multifaceted Chinese modernity. According to the historian Thomas A. Metzger, this public sphere not only existed but also functioned differently from the Western tradition of civil society, which has an un-utopian and bottom-up definition of political order. The Chinese sought a tradition-based, utopian, top-down structure with an intellectual leadership performing all political functions.[19] Such a civil society would ensure a Thirdspace or middle ground where a variety of contending ideologies—liberalism, democracy, capitalism, and socialism, among others—could coexist and interact with one another. After 1949, however, any intermediate groups or forums were completely subsumed under the Chinese Communist Party (CCP)'s totalitarian control.[20] From 1949 to the Cultural Revolution, the expulsion of the rational Thirdspace contributed to the pervading opposition against any means of reconciliation, creating extreme polarization that prompted simplistic judgments of right and wrong without any room for retractions.

The inclination toward radicalization that was subject to the logic of revolution also permeated the field of modern Chinese literature, gradually eroding Thirdspace, which shelters "the garden of one's own,"[21] "the third type of person," and the autonomy of literature from political manipulation. During the May Fourth Movement, one of its pioneers, Chen Duxiu 陳獨秀 (1879–1942), in his article "On Literary Revolution" ("Wenxue geming lun" 文學革命論), constructed antagonistic binaries such as aristocratic versus people's literature, classical literature versus realist literature, and eremitic literature versus social literature, unable to accept alternatives beyond the binary.[22] His radical declaration arbitrarily "denied any possibility that aristocratic and people's literature could coexist simultaneously,"[23] advancing a dogmatic either/or mentality that led to "totalistic cultural iconoclasm."[24] Even Hu Shi 胡適 (1891–1962), who used the word "reform" instead of "revolution" in his advocacy of the vernacular Chinese language as a writing medium to embody Chinese modernity, was still enmeshed in the binary mode of "living literature" (*huo wenxue* 活文學) versus "dead literature" (*si wenxue* 死文學), unreasonably rejecting two thousand years of literature written in Classical Chinese.[25]

Mainstream literature very quickly morphed from a literary revolution to revolutionary literature in the late 1920s, subordinating literature to politics and leaving less and less room for the diversification and thriving of individual creativity. When Zhou Zuoren 周作人 (1885–1967) wanted to retreat into his own personal space after the May Fourth Movement, he was viciously reprimanded by the leftists, who emphasized social responsibility and regarded literature as a tool of political purpose and national salvation. Taking an uncompromising stance of criticizing reality, Lu Xun 魯迅 (1881–1936) detested and ridiculed the position of hermits, who embraced Zhuangzi's transcendence of absolute "rights" and "wrongs" and contributed nothing to the urgent resolution of the nation's fate. As the ferociously antagonistic camps were increasingly drawn to leftist and rightist doctrines, Lu Xun and other writers became more and more intolerant of those who strove to remain neutral.

A typical case occurred in the early 1930s when Lu Xun scorned "the third type of person" as represented by Hu Qiuyuan 胡秋原 (1910–2004) and Su Wen 蘇汶 (1907–1964), who refused to side with either the rightists or the leftists, believing that literature should not be utilized as an instrument for the proletarian revolution. This brought Lu Xun's severe censure; he affirmed that writers are forever inextricable from their classes. He sarcastically mocked "the third type of person" for fantasizing about leaving the battlefield in a time of war. "To try to be such a man is like trying to raise yourself from the ground by tugging at your own hair—it can't be done."[26] In defense of the third type of person, the literary critic and essayist Liang Shiqiu 梁實秋 (1903–1987) explicated: "Either red or white, either friend or foe, either left or right, either proletarian class or capitalist class, either revolution or anti-revolution—this type of logic we have long heard before. Mr. Lu Xun's fundamental negation of the third type of person is nothing but a case of applying such logic to literature."[27] Liang was extremely concerned about the danger of the political coercion of literary creation on either the left or the right. The modern Chinese philosopher Zhu Guangqian 朱光潛 (1897–1986) also detected that the stringent dichotomy had solidified into the prevailing mode of thinking.[28] In his article "The Crisis of Chinese Thought" ("Zhongguo sixiang de weiji" 中國思想的危機), he criticized "the ethicalization of political thought" that did not allow any choice between "Left" and "Right" doctrines. This "ethicalization" boosted by dualism became an overbearing paradigm full of fixations, used to determine all thinking and attitudes toward personal and collective affairs.[29] Indeed, Lu Xun's delegitimization of "the third type of person" furthered the hegemony of the black-and-white binary mentality. This lack of tolerance was closely tied with the monist way of thinking, which stripped away a middle ground beyond political dichotomies and vindicated the dominance of radical worldviews for the rest of the century.[30] Although nonpolitical middle-ground literature existed in the 1930s, such as the leisure literature advocated by Lin Yutang 林語堂 (1895–1976), Zhou Zuoren's "little essays,"[31] and the school of new sensibility's experimental modernist writing,[32] it was repudiated by Lu Xun, who promoted the instrumentalization of literature. In his view, the little essays were useless ornaments resembling opiates, incongruent with the weaponized essays equivalent to javelins and daggers that can "hew out a blood-stained path to a new life."[33] This unyielding warrior spirit largely hindered the prospects for vivacious and heterogenous forms of literature disconnected from social utility.

After Mao Zedong's 毛澤東 (1893–1976) "Talks at the Yan'an Forum on Literature and Art" in 1942, the middle space was almost depleted because of the apotheosis of the either/or mentality within the central doctrine of class struggle. Mao's talks co-opted all literary discourses into a monopolized form serving political ideology. For instance, in 1948, Shen Congwen 沈從文 (1902–1988) tried to fight for literary independence from politics, Zhu Guangqian warned intellectuals to maintain a sober attitude free from the hysterical influence of mass movements, and the journalist and writer Xiao Qian 蕭乾 (1910–1999) put his hope in the third route between two major parties in the Republican period.[34] Their attempts to maintain Thirdspace all incurred severe criticism from the leftist writer Guo Moruo 郭沫若 (1892–1978), who wrote an article, "Denouncing Reactionary Literature and Art," in which he clearly demarcated revolutionary versus antirevolutionary literature. In the category of so-called revolutionary literature, he included pink literature as emblematized by Shen Congwen, black literature by Xiao Qian, blue literature by Zhu Guangquan, and yellow literature and white literature comprising most of the Chinese writers from the twentieth century's inception.[35] By doing so, Guo extirpated all voices that dissented or strayed from the party line. In response to the leftists' attacks, Xiao Qian wrote a fictional obituary, lamenting the unviability of the third route. He stated in a parodic manner: "My death is due to the collision of political philosophies, a shattering of the ideal of peace, an acknowledgment that coexistence and harmony will not work!"[36] This obituary thus symbolized the extinction of liberal Chinese literature or the middle space between the Left and the Right in the Republican period.[37] Under the brutal politics of the mid-twentieth century, the promoters of Thirdspace, such as the third-force intellectuals, were too weak to join together and break through the conflicts between the two parties and their political ideologies.

After 1949, the third route explored by Zhang Dongsun and his third-force companions in the Republican period, who struggled to find a middle politics to balance state power and personal freedom, socialism and capitalism, was virtually demolished under the totalitarian rule of the CCP, whereupon he was inevitably classified as an enemy—a counterrevolutionary and an insidious spy. This situation heightened during the Cultural Revolution, where factions fervently fought over ideological purity while trampling those who refused to join in. Even traditional options of exile and hiding in mountains and temples were excluded. At the same time, the Chinese Nationalist Party (KMT)'s one-party dictatorship in Taiwan perpetuated the same bifurcated thinking, eventually depriving Yin Haiguang 殷海光 (1919–1969) of a platform to voice his independent views. In Cold War-era Hong Kong, Jin Yong 金庸 (1924–2018) was constantly under attack from both the Left and the Right as he tried to fortify a neutral public space.

The philosophy of class struggle contingent on an us-and-them mentality was paramount in Communist goals, originating with attempted land reforms during the 1920s, reaching a mature form in Yan'an against intellectuals in the 1940s, and being taken to its apex during the Cultural Revolution. Toward the 1960s, while the either/or mentality presided over society, the literary monologic form expounding political ideology reached its summit of "socialist realism." Nuanced and morally gray literary characters gave way to easily defined heroes and villains who could only be used to magnify party propaganda. For instance, the rejection of the theory of "moderate characters" at that time was "in practice directed against those writers who tried to break away from absolute conclusions and seek moderate views."[38] The either/or value judgment embodying two oppositional classes exerted great influence on the Chinese mind, penetrating deep structures of national culture, or in Li Zehou's term, the human "cultural-psychological formation" (*wenhua xinli jiegou* 文化心理結構).[39]

The mid-1980s served as a turning point to a polyphonic era. Although still in "a very fragile embryonic form" overshadowed by political control, the avant-garde literary trend transferred the literary focus from mimetic realism to transcendental and diversified themes and motifs.[40] This decade thereby saw the resurrection of Thirdspace, where a vigorous "intellectual field" emerged between a historical structure of orthodoxies and heterodoxies,[41] altering the previous ideologically dominated monologic era. In the 1990s, economic advances in conjunction with the popularization of the internet in China gave rise to grassroots (*minjian* 民間) intellectuals, who, according to Sebastian Veg, existed between "officialdom" and "unofficial" borders.[42] Inspired by Anthony Giddens's book *The Third Way: The Renewal of Social Democracy*, Xu Jilin 許紀霖 (1957-) attempted to find a rational and moderate middle force between the two extremes to integrate a market economy with political democracy.[43]

However, the either/or mindset still lingered, as evident in the fact that the intellectual polemics of the 1990s were polarized between liberals and leftists, even if the two camps were well equipped with multifarious Western theoretical discourses and traditionalist ideas such as neo-Confucianism.[44] Even outside mainland China, when Liu Zaifu and Gao Xingjian 高行健

(1940–) chose a Thirdspace that could accommodate individual freedom in exile, they were still questioned by intellectuals aligned with either the CCP or the antigovernment democratic camp overseas. Unfortunately, the mentality that impeded the growth of Thirdspace between two extremes has been the overriding fact of most Chinese intellectuals' professional lives, despite how cyberspace encouraged multiple forms of debate and interaction unbound by physical constraints after the turn of the millennium. In the era of Xi Jinping, the dichotomic way of thinking that fiercely demarcates "us" and "them" has returned within a milieu of parochial nationalism, marked especially by a belligerent attitude. Therefore, it is not only necessary but pertinent to continue the unfinished project of Thirdspace in the twenty-first century.

The Philosophical Illuminations of Thirdspace

What does the philosophy of struggle permeated by dualism manifest in practice? Even when not under totalitarian rule, it could still devour all sense of mutual acceptance and dialogue. This is because a binary logic only allows two states of existence: domination and subjugation. The most distinctive quality of dualism is radical exclusion.[45] In contrast, at the core of Chinese Thirdspace, which is intimately interlinked with traditional Chinese philosophy, is the principle of tolerating contradiction. The Chinese intellectuals discussed in this book are mainly indebted to Chinese philosophical sources such as the "ancient notions of harmony in the One Universe," yin-yang metaphysics, the doctrine of the mean in Confucianism, Laozi's *Tao Te Ching*, and the concepts of nonduality and the middle way in Chan Buddhism. These indigenous philosophical sources echo Lefebvre's critical thirding, which aims to shatter "the hammerlock of binarist logic and to prevent any form of reductionism from constraining the free play of the creative spatial imagination."[46] However, the effectiveness of Chinese Thirdspace's method lies in its recovery of complementary paradoxes. By evading the pitfalls of reductionism that tend to confine individuals within rigid either-or categorizations, this method instead embraces an expansive perspective that seeks interconnectedness within a cosmological framework.

Recently, there has been a growing interest in the fields of management, cross-cultural studies, and psychology in how Chinese philosophical sources can provide sharply divergent views on paradox.[47] Chinese thought relies heavily on the interdependent nature of two opposites, seeking a both/and framework to transcend polarities, whereas traditional Western formal logic embodied by the philosophies of Aristotle, René Descartes, and Isaac Newton, as Marianne W. Lewis notes, is primarily "based on either/or thinking, incapable of comprehending the intricacies of paradox."[48] Similarly, in his research, Peter Ping Li identifies two core epistemological systems in the West. The first is represented by Aristotle's formal logic revolving around the permanent "either/or" framework with "an absolute and full separation of opposite elements (in both spatial and temporal terms) so as to avoid and deny paradox." It includes the law of identity, the law of noncontradiction, and the law of the excluded middle—all of which explicitly reject paradox. The second core system is exemplified by Hegel's dialectical logic, which "allows for the temporary existence of paradox in a transitional phase within a recursive process of 'negation' for the ultimate resolution of paradox at the higher level as sublation."[49] Peter Ping Li delineates Hegel's dialectical logic as "both/or" because it still belongs to a reductionist system designed to iron out paradox.[50] In contrast, Li describes the unique cognitive frame of the yin-yang balance as "partially complementary and partially conflicting" (*xiangsheng xiangke* 相生相剋) in the framework of either/and, or oppositions in unity, which has to perpetually seek holistic and dynamic balance without resolving paradox.[51] In a comparable spirit, Peng Kaiping and Richard E. Nisbett discovered empirically that Chinese participants in a study usually found the middle way to tolerate contradiction, while American participants tended to have polarized views on two apparently contradictory propositions.[52] Based on the Chinese middle way philosophy, the scholar Ming-Jer Chen proposed "paradoxical integration," underscoring the concept of interdependent oppositions in a both/and framework to transcend the conventional Western conceptualization of exclusive opposites.[53]

As early as the 1920s, Zhang Dongsun proposed the "logic of correlative duality" (*liangyuan xiangguanlü mingxue* 兩元相關律名學) to question Aristotelian logic, structured by dichotomous oppositions in the "either/or" frame.[54] Rooting his philosophical thinking in the correlative cosmological view, he considered the universe as a holistic and organic whole interlacing infinite interrelated structures, which unnecessarily has substance. Interweaving his philosophical thought with other ideas, Zhang Dongsun borrowed not only from Chinese Confucian, Daoist, and Chan Buddhist cosmologies but also from Alfred North Whitehead's philosophical thought as well as Western relativity and quantum theory.[55] His pluralist epistemology privileges an extraordinary openness of imagination and critical thinking, challenging the prevailing modern method restricted by essentialism or the linear cause-and-effect mentality. In interrogating the polarities of Marxist-historical thought, his theory resembles that of the postmodern and postcolonial theorists, such as Foucault, Said, and Bhabha, who aimed to create new pathways of analysis of heterotopologies and hybridities in relation to multiculturalism. Moreover, Zhang accentuated the middle ground as a pivotal and complex space to connect two extreme poles. By producing a kind of panstructuralism with correlative thinking, he threaded through interdisciplinary studies and engaged in concerted cultural interactions between the West and China. It is an emblematic Thirdspace where various cultural disciplines constantly collude and negotiate with one another and where the plurality of truth becomes possible.

Another facet of Thirdspace is concretized by the concept of *du* as articulated by the contemporary Chinese philosopher Li Zehou, which relays the ever-changeable and flexible nature of humans (and even animals). To be more specific, it alludes to individual adaptability, navigating "the middle way" in accordance with the complexities of a particular situation, thereby achieving the equilibrium of all life-sustaining needs.[56] Although Li Zehou never overtly associated his concept of *du* with the notion of Thirdspace, I perceive it as the discursive paradigm of "thirding" that possesses practical and empirical implications, in stark contrast to the "either/or" logic or the epistemological dualism prevalent in the Western philosophical tradition.

Li Zehou defines *du* as a moderate or artistic way to handle everything appropriately, exercising sound judgment in order to maintain the perfect balance. Embodying a vital attribute that can be aptly described as "a form of skill or even an art, closely approximating the Way (*dao* 道),"[57] *du* is even regarded by Li Zehou as the ontological issue of human existence. Interwoven with his own philosophical concepts such as "pragmatic rationality" (*shiyong lixing* 實用理性) and "reasonable and sensible" (*heqing heli* 合情合理), *du* eludes confinement within theoretical constraints. Instead, it gracefully arises and manifests its essence amid the intricacies of daily existence and the vibrant tapestry of life's myriad activities. Moreover, Li Zehou's characterization of *du* is buttressed by the traditional Chinese philosophical ideas of "moderation" (*zhong* 中), "harmony" (*he* 和), "craftiness" (*qiao* 巧), and "adjustment" (*tiao* 調), undergirded by what is known as "the culture of pleasure" (*legan wenhua* 樂感文化). In other words, *du* serves as a means to actualize moderation and harmony across various domains, including politics, music, the military, and literature, as well as our everyday lives. A concrete crystallization of practical operation, *du* is constructed by Li Zehou as an aesthetic ontology because acting appropriately and maintaining balance ultimately contribute to the establishment of beauty (*limei* 立美). However, the role of subjectivity or human consciousness in relation to *du* is paradoxical. On the one hand, cultivating a sense of *du* can be beneficial, as it aligns with the desired balance. On the other hand, the arbitrary nature of human consciousness has the potential to hinder and undermine the existence and development of *du* in practical scenarios.[58]

To further illustrate his idea, Li Zehou employs the curvaceous line that equally divides the black and white areas in the Taiji yin-yang diagram to symbolize and visualize *du*. It demonstrates that yin-yang cannot be sharply opposed and separated but is mutually dependent and permeable, perpetually in a metamorphosing process.[59] More importantly, such a dialectical model has "no negation, no sublation, and no higher stages or phases of development."[60] As such, Li Zehou's *du* decries a predetermined view of essence, causality, or a priori reason, emphasizing the art of maintaining balance in various evolving circumstances. Jana S. Rošker, a scholar of Chinese philosophy, accurately interprets it as equivalent to the "middle way": "Since it can only be applied within actual practice, this grasping of the 'middle way' is necessarily defined by particularity [rather] than by universal laws of some abstract principles. Hence, it involves dealing with situations differently according to their particular conditions."[61] Indeed, Li Zehou's *du* demands meticulous and precise judgments to effectively respond to particular historical practices and contexts. In essence, *du* serves both as a verb and a noun to describe the mobility and changeability encapsulated within Thirdspace.

Regarding the twentieth century, which was overshadowed by revolutionary ideology, Li Zehou trenchantly states: "I would like to highlight that all revolutions are harmful, irrespective of the question whether they are leftist or rightist. I have learned this from Chinese experiences."[62] His preference for gradual reform over violent revolution is contingent on his own historical experiences and understanding of Chinese political situations in the past. The wise implementation of *du* in different social and historical contexts proves very convincing and insightful. For instance, while discussing the question of public rationality and individual consciousness, Li Zehou has different opinions about the current Western and Chinese situations. According to him, if negative freedom is excessively emphasized in the

West, it will incite the problem of nonparticipation in politics, which might result in the impotence of the majority and an even more unfree condition. However, based on the Chinese historical experience and existing reality, the demand for individual freedom is more reasonable than that of collectivism.[63] Therefore, if *du* is used skillfully in specific historical contexts and sociopolitical practices, it will arouse an aesthetic sense corresponding to harmony.

The method of *du* Li Zehou emphasizes—close assessment of concrete situations and emotional responses—leads to his controversial statement that "harmony is higher than justice." For him, the highest level of human existence and continuity, as well as the "common good" and "good life," are sustained by harmony.[64] Touching on the ethical dimension of Thirdspace, his preference for harmony resulted from his skeptical attitude toward an absolute criterion for distinguishing right from wrong that bolsters the Western definition of justice. However, he also points out that, although harmony is higher, it cannot simply replace fair and reasonable justice but instead is built on that foundation. Again, his argument is framed in pragmatic reason instead of a priori reason, remaining sensitive to historical particularities and variations. While giving sufficient credit to harmony, he underscores the art of *du* because it relies on historicism and pragmatic rationality. As he argued, in the current Chinese situation in which justice and rule of law have not yet been realized, it is dangerous to talk about harmony.[65]

Another scholar of Chinese philosophy, Liu Xiaogan 劉笑敢 (1947–), similarly highlights the significance of integrating the sense of propriety (*fencun gan* 分寸感) while offering a stringent critique of the extremely polarized thought pattern prevalent in contemporary China. He vehemently condemns the rationale behind polarization, linear historical perspectives, and the glorification of struggle, perceiving them as a form of psychological ailment deeply embedded not only within the currents of modern Chinese elites but also within mass culture.[66] This compulsive mindset gave rise to oversimplified moral judgments, an exaggerated clash between two opposing factions, an outright rejection of rational middle ground for reconciliation and compromise, and a ludicrous aversion to objective analysis and evaluation of intricate circumstances.

The parallels between *du* and the sense of propriety are readily apparent. Both are established on a correlative model that fosters binary complementarities rather than oppositions. Furthermore, they are characterized as "operational rather than transcendental,"[67] addressing concrete problems under specific social conditions rather than conforming to a presumptive and absolute truth. Liu Xiaogan referred to the "middle action" (*zhongwei* 中為) as the key methodology for realizing the sense of propriety, which is analogous to the middle way espoused by *du*. As the treatment and rectification of the elite pathological mentality, the middle action combines the doctrine of the mean from Confucianism and the concept of "nonaction" (*wuwei* 無為) from Daoism. However, Liu Xiaogan diverges from Li Zehou by emphasizing a spectrum analysis approach, which identifies an appropriate point and mode of action within the transition zone between two opposite poles with the aim of achieving the optimal outcome.[68] This approach is comparable to Yin Haiguang's "colorless thought," synthesizing an intuitive way of experience and a scientific way of analysis. Furthermore, Liu Xiaogan visualizes a model of cosmology—a dynamic, spherical, and reticular structure highlighting interrelatedness—in contrast to a linear development as in Marxist historical determinism. The spherical image bears a resemblance to the Zahir, bypassing the dogmatic either/or dichotomy to embrace the all-encompassing Thirdspace.

The philosophical pathways of Thirdspace embody fundamental values rooted in balance and harmony. However, the undertaking of balance should not be misconstrued as a path toward unprincipled mediocrity and indifference. Instead, it signifies a deep appreciation for the intricate complexities and diverse nature of human existence. In addition, the quest for harmony does not equate to the pursuit of pristine utopias. In fact, Li Zehou once mentioned that historicism and ethicalism are an everlasting paradox that cannot be resolved. On the one hand, historicism, driven by the relentless endeavor of progress and development, often bears negative consequences regardless of the cost involved. On the other hand, ethicalism strives to uphold social justice and embodies positive attributes.[69] These two perspectives parallel each other, forming a pair of complementary paradoxes, acquiring the wisdom of *du* to balance it. Li Zehou's paradox resonates with Zhang Taiyan's 章太炎 (1869–1936) "dual evolution theory" (*jufen jinhua lun* 俱分進化論), which challenges the linear theory of evolution by suggesting that the seeds of good and evil coexist in human life from the very beginning, intertwining as they evolve. As goodness progresses, so does evil, making it unattainable for evolution to reach the utopia state of absolute benevolence.[70] Contrary to the Communist visions of a utopian society, both Li Zehou and Zhang Taiyan clearly recognize that the concept of an idealized utopia is merely an illusion. They understand that true harmony and coexistence can only be achieved through the interplay of complementary paradoxes. Therefore, the Thirdspace intellectuals amplify the concept of "harmony with differences" (*he er butong* 和而不同), which seeks not to obliterate contradictions and struggles but rather to achieve a state in which diverse perspectives and antagonistic forces can peacefully coexist through continuous adaptation and transformation. Moreover, they underscore the notion of "knowledge and action becoming oneness" (*zhixing heyi* 知行合一), suggesting that individuals must be equipped with tangible and appropriate pragmatic methods to solve problems.[71] Instead of relying on a predetermined standard of absolute right and wrong, these philosophers prioritize pragmatic, empirical reasoning and dynamic adjustments.

The Political Standpoints of Thirdspace

As the gaps have deepened between the two opposing factions in modern China, some Chinese intellectuals' adherence to Thirdspace has conferred invaluable insights for reexamining the multiple modernities that have been overshadowed in the process of radicalization. Even if the spectrum of thought between the two extremes is broad and diversified, their views are most consonant with the value of harmony and the ideals of modern liberalism. Those Thirdspace intellectuals were inclined to adopt more moderate political tactics—the doctrine of accommodation, a principle of value neutrality, an independent individual stance, and aesthetic transcendence—rather than radical and revolutionary means. Outstanding for their rejection of totalistic political feuding and either/or logic, they inaugurated a shared central ground, namely Thirdspace, on which multipronged ways of understanding the self and nation-building were displayed. In general, no matter how much they differ, they were greatly influenced by the Euro-American political liberal tradition, attempting to advance gradual reform instead of violent revolution.[72] Their voices addressing individual freedom and value pluralism were discordant with the twentieth-century mainstream Chinese politics that failed to promote and secure liberty. The dilemma all of them encountered, therefore, is that their choices of Thirdspace were greatly contested in the absence of a societal foundation for political pluralism.

Thirdspace in the Chinese political field has always been marked by acute paradoxes: it encompasses positive, promising qualities—such as tolerance, harmony, and balance—as well as negative characteristics—including compromise, vacillation, and the inability to commit to firm principles. While these intellectuals regarded Thirdspace as a discursive strategy for discernment of and resistance to reality, their theories also inevitably had contradictions and limitations. Whether they actively participated in the construction of public space or chose an individual withdrawal from politics, they found little support from society; they were destined to be marginalized because they refused to side with power, holding a dubious attitude toward any party's ideology. In the realm of Thirdspace, as visualized by Magritte's The *Castle of the Pyrenees*, the predicament of the political landscape is vividly revealed: boundless freedom is simultaneously accompanied by an enduring sense of uncertainty stemming from societal ostracization.

The first and most conspicuous political strand of Thirdspace is the doctrine of accommodation, which emphasizes the importance of establishing a common ground where conflicting political factions could engage in constructive negotiations. This notion harkens back to Chinese thinkers such as Zhang Shizhao 章士釗 (1881–1973) and Du Yaquan 杜亞泉 (1873–1933) in the 1910s, and was subsequently inherited by Zhang Dongsun. By mapping out less aggressive political directions for "a balancing democracy,"[73] this Thirdspace approach not only is buttressed by the quintessential Chinese concept of yin-yang metaphysics that pursues harmony and balance between opposing forces but also accords with the Western liberal political tradition, espousing a plurality of individual actions and interferences in civil society.

Inspired by James Bryce's work on the "centrifugal and centripetal forces of government," which "take account of everyone's emotions, opinions, and demands" to maintain a balanced constitution, Zhang Shizhao was critical of authoritarian and homogenized discourse.[74] His idea of accommodation not only emphasizes the oppositional forces (*duikang li* 對抗力) that stimulate the disparate opinions of others but also asserts the spirit of tolerance. In his own words, "I have heard that accommodation is born of mutual opposition and developed through mutual concessions. Without an oppositional force, one cannot speak of accommodation. Without the virtue of making concessions, one cannot speak of accommodation."[75] Therefore, Zhang's idea of balance is achieved by deliberately encouraging dualistic forces of competition, slightly different from the more passive and peaceful way of the Chinese yin-yang dialectics. Another important thinker, Du Yaquan, the editor-in-chief of *Eastern Journal* (*Dongfang zazhi* 東方雜誌), also championed the application of the doctrine of accommodation to the debates on Chinese culture versus Western culture from 1911 to 1920.[76] What emerged from his cultural criticism is a kind of "harmonious pluralism" or unity of diversity, with the purpose to deny the precept that a single, absolute principle can measure all values.[77] In addition, Du emphasized the dignity and power of the individual; he was critical of nationalism's denial of individual freedom in favor of the collective.[78] His open-minded worldview entails rationality and compromise, which could bridge the divide between tradition and modernity.

Building on their legacy, Zhang Dongsun underscored the significance of the doctrine of accommodation to properly grasp the plurality of truth and stimulate a diversity of ideas and knowledge for social benefit.[79] This stance remained essential within his corpus of ideas, motivating his opposition to Marxist ideology, particularly the rhetoric of class struggle that underlined a narrow either/or mentality that kept individuals from tolerating contesting opinions. He ardently voiced his critical opinions in various debates in the public sphere, carrying out middle politics to expunge the intoxication from partisanship and authoritarianism. From his beliefs in pluralism, Zhang Dongsun syncretized capitalism, socialism, and democracy, attempting to reconcile freedom with equality.

As the clashes of antagonistic isms and parties escalated after the May Fourth Movement, the doctrine of accommodation faced severe conundrums. Its implementation was thrust into the political spotlight due to the determined endeavors of Zhang Dongsun, who aligned with Zhang Junmai 張君勱 (1987–1969) and the other third-force intellectuals, attempting to mediate between the KMT and the CCP, particularly in the pre- and post-Chinese Civil War periods.[80] Their aim in building Thirdspace was to pursue an objective referred to as the "overlapping consensus," as later coined by the political philosopher John Rawls, who described how a consensus on a particular political principle of justice could be affirmed by believers in opposing religious, philosophical, and moral doctrines. Regrettably, this group effort faltered within political realities hostile to "reasonable pluralism."[81] Confronted with immense pressure, Zhang Junmai ultimately aligned with the KMT while Zhang Dongsun sided with the CCP during the 1940s. This raised doubts about whether the doctrine of accommodation is a viable proposition amid the fervid political feuding of two factions and whether middle politics was predestined to flounder in the modern Chinese context of overwhelming radicalization. But even if the third-force intellectuals failed and were deliberately buried by the official accounts, it does not mean their constructive and rational ideas were incorrect. Rather, their choice of "the third route" and middle politics pointed to an alternative and tangible historical trajectory, one that continues to reverberate in the contemporary political stances adopted by Chan Koonchung 陳冠中 (1952–) and Chu Tien-hsin 朱天心 (1958–).

Jin Yong successfully inaugurated Thirdspace based on the principle of value neutrality in the relatively free colonial Hong Kong in the 1960s. His *Ming Pao* 明報 journalism empire carved out a middle ground between the Left and the Right without prioritizing any one of a set of contrasting substantive political standpoints. Jin Yong aimed to cultivate a more moderate and pluralist view by refusing to be controlled by a given set of political ideologies; however, no matter how impartial he strove to be, his political commentaries on social events were still heavily value-laden and based on his subjective viewpoint. The value neutrality that Jin Yong endeavored to preserve within his empire can only be "a matter of degree," relative to a gradation within a specific spectrum of substantive political perspectives, the breadth of which may vary.[82] Therefore, to achieve maximum value neutrality in Hong Kong is to create a shared area among divergent and contrasting political groups, allowing for a consensus to emerge rather than eliminating all but one set of substantive political or ethical points of view. Jin Yong's neutral stance, not allied with any oppositional sides or parties, is a testament to his attempt to persevere and broaden the scope of Thirdspace with the individual and society closely bound. By providing a bridge between antithetical political groups with disparate value systems, his Thirdspace broke through the Cold War mentality and opened up new areas of inquiry and thinking, which had considerable impact on the ways people understand the world.

However, the polemics of Thirdspace at the political level persisted in a society that elevated class struggle and ideological conflicts over plural reconciliation. As the rivalry between the parties prevented any agreement on basic political rights and liberties, those who championed the doctrine of accommodation and the principle of value neutrality had to make certain compromises as they strove to defend a more inclusive and tolerant society. As a result, they were often accused by other Chinese intellectuals of obfuscating or even undermining judgments of right and wrong.[83] Although both Zhang Dongsun and Jin Yong, to a certain extent, had successfully constructed areas of intersection between two contrasting political sides, they were constantly questioned for promoting relativism to an excessive extent.

Nevertheless, Li Zehou regards the principle of value neutrality, along with the method of *du*, which is similar to the doctrine of accommodation, as the fundamental bedrock for contemporary social morality, aiming to promote the ideals of the "common good" and the pursuit of a fulfilling shared existence. For him, value neutrality is "a hard-won moral principle that has not been easy to achieve in the midst of the catastrophe caused by the absolute domination of traditional values in people's lives, and it is an important means of extricating oneself from the unification of the state and the church."[84] He emphasizes that it should be understood in accordance with concrete historical conditions. For instance, value neutrality may have already caused some compromising problems in the West, such as moral relativism and indecisiveness while facing crucial historical moments, but it remained an unattainable goal in modern China, especially during the Cultural Revolution. Again, it pertains to the pivotal and contentious issue of whether harmony should take precedence over justice, thereby questioning an absolute criterion of right and wrong under the party aegis, which overlooks the tangible realities at play.

Another political strand of Thirdspace is represented by the distinguished liberal Yin Haiguang, who steadfastly maintained an independently individual position without succumbing to either faction, repudiating any form of authoritarian rule. After moving to Taiwan in 1949, Yin strongly questioned the commitment of the third-force intellectuals who could not sustain their politically neutral position apart from the two combative parties and their inexorable authoritarianism. In contrast to both Zhang Dongsun and Zhang Junmai, he maintained an unflinching opposition to both the KMT and the CCP. His independent and unyielding liberal stance was even stronger than that of Hu Shi, who had been a pioneer of the Chinese liberal movement since the May Fourth events. Whereas Hu Shi was hesitant to break ties with the KMT in his later years, Yin Haiguang completely lost faith in Chiang Kai-shek's government in Taiwan and was cognizant of the CCP's totalitarian dominance. He noted how the majority of the May Fourth Movement thinkers wavered in their independent stance, feeling compelled to back one of the two dominant Chinese factions in the 1930s and 1940s. Critical of this fair-weather attitude, Yin Haiguang doubled down on the concept of individualism even more than other vocal Chinese liberals in the 1950s. Influenced by Western liberal classics such as John Stuart Mill's *On Liberty* and Friedrich A. Hayek's *The Constitution of Liberty*, he diagnosed the failure of the Chinese intellectuals to nurture individualism as rooted in collectivist cultural trends and polarized political pressure.[85] More importantly, Yin Haiguang specified the need for a pugnacious rationality to firmly distinguish right from wrong. As he repeatedly emphasized, uncompromising rationalism was indispensable in an era of zealous political trends such as dogmatism, pan-politicism, and pan-moralism. Yin Haiguang was a vociferous and virulent political fighter rather than a philosophical hermit. Nevertheless, drawn to the rigid sense of judgment between right and wrong, he was unavoidably caught in an either/or dilemma when he participated in the Sino-Western cultural disputes with scholars from the new Confucianist school in Hong Kong in the late 1950s. Maintaining the totalistic iconoclasm of traditional Chinese culture inherited from the May Fourth Movement, he was prevented by his complete Westernization from recognizing the "both/and" logic in these debates. However, his idea of "colorless thought" resembles Thirdspace because it sought a spectrum of rational objectivity to avoid political factionalism.

The exhaustive political struggle in modern China has inevitably made Thirdspace—a rational ground to contain disparate and opposing values—unstable and controversial. Such a polemical state compelled Liu Zaifu and Gao Xingjian to focus on Thirdspace's implications in the aesthetic realm instead, as far as possible from politics. Therefore, they called for aestheticizing Thirdspace while maintaining an independently individual political position. They shared the view that art must be separate from politics, not its handmaiden. This went against nearly a century of aesthetic and political thought represented by Liang Qichao 梁啟超 (1973–1929) and Lu Xun, who viewed literature as a primary instrument of national salvation. As the process of radicalization intensified during the revolutionary years, literature was completely hijacked by political imperatives, leaving no quarter for cultivating one's own aesthetic garden. Writers who wanted to utilize literature to influence politics were paradoxically ensnared by political ideology, vulnerable to losing their personal voice and space.

Choosing exiled lives overseas before and after the Tiananmen Square movement, Gao Xingjian and Liu Zaifu bid farewell to revolution and its either/or mentality. They not only kept their distance from the state but also were unwilling to join any expatriate dissident movements. This was due in part to their understanding that the overseas democratic force would "replicate the same revolutionary logic, uncannily solidifying the regime they meant to overthrow."[86] Instead, they chose to stand on the peripheries of the Western and Chinese cultures to nourish a cosmopolitan worldview and pursued an aesthetic transcendental goal by fully affirming Zhuangzi's spirit of individual freedom. Their political stance resonates with Isaiah Berlin's concept of "negative freedom," which not only proclaims a need for a minimum of personal freedom from external state interference but also celebrates the value of pluralism.[87] Running counter to Lu Xun's role model of a "spiritual warrior" that Yin Haiguang aspired to emulate, they aestheticized Thirdspace to enable literature's independence from politics and commercialization, protecting the potential for infinite creative possibilities.

In the aesthetic Thirdspace that is "a space of extraordinary openness,"[88] Liu Zaifu and Gao Xingjian have completely transcended the realm of judgments of right and wrong, showing how a playful thirding can lead to a multiplicity of approaches and visions of aesthetics. However, isolation from political and social trends relegated them to the periphery as calm observers and witnesses of society rather than proactive participants. They were politically ineffectual and consistently accused of being "escapists" within the intellectual field dominated by the "obsession with China,"[89] which is closely tied to Confucianism's ethos of social responsibility, throughout the twentieth century. Accordingly, regardless of the open and inclusive form Thirdspace presented, its proponents were often accused of being either "fence-sitters" or "escapists," demonstrating the insolvable quandaries in modern Chinese political history.

In short, the tumultuous political landscape of twentieth-century China witnessed the emergence of four distinct political stances—the doctrine of accommodation, the principle of value neutrality, the independent individual stance, and aesthetic transcendence—which showcased alternative pathways for Thirdspace politics. The doctrine of accommodation represented by Zhang Dongsun places great emphasis on the yin-yang dialectics that illustrate "partially complementary and partially conflicting," seeking negotiation and balance between two feuding and holistic political forces.[90] In a similar vein, the principle of value neutrality implemented by Jin Yong delineates a middle space of existence that stands entirely apart from the two feuding factions and is based on rationality. Although both Yin Haiguang and Liu Zaifu also longed for a public sphere that would permit democratic control of state affairs, they prioritized the ideals of individualism long absent in the intellectual political milieu after the May Fourth Movement. Where Yin Haiguang was prone to be a political fighter with a keen sense of right and wrong, Liu Zaifu was more inclined to embrace an apolitical, aesthetic transcendence, totally withdrawing from society after his flight in

1989. Altogether, these intellectuals have created a Thirdspace that implies or even proclaims an inherent affinity between the public and the private. This double-sidedness of Thirdspace—on the one hand, possessing an inclination to healthy public expression and on the other, having individualism as an integral part—points to a more complex image of creation. It aspires to not only a nation-building project protecting value pluralism but also assuring individual freedom without being subsumed under nationalist obsessions.

The Playful and Fantastic Thirding

How is Thirdspace represented in arts and literature? Although writers and artists desired the right to stay in their own garden, their works can still speak to the present with powerful and critical messages. Though there is no consensus about how to resolve the rigid polarization arising from the tendency to radicalization in modern China, Chinese writers and artists struggled to carve out a Thirdspace of individual creativity free from political distortion, with many passages to infinite possibilities and boundless richness in aesthetic creation. The very essence of the aesthetic Thirdspace is its transcendental and multidimensional visions, which cast reflexive light on the encroaching oppositions between the real and the imagined, the subject and the object. As such, Thirdspace is not merely a visible spatial construction with distinct political, cultural, societal, and material characteristics but also contains invisible, imaginary, surreal, and even quasi-theological layers that define the inner world of an artist. Such a realm offers enormous freedom to innovatively dissolve and transgress boundaries of genres, disciplines, and media. In the present study, I choose the following case studies to illustrate the variations of Thirdspace in the fields of literature and art: Zhang Dongsun's philosophical poetry, Jin Yong's literary fable of Thirdspace, Liu Zaifu's fragmentary writing, Gao Xingjian's playful and innovative thirding, Xi Xi's image-text reinvention, Chi Zijian's 遲子建 (1964–) epic portrayal of the Evenki group, Chu Tien-hsin's mapping of the heterotopias of Taipei, and Chan Koonchung's speculative political novel. I follow two trajectories, first treating intermedia practices—in-betweenness—as the typical Thirdspace in which new and diverse aesthetic meanings emerge and flourish. Second, I examine how the critical thirding is built into literary and artistic works that contain intrinsic allegorical meanings, successfully transforming "the categorical and closed logic of either/or to the dialectically open logic of both/and also."[91]

Zhang Dongsun's philosophical poetry (*zhexue shi* 哲學詩) written in the 1950s and 1960s is unequivocally the manifestation of intermediality. After he became a political dissident in 1952, he was forced to channel his personal feelings and philosophical knowledge into the classical Chinese poetic form. In the new genre of philosophical poetry that he invented, he transgressed the traditional formal and disciplinary boundaries of poetry and philosophy, experimentally invoking intensive interaction between poetic expression and scholarly connotation. The intermediality between the philosophical meanings and poetic expression not only expands our understanding of the new aesthetic form but also reflects the inner world of this sophisticated and controversial Chinese intellectual facing extreme political pressure. Inherently embodying a Thirdspace of intermediacy, his philosophical poetry interweaves his unique portrayal of certain eminent Western philosophers with his own theory of "plural epistemology." It formulates a critical interface, a middle ground where literature and philosophy constantly collide and negotiate, where individual rights, the spirit of tolerance, and freedom of speech are advocated and safeguarded. The interplay between aesthetic style and philosophical knowledge in this avant-garde literary form not only expresses the heart/mind and sentiment of the poet in response to the specific historical era but also exposes the unsettled tension between his ambition and cruel reality.

In Jin Yong's fictional world, he establishes and broadens the scope of Thirdspace through representative images of heroes who embody multifaceted cultural identities, mental vistas, and chivalrous hearts. Their personifications of Thirdspace go beyond the Manichean binary logic of dividing the world into absolute good and evil. This technique not only metaphorically reflects the political reality of the Cultural Revolution but also contains universal references that contribute to his criticism of the dichotomous principles prevalent in the modern world. Drawn from various traditional Chinese cultural resources, some heroes incarnate the Daoist spirit, retreating to a reclusive space to sanctify individual freedom; some embrace the Buddhist benevolent spirit to reinforce tolerance of difference; and others epitomize Confucian morality, actively engaging in salvation and undertaking social responsibilities to protect the people and country. Through those fictional images, Jin Yong not only calls for Thirdspace to transcend the dogmatic binary logic and mentality but also seeks to explore its complexity and paradoxes. With the cunning and intricate character of Wei Xiaobao 韋小寶, who excels at negotiating and mediating between oppositional forces without any principles, Jin Yong sarcastically discloses the negative side of Thirdspace as a kind of survival strategy and skill in the political and social context of modern China. As Wei Xiaobao becomes a fence-sitter not committing to any political and moral standpoints—a caricature of a certain Chinese character that is ubiquitous in officialdom—Thirdspace embedded in this image reveals the pitfall of completely expelling the judgment of right and wrong, trenchantly criticized by Lu Xun in his short story "Resurrecting the Dead" ("Qisi" 起死). Jin Yong's convoluted and paradoxical building of Thirdspace in his fictional world carries an allegorical criticism of both the social reality and the national character.

Liu Zaifu's fragmentary writing (*pianduan xiezuo* 片段寫作) is a unique form vacillating between poetic expression and metaphysical meditation, the lyrical and the pensive, the sensational and the rational. He became enthralled with fragmentary writing when he found himself at the crossroads of Western and Chinese cultures after the Tiananmen Square movement. Defining himself as a "gap man" (*xifeng ren* 隙縫人) who stands at the peripheries and intersections of both cultures, he finds that fragmentary writing, whose nomadic nature is in tune with his overseas drifting journey, gives him enormous freedom to float between oppositions and ruptures, breaking away from any fixations imposed by political ideologies and theoretical paradigms. The most distinctive feature of Liu Zaifu's fragmentary writing is its close association with the Chan Buddhist method of "sudden enlightenment" (*dunwu* 頓悟), which starkly contrasts with logical argument and evidence. Every piece springs from spontaneous intuition and lucid meditation, resonating with a sense of self-enlightenment in relation to his reflections on historical and cultural issues. Comparable to Walter Benjamin's notion of the "constellation,"[92] Liu employs fluid, ephemeral approaches to go between different forms and interweave disparate ideas and inspirations, maintaining skepticism about systematic and totalistic methodology. Most significantly, he not only uses fragmentary writing to cast light on his comprehension of philosophy and the predicament of exile but also applies it to literary reviews and cultural commentaries, bridging creative writing and literary criticism. His style often creates plural mental vistas resembling Gao Xingjian's state of Chan (*chan zhuangtai* 禪狀體), passing from heart to heart, soul to soul.

Gao Xingjian has excelled at implementing Thirdspace in his own works. He not only discovers a third broad space between two opposite poles but also employs various inventive methods, cognitive and emotive, to broaden and deepen new possibilities in this territory.[93] As a panoramic artist or a polymath, Gao Xingjian has successfully launched a new critical ground by calling for special attention to the "in-between" space, which amounts to Thirdspace in his transcultural and transmedia experiments and explorations. In Gao Xingjian's entire literary and artistic oeuvre, the innovative designation and implementation of Thirdspace have reached a climax, flourishing not only in specific genres such as drama, painting, fiction, and poetry but also in intermedial or transmedial phenomena such as cine-poems. He finds that the in-between space of transmediality possesses its own special sort of appeal, an immanent polyphonic effect that goes beyond the limit of a single register of one artistic form.[94] Akin to the Chinese correlative cosmological view that considers the whole universe as a holistic oneness with infinite interrelated things, Gao Xingjian proposes the approach of "the total theater" to interlink multifarious performance forms. Resembling the "complete drama" from Chinese traditional theater, "the total theater" is like a small universe including a range of artistic media such as singing, reciting, playing, dancing, and acrobatics.[95] His cine-poetry has the similar designation of "the total art," encompassing various media ranging from literature, drama, and poetry to dance, painting, photography, and music. It is analogous to what the literary scholar Werner Wolf defines as plurimediality,[96] a mixture of different and various medial forms, which enchants and stimulates viewers to perceive a diversity of meanings and aesthetic states generated from a vibrant and intertwined existence.

The celebrated and palpable image of Thirdspace is preeminently symbolized by Gao Xingjian's concept of "the third eye (figure 0.2)," which is strongly influenced by the Chan Buddhist sense of nonattachment.[97] For Gao Xingjian, the third eye is the intelligent eye of an artist that "overrides the self" as well as narcissism, capable of observing inwardly with lucid cognition.[98] It parallels the French philosopher Maurice Merleau-Ponty's concept of the third eye that emphasizes "a gaze from inside" to surpass the dualism of the subject and the object, the external and the internal.[99] But more significantly, it is closely related to the Chan Buddhist idea of nonattachment, no thoughts, and emptiness to completely free the subject from both worldly bondage and the narcissistic self.[100] Through a purification process, the subject temporarily withdraws from worldly traps and concepts as well as the chaotic self, achieving a Zhuangzian state of absolute spiritual freedom and then looking back to observe inwardly without any obstruction or attachment. Different from "the lyrical eye and mind,"[101] Gao

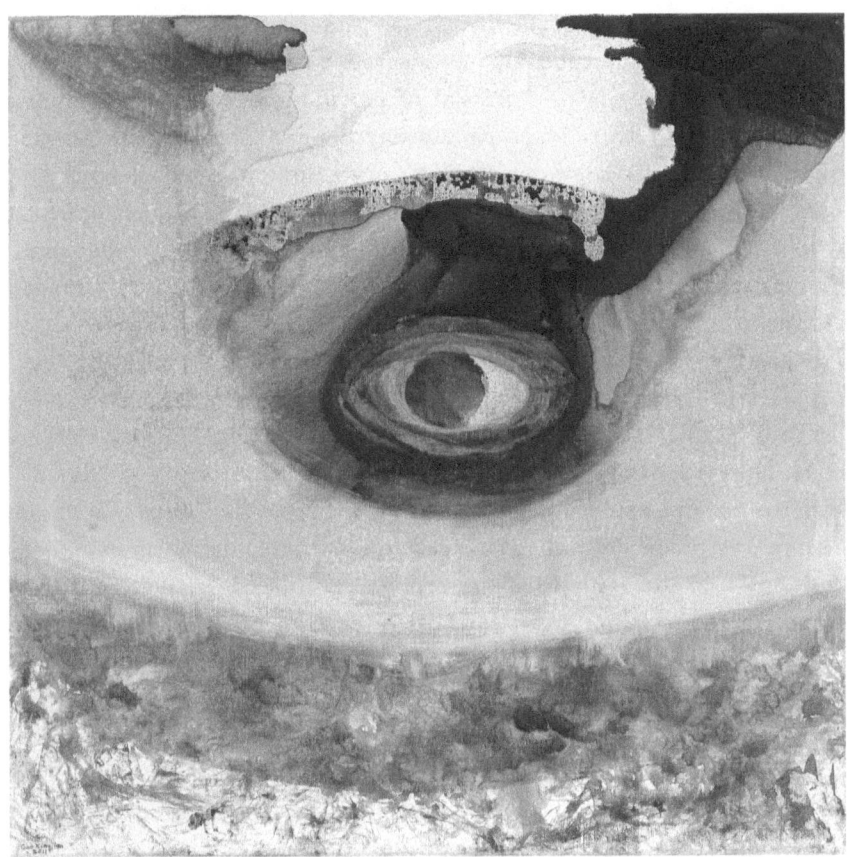

Figure 0.2 The Celestial Eye, 2011, by Gao Xingjian. Reprinted by permission of Gao Xingjian.

Xingjian's third eye is equivalent to "the neutral eye," which avoids any form of emotive self-indulgence by emphasizing Chan-like meditation.[102] Under the surveillance of a pair of lucid and cold eyes, the artist is able to detach from the self and calmly observe the surrounding world and the inner mind, kindling and cultivating the perpetual and ephemeral Chan state that is unattainable by verbal expression. In other words, Gao Xingjian's third eye becomes a premise for the emergence of a Chan state for higher spiritual and aesthetic fulfillment.

Xi Xi's experimental intermedial story "Marvels of a Floating City" combines René Magritte's thirteen paintings and her own interpretive texts, presenting a remarkable allegory of Hong Kong as well as Thirdspace in general. Her intermedial practice evokes "interactive narration" between artist/writer and audience, inviting viewers to imagine, think, and even tell a story of their own.[103] Instead of providing an integral relationship between image and text, Xi Xi circumvents the fixing of meanings, resisting mimetic representation of objects. The story clearly manifests the quandary signified by the aspiration and the disquiet of the residents of Hong Kong who simultaneously enjoy the privilege of cultural hybridity and fret about the unstable and unpredictable future that will be influenced by a sudden change in 1997.

Through poetically narrating the century-long history of the Evenki people, Chi Zijian in her novel, *The Last Quarter of the Moon* (*E'er guna he you'an* 額爾古納河右岸), assiduously constructs a unique Thirdspace from a contested borderland perspective. She grounds her imagination in the non-Han regionalism, exploring the shamanistic beliefs of the Evenki that sustain a unified worldview regarding all objects, human and nonhuman, as embedded with soul and spirit. Facing a formidable challenge from an aggressive Han-centered nationalism and modern civilization, her novel bears witness to the precarious ecology of a marginalized people unable to sustain their identity. Shamanism is important to this vista of Thirdspace because the shaman acts as a bridge between the physical and spiritual worlds, interplaying animism, modernity, and environmentalism. The utopian Thirdspace of the Evenki is loaded with a different set of cultural and religious components, yet it appears to inevitably dissipate due to the sweeping historical and modern forces. By singing a plangent dirge to this minority group, Chi Zijian trenchantly defies the hegemonic discourse of polarization between the Han Chinese center and its peripheral ethnicities.

In response to the politically divided ambience in Taiwan, Chu Tien-hsin creates a set of "heterotopias" ranging from her literary writing to political engagement and even the nonhuman world. Her novel *The Old Capital* (*Gudu* 古都) is a manifestation of a literary heterotopia that navigates nodes where intricate reality and memory interweave. Her political involvement in Taiwan primarily follows the footsteps of Zhang Dongsun's third route, intending to establish a third political party to break from the political gridlock of the KMT and the Democratic Progressive Party (DPP). She heightens the "freedom of non-identification" to uphold individual autonomy against any party's hegemonic control over a homogenizing Taiwanese identity. The multiple layers of her Thirdspace also extend to the nonhuman world, going beyond the entrenched anthropocentric worldview that has been dominant in the past few centuries. This interspecies Thirdspace encompasses a realm where animal protection volunteers and street cats embark on a constant struggle against the conventional boundaries of human versus nature.

Chan Koonchung's own political position is analogous to that of the third-force intellectuals, attempting to find an alternative way to balance liberalism and equality, capitalism and socialism, personal freedom and state power. In his fictional world, he delineates a heterotopia—a strategic metaphor of Thirdspace inspired by Michel Foucault—positioned between the optimistic utopian and the pessimistic dystopian, going beyond the stark demarcations between the physical and the metaphysical, reality and imagination. Belonging to the category of "political novel," Chan's speculative imagination of heterotopia is not necessarily an "oppositional novel," even if it is skeptical of "the fundamental principles and intrinsic logic of the Chinese model in certain ways."[104] Rather, Chan's views adamantly stand against the deadlock of extreme Left versus extreme Right, choosing a moderate and middle ground in which a truly plural and heterogenous society prospers.

In general, in the political and social context demarcated by the dichotomous thinking of "either you die or I do," the existence of Thirdspace is inevitably contested and complicated. Those Chinese intellectuals who sought to advance Thirdspace through diversified modes of intervention and mediation amid the national crisis were often disparaged as either vacillating between two extremes or attempting to retreat to the reclusive life. They unfortunately inhabited a world where dogmatism in the either/or framework rendered it impossible to find shared bases for launching and expanding Thirdspace. However, while literature can be used as an instrument to change society as Lu Xun advocated, it can also transcend reality by withholding Zhuangzi's absolute spiritual freedom.[105] Looking at the world with a "mundane eye" (*shisu zhiyan* 世俗之眼) requires making the judgment between right and wrong; however, looking with a Zhuangzian eye of the way (*daoyan* 道眼) would dissolve the bifurcations between gain and loss, self and world, right and wrong, life and death, truth and illusion.[106] Such a boundless vision is equivalent to the Aleph, which "was probably two or three centimeters in diameter, but universal space was contained inside it, with no diminution in size."[107] It is pivotal for literature to contain a profound third zone in which to understand the complexity of human nature, which cannot be solely and arbitrarily defined as either great benevolence or great evil. Only with such a transcendent perspective can

Thirdspace counter binary theories and reveal infinite creative possibilities without any restraints.

The Making of Thirdspace

Adopting an integrated methodology based on a dynamic interaction among different disciplines, this study probes the complexities of Chinese intellectuals' choice of Thirdspace in different historical contexts. An integrative approach—amalgamating historical narration, philosophical ideas, and literary analysis—helps to reveal the significance of Thirdspace against the grand narrative of Chinese political and cultural history, which is permeated by dogmatic ideological language and dominated by a variety of conventional paradigms in the either/or mindset. Thirdspace is a spatial politics or a resilient discourse to reflect the perplexing relationship between politics and aesthetics, the state and the individual.

The following six chapters focus on individuals' multidimensional and transdisciplinary endeavors in constituting Thirdspace in the Sinophone context. I set the periodization of the manuscript from 1946 to 2020 because 1946 was the time when Zhang Dongsun was most vigorous in concretizing his theory of the third route and putting it into action. The representative cases that I discuss stretch from 1946 to 2020, when Fang Fang's 方方 (1955–) *Wuhan Diary* was published in the midst of the concurrent COVID-19 pandemic.

Chapter 1 provides a critical reflection on Zhang Dongsun's theory of middle politics, which was simultaneously attacked by two extreme sides, the CCP and KMT, or the leftists and the rightists. Through investigating Zhang's philosophical system, political comments, and cultural criticism in the Republic of China, I seek to understand the motivations that compelled him to take the third route, which attempted to transcend binary oppositions but miscarried and perished in the new China. Moreover, I discuss Zhang Dongsun's "philosophical poetry" written after he was deprived of a political position in the central government as well as his position as a philosophy professor at Peking University in 1952.

Chapter 2 outlines the spiritual journey of Yin Haiguang, whose unyielding opposition to both the KMT and the CCP prevented him from falling into the same trap as the third-force intellectuals who failed to hold on to their independence under extremely polarized political pressure. Through selected political commentaries, philosophical treatises, and correspondence, I delineate how Yin Haiguang inherited and developed the self-reliant liberal legacy from Hu Shi and other May Fourth intellectuals, adhering to individualism as a fundamental stance to defy totalitarianism.

Chapter 3 discusses Jin Yong's great effort to position his own *Ming Pao* empire as neutral in response to the intense power struggles between the Left and the Right in colonial Hong Kong. By promoting value neutrality, he successfully constituted a Thirdspace that is tantamount to a civil society where political interactions stay outside the direct control of opposing political forces. In parallel, I will discuss how Thirdspace is symbolically imbricated in his martial arts novels, whose fictional world of "rivers and lakes" (*jianghu* 江湖) refers to Chinese history and political reality.

Chapter 4 gives a historical account of how Liu Zaifu consciously went beyond the dualist way of thinking in his literary subjectivity, theory of the composition of human character, and aesthetical transcendence from the 1980s through his post-Tiananmen exile life overseas. By choosing Thirdspace as his foothold in the diaspora, he not only chiseled out an alternative way to avoid being hijacked by either of the two extreme political sides but also found a richness and infinity of aesthetic meanings and forms that emerge from in-betweenness. His fragmentary writing, closely intertwined with his exilic journey, is testimony to a border-crossing among various literary and cultural forms.

Chapter 5 delves into Gao Xingjian's three innovative cine-poems—*Silhouette/Shadow*, *After the Flood*, and *Requiem for Beauty*—to scrutinize his unique transmedia aesthetics and philosophical meditations that characterize a profound and multifaceted Thirdspace. Gao Xingjian's inventive thirding not only provides insights into his postexilic plays and transnational and transcultural identities but also sheds light on all the genres he has experimented with, including cine-poems, fiction, painting, poetry, dance, and photography. His artistic undertakings in exploring Thirdspace have exemplified a personal renaissance in literature and arts in a time besieged by spiritual destitution.

Chapter 6 is devoted to how contemporary female writers from Hong Kong, mainland China, and Taiwan redefine Thirdspace in a disparate way. I first discuss Xi Xi's image-text story "Marvels of a Floating City," which hybridizes intermedia approaches to present an allegory of Hong Kong in between Western and Chinese political and cultural dominance. Then, I analyze mainland female writer Chi Zijian's novel *The Last Quarter of the*

Moon, which establishes the Thirdspace in borderlands from which she conjures up shamanism to go between the spiritual and physical worlds. Serving as an elegy for the declining Evenki ethnic minority amid the process of modern industrialization, this novel evokes an unfamiliar religious aura to grapple with a Han-dominant modernity and defy the disintegration of humans and nature. Third, I explore how Chu Tien-hsin situates the Thirdspace in a variety of "heterotopias" of postcolonial Taiwan, which has become an increasingly divided social and political space. The melding of social activism and literary representation exemplifies her emphasis on the Thirdspace political stance, which is incongruent with the prevailing Taiwan identity controlled by two antagonistic parties.

The book concludes with an epilogue reflecting the significance of Thirdspace in the global context. First, I reconsider the multifarious definitions of Thirdspace proposed by various writers and thinkers discussed in the book. I argue that their social practices, philosophical ideas, and aesthetic creations surrounding Thirdspace were alternative reactions to the political polemics of their times. The privileged and controversial positions they took were greatly challenged, exposing the unresolved tensions orchestrated by binary factions and their mentality. I also revisit and synthesize relevant insights from previously discussed concepts such as neutrality, pluralism, liberalism, aestheticism, positive and negative liberty, proper measure, and yin-yang dialectics. Thirdspace is thus not simply a word or idea but rather is intimately and eminently connected to not only Chinese wisdom such as Daoism, Buddhism, and Confucianism but also Western philosophical ideas as seen in the works of Immanuel Kant, Friedrich Hayek, Isaiah Berlin, etc.

Following that, I deal with Chan Koonchung's novel *The Second Year of Jianfeng: A Uchronia of New China* (*Jianfeng ernian: Xin Zhongguo wuyoushi* 建豐二年：新中國烏有史), which features Zhang Dongsun as one of the fictional characters and outlines a Uchronia of New China where the political ideas of Thirdspace have been successfully implemented. Lastly, I examine a polemic phenomenon that happened under Xi Jinping's regime in which narrow-minded nationalism resurrected the arbitrary either/or mindset that has largely polarized the existing booming cyberspace. Under political circumstances that entail the continuity of holistic or either/or language and logic, the discursive strategy of Thirdspace is still relevant for speaking to the pressing issues of our current time.

CHAPTER 1

Zhang Dongsun

The Predicament of Thirdspace

Time passes with a flick of the wrist as I approach eighty,
ashamed to possess this spirited body.
Sighing at the loss of my father at a young age,
studying at different places in the prime of my life,
embroiled in factional struggles in my waning years,
many times, alone, experiencing the world's heat and cold.
Released from capture and punishment,
preaching peace amid the besieged city,
what I should laugh at is my own overconfidence.
Don't gaze back at the past
as if dragging your tail through the mud,
as absurd as it is.[1]

彈指光陰，八旬將屆，愧此昂藏。
嘆早年失怙，壯年遊學，晚年錮黨，幾（獨）閱炎涼。
虜獄刑還，圍城勸解，應笑書生不自量。
休回首，似泥中曳尾，亦曰荒唐。

In 1964, Zhang Dongsun, one of the most important philosophers and public intellectuals in twentieth-century China, wrote a poem to celebrate in advance of his eightieth birthday, which was coming in 1965. His life was at its nadir, as he was politically and academically ostracized, accused of being an American spy and leaking national secrets during the Korean War. In the poem, Zhang briefly looked back at his turbulent life by using the classical form of *ci*—a literary genre at odds with all the new and revolutionary expressions in the new China. Although mourning a bygone career that saw dramatic ups and downs with hidden political causes, he seemed to replace a melancholic tone with a sense of ease and peaceful voice.

> The past flows away in vain;
> I should look to the future with joy,
> pouring wine to melt an iron heart.
> I know I am aging;
> the heavens have left me my weathered eyes,
> Still able to see peace and tranquility.[2]

> 去日空過，來朝且樂，有酒聊澆鐵石腸。
> 知衰矣，顧天留老眼，猶見和詳。

Even if the poem is designed around reminiscences, the poet was not entrenched in the mood of pain while facing the huge contrast between the glorious past and the humiliating present. However, had he known that a more violent political storm and spiraling crisis—the Cultural Revolution—would come in three years and relentlessly drag him into prison at the age of eighty-two, he probably would have written the poem in a completely different way.

Zhang Dongsun has been hailed in academic circles as one of the leading scholars of Western philosophy, an influential thinker, active political commentator, and trenchant cultural critic in the Republic of China period. As a well-established modern Chinese philosopher, he not only systematically introduced Western philosophy into China but also created his own theory of plural epistemology. Generally speaking, Zhang was regarded as the scholar of his generation who comprehended Western philosophy in the deepest and most profound way.[3] As a public intellectual, he vigorously participated in many significant debates, such as political reform versus revolution, science versus metaphysics, and Marxism versus democracy, and played a pivotal role in fostering a public sphere by launching and editing many magazines and contributing his political commentaries. His views on many important and enduring themes of culture and politics allow us to map the paths already trodden and those yet to be explored, especially his views on integrating capitalism and socialism as an alternative path for solving national problems. When the master narrative of Chinese political and cultural history of the past century was charged with a strong sense of either/or thinking and conflicts derived from opposing binaries, he intentionally created a critical interface of Thirdspace through which a spirit of tolerance, the independence of individuals, and freedom of speech could be protected.

Even if Zhang Dongsun never used the term "Thirdspace" in his political commentaries and philosophical works, he conscientiously explored an in-between space that could transcend the antagonistic conflicts between the CCP and the KMT, or the leftists and the rightists. Overtly claiming "a middle attitude" (*zhongjian taidu* 中間態度) to practice moderate politics, he rejected the long-established bipolar structure of class struggle formulated by Marxist followers.[4] More important, he promoted Thirdspace across his varied philosophical, cultural, and political system, in which his own creative intervention within the interstices or the in-between space opens up the possibility of coexistence and the negotiation of differences. His insistence on the principles of inclusiveness, rationality, and pragmatism distinguished him from radical leftists and rightists and even became one of the reasons he was purportedly named the first traitor in Maoist China. The study of Zhang's vital mode of Thirdspace, which is a testimonial to his effort to deconstruct binary logic in thinking and practice, can shed light on the dynamics among Chinese intellectuals facing a cluster of tensions amid national crisis.

Zhang Dongsun was an intriguing thinker because he embodied the contradictions of his time. He was both pedantic and radical, both old-fashioned and postmodernist, both political and apolitical, both responsive to and out of joint with his time. He was characterized as an idealist scholar trapped by the polar politics he strove to overthrow. Although his theory clearly drew from traditional Chinese philosophy, it unexpectedly anticipated postmodern philosophy, even influencing Western thinkers such as Julia Kristeva. It is not difficult to find affinities between Western postmodern philosophy and Zhang Dongsun's own system of the plurality of knowledge, including antiessentialism, antitotalitarianism, criticism of monism, the coexistence of multiple factors, and the subversion of authoritarian discourse.[5] Certain aspects of his ideas—the challenge of essentialism, the question of the one absolute truth, the innovation of cultural interactionism, the interrogation of metaphysical dualism and causality, the juxtaposition of multiple factors, and the dynamic envisioning of Thirdspace—are consonant with postmodern and postcolonial theories. However, we should be careful not to label him as a postcolonial theorist or a postmodern philosopher. His theory appears to be a pastiche, amalgamating the ancient and contemporary, Western and Chinese, philosophical thought and political commentaries, cultural interdisciplinary studies and cultural practices. On the one hand, he was extremely avant-garde in crafting a matrix of philosophical, political, and cultural patterns that constituted Thirdspace, where the plurality of truth, juxtaposition of two competing sides, heterogeneity, and otherness are deeply imbricated. On the other hand, on the broad spectrum of his interdisciplinary and intercultural studies, he persistently pursued individualism, democracy, and rationalism for the project of Chinese modernity.

How did Zhang Dongsun construct Thirdspace in his plural epistemology in addition to his views on the cultural conflicts between the East and the West? Why did Zhang Dongsun's notion of middle politics and his search for the third route, which aimed to constitute a shared existence between the left and the right in the modern Chinese political field, not come to fruition? Why can the intricate relationship between Thirdspace and Chinese modernity still be heard resonating even in our own time? To answer these questions, I will focus on exploring the Thirdspace embedded in Zhang Dongsun's thought and endeavors, which offers invaluable insights into the polemics of his time. Because Zhang Dongsun was a political dissident in the 1950s, he was relegated to oblivion in Chinese academic circles until the 1990s. Although many studies have emerged, revolving around his achievements in philosophical and political thought, there is a conspicuous lack of academic work drawing attention to Thirdspace, which he developed as a distinct discourse to truly speak to the complexity of Chinese modernity.

Adopting an interdisciplinary research method, I will scrutinize how Zhang's sensibility of creating and maintaining Thirdspace provides a new prism through which to reexamine a cluster of tensions associated with the dominant discourse of enlightenment and revolution. His philosophical system, political thought and comments, and cultural criticism in the Republic of China and his motivations to take the third route were simultaneously attacked by the two extreme sides of the left and the right. Intervening powerfully in modern debates on the ongoing role of nation-building, he attempted to transcend binary oppositions, but inevitably this led to his downfall in the new China. In addition, I will analyze his philosophical poetry, which was written amid his political quandary but became an innovative intermedia practice, combining Western philosophy with the classical Chinese poetic form. The case of Zhang Dongsun, who represents a group of liberal Chinese intellectuals, not only indicates the predicament of the discourse of Thirdspace in the modern Chinese context but also adds new insights to our understanding of the divergent spiritual journeys that Chinese intellectuals have taken in response to national crisis.

Acting out Middle Politics

Zhang Dongsun received a formal traditional Chinese education under the supervision of his brother, Zhang Ertian, who was a famous poet and scholar in their hometown, Qiantang County of Zhejiang. Confucian classical education was instrumental in shaping his later sense of political responsibility and social participation. At the age of nineteen, in 1905, he went to study philosophy in Japan, and after his return in 1911, he emerged as an important political commentator. Although he joined Sun Yat-sen's 孫中山 (1866–1925) Nanjing government, taking an administrative job in 1911, he ended his political career after Yuan Shikai 袁世凱 (1859–1916) usurped the government. As an influential political commentator, Zhang Dongsun was involved in many important public debates starting in the late Qing period. He exemplified those Chinese intellectuals who preferred to employ their own words and thoughts to influence society rather than physically plunge into political action.

From 1913 to 1916, he wrote many journal articles on the political systems suitable for the new Republic in China. His idea of elite politics (*xianren zhengzhi* 賢人政治) that aims to constrain dictatorship was an indispensable source of inspiration for the development of liberalism in China.[6] He also launched, with friends, his own magazine, *Righteousness* (*Zhengyi* 正誼), in 1914, along with *China Journal* (*Zhonghua zazhi* 中華雜誌) in the same year, both of which discussed sensitive political and national problems. In 1917, Zhang became the editor-in-chief of *The China Times* (*Shishi xinbao* 時事新報) and launched *Learning Light* (*Xuedeng* 學燈), the supplement of the newspaper that cultivated the Chinese public sphere for free discussion in the new Republic. As the scholar Nuan Gao pointed out, under Zhang Dongsun's leadership, the editors of *Learning Light* created a moderate, pragmatic, rational, and inclusive cultural milieu, which "enabled them to avoid arbitrariness or prejudice like that of the extreme left or right."[7] In contrast to the May Fourth pioneer Chen Duxiu's emotion-driven iconoclasm, Zhang Dongsun offered a path of moderation and rationality, advocating conciliation of values between science and philosophy and between Chinese culture and Western culture.

Inclined to identify with the reformist method rather than violent revolution, Zhang Dongsun had a close affinity with Liang Qichao, an influential Late Qing intellectual, but did not actually join his Progressive Party. In 1920, he secretly attended a meeting organized by Chen Duxiu to found the Chinese Communist Party, but he left the nascent party due to his preference for guild socialism. In the late 1920s, Zhang Dongsun participated in influential debates on socialism with the Communist leaders Li Dazhao 李大釗 (1889–1927) and Chen Duxiu; he was wary of the Leninist revolutionary vanguard model they espoused. He believed China needed to go through a process of industrialization but was critical of certain characteristics of capitalism, such as laissez-faire liberalism, materialism, and selfishness. He also recognized the socialist utopian idea of equality but strongly objected to the class struggle of Marxism. He believed that guild socialism, which allocates certain democratic rights to workers, was a moderate way to solve this dilemma amid debates with radical socialist advocates such as Chen Duxiu.[8] Zhang's criticism of Marxism continued in the 1930s when he launched a major debate about dialectical materialism, criticizing class struggle within Marxist theory and opposing the "dictatorship of the proletariat" promoted by the CCP. He also redirected his focus toward researching and teaching Western philosophy starting in 1917. Drawing on Kant's thought, Zhang Dongsun established his own philosophical system known as "plural epistemology."

Zhang Dongsun disavowed any political affiliations publicly, only forming the National Socialist Party with another notable liberal intellectual, Zhang Junmai, in 1932 in protest against the KMT's intolerant one-party government. Zhang Dongsun's famous political idea of the third route was formed as early as 1932 in his provocative article "The Words We Want to Say" ("Women yaoshuo de hua" 我們要說的話), jointly written with Zhang Junmai and published in *The National Renaissance* (*Zaisheng* 再生); they used the phrase "the revisionist democratic politics" (*xiuzheng de minzhu zhengzhi* 修正的民主政治) to designate a middle politics that could promote adjustments to reconcile two conflicting parties.[9] Since Zhang Dongsun and Zhang Junmai were very close friends and allies, it is unsurprising that both endorsed "a third kind of politics" or "a middle route," aiming to find a virtual balance between all-encompassing state power and valuable individual liberty. This political perspective was intended to construct a united government grounded in popular consensus that would safeguard the rule of law and thereby preserve human rights and individualism.[10]

During the Second Sino-Japanese War, Zhang Dongsun demonstrated strong patriotism and the unyielding spirit of Chinese intellectuals. He slightly tilted toward the CCP during the Japanese invasion due to his dissatisfaction with the KMT's corruption and malpractice during the national crisis. Endorsing Nationalist-Communist cooperation to properly defend against the Japanese, he helped establish a communication network with the Communists, encouraging his students to join the war effort. Both his fervent exertion and his high profile made him a valuable target for the Japanese, who captured him in 1941. During his captivity for four months and ten days, he attempted suicide four times to avoid humiliation by the Japanese, even fighting with his jailors. Repeatedly refusing to be intimidated by interrogators during the detention, he was later given an eighteen-month suspended jail sentence.[11]

In the 1940s, he belonged to the third force Chinese liberal intellectuals, who assiduously scouted the middle way, playing an important mediating role in reconciling the differences between two competing parties and two antagonistic ideologies. Edmund Fung penetratingly points out that those intellectuals, who were the elites of nonpartisan factions or minor parties and groups (MPGs), made a great effort to produce "the germs of a reformist, liberal order in the nationalist era." Furthermore, although they eventually failed to mitigate the struggles and conflicts between the two hostile sides, they vigorously "developed the democratic impulse of the May Fourth period, drawing strength from reason, tolerance, and a proclivity for negotiation and compromise."[12] As a representative figure of the third force movement, Zhang Dongsun constantly criticized the KMT for its one-party rule, political indoctrination, and corruption, but at the same time, kept a certain distance from the CCP, disagreeing with its ideology of class struggle and violent revolution. Different from most Chinese intellectuals, who were obsessed with dichotomous thinking, such as the rich versus the poor and divided themselves into opposing groups of rightists and leftists, Zhang Dongsun decisively chose the third route, searching for a middle ground to amalgamate capitalist industrial development, guild socialism, and democracy.[13] Advocating the theory of pluralist politics, he not only regarded democracy as a culture or a way of life with a cluster of values for an entire society but also integrated capitalist elements such as material incentives and the protection of private property with a socialist planned economy. He did not see any contradiction within the assimilation of all three qualities because he considered the road to socialistic democracy to be gradual, nonviolent, revisional, and open, in the course of which capitalism was a necessary phase.[14] But at the same time, due to his preference for a harmonious society, he was persistently critical of Marxism and objected to class struggle.

However, in the special historical situation that was bound to extreme polarization, the third route and middle politics were doomed to fail. Although Zhang Dongsun and Zhang Junmai were alike in certain political respects and held the same view of middle politics, embracing the democratic spirit and stressing moderation, independence, and compromise between two competing parties, they eventually differed, ending their friendship. Zhang Junmai became increasingly inclined to favor the KMT's cause, and Zhang Dongsun grew more sympathetic to the CCP. After the two parted ways, Zhang Dongsun became a leading spokesman for the Chinese Democratic League in 1946. His important essay "The Middle Way as a Political Route" ("Yige zhongjianxing de zhengzhi luxian" 一個中間性的政治路線) had a great impact on the intellectual circle at the time. Other Chinese intellectuals, such as Shi Fuliang 施復亮 (1899–1970), Chu Anping 儲安平 (1909–1966), and Fu Lei 傅雷 (1908–1966), endorsed his ideas and wrote articles enthusiastically supporting him.[15] By proposing the third route as an alternative political choice, they were making a last effort to emphasize the dynamic, multiple, and contested nature of democracy and liberalism, which were scarce in modern China.[16] In 1948, Zhang Dongsun served as a negotiator between the CCP and the KMT, helping achieve the peaceful liberation of Beijing.[17]

After the foundation of a new China in 1949, the middle route was wretchedly deprived of its right to exist. Not surprisingly, Zhang Dongsun became the victim of what he had long detested—dictatorship and class struggle. In the beginning, he held a high position in the Central Government Committee, but he became increasingly disappointed with the Communist dictatorship, which comprehensively suppressed democracy and freedom. In the nationwide assembly held to gather the votes for chairman on September 30, 1949, there was a mystery: everybody voted for Mao Zedong except one. Suspicion and scrutiny fell upon the typically outspoken and prominent Zhang Dongsun, regardless of a lack of evidence—another damning demonstration of how controversial Zhang Dongsun was under Mao's rule.[18]

His political and academic career ended abruptly in 1951 because he was charged with the crime of treason for leaking national security information to the United States. Ironically, even in the new China, Zhang Dongsun still naively tried to find a middle path, preferring moderation to ease the tension of binarism in the predominant Cold War mentality. During his attempt at accommodation between Communist China and the United States, the intermediary he found was a real American spy, creating a major scandal when the connection was exposed. Although Zhang Dongsun was deprived of his political and teaching positions afterward, he was exempted from severe punishment because Mao Zedong gave him the verdict of "a contradiction among the people." However, his case repeatedly caused him severe trouble during different political campaigns in the 1950s, which escalated when he was deemed a counterrevolutionary during the Cultural Revolution. At age eighty-three in 1968, he was arrested and thrown into Qincheng jail along with his eldest son.[19] His family members suffered enormously after his political downfall: his second son, third son, and third daughter-in-law committed suicide, and his eldest son developed schizophrenia in prison. Zhang Dongsun died at the age of eighty-eight in a guarded hospital in 1973, just a year after one of his greatest wishes was fulfilled—that of peace between the United States and China during U.S. President Richard M. Nixon's 1972 visit to the country. Zhang Dongsun's personal tragedy represents a compelling case epitomizing the contested advocacy of Thirdspace in the modern Chinese context dominated by a dichotomy of thinking.

The Political Implications of Thirdspace

Zhang Dongsun's idea of cultural interactionism is anchored in his political thought and permeates his political commentaries; it lies at the heart of his theory of plural epistemology and his synthesis of Western and Chinese cultures. Consistent with his skepticism about absolute truth in philosophy, Zhang Dongsun's political thought incorporates different and interrelated ideas, such as liberty and equality, individual freedom and guild socialism, democracy and rationalism. But most importantly, he discovered a middle ground where he could accommodate different ideas and antagonistic positions. His stress on this middle ground, or Thirdspace, enabled him to embrace the spirit of tolerance derived from democracy and liberalism. As a public intellectual who exuberantly participated in building the public sphere, he was controversial for his proclivity for moderate politics, which allowed him to make constant modifications in his thought to correspond with different historical and societal situations in modern China.

In his writings, Zhang Dongsun employs middle politics to reshape people's mindsets entrenched in binary oppositions. To bring a thought to fruition in society, he asserts, "there must be an ample measure of freedom to venerate and cultivate creative thinking. However, we must also possess the wisdom of compromise and be willing to yield to one another in the realm of practicality." He characterizes society as a "heterogeneous whole" (*yizhi de jiehe* 異質的結合) in which all components must coexist. By contrast, "the homogeneous whole" (*tongzhi de jiehe* 同質的結合) is against the nature of society.[20] No matter how fair a thought is, it cannot avoid being prejudiced because it will always have a kind of lens colored by certain cultural or social positions. Under this premise, Zhang strongly proposes to adopt the method of neutralization (*zhezhong* 折衷) from Karl Mannheim's theory of the sociology of knowledge to arbitrate among diverse ideas. He even elevates middle politics that esteems compromise to the foundation of nation-building because he views it as the only way peace and order can be maintained.[21]

In 1913, inspired by Liang Qichao's ideas, Zhang Dongsun addressed the theory of antagonism (*duikang lun* 對抗論), which attempts to tease out the relationship between society and politics. In his view, in a country governed by law, a variety of different and equivalent forces and components are fighting against each other, and such antagonistic forces (*duikang li* 對抗力) should reach equilibrium. If one force becomes overwhelmingly predominant, then it may break the harmonious balance and lead to dictatorship.[22] When he participated in the debate about the political system for the new Republic in 1915, he was influenced by Zhang Shizhao's doctrine of accommodation, which was inspired by James Bryce's political ideas in *Studies in History and Jurisprudence*.[23] Zhang Dongsun noticed two factors that constitute the political situation. The first is "the centripetal force" (*xiangxin li* 向心力), the cohesion that maintains the stability of a country, and the second is "the centrifugal force" (*lixin li* 離心力), which includes various complex thoughts and relationships. Zhang sought a balance between these two forces, which would not only ensure political stability but also encompass different and competing opinions and thoughts. The imbalance of these two forces would either cause the country to disintegrate or beget a despotism that could not accept dissident thought and schools.[24] In 1946, Zhang mentioned the balance between the centripetal forces and the centrifugal forces again and replaced them with two other paradigms: "social integrity" (*shehui zhengti* 社會整體), which always sees the society as a holistic whole, and "social antagonism" (*shehui duikang* 社會對抗), referring to class stratifications such as the ruler versus the ruled and the elders versus the young. What underpins these two paradigms is "authority versus freedom," which represents the fundamental problem for society.[25] Since one cannot exist without the other, it is necessary to maintain a balance between the idea of wholeness and the idea of antagonism. Starkly divergent from the tyrannical monism of revolution that propagates the illusion of one absolute truth, the ultimate purpose of Zhang Dongsun's approach is to maintain the harmony of society and foster plurality of values. Following those Chinese thinkers who advocated the doctrine of accommodation, such as Zhang Shizhao and Du Yaquan, Zhang Dongsun strove to lay the foundation of moderate politics in modern Chinese society.

In his article "Elite Politics," written in 1917, Zhang Dongsun took a critical step to emphasize the necessity of neutralization, which recognizes the plurality of truth and embraces different ideas and opinions, regarding it as a condition of evolution. "The more mediated, the more evolved. All modern thoughts are based on neutralization as a starting point, not only philosophical thought, but also scientific and political thoughts."[26] Through middle politics, Zhang Dongsun made his most engaged critique of Marxism. In particular, he severely criticized the law of opposition that is frequently exercised in the Marxist theory of class struggle. Zhang denigrated the logic of class struggle, which dogmatically follows the mindset of "either revolutionary or antirevolutionary," or "either good man or bad man," eliminating the neutral position. Such logic abolishes the option of the third route and only leaves two opposing routes: either break or maintain the status quo.[27] Averse to using prevalent terms such as "annulling" (*qing* 清), "countering against" (*fan* 反), "elimination" (*su* 肅), and "killing" (*jiao* 剿), he saw them as reflecting the mindset of class struggle, which could result in extreme damage, with society losing "the pure and clear air" (*qingming zhiqi* 清明之氣) as well as freedom and peace. He clarified that he was not completely against struggle, but he absolutely rejected the idea of perpetual struggle, which will deprive people of harmony in their daily lives.[28] In addition, due to the lack of liberal freedom, Zhang believed that communist education is similar to fascist education: both regard men as ore, trying to hammer them into the same template to forge the same kind of coins.[29] He strongly disavowed intolerance, narrowness, uniformity, and the either/or mindset, which would obliterate the diversity of opinions, freedom of thought, and versatility of individual creativity.

Deeply rooted in the quintessential Chinese idea of harmony and moderation, Zhang Dongsun's middle politics serves as a central method of finding a balance between oppositional forces in practical reality. Parallel to Li Zehou's concept of *du*, Zhang Dongsun emphasized the flexibility of practice according to concrete historical contexts by referring to the rationality (*li* 理) indoctrinated in the Chinese cultural sense, which depends on the self's changing relationships with the outside world to make necessary adjustments when things go awry.[30] According to him, the function of reasoning (*jiangli* 講理) is equivalent to rectification (*jiuzheng* 糾正) with ample plasticity. He also synthesized the Western connotation of rationality as protected by natural law, which acknowledges the existence of inherent human rights with the ability to distinguish right from wrong.[31]

In addition, by positioning Chinese intellectuals, including himself, as "the third persons" (*disan zhe* 第三者)[32]—the agents or subjects of middle politics who navigate between two extreme sides to maintain social harmony—he combined individual rights with intellectuals' public role, aiming to establish a utopia that would not only ensure the state's wealth and power but also protect freedom of speech and thought. As early as 1914, he introduced the important notion of "the third persons," who represent an organic entity resolutely independent from the government, parties, and the masses. The third persons are rational citizens in different social classes and fields; their participation reduces the danger of political power being misused and complements the system of checks and balances.[33] More importantly, the third persons are positioned between the political authorities and the masses, serving as watchdogs of the political power, speaking for the lower class of people who do not have a voice, and making changes whenever needed. In reality, Zhang actively played this role, voicing his own opinions in the public sphere and earnestly trying to reconcile the two extreme parties, helping to control the despotic government. In his argument for elite politics in 1917, he expressed suspicion of the masses, who usually lean toward a monophonic, repressive, exclusionary, and tyrannical form of governance. In contrast, he deferred to the strength of elite intellectuals, who are well educated and equipped with wisdom, courage, rationality, respectful morality, and a peaceful spirit, as the pillars of society.³⁴ Influenced by Robert Michel's political theory stipulating that all complex political organizations inevitably transform into oligarchies, he emphasized the elite's morality and ethics, polyphonic voices, independent thinking, and decisive judgment in order to avoid such consequences.³⁵ His insightful comparison between elitism and mass-ism connects the third persons with the role of modern Chinese intellectuals, which bears a conspicuous resemblance to that of the traditional literati (*shi* 士), whose social and political character he frequently elucidates in his discussions of the traditional Chinese political system.

Zhang Dongsun's most valuable insight is that the *shi* stratum, which required of its members a great deal of morality and wisdom, serves as an "antitoxin" (*fangdu su* 防毒素) to counter the poison of Chinese politics. "Tyrannical politics usually engenders self-intoxication," Zhang Dongsun expounded, "therefore people who belong to the *shi* stratum express their distinct opinions and make contested arguments that evoke 'the pure and clear air' within society from which to resist the allure of self-intoxication."³⁶ He drew an analogy between the *shi* stratum and members of Parliament in English constitutional history, noting their similar functions: to provide breathing room, prevent corrosion, and cleanse poison from the political system. To be sure, Zhang's definition of *shi* as widely diffused in society, with a high degree of autonomy, flexibility, and morality, cannot possibly make for a radical and revolutionary force. It can only become a force of reformers who intervene in politics through their opinions and discourse rather than direct involvement in governing. This unique historical mission has produced a kind of life philosophy that not only integrates personal interest with social interest but also engenders a cosmology of organic wholeness. Although the conflicts between the *shi* stratum and officialdom throughout Chinese history always ended in the defeat of the former and the success of the latter, the moral advantage of the *shi* is undeniable. In particular, Zhang recognized two inherent merits: "one represents rationalism, the other moralism."³⁷ No other social class can match the stratum of *shi*—Confucian-influenced modern intellectuals who prize self-cultivation, self-discipline, social conscience, and nonutilitarian ambition (*zhi* 志), utterly at odds with the pursuit of money and official rank. That is why Zhang Dongsun even found the spirit of *shi* equivalent to that of Christian martyrs or the American Puritans who were willing to sacrifice their lives for the sake of their beliefs.³⁸

Modern Chinese intellectuals who had been an outgrowth of the *shi* stratum, in Zhang Dongsun's opinion, still had their historical missions even though they lacked a financial foundation, which would inexorably undermine the stability of their social position. During the late Qing and early Republican period, he placed great hope in these intellectuals, who should be the third persons or the elites undertaking enormous social responsibility and promoting freedom of speech. In 1923, he even claimed that only the intellectual class, which had a courageously sacrificing spirit, could salvage China.[39] At the same time, he attributed all the problems in Chinese society within the previous thirty to forty years to the corruption of the *shi* stratum. Naming it the "middle-trend class" (*zhongliu jieji* 中流階級), he claimed that after being ruled by the foreign Qing dynasty for three hundred years, the mentality of *shi* had been transformed and degenerated: "They only know how to drag out an ignoble existence, catering to the political authorities, securing personal gains, becoming hypocritical and telling lies, and drifting along aimlessly."[40] He lamented that they had lost the historical mission they had inherited from Confucius during the Republican period. However, in 1946, in an attempt to make a compromise between democracy and socialism, he changed his tune about the *shi* class, which faced a great dilemma in the complexity of Chinese modernity and political reality. Zhang was disappointed that *shi* in China never obtained historical leverage and a consolidated financial position like the Western middle class, which arose within the Western Industrial Revolution.[41] Therefore, he envisaged that *shi* should go through a drastic reformation to find their position by taking technical jobs and implementing guild socialism.

No matter how many times he changed his remarks about the modern intellectuals, deep down, Zhang Dongsun was driven by the quixotic belief that China's future depended on restoring the historical mission of the *shi* class. Metaphorically speaking, he constantly described it as the organ that kept generating new blood for the whole body that symbolized Chinese society. This organ exemplified the vitality of the body, on which metabolism depended. Unfortunately, under the national crisis that hovered over modern China, Zhang's utopian orchestration could not be fulfilled. Although his political intervention of "the third persons" aimed to lay a significant foundation to increase China's democratic prospects, his demanding moral standards made the social prerequisites difficult to achieve. The ideals of "sages" and "martyrs" imposed upon "the third persons" would create more hypocrisy and fraudulence in practice. Furthermore, in a society lacking the basis for political pluralism, those who strove to be the "mentors of kings" (*wangzhe shi* 王者師) would be ironically transformed into the "slaves of kings" (*wangzhe nu* 王者奴).[42]

Under Mao's totalitarian society, the third persons were humiliated, tortured, marginalized, abandoned, or reeducated, along with Zhang Dongsun himself. They basically lost the mediating role between the governors and the masses and were instead enslaved by them. This situation was exacerbated during the Cultural Revolution when they were deprived of the last vestiges of dignity, tragically degraded as "snake-spirited cow-headed devils." Even the souls of the modern *shi* were owned by the state, and their minds were manacled and brainwashed by the party's ideology. Many even lacked the right to maintain "the freedom of silence," not to mention activate the function of checks and balances, but were collectively transmogrified into instruments of political propaganda.

The Philosophical Visualization of Thirdspace

Zhang Dongsun was ahead of his time because the system of plural epistemology or panstructuralism he developed can be described as a creative constitution of Thirdspace, which goes beyond binary logic in thinking about the complexities of modern life. At a time when antagonistic thinking—dichotomies such as the new versus the old, the rich versus the poor, the West versus the East, and the left versus the right—was deeply ingrained in the discourse of Chinese modernity, Zhang paid conspicuously more attention to the diversity of truths. Moving between Western and Chinese cultures, he revealed the relatedness of all things, rejecting monism and embracing a pluralism of values. He pioneered a multidimensional Thirdspace, an interconnected philosophical, cultural, and political system. Its purpose was twofold: to dismantle the entrenched cultural dichotomy of the East and the West and to challenge the imposition of arbitrary ideologies, refraining from imposing any singular, absolute truth or value upon others.

Although Zhang Dongsun made a great effort to systematically introduce Western philosophy to China, he started to construct his own coherent and unique theory that merged Western philosophical ideas and traditional Chinese thought in the late 1920s. In 1929, he raised the idea of cosmological "panstructuralism," emphasizing the interrelatedness of the subject and the object.[43] His definition of "thing" (*wu* 物) transcended the categorical boundary between objective phenomenon and subjective impression and recognized the correlation between them. Later he published a series of important articles on "epistemological pluralism" that were widely recognized by scholars of his time as the first attempt by a modern Chinese philosopher to create his own philosophical system.[44] Although he described his theory as "revised Kantianism,"[45] Zhang differentiated himself from Kant by combining cosmology with epistemology, going beyond both monism and dualism. He regarded five fundamental elements of cognition—sensation, external order, transcendental forms, postulates, and concepts—as parallel, without any hierarchical order.[46] By paying special attention to these five elements' independent existence as well as their interlocking connections, he abandoned Kant's theory of "things-in-themselves" (wu ziti 物自體) and focused on pluralist interactionism. In 1946, he delved into the field of the sociology of knowledge (zhishi shehui xue 知識社會學) and created a comprehensive system associating his pluralist theory of knowledge with cultural content, social problems, political thought, and moral theory.

The most important step Zhang Dongsun took to establish and bolster his Thirdspace was to espouse "mystic integralism" or the all-inclusive metaphysical view, embedded in ancient Chinese thought.[47] He stressed that Chinese thought is completely different from the substance philosophy (benti de zhexue 本體的哲學) and causality philosophy (yinguo yuanze de zhexue 因果原則的哲學) found in Western thought and leans more toward functional philosophy (hanshu zhexue 函數哲學).[48] Instead of the quest for a single essence or ontology hidden behind all things, what shapes Chinese thought is possible change and its correlative cosmology. This cosmology ignores substance and causality, instead valorizing the inherent relations that interconnect and exist in the whole. Zhang Dongsun characterized it as an "organismic philosophy" (youji zhexue 有機哲學),[49] which encompasses a myriad of things, allowing a person to achieve unity with the universe (tianren heyi 天人合一).[50] In other words, oneness is the whole, and the whole is oneness—they are essentially reciprocal. Mystic integralism laid the foundation for Zhang's philosophical system, which is closely related to Soja's concept of Thirdspace and comparable to the allegory of Borges's "the Aleph," postulating the infinite and unimaginable universal space.

For Zhang, the causality philosophy and the substance philosophy had blinded his contemporaries to traditional Chinese wisdom and rhetorical strategies of the integral whole for containing everything in the universe. Instead, he favored interrelations, adjustment, and negotiation among different or oppositional things and interpreted the truth from multiple perspectives. Zhang's idea was provocative at the time because he made the nonontological traditional Chinese philosophy a focal point to challenge the prevailing modern way of thinking constrained by causality and essentialism. In his plural epistemology, it is necessary to assume that the comprehension process is a continuous whole with multiple interconnections and that knowledge plays a vital role of differentiation (*fenhua* 分化).[51] Through mystic integralism, Zhang Dongsun validated the relatedness of different and countless opinions rather than haphazard unification, which usually leads to an arbitrary single, absolute "truth." He saw Chinese correlative cosmology as permeating politics, society, culture, and morality—the various disciplines belonging to the all-inclusive wholeness, with theory simply filling the gaps between them.[52]

Analogous to what Buddhism calls "relatedness" (*yinyuan* 因緣), Zhang Dongsun created the term "structure" (*jiagou* 架構) to denote the universe as a holistic and organic whole registered by and interwoven with infinite structures. He describes it as a big net that "comprises countless numbers of relations that are dependent on each other and combine in various ways and at various levels."[53] Drawing on the perspective of Buddhist cosmology, Zhang believed the universe has no substance, no independent being, no intrinsic and fixed nature but only the relatedness of structures; therefore, it is called "emptiness" (*kong* 空). Although his cosmology was very similar to that of Buddhism, Zhang added an idea of evolution.[54] As he explained, "Even if the world is a structure without substance and self-sufficient being, the structure itself can evolve and generate new things from time to time."[55] But what he meant by "evolution," as he went on to clarify, is more like "becoming" and changing. Therefore, his organic, changing, and interrelated cosmological view sheds light on the openness of Thirdspace that refuses essentialism and encompasses a multiplicity of perspectives.

One of Zhang Dongsun's most important ideas in relation to Thirdspace is transcending the oppositional dichotomy of power, questioning the binary logic of forms rooted in modern thinking to emphasize the dynamic, multiple, and contested theories of knowledge. As the scholar of philosophy Yap Key-chong aptly points out, "Chang [Zhang]'s rejection of dichotomy was not confined to new-idealism versus neo-materialism. Indeed, he rejected almost all famous dichotomies in philosophy such as subject vs object, mind vs body, monism vs pluralism, good vs evil, determinism vs freedom of will, rationalism vs empiricism, transcendentalism vs immanentism, and so on."[56]

However, Zhang's effort to avoid being confined to the oppositional dichotomy of power was vehemently attacked by Marxist critics. In 1934, Ye Qing's book *The Philosophical Criticism of Zhang Dongsun* (*Zhang Dongsun zhexue pipan* 張東蓀哲學批判) targeted Zhang's philosophical system.[57] Armed with Marxist materialistic dialectics, Ye Qing criticized the idealism, dualism, and eclecticism embedded in Zhang's system, which was strongly influenced by ideas from Plato, Hume, Kant, and William James. Zhang Dongsun compiled a book titled *Debates on Marxist Materialistic Dialectics* (*Weiwu bianzhengfa lunzhan* 唯物辯證法論戰) as a response to this attack by the Marxist camp.[58] For Ye Qing, the most problematic aspect of Zhang Dongsun's philosophical system was his relentless pursuit of eclecticism, which was intended to muddle demarcations between all kinds of oppositional entities. Nevertheless, by the 1990s, scholars such as Yap Key-chong saw Zhang's notion of eclecticism as an attempt to "include all aspects of truth," which echoes the more comprehensive knowledge that both Zhuangzi and Baruch Spinoza proposed.[59]

According to the scholar Jana Rošker, Zhang Dongsun's rejection of substance as well as the dualistic theories of idealism and materialism in his pluralistic epistemology not only recalls "classical Chinese (especially Daoist and Chan Buddhist) cosmologies, but also certain recent Western ontological systems based on the Theory of Relativity and Quantum Theory."[60] To go beyond binary thinking, Zhang Dongsun not only introduced Alfred North Whitehead's idea of interrogating the bifurcation of the objective world of facts and the subjective world of values but also formed his own unique interpretation of the Chinese logic system.[61] Essentially, he considered Chinese logic an alternative to the Western dichotomous division, which in his view is exclusive. In his argument, the Chinese logic system can be named "correlation logic" (*xiangguanlü mingxue* 相關律名學) or the "logic of correlative duality" (*liangyuan xiangguanlü mingxue* 兩元相關律名學),[62] which totally differs from the "logic of opposition" underlined in Western thought. The Chinese correlative logic argues that components of symmetrical pairs, such as yin and yang, up and down, good and evil, having and not having, are closely reliant on—rather than fighting against—each other. The ostensible evidence that Zhang provided is from Laozi's sayings: "Difficult and easy complement each other. Long and short exhibit each other. High and low set measure to each other."[63] Laozi also says: "Bad fortune is what good fortune leans on, good fortune is what bad fortune hides in."[64] The binary oppositions in Chinese thought were never featured as fixed, antithetical, and hostile but rather were designed as changeable, inseparable, and intrinsically bonded relations that supplement and depend on each other. Drawing from ancient Chinese philosophical sources, Zhang innovatively projected a thoroughly different vision of Western logic that is moored by the "logic of opposition."

In her article, "Word, Dialogue and Novel," Julia Kristeva notes Zhang Dongsun's insightful interpretation of the Chinese concept of duality and relates it to Mikhail Bakhtin's theory of dialogue: "It is no accident that the shortcomings of Aristotelian logic when applied to language were pointed out by, on the one hand, twentieth-century Chinese philosopher Chang Tung-Sun [Zhang Dongsun] (the product of a different linguistic heritage—ideograms—where, in place of God, there extends the Yin-Yang 'dialogue') and, on the other, Bakhtin (who attempted to go beyond the Formalists through a dynamic theorization accomplished in revolutionary society)." For Kristeva, the Chinese "Yin-Yang" dialogue that Zhang Dongsun postulates is attuned to Bakhtin's notions of ambivalence and dialogism: "*Dialogue* appears most clearly in the structure of carnivalesque language, where symbolic relationships and analogy take precedence over substance-causality connections."[65] In Kristeva's introduction of Bakhtin's theory, the Chinese "logic of correlative duality" that Zhang Dongsun singles out indisputably adheres to the logic of nonexclusive opposition, which solicits a dialogical relationship instead of a monological one restricted by causality.

Zhang Dongsun's comparison of the different attitudes toward duality in Chinese philosophy and Western philosophy tallies with what Charles A. Moore describes in *The Chinese Mind*: "Coupled with this is the somewhat difficult-to-understand attitude of 'both-and'—as contrasted with the Western tendency to think in terms of 'either/or,' such that the fine lines of distinction and exclusiveness so typical of Western life and thought and even religion are not common to the Chinese mind."[66] This attitude of "both-and" was not prevalent until the emergence of postcolonialism in the West, although it had been brought up by Alfred North Whitehead and Henri Lefebvre. In his book *Thirdspace*, Edward W. Soja points out that one of Lefebvre's most important ideas is a deep and thorough critique of "all forms of categorical or binary logic": "When faced with a choice confined to the either/or, Lefebvre creatively resisted by choosing instead an-Other alternative, marked by the openness of the both/and also . . ., with the 'also' reverberating back to disrupt the categorical closures implicit in the either/or logic."[67]

Among modern Chinese intellectuals who were deeply influenced by the May Fourth iconoclastic movement and absorbed in the binary logic of thinking about the complexity of the modern world, Zhang Dongsun was one of the few distinctly aware of the strength of the traditional Chinese attitude of "both-and" as well as its related ethical attitude of moderation. Comparing Marxism with Chinese thought in terms of dealing with dichotomies, Zhang asserts that the former is antagonistic but the latter reciprocal. By adopting the "law of contradiction" or "logic of opposition," Marxism advocates struggle or, more specifically, political struggle between two opposing classes. In contrast, Zhang notes that it is precisely in the logic of correlation—in which two bipolar points are conditional on and complementary to each other—that negotiation is inherently viewed as more important than struggle in Chinese thought.[68] This idea is echoed in Homi Bhabha's *The Location of Culture*, in which he advocates negotiation rather than negation. For him, only through negotiation between antagonistic and contradictory elements can a place of hybridity be opened up.[69]

While Zhang Dongsun recognized that duality or polarity has been widely and commonly used to describe Western thought, he stated that "Chinese usually do not pay attention to the two points of oppositions, but rather attend to the middle ground between the antinomies." The purpose of focusing more on the middle, Zhang noted, is to connect two points. Moreover, such connection, or thoroughness (*tong* 通) or go through (*guantong* 貫通), pulls two extremes closer to each other and eventually even makes them congruent and complementary instead of synthetic. As he further implied, this is similar to the dialectical attitude in the West against orthodox Western philosophy thought, which tends to push two antithetical extremes further apart, inevitably causing a struggle between them or, even worse, one to engulf the other. However, Zhang indicated that the progress of Western society may be impelled by this kind of constant struggle. Not until modern times did Western philosophers, such as Alfred North Whitehead, start to challenge the inveterate dualistic thinking by objecting to the bifurcation of nature.[70] In Zhang Dongsun's plural epistemology, he accentuates the prominence of the middle ground. Discussing the complex nature of comprehension, he posits a middle ground between the subject of cognition and the object of cognition: "People commonly think that there is nothing between these two poles, that between them there is only empty space. This would mean that the subject and object of recognition were in direct relation with each other. But I believe that there are many things between them, that this 'middle,' in other words, is very complex."[71] His emphasis on the middle ground is not simply eclecticism but a critical intervention in and reconciliation with the pressing social and political issues of his time. Moreover, it anticipates the dynamics of pluralism and otherness with which postmodern theories are concerned.

Zhang Dongsun wants to call attention to the middle ground because he believes the plurality of truth may reside there. For instance, he constantly claims that his epistemology is neither idealism nor materialism but a multiple-element interactionism (*duoyin jiaohu zhuyi* 多因交互主義). Between idealism and materialism, he discovers that more possible interactions can be undertaken among different elements, such as external things, sense, cognition, and concepts.[72] The middle ground is not an entity or solid thing but instead can be viewed as an unfixed and fluctuating relation depending on our own rules of measure (*chidu* 尺度).[73] His preference is based on his acceptance of the worldview of harmonization from ancient China. As Charles A. Moore observes, the Chinese synthetic attitude embodies the spirit of harmony that can be easily found in the realm of the intellect as well as in everyday life.[74] It is parallel to Zhang's theory in which the middle ground or Thirdspace purely serves the purpose of harmonizing the opposing sides.

In general, Zhang Dongsun's plural epistemology established a principal philosophical discourse for his Thirdspace, in which the central task is the comprehension and interrogation of the truth. Zhang's pluralist position distinguishes his theory from epistemological monism that combines the subject and the object and also from epistemological dualism that only recognizes the dichotomy between the subject and the object.[75] Furthermore, borrowing Karl Mannheim's theory of "neutralization," Zhang firmly asserts that the truth cannot be absolute or eternal. What he values is the process of neutralizing (*zhonghe hua* 中和化) or revision, which will not result in a final truth but will generate various possible perspectives. "As for which perspective is the most convincing to us, it depends on the situation we are in."[76] Through this process—in which different perspectives sprung from different conditions encounter, correct, and negotiate with each other— Zhang Dongsun most profoundly evokes the plurality of the truth. His interesting adaptation of Mannheim's notions of "perspective," "situation," and "neutralization" transforms his theory of knowledge as culturally conditioned, refusing to regard the truth as a given fact but instead viewing it as a constantly mobile state or a process of evaluation over the course of history and in the future. By acknowledging the truth as a very complex idea subject to "the traffic of opinions" (*yijian de jiaotong* 意見的交通),[77] he is able to reject the notion of fixed views on "right" and "wrong" yet avoid the relative position, as seen in Zhuangzi's transcendence of the sphere of judgments of right and wrong.

The Cultural Envisioning of Thirdspace

How can a person who promotes the middle way be radical? Intriguingly, Zhang Dongsun's idea of cultural interactionism is radically open, instilling Thirdspace with interdisciplinary dimensions. The overlaps between various disciplines, such as philosophy, politics, morality, and culture, opened more alternative possibilities for comprehending and exploring the truth. Stimulated by the interrelated thinking intrinsic within Chinese philosophy's mystic integralism, Zhang promoted an innovative model of multicultural interactionism.[78] To recognize the difference between Western and Chinese cultures, he tried to widen the scope of knowledge by extending it to "the determination of culturalism" (*wenhua zhuyi de jueding lun* 文化主義的決定論). As a result, his pluralist theory of knowledge expanded from social conditions to cultural grounding. He advanced a correlated and interdisciplinary cultural structure that included anthropology, political thought, social organization, religious life, philosophical ideas, morality, and ethics, which gave him unexpected insights regarding the zeitgeist and Carl G. Jung's concept of the collective unconscious.[79] In fusing epistemology and cultural history, he defined the social background of thought while simultaneously divulging cultural distinctions (such as the Western and Chinese differences) among the philosophical paradigms.

By engaging in multicultural interactionism, Zhang became a compelling vanguard for interdisciplinary studies, rejecting absolute and authoritative theoretical paradigms and viewing various cultural fields as an interrelated, organic, and changing whole. He refused to perceive the truth as stagnant, absolute, and prearranged. For him, the truth that satisfies certain cultural conditions is equivalent to the ideal, which brings a sense of "cultural satisfaction" (*wenhua manzu gan* 文化滿足感). Based on such definitions, he argued that "the intervals" (*jianxi* 間隙) between different cultural disciplines are crucial: "All the theories, whether social thought, political thought, economic thought, ethical thought, religious thought, or even metaphysical thought, are all for the purpose of filling in those intervals." By putting "the intervals" foremost as the testimony of the truth, Zhang Dongsun attempts to move beyond the binary opposition of right and wrong into the multiplicity of other places between different cultural disciplines. For him, whether a theory represents truth or falsehood is not a predetermined fact but instead depends on whether the intervals can be filled and cultural shortcomings overcome during a certain historical time. He states, "In the East, we generally address such filling of the intervals as 'making up a deficiency' (*bupian jiubi* 補偏救弊)."[80] In this way, the intervals become strategic locations between disciplines, conveying a theoretical critique that revolves around disruptions and disordering of the interrelated and organic whole of culture. By rejecting Marxist social economy and predictability, Zhang designated the operations of cultural intervals and related theories as uncertain, shifting, and contested. The veracity of theories is destined to be perturbed due to specific cultural environments. The intervals are equivalent to Thirdspace, which constantly invites new and different possibilities for knowledge of the truth.

The complex multicultural interactionalism enables a flexible mindset in interrogating Chinese and Western cultural conflicts. During the May Fourth Movement period, Zhang Dongsun insisted on importing Western knowledge, which, to him, exemplified the leading trajectory of world culture. This was in stark contrast to the view of another famous modern Chinese philosopher, Liang Shuming 梁漱溟 (1893–1988), which dwells on the innate essence of traditional Chinese culture. However, Zhang made a dramatic transformation in the 1940s by proposing the theory of mediation and interfacing between Western and Chinese cultures against any dogmatic closure and fixed totalizing patterns.[81] In other words, he did not support "Chinese essence and Western function" (*zhongti xiyong* 中體西用) or "complete Westernization" (*quanpan xihua* 全盤西化). Instead, he introduced Thirdspace between the two cultures, established on a tentative construction and reconstruction of cultural interactionism by absorbing the quintessence of both.

Among scholars who recognize Zhang Dongsun's effort toward openness, interdisciplinary viewpoint, and intercultural methodology, Zhang Rulun specifies that Zhang Dongsun regarded Western culture as "an equal other" (*pingdeng de tazhe* 平等的他者) taking part in an interesting dialogue with Chinese culture.[82] By doing so, he formed a positive and fruitful dialectical relationship between the self and the other, Chinese culture and Western culture.[83] To be more precise, Zhang Dongsun's cultural view epitomizes a kind of "grand mélange" (*da zahui* 大雜燴) juxtaposing and combining the ancient, modern, Western, and Chinese wisdoms.[84] This resonates with

Edward W. Soja's conceptualization of "thirding-as-othering," which interprets Lefebvre's theoretical strategy to transform the exclusive and closed logic of either/or into the inclusive and open logic of both/and.[85] Zhang explored Thirdspace as a particularly bountiful meeting ground in which the quintessential embodiments of Western and Chinese cultures encounter, mingle with, and communicate with each other. This is similar to Homi Bhabha's assertion of the "cultural hybridity" of Thirdspace, which emphasizes "the 'inter'—the cutting edge of translation and negotiation, the in-between space—that carries the burden of the meaning of culture. . . . And by exploring this Third Space, we may elude the politics of polarity and emerge as others of ourselves."[86] But unlike Bhabha, who situated Thirdspace in the condition of postcoloniality, Zhang Dongsun posited his interculturalism in the context of Chinese modernity. Through Thirdspace, he developed a new way to think about the positive comparison and amalgamation of Western and Chinese cultures. As a result, he meticulously devised an ideal blueprint for Chinese modernization, building on the strengths of both cultures while making up for the deficiencies in each cultural root.

The key to Zhang Dongsun's methodology was his keen attention to historical contextualization. He understood that both cultures have deep and accumulated cultural roots, constituted by a wholly different set of languages, logics, and paradigms that have penetrated people's worldview and daily habits, influencing their way of thinking as what C. G. Jung termed the "collective unconscious."[87] This resembles what Li Zehou calls "cultural sedimentation" (*wenhua jidian* 文化積澱) or "cultural-psychological formation" (*wenhua xinli jiegou* 文化心理結構), which means "the accumulation and condensation of the social, rational, and historical to become something individualistic, sensuous, and intuitive."[88] Acknowledging the factor of "cultural contextual structure" or "cultural demand," Zhang Dongsun not only acknowledged the historical dimension of cultural structures but also pressed for changing and supplementing intervals and the structures' inherent deficiency.[89] Thus, he consciously affirmed the fundamental importance of the pragmatic, democratic, and humanistic elements within the Western tradition, which he thought the Chinese should comprehend, learn from, and internalize as the basis for ongoing modernization. Different from the viewpoint of "Chinese essence and Western function," which regarded Western culture as a source of technical knowledge or an external instrument, Zhang treated it as a whole, rational, and beneficial culture that China must adopt and synthesize. In Chinese traditional culture, he appreciated the self-cultivation of morality embedded in the *dao* of Confucius and Mencius, which could rectify the laissez-faire individualism evident in capitalist societies.[90] His primary purpose was to remedy certain intrinsic gaps, distortions, and inadequacies ingrained in both cultures.[91] However, he was acutely aware of the time gap (*shijian cha* 時間差) between the Western and Chinese cultures, which Li Zehou and Liu Zaifu discuss in *Farewell to Revolution* (*Gaobie geming* 告別革命). Li Zehou and Liu Zaifu adamantly remind us that the development of Chinese modernization is almost one century behind that of the West, so to make up for the lag, China's culture needs to integrate post-Enlightenment theories and sciences that originated in the West long ago.[92] With the same objective of enhancing China's ability to modernize effectively, Zhang Dongsun identified the time disparity that has resulted in the lack of individualism, freedom, and humanism in modern China.

In particular, Zhang Dungun discussed the divergent and conflicting undercurrents of Western culture in both the nineteenth century and the twentieth century: the former embraced "naturalism, individualism, nationalism, rationalism, freedom, and empiricism," and the latter was focused on "socialism, humanism, internationalism, emotionalism, totalitarianism, and governance."[93] Inevitably, he favored the democratic culture of the nineteenth century and criticized the tendency toward antirationalism associated with imperialism and totalitarianism in the twentieth century, which caused enormous disasters such as World War I and World War II. The imperialism produced by colonization and nationalism, along with communist totalitarianism, were allegedly the modern predicaments of Western culture in the twentieth century. To avoid clashes between the Western and Chinese cultures, as well as the dilemma within Western culture, Zhang proposed a neutralized method to deal with the complexity of Chinese modernity. He pinpointed the ubiquitous shortage of individualism, freedom of thought, and rationality within his thorough interpretation and analysis of Chinese cultural tradition, calling for the implantation of nineteenth-century Western thought into China. Meanwhile, acknowledging the planned economy that had been successful in Russia, he highlighted the necessity of implementing the socialism prevalent in the twentieth century to ensure economic development in China. No matter how idealized it seems, his purpose was to establish a reasonable Thirdspace in which freedom of speech is assured and the socialist planned economy is adopted to strengthen national wealth and power.[94] This kind of Thirdspace intermingles various elements from different cultures and different historical stages to benefit the project of Chinese modernization.

For Zhang, Thirdspace also denoted a kind of "middle medium" (*zhongjian meijie wu* 中間媒介物) through which ideals could be actualized. He pointed out in *Democracy and Socialism* (*Minzhu zhuyi yu shehui zhuyi* 民主主義與社會主義): "We must realize that if we cannot discover the third thing as a medium to connect the ideal of liberty and equality with reality, everything will be in vain."[95] In his judgment, the middle channels that secured and built democracy in the West were the independent national state and individualism based on the system of capitalism. Taking into account both Russian socialist and American capitalist experiences, Zhang proposed to cultivate in the Chinese context a socialist planned economic industrialization, the national state, and individualism-based democracy.[96] After this political middle route encountered setbacks in reality, he adjusted it by making economic determinism the prerequisite for individual freedom. And once again, he gave the *shi* class a pivotal role in mediating all the social, political, and cultural conflicts and clashes.[97]

Although Zhang highlighted the flaws in the Chinese concepts of individuality, freedom, and rationality, he still stressed the reciprocity between Chinese and Western cultures. He sought to draw from their intersections or adjacent points to bridge disparities instead of fixating on conflicts, attempting to foreground the kinetic Thirdspace through which he could neutralize and adjust contesting cultural characteristics.

> The exchange and integration of cultures must start from their neighboring intersections. If China wants to transplant the Western concept of individuality and promote democratic values (which encompass not only a political system but also a holistic way of life), it is essential to first endorse the concept of individual within Confucianism and earnestly put it into practice. This notion shares some common ground with the Western concept of individuality. By blending these two cultures at their adjacent junctures, we can cultivate people's second nature.[98]

For Zhang Dongsun, the first nature is stipulated by one's birthplace and culture; the second nature is formed in Thirdspace by multiple cultural meanings. Finding the adjacent points, or the in-between space of two cultures, is a theoretical strategy to foster the emergence and development of otherness. "People who are born and raised in their own national culture need to use analogy to understand other cultures."[99] The in-between and the adjacent points give rise to cultural hybridity, which generates new meanings to alter the deep-rooted traditional culture. That is why Zhang asserted that Mencius's concept of individual was the point from which to develop the Western concept of individualism shielded by a democratic system. Meanwhile, he accentuated the reasoning ethos in Chinese tradition as the connecting point with Western rationalism associated with intellectualism. He proposed that the "Chinese not only should revitalize the method of reasoning but also should absorb merit from the West, regarding reason (*li* 理) as development instead of stagnation."[100] Since the capacity to perform the Chinese concept of *li* is intertwined with achieving all the social virtues such as love, benevolence, and humanity, it is parallel to the Western concept of reason that led to the ideal of democracy. Zhang sought to crystallize *li* so that one could simultaneously embrace intellectualism and enhance ideals of freedom and equality. On a larger scale, underlying his attempt to resuscitate the *li* vision in the twentieth-century Chinese and Western worlds was his earnest aspiration for world peace to be achieved. He stated, "The worldwide wartime disasters are exactly due to irrationalism," and therefore, "there will be no peace without rationalism."[101]

Zhang Dongsun's hankering for peace and harmony also motivated his obsession with the middle way method, usually seen in the moderation of Confucianism and Laozi's theory of the interreliance and complementarity of two opposing sides. Based on the traditional Chinese correlation that pursues the interdependent relationship of two ends, he questioned the logic of opposition and the law of identity that the Western mindset had grappled with. He suggested using the Chinese way of moderation to alleviate the detrimental effects of class struggle, intolerance, and mutual exclusiveness deeply embedded in Marxist ideology and revolutionary thought. In parallel, he found inspiration in Western philosophical ideas such as Samuel Alexander's notion of "compresence," R. G. Collingwood's perception of "the overlap of classes," and Alfred North Whitehead's concept of "concrescence." Whitehead's attention to the mutual immanence of every concrete being, regarding each as a nexus rather than an independently existing self, conforms with the Buddhist concept of relatedness. Both terms go beyond the polarity of thinking, paralleling the Chinese logic of interrelatedness. By making direct reference to the concept of "the overlap of classes" initiated by Collingwood in his book *An Essay on Philosophical Method*, Zhang Dongsun explicitly explained that the referent can be multiple, which he defined as having a variety of denotational content.[102] Since multiple referents have no clear boundaries, they will inevitably generate shifting meanings, a reminder of Jacques Derrida's definition of *différance*. Although Zhang Dongsun can hardly be described as a deconstructionist, he was a pioneer in noticing the multiple, shifting, and supplementary meanings that could be derived from the overlapping space. Western and Eastern cultural ideas provided him with significant resources to interrogate the fixation on dualism and criticize the Marxist theory that leaves "no middle position" for scholars like him who only want more room for freedom of thought and academic discussion.[103] As he once claimed in a public talk, if the world needs peace and human beings long for happiness, we should propel the leftists toward the right and the rightists toward the left.[104] The middle ground was his favorite place, in which an individual is shaped by healthy social relations while the tensions connected with perpetual class struggles and violence are eliminated.

Philosophical Poetry as Thirdspace

After Zhang Dongsun was accused of being a spy for the United States in 1952, he totally lost his political voice but still kept the right to remain silent without praising Mao Zedong and the party. At this extremely lonely and desperate time, he started to learn to write classical-style poetry,[105] which became an important, unique, and comforting spiritual home for him. From 1952 to 1955, Zhang Dongsun wrote two hundred poems in the classical poetic genre, naming himself as "an old man who takes joy in solitude" (*duyi laoren* 獨宜老人). The collection of these poems, entitled *Words from a Man Among Grasses* (*Caojian renyu* 草間人語), was never published, and only seventy poems remained after the catastrophe of the Cultural Revolution.[106] Amid the hyperbolic political milieu, he could not overtly express his personal opinions and feelings, so he chose the relatively repressed and obtuse classical-style verse forms to vent his loneliness, isolation, and despondence. Since the insurmountable political power still loomed, those poems were never meant to be seen by the public. Yet he still had the resolve to write so-called drawer literature (*chouti wenxue* 抽屜文學), which can be a means of self-salvation. His personal misfortune, loss, and trauma—all the emotional anguish that was unspeakable or forbidden to be uttered—are channeled and released in classical-style poetry. Furthermore, his self-reflexive tone is underscored by the combination of his poetic mind and historical experiences in those poems:

To whom can I reveal my centennial ambition?
Pouring the wine into the vast ocean,
I still raise the goblet several times.
Succeeding neither in misanthropy nor in mounting to the sky,
I will use the poetic vista to console my life.[107]

百年豪氣向誰傾,
倒海空尊亦數擎;
厭世攀天無一可,
但將詩境慰此生。

Without anyone to drink wine or discuss his political opinions and aspirations with, the poet was facing perpetual sorrow, loneliness, and nihilism. Luckily, he still had the poetic vista (*shijing* 詩境), an escape through which to engage with both his emotional impasse and his apprehension about the world. In the beginning, Zhang Dongsun inevitably lingered on pathos and pain, exemplified in lines such as:

The desolation of centuries is like a brush,
accompanied by the isolated lamp that envelops my tearful eyes.[108]

千秋寂寞如椽筆,
只伴孤燈掩淚眼。

Employing emotional tropes such as the coldness of autumn, a sleepless night, fallen leaves, the bitterness of summer drizzles, and endless tears, he clearly attempts to express dissent and bleakness (*yuan* 怨), discharging the accumulated humiliation and emotion. However, he gradually turned from weeping and self-pity to laughing and self-mockery in his poems by writing sentences such as, "It is worth laughing about that a scholar attempted to design a country" 書生謀國直堪笑,[109] and "Solitude anticipates the eternal laugh" 寂寞料知千古笑.[110] Such self-mockery repeatedly occurs in his other poems after 1955. For instance, when he encountered Liang Shuming in a hospital in 1959, who had been involved in the philosophical debate with him during the Republican period, he wrote about their laughter that ostensibly conveyed a sense of mutual understanding between friends in relation to personal disaster and the complicated political situation: "A laugh escapes our lips as we suddenly encounter each other in illness" 病中一笑忽相逢.¹¹¹ While he was rereading Liang Qichao's article responding to him during a debate about socialism, he was reminded of his late teacher and friend and wrote:

It is a pity we cannot connect from separated worlds,
yet I want to ask, did you laugh at me?¹¹²

獨憐隔界難通語,
慾問先生笑我無?

Looking back at his own political opinion and personal choices in the past, he often wrote about laughter with a sense of absurdity associated with philosophical existentialism. Those laughs also powerfully unveil and caricature the irrationality of the zeitgeist of new China that was swamped in hypocritical eulogies of Mao and the party as well as numerous deceptive promises to the people. Seeking spiritual strength from Buddhism, he eventually discovered a poetic vista he expressed as: "The finished poems are the self-made Chan" 詩成卻作自家禪.¹¹³

The most remarkable effort Zhang Dongsun made in writing classical Chinese poetry was to originate a new kind of poetic style, which can be called "philosophical poetry." After he gradually found peace and serenity in his heart, he began to conceive a new way to integrate Western philosophy into the classical Chinese poetic form. In total, he wrote fifty poems about selected eminent Western philosophers, ranging from ancient Greeks such as Thales of Miletus, Anaximander, Pythagoras, Heraclitus, Socrates, Plato, and Aristotle to modern philosophers such as Kant, Hegel, Arthur Schopenhauer, Friedrich Nietzsche, Henri Bergson, Edmund Husserl, Alfred North Whitehead, and Jean-Paul Sartre. Although some poems went missing, forty-six survived the calamity of the Cultural Revolution. The scholar Zhang Rulun compiled these in *Poetry of Philosophical History* (*Shi de zhexue shi* 詩的哲學史), accompanying each poem with an essay to explicate each philosopher in detail. There is no doubt that the strength of Zhang Dongsun's philosophical poems derives from the depth of his scholarship, the vastness of its scope, the profoundness of his vision, and the innovation of his literary writing. Even if the Chinese classical poetic forms greatly limited the freedom of his expression, he managed to explore Thirdspace, in which his erudite knowledge of Western philosophy and his own literary practice were experimentally hybridized.

In his own preface to these philosophical poems, Zhang Dongsun points out the quandary of combining classical poetic expression and philosophical noetics:

> Since I have taught the history of Western philosophy for twenty years, there is something worth recording as I reminisce about the past in old age, living in a predicament under a lamp in solitude. It has been a long tradition that Buddhist ideas were introduced into poetry, but we have never seen a similar way to convey Western philosophy. If this is such an attempt, it is the first. By teasing out some selective ideas of Western philosophers and adding my personal comments, I have written fifty poems. From there, I started to understand that poetry is suitable for expressing feelings and scenes but hard to articulate reason. What I have done cannot avoid criticism for acting in a Procrustean manner.[114]

> 因念講授西洋哲學史垂二十年，今老廢困居，一燈回憶，不無可記。蓋佛家義諦入詩者，由來已久，獨西方哲理迄今闕如，有之請自噲始。爰取其說，一鱗半爪，稍加私評得五十首。始悟詩適於言情言景，而艱於言理，誠不免有削足適履之誚也。

In an avant-garde experiment, Zhang Dongsun forges the link between his comprehension of Western philosophy and the indigenous literary form and gives this inventive combination rich play. The main purpose is to emancipate the "repressed" Western knowledge with which he had been so familiar and enamored in the past but that he was forbidden to continue to delve into in the present. Forsaken by the new regime, he was deprived of everything he had been previously enthralled with and good at—his political career, substantial philosophical scholarship, and beloved teaching position. However, what could not be stripped away were his honesty, integrity, knowledge, and literary talent that were intrinsic and developed inside himself. Therefore, he found solace in writing classical poetry even if the restrictions of language and form inevitably restrained his broaching of Western philosophy. As he wrote in the foreword poem:

I want to wash the turtle intestine and yet not abandon my writing;
the Western river is made into muddy water stepped in by hooves.[115]

慾洗龜腸未廢吟，
西江一水作蹄涔。

By employing "the turtle intestine"—a literary allusion to hunger that springs from "Book of South Qi: The Biography of Wang Zengqian" ("Nanqi shu Wang Zengqian zhuan" 南齊書·王僧虔傳),[116] Zhang Dongsun confesses his compelling craving for the Western philosophical knowledge that has been relentlessly subdued by the dominant political power. Although he modestly admits that his knowledge of Western philosophy is limited, which is represented by "the turtle intestine," his desire to write is still strong. He uses "the Western river" as an allegory of the enormity of Western philosophy over two thousand years; in contrast, his effort to recapitulate it in the classical poetry form is deemed as narrow and humble as "muddy water stepped in by hooves." Nevertheless, no matter how difficult it is to convey Western philosophical meanings in the restrictive Chinese classical-style poetry, Zhang Dongsun stunningly demonstrates his ability to carve an intersection for these two seemingly incongruent elements to dialogue and negotiate with each other.

Because of its unprecedented nature, Zhang Dongsun's inventive re-creation of philosophical poetry has a boldness of vision and a breadth of erudition hardly seen among his generation during the revolutionary period. The major goal of his experimental writing, as depicted in his afterword poem, is to expand his vision beyond China. Although there are only four lines in this poem, its original draft, discovered by his descendants, contains eight lines. Among the deleted lines, he virtually revealed his profound perspective:

When have orchid and mugwort ever self-perished at the same time?
Do not limit the loneliness and anger within China.[117]

蘭艾幾曾同自腐，
莫將孤憤限華夷。

Calling his predicament "a period of pure heart" (*suxin qi* 素心期), he transported his emotional pain into Thirdspace, in which he wholeheartedly indulged in the interplay between philosophical meanings and literary creation. More importantly, he cast a glance toward the world rather than being confined by the national boundaries of China. No matter how lonely and angry he felt, he attempted to find a way to elevate himself to the vista of the universe (*yuzhou jingjie* 宇宙境界) where he could be immersed in metaphysical thinking rather than fixating on national issues. The ambition behind his adaptation of the classical poetry form is to build a counterdiscourse with an extremely broad vision and a profound humanistic spirit, in contrast to Mao's socialist utopia and ideology in China. Such a cosmopolitan vision, easily traced back to his original political, cultural, and philosophical paradigm in the Republican period, enables him to transcend the cruel political reality surrounding him.

Among Zhang Dongsun's remaining forty-six poems, except the foreword poem and the afterword poem, forty-four are all "poetry expressing intent" (*shiyanzhi* 詩言志) with a palpable predilection toward expressing thought that is similar to Buddhist verse, a style visibly distinct from "poetry originating in *qing*" (*shiyuanqing* 詩緣情). Although in the lyrical tradition, most scholars have argued that *zhi* and *qing* are inseparable,[118] Zhang Dongsun's "philosophical poetry" has almost no space in which to interweave feeling. It is very different from the modern lyricism and "a history with feeling" (*youqing de lishi* 有情的歷史) that David Der-wei Wang delineated in his groundbreaking book *The Lyrical in Epic Time*.[119] Since condensing a Western philosopher's lifetime achievement into a classical form of heptasyllabic quatrain is already an enormously challenging job, he has to largely withdraw the lyrical expression of emotion from such a limited poetic space. According to Wen Yiduo 聞一多 (1899–1946), *zhi* has three important elements that revolve around the heart: memory, record, and inclusion (*huaibao* 懷抱).[120] Echoing this definition, Zhang Dongsun's philosophical poems are more oriented toward *shiyanzhi*, which undoubtedly comprises a personal memory of his previous comprehension, a record of his cognitive system, and a display of his inclusive vision. In rhetorical style, it vacillates between "direct articulation" (*zhibai* 直白) and "analogues and categorical associations" (*yinpi lianlei* 引譬連類), which would be "making the intent embedded in the words more subtle or indeterminable."[121] In general, the metaphysical thrust makes these philosophical poems significantly different from lyrical expressions that pay more attention to sensory concerns and feelings. The anguish of Zhang Dongsun, suffering during the severe political time, gradually recedes into the background. What surfaces are his placid and direct articulation of knowledge and thought, as well as the correlations between the ideas of selected Western thinkers and Zhang Dongsun's cryptic criticisms of the suffocating Maoist era.

If we read each poem carefully, it is clear that Zhang Dongsun's poetic sketches of selected Western philosophers resonate with his previous theoretical framework as well as his opinions about Chinese reality and turbulence. The most notable attribute of those poems is that he manages to incorporate his personal interpretation of the philosophers with his previous advocacy of Thirdspace. In his poem about Aristotle, he specifically points out that:

> People only mention his syllogism nowadays,
> but no one knows his golden proverbs about the middle way.[122]

今日但提三段論，
金箴中道沒人知。

Most scholars might pay more attention to Aristotle's contribution to the fields of metaphysics, politics, and logic, especially his syllogism, but Zhang Dongsun unreservedly appeals to Aristotle's opinions on ethics, especially his famous doctrine of the golden mean. Bertrand Russell summarizes this doctrine as the following:

> Every virtue is a mean between two extremes, each of which is a vice. This is approved by an examination of the various virtues. Courage is a mean between cowardice and rashness; liberality, between prodigality and meanness; proper pride, between vanity and humanity; ready wit, between buffoonery and boorishness; modesty, between bashfulness and shamelessness.[123]

However, Russell thinks this golden mean can only be applied to "the practical virtues," not to "intellectual contemplation," because truthfulness somehow cannot fit such a standard. In Russell's judgment, Aristotle's *Ethics* is not "intrinsically important,"[124] but Zhang Dongsun promotes the golden mean unstintingly, appreciating its moderate middle way and reasonable contemplation. It certainly is reminiscent of his selection of the middle route during the Republican period, which corresponds directly to moderation.

Zhang Dongsun goes on to praise Kant, William James, Samuel Alexander, Conwy Lloyd Morgen, and Alfred North Whitehead, whose philosophical thought greatly inspired him to contemplate how to construct his own plural epistemological system. About Kant, he wrote:

The fictional form of time and space is constricted by sensation,
for appearance is different from its origin.
With his own doctrine that became a popular principle,
he ushered in a renaissance era for philosophical schools.[125]

虛式時空限感官，
便知外物異其源。
自家立法成通則，
學派重開一紀元。

His poem about Kant resonates with his own polemical engagement with subjectivity and objectivity, idealism and materialism in an eclectic manner. Strongly influenced by Kant's thought in *Critique of Pure Reason*, particularly the idea that space and time only exist in the subjective perception, Zhang Dongsun made a great effort to overhaul the conventional dualism, attempting to find a middle way between rationalism and empiricism.[126]

In his poem about William James, Zhang Dongsun wrote:

Originally no distinction between self and matter but separate later,
human nature encompasses strength and gentleness in its own way.
It is said that knowledge and action are inherently one;
his different tune achieved the same goal as that of Wang
 Yangming.[127]

本無物我後才分，
性有剛柔各立論。
亦說知行原合一，
同工異曲比王門。

James's doctrine of radical empiricism denies the fundamental relationship between subject and object, instead discovering something like "knowing" in between. It exerted a great influence on Zhang Dongsun, who also questions the dualism of subject and object in his own plural epistemological system. Apparently, he appreciates James's philosophy of pragmaticism that aims to mediate between two extremes to resolve disputes; therefore, he relates it to Wang Yangming's 王陽明 (1472–1529) philosophy, which also combines speech and behavior as oneness.

Zhang Dongsun's philosophical theory of structure (*jiagou lun* 架構論) is derived from Samuel Alexander's idea that mind emerges from matter and Conwy Lloyd Morgen's "emergent evolution."[128] In his poem about these two philosophers, Zhang Dongsun wrote the following lines by borrowing the imagery of bamboo from traditional Chinese poetry:

In the realm of time and space, life layers emerged;
within the heart, mists of growth unfold.
Manifold order birthed from the abyss,
one layer gives rise to another.[129]

時空生物層層起，
心上增霧節節高。
條理萬端由底起，
一層突創一層包。

While Alexander and Morgen focus more on their views of the universe, Zhang Dongsun applies the law of involution arising from emergent evolutionism to his plural epistemology. However, he puts more emphasis on structure itself than on evolution. His theory of structure, according to Zhang Yaonan's 張耀南 studies, not only resembles A. N. Whitehead's idea of concrescence or nexūs but also draws inspiration from the Buddhist theory of interrelation.[130] Zhang Dongsun's, Whitehead's, and Buddhist ideas overlap in their repudiation of the most essential concept of "substance" in Western philosophy. According to Zhang Dongsun, his notion of structure "fundamentally neither regards 'matter' as a substantial entity nor considers 'heart' as a substantial entity."[131] Instead, it is more like Thirdspace that goes beyond causality and the dichotomy of matter and heart. In his poem about A. N. Whitehead, Zhang Dongsun wrote:

He once spoke of inspirations drawn from the East;
his thought expands relativity and spacetime.
Seeing his surroundings as interrelated like waves,
he has grown gray hair as have I become an old man.[132]

嘗說構思取自東，
擴充相對並時空。
萬緣周遍如波起，
欽倒白頭我亦翁。

Zhang Dongsun highly praises that Whitehead's idea of nexūs, developed from Eastern thought, has magnified space and time to the infinite. Since his own concept of panstructuralism shows equal interest in recapturing the infinite relatedness, Zhang Dongsun refers to Whitehead as his close friend who has accompanied him for years. Different from his other philosophical poems that avoid any specific description of his emotions, this one reveals his overt enchantment with Whitehead by including himself as a character.

Even if the philosophical poems adhere to a plain style to summarize each Western philosopher's major achievements, Zhang Dongsun frequently includes concealed messages pointing to contemporary politics. This requires the reader to decode the multifaceted meanings in association with the setting of Zhang Dongsun's own historical experiences. In his poem about Plato, Zhang wrote:

Using reason as the mold, all things take shape,
bestowing the wise man with the ruling power, the world revives.
How can we interrogate his idea of public wives and communal wealth?
The young ruler on the island is not yet ready to be supported.[133]

以理為型萬物模，
智人執柄世方甦。
公妻共產何堪問，
島上稚君未可扶。

Zhang Dongsun targets the *Republic*, Plato's famous designation of Utopia that is supposed to define and display justice. It is extremely ironic that Zhang Dongsun was living in a time when the collective Chinese were seemingly marching toward a Communist utopia, in which philosophers such as himself were exiled to oblivion. Zhang Dongsun admired Plato's philosophical thought, but in his later years, after experiencing Mao's socialist rule, he started to question the so-called utopian model that arbitrarily imposed the collective will upon individuals in the name of justice.[134]

It is not difficult to find connections between the historical figures and Zhang Dongsun's subterranean messages insinuating his previous political ambition. Writing about Thomas Hobbes, he highly esteems this great English political theorist's way of mediating between the state and its citizens during a time of political turmoil:

People are like wolves striving to safeguard themselves;
among different conflicting forces emerges mutual
    accommodation.[135]

人求自保各如狼，
力敵方知互讓強。

This kind of neutralization is parallel to the strategy of middle politics he employed to resolve conflicts in the political, social, and cultural realms during the Republican period. However, although he applauds Hobbes's advocacy of the social contract that begins with the individual right of self-preservation, he is suspicious of his political theory in *Leviathan*, which confers tyranny and its government enormous unchecked power. Therefore, he wrote:

Maintaining the social contract is attributed to the monarch;
freely leaves the madness of Leviathan.[136]

公約維持歸共主，
縱橫留得巨靈狂。

According to Bertrand Russell, Hobbes's Leviathan, which refers to the commonwealth, should be read as an analogy pointing to an artificial soul of the sovereign.[137] As Zhang Dongsun was experiencing the lunacy of the idolization of Mao Zedong after the establishment of the new China, he must have had an aversion to the unbridled political power that Hobbes guarantees to tyranny and the state. In comparison, his poem about John Locke is full of admiration and praise:

His heart is like a white board, leaving marks;
only with property can one have freedom.
The law of nature comes from man's given right,
which was regarded as a normal thing like mail in the West.[138]

心如白板印痕留，
有產方能有自由。
法定人權出天賦，
泰西奉此似傳郵。

Contrary to Hobbes's *Leviathan*, Locke attempts to limit the power of government and promulgate men's rights through the concept of natural law. By singling out Locke's influential idea of conferring individual rights to property, Zhang Dongsun intentionally contradicts the prevailing policy enacted by the Communist Party in modern China, in which communal wealth supersedes personal ownership. In Mao's regime, everything is in conflict with what Locke advocates. The political authority of the Communist Party has unlimited and overwhelming power not only to confiscate personal property but also to strip away an individual's natural rights. Zhang Dongsun's poem about Locke propounds a powerful counterargument to Mao's ideology that restricts individual freedom.

Probably because Marxism was the only legitimate and prevalent philosophical theory in China at the time, Zhang Dongsun avoided writing about Marx in his classical poems. Nevertheless, since some of his philosophical poems have disappeared, we cannot jump to conclusions. But at least from his poem about Hegel, we can tell that he is not a big fan of Hegel's dialectic. He wrote:

How can the dialectic be in conflict when there is antinomy?
Having and nonhaving were just changed names.
Thesis, antithesis, and synthesis are all empty;
whom does it help to mold warriors in the bosom?[139]

兩辭相悖豈成爭，
純有生無只異名。
正反合皆儱侗語，
助誰胸中造佳兵？

In the debates with the leftists in the 1930s, Zhang Dongsun stated that Hegel's dialectic of thesis-antithesis-synthesis had been mechanically utilized by Marxist believers as a universal model to apply to everything.[140] In his famous article "Various Kinds of Problems of Dialectic" ("Bianzhengfa de gezhong wenti" 辯證法的各種問題), he points out the flaws of Hegel's dialectic of opposites in unity, sarcastically mocking those who regard it as a fixed and unchanging principle or the absolute truth.[141] One of the most important legacies of Zhang Dongsun's plural epistemology is that he valorizes the "correlation logic" of the Chinese logic system,[142] which underscores that opposites are interdependent and complementary rather than antagonistic and contradictory. In this regard, he trenchantly criticizes that Hegel has confused "oppositions in unity" with "paradoxes," which, in his definition, should simultaneously accept both opposing propositions instead of eliminating one of them. Furthermore, he thinks Marx went even further astray by adopting Hegel's dialectic and applying it to historical materialism. As a result, everything is described in terms of war and conflict, be it class struggle or national problems, leaving no middle way to negotiate. "One should know that man and woman are not opposites; neither are heaven and earth, sun and moon, black and white, or red and green. They are absolutely not antagonistic to each other."[143] In his poem, he insinuates that Hegel's dialectic helped Marx to build his concept of class struggle, which stresses endless conflicts. It is truly unfortunate that his wise and rational ruminations on Hegel's dialectic and Marxism were never listened to and endorsed by those radical leftists in the 1930s, and in the end, he inevitably became the "enemy" of the proletarian dictatorship in new China, where Marxism is regarded as the absolute truth.

However, amid the political climate that excludes diversified opinions or "the plurality of truth" that Zhang Dongsun argues for in his own philosophical system, criticism of Hegel's dialectic and Marx's historical materialism would only cause personal misfortune. In his poem about Johann Gottlieb Fichte, Zhang Dongsun wrote: "But he can lift people's morale in forums" 但能講壇伸民氣. He had been desperately missing the opportunity to freely spread his ideas to a large and popular audience, like Fichte. Bereft of the public sphere where he could openly express his independent and liberating opinions, he could not belie his deep disappointment in Mao's so-called utopian China. His previous promotion of Thirdspace, which nurtures the public sphere, individual freedom, and diversified articulations, was brutally destroyed by authoritarianism. What was left was his poetic vista and the "self-made" Chan in his painfully struggling and lonely late years. Nevertheless, his creative synthesizing of Western philosophical insights with the classical Chinese poetic form reopened a poetic Thirdspace in which he could discuss forbidden topics and thoughts again. The significance of those philosophical poems lies not only in Zhang Dongsun's bold aesthetic innovation but also among the nuanced layers of political and philosophical meanings he attempts to underpin them with. This paradoxically newly created old poetry form is invaluable because it is where he could posit his heart.

Before the Cultural Revolution, Zhang Dongsun had begun to write his autobiography, *Politics and I* (*Wo yu zhengzhi* 我與政治), which he actually planned as early as 1948. Unfortunately, this unfinished autobiography did not survive the political havoc.[144] Although all traces of it were eliminated, one poem he wrote before the memoirs sounds like the reflection of his heart vista (*xinjing* 心境) at that time:

> Finishing writing, to whom should I give it to read in the future?
> As I face the lamp, drizzle falls relentlessly.
> Unrelated to the gains and losses of a demoralizing time,
> I know there were divergent routes long ago.
> Self-satisfaction and self-endangerment, resulting in self-narration,
> No gratitude, no resentment, and no extraordinariness.
> I have fully tasted all the flavors of life,
> In this life myriad ancient doubts exist forever.[145]

寫罷他年與誰看，
一燈相對雨如絲。
不關積毀失心期，
早識天涯本路歧。
自得自危因自述，
無恩無怨更無奇。
今生飽領人間味，
此世常存萬古疑。

Conclusion

Zhang Dongsun's philosophical, political, and cultural ideas, and even his literary creation, interact in an interdependent and interrelated way that he named "cultural interactionism." As an outstanding Republican-era intellectual actively engaged in nation-building and a polyphonic public sphere, he steadily presented himself as a reformist rather than a revolutionist. He valued harmony and negotiation over vehement strife. Deeply influenced by the philosophy of Kant, whose theory of antinomies sees that mutually contradictory propositions can be equally approved, Zhang was critical of the Hegelian dialectic that usually has three stages of development: a thesis, reaction (antithesis) that negates the thesis, and synthesis that resolves antithesis. Zhang's theory of plural epistemology creates an inherent incongruity with Karl Marx's materialist dialecticism because its rhetoric of class struggles and the identity of opposites is influenced by Hegelian dialects.

Zhang Dongsun's promotion of Thirdspace that stretched to the third route, middle politics, and the plurality of epistemology presented a daunting challenge to the prevailing paradigm focused on revolution and class struggle. However, rising above his Thirdspace is the Enlightenment spirit and rationalism that can be traced back to eighteenth- and nineteenth-century thought or even farther back to the classical humanistic spirit manifested in ancient Greece, Rome, and the Renaissance. Although experimental in his heterogeneity and antiessentialist fortitude, he was a stalwart proponent of the Enlightenment. Because he felt the lack of this spirit within the modern Chinese context, his Thirdspace with disclosive nature directly speaks to Chinese reality. Zhang Dongsun is indeed polemic, encompassing both conservatism and radicalism, traditionalism and postmodernism, political and apolitical tendencies, alignment with and divergence from the zeitgeist. Although the philosophical, political, and cultural trajectory he created for Chinese modernity is reasonable, it was expunged after the establishment of the new China. His personal tragedy not only symbolizes the loss of the public space where Chinese intellectuals could freely express themselves but also embodies the dire conundrums of Thirdspace in modern China. After the 1980s, this space was open once again during the rule of Deng Xiaoping 鄧小平 (1904–1997), who integrated capitalism with socialism, but personal freedom was still the sore point within the reforming China. This situation, stretching to the present, illustrates how China still falls short of Zhang Dongsun's call for Thirdspace.

CHAPTER II

Yin Haiguang

Colorless Thought as Thirdspace

In January 1967, two years before his death, Yin Haiguang, a well-known independent liberal thinker in Taiwan, wrote to his student Hu Yue 胡越 (1920–1980):

Many individuals engaging in discussions about national affairs, whether consciously or inadvertently, directly or indirectly, tend to align themselves with either the Communist Party or the Nationalist Party in various forms and manners; whereas those who are independent and genuinely argue for freedom and democracy on behalf of the Chinese people are exceedingly rare. In the past twenty years, this transformation engendered a focus on the right and wrong of the Party instead of the country itself. The gentleman's way is diminishing, while the scoundrel's way is growing. The voice of righteousness has ebbed, making people sigh wearily. For almost half a century, especially in the past two decades, China has endured tremendous turmoil, and the people have agonized and sacrificed massively. However, even these hardships cannot evoke a thorough awakening and sober cognitive concepts and opinions from normal intellectuals who remain entangled in the two-party framework. Even those intellectuals from the May Fourth Movement have virtually lost their independent spirit and thinking ability, and most of them are unable to go beyond the dichotomous standards of right and wrong imposed by the two parties.[1]

Yin Haiguang's harsh criticism reveals the brutal reality in which Chinese intellectuals have always been squeezed between the two hostile factions of the CCP and the KMT, unable to find productive solutions. Even for those intellectuals who were involved in the third force movement in the 1940s, attempting to play "a dual role as an agent of democratic change and a mediator" between the two major parties was predestined to end in failure.[2] Although Yin Haiguang sympathized with these third force intellectuals who endeavored to solve the conundrum through a middle way politics, he sharply criticized their "neutrality" as too weak to form a mainstream and maintain its own independence. With the outbreak of the Chinese Civil War, "these self-proclaimed neutral political groups were immediately affected by the social dynamic toward polarization and declared a rupture."[3] As a result, they succumbed to or defected to either the CCP or the KMT. After 1949, the majority of Chinese intellectuals could still hardly overcome the tensions between the two parties and remained haunted by great uncertainties and anxieties.

In this chapter, I explore the spiritual journey of Yin Haiguang, the emblematic and legendary intellectual figure of liberalism in Taiwan, who searched for an alternative way beyond the dualist party struggles. During his formative years amid the Second Sino-Japanese War and the Chinese Civil War, he exhibited unwavering opposition to Communism and staunch allegiance to Chiang Kai-shek and the KMT. He vehemently voiced his dissent against Marxist doctrine and adamantly rejected the concept of the "dictatorship of the proletariat." Around the time he moved to Taiwan in 1949, he gradually became disillusioned with the KMT while maintaining his trenchant opposition to the CCP. Changing from a defender of the "Three Principles of the People" (*sanmin zhuyi* 三民主義) to an independent liberal, he became a strident critic of the KMT and Chiang Kai-shek's dictatorial policies. As one of the main contributors to *Free China* (*Ziyou zhongguo* 自由中國), a vital journal propagating democracy in Taiwan, Yin Haiguang was an important thinker and fighter, carrying on the liberalism launched by Hu Shi in the May Fourth Movement. In his waning years, he defined the role he played within these turbulent times in China as that of "a post May-Fourthian" who was "ruggedly individualistic," insisting on being independent, neither belonging to nor wanted by any group.[4] He was a lonely "spiritual warrior" who promoted and ruminated on the stakes of individualism, liberalism, and democracy against the backdrop of the KMT-dominated ideology.

In addressing the proliferation of the dichotomic way of thinking bound by party struggles, Yin Haiguang originated a unique and fundamental perspective of "colorless thought," a kind of cognitive thinking that is free from the authoritarian, violent, bigoted, frantic utterances and voices prevalent in modern society.[5] It has the distinct nature of a solid Thirdspace, which accords with the Western liberal tradition—a more regenerative solution to the polarized deadlock that haunted Chinese intellectuals for several decades. Through select political commentaries, correspondence, and academic essays, I trace how Yin Haiguang grew to be in sharp contrast with the majority of Chinese intellectuals who aligned themselves with either of the two parties and how he strove to transcend this constricting and self-destructive political morass. I contend that his "colorless thought" entails a set of philosophical implications that bring to light the rational Thirdspace that is imperative in the context of the Chinese reality full of intense political battles.

The Stalwart Anti-Communist Stance

In 1952, having been settled in Taiwan for three years, Yin Haiguang was astonished and distraught to read his respected former mentor Jin Yuelin's 金岳霖 (1895–1984) article "Self-Criticism" ("Ziwo jiantao" 自我檢討) in a Hong Kong journal. To his dismay, Jin Yuelin, who chose to stay in mainland China after 1949, wrote: "Yin Fusheng 殷福生 [the original name of Yin Haiguang], who fled to Taiwan in opposition to the people, is a reactionary figure that I have successfully cultivated."[6] Under the extreme pressure of political circumstances after the establishment of the new China, Jin Yuelin's predicament was like that of other Chinese intellectuals, forced to give up their liberal positions, indoctrinated in Communist ideology, participating in self-criticism sessions to ensure their own survival. At that time, this kind of coercive and suffocating situation in the mainland was unfamiliar to intellectuals in Taiwan and Hong Kong because it far surpassed the political crises they were encountering.

In response, another of Jin Yuelin's former students, Mou Zongsan 牟宗三 (1909–1995), a representative figure of New Confucianism in Hong Kong, wrote an article satirizing his teacher's self-criticism and his rationale for remaining in the mainland. Yin Haiguang sympathized more with his teacher, seeing Jin Yuelin's lack of alternatives under totalitarianism and refusing to hold personal grudges. Using the pen name Mei Yunli 梅蘊理, Yin Haiguang published an article in *Free China* calling Mou Zongsan "self-enclosed" and an "idealist" for not understanding the plight of mainland intellectuals under totalitarian rule and making flippant and sarcastic remarks overseas.⁷ In addition, he published an article, "Why Do I Oppose the CCP?" ("Wo weishenme fangong" 我為什麼反共), explicating why he chose an unfaltering anti-Communist position from his germinal years to the present. This article, induced by his teacher's absurd and unwilling self-criticism, offers an invaluable introspection by dividing his anti-Communist career into three stages: fanatical criticism of the CCP according to the KMT's ideology from the late 1930s to 1948; promoting the juxtaposition of "economic equality" with "political democracy" while he was disillusioned by Chiang Kai-shek's one-party dictatorship from 1948 to 1952; and the totally independent liberal position that outstripped party doctrine after 1952. Yin Haiguang's three personal phases signify his increasing estrangement from the KMT and its ideology, unveiling his gradual identification with a politically and philosophically nurtured individuality that confronts intense internal and external conflicts.

Yin Haiguang became a student of Jin Yuelin, a prominent modern Chinese philosopher of logic, at Tsinghua University in 1936. When the Japanese occupied Beijing in 1937, Yin Haiguang followed Tsinghua University to Kunming, where he dedicated himself to philosophical studies at the National Southwestern Associated University in 1938 and completed a master's degree in philosophy in 1942. According to Yin Haiguang, Jin Yuelin had a decisive influence on him, not only guiding him to study logic and empiricism but also shaping his thought and worldview. In his own description, Jin Yuelin's "efforts and influence on the modernization of Chinese thought, his achievement in leading young Chinese scholars to the right path in the study of philosophy and logic, along with his introduction of Cambridge's analytic style, undoubtedly hold a significant place in history."⁸ Most importantly, because Jin Yuelin was educated at Columbia University, he fully embraced the Anglo-American democratic tradition, firmly believing that "individual freedom is a goal in itself rather than the means to achieve other purposes," so he strongly opposed the collectivist Bolshevik mentality.⁹ This exerted a tremendous impact on Yin Haiguang, whose anti-Communist stance was intrinsically linked to his mentor's view that individualism is inalienable and self-evidently inviolable.

During his seven university years, he identified with the ideology of the KMT and staunchly played an anti-Communist role. According to his own recollection, the student body at that time was divided into left-leaning, right-leaning, and neutral groups, so their activities were heavily tinged with political overtones. While most of the young people feverishly turned to the Left and embraced Marxism and the Communist ideology, he became a firm and loyal supporter of the KMT, frequently engaging in caustic arguments and disputes with the leftists. In his own words, "The philosophical education and analytical training I received successfully shielded me from the plague that is Communism." As he reflected, his anti-Communist posture evolved from both his liberal education and his active participation in the right-wing campus organization. In terms of theory, he was confident that he formed a powerful counterdiscourse against the ideological and affective impact of the CCP. Nonetheless, his fanaticism in action was polemic: whenever they encountered other anti-Communists, he and his friends would emulate the Nazi salute in a tongue-in-cheek manner of greeting. In his introspection at this stage, he soberly criticized such compulsive and zealous behavior as little different from that of the Communists. This testimonial of "an organization's prejudices or a collective stake" definitely belongs to the "colorful thought" he later delineated and reproached.[10]

Driven by political ardor, Yin Haiguang, at the risk of interrupting his own education, avidly responded to Chiang Kai-shek's call for the youth to fight the Japanese invaders by joining the KMT army in January 1945 and being sent to India to receive eight months' training in automobile driving. Unexpectedly, his career as a soldier was halted by the end of the Second Sino-Japanese War. However, instead of returning to the university to continue his graduate studies, he chose to enter society, working for a publishing house in Chongqing, where he met Xu Fuguan 徐復觀 (1904–1982), an ardent anti-Communist and a member of Chiang Kai-shek's staff at that time who later became one of the leading figures of New Confucianism in Hong Kong. With Xu Fuguan's help, Yin Haiguang had a brief meeting with Chiang Kai-shek and later moved to Nanjing in 1946; worked as writer-in-chief for *Central Daily News* (*Zhongyang ribao* 中央日報), a newspaper that best represented the KMT's official rhetoric; and taught philosophy courses at the University of Jinling. He published a series of articles and books bombarding the Communist ideology by means of multiple approaches, such as historical narrative, ideological structure, and comparative studies. At that stage, he spoke entirely from the standpoint of a passionate KMT loyalist, believing that only by following Chiang Kai-shek's policies would the country have promising prospects.

Though brutally right-tilted in tone, addressing the CCP as "a rare thing" (*juewu* 絕物) and "an incurable disease" (*juezheng* 絕症),[11] Yin Haiguang's writing at this stage marked a significant moment in the burgeoning of his public and intellectual life. While he attempted to set a heightened tenor for the KMT propaganda in competition with that of the CCP, which successfully enraptured people from different backgrounds, some of his analysis concerning the pitfalls of the Communist ideology and political practice proved prescient. Regardless of his rightist position, his analysis embodied a certain historical rationale and political prophecy based on his knowledge of liberalism. By digging beneath the tune of "democracy" enthusiastically chanted by the CCP, he lucidly revealed its "new ethics": "Whatever is in the interest of the proletariat is considered morally justifiable; conversely, whatever is not in the interest of the proletariat is regarded as morally unjust."[12] According to him, it was this new, arbitrarily determined set of ethics that formulated the so-called absolute and universal truth based on the benefit of the proletariat and "materialistic dialectics," which appear highly dubious. Yin Haiguang was keenly aware that the CCP's blatantly fraudulent rhetoric of "democracy" concealed a fundamentalist extirpation of dissent.[13] His liberal sensibilities led him to expose the intolerant spirit of a one-party dictatorship: "The Communists viewed culture as subservient to practical politics, wherein all aspects including science, philosophy, history, literature, and art should be developed in line with political imperatives. These elements were expected to reflect Marxism, Leninism, Stalinism, or they cannot exist within Communist-ruled territories."[14] Succinctly stated, Yin Haiguang argued that Marxism, Leninism, Stalinism, and materialist dialectics could only lead to political monism. He was sensibly clairvoyant in unveiling the monistic nature of Communist ideology, which subjugates literature, art, history, and philosophy to the political agenda.

One of his particular foci was that the CCP's political principle is imbued with an intolerant character that cannot accept freedom of speech. This discovery was paramount during the time when the CCP made enormous strides in uniting people from diverse classes and backgrounds, especially enticing members of the China Democratic League in the late 1940s. Yin's perception was very sharp and rational because even the third force intellectuals, such as Zhang Dongsun, were completely convinced by the Communist pretension of democracy. However, Yin carefully examined the insincerity of this democratic facade and observed the mutual exclusion between the two parties. As anticipated, this eventually led to totalitarian control after 1949. In Yin's acute observation, a semitotalitarian situation had already occurred within Communist territories such as Yan'an, where most of the purges were happening.[15] When speech was politically incorrect according to Marxist standards, it was labeled subversive, outdated, fascist, and reactionary by the CCP authorities.[16] The intolerance of newspapers from various groups in Yan'an, which aimed to enforce conformity of thought, was evident in the hyperbolic tone of the so-called democracy promulgated by the CCP.[17] While many prominent figures from the China Democratic League failed to discern the deceptive nature concealed within the CCP's propaganda, Yin Haiguang decisively disclosed the truth by quoting one of Mao Zedong's sentences in "Against Liberalism" ("Fandui ziyou zhuyi" 反對自由主義), written in 1937: "Liberalism, simply another form of opportunism, is fundamentally in conflict with Marxism."[18] What disturbed Yin Haiguang was the contradiction between liberalism and Communism, as in Yan'an, the CCP compulsorily subordinated individual freedom of choice to the demands of collectivism. Therefore, even if the CCP's propaganda of constructing a unified, powerful, democratic, free, modern nation-state was greatly appealing to leftists and some of the third force intellectuals, Yin Haiguang was never entranced by it.

In addition, Yin Haiguang rationally uncovered the CCP's "core axiom" based on its new ethics: "use any means necessary to achieve the ends" (*zhiwen mudi, buze shouduan* 只問目的，不擇手段). As he described, "From Marx to Lenin, from Stalin to the Communist Party cadres globally, this axiom became one of the basic teachings of the Communist Party. In order to give a 'theoretical foundation' to this basic dictum, they created seemingly esoteric statements."[19] The essential theories of the CCP revolving around "material dialectics" were to justify, legitimate, or even glorify various demeaning tactics, such as political propaganda filled with falsehoods, insistence on class struggle, favoring violent revolution, and dehumanization of opponents. Marx's claim in *The Communist Manifesto*—"The history of all hitherto existing society is the history of class struggles"[20]—laid the theoretical foundation for the CCP's worship of violent revolution, which for Yin Haiguang, was quintessentially incongruent with democracy.[21] Yin expressed this view unequivocally: "the CCP is a battle system (*zhandou tixi* 戰鬥體系) through and through, which not only could not coexist peacefully with people outside the Party but also butchered people inside the Party at every turn. After killing them, it still made a strong case for the so-called 'Trotskyism' or 'antireactionism.'"[22] In such a system, seemingly peaceful slogans such as "negotiation" and "democracy" are masks veiling deceptive schemes.[23] Yin Haiguang clearly foresaw the danger of putting ends before means, which would pervert benevolence into malevolence. Although Zhang Dongsun was also averse to the theory of material dialecticism and class struggle ingrained in Marxism, he was too naïve and idealistic in his faith of the CCP's "democratic" vision, and it inevitably ended in personal tragedy after 1949. Yin Haiguang, by contrast, foresightedly deduced the dogmatic nature of the CCP, which ruthlessly used various peremptory means to liquidate dissidents inside and outside the party. Moreover, he perceived that some of the third force intellectuals, who were "either dragonflies flying all over the sky before the storm or mayflies after the storm,"[24] were being manipulated by the parties and could not thrive in these conditions. Defying the democratic myth created by the CCP, Yin Haiguang was horrified to see how the grand, lofty Communist utopia was relentlessly built on endless class struggles and violent revolution, destined to turn into a dystopia, bringing heart-wrenching catastrophe and desolation for years to come.

At the end of 1948, Yin Haiguang changed his view of the KMT after a trip to Suzhou, where he witnessed hundreds of thousands of refugees from the Chinese Civil War. The devastating scene convinced him to emphasize people's welfare rather than party struggles, launching his second stage of anti-Communism, which sharply diverged from the first stage. He reflected upon his transformation at that specific historical moment: "I came to the realization that the challenges faced by China are far more complex than what the opposing factions' slogans would lead one to believe. It became clear to me how the partisanship is detrimental to the effective resolution of China's problems."[25] Moving beyond rubrics of party struggle, he unconsciously echoed the idea of mediation originating from the third force intellectuals, regarding economic equality and political democracy as correspondingly valid goals. In his article "Quickly Collect People's Hearts" ("Ganjin shoushi renxin" 趕緊收拾人心), he broke from the KMT upon seeing the aftermath of their corrupt policies and behavior, urging them to pay attention to the plight of ordinary people.[26] Apart from the CCP and the KMT, he did not advocate the path of neutrality either; instead, he propounded a new democratic socialist country that would keep its denizens nourished in addition to ensuring political freedom.[27] Although he sounded self-contradictory in his view of the third force intellectuals—criticizing their skeptical neutrality but adopting their proposal of a democratic socialist country—his intention of transcending party conflicts was obvious. However, even at this stage, he did not change his anti-Communist stance, seeing the realities of the CCP's rule on "fighting materialism" (*zhandou weiwulun* 戰鬥唯物論) as essentially incompatible with the rhetoric of political democracy. As he pointed out, the theories of "negation of negation" and "the unity of opposition" strongly insinuate "struggle," which builds up the solid ideological foundation of the CCP that contradicts democracy, whose philosophical base is peace.[28] All these vantage points were derived from his observations of recent Soviet history, that "the Communist Party of the Soviet Union over the past thirty years has been marked by a strict demand for ideological, organizational, and social totality."[29] Yin Haiguang believed that "in such a society, akin to Fascist regimes, the ordinary individual is treated merely as a means to an end, rather than as an end in themselves." As a result of this absence of political protection, the individual can be freely eliminated whenever he violates Communist law. In this environment, the people are stripped of their rights and become mere tools unable to challenge the Marxist-Leninist-Stalinist ideology. As Yin Haiguang predicted, "Once the CCP overthrows the KMT, they will definitely institute a more stringent, totalitarian regime on the ruins of the mainland."[30] Three decades of Mao's rule validated his intuitive prophecy.

In June 1949, Yin Haiguang moved to Taipei, continuing his job as writer-in-chief at *Central Daily News*. He later quit and became a lecturer in philosophy at National Taiwan University, where he gradually stood out as the most popular professor. He taught logic along with linguistic analysis and application for seventeen years. In November 1949, Hu Shi and Lei Zhen 雷震 (1897–1979) launched *Free China*, Taiwan's most important platform for discussing and publicizing democracy and freedom, and Yin Haiguang became a prominent contributor. From 1950 onward, he took a special interest in translating academic Western texts on Soviet totalitarianism written by Hans Kohn, Massimo Salvadori, and John S. Reshetar Jr. He even translated George Orwell's acclaimed dystopian classic, *1984*, an allegorical response to Stalinist totalitarianism. Friedrich Hayek's *The Road to Serfdom*, which Yin translated in 1953, tremendously solidified his position as an independent liberal. These translations provided a crucial impetus for Yin Haiguang's critical assessment regarding how totalitarian ideologies impinged upon the quotidian social life.

Based on his understanding of Soviet totalitarianism and Western political philosophy, he discovered that it was impossible to achieve economic equality and political freedom at the same time. As a result, he moved into his third stage of anti-Communism after 1952, which focused on vigorously bolstering political freedom. As he analyzed, "In China's present, political democracy should be considered more important than economic equality. Without political democracy, it becomes impossible to address any other issues. Individuals who have been deprived of their political freedom are reduced to serfs, labor slaves, commercial slaves, and literary slaves, losing their sense of human identity. They cannot act and risk their lives if they do not speak properly, so how can they fight for any economic equality?" He debunked that utopian dream of many Chinese intellectuals, particularly those deeply committed to the Communist ideology. He pointed out that the dearth of political freedom would inevitably give rise to a new form of modern serfdom, drawing inspiration from Hayek's ideas. Compared to his early mentor Jin Yuelin, who was forced to perform self-criticism in mainland China, Yin Haiguang felt extremely lucky that he at least still possessed the freedom of silence, the basic human right ensured by liberal principles.[31]

In general, Yin Haiguang expounded that resistance to totalitarianism was his primary motivation for opposing Communism.[32] Many of his viewpoints coincided with Hannah Arendt's arguments in *The Origins of Totalitarianism*, in which she not only noticed that Nazi Germany and Stalinist Russia were identical in terms of totalitarian forms but also emphasized the difference between a one-party dictatorship and total domination.[33] Developed from one-party dictatorship, the totalitarian government relied on mass movements, establishing a completely new political apparatus and discarding "all social, legal and political traditions of the country."[34] Similarly, Yin Haiguang pointed out that Mao Zedong's rule can be characterized as totalitarian dominance, "complete in all aspects, from spirituality to materiality, from clothing, food, housing, and transportation to the education of the next generation."[35] Resonating with Hannah Arendt's view, he concisely exposed that the totalitarian government not only destroys the public realm but also extends its hegemonic control into every corner of the private realm of life.[36] His shrewd and meticulous analysis is best demonstrated in his translation of John S. Reshetar Jr.'s *Problems of Analyzing and Predicting Soviet Behavior*, in which he added 48 percent of the notes in his own short free style, providing his astute understanding and criticism of Communist totalitarianism.

In his account of the very essence of the Communist state, he analyzed the nature of panpoliticization and panmoralization as preconditions for totalitarian domination. Disguised as equivalent to messianism, panpoliticization contains an overwhelming, near-religious power permeating every infinitesimal grain of human lives.[37] As he acknowledges, under totalitarian rule, everyone is transformed into a political engineer whose basic survival is political survival. "From the time people are born, they learn political slogans, sing political songs, recognize political symbols, and worship political figures. Their bleached mind is dyed with color."[38] In his opinion, panpoliticization is the most poisonous problem of totalitarianism, which is ubiquitous in everyday life, depriving the individual of breathing space. It breeds a way of thinking that only cares about political position regardless of right and wrong, using a singular and rigid "absolute truth" as the sole criterion for assessing compliance among individuals.[39] As he analyzed, "In the name of 'ism,' the most advanced modern governing techniques and instruments are used to coerce individuals into metamorphosing into mindless collectives, akin to swarms of bees, ants, and sheep. This manipulation serves to satisfy the primitive and barbaric desire for power held by a few fanatics." In accord with the doctrines of totalitarianism, individualism disappears completely, and the elements that define a person as a person are stolen away. These standpoints were derived from his critical observation of Russia's totalitarian environment in which party supersedes country, country trumps society, and society overrules individual. Yin Haiguang stridently pointed out: "Totalitarian rulers use the party as the goal, the state as the guise, and the people as the tool to carry out cultural, educational, military, economic, political, and even ideological control, with a planned economy and planned education." As a result, a paramount feature of totalitarianism is its utter intolerance of alternative political models and its relentless effort to negate the independent existence of all institutions, be they individual, community, societal, or national, outside the realm of its party sphere.[40]

Yin Haiguang's rational analyses and criticism of the CCP continuously fueled intense support for his later anti-KMT comments. After the Lei Zhen incident in 1960, Yin Haiguang halted his political commentaries and returned to academic research. However, he ended his political silence upon discovering Red Guard activities during the Cultural Revolution in 1966. He saw the Red Guards as emblematic of the problematic political tendencies he had once criticized. Their unprecedented fanatical, maniacal, and destructive actions reflected the lunacy of Mao Zedong and the Communist dictators, whose problems he characterized as "the psychology of the cave" (*yaodong xinli* 窯洞心理).[41] He used numerous words related to mental derangement to describe the mindset of the Red Guards—"fanaticism," "parochialism," "egocentrism," "paranoia," "megalomania," "sadism," "xenophobia," "vandalism"—manifestations of the Communist disease prevalent in mainland China and the world. By considering the psychosis exhibited by the Red Guards as a primary example of the malaise inherent in totalitarianism, he reaffirmed his previous assessments of totalitarian ideologies and movements. Yin Haiguang's critical understanding of the Communist political model reflected his liberal identity, enabling him to detect similar potential deficiencies within the KMT government in Taiwan. That led to another path in his spiritual journey, where he was critical of Chiang's policies that held people under the spell of semitotalitarianism.

A Trenchant Critic of the KMT

Beginning in 1948, Yin Haiguang transitioned from a staunch KMT loyalist into the party's most ferocious critic. In his political commentaries, he often urged Chiang Kai-shek's administration to examine all the follies and deficiencies that had led to its present defeated state. His 1948 article, "Which Road Should We Take?" already voiced stringent criticism of the KMT: that its government was founded by party dictators, warlords, plutocrats, and political moguls who were virtually in conflict with the majority of the people, who suffered enormously during the Chinese Civil War.[42] He was extremely critical of how the KMT leaders formed an oligarchy that solely benefited a prestigious minority at the cost of ordinary people. In another article, "Quickly Collect People's Heart," he advised the KMT to selflessly protect people's freedom and democracy in order to win popular support.[43] At that time, he started to reflect on how he had uncritically stood with the KMT in the past. Skeptical about the prospects offered by the CCP and the KMT as well as the neutral position taken by the third force intellectuals, who apparently lacked the strength to maintain true independence, he was conscientiously searching for an alternative to the antipodal party conflict.

After he moved to Taiwan in 1949, he initially worked for *Central Daily News*, writing articles eulogizing the "Three Principles of People" on the one hand and provocatively attacking Communist rule in mainland China on the other. But he soon quit because he was not in tune with the KMT's political policy anymore. After starting to teach philosophy at National Taiwan University, he began to write political commentaries for *Free China*, increasingly directing his criticism toward the KMT's one-party dictatorship, although his anti-Communist stance remained unaltered. The more he was acutely aware of totalitarianism's fundamental deprivation of human rights, such as freedom of thought and freedom of speech, the more he enthusiastically advocated liberalism in Taiwan. In his article "Against Bolshevism" ("Fan bu'er xiweike zhuyi" 反布爾希維克主義), he fervidly provided the remedy to the problem caused by the worldwide fanaticism of communism: "In fact, while it is necessary to use force to prevent communist activities, the most fundamental way is to foster democratic freedom. Democracy and freedom are the best antiseptics."[44]

Behind Yin Haiguang's anti-Communist narrative lies a zealous attempt at and an overarching vision of launching liberalism in Taiwan. Writing for *Free China*, he got off to a vigorous start, full of good intentions, and was eager to provide constructive suggestions against Communism. In a rhetorical tone that was mild and tactful, his political commentaries sought to persuade Chiang Kai-shek's administration to adopt the route of Western liberalism, which, in his opinion, would change the whole political and cultural milieu of Taiwan, forming the most efficient counterdiscourse to Communist totalitarianism. His argument was based on the global magnitude of the communist threat that stretched beyond Europe and Asia, so it was not merely a matter of country, party, or individual. Therefore, he proposed an effective antidote in the form of democracy to externally align with the free world and internally realize a new and genuine power. In his words, "anticommunism and democracy are two sides of the same coin and are inseparable in practice."[45]

Even though he criticized the KMT's rigged election in 1954, in which there was only one candidate in some cities and counties, he avoided radical rhetoric, urging party members to adopt Sun Yat-sen's tolerant spirit.[46] He had not given up hope for the KMT's ideological reorientation. In his article "It Is Time That the KMT Should Reflect" ("Zheshi Guomindang fanxing de shihou" 這是國民黨反省的時候), he applauded the party's effort to erect infrastructure in Taiwan but expressed his dissatisfaction with its political reform. His sharp criticism was partly on the grounds that KMT members should still have room to maintain human dignity instead of becoming "tools, gears, and statistics on a table," like CCP members under totalitarianism.[47] In essence, he likened the difference between KMT members and CCP members to that between man and beast, reflecting how he held out hope that the KMT would eventually enshrine human rights. Coincidently, his metaphor of "beast" was in conformity with the label of "cattle, ghosts, snakes, and gods" that the CCP assigned to Chinese intellectuals who suffered cruel degradation and humiliation during the Cultural Revolution. These individuals were deprived of their intrinsic human dignity, as their cognitive capacity was suppressed, and their right to express their thoughts and engage in artistic creation was ruthlessly confiscated.

However, to his disenchantment and frustration, instead of taking the democratic route, the KMT government exercised strict control over the freedom of speech under the guise or pretext of "national interests," "basic national policies," "extraordinary times," and "emergencies," preaching that individuals should sacrifice for the benefit of the nation.[48] Under such circumstances, along with his colleagues and friends from *Free China*, Yin Haiguang gradually transformed from writing in a restrained tone to a direct, confrontational manner, audaciously playing the role of social critic. In 1956, right after his one-year visit to Harvard University, he targeted his criticism toward Zhang Qiyun 張其昀 (1901–1985), the minister of education, who interpreted the three true meanings of democratic politics as to love the people, to teach the people, and to nurture the people. In Yin Haiguang's opinion, this testifies to what he terms "the democracy of the monarch" (*junzhu de minzhu* 君主的民主), with the presupposition of the ruler bestowing favors upon his subordinates. Furthermore, it relies on the "theory of an organic country" that resembles the all-devouring government envisioned in Thomas Hobbes's *Leviathan*, engulfing the individual. This "monarchical democracy," in his view, "contains militarism, fascism, ancient revivalism, narrow nationalism, national economic-ism, and, above all, 'pastoralism,' yet not a trace of democratic thought can be found."[49] Based on a hierarchical order rather than human equality, at its best, it is equivalent to "benevolent despotism"; however, he warned, once it adopts a modern domineering strategy, it can be easily transformed into harmful totalitarianism.[50]

In August 1957, *Free China* launched a series of editorials with the general title "Recent Issues," which comprehensively reviewed the political, economic, military, judicial, educational, and journalistic issues in Taiwan based on the attitude of "saying what it is"—a frank, rational way to explore the truth.[51] Yin Haiguang wrote several articles opposing party-oriented education, which in his opinion, approached the panpoliticism and panmoralization lionized by the Communist totalitarian rule.[52] In addition, he vehemently questioned the KMT's slogan of "counterattacking the mainland" (*fangong dalu* 反攻大陸), revealing it as a totally unrealistic and impossible goal. Under this self-deceiving slogan, the government requested the people to "put up with it for a while," brushing aside the more pressing social concerns. Instead, the KMT ignored human rights and freedom and impeded political development toward the democratic path.[53] Yin Haiguang likened this quixotic reclamation propaganda to the emperor's new clothes, putting forth an image of strength to hide weaknesses. This article incurred severe attacks from the KMT propaganda organs, which called it part of an international conspiracy, colluding with the Communists to undermine the KMT government.[54] Hu Shi, who had just returned from the United States, openly expressed his disagreement, stating that "'counterattack on the mainland' is a signboard and the most important hope and symbol, so it should not be touched."[55] At that time in Taiwan, even this forerunner and old guard of Chinese liberalism was inclined to support Chiang Kai-shek, albeit reluctantly and ambivalently. Hu Shi's support was pragmatic because it rested on the KMT's standing as the sole formidable force against the CCP-controlled mainland. Few intellectuals dared to voice opposition to KMT rule, unable to maintain their own independent spirit. The only consistently tenacious opponent was a group of intellectuals involved with *Free China*, among whom Yin Haiguang stood out as one of the most prominent leaders of liberalism in Taiwan.

When the editor-in-chief of *Free China*, Lei Zhen, was arrested on September 4, 1960, for attempting to start an opposition party, the New Party, Yin Haiguang came under immense political pressure. Before Lei Zhen's arrest, Yin Haiguang enthusiastically provided some constructive and pertinent suggestions for the opposition party. In proportion to Hu Shi's moderate proposal to replace the sensitive term "the opposition party" with "the party out of governance" (*zaiye dang* 在野黨), Yin set the basic goal for the new party: to pursue democratic freedom and guarantee basic human rights. He aspired to a brand new and healthy political and cultural ecology that could break the KMT's one-party dictatorship. After Lei Zhen was imprisoned and *Free China* was shut down, Yin Haiguang faced tremendous danger but intrepidly published an announcement along with another two colleagues taking responsibility for what they had written in *Free China* and exposing themselves to legal consequences. This reflected Yin Haiguang's heroic defiance as a liberal fighter and his last hope for the KMT's political reform, in addition to marking his cold distance from Hu Shi.

Yin Haiguang retired from politics to academia and maintained silence on political matters for the rest of his life, despairing of Taiwan's democratic future. The KMT authorities still treated him as a heretic and kept repressing him. His book *The Viewpoints of Chinese Culture* (*Zhongguo wenhua de zhanwang* 中國文化的展望) was banned from publication, and he was dismissed from National Taiwan University in 1966. This persecution endangered his family's basic survival, forcing them to rely on financial support from students and friends. Although later hired as a visiting scholar by the Yenching Society of Harvard University, he was officially prevented from leaving the country. In 1967, he was diagnosed with stomach cancer, and he died in 1969 at the age of fifty. Despite all the obstacles he faced in his later years, he never yielded to the political authorities and continued to explore the academic realm of political theory. Therefore, his student Chang Hao 張灝 (1937–2022) said, "Ten years of political persecution, social indifference, and vilification, long years of illness, and the threat of death did not hamper his characteristic idealism in any way."[56]

In his important paper titled "An Anatomy of the KMT" ("Pouxi Guomindang" 剖析國民黨), Yin Haiguang comprehensively and piercingly scrutinized the problem of the KMT from its launch to the Taiwan period, employing a research approach he termed "overlapping frames of reference" to examine various social and political entities.[57] As he explained:

> The KMT itself was neither communist nor fascist, nor did it closely resemble Japan. However, in solving its own problems and contending with these factions, the KMT has inevitably incorporated certain aspects of Russian Communist, Nazi Fascist, and Japanese militarist education to a greater or lesser extent. These elements coincided with patterns of monarchical tendencies, despotism, and secret gangsterism rooted in Chinese tradition.[58]

Dividing the KMT's transformation into three stages, Yin Haiguang recognized that in the first stage, the party under Sun Yat-sen was an idealistic pioneer that overthrew the Qing dynasty and established the Republic of China; in the second stage, the party became a short-lived strategic alliance of the CCP and the KMT that was appreciated by ordinary people; and the third stage was defined by Chiang Kai-shek's despotic manner all the way to Taiwan. There, the KMT's idealism gradually dissipated, replaced by a political cynicism that vindicated the perpetual acquisition of power. Yin Haiguang viewed the KMT's political predicament as reminiscent of the Nazis' and Communists' embrace of "ends justifying means," straying from their original republican goals. This precarious axiom often converts good intentions into evil consequences. In addition, its mimicry of panpoliticization and panmoralization intertwined with a Manichean dichotomy to distinguish its enemies made the KMT little different from the Communists.[59]

In particular, Yin Haiguang took umbrage with the KMT's deification of Chiang Kai-shek as a messianic national savior, similar to Mao Zedong's cult of personality. This created a political aura reminiscent of the totalitarian regimes of Adolf Hitler and Joseph Stalin, characterized by their absolute dominance. In tandem with the worship of the party leader, the political characteristics of the KMT were a combination of "the sadistic personality" and "the masochistic personality," or "the authoritarian type of personality" and "the subservient type of personality"—resembling the traditional master-slave mentality criticized by Lu Xun in the May Fourth Movement.[60] Similarly, Yin Haiguang despised the KMT's appropriation of Chinese tradition to sanctify a political myth and legitimize its repressive political policies. The party members fashioned themselves as protectors of Chinese cultural tradition from the iconoclastic Communists, and this political strategy impelled Yin Haiguang to take a position of "total Westernization," which inevitably put him in conflict with scholars of New Confucianism in Hong Kong, such as Mou Zongshan, Xu Fuguan, Tang Junyi 唐君毅 (1909–1978), and Qian Mu 錢穆 (1895–1990), who firmly valorized Chinese tradition albeit holding an anti-Communist stance.

In general, Yin Haiguang described Taiwan's government in a sarcastic tone as "a substratal totalitarian regime" that emulated the more powerful Communist regime by extinguishing individualism and treating human beings as livestock.[61] It maintained a propaganda machine that brandished the KMT party doctrine, hunting down heretical ideologies and presupposing that party authority equated to righteousness. Furthermore, the KMT's rule of Taiwan under Chiang Kai-shek was more of a reign of terror. The White Terror was a hallmark of the regime because it manipulated the ordinary people's fear and anxiety with ubiquitous informants and bellicose rhetoric of a war of reclamation against the Communist mainland. By doing so, the KMT essentially nipped the bud of Taiwanese democracy. Yin Haiguang composed his article analyzing the KMT in both English and Chinese, regardless of the perilous and repressive conditions prevailing in Taiwan. It most truly reflects his opposition to the KMT, which came from the same stock as the Communists and fascists. Facing the totalitarian horror that underpinned both the CCP and the KMT, he was extremely anxious to fight for freedom, yearning for a breathing space in which an alternative path would be possible.

Colorless Thought as Thirdspace

After a prolonged time of infatuation with politics, Yin Haiguang reflected on his anti-Communist and KMT-critical stance in 1967: "The experience of the past two decades has taught us that neither the CCP nor the KMT demonstrates a genuine commitment to patriotism or the well-being of the people. Consequently, it is evident that neither party is capable of guiding China toward a path of democracy and freedom. Instead, both parties are obsessed with pursuing power and personal gain."[62] He lamented that lofty words such as "nation, country, people" had all been ruthlessly utilized so that a monolithic "person, family, surname, and party" could procure private power and benefits.[63] As he underscored, his anti-Communist position was not simply against one party, group, or person but instead targeted the dogmatic thought and brutal behavior of any dictatorship. More importantly, he had been striving to pursue some intrinsic, basic values such as freedom, truth, justice, and love, which are common to all human beings.[64] Emphasizing his own status as an independent liberal, he detested any attempt to comply with the flagrant propagandistic style and intent based on party struggle, be it the CCP's or the KMT's. For the past two decades, he had earnestly yearned and searched for a new feasible route—a truly independent Thirdspace unfettered by party doctrines and founded on the authenticity of freedom and democracy—that would lead Taiwan and China toward a bright future.

For Yin Haiguang, the CCP and the KMT both were shored up by a binary logic that strictly demarcated allies and enemies. His philosophical knowledge and training enabled him to realize how detrimental such a mentality was, creating an unbridgeable chasm between factions. The afflictions of the world were deepened by such an oversimplified mode of thinking, which was engendered by the communist countries on a large scale. Essentially, the dichotomous way of thinking had inevitably become the backbone of their vision of the world, life, and society. Yin identified how communist regimes shape this binary mentality through their party ideologies and implement it through education, propaganda, and daily activities. In doing so, communism efficiently created a colossal system of "either/or" dichotomies: the antagonism between "materialism" and "idealism" on the philosophical level, the opposition between "bourgeoisie" and "proletariat" on the historical level, and the rivalry between "comrades" and "enemies" on the human level.[65]

According to Yin Haiguang, the Manichean dichotomy can be traced back to the Confucian ethical code focused on the moral choice between good and evil.[66] The prevailing Marxist ideology strengthened such either/or thinking by revolving around class struggles. It is not surprising that the CCP haphazardly invoked, promoted, and implemented it. However, it is uncanny that the anti-Communist party members in Taiwan vigorously emulated it, allowing the same dichotomy to pervade every aspect of the political landscape.[67] Yin Haiguang found that the KMT's obsession with binary logic made its ideology totalitarian, centering on exclusivism (*paichi zhuyi* 排斥主義) to maintain a homogeneous entity. The KMT leaders maintained a yawning abyss between us and them, friends and foes, even expelling American scholars researching Chinese problems such as Doak Barnett, Mark Mancall, and John King Fairbank.[68] This mentality of "either the KMT or the CCP" (*feiguo jigong* 非國即共) was closely associated with political monism, which inexorably "disturbs, divides, strikes, menaces, persecutes, represses, and eliminates" other anticommunist liberal beliefs.[69] Yin Haiguang believed that as long as this either/or thinking persisted, it was destined to annihilate the middle ground and repudiate the existence of nonpolitical members of society between the KMT and the CCP. Its "exclusivism" had virtually sanctioned a rigid and dogmatic party administrative apparatus, which not only extirpated the forces of liberalism in Taiwan but also alienated various anti-Communist organizations overseas. In his vivid description, "Binary dichotomy is like a sharp blade borrowed from enemies," but instead of killing the enemies, it is a self-destructive weapon that pulverizes the anti-Communist side with continuous usage.[70]

Along with his deep and profound critique of the oppositional dichotomy mentality, Yin Haiguang had a puzzling attitude toward "neutrality," a position taken by the third force intellectuals in the 1940s. In 1948, when he witnessed the emergence of the third force in the historical context of the opposition between the CCP and the KMT, he was very skeptical of the sustainability of their neutral position. He believed that those so-called neutral intellectuals failed to form a complete system or an actual force; therefore, they stayed in a shaky and broken state, constantly oscillating between the CCP and the KMT. Different from Hu Shi, a truly independent liberal, they played the role of peacemakers, advocating "peace talks," "cooperation," and "mediation," which for Yin Haiguang were indicative of their weakness, incompetence, and lack of independent spirit to firmly advocate for real freedom and democracy. They were mostly attracted by and dependent on the two oppositional poles of the parties, unable to truly hold on to "neutrality," and inevitably disintegrated. This opinion arose from his personal conviction that "they had a wrong way of thinking and shared a presupposition," which was to confuse the neutrality of personal identity with the neutrality of thought.[71] Yin Haiguang resolutely declared that in terms of personal identity, there existed a "neutrality"; however, in terms of thought, there was only right and wrong. The misperception or ignorance of such a distinction deprived the third force intellectuals of their independence and power. As a result, they only used liberalism as a decoration or subterfuge. Even though they claimed to be "plural" and "neutral," they turned out to be "non-neutral," leaning on one party eventually.[72]

When Yin Haiguang heard that Jin Yong and other journalists in Hong Kong espoused and promoted neutrality in their print media, he was also dubious. He thought that their goals were too ambiguous, without clear political visions and concepts, and therefore, they ran the risk of transforming into a "subconscious dependent worm" when facing political crisis. Again, he stated that the so-called neutrality was only valid in terms of party identities, human forces, personal feelings, and grudges; he strongly objected to the idea of a legitimate neutral space between truth and falsehood in an ethical sense. He endorsed the kind of neutrality that could transcend the party struggles between the CCP and the KMT but worried about an equivocal and muddled position that deliberately evaded the judgment of right and wrong and abandoned the basic principles of liberalism. For him, there was always a trap of neutrality that led people to embrace "village worthies" (*xiangyuan* 鄉願), delineated by Confucius as "thieves of virtue." According to Confucius, such individuals were commonly respected by their communities but acted as moral fence-sitters who lacked firm principles. These people claimed to take the route of "neutrality" but held vague moral standards, indifferent to the pursuit of truth. In Yin Haiguang's view, those "village worthies" were only good at surviving, not innovating new paths.[73] In contrast, the true Thirdspace that Yin Haiguang desired would rise above the values and ideologies of various authoritarian political parties, constructing a kingdom for the freedom of thought.

Though the term *Thirdspace* never occurred in his writings, Yin Haiguang made a great effort to galvanize the critical sensibility of the alternative space that went beyond the party struggle. In 1960, he proposed the concept of "colorless thought,"[74] creating a critical strategy to break out of all the binarisms preconditioned by both the CCP and the KMT. He divided thought into five different categories: aesthetic thinking, prescriptive thinking (including moral and ethical rules), emotive thinking, pictorial thinking, and cognitive thinking. In his definition, aesthetic, prescriptive, and emotive thinking belong to "colorful thought"; pictorial thinking is "color-neutral thought"; and cognitive thinking conforms to "colorless thought." Yin Haiguang employed "colorful thought" loosely to refer to the models emerging from ancestral teachings, tradition, religious structures, and various ideologies. In actuality, since no one can reside in a vacuum of thought, described by John Locke as the "tabula rasa," Yin Haiguang admitted that the majority of people most of the time lived in "colorful thought," which was unnecessarily harmful. However, those means that support, solidify, project, and disseminate "colorful thought" appeared emphatically detrimental. He mapped out the following means: (1) appeal to emotion—that is, institutionalizing the feelings of the group, inciting mass movements, and ushering the collective into a "nakedly incomprehensible" and frenzied state; (2) appeal to prejudice—that is, stereotyping emotion, hinging on ossified traditional concepts; (3) appeal to authority, which inevitably breeds totalitarianism and clamps down on academic freedom of thought; (4) appeal to big sticks, including direct violence and indirect violence, with the latter usually conducting persecution in the name of "doing justice for Heaven."[75]

In contrast, Yin proposed colorless thinking, which was intended to be separate from the contents, patterns, and paradigms of colorful thinking. As he defined it, colorless thinking is purely cognitive, relying more on logical and rational structures than on emotion, prejudice, authority, and violence—the means normally utilized for totalitarian domination. In response to potential criticism that Yin was creating his own dichotomy, he added a spectrum from colorful to colorless thinking, emphasizing the increasing or decreasing saturation of color. In this way, colorless thinking is not an arbitrary demarcation but an achromatic attitude liberated from emotionally charged, irrational, partisan, overpolitical, overmoral influence. For him, while colorful thinking is founded on ancestral teachings, tradition, religion, and ideology, colorless thinking only has one foundational pillar, which is Aristotle's observation: "To say of what is that it is not, or of what is not that it is, is false, while to say of what is that it is, or of what is not that it is not, is true."[76] To sum up in a phrase, it is "to say what it is," which was also the title of one of Yin's articles. Although this seems self-evident, it was gravely inapplicable in mainland China and Taiwan, where party interests sidelined the truth. Yin Haiguang clearly stated, "This basic standard is the pivotal watershed between totalitarianism and democracy, as well as the significant divide between science and metaphysics."[77] Whereas party politics in twentieth-century China has been a realm of frenetic sensation, perception, emotion, bias, lies, vehemence, and power, Yin Haiguang's colorless thought stemmed from empiricism and logic, paving the way toward freedom of thought and democracy.

Different from Zhang Dongsun and Jin Yong, whose "neutral" attitude was mingled with the idea of moderation derived from Confucianism, Yin Haiguang primarily emphasized both rationality and objectivity, clearly defining right and wrong with a firm antipathy to totalitarianism. He held a crucial scientific attitude to visibly and decisively distinguish veracity (*cheng* 誠) from truth (*zhen* 真),[78] against New Confucians in Hong Kong and Taiwan, who "insisted that Chinese culture could not be surpassed, and all scientific activities had to be constrained by the universal moral conscience of Confucian thought."[79] Yin Haiguang believed that the Confucian precepts of "benevolence, righteousness, and morality" delimited "sincerity," which was a necessary "attitude of being mentally prepared to accept true beliefs," but this attitude alone was woefully insufficient. It is vital to have scientific reasoning and knowledge in order to acquire the truth. As a solution, he propounded the use of cognition to avoid being influenced by various cultural, political, and emotional features such as "customs, habits, taboos, anathemas, reverences, insults, hopes, disappointments, joys, pessimism, self-exaltation, inferiority, and self-centeredness." Only by gradually "getting rid of the mud of colors" can we acquire objective knowledge. According to him, "If we are to be able to solve the problem of ethical norms and values, we must establish a moral science based on empirical facts, with a clear and colorless mind."[80] Apparently, emanating from his persistent endeavor to deconstruct the dichotomy of thinking, his colorless thought was intended to configure Thirdspace, in which the individual experience did not have to be closely intertwined with prevalent ideologies and existing party struggles.

The achromatic thought he advocated was centered on "the cognitive use of language," which was based on scientific hypothesis, evidence, and verification. It clearly targeted political language, or more specifically, the language of violence charged with high-strung "emotive-centric language" in alignment with all kinds of fallacies such as banking on argumentum ad populum, psycho-engineering, idolization of authority, application of violence, maneuvering empathy, ad hominem attacks, oversimplification, and egocentrism.[81] He noted that the prevalent "ideological struggle" was constantly generated because multifarious intellectuals were bound by the "emotive use of language" that begot myriad irrational states comprising frustration, anxiety, longing, pursuit, fantasy, and fervor. Such "ideological struggle" inevitably widened social divisions, which only benefited powerful groups without substantially solving any social problems. Therefore, as an antidote, he pitched a "system of public right and public wrong" (*gongshi gongfei de zhidu* 公是公非的制度) separate from personal political identity and social status that would cloud objective judgment. The purpose was to stress the intellectuals' role as independent thinkers who are able to unravel the web of complicated social problems.[82]

Yin Haiguang's concept of colorless thought underscored the neutrality of scientific knowledge, reasoning, and analysis, posing a serious challenge to the panpoliticization and panmoralization that permeated both the mainland and Taiwan. He declared, "What makes science invaluable is that it is free or neutral from any isms."[83] As an effective mode of thinking, colorless thought incidentally parallels Max Weber's methodological postulate of "ethical neutrality" in social science, a separation of "purely logical deducible and empirical factual assertions on the one hand, and practical, ethical or philosophical value-judgments on the other."[84] Weber's postulate essentially calls for the researcher to set aside emotional biases that could interfere with research. By forming a new third pathway, colorless thought called attention to value neutrality, which laid the foundation for the individual's independent and objective judgment to emerge. To a large extent, Yin was in tune with Karl Popper and Hans Albert's defense of the principle of value freedom as a necessary condition to avert social science from devolving into ideologies.[85] His critical approach is, as far as we know, a strong reaction to the holistic aberrations of party ideologies associated with the problems of determinism, essentialism, and irrationalism. As a result, his exploration of Thirdspace was extremely significant during this historical time of ideological fanaticism and extravagant expressions.

However, while Yin Haiguang was involved in a series of debates with the New Confucians regarding whether Western democracy and science were well matched with the spirit of Chinese cultural tradition in the 1950s, he fell into another trap of dichotomous thinking by taking the position of complete Westernization against the traditionalistic group. The unbridgeable chasm between Yin Haiguang and the New Confucians was understandable because he feared that the panmoralization arising from Chinese tradition would adversely affect his scientific outlook. Furthermore, since the KMT utilized Chinese tradition as a key strategy of political legitimacy to justify its power and oppose Communism, the morality of Confucianism became a persistent source of colorful thought for the one-party dictatorship, which was a red flag for him. Nevertheless, in his later years, Yin Haiguang gradually withdrew from such either/or thinking by reflecting on his previous totalistic rejection of Chinese cultural tradition.[86] He recognized that a good political system, including democracy and freedom, "will be used for dangerous and contrary aims if the original motivator provided by moral ideals and ethical standards is not in place."[87] He even lamented that if he were not hindered by his poor health, he would contemplate how to find a theoretical link that bound Chinese culture and liberalism together.[88] This self-reflection and self-adjustment on the issue of Chinese culture testified to the openness of Thirdspace signified by the spectrum he created for colorless thought. As an alternative way of thinking, achromatic thought innovatively provided a powerful remedy, a means to go beyond the formidable rigidity of dualism favored by totalitarian dominance.

On Liberty and Individuality

Caught between the opposing camps of the KMT and the CCP, Yin Haiguang discovered that the most efficient way to set aside an either/or mindset was to embrace a third path, which involved vigorously instilling liberalism in Taiwan. When he arrived in 1949, he attempted to seek political democracy and economic equality simultaneously. But, influenced by Friedrich A. Hayek's *The Road to Serfdom* in 1953, he started to realize that a planned economy could easily result in totalitarian rule and undermine political democracy.[89] More importantly, it usually ended in subjecting all individual desires and rights to the hegemonic demands of the state and its government. Consequently, he devoted himself unwaveringly to advancing the ideals of liberalism, channeling his efforts toward the promotion of democracy in Taiwan. Following Western liberal political theorists such as Hayek, John Locke, John Stuart Mill, Bertrand Russell, and Karl R. Popper, he emphasized individualism, for "among the various attitudes and value systems in life, individualism and communism stand out as fundamentally incompatible from beginning to end."[90] In the 1950s and 1960s, Yin Haiguang's discussion of liberalism was extremely concerned with individualism. Unlike other Chinese intellectuals such as Hu Shi, who had subordinated the individual (*xiaowo* 小我) to society (*dawo* 大我) since the May Fourth Movement,[91] Yin Haiguang resolutely advanced the ontology of the individual without entangling it with the ontology of the collective. He viewed individuals as *prior to* the state, the society, the party, and any other groups, stating that the difference between the ontology of the individual and the ontology of the collective was "one of the basic distinctions between democracy and nondemocracy."[92] As the majority of Chinese people still lived under the shadow of Confucianism, which restricted the individual beneath collective responsibilities, Yin Haiguang stood out as a unique intellectual who audaciously and lucidly asserted, "In a democratic system, the individual is not seen as a tool to achieve any goal: each living individual is the ultimate goal in itself."[93]

The scholar Qian Yongxiang 錢永祥 (1949–) noticed a deep-seated "negative" predilection in Yin Haiguang's democratic viewpoints, which approached the so-called protective democracy represented by Jeremy Bentham and James Mill.[94] Other scholars attempted to uncover the balance between negative freedom and positive freedom underlying Yin Haiguang's political commentaries.[95] Pursuant to the previous scholarship, I want to clearly point out that even if Yin Haiguang inherited the national "fighting spirit" prescribed by Lu Xun since the May Fourth Movement period, he nevertheless understood the importance of negative freedom that was largely absent in modern Chinese history. Singling out individualism as a radical perspective against totalitarianism, Yin Haiguang's liberal thought strongly echoed Hayek's distinction between two individualisms, the true and the false. As Hayek defined it, "true individualism" is represented by John Locke, Bernard Mandeville, David Hume, Josiah Tucker, Adam Ferguson, Adam Smith, Edmund Burke, Alexis de Tocqueville, and Lord Acton, who affirmed the sanctity and uniqueness of individual rights.[96] In contrast, the second type of individualism was mainly exemplified by French and other continental writers, such as the encyclopedists, Rousseau, and the physiocrats, and often metamorphosed into socialism or collectivism. According to Hayek, it belongs to a "pseudo-individualism" that simply lays the groundwork for socialism due to its collectivist traits.[97] Hayek explained that while theories of the second strand of individualism "necessarily lead to the conclusion that social processes can be made to serve human ends only if they are subjected to the control of individual human reason, and thus lead directly to socialism, true individualism believes on the contrary that, if left free, men will often achieve more than individual human reason could design or foresee."⁹⁸ Based on his political commentaries written after 1954, it becomes evident that Yin Haiguang strongly identified with what Hayek defined as "true individualism," which resists any attempts to be shaped into collectivism. The influence of Friedrich Hayek brought Yin Haiguang intimately close to the concept of negative liberty, ensuring that there must be a certain basic amount of personal freedom that cannot be violated.

Yin Haiguang noticed Isaiah Berlin's concepts of negative freedom and positive freedom, especially the idea that noninterference is an integral component of personal freedom. At a time when the majority of Chinese intellectuals had no clue about what negative freedom meant, he completely understood its importance because it corresponded with his goal of warding off interference from totalitarianism. His anti-Communist and anti-KMT stances were closely associated with the defense of negative liberty, as resisting totalitarian pressures entails combating the coercion of individuals. Regarding the word *negative*, Yin Haiguang explained:

> Some may argue that the notion of freedom is inherently negative, and it surely is. Peace, tranquility, and the removal of obstacles can all be considered negative aspects. By contrasting freedom with its fundamental opposite—slavery—it becomes conspicuous that the negative aspect of freedom, specifically "freedom from coercion," is of utmost importance. At the very least, individuals or groups should not live in constant fear of being restrained in order to experience true freedom. In fact, negative freedom serves as a prerequisite for positive freedom, and without it, positive freedom will lose its foundation.⁹⁹

Yin Haiguang also borrowed Christian Bay's concept of "potential freedom" to explain negative freedom, pointing out that it counters the external pressures on the individual.¹⁰⁰ He recognized that although premodern China was an authoritarian society, "the freedom of silence" was still allowed to exist, as for some aesthetic hermits such as the Seven Sages of the Bamboo Grove, who refused to serve at court and retreated to their own individual space. However, under high-pressure modern authoritarian regimes, even "the freedom of silence" that could protect "the freedom of conscience" has been callously stripped away. Everyone has been reduced to loyal cheerleaders of the totalitarian regime; there is no minimal area of individuality as a shield from the totalitarian power.¹⁰¹

Although Yin Haiguang did not fully identify with Isaiah Berlin's specific concern regarding the precarious potential for positive freedom, he highlighted his disquiet about how the totalitarian pursuit of a common utopia would submerge the self into the collective sea of human beings. As a result, individuals would be transformed into "the instruments of power seeking, the sacrifices of the old times, the bricks of the new tyranny." Under the aegis of Hayek's philosophy, Yin Haiguang regarded the Whig Party in England as pure individualists because of their ironclad liberalism that values individualism as sacrosanct. He firmly stated, "individualism is both the truest starting point and the truest ending point of liberalism. Genuine liberalism starts from individualism, goes through the social process and cultural integration, and then returns to individualism. In fact, apart from adhering to the path of individualism, there exists no viable approach to fostering peace, facilitating sustainable development, and safeguarding humanity from regressing into a collective mindset akin to that of ants."[102] This had great significance in reference to mainland China because the authoritarian state has always denigrated individualism as a product of the petit-bourgeoisie discourse. Yin Haiguang steadfastly opposed using the so-called highest level of collective freedom to substitute for the so-called lowest value of individual freedom.

Although Hayek's and Mill's definitions of individualism both allude to negative liberty, they differ in the choices made by individuals regarding their freedom. While Mill is more concerned with utilitarianism, which is related to maximizing popular welfare, Hayek affirms the right of the individual to wield their own material wealth. Due to Hayek's influence, Yin Haiguang completely supported the idea of protecting individual property, but he also deeply admired Mill's powerful defense of free speech. Regarding the precondition to ensure liberty, Yin Haiguang discussed two quintessential principles: the protection of private property and the preservation of the rule of law. The rule of law enables individuals to see how the state's institutions and tools could be used against ordinary individuals; therefore it "implies limits to the scope of legislation."[103] Apparently using insights from Hayek, Yin Haiguang's discussion of private property and the rule of law was self-consciously preoccupied with how to restrict the government from infringing upon individual freedom. However, different from Hayek, Yin Haiguang reaffirmed liberal political theory rooted in utilitarianism, which includes the thought of Thomas Hobbes, John Locke, David Hume, William Godwin, Jeremy Bentham, James Mill, and John Stuart Mill, and considered the individual as the basic element of society. These theorists share a liberal concept of freedom as negative, without coercive interference by other people, the state, or society. In comparison, Yin Haiguang was averse to Hegelian social and political thought, which emphasizes the state and great men over normal individuals. He criticized Hegelian philosophy for adopting a totalitarian perspective on history, society, and culture, placing state and morality higher than the individual. Yin believed that Stalin and Hitler both favored the world-spirit or *weltgeist* as illustrated by Hegel, which subsumes the individual spirit into the so-called ethical life dominated by the state.[104]

In essence, Yin Haiguang tended to presuppose a negative definition of liberty because he directed a large amount of criticism toward the constraints of totalitarianism. In his words, "The biggest nemesis of freedom is suppression."[105] Quoting Hayek's definition of "freedom as the absence of coercion,"[106] Yin Haiguang identified three types of political compulsion: naked violence with physical force, mystifying ideology, and a planned economy. Through these forceful and repressive elements, modern totalitarian dominance is like "a gigantic spider web engulfing a garden analogous to a formidable central control system." Individuals are even denied the right to retreat from society to enjoy a personal freedom comparable to that of ancient hermits. Without political checks and balances, the individual becomes vulnerable, akin to "a wretched and helpless goat," easily manipulated and subjected to the oppressive exercise of power.[107]

In addition, Yin Haiguang deliberated on the two types of freedom, external and internal, which he deemed intimately interconnected, although existing on different tiers. For him, external freedom is guaranteed by legislation, or more specifically, the rule of law, enshrining freedom of speech, personal property, and private space as advocated by the utilitarian liberals. While external freedom depends on the outer space's political and social insurance, internal freedom relies upon the individual's inner strength and self-awakening, which adumbrate the "freedom of open-mindedness" or "liberty from mental enslavement."[108] Even when one is imprisoned, he may still be internally free as long as he is willing to transcend his time and environment. However, when someone is accustomed to "the prison of the heart," it is just like the metaphor of the iron house described by Lu Xun, where some inhabitants refuse to be awakened even when the door is opened by the enlighteners. Yin Haiguang's discussion of internal freedom is very similar to that of Gao Xingjian, who emphasized the soul mountain as a state of inner awakening: "freedom is self-given rather than given by others."[109] However, Yin Haiguang still stressed that the modern political system and institutions can only be developed through attaining external freedom. If one has only internal freedom, it is limited, residing in "the inner citadel," as Berlin describes.[110] Therefore, differing from Gao Xingjian, Yin Haiguang regarded both types of freedom as equally important. In his lifelong journey, he devoted all his passions and energies to fighting for external freedom to counteract authoritarian coercion.

Conclusion

In response to intense authoritarian conflicts that gave no quarter to the common individual, Yin Haiguang wholeheartedly embraced Western liberal political traditions. But at the same time, he realized that liberalism had been transformed in multifarious ways in the Chinese context. Reflecting on the Chinese liberals' precarious situation, he pointed out, "For about fifty years, liberalism in China has been attacked from the right by conservatism, and from the left by Bolshevism. As far as I know, very few liberals have been able to cope with the attacks from the right and the left while remaining upright as mountains."[111] In terms of the rebukes from the left, he alluded to the totalitarian mindset of the political party, which includes not only the CCP's totalitarian rule but also the KMT's one-party dictatorship. As for the strikes from the right, he referred to the Chinese traditional cultural influence mainly centered on the Confucian moral system, which, in his view, would beget panmoralization and cloud liberalism. In his judgment, even Buddhism and Daoism failed to provide a true path to individual freedom because they superficially seemed to conform to Western liberalism but actually offered a defeatist and escapist mentality. Only in his later years did he turn to affirm Zhuangzi's concept of inner spiritual freedom that propels rebellions against and transcendence of the dogmatic reality.[112] In short, he concluded that the Chinese liberals were stunted in their growth. On the one hand, it was due to the political and historical environments that persistently quelled the individual in the name of the collective; on the other hand, they were easily lured by domineering political trends and lacked independent thinking. He lamented that Chinese liberals had never produced any substantial works equivalent to Western liberal classics such as John Stuart Mill's *On Liberty* and Friedrich Hayek's *The Constitution of Liberty*.[113]

Positioning himself between the dual authoritarian forces, Yin Haiguang insightfully constructed his own Thirdspace by promoting colorless thought based on cognitive thinking unencumbered by habitual concepts, ideas, and paradigms derived from tradition, modern ideologies, and mass pressure. With a scientific attitude, colorless thought, by its very nature, is intrinsically inclined to defend an independent and critical way of thinking for individuals, relying on value neutrality to safeguard fair and objective judgment. By identifying with the core tenets of liberalism, he particularly underscored the importance of a skeptical mindset and the power of logical analysis inherent in colorless thought. This enabled him to question the notion of absolute truth propagated by political propaganda apparatus or any individuals, including sages, great men, or other leaders, who claimed to possess a singular and universally applicable truth. The unique attribute of Yin Haiguang's Thirdspace is that he propounded a resolute judgment of right and wrong rather than simply talking about "tolerance" as Hu Shi did. Yin was influenced by Karl Popper, who delineated a "Paradox of Tolerance" in a clear way:

> Unlimited tolerance must lead to the disappearance of tolerance. If we extend unlimited tolerance even to those who are intolerant, if we are not prepared to defend a tolerant society against the onslaught of the intolerant, then the tolerant will be destroyed, and tolerance with them.[114]

While Hu Shi valued tolerance as more important than freedom, Yin Haiguang questioned whether too much tolerance from the subaltern would give the authoritarians room to impose more repressive ideologies and policies.[115] He was worried that without fending off dogmatism and narrow-mindedness, unlimited tolerance would only foster intolerance from those in power. Beyond acceptance of different opinions, he clearly distinguished between tolerance toward the wielders of power and toward the powerless.

Unlike the third force intellectuals, Yin was always cautious about any state-led collectivism organized by political parties. He made a pioneering effort in developing a rigorous Thirdspace to transcend the constricting dichotomy of party ideologies. His Thirdspace held unyielding individualism as the greatest alternative, especially delineating negative freedom to place strong limitations on the activities of the state, ensuring a basic individual freedom from constraints. Since individualism had never been a potent force in Chinese culture and politics, this emphasis initiated another significant pathway of exploration. Meanwhile, Yin rejected any ambivalent attempt at mediation, the approach employed by some third force intellectuals in the 1940s. Instead, he blatantly stated that the individual should maintain an independent spirit and open mind, using cognitive thinking to acknowledge ignorance, distinguishing right from wrong, and telling the truth without being swayed by any dominating trends. For him, there only exist relative truths rather than absolute truth, so the individual must analyze, distinguish, and judge in accordance with different social and political contexts. Although his Thirdspace was slanted toward Westernization, he introduced a critical awareness of rational and logical methods in reaction to the prevailing obscurantism and dogmatism. With his tremendous effort and sacrifice, liberalism in Taiwan flourished in spite of the KMT's political repression, blossoming three decades earlier than in the mainland, where it was only seriously discussed among intellectuals following Deng Xiaoping's reforms. Despite the Tiananmen crackdown, such political debates proliferated, only to be prohibited and squelched under Xi Jinping's rule. Therefore, Yin Haiguang's political thought is both unique and continually relevant in the modern Chinese context.

CHAPTER III

Jin Yong

Thirdspace as a Political Stance and Fictional Transgression

On September 3, 2001, Liu Zaifu published his article "Searching for the Survival of Thirdspace," overtly seeking an independent and liberal space between the authoritarian government and the antigovernment forces. This article immediately aroused particular interest from Jin Yong, who wrote a letter to Liu Zaifu on October 31, 2001:

Dear Zaifu,

After I read your article about Thirdspace, I found it resonated with me. In my novel *The Smiling, Proud Wanderer* (Xiao'ao jianghu 笑傲江湖), Liu Zhengfeng 劉正風 attempts to flee the factionalism of the *jianghu* 江湖 by "washing his hands in a golden basin," which equates to striving for Thirdspace. But instead, his attempt ends in tragedy because the leaders of the orthodox schools interdict it and massacre his entire family, even forcing his young son to subject him to a struggle session. Chen Jialuo 陳家洛 eventually returns to a reclusive life in Xinjiang; Yuan Chengzhi 袁承志 flees far away overseas; Zhang Wuji 張無忌 refuses to be the head of the Demon Sect—those actions parallel Wei Xiaobao's 韋小寶 attitude of "I'm done." You have essentially found Thirdspace, and it is especially worth celebrating.

All the best,
Jin Yong

P.S. This letter is only for you to read, which means we are kindred spirits. Please do not bring it to the public; otherwise, I will be compelled into the X-space.[1]

Liu Zaifu kept this letter secret until Jin Yong passed away in 2018 and eventually decided to publish it for the historical record, including it in his own book, *The History of My Thought* (*Wode sixiang shi* 我的思想史), in 2019. The letter reflects Jin Yong's frank and unstinting identification with and endorsement of Thirdspace, in which an individual has the right not to participate in the exercise of power if that is his/her wish. He concluded that by launching the concept of Thirdspace, Liu Zaifu found an alternative solution to the Chinese intellectuals' long-standing, problematic experience of the endless political struggles between opposing sides. However, although Jin Yong acknowledged the significance of safeguarding "the minimum area" that individuals require to resist the interference of the state power or other forces, he was primarily inclined toward establishing a platform to support a diverse array of public opinions.[2] More precisely, he formulated Thirdspace as an organic public sphere that would stay neutral in journalism, fostering the critical exertion of public reason no longer steered by any political authorities.

Nevertheless, having long been revered as the most prominent Chinese martial arts novelist of the twentieth century and the extremely successful founder of *Ming Pao*'s publishing empire, Jin Yong never openly discussed his validation of Thirdspace, although he configured it assiduously in his fictional writings and political commentaries. Such caution reveals the subtle and complicated political situation in Hong Kong and modern China. In spite of living and writing in a relatively free social space, Hong Kong, Jin Yong was still afraid of being put in the "X-space," the restriction that could be imposed upon him by the oppositional forces of the left and the right. His postscript to the letter shows his lack of self-confidence about the public reception. Was the political ecology in Hong Kong manifestly a recurrence of the binary struggle between the rightists and the leftists that Jin Yong had dedicated himself to overcoming since the 1950s? How did he employ the martial arts novel as a quintessential tool in response to the political and cultural situation of modern China, bound by the dichotomous way of thinking? How did he deal with the inherent tension between fiction and the political reality? To what extent had he opened up Thirdspace in his fiction as well as in *Ming Pao*, which he established in Hong Kong in 1959 and for which he served as editor-in-chief and wrote as a political commentator for thirty-three years? These questions are not only closely related to Jin Yong's devotion to journalism and publishing undertakings in Hong Kong but also bear on the convoluted interplay between politics and fiction.

Jin Yong, the pen name of Zha Liangyong 查良鏞 or Louis Cha, emerged as a leading writer of "new martial arts fiction" (*xin wuxia xiaoshuo* 新武俠小說) in 1955. Since revision and canonization, his fifteen martial arts novels, originally serialized in newspapers (1955–1972), have had an enormous cultural and literary impact on Chinese readers globally.[3] Regarded as "the common language of Chinese around the world," his novels were widely circulated and adapted into films, television dramas, comic books, video games, and many other cultural media. In the 1990s, he was recognized as a literary writer comparable to the top-ranked modern Chinese literary masters such as Lu Xun, Shen Congwen, and Zhang Ailing 張愛玲 (1920–1995) by academic circles in mainland China, Taiwan, and overseas.[4] Although his novels are set in the context of colonial Hong Kong and inherently touch upon the issue of Hong Kong identity, they have traversed the geopolitical boundaries of the nation-state, contemplating the underlying problematics of Chinese politics and the ingrained complexity of national identity.[5] Equally important is Jin Yong's role as a political commentator and his active intervention in building the public sphere by means of his influential *Ming Pao* empire. As the literary scholar Chen Pingyuan 陳平原 (1954-) elucidated: "Mr. Cha was a writer with political ambitions and it is precisely this quality that makes him stand out from the multitude of martial arts writers of the twentieth century."[6] In the academic field, most scholars confirmed that Jin Yong's anti-Europeanized Chinese writings not only rejuvenated the long-neglected Chinese native literary tradition but also filled the gap between elite literature and popular culture. However, few have paid attention to how his political aspiration impelled him to shape and reshape the public sphere in Hong Kong through his consistent contribution and commitment to social and cultural criticism. He achieved what most Chinese literati have dreamed about but failed to actualize in terms of expanding Thirdspace through his newspapers and other media in the political society.

While addressing issues such as individuality, the state, national boundaries, Hong Kong identity, freedom, and responsibility, this chapter works to open a new critical dimension by locating and highlighting Thirdspace in Jin Yong's political commentaries and fictional imagination. Although his novels are extremely entertaining, fabricating a self-sufficient and imaginative universe, namely "rivers and lakes" (*jianghu* 江湖), they nonetheless embody serious engagements with Chinese history and political reality. To a remarkable degree, the power struggle between opposing forces, along with an individual's irresolvable aporia amid such conflicts and contradictions, is a persistent theme in Jin Yong's novels. Whenever individuals attempt to eschew the dilemma of the binary political situation, they usually seek another possibility—Thirdspace—in order to transform the closed logic of either/or to an "in-between" position, or all-inclusive prospects. While his martial arts novels are suffused with profound allusions to modern politics, Jin Yong as a journalist had to audaciously face the realities of everyday life, mediating between opposing political forces. His political essays, which were praised as "knowledgeable, insightful, tactical, strategic, full of foresight,"[7] contributed to an unusually intense period distinguished by the Cold War mentality. Jin Yong positioned himself not only as an outspoken intellectual proactively involved in political debates but also as a successful journalist entrepreneur capable of powerful and original conceptual innovations that shaped public opinion. Instead of being trapped by factionalism, he set up a space of critical and strategic neutrality as a necessary precondition to coordinate communities and nations. Examining his political commentaries and martial art novels side by side will provide a new paradigm and language for understanding Jin Yong's political ambition and vision in nation-building and his multiple literary representations of Chinese societies as a novelist, journalist, publisher, and entrepreneur. By continuously and consciously selecting Thirdspace as a political stance and fictional intervention, he not only offers a profound understanding of the Chinese literary and cultural legacy but also develops a feasible way to augment the role of intellectuals in the political realm.

The Salient Standpoint of Neutrality

Despite considerable attention to Jin Yong's martial arts novels, his political stance of Thirdspace, which spotlights the position of value neutrality, is probably not immediately familiar to many readers. Starting in the late 1950s in colonial Hong Kong, Jin Yong was determined to carve out a distinct, neutral public sphere in defiance of the Cold War mentality. After launching *Ming Pao* with Shen Baoxin 沈寶新 (1921–2018) on May 20, 1959, Jin Yong strove to maintain the paper's neutral position without yielding to the control of any parties.[8] In the editorials, he again and again called for renewed attention to the political standpoint of *Ming Pao*—the painstaking discipline of independence and neutrality. This assertion, difficult at the time, became his practical political strategy, which filled the enormous gap between the competing political adversaries and ensured that *Ming Pao* enjoyed a vibrant and unique existence. Completely unbiased objectivity seems impossible to achieve because journalists are constantly involved in debates over their commitment to value judgment. Nevertheless, Jin Yong succeeded in adopting an empirical approach that is unfettered by any stipulated political positions from either the left or the right.

As Jin Yong recalled his experience in building the *Ming Pao* empire, he indicated that although Hong Kong was a completely open and hybrid society, it was suffused with intense political struggle. Among the complicated and competing political forces, *Ming Pao*'s main goal was to achieve "true independence" without being influenced and maneuvered by any side.[9] He also frankly confessed that it had not been easy to maintain this principle for more than twenty years against many kinds of coercion and inducements.[10] He had to resist not only the factional political menace but also financial enticements in Hong Kong society. Regardless, he firmly defended and validated the political stance of neutrality for *Ming Pao*— initiating a significant Thirdspace that is associated with liberty to express and publish one's opinions. As a nonpartisan and nonaffiliated person who ran the newspaper according to his conscience, Jin Yong strove to defend the utilitarian principle in favor of promoting and maximizing people's happiness. Opposing political extremism and intellectual fanaticism, he embraced utility on the basis of the fact that people should naturally pursue wealth and pleasure. This pragmatic goal is perfectly consistent with the common pursuits of Hong Kong citizens.

Behind *Ming Pao*'s policy of impartiality lay a sustained struggle over what journalism should be, for many newspapers carried a more or less explicit political agenda supported by either the Communist Party or the Nationalist Party. Jin Yong understands that journalism plays a crucial role of "checks and balances" of government, which has held seminal significance in Western political thought for centuries.[11] Maintaining the newspaper's impartiality is vital in terms of supporting a public sphere that can steer government policies to benefit the wider society. While the majority of presses in Hong Kong were attuned to the Cold War mentality, Jin Yong called for a general transformation of that either/or logic by clinging to the position of neutrality. However, under different historical circumstances, his stance was constantly thrust into a crucible because even in the ostensibly free and hybridized society of Hong Kong, Thirdspace is not a ready-made and safeguarded zone. It demands a great effort of struggling and endurance to keep it alive.

Due to his neutrality and pragmatism, Jin Yong refused to hold any ironclad political affiliations, changing and adjusting his statements based on historical and situational necessities. Whether facing the heightened radical environment during the Cultural Revolution in the 1960s, interviewing the KMT leaders in Taiwan in the 1970s, or participating in the lawmaking before Hong Kong's handover to mainland China in 1997, Jin Yong consistently reinforced his middle stance between two hostile forces. His political commentaries have a clear goal: to transcend the perpetual internecine feuds. However, he was constantly questioned for the scope of his relativism, suspected of catering to both the right and the left. Regardless of the political pressure and controversies that entangled him, Jin Yong remained a staunch advocate for neutrality, providing a shared and organic public sphere to protect freedom of speech and individual political rights.

The 1960s: On the Problems of China

The period from 1959 to 1961 was the most difficult time for *Ming Pao* in establishing its reputation. Jin Yong's editorials supported China when it was in conflict with the Soviet Union and India but criticized the Great Leap Forward for shackling ordinary people in forced labor. Nevertheless, the newspaper did not catch many readers' attention until the refugee crisis of 1962, when thousands of people flooded into Hong Kong from Guangzhou. Under Jin Yong's leadership, *Ming Pao* actively covered and commented on the devastating conditions and won a large number of readers. In John Christopher Hamm's description, "*Ming Pao*'s extensive coverage and aid efforts (the uniqueness of which the paper lost no opportunity to trumpet) allowed it to give a concrete demonstration of 'nonaligned' solidarity with the Chinese people, won it greater journalistic authority than it had hitherto enjoyed, and paid off in a dramatic rise in daily circulation, from slightly above twenty thousand before the crisis to over thirty thousand during its height."[12] During this period, Jin Yong published many important editorials, openly reprimanded the Chinese government for its insouciance, and trenchantly specified that the massive exodus was caused by three consecutive years of famine in mainland China. Such criticism brought hostility from the leftist forces.

After the refugee crisis, Jin Yong continually criticized mainland politics, and his moderate and outspoken tone incited vehement attacks from *Dagong bao* 大公報 and other leftist newspapers. In 1963, Jin Yong addressed the so-called socialist education movement in China, opposing the Chinese Communist Party's elimination of the system of private ownership (*siyou zhi* 私有制). Valuing the economic living conditions of the majority of people more than any ideologies, he basically adopted a pragmatic attitude: "We believe that any economic system, be it capitalism, socialism, or the primary communist people's commune, should be judged based on its ability to provide the majority of the people with sufficient food and clothing. Such a system should merit our full support."[13] This pragmatic tone was reverberated later in Deng Xiaopeng's political policy. Striving to free the existential condition of humanity from abstract codes and concepts, Jin Yong asked: "Is it worth sacrificing the interests of economic development for the sake of adhering to a certain ism or ideal, and making tens of millions of people suffer unnecessarily?"[14] Jin Yong's realistic attitude is also exemplified in his incisive criticism of Foreign Minister Chen Yi's 陳毅 1963 remark that China was determined to produce atom bombs even if the people had to pawn their trousers. His explicit and sharp criticism inevitably put him in direct confrontation with left-wing newspapers such as *Dagong bao*, *Wenhui bao* 文匯報, *Xin Wanbao* 新晚報, *Shangbao* 商報, and *Jingbao* 晶報, who accused him of being a "traitor" with "anticommunist and anti-China" and "pro-British and pro-American" inclinations.[15]

As the hostile and prolonged pen wars between *Ming Pao* and leftist newspapers continued through 1964 to the Cultural Revolution, Jin Yong's editorials drew local and international fame, which helped to boost the paper's visibility and credibility. Compared to Jin Yong's rational and analytical style of writing, the editorials in *Dagong bao* were infused with violent and vicious statements, attempting to demonize the opponent. In 1967, when the leftists joined the anti-British colonial movement under the influence of the Cultural Revolution, involving dangerous and fierce actions such as strikes, riots, and bombings, the pen wars transmogrified into direct personal attacks. Jin Yong received a package bomb at his residence and became an assassination target in the summer of 1967.[16] Despite facing increasing danger and extremist violence from the left, he never changed his neutral stance and moderate tone in his political commentaries, avoiding the violent language prevalent in mainland China and Hong Kong leftist newspapers. His commitment to honestly criticizing the problematics of fanatical idolization and the petrified social system of mainland China under Mao's rule made him an independent and prominent voice that attracted readers who lived in colonial Hong Kong but were attentive to the political situation in China.

Among many of Jin Yong's political commentaries that emerged in the 1960s was a long article, "On the Problem of the Home Country" ("Lun zuguo wenti" 論祖國問題), published under the pen name Huang Aihua 黃愛華, which analyzed the general conundrum in China.[17] This article in *Ming Pao* aroused enormous interest among readers and tidal waves of discussions. The article showcased Jin Yong's political ambition in a comprehensive manner by covering a range of topics, from Marxism to many concrete national affairs. It meticulously and objectively scrutinized the CCP's governing oversight in various aspects ranging from ideological hegemony to industrialization, international relationships, the People's Commune, the Great Leap Forward, agriculture, the education system, population control, hygiene, nuclear weaponry, the position of intellectuals, the idolization of leaders, overseas Chinese, propaganda and media, etc. This style of fact-based and rational analysis distinguished him from the essentially antagonistic partisan world, imbued with an exaggerated emotional tone and language, in which he lived.

After tangibly and fastidiously tackling multifarious facets of the CCP's governance, Jin Yong concludes with some pivotal and basic issues that summarize its many flaws. The first and foremost problem is the CCP's imperious superstition about Marxism-Leninism that resulted in its ironic disbelief in and ignorance of common sense and facts. Although the facts and past experiences proved that Marxism-Leninism was not entirely suitable to China, the Chinese Communist leadership still believed that its ideological system was a universally applicable and absolute truth. The second problem is that the party supersedes the state and the government. Since the party's authority was regarded as paramount, it relentlessly pulverized anything that might jeopardize its hold on power. By centralization and the "dictatorship of the proletariat," the CCP completely rejected the principles of democracy and freedom, persecuting intellectuals who articulated different opinions. This privileging of ideology begot the absurd phenomenon that amateurs led experts who were well-educated and trained in many specific fields. The third problem is the true blight on the Chinese scene: that the positions of the party and the people were reversed: "The CCP's overarching agenda was to solidify the Party's control and governance over the people, with the primary focus being on consolidating power rather than working toward the people's well-being and happiness."[18] Underlying the prevailing slogan of "serving the people" was the verity of "serving the party," and as a result, Chinese citizens were deprived of fundamental civil rights and their quality of life was not guaranteed. In addition, Jin Yong derided the CCP's overly ambitious aid given to third-world countries while disregarding the Chinese people's impecunious livelihood; he also blamed the party's rush for quick success and profit without a hundred-year plan, which unavoidably resulted in the catastrophe and adversity of the Great Leap Forward and the famine.[19] In short, Jin Yong stridently lambasted the essential flaws of the CCP, which superstitiously deified the Marxist ideology in order to systematically and exhaustively hijack people's normal lives.

As a political commentator for *Ming Pao*, Jin Yong was one of the harbingers in Hong Kong who prophesied many disastrous political movements in China. Unlike the rightists' more radical approach, which totally negated the CCP's government, or the leftists' unconditional and flattering exaltation and emulation of the mainland's propaganda, Jin Yong's criticism with a sober and down-to-earth tone took the utilitarian concern with people's welfare as the standard for right and wrong actions. His political commentaries became extremely influential because he adopted a practical method rather than swearing allegiance to any political party. In other words, he directed his criticism toward concrete and realistic matters in various fields and against ideological domination. His persuasive approach coincides with that of Western utilitarian philosophers, such as Jeremy Bentham and John Stuart Mill, who consider good and happiness as reciprocal, employing the principle of utility to promote people's well-being.[20] According to Julia Driver, utilitarianism, which believes in the right action maximizing the good, is "probably the best-known version of consequentialism."[21] Jin Yong's approach also affirms that the right action is vindicated by the consequences produced.

Jin Yong's neutral position was bolstered by his patriotism as an overseas Chinese, more dedicated to the people than to the party, unfalteringly enunciating the truth and common sense. At the beginning of his article "On the Problem of the Home Country," he first affirms the capability and idealism of the majority of the CCP leaders, who, in his eyes, have an indisputably good intention to contribute to nation-building.[22] Meanwhile, he ridicules the idea that the KMT government in Taipei was calling for a counterattack on the mainland and a fundamental overthrow of the Chinese Communist regime, which "is at least for the time being, close to a fantasy and completely unrealistic."[23] Rooted in such a position, he then unfolds his acumen and astute arguments against and criticisms of the CCP's problematic governance. His lucid and rational statement is designed to open the possibility of innovative thought, allowing readers to have a dialogue with him. Among his many insightful viewpoints, his denigration of the CCP's way of handling newspapers, publishers, and other media, which were strictly restrained and utilized as the mouthpiece of the party, reflects his resolution to speak the truth and present the facts through his own *Ming Pao* system.

Without aligning with either the left or the right, Jin Yong believed politics is instrumental, intended, and pledged to invigorate the people's prosperity and happiness. Although fact and value are entangled and cannot be completely separated, Jin Yong's political commentaries attempted to maintain ethical neutrality by clinging to "object-language" rather than the "meta-language," as Hans Albert distinguished.[24] It is unsurprising that the leftist newspapers adamantly attacked Jin Yong's criticism of the Cultural Revolution, labeling him a "cultural wolf-traitor" (*wenhua hanjian lang* 文化漢奸狼) and "jackal and wolf Yong" (*baolang Yong* 豹狼鏞).[25] However, his insightful and impartial reports and analyses of mainland affairs in the 1960s continued to draw a broad readership, which allowed his *Ming Pao* empire to shine and prosper.

The 1970s: On Taiwan's Affairs

In 1971, when The People's Republic of China was allowed to join the United Nations, Jin Yong changed the original denotation of the ideologically tinged "Chinese Communist" (*zhonggong* 中共) to the standard reference, "Chinese government" (*zhongguo zhengfu* 中國政府), in his political commentaries. As a result, the right-leaning newspapers charged that *Ming Pao* was an "opportunist newspaper" that "alternates from the Left to the Right, then the Right to the Left, currying favor with the Communist Party on a daily basis."[26] On April 18, 1973, Jin Yong accepted an invitation from Taiwan's Nationalist government to visit for ten days. Since his martial arts novels had long been banned in Taiwan, his visit marked a new beginning of his relationship with the Taipei government. This resulted in his long article "What I Saw, Heard, and Thought in Taiwan" ("Zaitai suojian, suowen, suosi" 在台所見所聞所思), which was serialized in *Ming Pao* consecutively for ten days and became an instant sensation. At the beginning of the article, Jin Yong solemnly clarifies: "I desire to gain nothing from either Taiwan or China personally. I sincerely and earnestly wish for the good of the whole country and the happiness of all my compatriots." He stresses that his report follows the famous saying from C. P. Scott, the editor of the *Manchester Guardian*: "comment is free, but facts are sacred." In particular, he reaffirms and strengthens his objective and neutral stance by mentioning that although he does not oppose the Taipei government, he purposefully maintains a certain level of distance from it.[27] After interviewing Chiang Ching-kuo 蔣經國 (1910–1988) and other top Taiwan leaders, he understood that although they staunchly refused to accept the peace talks offered by the CCP, they denounced any attempt to be an independent nation. This tallied with Jin Yong's political belief in one China.

What impressed Jin Yong most was the psychological state of Taipei's leadership, who abandoned the attitude of "pompous boasting" (*fukua chuixu* 浮誇吹噓) and self-deception and instead adopted a realistic attitude to seriously focus on the improvement of infrastructure, the people's livelihood, and moderate military defense. Jin Yong applauded that Taiwan leaders preferred to dispatch financial resources to build people's lives rather than produce atom bombs. As a result, Taiwan's economic development was an incredible success. However, when he observed that the Taipei government was still stalwart in exalting "Three Principles of the People," he commented, "I believe that in politics, there are no absolute rights or wrongs, but rather distinctions between good and bad. The measure of what is good or bad lies in achieving the greatest benefit for the majority of people." He rightly points out that neither the "Three Principles of the People" nor Marxism-Leninism-Maoism embodies the absolute truth. What matters is results rather than beliefs—this is the spirit of science.[28] An equivalent view was expressed by Jeremy Bentham when he stated that the principle of legislation should be to promote the happiness of society and avoidance of pain. Jin Yong's assertion that the consequences of any action should serve as the sole criterion for determining right and wrong aligns impeccably with the long-standing tradition of utilitarianism inaugurated by Bentham and upheld by notable philosophers like John Stuart Mill, Henry Sidgwick, and Peter Singer. Again, Jin Yong echoes the Western precursors of consequentialism, who believe that the rightness of action "is completely determined by the action's consequences, relative to the consequences of alternative actions open to the agent."[29] He points out that within any political framework, be it the "Three Principles of the People" or Marxism-Leninism, there are always elements that are reasonable and elements that are not. Therefore, it is very important to adopt the method that can best serve the happiness of the Taiwanese, the method that is most welcomed by them, so that their greatest numbers can live happiest.[30]

Jin Yong highlights that Taiwan should compete with the CCP in terms of achieving popular welfare instead of dogmatic truisms. Furthermore, he argues that happiness includes many specific and concrete matters ranging from adequate public services to individual freedoms, not only material prosperity but also spiritual freedom. In his opinion, freedom of speech was still relatively limited in Taiwan, unlike in Hong Kong, because criticisms of the government were strictly prohibited. Jin Yong counsels the Taiwan government to take a different stand from the CCP's hegemonic control of the public sphere and freedom of speech. He writes: "I personally do not agree with Marxism-Leninism, and what I oppose is not the improvement of workers' lives and fair distribution of wealth as advocated by Marx, but the deprivation of freedom of life, the idea of class struggle, and the supremacy of government power imbued within it."[31] The advice he gives to the Taipei government—rationality, tolerance, fairness, and gradual reform—recapitulates the conventional wisdom of Western utilitarian thinkers. At the end of the article, he states that his greatest wish is to see China and Taiwan eventually unified peacefully to form an "independent, democratic, neutral" government whose primary goal is to ensure that the rights of the people are fully protected, which means "people can enjoy freedom of religion, belief, speech, publication, enterprise, residence, action, assembly, association, and property rights."[32] By emphasizing the neutrality of such a government, he intended to put aside disparate political ideologies and promote liberalism rooted in utilitarianism. Unfortunately, this is still a quixotic ideal, a transpartisan unity that cannot be manifested even now.

The 1980s and 1990s: On Hong Kong's Future

Nothing at the beginning of the 1980s galvanized public controversy more than questions related to the impending handover of Hong Kong in 1997. While the public was haunted by grave uncertainties, Jin Yong's editorial on February 19, 1981, manifested his political wisdom, prescribing essential principles for the negotiation between the Chinese and British governments. He presciently points out that an arrangement made by both sides should comply with the following requirements: first, the Chinese government should take over the sovereignty of Hong Kong to preserve its territorial integrity; second, the rule of law, freedom, and human rights principles should be maintained; third, Hong Kong's political, economic, and social status quo should remain untouched.[33] The three fundamental prerequisites were based on his genuine purpose of finding goodwill and common wishes between the two sides to maintain the prosperity and stability of Hong Kong. The editorial reflects his distinct judgment of the general tendency based on his erudite historical knowledge and cultural imagination.

Jin Yong's iconic status as a great martial arts novelist and his sensible and concise editorials proved durable enough over the next decades to survive the harsh public reaction to the complex Hong Kong situation. His editorials were so influential in the 1980s that they elicited special attention from both Chinese and British political leaders. He was a constant guest of several Hong Kong governors and met with British Prime Minister Margaret Thatcher to voice his opinions in September 1982 before she went to Beijing for negotiations. On July 18, 1981, Jin Yong was invited to Beijing by Deng Xiaoping, whom he admired and gave high praise in many of his political commentaries. Based on their conversation published in *Ming Pao Monthly*, both of them embraced utilitarianism, allowing the ends to justify the means.[34] The old proverb that Deng used to quote—"It doesn't matter if a cat is black or white, it is a good cat as long as it catches mice"—resonates with consequentialism, the teleological ethic endorsing how the effects of an action determine its moral quality. Rather than rigidly abiding by binary distinctions like good versus bad or right versus wrong, Deng Xiaoping conveyed a pragmatic approach premised upon flexibility. Deng and Jin had in common the resolve to search for an appropriate approach to alleviate and solve real problems without obstinately adhering to any dogmatic ideologies.

Between February 12, 1980, and April 23, 1984, Jin Yong wrote copious editorials enthusiastically discussing the future of Hong Kong. The most important idea he expressed throughout is that stability and prosperity can only be maintained through "freedom and the rule of law."[35] Intrinsic good would be realizable if the Chinese government were to prioritize the welfare and happiness of the Hong Kong people "to keep the present way of life," as indicated in his editorial on August 31, 1982. He believed that freedom in every aspect of man's life was the very condition for Hong Kong to continue to thrive. "Prosperity of the Hong Kong type has been due to freedom of the Hong Kong type. The latter is so indispensable that it cannot be removed, restrained, slashed, or partly kept after careful selection. And this is fundamental to Hong Kong's economic growth and prosperity."[36] Much emphasis has been put on freedom of speech, the right to speak out, criticize, and supervise the government, to amend any unfair and unreasonable state of affairs. According to Jin Yong, the rule of law is closely related to freedom because it frees people from fear, curtailing the government from transgressing individual rights.

Jin Yong's editorials are of paramount significance in comprehending the public's anxiety and his political approach during the transitional phase of Hong Kong's handover. The rhetoric of his political commentaries in the 1980s is closely tied to the pragmatic method, which valorizes common sense and practical experience at the expense of denying the metalanguage in relation to political ideologies and doctrines.[37] Jin Yong insisted on pursuing a middle way to reconcile the differences between China and Britain, calling for a "sensible, reasonable, and legally justifiable solution"[38] that would be multilaterally acceptable. Throughout his political commentaries, he constantly propounded that both sides should "adopt a fixable line," "involve mutual accommodation and concession on an equal basis," and "seek common ground while preserving differences" (*qiutong cunyi* 求同存異).[39] On the one hand, Jin Yong's method echoes John Rawls's idea of "an overlapping consensus" that looks for "an agreed basis of public justification in matters of justice."[40] On the other hand, his frequent core words in political commentaries, such as "sensible," "reasonable," and "flexibility," recall Li Zehou's philosophical concept of *du*, which embodies pragmatic rationality embedded in Confucianism. Precisely because of practical concerns, Jin Yong did not support an idealized democracy in Hong Kong with a direct election system of one person, one vote. In his defense, he was not skeptical about the value of democracy, nor did he intend to "negate the political wisdom of the lower income groups." However, in order to "give more weight to reality than to theory,"[41] he considered it unnecessary to fight for an unrealistic election system doomed to be anathema to the Chinese government.

Jin must have sounded contradictory in advocating freedom and the rule of law yet objecting to democracy with the direct electoral system. However, he never lost an overarching vision of the specific time and conditions and had a keen intention of finding a middle ground for China, Britain, and Hong Kong to reach an agreement. In his editorial "Can Democracy Be Practiced?" he ostensibly broached the guild system, "whereby members of the legislative council are chosen through consultations by various trades and circles" and then "formally appointed by the central government."[42] According to him, the guild system or the system of consultation is more applicable than the one-person, one-vote direct electoral system. By reiterating how crucial it was to preserve the existing and prevailing system in Hong Kong, he expressed his stance for not fully endorsing either Western democracy or one party's dictatorial rule, as had been imposed in mainland China and Taiwan. All he asked after China regained its sovereignty over Hong Kong was that the extant economic and social system and lifestyle be maintained—a practical request that was relatively uncomplicated to implement.[43] His most fundamental commitment, the driving force of all his thought and writing, was safeguarding Hong Kongers' happiness. His prioritization of liberalism, which includes freedom of speech, public opinion, and individual rights, was established on the grounds of utilitarian justifications. However, once he put those political utterances into practice, he encountered unanticipated setbacks, which demonstrate the intricate predicament of Thirdspace in political reality.

Real political action was far more complex than writing political commentaries, and Jin Yong found himself in an unexpectedly agonizing and equivocal situation. After the Sino-British Joint Declaration with the key designation of the "one country, two systems" principle was signed on December 19, 1984, in Beijing, Jin Yong was appointed as one of the members of the Basic Law (jiben fa 基本法) Drafting Committee in 1985. It was the first time he plunged into actual political activities as a government policymaker instead of merely a political commentator. Between 1985 and 1989, Jin Yong earnestly participated in the drafting committee meetings, fostering vigorous and intense debates and negotiations while adeptly mediating between diverse groups and members who held disparate political opinions. The mainstream proposal he initiated was finally adopted by the committee, choosing a gradual approach of election rather than direct votes.[44] However, it ran counter to the wishes of many Hong Kong citizens and the prodemocracy camp, who considered it too conservative for not establishing a direct electoral system. Although Jin Yong wrote three editorials in *Ming Pao* explaining the shortcomings of the system of one person, one vote, which is not even commonly implemented in democratic countries, he failed to convince his readers. The proposal resulted in a series of full-blown, defiant protests in Hong Kong. On November 30, 1988, more than twenty college student representatives furiously burned *Ming Pao* in front of Jin Yong's office building and accused him of "pandering to the demands of the Chinese Communist Party and betraying the interests of Hong Kong people for his own personal gain."[45] On December 3, 1988, the prodemocracy camp in Hong Kong organized a massive twenty-four-hour hunger strike for democracy, which rapidly escalated into a marathon hunger strike that lasted for more than two months and made Jin Yong the main target of protest.

Insistently, Jin Yong confronted the public protests by writing twelve editorials, patiently defending the gradual approach to elections that he had put forward in the mainstream proposal. In addition, he reemphasized that he was merely a mediator in the Basic Law Drafting Committee. Caught between the prodemocracy camp and the conservative group, he was in an exceedingly awkward predicament, destined to face doubt and criticism. The Basic Law based on the mainstream proposal was finally approved by the National People's Congress on February 21, 1989. Nevertheless, due to his frustration over the CCP's stamping out the students' protests in Tian'anmen Square as disturbing (*dongluan* 動亂), Jin Yong formally resigned from the drafting committee on May 20, 1989.[46] His five-year political career attests to the fact that he was a pragmatist who took into account what was feasible within political constraints. Recognizing the limits of the Chinese government's concessions and the bottom line, he did not intend to pursue lofty ideals that seemed impossible to actualize. His proposal that advocates a gradual and orderly progression to full democracy appears realistic and feasible, although it remains controversial. Jin Yong's decisive and arduous involvement in the drafting of the Basic Law went beyond merely reflecting the intricate situation in Hong Kong, as he carried a profound sense of social responsibility derived from Confucianism. His political approach of working for consensus between the radical and the conservative represents a strategy of moderate politics imprinted with the Thirdspace mentality of avoiding the either/or way of thinking. However, his flexible way of attending to the contradictory and problematic features of politics was severely interrogated by the public in Hong Kong. When he was accused of taking a pro-Chinese position, he explained in an interview:

> In the past, the political policies of both the Chinese Communist Party and Taiwan were deemed unsatisfactory, or even detrimental, leading me to disagree with both sides. As a result, I was described as someone who was "unpleasant to neither the left nor the right" (*zuoyou butao hao* 左右不討好). However, I now perceive that the political policies of both sides are showing signs of improvement, which has led to accusations of me "catering to both the left and the right" (*zuoyou fengyuan* 左右逢源). In fact, if a person does not seek anything from others, what is the need to please them? What is the need to pander to them?[47]

This statement precisely attests to the ineluctable dilemma surrounding the position of Thirdspace within political reality, inevitably subject to criticism from both the left and the right. Each side usually affirms a singular command, adhering to rigid ideological doctrines and rules. But Jin Yong saw pragmatism as an avenue to validating true opinion and knowledge; he would adjust his tactics depending on the changing realities. While two combative opponents were facing a widening gulf of distrust and disagreement, he strived strenuously to bridge the gap by paving the way for a more constructive and flexible solution. In his own response to the criticism of his changing attitude toward mainland China from the 1960s to the 1980s, he explained: "My stance, akin to a straight chopstick, remains unwavering. The only alteration lies in the plate upon which the delectable feast rests."[48] The unaltered position he meant is the Thirdspace discourse that takes the stance of neutrality, independence, and tolerance coupled with the means of negotiation and adjustment that had been the main principles of *Ming Pao*. What fluctuates is the immediate social circumstances that prompted Jin Yong to modify his approaches and attitudes. His neutral political stance is a testimonial to his attempt to persevere and broaden the scope of Thirdspace with the individual and society closely bound. By providing a bridge between antithetical political groups with disparate value systems, his Thirdspace broke through the Cold War mentality and opened up uncharted realms of inquiry and thinking, which wielded profound influence on the way Hong Kongers perceived the world around them.

A Manifold Thirdspace in Jin Yong's Fictional World

As Jin Yong created a real Thirdspace—a tangible public realm for the freedom of self-expression and free thought in Hong Kong society—he simultaneously developed a fictional Thirdspace brimming with a variety of cultural meanings. In his fictional world, the power struggle of the rivers and lakes always metaphorically melds historical and contemporary aspects of the real world. The male heroes or protagonists in his novels, such as *The Heaven Sword and the Dragon Saber* (*Yitian tulongji* 倚天屠龍記), *The Semigods and the Semidevils* (*Tianlong babu* 天龍八部), *The Smiling, Proud Wanderer* (*Xiao'ao jianghu* 笑傲江湖), and *The Deer and the Cauldron* (*Luding ji* 鹿鼎記) usually embody his own political ambition of expanding Thirdspace. The way to conceive of the ideal hero, according to Jin Yong, is by envisioning the cultural significance of that singular person, a spiritual paragon who is able to initiate, forge, and give voice to Thirdspace. As a result, Thirdspace, as depicted in his fiction, does not solely refer to the physical space where the heroes eventually choose seclusion to escape from endless political struggles and chaos. In addition, it signifies a cultural and spiritual space that holds a deeper significance encompassing the heroes' diverse personality traits—heroic deeds (*yingxiong xingwei* 英雄行為), chivalrous heart (*xiayi xinchang* 俠義心腸), emotional embraces of culture (*wenhua qinghuai* 文化情懷), and mental vistas (*jingshen jingjie* 精神境界). Through these traits, the heroes bring to light the inclusive perspectives and profound implications of Thirdspace. In a world characterized by an infinitely complex network, plagued by singular and dogmatic either/or thought patterns, Jin Yong's heroes opt for an alternative, seeking Thirdspace as a gateway to break free from the conflicts between orthodoxy and heterodoxy, good and evil, right and wrong, Han and non-Han people. They personify multifarious cultural embodiments, which, to a certain extent, incarnate traditional Chinese thought and spirit, such as Daoism, Buddhism, and Confucianism. Since most of Jin Yong's martial arts novels were written from 1955 to 1969—a historical context in which the binary oppositional mentality reigned in the political arena and people's daily lives—their Thirdspace contains significant cultural connotations in dialogue with the problematics of the politics at the time.

Discussing the utopian spirit invoked in Jin Yong's fiction, the literary scholar Song Weijie points out that it is "the union of the double identities—savior and hermit."[49] As he explains, "On the one hand, the 'men- and women-at-arms and outlaws' often maintain a yearning for seclusion, insofar as they yearn for the possibility of a life beyond reality, for an immediate idyllic life and mystical destination. On the other hand, the significance of the knights-errant lies in reordering the *jianghu* without order, and exhausting themselves to prevent the *jianghu* from succumbing to crisis."[50] Indeed, most of the heroes in Jin Yong's novels retreat to a reclusive space to embrace individual liberty after making a great effort to save people from the cruelty of political struggle.[51] Favoring individual freedom and individual sentiment over the dimensions of history, nation, and state, a secluded life is a galvanizing form ingrained with the message of Thirdspace. Loathing the viciousness and atrocity of power struggles between two opposing sides, Jin Yong's heroes, by and large, find the third option—seclusion—to preserve personal space for their actions and choices. Apparently permeated with Zhuangzian freedom that is mainly concerned with the spiritual domain, the innate quality of seclusion gives up on intervening in politics and cannot be "forcefully carried into the political discourse in reimagining new possibilities with regard to the state."[52] The pursuit of individual liberty in the form of seclusion typifies Isaiah Berlin's negative freedom to request personal space while criticizing moral monism in favor of value pluralism. Nevertheless, Jin Yong did not want to relinquish his involvement in the political realm. By emphasizing seclusion in its implication with negative freedom, he affirms and appeals for the social legitimacy of an individual choosing to escape from the largely dualist political world in which he lived.

Furthermore, I argue that in his fictional world, Jin Yong maximized the connotation and vision of Thirdspace, vigorously defending the value of positive freedom while shielding negative freedom. One of the most trenchant critics of Isaiah Berlin, Charles Taylor, in his article "What's Wrong with Negative Liberty?" claims that Berlin's espousal of negative freedom "leaves no place for a positive theory to grow."[53] In his view, Berlin's elevation of negative freedom sidelines "one of the most powerful motives behind the modern defence of freedom as individual independence, viz., the post-Romantic idea" that every individual's path to liberty is unique to themselves.[54] Taylor thereby rebukes Berlin for emphasizing the external freedom at the expense of ignoring the internal one, as doing so hinders an individual's unique and independent pursuit of liberty. Although Jin Yong follows Berlin's defense of basic individual rights from interference, he maintains a middle ground by identifying with Taylor's affirmation of individuals' self-determination and self-realization within a broader societal framework.

Because the valor of the knights-errant consists of gallantry, altruism, and salvation, Jin Yong's fictional heroes and heroines intuitively embrace positive freedom that promotes self-fulfillment in shaping society regardless of external obstacles. While rescuing people from chaos and crisis, they endeavor to apply prominent tenets of Thirdspace—individual liberty, tolerance, benevolence, and harmony—to the political field suffused with dualist tensions.

Therefore, in Jin Yong's fantastic imagination of the rivers and lakes, the essence of Thirdspace is perceptible in both the "positive" and "negative" senses of individual freedom. The variety of different spiritual undertones among the heroes is the reservoir of Thirdspace, which not only is attached to the social production of time pointing to history and reality but also evokes a profound and provocative connection with traditional Chinese thought. More intriguingly, by creating the antihero image of Wei Xiaobao in his most controversial novel, *The Deer and the Cauldron*, Jin Yong employs paradox as a key to understanding the complicated aspects of Thirdspace. Wei Xiaobao's cunning and chameleonic character allows him to effectively subvert and parody the binary oppositions between the governor and the resisters, the colonizer and the colonized; his lack of principle and commitment to value judgment contains "the dissolving power of irony,"[55] leading to the predicament of Thirdspace—the possibility of degenerating into the nihilism of relativism.

Fighting for the Right of Wandering

Jin Yong's novel *The Smiling, Proud Wanderer* emerged in the historical time of the Cultural Revolution, which spread to Hong Kong and led to a series of large-scale demonstrations against British colonial rule in 1967. Serialized in *Ming Pao* from 1967 to 1969, *Wanderer* was commonly regarded as a political allegory responding to the current chaotic historical period,[56] when people's mentality was gripped by dictatorial and petrified ideological binaries such as revolution versus antirevolution and Communist versus anti-Communist. Although Jin Yong admitted, "My violent reaction against the sordidness of political events was naturally reflected in the daily installments of my martial arts fiction," his ambition was apparently bigger. In his own words, "This novel does not, however, intentionally allude to the Cultural Revolution. It intends rather to employ characters within the novel to depict certain universal phenomena from the three thousand years of Chinese political life."[57] Indeed, it is not difficult to find the affinity between political reality and the fictional imagination, but Jin Yong aimed to transcend his own time and outline a political model that has dominated the Chinese mindset from ancient times to the present.

To be sure, Jin Yong was impelled to reflect in *Wanderer* the extant paradigm of political struggles, dominated by the exclusive and dogmatic either/or mindset, which not only is strongly relevant to reality but also reveals the universal problems that arise from binary vindictive partisanship. As a contemporary Chinese novelist in Hong Kong, Jin Yong was the first writer to consciously realize how destructive binary logic had been in modern Chinese society. In *Wanderer*, the dichotomy of power is clearly drawn between the five orthodox martial arts schools and the Sun-Moon Sect (*Riyue shenjiao* 日月神教), derided as the Demon Cult (*Mojiao* 魔教) by the so-called righteous people. The ceaseless and formidable conflicts between these two opposing camps represent the endless struggles between the forces of good (*zheng* 正) and the forces of evil (*xie* 邪). The novel aims not only to question the doctrines behind the moral judgment of good and evil but also to expose how difficult it is for an individual to find a breathing space amid perpetual power struggles. The characters can only side with either the orthodox schools or the Demon Cult and have no other way out. This typifies the vicious antipodal logic of "either you die or I live" that was prevalent during the Cultural Revolution as well as the worldwide Cold War period.

Jin Yong's humanistic position unveils what is lurking behind that model. On the surface, the ceaseless war between the forces of good and the forces of evil seems unavoidable and lofty. However, by uncovering the iniquity of human nature in the leaders of both camps, animated by a voracious desire for power and willing to employ any malicious means to achieve their goals, Jin Yong plausibly obliterates the sharp dichotomy between absolute "rights" and "wrongs" in the moral sense. One leader from the orthodox martial arts schools is Yue Buqun 岳不群, who initially appears austere and sagely, only to be exposed as an opportunistic hypocrite who values power above all else. This fictional façade was so successful that it became a byword for righteous hypocrites or false gentlemen (*wei junzi* 偽君子) in real-life Chinese politics. It effectively deconstructs the fixed, stark contrast between the gentleman (*junzi* 君子) and the petty man (*xiaoren* 小人) propounded by Confucianism. The other leader, Zuo Lengchan 左冷禪, who wants to be the head of all five orthodox martial arts schools, proves to be wily and perfidious. Dongfang Bubai 東方不敗 and Ren Woxing 任我行, the leaders of the Demon Cult, are no different, simply totalitarian power seekers who demand a cult of idolization from their followers akin to Mao Zedong's cult of personality. Their semireligious behavior and ritualistic idolatry mark them as stand-ins for Mao and the Chinese Communist Party. The moral gray areas are reinforced by the presence of the *Evil-Quelling Sword Manual*, which is a powerful metaphor for political corruption. Every holder of the manual, from antagonists such as Dongfang Bubai, Zuo Lengchan, and Yue Buqun to protagonists like Lin Pingzhi, becomes corrupt and abnormal. The manual brings great political advantages to Yue Buqun and Zuo Lengchan, who receive wide acclaim and praise among the orthodox martial arts schools, but this simply veils their amoral personalities. Instead of quelling evil, the manual perverts the original nature of its holder. Dongfang Bubai and Yue Buqun become indistinguishable in gender upon obtaining it, disgusting and shocking their followers. Although the transgender description appears to be "political incorrectness" in our time, Jin Yong employed it to suggest the metamorphosis of human nature caused by corrupt power in his time. By vividly divulging the evil human nature in those power holders, Jin Yong vehemently interrogates the moral standard of good and evil stipulated by the dogmatic political struggles.

  The fatal repercussions of that binary logic are illustrated by the fate of Liu Zhengfeng 劉正風, who intends to withdraw from the conflicts of the rivers and lakes but falls afoul of the orthodox schools' fanaticism. When he is interrogated about his motive for retiring from the martial world during the hand-washing ceremony, he explains: "The Demon Cult and the righteous sect have been entangled in a bitter struggle and feud for over a century. The complexities of rights and wrongs cannot be fully elucidated at this moment. I only wish to quit this bloody struggle and retreat to the ancient forest spring, where I can play the flute and live as a peaceful and virtuous man. I think this wish does not violate the fundamental principle of my own school nor the alliance of the Five Yue Schools." However, his wish is ruthlessly denied by Fei Bing 費斌, one of the leaders of the orthodox schools: "If everyone were to follow your example in times of crisis, fleeing from the battlefield, would it not enable the Demon Cult to freely roam the rivers and lakes, causing harm to innocent people?"[58] This tone is reminiscent of Lu Xun's pungent and harsh derision of hermits, whose flight from the battlefield, in his eyes, reveals a "deadwood heart" (*gaomu zhixin* 槁木之心) lacking courage to face reality and extend sympathy toward those who are suffering.[59] Under the righteous principle of "fighting for justice in the name of heaven" (*titian xingdao* 替天行道), no one has the right to be a hermit. This certainly infringes upon individual liberty and the private domain. For Western philosophers such as John Stuart Mill and Isaiah Berlin, there is a certain minimum area of the individual's life that should be free from interference by others. However, Liu Zhengfeng is compelled to do what is right in others' opinions and deprived of his sacrosanct individual rights.

The revelation of Liu Zhengfeng's friendship with Qu Yang 曲洋, one of the leaders of the Demon Sect, prompts those from the orthodox schools to slaughter Liu's family down to the last child, a brutal scene that commonly occurred during the periods of land reform and the Cultural Revolution. It not only demonstrates that adherents of dogmatic dualism commit the most heartless and debauched atrocities in the guise of uprightness but also denounces the violence normally practiced in revolution. Interestingly, it is music that connects Liu Zhengfeng and Qu Yang, who cross the rigid demarcation of the forces of good and evil to jointly compose and perform the song "The Smiling, Proud Wanderer," which signifies the alternative way to transcend either/or thinking. This alternative is precisely the kind of Thirdspace defined by Liu Zaifu as a "personal space," or a survival zone where individuals are liberated from the extreme antipodal politics that ravage society.[60] This Thirdspace is essential for literary and artistic activities to thrive, keeping political power from arbitrarily intervening and distorting the literary/artistic effort. Jin Yong seems to celebrate music, the symbol of artistic creation, as the essential form that serves as a vehicle for the implementation of Thirdspace. By doing so, music highlights "the Daoist yearning for spiritual freedom" and signifies a stance of "apolitical transcendence" that cannot be tolerated by the dominant political authorities.[61] In inheriting the script of "The Smiling, Proud Wanderer"—a pure and highly creative piece of music yet useless in terms of martial arts—the central figure, Linghu Chong 令狐冲, who strives strenuously to free himself from the impasse of the dualistic political struggle, is the major carrier of the eremitic spirit. According to the scholar Chen Pingyuan, the Daoist qualities of individual freedom and the Confucianist sense of responsibility for the nation are evident in both the personalities and actions of Jin Yong's fictional heroes and his commentary on real-world politics.[62] However, the Daoist thematic elements are the most pronounced in *The Smiling, Proud Wanderer*. The ambiguity of the historical era provides an allegorical atmosphere unconfined by the contingencies of specific political events, even if the plot is most applicable to the Cultural Revolution era.

Jin Yong, in his afterword to *Wanderer*, states that in politics, there are always the wielders of power, the rebels, the reformers, and the hermits. The hermits do not want to be contaminated by political power, so they prefer to be left alone to enjoy personal virtuous cultivation. Jin also notes that many hermits were recorded in Confucius's *Analects*. Although Confucius did not fully agree with their stances, he paid great respect to three categories of hermits: "those like Bo Yi 伯夷 and Shu Qi 叔齊, who did not give up their will nor sacrifice their dignity; those like Liu Xiahui 柳下惠 and Shao Lian 少連, who sacrificed their will and dignity, but whose words and actions were reasonable; and those like Yu Zhong 虞仲 and Yi Yi 夷逸, who abandoned the world and resided in seclusion, and spoke liberally and frankly, without committing misdeeds or partaking in politics."[63] In general, Jin Yong signals that Confucius had a good opinion of them all and obviously thought that being a hermit had a positive side.

Jin Yong acknowledges that in the Chinese tradition, hermits who endeavor to achieve spiritual freedom without obligations to others are fully respected, for their reclusive tactic is unambiguously a form of resistance to the overwhelming political hegemony. In contrast, Jin Yong laments that in contemporary society, to be hermetic is not easy because it is absolutely forbidden by the rules and apparatus of political struggle.[64] Gao Xingjian also observes: "During the years when Mao Zedong implemented total dictatorship even fleeing was not an option. The monasteries on faraway mountains that provided refuge for scholars in feudal times were totally ravaged and to write even in secret was to risk one's life."[65] The occlusion of the right to wander is the absence of negative freedom in modern China. The country simply lacks a sphere of private life free from intrusion by the state or society for the majority of people. This is why Liu Zhengfeng's aspiration to retire to the rivers and lakes and pursue the arts and pure friendship only leads to a tragic end. In the novel, the four friends of the Plum Manor want to enjoy the pleasures of delving into musical instruments, calligraphy, chess, and painting but have no way to materialize that goal and eventually commit suicide. Jin Yong singles out a central theme of *Wanderer* where Linghu Chong is similar to a hermit like Tao Qian 陶潛 (365–427), who pursues individual liberty and emancipation instead of embracing Confucius's doctrine of "doing what is known to be impossible" (*zhiqi bukewei er weizhi* 知其不可為而為之). As Jin Yong elucidates, "Linghu Chong is a natural hermit, not interested in power. Yingying is also a 'hermit'; she has the power of life and death over the martial art giants, but she prefers to live in a secluded alley in Luoyang and entertain herself with the flute. In her life, she only values her personal freedom and the expansion of her individuality, and the only thing that matters to her is love."[66] What Jin Yong fights for most within *Wanderer* is the right of seclusion for hermits, which was forfeited, disdained, and belittled in the modern revolutionary context.

As an incarnation of the eremitic spirit, Linghu Chong is weary of political power struggles, voluntarily keeping distance from the political center. When he witnesses Dongfang Bubai and Ren Woxing enjoying their followers' cultish and ingratiating chants—nearly verbatim from the Cultural Revolution—he is extremely averse to those nauseatingly hyperbolic and groveling slogans. Realizing the alienation of political corruption, he refuses to be a political leader for the Demon Sect, turning down high positions offered by Ren Woxing, the head of the sect, regardless of death threats. Even as the head of the Buddhistic all-nun Hengshan sect, he employs Laozi's "governance without action" (*wuwei erzhi* 無為而治), basically doing nothing but selecting his replacement early on to pave the way for his own retirement. His ideal is to eventually withdraw from the complexities of the rivers and lakes and live a liberated and carefree life as a hermit.

Linghu Chong's subjectivity and individuality closely conform to Zhuangzi's "free and easy wandering," which holds on to genuine self-sufficiency, relying on nobody and nothing to attain absolute freedom. Shedding political power, he makes every effort to keep his naturalness unpolluted, transcending notions of good and bad, right and wrong, which are externally imposed. Even his martial arts skill, "the Lonely Nine Swords" (*dugu jiujian* 獨孤九劍), passed down from a reclusive master, contains a Chan-esque spiritual comprehension and enlightenment. After fully mastering this special sword technique, he achieves a state of free frolicking unfettered by any code of the martial arts. Therefore, every time he fights with the enemy, "there is not a trace left, it is as if a poet suddenly gains inspiration to write a masterful poem."[67] This unique skill refers to Zhuangzi's parable of Butcher Ding's dissection of the Ox, which epitomizes an extraordinary level of artistic and spiritual excellence. Even his romance with Ren Yingying bridges the chasm between the forces of good and the forces of evil that incited a century of sectarianism. Before he retreats to the reclusive life with Yingying, his personification of the Daoist spirit of the wanderer has created a path for Thirdspace to break free from the perpetual political feuds.

The Power of the All-Encompassing Heart

In 1961, Jin Yong's novel *The Heaven Sword and the Dragon Sabre* started to be serialized in *Ming Pao*. Similar to *Wanderer*, this novel aims to deconstruct "the Manichaean axis of good and evil" analogous to the opposing sides of the orthodox forces and the Demon Cult.[68] In the afterword, published in 1977, Jin Yong explicitly elucidates his intention to subvert a totalizing tendency to divide human beings into two contrasting categories of good and evil:

> I believe that in human society, good and evil are intricately intertwined, and no individual can be entirely virtuous or utterly debauched. Even evildoers have a kinder side, while the righteous possess their own shades of darkness, albeit to a lesser extent. What the writer has to consider is how to write authentically. When I wrote *The Heaven Sword and the Dragon Sabre*, I expressed a view of life that is: good and evil, right and wrong are generally difficult to judge, and sometimes impossible to distinguish clearly. Life does not necessarily adhere to the idiom that "good actions yield good rewards, and evil actions yield evil consequences." The demarcation of good and evil is not as clear as a glance at the Chu-Han boundary. Life is really convoluted, and fate is undeniably ever-changing.[69]

Jin Yong clearly rejects the fixed principles or rigid antitheses of absolute good and absolute evil in depicting human characters. His viewpoints find reverberation in Liu Zaifu's *A Treatise of Character Compositions*, which challenges the dualism of stereotyped good and evil characters imprinted in revolutionary morality and explores the complexity and heterogeneity in the literary construction of fictional characters. In addition, Jin Yong's attitude resonates with Liu Zaifu's *Reflections on Dream of the Red Chamber*, which argues that Cao Xueqin 曹雪芹 (1715–1763) actually adopts the Middle Way approach devised by the Buddhist philosopher Nagarjuna to oppose dualism.[70] With high aesthetic values, *Dream of the Red Chamber* (Honglou meng 紅樓夢) cuts across the distinctions between truth and fiction, right and wrong, good and evil, cause and effect.[71] By questioning whether great benevolence and great wickedness truly exist, Jin Yong essentially aligns with Cao Xueqin in affirming the complexity of human nature, which cannot be adequately encapsulated within binary moral standards. Even Lu

Xun acknowledges that the greatness of *Dream of the Red Chamber* lies in its defying the absolute distinction between good and bad characters.[72] The versatile, changeable, and complex codes of human nature are efficaciously integrated into Jin Yong's exploration of Thirdspace, which breaks through the framework of an unbreachable divide between good and evil.

Parallel to *Wanderer*, a central theme in *Dragon Sabre* is the disruption of the dichotomous moral logic of good and evil strictly defined by the feuding factions. The orthodox martial arts schools (the good forces) and the Demon Cult (the evil forces) are both capable of heroic valor and despicable atrocities. When Master Nun Miejue 滅絕師太 from the good forces discovered that her apprentice Ji Xiaofu 紀曉芙 bore children with Yang Xiao 楊逍, one of the leaders of the Demon Cult, she swiftly slays the apprentice with one clap. Despite her allegiance to the banner of supreme righteousness, she mirrors the Demon Cultists, who are alleged to "kill without blinking an eye," lacking empathy. Her unbendable attitude illustrates a violent intolerance chained by dualist dogmatism. Those from the Demon Cult show complicated personalities that cannot be easily labeled as good or evil. The seemingly demonic cult actually plays a significant role in resisting the invasion of the Mongols. When their center—Bright Summit (*guangming ding* 光明頂)—is surrounded and assaulted by the orthodox martial arts schools, which represent the good forces, various demon warriors sacrifice themselves to aid their companions and demonstrate the sacrosanct bonds of brotherhood. Vacillating between good and evil, the leaders of the cult exhibit courage, loyalty, and honesty, making a marvelous show of affection and heroism in times of crisis.

However, Thirdspace finds its most emblematic expression in the personality of the central protagonist of *Dragon Sabre*, Zhang Wuji 張無忌, who embodies open-mindedness and embraces all political sides with an all-encompassing heart. Zhang Wuji was born from a union between members of the two opposing sects, his mother from the Demon Cult and his father from the orthodox schools. With this unique heritage, he is the symbol of "hybridity," similar to Homi Bhabha's definition of the "third space which enables other positions to emerge."[73] The image of Zhang Wuji forcefully defies the essentialism and rigidity of the good forces and the evil forces, establishing new ground for multiple values and identities to come to light. His most impressive characteristic is that his mind and heart are free of discrimination and full of tolerance, empathy, and inclusiveness—a spiritual state that crystallizes the Thirdspace epistemology of openness and unboundedness. Describing his personality as "moderate" (*zhonghe* 中和), the scholar Chen Mo 陳墨 acclaims him as a hero who is a profound humanist with a strong life consciousness and benevolent heart.[74] Jin Yong bestows Zhang Wuji with a superb medical ability—the metaphor of a cure to alleviate all the historical traumas, damages, and injuries caused by the unrelenting disputes and battles between the opposing factions. He is a very trusting and warmhearted individual who accepts the virtues and vices of the people he meets, trying to surpass the sects' fractious feuding. Treating all patients equally regardless of their positions and identities, he effortlessly replaces the either/or mindset with that of "both/and also." Moreover, he is extremely unbiased and tolerant, not suspicious of Xiaozhao 小昭, a beautiful Persian spy attempting to steal an important martial arts script from the Demon Cult. Even when Xiaozhao is disguised as an ugly slave, Zhang Wuji treats her magnanimously. This nondiscriminatory attitude echoes Jia Baoyu 賈寶玉 from *Dream of the Red Chamber*, who treats everyone in the Jia household equally, be they servants or aristocrats.

According to Jin Yong, Zhang Wuji is a weak character who lacks the political ambition, will, and guile to be entangled in intricate and intense power struggles.[75] He is easily influenced by others as well as the specific environment surrounding him. Hesitating to choose a lover among several beautiful women like Zhao Min 趙敏 and Zhou Zhiruo 周芷若, he seems to be easily manipulated by them. However, despite his indecisiveness, Zhang Wuji is the only true person who can unify the feuding factions, encompassing and balancing forces from different racial, ethnic, and political backgrounds. As a vital embodiment of Thirdspace, he has no desire to be the foremost political leader. Able to tackle issues from multiple perspectives, he shows compassion for others' suffering, having great sympathy and a keen willingness to rush to help the downtrodden. Zhang Wuji exhibits Mencius's "benevolent heart" (*buren zhixin* 不忍之心),[76] which empathizes with human suffering and manifests compassionate predilections. In contrast, one cult leader, Zhu Yuanzhang 朱元璋 (1328–1398), starts out in a very lowly peasant position, only to emerge as a fierce rival to Zhang Wuji upon rising to power. Because of his political ambition and schemes, Zhu Yuanzhang triumphs as the founder of China's Ming dynasty who overthrows the Mongol Yuan dynasty, whereas Zhang Wuji retires from the rivers and lakes and abandons his position as the primary leader of the cult. In seclusion, he lives with Zhao Min, the Mongol royal, even if their biracial union is disapproved of by most Chinese knights-errant. Zhang Wuji audaciously crosses racial boundaries in addition to sectarian lines, showing his profoundly inclusive and impartial mind/heart, which is the hard core of the spirit of Thirdspace.

The Embodiment of the Mahayana Buddhist Spirit

The Semigods and the Semidevils was serialized in *Ming Pao* between 1963 and 1967. The novel is set against the historical backdrop of the late Northern Song (960–1127), when the Song dynasty was fiercely menaced by both the Liao empire of the Khitans and the Western Xia kingdom of the Tanguts.[77] According to the scholar Chen Shixiang 陳世驤 (1912–1971), although its structure is relatively loose, behind the multiple characters and events is "the boundless transcendence of the Buddha's teachings" (*fofa de wubian da chaotuo* 佛法的無邊大超脫).[78] Affirming it as a benevolent book (*beitian minren zhizuo* 悲天憫人之作), Chen especially praises the depth, height, and breadth of the mental vista that Jin Yong creates by imbuing every figure and event with "karmic debts and salvation/transcendence" (*yuannie yu chaodu* 冤孽與超度). There is no doubt that Buddhist thought permeates the whole novel, whose title, *Tianlong babu*, is "a Chinese translation of the Sanskrit *deva-nāga*."[79] The various predicaments and conflicts are internally intertwined and entangled, with a series of uncannily interrelated relationships closely and mysteriously binding the characters together. The characters are all suffused with the "three poisons" of Buddhism—*Moha* (delusion 痴), *Raga* (greed 貪), and *Dvesha* (hate 瞋)—which are the fundamental causes of torment, pain, and grief. Those with wisdom eventually seek a way to solve these problems, while others are deeply trapped and ruined.

The novel is structured around three main protagonists, Duan Yu 段譽, Xiao Feng 蕭峰, and Xu Zhu 虛竹, each of whom "represents a different ethno-political entity."[80] Beyond the geopolitical and ethno-racial concerns, what is more important is that the stories unfolding around them are pertinent to different Buddhist values. Duan Yu, the crown prince of the Buddhist Kingdom of Dali 大理, resembles Jia Baoyu from *Dream of the Red Chamber*, who signifies an obsession with feeling (*qingchi* 情痴). The irony lies in that the beautiful women with whom he is enthralled turn out to be his half-sisters, the offspring of his father's various love affairs. Although the truth is eventually revealed that he is not his father's biological child, those intricate and entangled relationships are a testimonial to the fact that desire and feelings are nothing but an illusion. Xiao Feng, the leader of the Beggar Gang, is raised in a typical Han Chinese cultural environment but discovers that his biological parents are Khitans, enemies of the Han. Framed for a series of murders he does not commit, he is ensnared in a cycle of revenge and has to live among the nomadic Khitan people. Despite his promotion to the role of generalissimo by the King of Liao, he chooses to sacrifice his own life in order to save people from the brutal war between Song and Liao. The anger and anguish embedded in him transform into a benevolent heart. Xu Zhu, a monk in the Shaolin monastery, desires nothing from the mundane world but miraculously obtains everything. Not only does he master the preeminent martial arts skill, he also marries the princess of the Western Xia Kingdom and becomes the leader of a powerful martial clan. In contrast, Murong Fu 慕容復, a secondary protagonist who dreams of revitalizing the Yan kingdom by whatever means, ironically ends up bereft of everything. One can see a parody in the contrast: nonaction and nondesire reward Xu Zhu with everything, but avarice leads to Murong Fu's final ruin. It is apparent that the Buddhist teaching conveyed through these main protagonists is about how to get rid of *Moha* (delusion), *Raga* (greed), and *Dvesha* (hate), and rescue oneself from the abyss of pain and suffering.

The most impressive personification of the Mahayana Buddhist spirit is Xiao Feng. The central concern he represents is "the burden of double identity of being both Han and Khitan."[81] Caught in the extremely hostile opposition between those two sides, Xiao Feng is torn asunder by his hybrid identity, which adds a tragic sense to the story. Originally, he is a highly acclaimed heroic leader of the Beggar Gang, identifying with the orthodox Han culture, but after his Khitan bloodline is revealed, he is plunged into a tormented splitting stage, full of questions like "Who am I?" "Where did I come from?" Such interrogations elevate Jin Yong's fiction to the existential dimension, which is lacking in the majority of Chinese martial arts works. While Xiao Feng is entrapped in the mysterious schemes and cycle of vengeance by his still-living father and other martial arts masters who wronged his Khitan family, his agonizing individual experience embodies a metaphysical stance that is closely related to existentialist philosophy. All the things he once regarded as absolutes—the Han-centered cultural identity, reason, and history—have been relentlessly shattered. He can no longer rely on any ultimate authority to prescribe how he should live his life. Confronting a political and cultural predicament bound to the polarized either/

or mindset, he must make his own choice. The dramatic tension between a shared collective experience of patriotism and the isolation of this suffering hero develops a unique sense of tragedy. It is no accident that Xiao Feng finds personal enlightenment through a Buddhist principle. In the novel, Jin Yong intentionally provides an antidote to this racial antagonism in the dying words of the master monk Zhiguang 智光:

> All things are nondiscriminatory, all beings are inherently equal. Han Chinese and Khitan should be treated as equals. Gratitude and resentment, honor and disgrace, possess a mysterious and intricate nature that is difficult to comprehend. We should always have a benevolent heart in thinking of all sentient beings with compassion.[82]

> 萬物一般，眾生平等。漢人契丹，一視同仁。恩怨榮辱，玄妙難明。當懷慈心，常念眾生。

These insightful words reflect the core values of Buddhism, which find no difference between Han and Khitan, gain and loss, from the perspective of a compassionate and benevolent heart within which Thirdspace is embedded. In Buddhist philosophy, everything is an illusion that will eventually turn into dust. This principle not only casts doubt on the importance of adhering to ethnic distinctions and hostility but also presents a daunting challenge to dogmatism by offering an all-encompassing mindset. By invoking the profound cultural meanings of Thirdspace, this Buddhist remedy straddles the breach between Khitan and Han Chinese. More importantly, Jin Yong incorporates the spirit of positive freedom into Thirdspace, entailing individuals' capacity for self-determination and self-realization within a broader societal framework. Unlike negative freedom, which focuses on the absence of external constraints, positive freedom emphasizes the ability of individuals to actively take part in shaping the social and cultural conditions that define their lives. Instead of choosing a secluded life as a free-spirited hunter and shepherd with his lover Ah Zhu 阿朱 in the northern wilderness, Xiao Feng courageously confronts the brutal reality, sacrificing his life to bring a ten-year peace in the Song-Liao war. Viewing people from Song China and the Khitan Liao not as inveterate foes but as human victims of vicious wars, he deals with the conflicts between the two groups by demonstrating boundless benevolence and love (*ren'ai* 仁愛). The famous modern writer Zhou Zuoren discovered that Buddhism and Confucianism share a similar benevolence and love. He was touched by the great spirit embedded in "The Scripture of the Bodhisattva Who Sacrifices Herself to Feed the Hungry Tiger" ("Pusa toushen si ehu jing" 菩薩投身飼餓虎經) and thought that such a benevolent spirit also existed in Confucianism. In his words, "The Mahayana spirit of entering the world is similar to that of Confucianism, and perhaps more thorough."[83] Xiao Feng's peacemaking effort reflects a quintessential value of Buddhism and Confucianism, which are universally compassionate and generous toward others. It is the benevolent heart that allows Xiao Feng to escape the quandaries of ethnic loyalties, transcending political and racial differences. At the expense of his own precious life, he is sublimated into a "superhero," devoted to a broader humanistic purpose. His actions achieve a "bigger I" by sacrificing "the smaller I"—a choice of self-realization that is exactly what positive freedom is about.

One incident in the novel contains a strong message of Thirdspace bearing on Buddhist thought, which upholds a tremendous power to transcend and resolve antipodal rivalry. Due to accumulated historical and personal problems, Murong Fu's father, Murong Bo 慕容博, and Xiao Feng's father, Xiao Yuanshan 蕭遠山, are archenemies determined to kill each other and achieve vengeance. Although both individuals' martial arts skills are extremely advanced, both have deep inner wounds that are serious enough to lead to their death. However, an old abbot who is advanced in both Buddhist knowledge and martial arts knowledge appears to enlighten them by suddenly shouting: "Join hands in unison, attune to your inner breath, let *yin* empower *yang* and *yang* dissolve *yin*. The ambition of establishing a kingdom, the profound animosity that spawns a sea of blood, all converge back to dust and fade into shapelessness."[84] Miraculously, after Murong Bo and Xiao Yuanshan hold hands, they achieve a spontaneous epiphany that not only cures their inner wounds but also removes their enmity. The flow of *qi* between them is the supplement of yin and yang, which brings unexpected balance and peace to the two opponents. Furthermore, they both become the old abbot's apprentices, embracing Buddhism wholeheartedly. This incident attests to how Buddhist principles embody the cultural connotations of Thirdspace and effectively resolve binary conflicts and hatred by championing the balance of yin and yang. Parallel to Zhang Dongsun's correlative theory of yin and yang, the old abbot productively transmutes the intolerant opposition into mutual complementarity, reliance, and support. Therefore, the mental vista of this novel, as Chen Shixiang reminds us, is extremely broad and inspirational.

The Cunning Chinese National Character

The Deer and the Cauldron was serialized in *Ming Pao* from 1969 to 1972. It attracted great attention mostly because the main protagonist, Wei Xiaobao, is portrayed as a typical antihero, equivalent in significance to Lu Xun's Ah Q, symbolizing the problematics of the national character that is ubiquitous in China. The novel contains a strong sense of irony that relentlessly deconstructs the venerable and lofty moral qualities steeped in the ideal male heroes that Jin Yong previously created.[85] However, I contend that the national character represented by Wei Xiaobao emphasizes the question of survival. In the context of extreme binary antagonisms, Wei Xiaobao shows a superb survival skill, "unprincipled adaptability,"[86] relying on various dishonorable means such as lying and scheming to go around different forces and climb to the top of society. This strategy is enacted amid harsh dichotomic oppositions, omnipresent in both traditional and modern societies. The image of Wei Xiaobao shows a polemical paradox of Thirdspace: it effectively dissolves the strict distinctions between the Han and Manchu, the government and antigovernment. Yet it fosters a kind of moral ambiguity based on utilitarianism and pragmatism, which inevitably cultivates a dubious national character that is dishonest, lacking in principles, and masquerading in disguises.

Consistent with Jin Yong's usual character composition, which does not posit absolute right and absolute wrong, Wei Xiaobao is an unscrupulous character who rests in a moral gray area. Born and raised in a brothel in Yangzhou, he behaves like a little hooligan and is good at gambling, deceiving, and scheming. What he cares about most is not political ideals or social responsibilities but his own profit and desire. Muddling through, rather than taking a side in the rivers and lakes, he has neither martial arts skills nor erudite scholarly knowledge, yet he is extremely adroit in the mundane world. He is virtually an illiterate who learns history in teahouses and theaters instead of in the Confucian Classics. From a very lowly background, he is not a complete scoundrel due to his loyalty to friends and valor. After he bumbles into the Forbidden City as a fake eunuch, he befriends the young Kangxi Emperor 康熙皇帝 (1654–1722) and helps him secure the emperor's throne by killing Minister Oboi. The most intriguing aspect of Wei Xiaobao is his double role: he not only befriends the Manchu emperor, occupying vital official positions in the Qing court, but also maintains an intimate relationship with the anti-Qing resistance group, the Heaven and Earth society, apprenticed to its leader, Chen Jinnan, and controlling its Beijing division. While normal people would regard such a double role as contradictory, Wei Xiaobao's strong survival skills enable his adept success in both factions. He blends in like a chameleon, able to shift between ostensibly clashing loyalties.

Between the two opposing worlds, Wei Xiaobao seems to represent a certain kind of Thirdspace with a hybrid identity proposed by Homi Bhabha. Because his mother was a prostitute, Wei Xiaobao's father could be Han, Manchu, Mongol, Muslim, or Tibetan. As Song Weijie argues, "The so-called distinctions of a pure race/nation/state identity of Wei Xiaobao are collapsed, questioned, and parodied."[87] Wei Xiaobao's hybrid identity puts narrow-minded nationalism and the oversimplified division of right and wrong into question. He even causes the anti-Qing leaders to reflect on the viability of their own movement, as the Kangxi Emperor exemplifies many Chinese cultural virtues and works to improve the people's welfare, acting more capable than the ruthless and incompetent emperors in the Ming dynasty. In contrast, the anti-Qing leaders are trapped in various internecine and chaotic organizations, competing for power and profit rather than uplifting and loving ordinary people. The rebels' predicament mirrors a situation described in Jin Yong's earlier novel, *The Sword of Loyalty* (*Bixue jian* 碧血劍), where anti-Ming rebels led by Li Zicheng 李自成 (1606–1645) succeed in wresting Beijing from the corrupt Ming, only to fall into infighting. In the march to Beijing, the rebels claim to fight righteously in the name of heaven. But after they seize the imperial capital, their rhetoric is proven hollow when they indulge in debaucheries such as chasing and raping women, looting goods and houses, and massacring the populace. These hypocrisies indicate Jin Yong's suspicion of political movements that espouse righteous rhetoric only to squander power and fight among themselves.

Wei Xiaobao's hybridity destabilizes and deconstructs the system of national identity and the rigid polarization of good and evil, which have always been Jin Yong's target of criticism. However, the novel poses an intriguing and important question: As Wei Xiaobao employs a variety of unethical means to undermine the ideals of salvation, negotiating between the personal and the political, does he not also symbolize the pseudo-model of Thirdspace? His hybrid identity combining two opposing forces not only parodies exalted national ideals but also mimics the Thirdspace that Jin Yong endeavored to establish and expand in real life. Since masking and deception are necessary for Wei Xiaobao's survival, he embodies an embarrassing situation in which an individual has to be very crooked in order to adapt to a conflicted political milieu. Such a twisted way of life is a compelling caricature of many Chinese people's existence under ceaseless polarized struggles. While Wei Xiaobao is adeptly floating and maneuvering between various positions, he typifies the enduring popularity of "the thick and dark science of officialdom" (guanchang houhei xue 官場厚黑學), even in post-Mao China. With this protagonist, Jin Yong efficaciously continued Lu Xun's profound reflections on the problematics of the Chinese national character.

On the surface, Wei Xiaobao's adaptability is in tune with the philosophy of change in the *Book of Changes* (*Yijing* 易經). According to Benjamin I. Schwartz, this is a text "closely associated in its present form with a correlative cosmological outlook." To a certain extent, Wei Xiaobao's mode of behavior resonates with the *Book of Changes* in terms of using flexible patterns to cope with "the vastly varied and contingent world of shifting situations and circumstances." However, the *Book of Changes* reflects the strong influence of *yin/yang* cosmology and asserts a "numinous or divine" looming behind the unfathomable.[88] Wei Xiaobao has no connections to Daoism or correlative cosmology but instead comports himself in extremely pragmatic fashion, without concrete ethical principles. His sense of playfulness shows that he does not fully abide by Confucian virtues either. Being so easily integrated with whatever faction he encounters, he wears the façade of loyalty. He parrots the appropriate slogans, proclaiming loyalty to the Qing dynasty or willingness to restore the Ming. His unprincipled adaptability to different circumstances uncannily legitimates dishonesty by affirming that survival imperatives trump all. Ironically, due to his sneaky survival tactics, Wei Xiaobao prevails in the mundane world by achieving high official positions, becoming extremely wealthy, and marrying seven beautiful women. According to the writer Liu Xinwu 劉心武 (1942–), Wei Xiaobao epitomizes the philosophy of survival (*huoming zhexue* 活命哲學) and the philosophy of pleasure (*xiangle zhexue* 享樂哲學) that many Chinese people embrace. Both philosophies lack metaphysical sublimation; they dwell on what Feng Youlan 馮友蘭 (1895–1990) describes as the state of nature and the state of utilitarianism but have no way to elevate the self into the state of morality and the state of the universe.[89] Lacking any moral yardstick, Wei Xiaobao has remarkable flexibility, maintaining a purely commercial and opportunistic mindset. For him, there is nothing that cannot be negotiated, no boundary that cannot be crossed, no can of worms that cannot be closed. Entrapped in the state of nature and the state of utilitarianism, no matter how absurd and muddled it is, he enjoys the shallow and vulgar happiness brought by material life. In essence, Jin Yong provides a burlesque of a national character who is always living in a profit-oriented and unprincipled way, putting on various masks whenever needed, with no interest in or ability of metaphysical contemplation, nor the grand ideal of nation and people.

In his political commentaries, Jin Yong idealistically propounds Thirdspace, through which he aims to strike dissonant notes to the historical context of binary struggle. Behind his promotion of negotiation and mediation between different forces, as well as his validation of "pragmatic rationality" rather than isms and concepts, is his profound concern with the affairs of the nation and people. During the Cultural Revolution, Jin Yong criticized those who were too idealistic, totally disregarding pragmatism and real-world concerns. But Wei Xiaobao exemplifies the opposite extreme, totally immersed in the real world to the extent that ideals and principles are nonexistent. In his previous novels, Jin Yong's ideal heroes personify different spiritual vistas of Thirdspace through various ways of self-cultivation and self-realization: Linghu Chong makes a great effort to strive for the right to be a hermit, embracing Zhuangzi's "free wandering"; Zhang Wuji is an incarnation of the tolerance that is extremely deficient in the bipolar conflicts; Xiao Feng's heroic sacrifice for the Han and Khitan people epitomizes the spirit of benevolence, which can be traced to Buddhism and Confucianism. In contrast, Wei Xiaobao is the falsified version of Thirdspace because he is simply void of any spiritual views and acknowledges only monetary value and carnal desire. It is no surprise that Jin Yong specifically notes in the afterword of *The Deer and the Cauldron*: "I strongly discourage modern teenagers from emulating Wei Xiaobao: he not only fails to oppose his mother's occupation as a prostitute, lacking proficiency in the Chinese language, engaging in bribery and corruption, exchanging people in the execution square, flouting the law, killing people and then using drugs to intoxicate their bodies, but also partakes in a series of consecutive marriages to seven different spouses."[90]

The image of Wei Xiaobao emphatically shows Jin Yong's intention of elucidating and ridiculing the absurdities of the oppositional dichotomy of reality in which individuals must wear several masks in order to survive. But in tandem, it reminds us of the pitfalls of the fallacious Thirdspace that sanctions unethical adaptability. As Wei Xiaobao becomes a fence-sitter, not committing to any political and moral standpoints—a burlesque of a certain Chinese character that is ubiquitous in officialdom—the Thirdspace embedded in this image reveals the peril of completely expelling the judgment of right and wrong that Lu Xun trenchantly criticized in his short story "Resurrecting the Dead" ("Qisi" 起死). As a result, Jin Yong's convoluted and paradoxical building of Thirdspace in his fictional world carries an allegorical criticism of both the social reality and the national character. While Wei Xiaobao's astute guile and ever-adapting nature skillfully undermines and satirizes the dualism, his deliberate lack of value judgment encapsulates the quandary of Thirdspace—the precarious prospect of devolving into the abyss of nihilistic relativism.

In general, although he writes popular martial arts novels, Jin Yong imbues this genre of fiction with extensive and rigorous cultural and spiritual meanings in reference to Thirdspace. On the one hand, he recognized the advantage of Thirdspace, symbolized by heroes such as Linghu Chong, Zhang Wuji, and Xiao Feng, who go beyond the dogmatism of the Manichaean mentality by embracing the spirit of Daoism, Buddhism, and Confucianism. On the other hand, he remained acutely aware of the contentious and problematic aspects of Thirdspace rendered by Wei Xiaobao, who forsakes moral and social obligations and spiritual commitments for personal gain. With an explicitly metaphorical quality, Jin Yong's martial arts novels delve deeply into the paradoxes and intricacies of Thirdspace, exploring its nature of openness and inclusiveness while also contemplating the potential pitfalls it may face in the real world.

CHAPTER IV

Liu Zaifu

Envisioning Variations of Thirdspace

My existence became peculiar: on the one hand, I was sundered from my Eastern mother's womb, and on the other, I did not coalesce into the relocated Western mother's womb. Thus, I was vacillating, wandering, drifting in the crevices between two mothers' bodies. Instead of being reincarnated into a singular new womb, my ethereal self was plunged into the desolate wilderness between two wombs. The originally deformed fetus had grown even stranger, and both thought and words are imbued with a whiff of the uncanny and wild grasses found in those crevices.

我便成了一種特殊的生命，既脫離了東方的母體，又未進入西方的母體，於是，就在兩個母體的隙縫之間徘徊、漂泊、遊蕩。"投胎"變成"投荒"，生命就在兩個母體之間的荒野地裡存活，本來就怪的胎兒變得更怪，思想與文字大約都帶著隙縫中的怪味與荒草味。[1]

Liu Zaifu, one of the prominent contemporary Chinese intellectuals, wrote the above words when he chose to go into exile in the United States after the Tiananmen Square movement in 1989 that marked China's tryst with freedom and democracy. Caught in an unexpected quandary—homeless, lonely, perpetually roaming in the expanse of wilderness between Chinese and Western cultures—he ridiculed himself as the "man of the gaps" (*xifeng ren* 隙縫人).² While he failed to completely immerse himself in Western culture overseas, he was unable to return to his home country and had to face the aporia saturated with melancholia and a solitary feeling. At a pivotal historical juncture, he had a strong desire to seek a space that could once again be his home, providing solace for his heart and nurturing his spiritual contemplation. Instead of plunging into despair, he solved this quandary by transmuting "the gaps" into the Thirdspace from which to secure a foothold in foreign lands. More importantly, he developed Thirdspace with very unique and salient multidimensional forms and meanings.

Before he had to flee China, Liu Zaifu was the director of the Institute of Literature at the Chinese Academy of Social Sciences and one of the most influential literary critics and elite intellectuals in the 1980s. He was very innovative and bold in launching new literary theories and organizing national cultural events that exerted enormous impact upon the so-called new literary era after the Cultural Revolution. Parallel to this process, he actively and enthusiastically engaged in social reform, which brought about a radical disjunction of culture and social structure distinct from the previous historical period enshrouded by revolutionary ideology. Therefore, it is not surprising that one of the broadest and most perceptive discussions of the literary and cultural discourse amid the "culture fever" in the 1980s was found in his works, such as *A Treatise of Character Composition* (*Xingge zuhelun* 性格組合論) and *On Literary Subjectivity* (*Lun wenxue zhutixing* 論文學主體性). Since his literary theory effectively opened ways for Chinese writers to experiment and thrive, his name is indelible in contemporary Chinese literary history. However, historical contingency—the unexpected political event on June 4, 1989—drove him out of his home country and forced him to embark on the floating odyssey that has continued ever since.

During the difficult time of his second life voyage, Liu Zaifu was invited by Leo Ou-fan Lee 李歐梵 (1939–) to be a Henry Luce Visiting Scholar at the University of Chicago from 1989 to 1991. Afterward, as he was still facing an uncertain future, he was approached by Liu Binyan 劉賓雁 (1925–2005) and Chen Yizi 陳一諮 (1940–2014), two famous Chinese intellectuals who were also thrust into exile and had become active figures in organizing the expatriate democratic community against the Chinese government. They were hoping Liu Zaifu would join them in building a solid counterforce to continue the democratic movement overseas. However, after careful consideration, Liu Zaifu firmly declined and chose to retreat to a personal space in order to concentrate on his own scholarship and literary creation. Whereas Chinese intellectuals are largely characterized by collectivism, being starkly divided into the loyal followers of the party and the rebellious counterforces, Liu refuses to join either side. He wrote, "After I entered middle age, I refused to be chained to any kind of chariot, be it labeled by the emperor or the people. All kinds of political groups were attached to the war chariots, which would only tie you to their goals and deprive you of your freedom."[3] Rendering his reflections in aphoristic remarks, he was keenly aware that modern Chinese intellectuals lacked a place to be unfettered by political control. At this moment, he formally proposed the concept of Thirdspace, which, in his definition, is "a personal space with sovereignty of thought or a space that endows the individual with the right of independent thinking."[4] Liu's uneasy choice of Thirdspace may be viewed as haphazard in light of the Confucian tradition that advocates positive participation in social undertakings. However, in the broader context of Chinese modernity, his choice reveals a more complex picture in which his fate is emblematic of many modern Chinese intellectuals who have very little space to themselves.

By reopening Liu Zaifu's first and second voyages in life, this chapter analyzes how he nurtured a vivid exploration of Thirdspace, which is suffused with cultural, philosophical, and literary connotations. Emanating from his insistent search for the Thirdspace is his strong intention to break away from dualism. Different from Zhang Dongsun, who attempted to disentangle himself from factionalism through the third route but instead was ensnared, Liu Zaifu has conceivably escaped political discourse. By consecrating a remarkable dedication to individual freedom, the wisdom of the middle way, and the ontology of mind/heart (*xinxing benti lun* 心性本體論), he has reconstructed Thirdspace revolving primarily around the aesthetic spirit, extending beyond a lived space determined by dogmatic dualism. However, his seemingly depoliticized stance in his life overseas cannot be stripped of its historical specificity, as it resulted from his previous political confrontations with the dominant ideology in China. Hence, his search for Thirdspace in diaspora has perpetually been a journey of self-discovery and self-salvation.

Reflection on Polarization

Before he went into exile in the United States, Liu Zaifu had already begun to challenge the authority of literary discourse ensconced in dualism in a multitude of ways. During the period of "high cultural fever," he published *A Treatise of Character Composition*, which not only stirred the literary field by criticizing the theory of reflection (*fanying lun* 反映論) and theory of typicality (*dianxing lun* 典型論) shaped by the Soviet literary theoretical model but also became a best-seller to readers who felt suffocated by the revolutionary ideology in the 1980s.

In this book, Liu Zaifu points out that in the realm of modern and contemporary Chinese literature and arts, there has been a tendency to prioritize political value and concepts over the aesthetic value of art. This approach has often led to neglect of the richness of character, giving rise to "the syndrome of anemia in terms of portraying fictional images and characters."[5] As a result of political value dominating aesthetic value, revolutionary literature can only produce completely beautified and godlike images, which embody hypocritical and grandiose concepts and ideologies, utterly lacking the complexity of human nature. In this way, literature has been transformed into theology or vulgar class sociology. Liu Zaifu discovers that revolutionary authors unanimously adopt "the law of the excluded middle" (*paizhong lü* 排中律) in portraying fictional characters who abide by political ideology. Such characters are shackled with an either/or mindset—being either class heroes or class enemies—which completely eliminates any neutral ground on which a subtle and complex subjectivity can be truthfully presented.

The character composition he initiated aims to transcend "the law of the excluded middle" and the either/or mindset. For Liu Zaifu, character composition is governed by multifaceted and contradictory elements with bipolar traits, perpetually partaking in a dynamic and dialectical process to reveal the innate complexity of human nature. "The profound significance of the dualist composition lies in the deep and inherent structure of character, which refers to contradictions and struggles of the inner world of human beings along with various convoluted feelings such as anxiety, perturbance, and agony incurred by such conflicts."[6] Firmly believing that "literature is the study of human beings" (*wenxue jiushi renxue* 文學就是人學), Liu Zaifu claims that the profundity and fathomlessness of interiority cannot be simply described by the concept of class struggle. He especially underscores the ambiguity, fissures, and contingency underpinning humanity's intricate nature, showing readers that the human world is imbued with infinite possibilities.

It is not difficult to detect that Liu Zaifu was influenced by Hegel's concept of "medium," a dialectical mode of thought through which contradiction and paradox turn out to be the tangible and conspicuous juncture to understand the world.[7] Following Hegel, Liu Zaifu discusses the interrelatedness between a variety of character elements and "a core character" (*xingge hexin* 性格核心) as well as the entangled intermediate zone between two extreme characters. However, he was too captivated by Hegel's dialectical theory that asserts "thesis-antithesis-synthesis,"[8] meaning that the conflicting elements of paradox only coexist temporarily in a transitional phase and are eventually resolved at the higher level as sublation through the process of negation. Therefore, Hegel's dialectic logic only briefly embraces and tolerates conflicting elements but eventually seeks unity, which is "comparable with Aristotle's 'either/or' logic."[9] In accordance with Hegel's dialectic logic, even if Liu Zaifu notices the ambiguity and contingency of characters as well as the interpenetration and dependence between the two competing sides, he still accentuates unification after multiple permutations and recombination.

After he entered his second life in exile, Liu Zaifu started to reflect upon his previous obsession with Hegel's dialectics. He wrote: "Although the entire book extensively discussed the antinomy and explicated that two opposing sides of character align with 'the law of sufficient reason' (*chongfen liyou lü* 充分理由律), I found myself reluctant to abandon the concept of uniformity of multiplicity (*zaduo guiyi* 雜多歸一)." He then overtly questioned whether he needed to discuss uniformity in his exploration of character composition, which emphasizes the coexistence of multifaceted, often bipolar elements within individuals. As he pointed out, "Hegel focuses on the concept of 'one,' while Kant grapples with the notion of 'two,' and contemporary philosophers are wrestling with the complexity of the 'manifold'; what kind of position should I consider in terms of character composition?"[10] In self-reflection, he precisely and honestly deliberated the limits of his previous literary theory of character composition. According to him, because he embraced Hegel's philosophy more than Kant's, being too deeply invested in Hegel's definition of the dialectic as "thesis-antithesis-synthesis," he did not give Fyodor Dostoyevsky, who never pursues "oppositions of unity," a very high evaluation in the 1980s. Only after he went overseas in 1989 did he realize the depth and profoundness of Dostoyevsky and start to embrace Mikhail Bakhtin's theory of dialogism or a polyphonic interplay of multiple voices. For instance, right after he left China, Liu Zaifu adopted Bakhtin's theory to delineate modern Chinese literary history, arguing that literature from the 1950s to the 1970s in mainland China was generally "in an era of monologue and on the way toward literary dogmatism and monopoly." The early 1980s saw the development of mainland Chinese literature begin to transform into a polyphonic mode with the emergence of heterogeneous writings.[11]

After advocating "roots-searching fiction," in which Chinese writers searched for their own cultural source, freeing themselves not only from political constraints but also from Western influence, Han Shaogong 韩少功 (1953–) wrote his celebrated novel *Dad, Dad, Dad* (*Ba ba ba* 爸爸爸). Soon after it was published, Liu Zaifu wrote a critical article, "On Bingzai" ("Lun Bingzai" 論丙崽), which was well-received in the literary field at that time. He considers the image of Bingzai, who can only utter two sounds—one is "Ba Ba Ba" and the other is "F-your mom"—as "a prototype of Chinese psychological malaise."[12] Following in the footsteps of Lu Xun, who employs the image of Ah Q to criticize the Chinese national character, Liu Zaifu's interpretation regards Bingzai's simple and dichotomous mindset as a significant metaphor for the Chinese either/or binary judgment. Such an extremely essentialized and meager way of thinking and spiritual trait not only represent the mindset of Bingzai's fellow villagers but also symbolize the whole Chinese national character and mentality: "Not only do we carry the shadow of Bingzai in us, we can even say that, judging from our mode of thinking, we have lived our lives in as simplistic and vulgar a way as Bingzai."[13] Liu Zaifu alludes to the problematic dichotomy of thinking and judgment in Chinese mentality during the revolutionary years. Not only did abundant literary works adulate the polarity of black versus white, good versus evil, and revolution versus antirevolution, but numerous people also acted, thought, and judged in a horrendously simplified, dualistic way. The political system was solely and arbitrarily centered around class struggle, underscored by the extreme concept of "either you die or I live." Liu Zaifu traced the either/or mindset represented by Bingzai back to Confucius's moral doctrine of "noble man versus little man" (*junzi yu xiaoren* 君子與小人) that has deeply pervaded the national psychology. He believed that once this kind of traditional moral indoctrination was incorporated with despotism and authoritarianism, it would be exceedingly detrimental to the Chinese national character.[14] Chinese people, similar to Bingzai, would never grow up, forever taking an oversimplified view of the world, unable to engender their own independent subjectivity and value judgment.

The Method of Antinomies in *Farewell to Revolution*

In 1995, Li Zehou and Liu Zaifu published *Farewell to Revolution* (*Gaobie geming* 告别革命), which is still prohibited from being published in mainland China yet has had tremendous influence in Hong Kong, where it was reprinted eight times, and overseas. In the preface, Liu Zaifu unwaveringly declares that "we are resolved to bid farewell to revolution, not only bid farewell to revolution from the leftists, but also bid farewell to revolution from the rightists."[15] He and Li Zehou were striving to undertake a comprehensive reflection upon the fundamental currents of thought that permeated the entire twentieth century. They advocate for a reevaluation of what they perceive as the detrimental tendencies of thought embedded in the modern Chinese mentality: violent revolution and class struggle, historical determinism, dialectical materialism, the political-ethical-religious trinity, the mindset of binary opposition, and the worship of ideology. Instead, they propose a series of new strategies: the essentialization of the economy, the coexistence and cooperation of multiple political forces, gradual reform, the opening of the public sphere, the differentiation of society and government, the antinomy of historical development, and the re-establishment of subjectivity.[16]

Conspicuously, Li Zehou and Liu Zaifu are determined to split from the revolutionary mindset and its violent ethos of "either you die or I live." *Farewell to Revolution* serves the explicit purpose of expressing their trenchant concerns about and reflections on a bygone era and its dominant political, cultural, philosophical, and literary discourses. When the political scientist Tsou Tang 鄒讜 (1918–1999) first read the book, he applauded its innovative way of thinking and its unique cultural and political insights and significance. In his article analyzing *Farewell to Revolution*, he incisively points out that the system of thought imbricated within this book starts from the concept of "antinomy" (*erlü beifan* 二律背反). This not only is its research methodology but also serves as a particular historical view and epistemology. Rather than the Hegelian dialectic in which one of the two extremes overwhelms the other, Li Zehou and Liu Zaifu favor the coexistence of opposites.[17] The purpose of their retrospection on the currents of thought in the twentieth century is to transcend the entrenched dualism and aspire toward a multifarious and coexistential way of thinking. According to Tsou Tang, the method of antinomy in *Farewell to Revolution* is undoubtedly derived from Kant's philosophy. To support his argument, he intentionally quotes a paragraph from Li Zehou's interpretation of Kant's concept of "antinomy," in which a nonlinear and nondeterministic understanding of cause and effect is evident.

> Causality is not entirely guided by linear and mechanical determinism. The intricate structure of a system has formed multifarious and reticulate causality, generating extremely vast numbers of possible selections, and each choice would influence the whole system and structure. Therefore, it is inadequate to view the holistic process as the ultimate result of mechanical determinism; instead one must pay enormous attention to contingencies and multiple viable choices.[18]

Tsou Tang highlighted the core philosophical thought of *Farewell to Revolution*, which aims to shatter the narrow-minded and one-dimensional vision of mechanical determinism and causality. Instead of the mindset of totalization that essentializes the dogmatic way of one force engulfing another, Liu Zaifu and Li Zehou pronounced that multiple and heterogeneous forces should rely on and relate to one another. As Liu Zaifu wrote, "Our [twentieth] century is loaded with antagonistic struggles between two sides, from which the way of survival and the way of thinking are rife with 'either you die or I live.' This century is coming to an end. It would be our nation's good fortune if this antagonistic way of two extremes could end with it."[19] Based on such reflection, Liu Zaifu and Li Zehou eschew the revolutionary ideology permeating Chinese politics that is readily aligned with negative values, such as despotism, dogmatic doctrine, the dismissal of different opinions, and the absence of neutral ground. Instead, they endorse slow-paced reform and constitutionalism that can be traced back to the political reform of Kang Youwei 康有為 (1858–1927) and Liang Qichao of the late Qing. Rather than employing violent and extreme means, political and social reform require a more tolerant, rational, subtle, and open attitude to deal with unresolved tensions. The authors capture the historical situation by creating a rational and dialogical public space to foster diversified political, philosophical, and cultural activities and abolish political hegemony.[20] Such a public space is precisely equivalent to Thirdspace, which ratifies an all-embracing plural existence of opposing views rather than the monist way of thinking.

Many topics discussed in *Farewell to Revolution* are tinged with Kant's concept of antinomy. For instance, Li Zehou's theory of the antinomy of historical process (*lishi xingcheng de erlü beifan* 歷史行程的二律背反) argues that history is always going forward with contradictions. There has continuously been a mutual implication between historicism and ethicism. The advent of historicity, which pursues progress by any means, whether good or bad, is always in tandem with the complexity of ethics, which asks for social justice and equality. These two contradictory and complementary propositions have been proved through reason and logic.[21] This inevitably recalls Zhang Taiyan's "dual evolution theory," which posits that on a moral level, the evolution of goodness and the evolution of evil occur alongside each other. As a result, the culmination of these simultaneous evolutions falls short of achieving the utopian ideals of perfection and absolute goodness.[22] Following the idea of antinomy, Liu Zaifu developed the idea of literary history as paradox, "containing multiple trends and multiple motifs, in which various ideologies and discourses converge and dialogue."[23] As a result, the rewriting of literary history he proposes should not be confined to a linear evolutionary framework; instead, it can embrace a circulatory and paradoxical approach that does not overly prioritize social reality.

Upon publication, *Farewell to Revolution* was simultaneously attacked by the radical democratic activists overseas and the leftists from the Chinese Academy of Social Sciences in mainland China, where Li Zehou and Liu Zaifu worked before their exile. The awkward situation in which this book was placed compactly refers to the predicament of Thirdspace in the Chinese political and cultural context and testifies to the urgency of transcending the binary logic. The criticisms by leftists from mainland China persist in the dichotomy of "revolution versus antirevolution" or "Marxism versus anti-Marxism," decrying Li Zehou and Liu Zaifu for plunging into the so-called historical nihilism. Democratic activists such as Liu Binyan and Hu Ping 胡平 (1947–) accused them of abandoning the critical spirit of Chinese intellectuals and their proposition of moving the intellectual role from the center to the margins of society as catering to the Communist Party.[24]

In *Farewell to Revolution*, Li Zehou recalls the discomfiting situation of being wedged between the government and the protesting students during and after the Tiananmen Square movement in 1989: "I vividly recall the letter we signed on May 14th, which was sharply criticized by students who labelled us weaklings aligning ourselves with the government. However, starting from June 4th, we encountered the government's severe accusations against us as supporters of the students, and they were mouthed more fervently."[25] When Li Zehou and Liu Zaifu were involved in the movement, they originally intended to mediate between the government and the student protestors. On May 15, the renowned journalist Dai Qing 戴晴 (1941–) summoned fourteen elite Chinese intellectuals, including Li Zehou and Liu Zaifu, trying to persuade the students to stop their hunger strike and requesting that the government meet the students' demands.[26] Such attempts at negotiation between the two sides ended in vain, and ironically, both Li Zehou and Liu Zaifu were then deeply embroiled in the movement and had to go into exile overseas. This gives evidence to the bewildering reality in which the elite intellectuals were caught in a dilemma of polarization, not only shunned by the government but also inhibited by the majority of resisters. Their tenuous predicament exhibits how difficult it was for Thirdspace to survive in the Chinese-speaking world, which was unable to contain and tolerate multiple and rational voices. Later, Liu Zaifu responded to both the leftists in mainland China and the opposition groups overseas at the same time, considering that the criticisms from both sides had some uncanny similarities: "Because they regard violent revolution as sublime and righteous from different stances and perspectives, of course they are infuriated." He continued to emphasize that not pandering to anyone is the essence of independent thinking. The greatest maxim of a thinker is to neither ingratiate authorities nor cater to the opposing side but only face the truth while speaking.[27]

Although Liu Binyan from the democratic activist group overseas was a very respected Chinese intellectual who audaciously fought the hegemonic power, he nevertheless did not understand the necessity of Thirdspace that Liu Zaifu and Li Zehou strove to construct and cultivate. Liu Binyan even denounced the spirit of rationality underpinning the trajectory of thought in *Farewell to Revolution*, charging that it is their deliberate veil for avoiding Chinese intellectuals' historical duties, turning away from criticizing social misery and injustice. One can quickly point out the shortcomings of Liu Binyan's observation. His invoking of lofty morality and responsibilities, traceable far back to Confucianism's designation of the *shi* class, fails to acknowledge the individual's free choice that is not grounded in the collective. More importantly, he neglects that the exploration of Thirdspace is as important as the "spiritual warrior" mentality ingrained in the thoughts of the majority of Chinese intellectuals. Liu Zaifu and Li Zehou cried out for "the ethics of multiple elements and coexistence"—a kind of Thirdspace that encourages neutralization between antagonistic powers, dialogues in the public sphere, harmonious competition, and the safeguarding of individual rights. This is exactly what was deficient in China of the twentieth century, tightly constrained by the mentality of class struggle, violent revolution, and collective consciousness. Therefore, the new pathway designated by Liu Zaifu and Li Zehou to diverge from the dichotomic mentality of the twenty-first century is very evocative and precious.

Thirdspace as a Political Survival Space

Although Homi Bhabha's theory of Thirdspace emerged in the 1990s, Liu Zaifu did not acknowledge it due to his distance from the English-language academic community.[28] Compared to Bhabha's "Thirdspace," assertively situated within the postcolonial context, Liu Zaifu's "thirding" speaks directly to the fate of modern Chinese intellectuals who have been perpetually constrained by an abundance of binaries such as revolution/antirevolution, self/collective, Marxism/anti-Marxism, leftist/rightist, materialism/idealism, modernity/tradition, and East/West for more than a century. Being profoundly preoccupied with the binary logic, modern Chinese intellectuals seldom have the luxury to think beyond the immediate impasse.

In "Searching for the Survival of Thirdspace" ("Xunzhao shengcun de disan kongjian" 尋找生存的第三空間), Liu Zaifu confessed that he had contemplated Thirdspace for a long time. In the article, he first gives a brief historical outline of the dilemma of Thirdspace and the third type of person in modern China. After the leftist ideology gradually dominated the mainstream literary field in the 1930s, Chinese writers and scholars were belittled if they chose Thirdspace, which encompasses the appeal of an individual voice as well as a multiplicity of perspectives. Even the towering cultural and literary figure Lu Xun vehemently assailed the "third type of person" in the 1930s, stripping Chinese intellectuals of Thirdspace in the name of national salvation. The situation deteriorated further during the Cultural Revolution. Individuals who abstained from taking sides in the conflict were stigmatized as part of the "school of wandering," subject to ridicule and condemnation. Interestingly, Liu Zaifu finds an analogy between Chinese intellectuals' predicament and that of Lu Junyi 盧俊義, a literary character from *Water Margin* (*Shuihu zhuan* 水滸傳), a famous gentleman belonging to neither the loyalists of the emperor and the court nor the rebels and bandits. For the lofty reason of "carrying out justice on behalf of heaven," the Liangshan heroic warriors extort him to join them against his own will. Lu Junyi's situation incarnates that most Chinese intellectuals are hijacked by high moral standards, bereft of individual freedom, and coerced into something not their own choice.[29] In his exile, Liu Zaifu no longer wanted to be beguiled by either the officials or the rebels but sought to build Thirdspace:

> The so-called Thirdspace is actually a "personal space." To put it more specifically, it was a surviving space beyond dualism for an individual's free activities during the confrontation of two political extremes within society. "The garden of one's own" that Zhou Zuoren excavated is exactly this kind of personal space. To respect human rights, one should primarily assure the legitimacy of this kind of private space and its noncoercive rights. Besides private space, Thirdspace also includes the kind of public space that instills individual freedom in the society, such as newspapers, journals, schools, churches, forums with value neutrality.[30]

In very resolute terms, Liu highlights the idea that Thirdspace serves to endorse the independence of the individual in the private space and value neutrality in the public space. His goal is to free both private and public spaces from the constraints of absolute rules about what an individual must do by reminding us how important it is to tolerate individuals' unforced choices and diversified voices. As Liu laments, the ancient Chinese intellectuals at least had the right to retreat to a reclusive life in order to preserve their individual dignity and freedom; after 1949, modern Chinese intellectuals were denied both secluded private space and rational public space to express their opinions without fear. The mindset of binary struggles is ubiquitous and overwhelming. By redefining Thirdspace, he prods us to rethink whether modern Chinese intellectuals must undertake social responsibility, be the spokesperson for any group, or epitomize high morality. According to him, after the end of the Cultural Revolution, the intellectual pursuit of freedom manifested as the quest for Thirdspace—an individual realm untainted by political interference.[31] However, during the past thirty years, although Thirdspace stealthily expanded, people did not realize its importance. Whether inside China or overseas, the majority of people still think intellectuals must wear certain political coats and align with certain political collectives. After his exile, when Liu Zaifu chose to maintain an independent and neutral position, transcending polarization, becoming neither the government's docile tool nor the counterforce's puppet, he received harsh criticism from both sides. He realized it was a daunting challenge to uphold Thirdspace within the absolute binary structure of society.

Ostensibly, the idea of Thirdspace that Liu Zaifu proposed not only is closely related to the Chinese recluse culture and literature that were obliterated during the Mao years but also conforms to the "negative freedom" that Isaiah Berlin defines. As Berlin emphasizes, "There ought to exist a certain minimum area of personal freedom which must on no account be violated; for if it is overstepped, the individual will find himself in an area too narrow for even that minimum development of his natural faculties which alone makes it possible to pursue, and even to conceive, the various ends which men hold good or right or sacred."[32] Drawing on the classical liberalism advocated by John Locke, Jeremy Bentham, John Stuart Mill, and Isaiah Berlin, Liu Zaifu, in fact, singles out the value of negative liberty in defense of a private life free of coercion by state and society. While "negative freedom" is a long-standing tradition in the West, it was extremely vulnerable in modern China. As the country was mired in the national crisis, individual rights had been relegated to oblivion ever since the revolutionary ideology dominated the cultural and literary field. Negative freedom existed, barely, in the Republican period but was largely relinquished after Mao's "Talks at the Yan'an Forum on Literature and Art" in 1942. Eventually, it was completely eradicated under the hegemonic control of the Communist Party after 1949.

Liu Zaifu comes to the realization that, while negative freedom faces the significant risk of being overlooked, there has been an excessive extolment of positive freedom among modern Chinese intellectuals. Amid the demands for national salvation, the positive freedom about which Berlin has certain reservations inevitably became the definitive truth in modern China. What has been largely ignored is Berlin's warning that the so-called positive self "may be inflated into some super-personal entity—a State, a class, a nation, or the march of history itself."[33] Unfortunately, this situation has prevailed among the cultural and literary circles in the post-May Fourth period. Consequently, Chinese intellectuals were usually designated for particular roles, such as the savior or reformer of the society, the spokesperson of the subordinate group that does not have a voice. Underlying this demand is the cultural psychology derived from Confucianism, which requires Chinese intellectuals to participate in political and social activities that have educational effects. In contrast, the reclusive culture associated with Daoism and Zhuangzi's "free and easy wandering," even if it provides an individual absolute freedom to engage in artistic creation, is largely demeaned and even equated to "Ah Q spirit."

Before his exile, Liu Zaifu continued in Lu Xun's footsteps to provide a general examination of traditional Chinese culture's pernicious impact on the national character. In his eyes, the spirit of Ah Q can be traced back to Zhuangzi and Chan Buddhism, which seek a hallucinatory spiritual escape from reality, by and large hindering the modern sense of self-realization.[34] However, after Liu Zaifu went into exile in the United States in 1989, he deeply reflected on his previous unquestioning embrace of Lu Xun's prejudice and intolerance of the reclusive spirit and pointed out that the ousting of negative freedom "in practice blocked up writers' free spiritual space."[35] Based on his own experience, he began to comprehend the cultural value and spirit of Zhuangzi and Chan Buddhism, which eventually laid the very foundation for his definition of Thirdspace and his independent aesthetic pursuit.

In addition, Liu Zaifu's proposal of Thirdspace provides another theoretical level to accentuate value neutrality, reminiscent of Yin Haiguang's colorless thought and Jin Yong's valorization of an absolutely impartial and nonpartisan position. As Liu points out, "The fundamental role of intellectuals should be impartial. Their distinctive expertise lies in undertaking spiritual creation from the position of value neutrality, offering constructive criticism of societal flaws and self-examination with a selfless attitude." However, in modern Chinese history, Chinese intellectuals had a very difficult time circumventing the intense conflicts between two opposing sides, such as the CCP versus the KMT, leftists versus rightists, revolution versus antirevolution. After the establishment of the new China in 1949, struggles emerged between the two classes and two routes. As a result, some intellectuals who belonged to the party happily indulged in the privilege, while other intellectuals were living in an everlastingly disquieting state and unable to maintain a neutral position.[36]

Liu Zaifu's call for Thirdspace with value neutrality indisputably resonates with Max Weber's famous concept of "Wertfreiheit" or "value-freedom."[37] Inspired by the impartiality of the scientific endeavor, Max Weber postulates Wertfreiheit as a general methodological sense of social science study. "By 'value-free' (Wertfrei), with the emphasis on free, Weber is referring to 'the reality of life that surrounds us.' 'Value-free' here means facing reality with an open countenance, unprotected by the soothing certainties of tradition or the optimism of modern ideas, clad with a thin armor of hope, carefully keeping a distance from all illusions and desires of the period, with its 'colorful medley of values' among the mass offerings of modernism." It is clear that Weber's application of the impartiality of scientific methodology to social facts is targeting the world "driven and torn by the antinomies of modernism."[38] However, Liu appropriates Weber's "value-freedom" to pointedly disrupt a persistent tension caused by two hostile forces that have been relentlessly hovering over the modern Chinese mindset. He emphasizes that Thirdspace is not only "a nonpartisan, nonaffiliated, and non-manipulative space" for people to survive in between hostile antagonisms but also an independent and unrestricted discursive platform that goes beyond the binary thinking paradigm.[39]

In particular, Liu Zaifu employs the image of Wei Xiaobao from Jin Yong's *The Deer and the Cauldron* to exemplify the awkward and distressing situation in which modern Chinese intellectuals were placed. Ensnared between the Kangxi Emperor and the anti-Qing forces, Wei Xiaobao is constantly living in a dilemma and has to rely on all kinds of cunning skills and schemes to survive, inevitably metamorphosing into a sleek, agile, and very alert political animal, wearing several masks simultaneously. Like Wei Xiaobao, who has no way of reconciling two opposing forces, Chinese intellectuals were constantly plunged into struggle and strife, completely lacking their own independent space. Their existential state hinged on the ultimate tension of class struggles, which usually boiled down to their loyalty to state, party, and people other than themselves.[40]

Essential here is Liu Zaifu's attempt to legitimize elbow room for Chinese intellectuals to turn away or escape from radical politics, ensuring other alternative possibilities and fostering the freedom of aesthetic and artistic creation. In his words, "although on the surface the reclusive literature and negative freedom are 'supple and nonbelligerent' (*rouhe wuzheng* 柔和無爭), they contain the intrinsic power to guard freedom and refuse the dark politics."[41] His exploration of Thirdspace, however, is emphatically related to the question of historical contextualization, and particularly "a serious discrepancy in demands between Eastern and Western cultures."[42] While in the West, unbridled individual freedom has caused another kind of social problem, it is still very difficult in China to affirm the essence of freedom, such as the value of individual subjectivity. Therefore, his concept of Thirdspace is intricately bound up with historical specificity, which ostensibly distinguishes it from the alternative space proposed by postmodern and postcolonial theories.

Unfortunately, the dream of individual freedom is still prohibited in the tyrannical and authoritarian society under Xi Jinping's regime. Liu sharply pointed out: "One of the most significant cultural lessons or, perhaps, the most severe error in cultural understanding of the twentieth century is the eradication of Thirdspace, which imposed simplistic and essentialized polarization upon people, such as black versus white, good versus evil, revolution versus counter-revolution." Due to such simplification, Chinese intellectuals have forsaken "value neutrality," abnegating the vision of a middle ground that transcends different factionalisms. Using "the situation of Linghu Chong" ("Linghu Chong chujing" 令狐沖處境) from Jin Yong's novel *The Smiling, Proud Wanderer* as an example to illustrate the typical situation of modern Chinese intellectuals, Liu Zaifu calls for the recognition of three fundamental rights: "the right of criticism, which pertains to the freedom of nonconformity and independence; second, the right of silence, which touches on the freedom of nondeclaration; and third, the right of wandering, which implies the freedom of nonparticipation." According to Liu, in Chinese cultural history, it was precisely the rights of silence and wandering that ignited remarkable creations like *Dream of the Red Chamber*, which stands as the pinnacle of the nation's culture and arts. The Thirdspace where intellectuals could survive, breathe, and create freely confirms the existence of these basic rights.[43]

The Thirdspace is emblematic of Liu Zaifu's persistent demands for tolerance, opening more paths for the individual, revolting against the orthodox stipulations of Chinese intellectuals. It allows individuals to choose a marginal position distinct from the center overshadowed by the party and the collective. It is just like his own personal choice in exile, floating from the center to the periphery, repudiating the delusion of being "the emperor's teacher" or a "tide player" (*nongchao er* 弄潮兒) of the era. In *Farewell to Revolution*, Liu Zaifu and Li Zehou intensely criticize the mentality of the traditional Chinese intellectuals—the *shi* class—which is to aspire to be "the emperor's teacher," yearning for an opportunity from above to contribute to nation-building. Such an illusion has ironically transformed the *shi* class into "the emperor's slaves," willing to be subjugated by the court. Not distancing themselves from the center of political authority, the *shi* class has to depend on the emperor's favor or join a political group, becoming the spokespersons of the dominant ideology, such as the royal doctrine or the moral doctrine. As a result, the *shi* class is usually deficient in the capability of self-reflection and constructive criticism of society. In Liu Zaifu's words,

"This kind of intellectuals can only be the representatives of the monism of political ideology; it is impossible for them to be the protectors of the multifarious structure of society." Without getting rid of this mentality of the *shi* class, there is no way to transition from the practice of "speaking for the saints and nobles" (*dai shengxian liyan* 代聖賢立言) to expressing one's own thoughts and opinions.[44]

Unlike Zhang Dongsun, who enthusiastically relegated the *shi* class to the significant role of the third persons to mediate between political authorities and the masses, Liu Zaifu confronted the issue that the crisis of the elite was exacerbated rather than alleviated in the socialist context. Under the despotic rule, the *shi* class was unprecedentedly deprived of its subjectivity and became intoxicated by tyrannical politics. Unyielding and confident as ever, Liu Zaifu asserts that an invaluable independent spirit can only be derived from marginal positions, such as Jia Baoyu's identity as "a person outside the threshold" (*kanwai ren* 檻外人) in *Dream of the Red Chamber*, defying the social responsibilities of the *shi* class. This position coincides with Edward Said's affirmation of the intellectual role as "the exile-immigrant, the expatriate, and the amateur" who is "speaking truth to power,"[45] and also echoes Leo Ou-fan Lee's espousal of the cultural meaning of the periphery.[46] Despite being a "man of the gaps" between Eastern and Western culture, Liu Zaifu viewed it as an advantageous zone, equivalent to Thirdspace, as it enabled him to stretch his worldview to a cosmopolitan extent.

The Wisdom of the Middle Way

Regarding Thirdspace as a discursive survival space for Chinese intellectuals, Liu Zaifu gives it very unique and salient multifarious forms:

> From "the doctrine of nonduality" of Chan Buddhism, I go forward to "the thirding" and "ten thousand" revealed by the *Tao Te Ching*, which is "one generates two, two generates three, three generates a myriad of things." This is to say, an infinite and fruitful myriad of things and substances are all derived from "the thirding." I regard three as the zone between two opposite poles and realize its vast, boundless breadth is ineffable. Therefore, I chose Thirdspace as a ground to stand on while overseas. In terms of politics, I do not stand at either extreme of left or right, but rather on the middle ground between two opposites. In

terms of morality, I do not worship either grand benevolence or grand wickedness, because neither is bona fide. Conversely, many people who are in between grand benevolence and grand wickedness, such as "the third type of person," are more genuine.[47]

Distinct from Western theorists of "the third space," Liu Zaifu invests it with political, philosophical, aesthetic, and moral dimensions. On the political level, Thirdspace is based on the middle ground between polar opposites, with a broad spirit of tolerance, not only allowing individuals to return to "their own garden" but also encouraging value-neutral civil society or public spheres of all kinds. On the philosophical level, Thirdspace is based on the wisdom of "the middle way" and the doctrine of nonduality in Chan Buddhism, bridging the truth of the transcendental world and the truth of the secular world, embracing both the otherworldly spirit and the diversity of human existence. On the literary level, Thirdspace is the haven where literature and art may truly thrive and gain genuine independence and freedom, where actual artistic and literary innovation can be cultivated, preventing any kind of political enslavement or commercial commodification. On the level of morality, it refers to the morally gray human characters in between the strict contours of great benevolence and great evil. In consequence, his worldview, which hinges on Thirdspace, appears to be far more inclusive and compassionate than slotting human beings into simple categories.

Liu Zaifu's concept of Thirdspace is firmly rooted in the foundational principles of Buddhist "Middle Way wisdom." Taking a retrospective look at the mindset of "one partitioned into two" (*yifen wei'er* 一分為二) and "unity of oppositions" (*duili tongyi* 對立统一) embedded in the Marxist ideology he used to believe in, he turned away to choose "the middle way," neutrality, and moderation that directly stem from Chinese religious and philosophical resources. Although advocating moderation and harmony, Li Zehou's ontology of *du* is firmly based on the mundane world in which pragmatic operation is adjusted to apt and applicable degrees, whereas Liu Zaifu's Thirdspace, profoundly influenced by the Middle Way, is prone to juxtapose the transcendental world and the realistic world. In other words, his passion for literature leads him to surmount Li Zehou's pragmatic rationality, employing a "double vision" that reflects upon both this shore and the other shore, the inner universe and the outer universe. In his autobiography, he describes himself as perpetually vacillating between materialism and idealism, sudden enlightenment and gradual enlightenment, theism and atheism.[48] For him, only the Middle Way, which encompasses both the ultimate truth and the mundane truth, can embody the spirit of benevolence. His interpretation amalgamates Western and Chinese wisdom: in a way, he interprets Kant's concept of "antinomy" as embracing both opposing sides, attributing to them sufficient reason; in another way, he is attentive to the fact that many ancient Chinese belief systems, from the *Book of Changes* to Confucianism, stress moderation, the mindset of "both/and," and the sense of appropriateness. Therefore, he is keenly aware of the importance of sustaining the Middle Way, which renders him immune to the partiality of any collective ideological or religious groups.[49]

Before his exile, Liu Zaifu did not totally distance himself from Marxist materialism, which deceptively simplifies the whole nation's philosophical mind, degrading idealism to a bourgeois or antirevolutionary ideology. But after he was thrown out of China, he started to realize the power of idealism, which galvanized him to build a spiritual home on his floating journey. However, he did not want to valorize one at the expense of the other. Instead, he shifted back and forth, regarding them as complementary without the presupposition that one represents the absolute truth.[50] As he entered his life in the United States, he transformed from embracing materialism to idealism simply because he needed to mobilize the power of the heart against the enormous pressure from the completely new and alienating environment. Later on, he and Li Zehou advocated "the philosophy of eating" (*chifan zhexue* 吃飯哲學), which sprang from a Marxist base and superstructure model, to replace the prevailing "struggle philosophy" in China. However, after the majority of Chinese people had been besieged by materialism and money-driven desire resulting from thirty years of economic reform, he again called for a return to the spiritual home through reinterpreting Chan Buddhism. Fluctuating between materialism and idealism, his adaptation of the Middle Way allows him to view both as concomitant and interdependent. In his comprehension of Chan Buddhism, he was captivated by Huineng's method, which represents the southern school's sudden enlightenment, but later, he also reckoned with the northern school's gradual enlightenment. For him, there is no need to uplift one and denigrate the other since both have ample reasons for existing. The Middle Way is also reflected in Liu Zaifu's wavering between theism and atheism. Unlike Li Zehou, who is a determined rationalist, completely denying the existence of God and other deities, Liu Zaifu regards God as an entity of heart and emotion.[51] Inspired by Kant's antinomy, he regards the existence of God as a paradox, which means the existence and nonexistence of God have apposite reasons to endorse and buttress each other.

Influenced by Nāgārjuna's *Fundamental Verses on the Middle Way* (*Zhonglun* 中論), which refrains from any extreme practices or perspectives, Liu Zaifu finds the middle path a powerful repellent of narrow-minded and essentialized positions. Accepting Nāgārjuna's two truths doctrine, he simultaneously endorses the conventional truth and the ultimate truth, taking account of not only the inherent quality of excellence registered in the mundane world but also the transcendental values that are often emblazoned in arts and literature. The Middle Way of Buddhism with which Liu Zaifu identifies is different from the moderation of Confucianism to which Li Zehou attributes the ontology of *du*. Although both regard neutralization as the purpose, moderation usually sacrifices some principles in order to compromise between opposites, whereas the Middle Way does not need to sacrifice any principle. That is to say, the Middle Way, which is derived from the Buddhist concept of "emptiness," allows one to transcend conflict by taking a position on "a higher spiritual level to observe the two sides, understanding the reasons for their conflict, seeing both with profound and benevolent eyes, and searching for possible consonance to link the two extremes."[52]

The Middle Way is deeply ingrained in Liu Zaifu's interpretation of *Dream of the Red Chamber*. He contends that there are two ways to "return home" (*huanxiang* 還鄉): one is epitomized by Lin Daiyu 林黛玉, who eventually goes back to heaven, as well as emptiness—the place of absolute freedom and idleness; the other is embodied by Qiaojie 巧姐, who returns to land—the original and solid source of life.[53] Obviously, the former refers to the transcendental truth that highlights a spiritual dimension of existence, and the latter alludes to the mundane truth with an emphasis on secular pursuits; both routes of returning home carry equally important philosophical connotations and significances. Moreover, making an effort to connect two-sided truths, Liu considers that two major female protagonists from *Dream of the Red Chamber*, Xue Baochai 薛寶釵 and Lin Daiyu, respectively represent the mundane truth and the transcendental truth, the Confucianist spirit and the Daoist spirit, constituting a complementary structure. Furthermore, he reveals that this great masterpiece of Chinese literature is loaded with profuse cultural significances that forge an essential link with the Middle Way. As he elaborates, "Cao Xueqin's famous lines 'truth becomes fiction when fiction is taken for truth. / Being becomes nonbeing when nonbeing is taken for being' 假作真來真亦假, 無為有處有還無 show that he adopts a Middle Way approach and is opposed to dualism." Taking a cue from Cao Xueqin's unique formulation of human character, he also notes that it is based on the model of avoiding both grand benevolence and grand wickedness, which paves the way for a deeper understanding of the complexity of human nature.[54]

The juxtaposition of the mundane truth with the transcendental truth can also be seen in Liu Zaifu's theory of "the subjectivity of literature." In discussing the subjectivity of writers in 1985, he described two different roles: "the realistic subject" and "the artistic subject." In reality, writers are inevitably constrained by the politicized status quo and encumbered by all kinds of stipulated social burdens. However, once they venture into the realm of artistic creation, their mundane role must give way to their genuine role, which allows them to immerse themselves in artistic creation with absolute spiritual freedom, going beyond their social engagement and political commitment. Different from Hu Feng's 胡風 (1902–1985) theory of "subjective initiative" (*zhuguan nengdongxing* 主觀能動性), which underlines the subject's embrace of the object in order to stimulate the subjective fighting spirit,[55] Liu Zaifu's theory emphasizes the subject's transcendental capacity to unshackle literature from the restrictions of worldly matters.

As the majority of modern and contemporary Chinese writers are obsessed with the mundane vision (*shisu shijiao* 世俗視角), exemplified by their persistent infatuation with the form of realism, Liu Zaifu vigorously augments the transcendental vision (*chaoyue shijiao* 超越視角). His literary theory aims to dissolve the deep-rooted ontology of monism, which drives people to cling to the either/or mindset. He finds that most modern and contemporary Chinese writers singularize the dimension of "nation, society, and history" but neglect the polyvalent dimensions, such as "nature, philosophy, and religion," in their literary representation.[56] In his coauthored book with Lin Gang 林崗 (1957–), *Sin and Literature* (*Zui yu wenxue* 罪與文學), he delves into the dimension of the soul, metaphysical reflection, and transcendent vision to surpass the criticism of social reality by which Chinese writers were so gripped. By opening up a whole new area of inquiry, Liu Zaifu's definition of sin differs from "secular sin" aligned with the visible and virtual law and punishment, but is associated with conscious responsibility (*liangzhi zeren* 良知責任). More specifically, it is "a sin without sin" (*wu zui zhi zui* 無罪之罪) committed by a person who is unconsciously and innately enclosed in the "structure of complicity" (*gongfan jiegou* 共犯結構) and seeks salvation through repentance. For instance, he states that one must have a consciousness of repentance even if he inadvertently takes part in a cataclysm such as the Cultural Revolution. As Tu Hang astutely points out, "Liu's repentance is always oriented toward the mundane world yet must find a transcendental horizon to assert itself above and beyond the secular realm." Creating "a quasi-theological path" combined with a Kantian moral principle, Liu Zaifu stages the inner conscience in between the moral responsibility of the mundane world and the spiritual salvation of religion as a way to interrogate the self and engage in soul-searching.[57] As a prelude to his envisaging of the aesthetic Thirdspace, the inner conscience formulates a spiritual court of law inside individual subjectivity to give rise to a transcendental vision much grander than the mundane vision bundled with utilitarianism and teleology. The transcendental vision illuminates Thirdspace, where variegated dimensions such as the natural and the human, the sensual and the rational, the otherworldly and the secular world, and the inner and the outer can coexist and dialogue; a neutral character between grand benevolence and grand wickedness becomes exceptionally fruitful; and a simplified moral judgment of right and wrong as well as a causal relation are doomed to be questioned.

The Aesthetic Thirdspace

In the realm of literature, Liu Zaifu distinctly postulates that only Thirdspace can shelter individualistic strains in artistic innovation. By positioning literature in Thirdspace, he has endowed it with wings—aesthetic transcendence—to freely soar above the limitations of the mundane world, transgressing the boundaries between reality and imagination, the sublime and the abject, the center and the margin. Literature, as he characterized it, should possess an expansive realm of imagination and offer a vista of the universe, thereby transcending the limitations of utilitarian reality. Moreover, he underscores that freedom usually exists in Thirdspace, but it depends on one's own epiphany and awakening.[58] To attain the freedom of speech and writing, a writer should avoid self-censorship or any kind of prerequisite from politics and religions. Drawing from traditional Chinese cultural resources such as Laozi, Zhuangzi, and Chan Buddhism, Liu Zaifu has produced the aesthetic Thirdspace as a spiritual haven for literati. It is saturated with multifarious symbolic meanings, extending beyond restrictions of factionalism, politics, causality, and morality. In the light of "purposiveness without a purpose" in Kant's *Critique of Judgment*,[59] Liu Zaifu recognizes that literature and art in one way resist any kind of utilitarian purpose and conceptual reduction and in another way suit the ultimate kindness and beauty as well as the essential purpose of human beings.[60]

Residing in the Thirdspace that is as infinite as the universe, literati and artists no longer need to be the instrument or spokesperson of any political ideology. Instead, they can explore the boundless literary world, incorporating the social space with the imaginary space, the outer world with the inner world. Only this kind of ideal Thirdspace can engender a state such as that of *Dream of the Red Chamber*—transcending not only the value judgment of good and evil from the mundane world but also the religious causality judgment and the epistemological judgment of right and wrong. It reaches "the state of ultimate artistic freedom of 'nonrealness and nonfalseness' (*wuzhen wujia* 無真無假), 'nongoodness nonevilness' (*wushan wu'e* 無善無惡), 'nonrightness nonwrongness' (*wushi wufei* 無是無非), 'nonreason nonresult' (*wuyin wuguo* 無因無果)."[61] In this Thirdspace, a writer should not judge his fictional characters either politically or morally but rather bear witness to complex and contested human nature with an all-embracing heart.

In addition, by surpassing the idea of "one partitioned into two" that was prevalent in Marxist-dominated modern China, Liu Zaifu reappropriates and refashions the Chan Buddhist "doctrine of nonduality." While analyzing the philosophical thought rooted in *Dream of the Red Chamber*, he paid special attention to Jia Baoyu's "heart of nondistinction" (*wu fenbie xin* 無分別心), which exemplifies "the doctrine of nonduality." He notices that Jia Baoyu innately disregards social hierarchy, class differences, and even the distinction between good and evil, treating every human being equally and sincerely, demonstrating a "life miracle of grandiose integration and harmony."[62] His heart of nondistinction is consonant with Laozi's philosophy of "good governance does not divide people into separate groups" (*dazhi buge* 大制不割), as well as Zhuangzi's transcendence of distinctions between opponents, subject and object, and life and death. Liu Zaifu even finds an analogy between Jia Baoyu and Siddhartha Gautama because both love and embrace all beings regardless of distinctions, manifesting the benevolent spirit of Buddhism. In his eyes, the difference between Jia Baoyu and the female protagonist Miaoyu 妙玉 is that the former has no heart of distinction, but the latter firmly upholds the hierarchical social standard and peculiarity; therefore, the former is profoundly benevolent but the latter has not yet gone beyond all the mundane rules and boundaries. According to

Liu Zaifu, "Benevolence comes from 'the doctrine of nonduality' instead of the mentality of dualism."[63] Therefore, adopting this approach, his aesthetic Thirdspace parallels the correlative cosmology, not only expanding infinitely but also reaching the state of the universe and the state of clarity (*chengming zhijing* 澄明之境) in which countless colors, gestures, models, and lives are interrelated.[64] Such a Thirdspace is closely associated with the grand view (*daguan shiye* 大觀視野) through which Liu Zaifu deciphers Cao Xueqin's transcendental worldview and perspective. "We can use a modern word to describe Cao Xueqin's grand view as a 'macrocosmic' view, a boundless view on the universe. He has what *The Diamond Sutra* (*Jingang jing* 金剛經) calls the 'divine eye' and the 'Buddha eye.'"[65] Just as "the Aleph" is the allegory of Soja's Thirdspace, the "grand view," "the divine eye," and "the Buddha eye" are the most vivid and powerful metaphors of Liu Zaifu's Thirdspace, with infinite space and time to encompass a myriad of beings and lives as well as multifarious cultures, feelings, and existences.

Li Zehou has grounded the ontology of *du* in the secular world, linking it closely with the pragmatic rationality of Confucianism, but Liu Zaifu intentionally centers his provocative Thirdspace around the ontology of the heart, through which to implement "aesthetic transcendence." The ontology of the heart dovetails with the allegory of Borges's "the Aleph"—the ineffable core that contains the infinite universe. As Liu Zaifu describes, "This inner universe is as vast as the outer universe, without boundaries and destinations."[66] Drawing inspiration from Lu Jiuyuan's 陸九淵 (1139–1193) saying, "my heart is the universe, and the universe is my heart" (*wuxin ji yuzhou, yuzhou ji wuxin* 吾心即宇宙，宇宙即吾心), Liu refers to the inclusive scope of time and space, attempting to go beyond the opposition between heart (*xin* 心) and material (*wu* 物).[67] There is no doubt that Liu Zaifu has created a quasi-religious system akin to Cai Yuanpei's 蔡元培 (1868–1940) idea of "replacing religion with aesthetics" (*meiyu dai zongjiao* 美育代宗教), with which Li Zehou also identifies. While Li Zehou's ontology of aesthetics must deal with "the reconciliation between spiritual cultivation and the rationalist ideal of enlightenment,"[68] Liu Zaifu's ontology of heart always points toward aesthetic transcendence beyond sociopolitical reality. Clearly, Liu was stimulated by traditional Chinese cultural resources, ranging from the absolute spiritual freedom of Zhuangzi to the original and unadorned heart of Laozi, the self-reflexive heart from *The Platform Sutra of the Sixth Patriarch* (*Liuzu tanjing* 六祖壇經), the true and unobsessed heart from *The Diamond Sutra*, the conscious heart from the school of the heart/

mind (*xinxue* 心學) of Confucianism embodied by Lu Jiuyuan of the Song dynasty and Wang Yangming of the Ming, and the poetic heart from *Dream of the Red Chamber*.[69] In other words, constructing the aesthetic Thirdspace is not for the purpose of national salvation or pursuing personal benefit and success in the mundane world but for the sake of establishing the heart (*lixin* 立心) for heaven and the earth as well as for the self.[70]

Why does Liu Zaifu make the ontology of the heart the most pronounced feature of his conceptualization of the aesthetic Thirdspace? The answer lies in his traumatic experience during the harsh and turbulent revolutionary years, the memory of which arises to his powerful reflection. In *History of My Heart*, which is barred from publication in China, Liu Zaifu copes with the fact that his heart was gradually contorted and torn asunder after the establishment of New China in 1949. During numerous political campaigns, there was a persistent propensity to shrivel the individual into a fanatical, heartless political animal. The centralized socialist government utilized all kinds of means to actualize "the nationalization of the heart" (*xinling guoyou hua* 心靈國有化), the term devised by Liu Zaifu to vividly describe that specific historical situation. Heralding a bright communist future for the people, the party requires an individual to "submit the heart to the Party" (*xiangdang jiaoxin* 向黨交心), "fight against selfishness and lambast revisionism within a flash of thought" (*dousi pixiu yishannian* 鬥私批修一閃念), "launch a revolution in the depths of our souls" (*linghun shenchu nao geming* 靈魂深處鬧革命). Through endless voluntary self-criticism and self-accusation, the individual no longer harbors a genuine and complete heart but is flattened into a political instrument. While Liu Zaifu witnessed renowned intellectuals being brutally persecuted and humiliated during the Cultural Revolution and had to shout slogans alongside the masses, he felt his heart was incarcerated by the ideological hegemony, being ripped apart by the dominant power.[71] The happiest thing for him since he chose exile is that he has recuperated his complete personality, heart, and soul.

While Liu Zaifu's ontology of heart is clearly a powerful response to the traumatic political history in China, it simultaneously launches a critique of the prevailing global myth of materialism. As the postmodern individual's heart has been tightly gripped by commodities and driven solely by desire and money, they have inevitably succumbed to objectification and instrumentalization. As early as 1908, Lu Xun in "On the One-Sidedness of Cultural Development" ("Wenhua pianzhi lun" 文化偏執論) sounded the alarm about the aberration of materialism brought by Western modernity.

He advocated to "cultivate spirit but downplay the material, promoting the individual but repelling the collective."[72] Echoing such a critique, Liu Zaifu detects that the problem of our current society is the obsession with "the world of materials" (*qi shijie* 器世界) and obliviousness to "the world of heart" (*xin shijie* 心世界); therefore, he feels impelled to address and restore the heart to the aesthetic Thirdspace.

Although his evocation of the heart provides a remedy for the particular historical situation in China, there is no doubt that Liu Zaifu's aesthetic Thirdspace is universally applicable. His definition of literature includes three core components—heart, aesthetic forms, and imagination—among which he regards heart as the first and most important. More specifically, he has defined literature as "the aesthetic form of the free spirit's existence" (*ziyou xinling de shenmei cunzai xingshi* 自由心靈的審美存在形式).[73] In such an aesthetically loaded arena, he has embarked on a journey to interpret the state of the heart of many selected literary products. In his famous interpretation of the four Chinese classics, "the heart of brutality" and "the heart of misogyny" of *Water Margin* and "the heart of scheming and trickery" of *Romance of the Three Kingdoms* represent "the gate of hell" and have a detrimental impact upon Chinese people. Since these two classics' poisonous influence still lingers in contemporary Chinese minds, Liu Zaifu treats them not only as literary products but also as a sedimented national psychology. In contrast, he highly appreciates "the heart of Buddha" and "the heart of benevolence" in *Dream of the Red Chamber* and "the childlike heart" and "the heart of freedom" of *Journey to the West*, which represent "the gate of paradise" and leave splendid cultural legacies that will continue to illuminate modern readers.[74]

Distinguished from "the 'first place' of China and 'second place' of the world of expatriates," David Der-wei Wang notes, Liu Zaifu's Thirdspace not only is "a virtual world of sorts that comes into shape in multiple conditions and forms" but also has provided an ideal space for Chinese intellectuals to both settle their physical bodies and strengthen their spirits.[75] Furthermore, Wang has astutely identified freedom and compassion as the two most significant attributes that underlie Liu's definition of "the literary heart": "If compassion means all-embracing acceptance of the other, freedom means total autonomy regardless of external interference."[76] These two attributes form a compelling dialectical relationship that values the transcendent quality of literature, surpassing the boundaries of political ideology and morality. As a result, the formulas of typology and realism disintegrate.

Indeed, if Gao Xingjian regards freedom as the first and most prominent value of literature, then Liu Zaifu has supplemented it with compassion, tolerance, and benevolence. In terms of freedom, Liu Zaifu not only endorses the positive freedom epitomized by Sun Wukong from *Journey to the West* but also underscores the negative freedom that respects the individual's uncoerced rights. While he strived to gain Zhuangzi's absolute spiritual freedom through self-awakening and self-enlightenment, he was also keenly aware of the dialectic relationship between freedom and restriction. For instance, in his interpretation, the relationship between Sun Wukong 孫悟空 and Xuanzang 玄奘 is exactly the relationship between freedom and restriction, which signifies the mutually dependent and mutually coexisting structure of the rights of freedom and social responsibility. Regarding compassion, Liu Zaifu is highly influenced by Zhuangzi's "On the Equality of Things" that eschews absolute and fixed views on right and wrong to transcend all kinds of differences and oppositions. By asserting the benevolent heart or the buddha heart, he advocates that writers should possess the heart of nondistinction when facing the discrepancies determined by social status, political ideology, and moral doctrines. With a "boundless heart of benevolence" (*ci wuliang xin* 慈無量心), "boundless heart of empathy" (*bei wuliang xin* 悲無量心), "boundless heart of love" (*ai wuliang xin* 愛無量心), the writer can fully understand the complexity of human nature.

Implementing Liu Zaifu's Thirdspace would definitely encounter substantial challenges at both the political and social levels, as it becomes constrained within the framework of Zhuangzi's concept of dependence (*youdai* 有待). This framework necessitates reliance on external factors such as governments, the public sphere, liberal groups, and social systems. However, on the literary and aesthetic level, it remains as liberated as Zhuangzi's concept of nondependence (*wudai* 無待), without relying on any outer forces. As a result, it has an infinite and absolute freedom that invites individuals' exuberant and innovative literary imagination and adventure. As long as writers are able to discover their enlightened inner self—reaching self-awareness, self-illumination, self-comprehension, self-transcendence—they can free themselves from political manacles and the material world and obtain tremendous happiness, freedom, and creativity.

Although all intended to surpass the bipolar logic, Liu Zaifu's concept of Thirdspace is different from that of Homi K. Bhabha and Edward Soja. First, by constituting Thirdspace, Liu Zaifu aimed his criticism at the historical and cultural reality in twentieth-century China, attempting to bypass the Marxist politicization of social life. Through Thirdspace, he initiated and reproduced a new kind of discursive space very different from spatial politics in the postcolonial context. Second, Liu Zaifu synthesized a variety of traditional Chinese principles with "the Kantian aesthetic autonomy of disinterestedness" in order to uphold independence of spirit and freedom of thought.[77] In particular, distinct from Western theorists of Thirdspace, Liu Zaifu has expanded the critical strategy of thirding to multifarious levels, aiming to criticize the despotic social environment in China that perpetuates and reinforces a rigid dichotomy of thinking. With specific Chinese historical problems in mind, he strived to inaugurate an encompassing cultural and aesthetic Thirdspace for Chinese intellectuals to dwell and prosper in.

Fragmentary Writing

Liu Zaifu is not only a distinguished literary theorist and critic but also a prolific writer who has produced a large amount of prose poetry, prose essays, miscellaneous essays, memoirs, letters, dialogues, and fragmentary writings.[78] He prefers to transgress the boundaries of different literary genres and styles, as is evident in his ten volumes of prose, *Drifting Notes* (*Piaoliu shouji* 漂流手記), in which he assiduously quests for a spiritual home during the floating journey. Among the multigenre creative writing forms that he has experimented with and adopted, fragmentary writing (*pianduan xiezuo* 片段寫作) stands out as a new and unique literary style, which can be considered an exemplary artistic embodiment of Thirdspace.

Although each piece of Liu Zaifu's fragmentary writing is short and independent, filled with luminous and exciting messages and floating between multifarious genres—essays, prose poetry, aphorism, and cultural criticism—it succinctly expresses the author's improvised thought without tending toward cause-and-effect logic. It is comparable to Walter Benjamin's notion of the "constellation" that breaks out of the dualism between noumena and phenomena. As stated in his *Origin of German Tragic Drama* (1925), "ideas are timeless constellations," and every idea "is a sun and is related to other ideas just as suns are related to each other."[79] With such "astronomical metaphors,"[80] Benjamin reveals that fragmentary writings are similar to constellations, with independent and mutual existence, gleaning the essence of truth. Benjamin's concept of constellations is indebted to the architectural historian Siegfried Giedion, who likened a historian developing their views to building a constellation from fragments "scattered" and "ceaselessly in change" like "stars across the firmament."[81] In tandem, Liu Zaifu's fragmentary writings exhibit an intermedia style incorporating different literary genres, and they are also like constellations in their aggregation of disparate ideas and inspirations. Employing this nonhierarchical and coalescent format, Liu Zaifu's fragmentary writing generates Thirdspace, reflecting Marshall McLuhan's description of the galaxy or a constellation as "a mosaic of perpetually interacting forms that have undergone kaleidoscopic transformation."[82] Every piece of fragmentary writing is a constellation related to an assortment of other constellations, containing an alternative model for understanding an inclusive and diverse universe of truth.

During his life in mainland China, Liu Zaifu started creating this new aphoristic and fragmentary style of writing in his book *Collection of Drizzles* (*Yusi ji* 雨絲集). After he embarked on his journey overseas, consciously and unconsciously he frequently chose this new style of writing, whose formal flexibility and dynamic perceptiveness fit perfectly with his exilic experience that shattered the previous vision of state, worldview, and academic system.[83] Short, irregular, and disconnected, these starlike pieces are in a mode of becoming, tallying intuitively with the thoughts that inspired them. Derived from the inner self's meditation, each piece stresses an eye of an article (*wenyan* 文眼), the heart of an article (*wenxin* 文心), or the core of a thought (*sixiang zhihe* 思想之核), expressed in a clear, straightforward, and unembellished style.

Liu Zaifu once described his fragmentary writing as a style of reflective words (*wuyu* 悟語). Such "reflective words" are similar to "a record of random thoughts" (*suixiang lu* 隨想錄) and prose poetry. However, they are not random and casual: reflective words are underlined by enlightened feeling and thought. Therefore, every piece of reflective words must contain some "awakening" (*jue* 覺) derived from "illuminating the heart and witnessing human nature" (*mingxin jianxing* 明心見性). According to Liu, a record of random thoughts is more akin to Wang Yangming's *Record of Practical Living* (*Chuanxi lu* 傳習錄), whereas reflective words are tantamount to Huineng's *The Platform Sutra of the Sixth Patriarch*. Compared with prose poetry, reflective words do not intentionally pursue rhetorical artifice and inner emotional rhythm but only follow thoughts and opinions. Of course, some reflective words with lyrical emotion also contain certain ornamentation. However, Liu underscores that "one must strictly maintain the proper standard and avoid letting overly decorative words overwhelm the essence, which would only leave an empty beautiful shell."[84]

Featuring a compilation of unsystematic thoughts that are given either poetic expression or metaphysical meditation, Liu Zaifu's fragmentary writing vacillates between, and sometimes even combines, the sensational and the rational, the lyrical and the contemplative. Most importantly, it bears witness to the Chan Buddhist methods of "sudden enlightenment" and "enlightening verification" (*wuzheng* 悟證), accentuating a moment of epiphany or a flash of thought, which is completely different from the conventional approach of logical argument and evidence. Enlightenment (*wu* 悟) is not only a method but also a destination; therefore, Liu Zaifu interprets it as such: "Once you are enlightened, you have become a buddha; if you are still bewildered, you belong to the masses" (*wu ji fo, mi ji zhong* 悟即佛，迷即眾).[85] The route he chooses is exactly the opposite of that of some Chinese intellectuals who regarded "joining the crowd as a moment of self-transcendence" during the revolutionary period.[86]

Taking recourse to Laozi's "returning back" in the *Tao Te Ching*, Liu Zaifu strives for a reverse effort of going back to infancy (*fugui yu ying'er* 復歸於嬰兒), going back to simplicity (*fugui yupu* 復歸於樸), and going back to the infinite (*fugui yu wuji* 復歸於無極). In accordance with such discursive directions, the language he espouses is also unembellished, pointing directly and clearly to the simple and unadorned heart. In addition, in light of Chan Buddhist master Huineng's "illuminating heart and witnessing human nature" and "passing from heart to heart," Liu Zaifu's fragmentary writing is ignited by spontaneous intuition about the nature of human existence, literature, the self, and many other topics. It unswervingly reaches the depths of thought that are hard to capture by the logical and systematic way of thinking. Since all the small pieces are dispersed in a plural and nebulous way, they automatically constitute a sense of fluidity. As he wrote, "Certainty is a form of despotism, and to nominate is an act of violence" (*queding shi yizhong zhuanzhi, mingming shi yizhong baoli* 確定是一種專制，命名是一種暴力).[87] He is up against a variety of fixed concepts and paradigms imposed by the dominant political ideology. In addition, he is suspicious that those theoretical concepts, along with systematic and totalistic approaches, however dazzling they may seem, are obstacles to accessing the truth. Therefore, lingering less in ornamental descriptions, lyrical sentiments, theoretical conceptualizations and arguments, or the process of parsing, his new writing style corresponds to what he phrases as "breaking through all the obsessions, maintaining a heart" (*po yiqie zhi, liu yike xin* 破一切執，留一顆心).[88] It attests to revealing the truth amid all the delusions in the secular world, entailed in *The Diamond*

Sutra and *The Platform Sutra of the Sixth Patriarch*. Ostensibly, the conventional ways of academic systematization belong to one kind of obsession he attempts to break through.[89]

The Swedish scholar Horace Engdahl points out that every piece of the lively and amiable fragments in such writing can be as refined as real life, sometimes even more beautiful than a regular and complete work. Opposing logic and systematic construction, fragmentary writing is like spirits wandering. On the surface, it seems disconnected and irregular, but the truth will be precisely engendered from numerous individual centers. For him, fragmentary writing is like a flying encyclopedia, creating the possibilities of different thoughts freely moving between different fields, and such roaming resembles a spiritual journey, taking the form of going back home.[90] Comparably, Liu Zaifu's fragmentary writing offers an innovative and distinctive way to cope with the far more complicated and speedy world we are currently facing. Buttressed by an eye or a heart of an article, his pieces with a core of thought are like torches irradiating the crowds submerged by the endless tide of digital information. By constructing a unfixed and shifting style, he is able to create enlightening pieces capable of expressing intuition based on self-reflective contemplation, delimiting the possibilities of meaning, and opening capacious transgressive space to surpass all kinds of differences, be they of class, race, nation, or culture.

Although Liu Zaifu has touched upon many diverse topics, there are two distinct trajectories embedded in his fragmentary writing: one looks internally at the exilic self, who was previously pulverized and traumatized by the dominant revolutionary ideology and thereby endeavors to collect pieces of enlightenment to rejuvenate a complete self; the other looks externally at the world, especially the Chinese mind/heart and cultural psychology that have been accumulated and underlined in the four famous Chinese classics. Emphasizing his exilic experience with an aspiration for freedom, Qiao Min points out that there is always an image of a wanderer hidden in Liu Zaifu's fragmentary writing. Such an image "not only responds to Jean-Jacques Rousseau's image of the walker, Andre Gide's image of the traveler, and Walter Benjamin's classical *flâneur* image in the era of high capitalism, but is intimately associated with Zhuangzi's 'wandering free and easy' and Zen's purest state in which one has 'no ground to stand on' (*wu lizu jing* 無立足境)."[91] Indeed, this new style of writing is extremely closely tied with Liu Zaifu's life in exile, in which he has obtained an absolute spiritual freedom that can no longer be fettered by political power and national boundaries.

Immersed in such joyful freedom, he needed a more emancipated and inclusive style that would grant him a certain power to fight against any kind of fixed and despotic naming and definitions.[92] "Without ground to stand on" in the secular world is parallel to "a heart is generated in the condition in which there is nowhere to reside" (*yingwu suozhu er sheng qi xin* 應無所住而生其心) from *The Diamond Sutra*.[93] Such a highly paradoxical nowhere-yet-everywhere state becomes an allegory of his spiritual roaming, which is suffused with a sense of enlightenment and euphoria rather than melancholia and sadness triggered by nostalgia for his home country. Exemplifying this state, the fragmentary writing that carries "a philosophical metaphor of free wandering and flowing" (*ziyou liudong de zhexue* 自由流動的哲學) becomes the perfect means for him to reflect on the plurality of the self, saving him from the void as he was physically ostracized from his original home.[94]

More innovatively, Liu Zaifu has expanded his fragmentary writing into the field of literary review and cultural criticism. In fact, he is the first person to bring the Chan method of "sudden enlightenment" into the field of cultural studies. By applying this new style of writing in cultural anthropology and cultural criticism, he emphasizes that his reading of *Dream of the Red Chamber*, *Journey to the West*, *Water Margin*, and *Romance of the Three Kingdoms* is "not conducted by the head but by life and the soul."[95] Correspondingly, his writing is not "a decoration outside of his body, but the necessity to sustain his life."[96] Gao Xingjian comments: "Unlike countless studies of *Dream of the Red Chamber* that employ the method of evidential research and analysis, *Reflections on Dream of the Red Chamber* [Liu Zaifu's work] uses the intuitive approach of Zen to get to the heart of the novel."[97]

In the field of Redology in mainland China, there are two popular branches of research: one is the school of comments (*lun* 論), represented by Wang Guowei's 王國維 (1877–1927) *Criticism on Dream of the Red Chamber* (*Hongloumeng pinglun* 紅樓夢評論); the other is the school of disputations (*bian* 辯), which includes analysis, annotation, evidential scholarship, and contextual collation.[98] Regarding the school of comments, although Wang Guowei made a groundbreaking effort, it was eventually contaminated by political ideology and concepts during Maoist rule. As for the school of disputations, especially with the focus on evidential research, it has thrived, trying to solve the historical puzzles surrounding the author Cao Xueqin and his family. Different from these two conventional ways of reading, Liu Zaifu adopts the way of intuitive reflection—"the method of Chan"—to transcend conceptuality, theory, evidential proof, and logical argumentation.

This is unprecedently experimental because no one has ever employed an intuitive approach as the basic and main reading method. However, such an approach has connected the past and the present, the literary texts and the self, breaking through the boundaries of literature, history, and philosophy. As he points out, "Instead of taking *Dream of the Red Chamber* as an object of scholarship, I treat it as an object of aesthetic appreciation, an object that inspires, in particular, reflections on life and spiritual exploration."[99] Such a method has created an infinitely expandable, ethereal, and mysterious third aesthetic space, granting him a true freedom of literary criticism. In terms of microscopic vision, he has uncovered the cultural archetype of *Dream of the Red Chamber*, as well as its close relationship with Confucianism, Daoism, Buddhism, and Chan Buddhism, and even its comparison with Western philosophies such as those of Schopenhauer, Nietzsche, Spinoza, Marx, Martin Heidegger, and Friedrich Hölderlin. From the macroscopic vision, he has produced many insightful analyses that are impossible to find in any systematic academic works. For instance, when he talks about Lin Daiyu's bodily fragrance, he interprets it as the fragrance of the soul, which cannot be verified by logical scholarship but is derived from his intuitive judgment.

Inadvertently, fragmentary writing is closely aligned with the rapidly changing society because it provides a multifaceted prism through which to look at the world. But for Liu Zaifu, it is primarily a means of self-salvation. The complex interplay between the broken heart resulting from historical trauma and the complete heart enlightened by self-reflection is infused in his fragmentary writing. What is more, his reflective reading of four famous Chinese classical novels contains a triad of spatiality: the historical-social space, the cultural space, and the transcendental space with an inspirational reinterpretation of the Chinese aesthetic spirit. On the surface, all the pieces of fragmentary writing look loose, random, and disconnected, but in fact, they are closely interlinked in a multidimensional model, constituting a sharp criticism of Chinese cultural psychology, character, and mind. While Liu Zaifu is engaging in dialogues with his internal plural selves—the Eastern self and the Western self, the old self and the new self—he simultaneously comes across all the different souls from the four Chinese classics. As a record of his spiritual awakening, his fragmentary writing is a flying stream of thoughts, a floating aura, and a way of self-salvation, delivering the humanistic spirit that has been lacking in modern society.

In regard to the literary form, Liu Zaifu's fragmentary writing has created a stylish divergence from established norms, traveling between manifold genres: prose poetry, literary criticism, and philosophical contemplation. Each piece is as inspirational as a Chan proverb and shows a kind of reading passing from heart to heart: "The so-called awakening is a moment when one's heart reaches a state of truth, encountering Buddha in the heart, joining with Buddha as one."[100] Lurking behind the Chan approach is a sense of suspicion of language itself, or an attempt to get free from "the prison-house of language."[101] As Liu Zaifu wrote, "Laozi's saying that 'Great music has the faintest notes' (*dayin xisheng* 大音希聲) is the ultimate inquiry of language.[102] The real outstanding voices are modest, humble, and even wordless. Chinese poetic verse—'at this moment soundless is better than sound'—is the truth, because the most beautiful music usually emerges in the transition of two notes. In an instant of silence, one can hear the resonance of thousands of voices."[103] Although Liu Zaifu's fragmentary writing is a kind of minor words (*weiyan* 微言), it successfully prompts us to see the world via the macroscopic vision and the Buddha eye, comprehending the ultimate meaning of life. It is literary criticism as well as a literary creation, belonging to a life of heart (*xinshengming* 心生命), a kind of liberated language and literary experiment.

In general, Liu Zaifu's fragmentary writing is a unique form epitomizing Thirdspace, in which the "man of the gaps" who was caught in between Western and Chinese culture has found a new literary practice and deliberation to fill the rupture. It allows him enormous freedom to vacillate, float, and create between the sensational and the rational, the lyrical and the pensive, escaping from any confinement of concepts, systems, paradigms, and ideologies. It is not only a way of "self-salvation" by "using the genuine words to fill the unfathomable abyss" but also an innovative literary creation that imbues the interstices and intervals between two cultures with a significant plurality of personal insights.[104] His fragmentary writing skillfully "grafts" (*jiajie* 嫁接) the quintessence of two cultures in the sense that "the Sixth Patriarch Huineng's thought can be grafted onto that of Jesus Christ and Kafka."[105] In addition, by initiating Chan's sudden epiphany in a modern way, he has freely traveled between various literary forms ranging from prose poetry to philosophical illumination to cultural commentaries. Fragmentary writing has thus constituted Thirdspace—a particular meaningful locale communicating between outer reality and the interiorized universe, transposing historical experiences into manifold subjective mental vistas equivalent to Gao Xingjian's Chan state, which has a mysterious power to pass messages from heart to heart, soul to soul.

CHAPTER V

Gao Xingjian

Transmedia Aesthetics of Thirdspace

In his poem "Wandering Mind and Metaphysical Thoughts" ("Youshen yu xuansi" 遊神與玄思), Gao Xingjian wrote:

Perhaps you could try to re-create
A weightless Nature
A Garden of Eden in your heart
A place where you could freely roam
And enjoy yourself to the full[1]

你不妨再造
一個失重的自然
心中的伊甸園
可以任你優遊
由你盡興

The purpose of Gao Xingjian's exile is to rebuild "a Garden of Eden" where he no longer is subjected to political, social, and commercial pressures and can be immersed in artistic creation. The most distinct characteristic of this ideal is freedom, which is analogous to Zhuangzi's absolute spiritual freedom. Gao Xingjian is clearly aware that the individual is restricted by a variety of regulations in daily life; therefore, "It is only in the realm of the purely spiritual that humankind can possess an abundance of freedom."[2] Because he understands that freedom resides internally rather than externally, his conceptualization of the Garden of Eden stands in contrast to the grand vision of a utopian nation that captivated and preoccupied many Chinese intellectuals. Instead, it is rooted solely in his own heart, intimately intertwined with the state of Chan. Taking advantage of his freedom after going into exile in Paris, his artistic and spiritual endeavors are thriving and successful. Few Chinese artists have extended their creative potential to so many fields: poetry, film, fiction, drama, painting, photography, and literary criticism. The garden of this polymath artist is unlimited, equivalent to a broad, infinite, and prolific Thirdspace that has crossed many boundaries, as manifested in his transnational, transcultural, transdisciplinary, and transmedia aesthetic activities.

Drawing on Homi Bhabha's and Edward Soja's theories of Thirdspace in combination with William Storm's idea of the tragic field as a "fabric connection" between characters, Letizia Fusini, in her book *Dionysus on the Other Shore: Gao Xingjian's Theatre of the Tragic*, coins the term "thirdspace tragedies" to describe Gao Xingjian's postexile plays.[3] In her definition, "These are tragedies that, by working between opposite polarities—Self and Other, cohesion and division, reality and imagination, antiquity and modernity—actually occur within a less visible thirdspace, a dynamic realm of potentialities akin to Hölderlinian caesura, that can be fully brought to the surface only through an *ad hoc* methodological exploration."[4] Fusini vividly delineates Gao Xingjian's dramatic space, in which the psychic energies between opposite polarities constitute a dynamic "polyphony of selves."[5] It is indubitably important that Fusini has discovered a Thirdspace in Gao Xingjian's "psychological field" with dialectical interchanges between the character's internal opposite selves. However, Gao Xingjian's Thirdspace is not limited to his postexile plays but rather permeates every aspect and genre of his artistic creation. Another scholar, Sau Ching Janet Shum, also applies Homi Bhabha's concept of Thirdspace to her study of Gao Xingjian's transnational identity and translations. Although her study frees Gao's work from the Eastern/Western dichotomy, it mainly focuses on transcultural and transnational identities.[6]

In fact, through carving out his personal path between Chinese and Western resources, Gao Xingjian has shown that the innovative Thirdspace has become one of his extraordinary and powerful modes of aesthetic representation. With strong personal imprints, the Thirdspace not only exists in Gao Xingjian's postexile plays and transnational and transcultural identities but also is intriguingly embedded in all the genres he has experimented with, including cine-poems, fiction, painting, poetry, dance, and photography. What needs to be further explored is why Gao Xingjian is so fascinated with "thirdings" and how he has created a unique, profound, and multifaceted Thirdspace full of imagination and poetics. His Thirdspace concentrates on artistic creativity, which is a vigorous reaction to the flat, utilitarian, monologic, and repetitive artistic products regulated by the ubiquitous political and commercial ideologies. In this chapter, I will first survey Gao Xingjian's thirding as expressed in different genres and then focus on discussing his three cine-poems—*Silhouette/Shadow*, *After the Flood*, and *Requiem for Beauty*—to review a number of interrelated themes and philosophical meditations that run through his poetic Thirdspace. Since the genre of cine-poems involves dynamic interrelations among a variety of media, such as poetry, photography, film, dance, and music, it intrinsically constitutes Thirdspace with emphasis on "intermediality" or "plurimediality,"[7] allowing innovative aesthetic meanings to emerge from the interaction and mutual influence of different art forms. In between the plural media, different independent artistic forms not only have their "self-reflexive" traits but also weave a mutually supplementary and dialogical relationship.[8] Gao's "plurimediality" generates a vista of heart (*xinjing* 心境), visualizing a milieu of ethereal emptiness (*kongling* 空靈), which evokes a creator/audience's poetic imagination and soul-searching while confronting the complexity of the world and the self. It conscientiously enhances the reciprocal communication among the author, audience, and performers, leaving plenty of room to prevent "the loss of aura" that Walter Benjamin foresaw in art during the age of mechanical techniques of reproduction.[9]

Thirding as an Alternative Aesthetics

Although Gao Xingjian has never formally brought up the concept of Thirdspace as Liu Zaifu did in the early 1990s, he clearly emphasizes "thirding" in his article "Freedom and Literature": "Laozi's one gives birth to two, two gives birth to three, and three gives birth to the myriad things is ancient wisdom that can act as a cooling elixir to help people escape the vicious circle of endless revolutions inherent in the negation of negation."[10] Parallel to Liu Zaifu, Gao Xingjian derives his idea of thirding from traditional Chinese resources rather than Western ones. Although both have been inspired by Laozi's "thirding regenerating the myriad things," the openness they embrace and recompose is consonant with Soja's Thirdspace "that invites further expansion and extension, beyond not just the binary but beyond the third term as well."[11] However, different from Soja's Thirdspace, which is based on Lefebvre's trialectics that link the perceived space, conceived space, and lived space dialectically, Gao Xingjian's thirding has its own perceptional structure centering around the inner world of self by conjuring up all kinds of new and alternative methods in his aesthetic practice. The thirding in his oeuvre highlights his commitment to expanding the horizons of his personal artistic imagination and creative output rather than solely focusing on cultural politics within the postcolonial context.

Since Liu Zaifu and Gao Xingjian are very close friends and belong to the same generation who experienced the Cultural Revolution, they were compelled to distinctly direct their criticism toward the prevailing either/or mindset indoctrinated in the revolutionary ideology. When Liu Zaifu analyzes Gao Xingjian's notion of freedom, he expounds on his thirding in this way:

> He [Gao Xingjian] consciously breaks away from the established philosophical model of binary oppositions and paradoxes, going from "two" to "three," from three to infinity. Enlightened by Laozi, the great Chinese philosopher, and Huineng, the prodigious Chan Buddhist thinker, he found that their thinking gave up binary opposites long ago and that they went from two, to "not two," to "three representing everything" and to all phenomena. Gao Xingjian's free state of mind challenges the "either/or" and "both" way of thinking. As a result, in painting he creates new visual images using a third possibility that is neither figurative nor abstract. In drama, he discovered a third possibility that is neither Stanislavski nor Brecht: by introducing his concept of tripartite performance and the neutral actor, he created a new form of drama. He also created a new form of novel that uses a form of narration that is neither character-driven nor plot-driven, and that replaces characters with personal pronouns and plot with psychological rhythms.[12]

According to Liu Zaifu, one of Gao Xingjian's significant discoveries is a broad third zone between two opposite poles from which all of his innovative literature and art forms are sprung.[13] In fact, Liu Zaifu and

Gao Xingjian have a lot in common in terms of drawing from traditional resources to define their thirdings. Both have a profound humanistic concern, regarding Thirdspace as a method to diverge from the compulsive revolutionary cycle inflicted upon the preponderant intellectual mentality of the twentieth century. However, they are different in two aspects: first, Liu focuses more on literary and cultural critique, while Gao accentuates art creation; second, Liu intends to have a dialogue with Chinese intellectuals who are still possessed by the arbitrary, dichotomous way of thinking, but Gao has palpably set his thirding in the context of contemporary art history all over the world. Different from Liu Zaifu, who lingered in his definition and redefinition of "home" during the early years of his exile, Gao Xingjian made an unwavering declaration right after he arrived in Paris in 1987 that he would never go back to his homeland where freedom of speech is not permitted.[14] Probably because of his resolute manifesto, his home country—China—has strictly banned all publication of his oeuvre. Even academic articles or books about Gao Xingjian are forbidden to be published in mainland China, especially under the Xi Jinping regime. Repeatedly refusing to be nostalgic about the "Chinese dream," Gao Xingjian has vigorously identified with the cosmopolitan position, embracing universal values (*pushi jiazhi* 普世價值) and considering his own work as purely an individual's voice. He has never again set foot in China and only visited Hong Kong to attend some cultural events. While Liu Zaifu's Thirdspace speaks unequivocally to modern Chinese history and reality, Gao Xingjian's thirding points more toward the worldwide art revolution of the twentieth century besieged with "antinomy and dialectics that are binary theories that simplify and stereotype things and questions."[15]

Since Gao Xingjian experienced the Mao years, dominated by a stifled mode of thinking full of divisions and opposites, he abhors seeing the same logic pervading the postmodern artistic field internationally. Relentlessly pursuing the so-called new, avant-garde, or one-linear progress, Western art history becomes entangled in an incessant cycle of artistic revolution, employing tactics reminiscent of political struggles. "When artists entered the battle of views on art, the aesthetic evaluation of artworks was replaced by the endless proclaiming of new concepts, and this, too, was a strategy."[16] Just as Zhang Dongsun is poignantly critical of Hegel's dialectics that nurture Marxist historical materialism, Gao Xingjian finds the template of the "negation of negation," which is derived from Hegel's philosophical concept of "sublation," particularly problematic.[17] During the revolutionary years, the "negation of negation" promoted a malicious cycle expressed by Lu Xun as "revolution, anti-revolution, revolution of revolution, revolution of anti-revolution, anti-revolution of revolution. . . ."[18] Lurking behind such a spiral and ceaseless negation is the historical determinism of Marxism, which is preferred by totalitarian regimes. Gao Xingjian calls into question the "either/or" dichotomous thinking pattern: "The numerous divisions and opposites—such as progressive and reactionary, revolutionary and anti-revolutionary, innovative and conservative—that came with the flood of twentieth-century ideologies were used as the prevalent mode of thought and even for making value judgements, and they profoundly interfere with people's thinking."[19] He not only compels us to rethink the conundrum of art revolution that is imprisoned in the analogous political logic of endless overthrow, as he mocked in *The Man Who Questions Death*, but also proposes the alternative path that is not bound to the "either/or" mindset.

According to the French philosophy scholar Jean-Pierre Zazader, Gao's attack on Hegel's sublation is adjacent to contemporary philosophy, such as that of Derrida and Gilles Deleuze, which incessantly confronts the totalitarian way of thinking. In addition to challenging "the totalizing power of Hegelian reason," Zazader points out, Gao pays attention to "an exteriority of the in-between, not only when he insists on the importance of the margins but also when he continues, concretely and consistently throughout his work, to go beyond all established categories and all oppositions."[20] It is true that Gao Xingjian's thirding coincides with that of theoretical thinkers, such as Derrida, Deleuze, Luce Irigaray, Emmanuel Levinas, Jean-François Lyotard, and Homi Bhabha, who regard the "in-between" as an important alternative path to the Hegelian synthesis.[21] Resisting predetermined totalization, Gao Xingjian's concept of "another kind of aesthetics" (*lingyizhong meixue* 另一種美學) is constructed in tune with the "in-between" path, challenging a bifurcation of experience such as object versus subject, the West versus China, the new versus the old. In his own words, "the medium between the two is impregnated with mechanisms for producing the myriad things. Freedom of thought is like this, too. Fresh thoughts often are born at the boundary between two things, and the long accumulated history of human culture is the continual discovery of new understanding on the foundation of predecessors. Literary and art creations are also like this."[22] By transgressing all boundaries and genres, Gao Xingjian goes even further, forging his own aesthetic space.

The "in-between" path gives rise to Thirdspace, in which Gao Xingjian draws special attention to the Chan state (or, in his own words, the Chan

Buddhist realm[23]) that is visibly and invisibly implanted in his fiction, drama, poetry, painting, and cine-poems. "Chan cannot be spoken of and once spoken of no longer exists; it can be comprehended only by direct perception."[24] The image of a frog appearing in the snow in *Soul Mountain* epitomizes the Chan Buddhist realm, which involves meditation, retrospection, and eventually enlightenment.[25] The importance of this all-powerful Thirdspace has, of course, strong Chan Buddhist connotations, blurring the demarcation between the aesthetic subject and the aesthetic object, the fictional and the real, the invisible and the visible. Aligning with the psychological process of aesthetics, it cultivates poetic meanings that are directly related to the soul, inviting both the artist and the person who appreciates the work to participate in seeing and listening, primarily to gaze and contemplate inwardly, allowing their perceptions of world, art, and self to intermingle and communicate.

Gao's Thirdspace stands as an effect of the openness of becoming, fostering polyphony, or multifaceted dimensions, against the causality stipulated by the ascertained, monologic, and static way of thinking. In other words, the vista of heart—the soul of Thirdspace—that Gao Xingjian attempts to amplify and reproduce in various artistic forms is directly linked to the poetic image of an individual consciousness. The variety of subjective, intersubjective, and trans-subjective consciousnesses is so unpredictable and heterogeneous that it inevitably contrasts with the logic of causality. In *Soul Mountain*, the protagonist contemplates: "Ways of sequencing, logic or karma, have been established by people in this vast unordered world in order to affirm oneself, so why shouldn't I invent my own sequencing, logic or karma? I can then take refuge in this way of sequencing, logic or karma, and be secure in my own actions and have peace of mind."[26] Instead of following the ready-made causality provided by other individuals, groups, the state, or society, Gao Xingjian takes the initiative to freely establish his personal and all-inclusive realm and order—his individual Garden of Eden. In fact, his own artistic creations are so intangible and complex that they never depend on a single and linear causality. In his postexile plays, he has developed a psychological field in opposition to "a consistent, linear plot featuring a logical sequence of cause and effect, dictated by the principle of possibilities."[27] In contrast to the prevailing realistic mode in modern Chinese fiction, drama, and painting that usually unfolds in a linear sequence following precise rules, Gao Xingjian's Thirdspace is imbued with variations and uncertainties, filled with a flux of consciousness and perception rather than a supposedly definitive logic and rationality. As he points out, "consciousness illuminates the chaos of the self and is not restricted by cause and effect, and at the same time both controls and directs a person's behavior."[28] In contrast to regulated causality, the philosophical message conveyed through his poetic imagery of the Chan state is aimed at dismantling the absolute truth proclaimed by those who are deluded by historical materialism. In doing so, it engenders greater artistic freedom by liberating creative expression from the shackles of Marxist material determinism, which asserts that individual actions are ultimately dictated by the underlying material conditions in which they exist.

The Poetics of Gao Xingjian's Thirdspace

Before delving into Gao Xingjian's cine-poem form, which hybridizes poetry, cinema, painting, dance, music, and photography, we need to take a closer look at how he instigates the thirding in each art genre he has experimented with. In his fictional writing, thirding is demonstrated in the shifting among tripronouns—*I, you, he*—which discloses an ephemeral and multidimensional mental landscape. In this narrative structure, the self is no longer a single and unchanging entity but rather an unfathomable and fluctuating plurality, always in a fluid, continuous consciousness. According to Gao Xingjian, the tripronoun narrative structure, which replaces the conventional narratology that emphasizes story, plot, and character, represents the same character, enlarging and complicating the inner space of the self. As the first-person pronoun *I* designates a fictional character/narrator, the second-person pronoun *you* is "the external projection of the narrator's ego," functioning "as adversary when the narrator engages in interior monologue," and the third-person pronoun *he* refers to the same fictional character but "becomes the object that *I* is considering."[29] Such a complicated narrative designation constitutes what Jessica Yeung defines as a "tripartite reality structure" in *Soul Mountain*: in the first-level reality, *I*, the authorial self, travels along the Yangtze River region; in the second-level reality, *you* indulges in imagination, memories, and dreams prompted by what *I* experiences in the external world; and in the third-level reality, *he* performs "on the meta-narrative level."[30] These three realities construct an interrelated social space, mental space, and metafictional space.

Here, I would like to go one step further, unraveling profound and intricate layers of meanings intricately woven into Gao Xingjian's poetic

Thirdspace by adumbrating his trispatialities of self-consciousness as the outer universe, the inner universe,[31] and the Chan state. The first space is the outer universe experienced and perceived by the self. It refers to the real, visible, concrete material world that exists outside human beings, including social space, political space, national space, cultural space, and natural space. For instance, when dealing with the real space, Gao Xingjian intentionally sets it on the periphery of the political center in *Soul Mountain*. Traveling in the Yangtze region in southwestern China, within the marginal culture that stands counter to the hegemonic culture of the Yellow River region suffused with Confucianism, the protagonist roams into primeval forests, non-Han ethnic minority territory, and Buddhist or Daoist temples. The second space is the inner universe, the dynamic psychological field, in which the multiple dimensions of self actively interact and dialogue with one another. It overflows with consciousness and unconsciousness, dreams and memories, feelings and desires. Gao Xingjian displays the contradictions and struggles, pains and agonies of the inner universe on the stage as well as within fiction, poetry, films, and ink paintings. The third space is a Chan state that transcends the dichotomy between the outer universe and the inner universe, enabling one to observe both the world and the self from a detached perspective. By doing so, it allows individuals to avoid the quandaries of the political and social world as well as the chaos of the inner psyche. The configuration of the Chan state paves the way for the plurality of self to engage in comprehensive observation and contemplation. It has transformed into a site wherein the self can experience moments of sudden enlightenment or profound epiphany. Within the unique nexus of trispatialities, not only are the self's multifarious psychological layers revealed, but the self is also endowed with a reflexive attribute and looks back at himself/herself from a distance. Moreover, the Chan state also invites and conjures readers' resonance with, interpretation of, and reflections on the novel based on their own personal experiences and emotions.

What is striking about Gao Xingjian's thirding is that it is also highly traceable in his other artistic forms. In Gao Xingjian's poem "Wandering Mind and Metaphysical Thoughts," the pronoun *you* actually stands for three subjective spaces. The first is represented by the authorial self, who has just attained his freedom by leaving his home country. Although fully enjoying spiritual sovereignty as a wanderer all over the world, he is as fragile as "a blade of grass between rocks, surprisingly surviving repeated trampling,"[32] and has to face disease and death like every normal person. The second subjective space implies another inner self that constantly engages in dialogue with the authorial self and even has a conference with God and the devil. In other words, both God and the devil simultaneously exist in the complicated inner mind. This shows the contradictory and riven facets of the self, such as heaviness versus lightness, narrow-mindedness versus magnanimity, and restlessness versus calm. The third subjective space is crystallized by "a big mass of consciousness" that is "clear and limpid,"[33] or "an eye which has no tears," tranquilly gazing at oneself.[34] This Thirdspace, provoked by acute aesthetic sense, points directly to a Chan-esque vista gained through reexamining oneself and banishing all delusions:

> You
> You exist if you say so
> You don't exist if you don't
> You transcend the transience of life
>
> You
> You have no birth and no death
> You have neither life nor extinction
>
> You
> You are the light that can't be seen
> The voice that can't be heard
> You could be far or near
> Close by or at infinity-and-beyond[35]

> 你
> 說有便有
> 說無便無
> 超越生命的短暫
>
> 你
> 無生無死
> 不生不滅
>
> 你
> 看不見的光
> 聽不見的聲音

可近可遠
咫尺到無限

By entering the Chan state, the self transforms into an exalted individual estranged from the physical and material world, independent and free from all restraints. Comparable to Zhuangzi's liberated realm of spiritual euphoria, the frame of time and space in the Chan state is infinite, allowing *you* to immerse his spirit in the eternal cosmic order, transcending the boundaries of life and death, being and nonbeing, distance and proximity. As a result, *you* has been transmuted into "the invisible light" and "the inaudible voice," amalgamating into the universe. This indicates that the spirit of liberty is infinite, and all the differences can be encompassed in the all-pervasive Thirdspace endowed with the Dao.

The paintings of Gao Xingjian are defined by Daniel Bergez as the visualization of the soul. "In a kind of hand-to-hand combat that paradoxically remains meditative, Gao Xingjian constructs from inner images a homogeneous yet varied universe that remains completely open to the viewer's interpretation."[36] Gao emphatically declares that his water-and-ink paintings explore a middle ground between figurative and abstract, evoking visual images of the inner mind. Rather than viewing figurative and abstract as opposites, he prefers to discover a Thirdspace, wherein he either melds the two qualities or forges a unique path that lies between them.[37] This is akin to traditional Chinese suggestive (*xieyi* 寫意) paintings, which seek expressive aesthetics and vista of spirit in contrast to the mimetic realism of realistic (*xieshi* 寫實) paintings. It also bears a similarity to Western abstract paintings but never completely abandons images. Instead of being confined by a specific historical reality, Gao Xingjian's paintings embody a concept of "omniscient Chan" and explore the intangible and fluctuating nature of time and space that emerges from the depths of the heart. As he points out, "Space and time in art are in the mind of the artist, and this psychological space and time have endless changes."[38] In order to forge a vista of heart or "inner landscape,"[39] his consciousness of time and space is directly linked to the painter's inner eye, employing traditional Chinese paintings' "multiple scattered perspectives" rather than the single and "consistent perspective" of Western painting.[40] In this way, both space and time follow a fluid state of mind, representing an internalized sense of cosmology. It enacts a mythical and active interaction among the painter, the artwork, and the person who appreciates it, leaving a large blank space for the seer's perceptions and interpretations.

In his theatrical world, if the first space signifies the performance's stage and the second space indicates the audience's place, then Gao Xingjian is attempting to construct Thirdspace, a psychological space for free and vibrant interaction between the performers and the audience.[41] It is exactly in this Chan-esque Thirdspace that the idea of *xieyi* drama, originating from Huang Zuolin's 黃佐臨 (1906–1994) theatrical theory in opposition to the conventional idea of *xieshi* drama, can be realized. It is also in this highly fluid and arcane Thirdspace that Gao Xingjian could implement his theory of total theater that highlights suppositionality (*jiadingxing* 假定性), facilitating both a performer's intuitive spontaneity and the audience's liberated imagination. In his postexile plays, Gao Xingjian's strategy of "tripartition of performance" and the neutral actor amounts to the tripronoun narratology. As he explicates, "The tripartite nature of performance—from self to neutral actor status to character—coalesces as three pronouns because these three pronouns are constructed on three levels of human consciousness."[42] In contrast to Stanislavsky's system that suggests the actor should be completely immersed in the character, Gao Xingjian's approach of the neutral actor has created a middle ground between the actor's everyday self and the role he plays. On such middle ground, "the consciousness of self is refined into a third eye or, in other words, is the lucid observation of one's own body." This third eye is simultaneously a "neutral eye," with a sense of detachment from the self, establishing a distance from which to see inwardly without a narcissistic complex. Through this kind of "detached-from-self observation," the actor observes both the everyday self and the performing self, gaining enormous freedom to create a dialogue between the onstage performance and offstage spectatorship.[43] In line with the Buddhist concept of nonattachment, as Gilbert Fong and Shelby Chan argue, "the actor is no longer 'attached' to the 'I' consciousness"; instead, he extricates himself from the bondage, predicament, and trap of self-obsession to obtain unbounded freedom.[44]

Gao Xingjian's most innovative aesthetic creation lies in the Chan-esque Thirdspace, which is both crystallized and illuminated by the third eye. In Gao Xingjian's theory in "Another Kind of Aesthetics," the painter's visual perception includes three layers of self-consciousness: *I* is observing the external world, *you* is scrutinizing *I*, and *he* has a third eye simultaneously looking at *I* and *you*.[45] With a sense of detachment, the third eye calmly observes the subject's perceptions of the external and inner worlds, neither making moral judgments nor indulging in the narcissistic, chaotic, and struggling state of the self. Gao Xingjian's third eye reminds us of the French philosopher Maurice Merleau-Ponty's "the third eye," which, in his famous essay "Eye and Mind," denotes "a gaze from the inside," seeing "the pictures and even the mental images." It is like a "third ear" that receives "messages from the outside through the noises they caused inside us."[46] Intertwining art and perception, Merleau-Ponty's notion of the third eye has a double vision—a painter's view of the landscape and the inner vision that arises from the painter's contact with the landscape—that creates a reflective condition for the artist's consciousness to emerge. Apparently, both Gao Xingjian and Merleau-Ponty emphasize an inner vision that crosses the boundaries of the gazer and the visible, subject and object, attempting to awaken a sense of reflexivity, "turning inward" or looking back at both the gazer and the visible.[47] However, Gao Xingjian puts more effort into the purification of the self through introspection, which is directly associated with the Chan Buddhist concept of observation (*guan* 觀). In other words, observation creates a certain distance between the multiple selves, constituting a Chan state or a Chan Buddhist realm from which a higher spiritual fulfillment—self-illumination, self-awakening, and self-enlightenment—can be actualized. In other words, it transforms the self's complicated and unreconciled impulses and desires into a high level of spirituality.[48] As Gao Xingjian puts it, "Perception can transform into enlightenment, thought can be sublimated into the spiritual, and conscious observation and contemplation of existence do not lead only to religion but can also lead to aesthetics."[49] High spirituality in relation to aesthetics, in Gao Xingjian's view, is an elevated state achieved by purifying the self from impulses and attachments in order to embrace pristine experience.

Inspired by Merleau-Ponty's theory on the visual medium, Wu Shengqing proposes the notion of "the lyrical eye and mind" to delineate early twentieth-century Chinese visual culture. The lyrical eye fuses the self and world, the subject and object, in contrast to the dualistic Cartesian perspectivism that separates body and mind.[50] Although Gao Xingjian's third eye is comparable to "the lyrical eye and mind" in terms of focusing on the subject's inner perspective, it adds another layer—a sense of detachment from the self and a distancing from the mundane world. In contrast to "the subject's sensorial response to both the inner and outer world,"[51] Gao Xingjian's third eye is more inclined to perception than sensory vibrations, having the propensity to cool down rather than enact feelings while engaging in calm observation. It expels entangling emotions and narcissistic egos because it is preconditioned on Tao Yuanming's "pure-hearted person" (*suxin ren* 素心人), whose poetic ingenuity originates in a withdrawal from the mundane world.[52]

In the Buddhist and Daoist meditation tradition, *guan* plays a pivotal role in helping the self reach a state of purification and attainment.[53] Similarly, the starting point of silent observation (*jingguan* 靜觀) is derived from emptiness (*kong* 空), which denotes that one is temporarily detached from all worldly affairs in order to obtain inner freedom.[54] The distance of observation and the realization of emptiness allow Gao Xingjian to create the vista of art (*yijing* 藝境) or, more precisely, the Chan state. In his article "The Position of Writer," Gao Xingjian writes: "The writer uses a third eye that overrides the self, and it can be called an intelligent eye. In other words, it is awareness, a form of lucid cognition. It is of course subjective, but it does possess an aesthetic filter."[55] Through visualization and meditation, this wisdom eye is exactly like an inner light radiating the various and complicated phenomena of reality, allowing the self to comprehend the real and unreal of the Buddha in the heart. For Gao Xingjian, emptiness in art does not signify nothing; instead, it is "the spirit that illuminates the artwork and presents an inner mind state that is experienced by the artist."[56] As he further illustrates, "Emptiness is within the painting and outside it, and it is both an explanation and a spiritual state."[57] The concept of emptiness in art enables him to visualize the infinity of the spiritual world, comprehending the sense of ubiquitous Chan hidden in myriad phenomena.

This dispassionate attitude positions writers and artists on the periphery of society, refusing to be strangled by state affairs or social responsibilities. In contrast to the majority of modern Chinese writers, who are so "obsessed with China,"[58] Gao Xingjian firmly extracts himself from worldly concerns, defining his own writings as "cold literature": "This sort of literature that has recovered its innate character can be called cold literature to differentiate it from literature that promotes a teaching, attacks contemporary politics, is involved with changing society or gives vent to one's feelings and ambitions."[59] Linked to the notion of "no-ism" (*meiyou zhuyi* 沒有主義),[60] which demands the minimum right for individuals to be free from enslavement to any particular ideology, cold literature emphasizes adopting a serene perspective and taking a marginal position that is detached from the complexities of social reality. Both no-ism and cold literature are prerequisites for the vista of ethereal emptiness that Gao Xingjian intends to create in his manifold artistic and literary forms. Before producing the vista (*zaojing* 造境), an artist needs certain psychological preparations. The gesture of standing solitary and alone without passing any moral judgment of good and evil makes Gao Xingjian's vista of *kongling* possible. Excavating Thirdspace in fiction, poetry, plays, paintings, or films, Gao Xingjian has successfully bestowed it with spirit and aesthetics, making it a typical "space of spirit" (*lingde kongjian* 靈的空間) that encompasses myriad phenomena of the inner landscape.[61]

Silhouette/Shadow: The Vista of Ethereal Emptiness

Gao Xingjian's first cine-poem, *Silhouette/Shadow*, is about a poetics of inner space in which thirding in his tripartite film theory is exemplified. As he defines, "By isolating audio-language from the concept of audiovisual, one creates a third important component for film. What I call a tripartite film refers to the picture, sounds, and language, each having independence and autonomy, but each complements, combines with, and contrasts with the others to produce new meanings." The most prominent feature is that Gao Xingjian has incorporated literary sensibility (*wenxue xing* 文學性) into the filmic world by adding the third component—language. According to him, "Words and phrases are conceptual: they involve a thought process and are therefore abstractions." By inserting language into "the usual two-element composition of picture and sound in films," he attempts to arouse viewers' conscious and reflective mind, inviting them to participate in aesthetic meditation and philosophical thinking.[62] In contrast, popular films that pursue commercial value normally focus on telling an intricate and captivating story with a distinct narrative, accentuating shocking effects in order to mesmerize the audience. While watching a popular film with the logic of linear narrative, viewers' attention is ensnared by external cause and effect, as they indulge in the pleasure of entertainment without the need to contemplate. Gao Xingjian's cine-poem moves in another direction by defying the causality that is largely privileged by commercial films. He intends to locate his art film further from the spectators' horizon of expectations, making it more unfamiliar and challenging to decipher yet, at the same time, indelibly rich and intriguing. It is not for the purpose of entertainment but instead to provoke viewers' aesthetic appreciation and comprehension. By encapsulating the distinctive feature of a fluid consciousness, which is displayed through poetic images, experimental music and sound, and even real poetry, he has created a special filmic language that equates to "a commitment of the soul,"[63] demonstrating that space can be spiritual. It induces free thinking that is unfettered by exterior causality.

It is evident that Gao Xingjian prefers to navigate between different media. Even in the fictional form, he juxtaposes and intermingles different genres, language moods, and rhythms to express psychological activities that integrate the self's cognition of the outside world and the inner world full of desire and emotion. In *Soul Mountain*, he not only traverses the boundaries of fiction, prose, poetry, fable, legend, and historical records but also discovers an intersection between words and sounds by emphasizing the musical feeling of language. In his drama, he advocates "total theater" that synthesizes traditional Chinese drama elements such as singing, reciting, playing musical instruments, and acrobatics. His idea of total theater promotes various cross-cultural methods ranging from traditional Chinese storytelling to Beijing opera's performing technique and designation of mise-en-scène, Japanese noh theater, and Western absurdist plays. In general, an entire range of phenomena displayed in Gao Xingjian's creative endeavor crosses borders between media. It comprises the musicalization of literature, the total theater, and visual poetry, which are well qualified as intermedial.

Since the acoustic, pictorial, and linguistic aspects of Gao Xingjian's cine-poem are derived from diverse art forms, including literature, drama, dance, painting, photography, and music, he defines it as "total art."[64] By engaging in intermediality or plurimediality of artistic practice, he has created a milieu for the sense of poetry to come to light through a border-crossing of different art forms. This milieu not only comprises a rich and intricate synthesis of multidisciplinary and polyphonic factors with hybrid spectacles but also nurtures what Irina O Rajewsky defines as "intermedial reference"—"an illusion of another medium's specific practices." It certainly creates an "'as if' character and illusion forming quality" of one medium in relation to another.[65] Rajewsky further explains, "Just as a literary text can evoke or imitate specific elements or structures of film, music, theatre, etc., so films, theatrical performances, or other media products can constitute themselves in various complex ways in relation to another medium."[66] In Gao Xingjian's cine-poem, the strategies of intermedial reference have been applied to the fullest: we see poetry in Gao Xingjian's paintings and pictorial elements in his poetry; we hear music in his visualization of mental activities and perceive the spiritual space through the vitality of rhythm; we detect the sensibility of literature in his films and connect his films to paintings. He has transgressed the conventional cinematic boundary by unfolding multiple layers of fresh meanings.

Filmed in 2002 and 2003, *Silhouette/Shadow* is about Gao Xingjian's exilic life in Paris, his artistic practice, and his psychological state. Although the semiautobiographical aspect undergirds it, this film provides free, open, and spontaneous venues for multiple interpretations. A distinct feature is its ambiguous and open format. The strategy Gao employs is the half-made film or open cinema mingled with the sensibility of literature, which is very reflexive on the reality, the subject, and the transmediality of cinematic forms. According to the film scholar Leo Braudy, open films offer "a privileged view on a world of which other views are possible," inviting external influences to shape the storyline.[67] The film clearly gives rise to Gao Xingjian's tripartite cinematic aesthetics that stimulate interactions among visual, acoustic, and linguistic presences. Moreover, it reveals trispatiality or tetraspatiality that is closely related to subjective positions and consciousnesses. According to Gao Xingjian's own explanation in his article "Concerning *Silhouette/Shadow*," the first spatiality denotes the factual background where he was involved in a series of artistic activities during "The Year of Gao" held in Marseille in 2003. Portrayed in color, this level of space focuses more on the objective reality where Gao Xingjian is working and traveling between several cultural and artistic events, such as directing and staging his plays *The Man Who Questions Death* and *Snow in August* as well as preparing to exhibit his ink paintings. "The artist at work, the play rehearsals, the exhibition, and the stage performance are interwoven with the artist's psychological activities during the inception and production of his works—in other words, from reality to imagination—and then the emergence of the works all constitute the film's first level."[68] During the festival, Gao Xingjian fell seriously ill, so the film shows him lying in the ambulance heading to the hospital. On this reality level, his health is fragile, and his near-death experience triggers his contemplation of death in film.

The second spatiality points toward "the materiality and mediality of artistic practices" or the process of the artist at work in relation to his psychological state.[69] If the first space pertains to the artist's objective reality—his actual life in real surroundings, such as living in Paris, visiting a temple in Taiwan, attending international art festivals, and being hospitalized—then the second space represents his artistic creativity. Shot in warm or cold hues, it allows viewers to glimpse the artist's subjective reality while he was immersed in art creation. In his studio, Gao Xingjian visualizes before he paints, pours the ink, and then follows its flow to find inspiration to create, attempting to capture the aura of art that lies in instantaneous awakening. While directing his play *The Man Who Questions Death*, he communicates with the actors, constantly making changes according to the effects of performance. As he directs his play *Snow in August*, he attempts to seize insights from the movements of dancers and performers. Whether in ink painting or directing plays, spontaneity and immediacy are intentionally showcased in the film, inviting viewers to encounter a world full of mysterious creative experiences.

According to Gao Xingjian, "The film crosses over to a third level, as the picture turns black and white when entering the world of the imagination, the pure inner mind."[70] The third spatiality explores the artist's personal desire, emotion, and thought through painterly, musical, and poetic qualities, making a concerted effort to gauge and comprehend the depth of the inner universe. The way he portrays desire and emotion resembles the narratology in *Soul Mountain*, where various female images all allude to manifold variations and compositions of *she*, either real or illusory, melded with the artist's imagination. It is at this point that the film unfolds the third spatiality in which the artist calmly observes the inner mind from a distance, showing a sense of nonattachment. While a nude woman stands in front of one of his paintings, which symbolizes the abyss of desire, the artist covers one eye to observe her and the artwork. This captivating scene implies the Buddhist notion of "attaining emptiness through sexual experience" (*yise wukong* 以色悟空), hinting at a path of enlightenment through the exploration of passion and sensual encounters. The one-eye gesture evokes different layers of interpretation: it can signify "two different personalities," one unveiled and the other hidden;[71] it can also be the metaphor of the third eye, which embodies an inner gaze of cold observation as prelude or precondition to ignite self-enlightenment.

Although the film vacillates among these three spatialities, lacking a coherent narrative line, it is not hard to garner the main themes scattered in the fragments of the poem "Carefree as a Bird"; the two plays, *The Man Who Questions Death* and *Snow in August*; and some of Gao Xingjian's paintings. They resonate with the position with which he always identifies—that of an exiled artist who chose to live in solitude and serenity, withdrawing from the obstreperous political and commercial centers and fully enjoying spiritual freedom. In the film, the image of the flying bird and the reciting of some lines from "Carefree as a Bird" contentiously reflect Zhuangzi's absolute spiritual liberation, the central theme running through many of Gao's works. He is deeply suspicious of the prevalent role of Chinese intellectuals, who usually aspire to be "the savior of nation," "the incarnation of justice," "superman," or "the conscience of society";[72] they ironically squander their individuality. In contrast to worldly duties, he only wants to identify with Huineng, who has great wisdom and the ability to realize the emptiness of the fame and power most people aspire to and pursue. Inventing an interesting way for Gao Xingjian to see himself, despite overwhelming evidence that the majority of contemporary Chinese artists and writers prefer to project their vision on the objective world rather than the subjective one, this film incarnates his insight that "free will is determined by the awakening of the self."[73]

The philosophical dimension is conveyed by Gao Xingjian's representation of death in the film. In his own explanation, death is manifested in three modes. In addition to his own near-death experience in real life, the artist visualizes the god of death, dressed in black by the mountain, as "a black shadow, and its coming and going is not as one wills."[74] Then, the artist confronts and gazes at the god of death from a certain distance, as if looking at an image of the inner mind in a stolid and emotionless mood. The distance of observation leads viewers to reflect on the meaning of life; at the same time, it is closely linked with the artist's acuity of emptiness—a stance that generates the vista of *kongling* in the film. Employing black humor and farcical elements to explore the theme of death, Gao Xingjian assumes a stance of nonattachment, provoking self-reflection and preventing the trap of perceiving oneself as a superhuman or the world's savior. Despite his pessimistic view of the predicament of human existence, he finds resonance in Huineng's idea of "living in the moment," a concept vividly portrayed in the opera *Snow in August*. In the film, Gao Xingjian selectively presents parts of the play, allowing Huineng to give a Chan maxim: "As for my way to enlightenment, its principle is no thought, its essence is no form, and its foundation no attachment." As the scene switches to offstage, where actors stand in a building with numerous archways, they chant, "The way of Heaven, the law of Buddha, is only a mass of nothingness." After Huineng passes away, what is left on the stage is the final scene of the opera, with the storyteller featured as a geisha and the writer giving a summary of the master's life, two roles that function more like a metadrama with retrospection by Gao Xingjian himself. In the film's climatic burning scene, the carnivalesque atmosphere serves as a metaphor for the profound message that Buddha's presence transcends physical structures such as a temple and abides only in one's heart. This poignant portrayal shows that one who is awakened and enlightened will eventually embody the essence of a buddha. Embracing Chan Buddhism dissipates the fear of death; instead, death becomes a vessel for transcendent significance. The scenes related to this theme encompass the profound realization of emptiness, awakening from ceaseless mundane pursuits, and the understanding of a universe that is in a constant state of change and evolution.

The film is ostensibly in "the documentary mode," which shows the real life and the artistic process of Gao Xingjian in 2003 and features the artist and his wife as the main performers. As nonactors, they certainly add a natural and authentic effect. However, Gao Xingjian never intends to pursue the daily reality; he is consciously aware of the artificiality of the film, situating the installation of his own paintings in specific indoor spaces. His implementation of minimalism in those spaces is vital for the audience's participation and imagination, shaping an atmosphere in which to question restrictive realities. The most fascinating part of the film—and the one most clearly visualizing the Chan state—is the representation of the infinite within limited spaces. Within the restrained spaces of the objective world, such as the studio, the exhibition lounge, and the church, the camera moves slowly to display Gao Xingjian's mystifying and esoteric paintings in *xieyi* style on the wall. Close-up shots following the lines of the "landscape" coupled with environmental sounds seem to incessantly push the boundaries of limited space, inviting the viewer to step into the invisible and infinite world of meandering that is permeated with the stream of consciousness. This sequence gives the viewer an illusion of the boundless universe in everlasting transformation, allowing them to effectively rise above the predicaments of reality. Employing Merleau-Ponty's phenomenology to discuss *Silhouette/Shadow*, Rosalind Silvester stresses that Gao Xingjian "works towards a space of becoming, recognizing that the relationship between space and being is a dynamic, relational and prospective process linking inside and outside, self and other, past and present."[75] Within this "space of becoming," the sensuous and the rational are intermingled and the interactions among the artist, the artwork, and the viewers happen.

There is a scene set in the limited space of the church, with the *xieyi* paintings installed to replace the stained-glass windows, achieving the effect of a *kongling* state in which a truly aesthetic attitude toward life and art is about to surface. Inside the church, the front and central place that typically enshrines a crucified Jesus instead contains Gao Xingjian's painting *Past Charities no. 1, 2000* (fig. 5.1), where a crosslike image stands desperately and

Figure 5.1 Past Charities no.1, 2000, by Gao Xingjian. Reprinted by permission of Gao Xingjian.

forlornly against the vastness of the background. Resting on the cross are apparently four little birds, which raise the question of whether Christianity can still provide a place for human souls to rest. This scene also harkens to a similar dreamlike vista of a church within Andrei Tarkovsky's film *Nostalgia*, where the protagonist, Andrei Gorchakov, reminisces about his bygone home in the hollow husk of a cathedral. The cathedral lacks a roof and has been long abandoned and overtaken by nature, but Gorchakov still finds a spiritual joy in examining it. In fact, his last vision and the film's final scene show the forsaken church melding into his nostalgic memories. Using such elements, Tarkovsky searches for a continual spirituality within the building's desolation. Even after abandonment, the cathedral still manages to fulfill its religious role. However, Gao Xingjian is suspicious about this religious residue and abandons Christianity for Chan Buddhism. In contrast to a desolate but verdant church, the cathedral in Gao Xingjian's film is more like a self-made church standing in as a specific place for meditation. It is full of Chan ambience to invoke inner reflection. Unlike Tarkovsky's church, Gao's church appears unrooted, as if existing in an otherworldly immaterial dimension.

As Daniel Bergez argues, "Paradoxically, Gao Xingjian's conscious choice of a 'limited' medium gives his art its inexhaustible richness."[76] The aesthetic minimalism represented in the church scene transforms the sublime of Christianity into the Chan state permeated with a sense of ethereal emptiness. The artist finds that Chan Buddhism carries more promise for individual salvation compared to the totalizing mentality of Christianity. Sitting in the middle of the church, he grapples with the boundlessness of the inner mind portrayed by his black-and-white ink paintings. It is as if he is immersed in his own meditation while inviting viewers to contemplate whether there exists a religious belief that can truly rescue human beings from the agonizing life. In accordance with his novels and plays, he is prone to embracing self-salvation in the context of ordinary life inspired by Chan Buddhism rather than God and Jesus on the other shore. The four little birds vividly symbolize the existence of everyday life or the normal heart from which one can discover transcendence and enlightenment. In other words, Buddha/God is inside oneself rather than outside in organized institutions such as temples and churches. It is only accessible through one's self-awakening.

This church scene containing the direct experience of mysterious awakening has an interesting effect of transmedia illusion, which immediately recalls certain lines from Gao Xingjian's poem "Carefree as a Bird," in which he delineates his special *kongling* vista. Some of those poetic lines are displayed along with moving shots of the massive paintings prior to the church scene, allowing the paintings to directly engage in the dialogue with poetry.

So big is the eye of wisdom
It guides you going forward
To a place unknown

With this vision
You become like a bird
Rising up from meditation
To escape the predicament of words
With difficulty does imagination arrive
At this fuzzy and hazy place
But right at this moment, in front of your eyes
Up it springs, one after another

The realm of metaphysical thoughts
It's neither near nor far
It's interminable
It's vivid and bright[77]

諾大一隻慧眼
引導你前去
未知之境

憑這目光
你便如鳥
在冥想中升騰
消解詞語的困頓
想像都難以抵達
那模糊依稀之處
霎時間在眼前
一一浮現

玄思的意境
無遠無近
也沒有止盡
清晰而光明

The eye of wisdom is synonymous with the divine eye or the Buddha's eye, which "neither exists beyond the human mind nor can be perceived by a clouded mind."[78] By finding the divine eye or a sober eye within his own mind, Gao Xingjian is able to transcend the chaotic self, going to the unknown world with infinite possibilities. The Chan state that he has created takes on even more metaphorical weight by emphasizing "eternity in a moment." In this state, "eternity" refers to "an imperishable original buddha nature," which contrasts with "the ever-changing, chaotic, and multifarious phenomenal world." As Li Zehou explicates, "Buddhism advocates meditation and nonconventionality in order to escape the 'false front' of the phenomenon-world that is ever in motion, and thereby to approach the original Buddha-nature."[79] It is in such moments, when words fail to capture the essence, that the ambivalent meanings undergo a transformative journey into a vibrant and luminous "realm of metaphorical thoughts." Within this spiritual realm, one can attain a profound sense of eternity through the experiential fusion of self and buddha.

As the Chan state is manifested in the church scene where Gao Xingjian is meditating surrounded by his paintings that denote the richness and profoundness of inner vision and mindscape, it is simultaneously exhibited in his poem that aims to comprehend momentary awakening. The intermediality of Gao Xingjian's paintings and poetry, one art form embedded within the other, captures a sense of condensed eternity in a fleeting moment. This artistic fusion showcases the mind's profound realization and enlightenment of transcendence. In contrast to the bright realm of thought, those "shadows and cracks" that are closely related to light and darkness point to the fluctuating unconsciousness and the phenomenal world that await further illumination from the viewers.[80]

"It's empty but it's full"[81]—Gao Xingjian's line is similar to Su Shi's 蘇軾 (1037–1101) "silence therefore ends numerous movements, empty therefore contains myriad vistas" 靜故了群動，空故納萬境.[82] To reach the vista of *kongling*, one needs to temporarily isolate oneself from worldly affairs, have no attachments, and observe everything with a sober mind. As an intimate portrait of Gao Xingjian's personal life, *Silhouette/Shadow* is most successful in the state of ethereal emptiness he has created. Such a state embraces a multitude of liberated and self-contained elements, encompassing dynamic interplay between light and darkness, black and white, as well as the intermingling of inner and outer realms. It is also the cause of the awakening heart of an individual, which avoids falling into the trap of narcissism normally seen in typical autobiographic portraits.

After the Flood: The Vista of Desolation

Shot in 2008, *After the Flood* is Gao Xingjian's second cine-poem, twenty-eight minutes long. If *Silhouette/Shadow* is more autobiographically oriented and full of traces of the director/artist/actor, such as his deeds, actions, and stream of consciousness, then *After the Flood* casts a pessimistic look at the collective humanity, representing their postapocalyptic psychological state. Instead of focusing on the solitude of an individual, Gao Xingjian confronts natural and human-made crises and disasters affecting all of humankind. Natural disasters such as earthquakes, tsunamis, and tornados can be devastating, engorging "heaven and earth like scenes of the end of the world in the Old Testament of the Bible."[83] However, even more formidably disturbing are the disasters caused by human actions, including merciless and protracted wars, the devastating impact on the environment, widespread famine, economic inequality, disruptive technological advancements, the looming threat of nuclear weapons, and the recent overwhelming and distressing COVID-19 pandemic. All those menaces form the bleak landscape of our present, summoning up an apocalyptic mood that is manifested in *After the Flood*.

While discussing concepts of the end, Frank Kermode envisions that the "imminent" sense of apocalypse has been altered toward the "immanent" sense of postapocalypse both in religion and in modernism.[84] As James Berger further argues in his book *After the End: Representations of Post-Apocalypse*, "Modernity is often said to be preoccupied by a sense of crisis, viewing as imminent, perhaps even longing for, some conclusive catastrophe."[85] Although this sense of crisis lingered on and loomed large in the late twentieth century, Berger considers that it was transformed into "a complex form of stasis,"[86] becoming an immanent state of both the individual and the collective influenced by crisis. As an art film about the postapocalypse, *After the Flood* is more like a modern fable with a compelling expression of human feelings and psychology while tackling disasters. As Gao Xingjian points out, "The film is different from usual disaster films in that it constitutes painting and performance and is devoid of reality."[87] Unlike disaster films, which typically understand history as a linear progression from the beginning to a circumscribed end, the film does not refer to the end of the world as an impending actuality but as an intrinsic and poignant state relentlessly haunting human existence. Gao Xingjian is concerned with the tendency of the whole civilization and its values; the film is not grounded in any specific political, social, cultural, or religious contexts. Instead, *After the Flood* focuses more on what Walter Benjamin calls "the time of the now [Jetztzeit]" or even suspended time, a psychological state or moment that cannot be defined by linear time.[88] Even if it has a pivotal purpose of revelation and premonition that challenges the problematic civilization at large, the film does not follow the logic that the end of things heralds a new beginning but hangs around or procrastinates in a state of anxiety, shock, rage, fear, and despair, presenting a traumatizing situation that is impossible to escape. Moreover, the film also contests the dualistic thinking that is inherent in certain apocalyptic narratives, characterized by the "tendency to view the world as a battleground between pure good and pure evil."[89] Gao Xingjian has turned his gaze toward the imagination offered by the inner world of the humanities.

Different from *Silhouette/Shadow*, in which language plays a significant role in rendering abstract thinking, *After the Flood* deliberately contains no language elements in either subtitles or speech. Instead, music and dance have replaced the potential of language in written and audio forms. Again, Gao Xingjian's theory of tripartite film is evident: his ink paintings, the dancers' bodies and performance, and the sounds created by stage acoustics expert Thierry Bertomeu are three independent elements that contrast with and supplement one another. As Megan Evans points out, "Providing the setting for *After the Flood*, Gao's suggestive paintings employ Chinese ink but through innovative techniques so that they evoke an every/no-placeness, becoming an archetypal signifier for 'Earth.'"[90] Viewers may perceive a sense of "an every/no-placeness," but it is not only a reference to the earth. Actually, different layers and shapes of black ink strokes and the white blank space in between have forged a boundless and profound scene, which corresponds to the state of heaven and earth (*tiandi jingjie* 天地境界) or the state of the universe. It is directly connected to Gao Xingjian's identification with the universal values that transcend national and cultural boundaries. Among fifty ink paintings featured in the film, Gao Xingjian explains that "only six directly manifest disaster; the others have their own individual themes, either the vast cosmos with its undefined space or isolated men and women who manifest certain mental images: these are all visions of the inner mind that are often evoked when one loses oneself in deep thought."[91] It is exactly that "vast cosmos with its undefined space" that elevates Gao Xingjian's apocalyptic film from the reality level to the metaphorical level, by and large targeting the essential values of civilization and the human psyche in the midst of crisis.

By dispensing with the usual narrative structure of film, *After the Flood* creates the illusion that each scene is like a painting (fig. 5.2). As Megan Evans says, the film is more like a "close form": "The frame of the short is emphasized and operates similarly to a proscenium arch, blocking off expectation that viewers will be given access to additional information that they might expect in 'open form' composition about a world continuing beyond the frame."[92] By using a close form, Gao Xingjian employs a stylized design, encapsulating all the information, such as mysterious settings and psychic reactions, within a frame, bestowing the film with the intermedial reference of painting. However, the six dancers' performance and movement augment "the rhythm of life" (*shengming de jiezou* 生命的節奏) in each painting

Figure 5.2 The End of the World, 2006, by Gao Xingjian. Reprinted by permission of Gao Xingjian.

and generate variety and diversity that inevitably stretch beyond the frame. When Zong Baihua 宗白華 (1897–1986) discusses the relationship between dance and Dao, he regards dance as a perfect means to visualize and incarnate the unfathomable state of heaven and earth. As he writes, "Dance—its highest degree of cadence, rhythm, sequence, rationality, which at the same time is the highest degree of life, swirling, power, enthusiasm—not only expresses a fundamental state of all artistic representation but also symbolizes the process of the cosmos' birth and transformation." Only dancing postures can concretize and visualize Dao embedded in silent illumination (*jingzhao* 靜照), which is the endless resource of the vitality of dance.[93] Gao Xingjian understands the spirit of Chinese aesthetics; therefore, he employs dance—the movement of human bodies—as a special language of visualization (*juxiang hua* 具象化) and incarnation (*roushen hua* 肉身化) of the ingrained Dao to negotiate with the space inside his own paintings. Fiona Sze-Lorrian's analysis of the dancers in the film notes that "within his or her time-space, each dancer is capable of executing choreographed moves by using a vocabulary of body gestures that seems at once contingent upon and liberated from the painting behind."[94] The dancers' gestures, movements, and facial expressions open additional layers of meaning in the paintings by expressing the individual's anguish, sorrow, grief, and despondency while facing the end of the world. Melting into the infinite background of the painting, the dancers undoubtedly craft a painterly mirage, but their representational mode constantly moves beyond the paintings' frames. To be more precise, they are the embodiment of the "state of being," which vividly displays human postapocalyptic psychology. In Gao Xingjian's own explanation:

> State of being is within the painting yet overflows beyond the painting. The interest and rhythm of the ink and the brush in the painting can be realized in the painting through visual-art strategies. When a person observes, he or she is enticed into the painting and also experiences a psychological state that is akin to that of the artist engaged in the making of the painting.[95]

The dancers have become part of the painting process, using bodily and facial expressions to transmit the image of the mind. At the beginning of the film, the viewer can only see the painting through an image of a dancer's back. It is as if both the dancer and the viewer are joining in "the making of the painting" through their distant observation. As the dancers' bodies are interwoven into the fabric of the paintings, the sensibility of images that carry the psychology of apocalypticism is immediately expanded, making the experiences between the performers and the viewers communicable and sharable. Following the slow-moving shots, the physical appearance of the dancers and the painterly vision of the end of the world are perceived by the viewer as one. However, there is a middle ground or Thirdspace that instantly emerges from the dancers' distant observation of the self. Contrary to conventional approaches that view dance as the vehicle to express the performers' subjective emotions, Gao Xingjian argues that a form of poetry can emerge from the dancers' contemplative exploration of the self, "focused, unemotional, quiet, silent, and concentrated observation of the movement of the body, or listening intently to the sounds of the inner mind."[96]

Gao Xingjian's dramaturgical method of "the neutral actor" is also applied to the dancers in *After the Flood*. As they conduct the conscious "detached-from-self-observation," they are concurrently communicating with their role and the audience.[97] The dancers have become self-perceptive and even self-purified before the performance, keeping a wide berth from their egos. Before they act out their roles, they will gaze within the psyche. This not only enlarges the representational scope of the dancers' inner mind but also stimulates the audience's reflective thinking. The dancers' self-illumination enhances the inspiration of their performance, but simultaneously, their bodily expressions vividly visualize the depth of human psychology in the face of the end of the world.

The acoustic element registers the extent of shocking and crestfallen effects, repelling viewers from their comfort zone to interrogate why conundrums and disasters have been suddenly imposed upon them. Gao Xingjian's ink painting is suggestive, provoking further interpretations; therefore, the sounds function as a special means to elucidate the meaning and mood inherent in the paintings. Following the flow of ink in each frame of the painting, the sounds strengthen the representation of the human psyche with internal force, interfacing with the dancers' body language that expresses the subtlety of emotions. Enriching the process of involvement with dance and paintings, the sound design attempts to simulate the viewer's comprehension of the present apocalypse, exerting a pull on their nerves with an emphasis on trauma and personal crisis by awakening them from the benumbed state. It is the kind of sound that penetrates both "body" and "soul" with vibrations of prolonged frustration and devastation caused by massive destruction.

The intermediality among sound, dance, and painting is a site of genesis for the senses of poetry to incubate. To be more specific, Gao Xingjian has devised a vista of desolation (*cangliang de yijing* 蒼涼的意境) in which tragedy and crisis are inherent. The suggestive paintings illustrate the inner universe, or the mindscape, as vast, encompassing, and abyssal as the outer universe, implying that disasters and crises infringe upon the inside and outside of human bodies. Regardless of religions, cultures, and races, human beings are all forced to be involved in a continual struggle with and adjustment to the intimidating and dreadful obliteration of civilization. The film is remarkable for its inclusiveness in embodying the universal feelings of crisis in a new and powerful light. The feelings of desolation render the outside world a plutonian hellscape, yet this mood exists simultaneously in the human psyche. Gao Xingjian touches, at this point, what is undoubtedly our central postapocalyptic preoccupation. Placing an abstraction above actual life, he predicts the gloomy and forlorn future of civilization, which will end in its own deadlock. This prediction echoes Walter Benjamin's image of an angel, inspired by the Klee painting, *Angelus Novus*: "This storm irresistibly propels him into the future to which his back is turned, while the pile of debris before him grows skyward. This storm is what we call progress."[98] Likewise, Gao Xingjian's postapocalyptic message uses a strike and a shout (*banghe* 棒喝) to evoke Chan's sudden awakening. It is a metaphysical warning and revolt against a disintegrating world suffused with modern and postmodern crises such as eternal injustice, hidden menaces, and endless violence.

The visions of the end of the world in *After the Flood* are an assertion of human dignity on both an individual and a collective level. Human beings may be weak and helpless in the face of natural and man-made disasters, but as Gao Xingjian underscores, "it is possible to live without loss of dignity, and it is this that is the affirmation of the human that is the source of art and literature."[99] Although the concept of the end of the world is primarily designated as "revelation" in religious contexts, especially Christianity, Gao Xingjian is determined to recontextualize it in aesthetics. What he attempts to transpose into his own cinematic practice is aesthetics instead of religion. Comparable to Cai Yuanpei's theory of "replacing religion with aesthetics," Gao Xingjian seeks a spiritual, purified form in literature and art in which poetic sense and beauty become the fundamental means of salvation and redemption. That is why he describes *After the Flood* as "an appeal for the spiritual, the poetic, and the beautiful," which "symbolize hope" in the postapocalyptic mode of confronting the fragility of human civilization.[100]

Requiem for Beauty: The Vista of Melancholic Absurdity

Gao Xingjian's third cine-poem, *Requiem for Beauty*, took him seven years to finish and was released in 2013. Based on his poem "Requiem for Beauty," it unmistakably bears "intermedial references" to poetry. Like his other two cine-poems, this film abandons the narrative mode; it lacks both a linear storyline and characters beyond symbols. Gao Xingjian explains, "The shots and scenes, which are connected merely through poetic lines or music, are almost unrelated."[101] His cinematic theory of "tripartite film" highlights three elements—picture, sound, and language—that serve to visualize poetic forms on screen without following the logic of linear narrative or external causality. In between the isolated images and fragmentary scenes, a floating mood and wandering thoughts transmute verses in the shots. The way subjects and objects are framed within each shot has vital symbolic value with a certain degree of abstraction, which contains philosophical meanings. Going counter to dominant cinematic practice in the postmodern era, all aspects of the film—settings, gestures, movement, poetic verses, music—are incorporated thoroughly to create an aura of poetic enchantment.

At the beginning of the film, the Poet comes into the room, suddenly claiming that beauty has vanished, but no one understands him. Such an abrupt announcement echoes the first paragraph of the poem *Requiem for Beauty*. Earlier, in his play, *The Man Who Questions Death*, Gao Xingjian revealed the brutal fact that beauty has been destroyed in the modern museum due to the art revolution of the twentieth century that is subservient to political strategies influenced by Marxist dialectics. The film *Requiem for Beauty* expands the scope of clairvoyant criticism to the whole contemporary world, in which beauty is largely annihilated by the prevailing consumer culture, endless political battles, and environmental pollution. The vulgarity, kitsch, inanity, and meaninglessness are like a virus, contagious and ubiquitous, spreading and permeating every corner of daily life.

> This is the age which has no redemption
> Except all kinds of trademarks
> This is the age of unequaled grandiosity

Huge buildings built taller and taller
But the human spirit gets smaller and smaller[102]

這是一個沒有救贖的時代
有的只是各種各樣的商標
這是一個無比偉大的時代
大樓一座比一座蓋的更高
精神一個比一個更矮小

The death of beauty is the loss of the human spirit, and such a sense of prescience echoes the postapocalyptic style of warning. "A lonely man/Where can he find a woman/Who's just as lonely/On the margins of society/To face Doomsday's trials?"[103] Again the immanent sense of postapocalypse reverberates, pointing to an increased prevalence of the condition in real life.

In his article "The Aesthetics of the Artist," Gao Xingjian distinguishes the philosopher's aesthetics from that of the artist: the former is abstract, transforming beauty and art into concepts, categories, logics, discourse, and theories; the latter "is always concrete and must be verified in the work." Moreover, the artist's aesthetics is hard to define, because it is individual, nonhistorical, nonutilitarian, and reliant on the instant inspiration of creative experience.[104] As a concept of aesthetics, beauty, personified as "she" in the poem, is killed and strangled in our present time all over the world, yet there is no way to find out who has committed the crime. It seems everyone in the contemporary world is implicated as accomplices in such "murder." In the film, beauty is personified by women and men such as a poet, a thinker, and Venus, who signify spirituality and aesthetics. More importantly, beauty is visualized and orchestrated by what Daniel Bergez calls "a Baroque aesthetic": "A 'black' Baroque that culminates in the splendour of a death sentence and eternal grief; a 'white' Baroque, festive, with moments of humour, irony and a carnival."[105] Indeed, in contrast to *After the Flood*, which is structured around minimalism and black-and-white tones, *Requiem for Beauty* adopts an increasingly elaborate and extravagant style. Beauty is captured by a rich, radiant, and feast-like color palette, "a kaleidoscope of images,"[106] and a mixture of various art forms. By employing a Baroque aesthetic that is epitomized by the ornate, humanistic, and spiritual, Gao Xingjian attempts to encourage the Renaissance spirit that is derelict in the contemporary world.

The film consists of three distinctive spatialities. The first is background projections, including a large amount of video clips and pictures Gao Xingjian collected all over the world and his own paintings. Those pictures gleaned from different locations, from Europe to the United States and Asia, construct a "museum without walls," as defined by André Malraux in *The Voices of Silence*,[107] prompting a dialogue between the phantoms of artwork and present daily life. Although the film was shot in Gao Xingjian's studio, the images move beyond limited space and time, shuttling between profound European cultural traditions and forest-like contemporary urban architecture and settings.

The second space is displayed by performers of different nationalities, improvising against the backdrop of either simulated reality or the "Imaginary Museum" from the past.[108] The diverse racial identities of the performers stand for people all over the world regardless of national boundaries. Their instantaneous gestures, vivid movements, and facial expressions interpret human psychological reactions to the perceived world behind them. Such improvisation with dancing postures, akin to installation art, gives the background a human form with a sense of mobility and temporality. The tension between the performers and the background, accompanied by music, "not only conveys emotion, but also evokes wave after wave of ideas,"[109] presenting the complexity of human existence. In Jean-Pierre Zarader's comment, "Gao has achieved, in a very different way, what Malraux could only dream of: a film where *The Voices of Silence* comes to life, a film that animates not only the artworks' historical context and the 'real' museums they find themselves in—but also the subjects of the artworks, personified by actors, who re-enact, in a contemporary language, the roles the artworks played in the history of art."[110] The actors' postures and dance movements are indeed a contemporary construal of the world's masterpieces and the expressiveness of human emotions. The bodily movement integrated with musical sound endows the space with rhythm, rhetoric, and lyricism, constructing a parade of the imaginary and the symbolic with a strong emphasis on the relationship between art and contemporary society.

The third spatiality is manifested by the mind's eye—the third eye that calmly observes both the background and the roles in the film. Wah Guan Lim astutely points out that the actors employ Gao Xingjian's theory of the neutral state of performance, which enables them to keep a distance from their roles.[111] As he analyzes, the Poet and the Thinker in the film always stand at the periphery of the mise-en-scène; such a distance empowers the actors' cogent and conscious observation of themselves. This peripheral position is that of an exterior third eye, which not only allows the actors to conduct self-scrutiny but also provokes the spectators' reflection on their own existential situation.[112] Indeed, the countenance of the third eye is consistently put into practice in Gao Xingjian's three introspective cine-poems. It generates a reflective tension between the performance and the viewers' involvement in the work. It encourages the audience to participate in the ongoing realization of the film, opening a door for their free readings against the grain. With a gaze that looks objectively at the film and turns inward at the same time, the audience's aesthetic experience is able to transcend the bifurcation of the intellect and the senses. Gao Xingjian prefers that his film be experienced as an operating structure which interweaves with sensory memory, perceptual capacity, and imaginative pattern, provoking the audience's cognitive understanding of aesthetics and an inner state of spiritual realization.

As in *Silhouette/Shadow* and *After the Flood*, intermediality or multimediality becomes the fundamental condition for Thirdspace to emerge in *Requiem for Beauty*. By integrating several media—dance, music, poetry, painting, photography—into an intensifying and symbolic process, Gao Xingjian has created Thirdspace sprung from multimediality, which is saturated with "the rhythm of life," the music of thought, and the poetry of gesture. We vividly sense the musical quality in the lyrical poetry, the painterly quality in the background projection, and the poetic quality in the dancers' movement. The intermedial or multimedia tension and interaction incite an aesthetic gesture that is not limited to social criticism but instead renders the psychological inner world of the film into an extension of cosmic realities, transcending space and time.

When Zong Baihua discusses the inimitable characteristics of Chinese landscape paintings, he points out that Chinese spatial consciousness (*kongjian yishi* 空間意識) is closely related to musicality, dance, and rhythm.[113] He wrote: "What the painters want to represent in the frame is not only a house (*yu* 宇) in an architectural sense of space but also a musical sense of present and future (*zhou* 宙). A universe with the unity of time and space that is full of musical temperament is a vista of art for Chinese painters and poets."[114] Obviously, this kind of spatial consciousness is closely intertwined with time, referring not only to physical space but also to aesthetic space that is channeled through "the rhythm of life." In *Requiem for Beauty*, Gao

Xingjian intends to create exactly this kind of aesthetic space where rhythm is embedded in all the media, visible and invisible coexist, and the flow of time is sensationally framed in the shot. For instance, the dancers' postures and movements in the film simultaneously and dialectically embody fantasy and reality, the representational and the verisimilar, displaying an ethereal and suggestive space that is typically inbred in many Chinese art forms such as calligraphy, poetry, drama, architecture, and paintings.[115]

The shots in the film also adopt the Chinese multiple perspectives of paintings that intrinsically comprise beats and cadences of seeing. Different from the Western perspective, which has only one focus, Chinese paintings usually consist of multiple perspectives that foster a rhythmized space. The Song dynasty painter Guo Xi 郭熙 (1020–1090) once described three types of distance of mountains: "Looking up to the mountain's peak from its foot is called the high distance. From in front of the mountain looking past it to beyond is called deep distance. Looking from a nearby mountain at those more distant is called the level distance."[116] Usually, Chinese painters aim to create a poetic and innovative artistic space that is inclined toward the musical realm, imbued with the rhythm of time. Such rhythmic and musicalized space is also exemplified in *Requiem for Beauty*. In the film, sometimes when the actors are performing in the foreground, their images eclipse and overwhelm the buildings or sculptures behind them. When they look at those buildings from an aerial perspective (or the bird's-eye view), the hustle and bustle of contemporary life becomes demeaned and diminutive—it is analogous to the deep distance. While they are walking on the streets, it is similar to the level distance. As they look up to the sky, their gaze is akin to the high distance. Those different distances form a rhythm of observation, delineating an intriguing interchange among the self, society, and cosmos.

In *Theory of Poetry* (*Shilun* 詩論), Zhu Guangqian points out that poetry, music, and dance are derived from the same source—rhythm in ancient time. Inspired by R. P. Blackmur's theory of language as gesture, Chen Shixiang discusses the close intermedial relationship among body, sound, and language. He expounds that prior to language, the rhythm of bodily gesture is the primary resource from which the poetic imagination is generated. Furthermore, he uplifts the principle of gesture as a general concept of art theory, extending it to various art forms rather than limiting it within the territory of language. Like Blackmur, he asserts that the vitality of gesture lies in recapturing "the most significant moment" of the artistic creation.[117] In *Requiem for Beauty*, Gao Xingjian uses the principle of gesture lavishly in various art forms, vindicating a rhythm of heart and emotion in its resonance with worldly and universal tumult. In other words, gesture can be regarded as a heuristic metaphor of the intermedial space of dance, music, and poetry. The film is crowded with a kaleidoscope of gestures from showgirls, singing stars, Don Quixote, Hamlet, Venus, Jesus, God, a prince, a queen, the Madonna, a modern Lolita, a poet, a thinker, an old man—all together showcasing the deformity and waning of beauty and the human spirit in the contemporary world. But more importantly, music—Mozart's *Requiem*, dance—the performers' bodily postures and movement, and language—the poem "Requiem for Beauty," come together to register a spectacular poetic gesture that is against the tide of time.

In addition, by employing masks in the film, Gao Xingjian develops a symbolic gesture showing a transition from imitative to representative effect. As Izabella Łabędzka illuminates, masks are used in *Soul Mountain* as a unique prop for seasonal exorcism rituals, functioning as symbols that guide the reader to temporarily withdraw from the routines of everyday life and enter a completely different space and time.[118] In the scenes of the carnivalesque in Venice, masks have become part of the tradition, which, for Bakhtin, is the site of resistance to traditional hierarchies and values. Behind masks, one is at liberty to lampoon and overturn the existing order of daily life where beauty is largely trampled.[119]

Through the medium of the mask, one may ask: How to distinguish reality and illusion? Who is behind the mask? Is it the Poet who is searching for beauty or the god of death who kills beauty? Is life simply a play? All these questions are intensified in the intriguing image of Janus—the god of gates, transition, duality, beginning, and ending in ancient Roman religion and myth—covered in two face masks staring in opposite directions.[120] The Janus mask can be characterized as a polarity: one faces toward the past and the other toward the future; one gazes at death and the other at life; one mourns the extinction of beauty, the other anticipates the resurrection of Renaissance. There is a scene in which Janus even wears four masks, symbolizing the opening of the gates to more possibilities and crossing more spatial boundaries. The multiple symbolic gestures in *Requiem for Beauty* generate a variety of literary traits, from irony, farce, absurdity, and playfulness to sorrow, melancholy, and despair. The mixture of different poetic styles is just as Gao Xingjian articulates in the poem: "This is mankind's most profound tragedy/Surely it's also a wonderful comedy/Sorrow and happiness are blended together/As are the absurd and the grotesque."[121]

The mélange of aesthetic gestures in the film produces dazzling and paradoxical effects: "Beauty while mourned is equally celebrated and resurrected";[122] the absurd comedy goes hand-in-hand with tragedy. Daniel Bergez insightfully notes that the themes are "polysemic": "The film is structured around inversions as implicit as they are active: death and splendour, loss and its aesthetic inversion, pictorial logic and the musical score, as well as a carnivalesque reversal of the visual syntax." Swinging back and forth between reality and illusion, modernity and tradition, the film is, as Gao Xingjian describes, a "cinematic poem structured like a symphony."[123] This symphonic or polyphonic cine-poem has forged a vista of melancholic absurdity, which lies in the striking contrast between revelry and sorrow, life and death, irony and elegy.

The whole film is preoccupied with a grand funeral ritual, which is permeated with intense melancholic and elegiac feelings. It bears witness to the extravagant yet shattering images of beauty drawn from residues and fragments of epic, myth, religion, and nature. As Gao Xingjian wrote in his poem: "No matter how changeful the face might be/It's only a phantom in the mind/Only sorrows are real enough/To prompt successive associations."[124] Behind the glamorous mask is the Poet's sorrow and melancholy: "No one can understand this sorrow/It runs so deep/The gravity."[125] Unequivocally, as beauty is being disfigured and destroyed, human subjectivity is vivisected under the geometric, rigid oppressiveness of contemporary urban skyscrapers, endless commercial advertisements, and ubiquitous political propaganda and kitsch. Under such circumstances, there is no way to recover "the fresh and novel feeling," "the resonance in our hearts," "the throbbing of the soul."[126] As Gao Xingjian laments in the poem:

> You have nothing
> Except disconsolation
> Nonetheless, you're very rich
> You still have this precious feeling
> But the world is poor
> It has lost its sorrow[127]

> 你一無所有
> 只剩下惆悵
> 可你好富裕
> 這珍貴的情感

世界卻如此貧困
失去了哀傷

In his famous 1917 essay, Sigmund Freud distinguished mourning from melancholy: the former is a normal response to loss and can end grieving by liberating libidinal desire, but the latter reacts to reality in a pathological manner by remaining entrenched in loss.[128] According to Ilit Ferber, by regarding melancholy as a philosophical mood, Walter Benjamin transformed "the Freudian melancholic's passive stance into that of activity and, more important, of productivity."[129] In the film, Gao Xingjian does not demarcate the difference between mourning and melancholy in explicitly binary terms. Instead, he regards mourning and melancholy as interchangeable because they are both precious and poetic feelings that are no longer cherished in the present world. This view harks back to the Chinese lyrical tradition that employs mourning and melancholy as a rhetorical medium bonding the wounded self and the devastating external world. By putting aside the distinction between normality and pathology, Gao Xingjian prolongs the process of mourning and externalizes melancholy in the ritual of requiem. Similar to Benjamin, Gao invokes melancholy as "a productive rather than a passive and paralyzing mood."[130] As a result, melancholy embodies not only an internalized individual experience but also a shared collective experience, which can be viewed as both a metaphysical stance and social criticism. In other words, melancholy in the film is presented not as an illness but rather as an important aesthetic gesture or a critical attitude toward the decaying and meaningless reality.

At the same time, the film sarcastically mocks the loss of beauty in the contemporary world by displaying a series of uncanny, grotesque, farcical images, such as Don Quixote holding a broken umbrella in the rain, Hamlet with no enemy to confront, Ophelia's corpse drifting in the water, God transformed into a beggar, Jesus replaced by a superman, the Queen trapped in a spider's web, the alienated Lolita having lost her innocence, etc. A sense of absurdity penetrates those familiar yet twisted images along with the carnivalesque atmosphere. On the one hand, a sense of harmony prevails while the bodily movements of actors and dancers amalgamate Baroque architecture and sculptures, but conversely, the eerie feeling is reflected as they perform in front of overly practical and rational contemporary buildings. As Jean-Pierre Zarader describes: "The film is not a nostalgic mourning for Beauty; it simply states that life cannot exist without death. *Requiem for Beauty* is then a metamorphosis; it is timeless, in contrast to the classical aesthetic where Beauty rimes with immortality."[131] The metamorphosis of beauty is a testament to how absurd the contemporary world has become. It has inevitably transfigured the sublime into farce: "In a parody of the biblical scene of the *Last Supper*, farce suddenly deflates pathos while at the same time crowning it."[132] The element of laughter juxtaposed with sadness has produced a vista that cannot be simply characterized as melancholy in terms of lyricism; instead, it should be encapsulated as melancholic absurdity. This blending intertwines humanity's profound tragedy, comedy, the absurd, and the grotesque, placing sorrow and happiness in close proximity. More specifically, the film unfolds a paradoxical complex that seems self-contradictory, yet incites the unresolvable and indubitable sense of sadness and irony.

In the concluding scenes, the cinematic melancholy reaches a peak. Following footage of war, misery, and pandemonium, the film ends like a sublime funeral. The mood is exemplified by a bevy of black-clad actors against the backdrop of one of Gao Xingjian's black-and-white ink paintings. The *xieyi* painting is filled with a deep and profound cosmic wilderness in addition to an empty, abyssal cave-like space, denoting the beginning and the end of life. The "multi-dimensional structure of time and space"

Figure 5.3 Requiem for Beauty, by Gao Xingjian. Reprinted by permission of Gao Xingjian.

embedded in Gao Xingjian's paintings is saturated with inconsolable sorrow but simultaneously accompanied by an ambiance of ethereal emptiness, which prevents the audience from projecting personal feelings.[133] Lurking behind the mourning procession is the vestigial hope of beauty's reincarnation. The actors reach skyward toward the sun and the moon as if to represent the ebbing of one and the ascent of another (see fig. 5.3). Despite the mourning, the reverential composition of the actors beckons for beauty's rebirth in a new form.

In general, through deep mourning and sarcastic irony, *Requiem for Beauty* goes beyond simple social criticism by calling for a renaissance—a return to humanism, aesthetics, and spirituality, everything that has diminished in the contemporary world. It is an apocalyptic warning, but at the same time, it also lays "another kind of aesthetics" as the precondition for new beginnings. Unlike the Judeo-Christian tradition's linear and teleological time, it juxtaposes moon and sun, death and rebirth. Since time and space are structured freely, flexibly, and multifariously according to the artist's inner mind, the call for a renaissance is undergirded by the prolonged requiem, which transforms death from a frightful event into an aesthetic ritual, inspirational ceremony, and dramatic performance.

CHAPTER VI

Chinese Female Writers' Construction of Thirdspace

In her seminal work *Feminism and the Mastery of Nature*, Val Plumwood elucidates a concept of the "third position" in ecofeminist theory to resolve the conflicts between "deep ecology" and "social ecology."[1] Embedded in this "third position" is her ambitious philosophical challenge against the prevailing structure of dualism that undergirds the Western political landscape, which not only can be traced back to ancient Greece but also holds a central position within the discourse of modernity. Rooted in the modern and post-Enlightenment consciousness, this dualistic logic system is defined by its propensity for "radical exclusion," which maximizes distance and separation between dichotomous spheres while simultaneously denying or downplaying any "overlap qualities and activities."[2] Consequently, rigid adherence to dualism not only "naturalises domination" and "ground hierarchy" but also tends to dismiss or overlook alternative theoretical pathways.[3] Plumwood's "third position" of ecofeminism is a tremendous counterpoint to this dominant paradigm, serving as a catalyst for reevaluating and transcending the constraints imposed by dualistic thinking. The evasion of dualism she proposes opens a door to the exploration of Thirdspace in which a nonhierarchical concept of differences is espoused.

The trajectories pursued by Chinese female writers in their navigations of Thirdspace strikingly resemble Plumwood's critiques of dualism, a framework that serves as a significant link among various forms of oppression. In this chapter, I select three representative female writers—Xi Xi from Hong

Kong, Chi Zijian from mainland China, and Chu Tien-hsin from Taiwan—to delineate their purposeful inquiries into Thirdspace within their respective situations, entrenched in various dichotomies engendered by different and complex historical and cultural contexts. Instead of adhering to a radical feminist perspective that rigidly separates men from women, these female writers approach the gender dichotomies with skepticism, acknowledging how they reinforce and intertwine with the broader network of dualisms. None of these authors can be neatly categorized as a radical feminist. In her works set in Hong Kong, Xi Xi often assumes a neutral, open stance when exploring gender relations. She does not claim gender neutrality but rather advocates a more independent and self-reliant feminist choice of urban lifestyle that is not defined by the traditional gender view.[4] Although Chi Zijian portrays numerous female characters in her writing, she resists being labeled a "feminist" and emphasizes the complementary relationship between men and women.[5] Chu Tien-hsin consistently features outspoken and individualistic female narrators who behold multiple subjectivities while encountering different and dominating political forces. For her, gender plays an important role in social construction, but it is not the sole and essentialist issue linking political and historical cultural identities. All three female writers reject a reductionist viewpoint that regards "women's oppression as the fundamental form of oppression from which all others are derived."[6]

Their commonalities, despite different cultural and political locations, are their diverse methods of breaking dualism. By navigating two opposing positions, they perceive the binaries in a more interconnected, dialogical manner that embraces the differences in a nonhierarchical fashion. In her intermedia story, "Marvels of a Floating City," Xi Xi portrays Hong Kong as a Thirdspace where its inhabitants relish openness and freedom yet simultaneously cope with the perplexities of an uncertain future. By interweaving indigeneity, modernity, and environmentalism in her novel *The Last Quarter of the Moon*, Chi Zijian employs the shaman of the Evenki group as a medium between the spiritual and physical realms—an extraordinary embodiment of Thirdspace—to defy a commodifying and homogenizing modern civilization. Chu Tien-hsin steadfastly refuses to surrender to conformist pressures for Taiwanese identity and instead activates heterotopias in the form of both the democratic movement and protecting the interspecies human/nonhuman kingdom. As these authors deal with the complexities of their own positioning, they present a potent critique of hegemonic cultural practices and carve out a creatively expansive Thirdspace.

The Floating City as a Thirdspace

Many, many years ago, on a fine, clear day, the floating city appeared in the air in full public gaze, hanging like a hydrogen balloon. Above it were the fluctuating layers of clouds, below it the turbulent sea. The floating city hung there, neither sinking nor rising. When a breeze came by, it moved ever so slightly, and then it became absolutely still again.[7]

This is the opening paragraph of "Marvels of a Floating City," a story that interconnects thirteen paintings by Belgian artist René Magritte and Xi Xi's text. By constructing the story on the dialogical and intermedial level of image and language, Xi Xi grasps allegorical meanings to conjure emotions, dreams, and illusions related to space and time. Hanging in midair, drifting between the sky and the sea, the floating city expressed by Magritte's The Castle of the Pyrenees is interwoven with Xi Xi's language. The drifting castle not only implies the historical situation of Hong Kong in between British colonialism and Chinese nationalism but also characterizes one form of the imagery of Thirdspace. This illustration is powerful in two respects. First, it presents the freedom of Thirdspace graphically, capturing the epitome of breathtaking existence and unexpected possibilities in the boundless space while linking it to the linguistic expression of feelings from the city's residents. Second, it provides a rootless figure in isolation that is related to the predicament of Thirdspace, where one encounters unsettling problems of personal identity and belonging. The intermediate relationship is formed between the figure and the text, rendering a richness of meanings in allegory that can be applied to both the specific context of Hong Kong and the universal referent of Thirdspace at the same time.

Xi Xi was one of the most famous Hong Kong female writers to emerge in the 1970s. Her writings, intermingling multifarious genres, styles, perspectives, and media, have successfully evoked the new identity of this unique city. Her sketches of urban spaces in novels such as *My City* (*Wocheng* 我城) and *Flying Carpet* (*Feizhan* 飛氈) treat ordinary people and their daily lives as "the rich mosaic that constitutes the vast synthesis of urban reality."[8] In contrast to the detailed tapestry of urban daily life she used to portray and weave, "Marvels of a Floating City" suggests allegory, "expounding on the problem of the contrast between the two models of meaning—self-sufficient and self-contained meaning versus constantly oscillating meaning." According to Ilit Ferber, "One of the most important features of allegorical form, for

[Walter] Benjamin, is its unique structure of meaning, unstable and fluctuating, in a constant state of deferral—the complete opposite of self-sufficient meaning."[9] Similarly, Xi Xi's own subjective interpretation is unsteady even as she attempts to stabilize the constantly oscillating meanings expressed by Magritte's surrealist paintings. While the paintings "short-circuit the sociolinguistic fixing of meaning or narrative continuity,"[10] Xi Xi's texts break down the mimetic representation of the objective city, exuding open and heterogenous levels of messages to inspire thinking. The interactive dialogues between image and text invite the viewer/reader to piece together the story against conventional habits and thoughts.

Written in 1986, when most Hong Kong citizens were extremely concerned with the impending handover of Hong Kong in 1997, Xi Xi's "Marvels of a Floating City," along with her series of Fertile Soil Town tales, were considered a direct response to the anxious mood of the city triggered by the uncertain future.[11] In her interpretation of Magritte's painting *The Mind's Gaze*, Xi Xi depicts the promising and positive side of the floating city: its citizens' willpower, faith, courage, pioneering spirit, and hard work have created a vivid and flourishing metropolis. The miracle not only encompasses diverse facets, including economic prosperity, social welfare, and cultural flourishing, but also is epitomized by its most quintessential characteristic—a guarantee of individual political freedom. The sense of self-fulfillment and happiness is indisputable because "buildings in the floating city can float in the air; that flowers grown in the floating city are each big enough to fill a whole room."[12] A joyful feeling carried by flowers in conjunction with the marvelous achievement of the city corresponds to what Xi Xi celebrates in her novel *My City*, in which she proudly proclaims her citizenship rather than her nationality,[13] exulting in her identity as a resident.

The miraculous city is enhanced by the revelation in Xi Xi's interpretation of Magritte's painting *Golconda*, which explores the subconscious of its citizens, who transform into "floating men" in their dreams in the windy season from May to September every year. Accompanied by a mysterious atmosphere, the image of numerous "floating men," depicted by Magritte as a mass of stereotyped, bowler-hatted men that alludes to a crowd rather than an individual, appears to remain suspended in midair or, alternatively, to ascend and descend. In a letter to Gaston Puël, Magritte himself uncovered two different ways of interpreting *Golconda*: the picture is "an instantaneous vision," but at the same time, "it might have been the result of an investigation starting from 'the problem of space.'"[14] For Xi Xi, the city's common dream with everyone floating in the air testifies to "a collective manifestation of the Third-Side-of-the-Straits Complex."[15] This complex signifying citizens' relationship with space is to be understood metaphorically as the state of mind and psychology derived from the political and cultural situation of Hong Kong caught between Britain and China. It intrinsically contains paradoxical meanings: the advantage of in-betweenness opens up not only more possibilities for cultural innovation and flourishing but also the disquieting uncertainties of being adrift. Closely aligned with the discourse of Thirdspace, the "Third-Side-of-the-Straits Complex" conjoins promising and negative attributes: it dislocates the colonial authorities—be they British or Chinese—and, at the same time, encapsulates the vexed nature of identity.

Confronting a world devoid of essential meanings, Xi Xi continues to employ paradox as a prominent rhetorical figure to encompass all deviations from the outer and inner space of the floating city. Magritte's *This Is Not an Apple* displays the titular words over an apple, highlighting the illusory nature of painting itself. The apple in the painting can never be an actual apple, even if it resembles the fruit in verisimilitude. Xi Xi applies this reflexive awareness to Hong Kong, asking whether its prosperous existence is ultimately illusory as well. Following with Magritte's *The False Mirror*, which is about the "true nature of seeing and interpreting reality,"[16] Xi Xi reflects the citizens' internal thoughts rather than external phenomena. Thus, her writing reinforces that Hong Kong's marvels are both real and illusory. Despite the prosperity exemplified by advanced technology such as the best microscopes and telescopes—the eyes to observe—there is a constant anxiety that these marvels are ephemeral, ready to dissipate at a moment's notice. It is articulated in Xi Xi's story, where the inhabitants do not know if the city will "soar upward, or sink, or be blown away to some unknown place."[17] This dilemma reflects Hong Kong's destiny, which is never in its own hands, bound to either its British colonizer or ancestral Chinese land. A sense of joy and pride embedded in the miracle is accompanied by the consciousness of precarity that perpetually haunts residents' minds.

Magritte's *Hegel's Holiday*, portraying a glass of water on an umbrella, plays a significant role in Xi Xi's story because it succeeds in visualizing a "both/and" logic that represents the core value of Thirdspace. The coexistence of two opposing functions—"acceptance and rejection, external and internal"[18]—has deconstructed Hegel's dialectical logic, which resolves the conflicting elements in a process of recursive negation or sublation to ultimately embrace the "either/or" system. Both Magritte's painting and Xi

Xi's text aim to balance opposing elements as complementary and interconnected without reaching a conclusive resolution. The "both/and" logic that Thirdspace embodies consequently goes against the idea of self-enclosed images and language. Accordingly, a series of paradoxes underpinning the "both/and" logic are carefully woven together through the intermedial image-text, providing multidimensional and allegorical views of the complexity of the floating city. In his painting, *The Ready-Made Banquet*, Magritte combines Botticelli's famous Flora from *The Primavera* with a rear view of his typical bowler hat man, and Xi Xi explains it as the juxtaposition of a wealthy modern society and "the black hole of material possessions."[19] The Goddess of Spring who sprinkles blossoms signifies the material temptations of the prosperous floating city, and the bowler hat man who carries her on his back was inevitably enticed and enslaved by her, hollowing out his soul. This situation of interspersed creation and loss represents the complementary complexity of Hong Kong's spiritual existence. Without the hard work of the citizens, a prosperous society is impossible, yet the materialistic attitude entwined in that wealth is similar to a black hole, which will drain the citizens' souls.

The mental essence of the floating city is closely associated with the critical moment of the handover of Hong Kong in 1997. Using Magritte's painting *Time Transfixed*, Xi Xi demonstrates that what determines the dividing line between the past and the future is exactly this absolute moment, when a train engine abruptly intrudes through the fireplace of a normal private room. The intrusion infuses time and space in a dramatic way, evoking a shocking and unfamiliar effect. Corresponding to the mentality of the city affected by this specific historical moment, Xi Xi finds answers in Magritte's painting *Not to Be Reproduced*, which features an unusual mirror by which the viewer can only see his back. Symbolizing history, the most honest mirror of reality, Xi Xi insinuates that the unknown future of the floating city is embedded in its past. What is communicable through this uncanny mirror is the mental being of the city, which crosses the unresolvable divide between the past and the future, the positive and the negative.

Because of the floating city's complex and diverse existence, pulling in all possible directions, it is crucial for Xi Xi to pinpoint that the central theme of her story is freedom. This means, in effect, that the floating city—the model of Thirdspace—is not in the chain of the evolution of thinking about its past, present, and future but rather attempts to reveal that the city's innermost spirit lies in the concern of freedom. In this regard, the paradox of freedom and restriction goes hand-in-hand in Magritte's painting *The Healer* and Xi Xi's text "Wings." The headless figure in the portrait with a cage of birds in the place of a human body signifies mental cages, implying that a mindless force binds inhabitants of the city. Although they have enormous freedom to choose any place to immigrate by various modes of modern transportation, they can never embrace the absolute spiritual freedom genuine to Zhuangzi because they are afraid of ending like the Greek myth of Icarus—flying too close to the sun and falling to abyssal lows. In Xi Xi's interpretation, "Though the people of the floating city long to be winged pigeons, in their hearts they are repressed, caged birds."[20] The intermedial image-text dialogue displays the forceful transgression of the boundary between the internal and external, challenging the stark demarcation separating freedom and restriction. If one lacks sufficient awareness of internal freedom, one will unequivocally be fettered by mental cages. Xi Xi's text of "bird-grass" in connection with Magritte's *Natural Graces* further reinforces the theme. The unusual and strange plant of the floating city, the bird-grass is a hybrid with bird-shaped leaves that carry the citizens' dream of flying and stems that are firmly attached to the soil. Two completely different and opposite directions—aspiration for freedom and being perpetually bound to the ground—are simultaneously embodied by this local plant, hinting at both hope and conundrum generated by the position of Thirdspace.

It seems that Xi Xi puts hope in the "child prodigies," whose exceptional intelligence unexpectedly surpasses that of their mothers, as if their roles have been uncannily swapped. In Magritte's painting *The Spirit of Geometry*, the exchange of faces between mother and infant gives rise to a captivating paradox. On the one hand, the mother, representing China, with an infantile visage and an adult physique, implies that Chinese leaders from the homeland remain immature and are uncertain about how to nurture the infant in their care. On the other hand, the embraced infant, Hong Kong, despite its physically delicate stature, possesses a remarkably mature mind, akin to that of an adult, highlighting the social system's maturity in Hong Kong. This paradox encapsulates a profound sense of irony. However, Magritte's painting immediately calls into question Hong Kong's promising future by portraying the reciprocal dependency between the parent and the child. No matter how intelligent the prodigies are, they cannot be truly independent from their parents and still rely on maternal care. If we extend the intermedial image-text to the context of Hong Kong, the fast growth of the floating city is always contingent on and controlled by its superior authority, whether

British colonizer or Chinese motherland. Full of hope for the city's future, the mutual dependence of the mother-child relationship is not tinged with the melancholic mode in Xi Xi's story. However, with the advantage of historical hindsight, we know that child prodigies of Hong Kong under Xi Jinping's regime are almost suffocated by the motherland's supervision and overprotection, which have relentlessly pulverized their dream of flying.

Magritte's *The Month of the Grape Harvest*, the last painting in Xi Xi's "Marvels of a Floating City," depicts a mass of stereotypical bowler-hatted men who gaze into a room through a window, blocking the view outside. It inverts the typical relationship between artwork and audience, giving the painting a subjective role in communicating with the viewers. As Lisa Lipinski points out, "Magritte explains that what the paradox achieves is an animated and active painting, which is not simply a mirror or reflection of the world but has agency itself; the painting activates not only *our* thinking but also its own."[21] Xi Xi's text also focuses on the reciprocal gaze and scrutiny between the bowler-hatted men in the painting and the viewers of the painting, as if the inhabitants of the floating city and outsiders look at and think through one another. Obviously, Xi Xi strived to maintain the balance of insiders and outsiders when writing "Marvels of a Floating City" because her peaceful and rational tone parallels the mode of melancholy, rendering her complicated perception of and apprehension about the destiny of Hong Kong. Nevertheless, since the Anti-Extradition Law Amendment Bill Movement broke out in 2019, in protest of increased political encroachment by mainland China in Hong Kong, the relationship between insiders and outsiders has been completely changed. If we recontextualize Magritte's *The Month of the Grape Harvest* in the present time, those identical bowler-hatted men who obstruct the view outside the window are no longer emotionless but rather show "an almost threatening expression despite their passivity."[22] The balance of Thirdspace was unfortunately disrupted after 2019, and the outsiders of the floating city have become an aggressive governor, committing exclusively to watching, supervising, and controlling the insiders, whose feelings have been utterly neglected.

Building a Thirdspace from Borderland

Chi Zijian has established herself as one of the most celebrated contemporary Chinese female writers. Following in the footsteps of Shen Congwen, the leading figure of the "native soil literature" (*xiangtu wenxue* 鄉土文學), Chi Zijian has grounded her imagination in the borderlands of northeast China, a landscape ensconced in snow, ice, and forests unfamiliar to Chinese readers. Despite her ethnic Han background and her official position in the Chinese Writers' Association, Chi Zijian cast her gaze toward the Evenki people, capturing their essence in her acclaimed novel, *The Last Quarter of the Moon*, in 2005. Through her poetic portrayal of their tragic decline in the face of modernization, she poignantly criticizes the hegemonic discourse of polarization between the Han Chinese center and its peripheral ethnicities.

By placing the nomadic Evenki clan at center stage, she creates a natural and social borderland nurtured by shamanism, establishing a new Thirdspace that strikingly resembles Edward W. Soja's critical "thirding-as-Othering." Drawing on bell hooks's feminist theory, Soja's concept of "thirding-as-Othering" simultaneously centralizes and marginalizes and thereby sculpts an inclusive location imbued with "radical openness and possibility."[23] Chi Zijian chooses the Evenki culture as this inclusive space where marginality presents an alternative worldview toward nature, human, and universe, urging us to interrogate the dichotomous model of nature versus humanity and barbarian versus civilized under the modern nation/state.[24] In other words, *The Last Quarter of the Moon* stands out from other mainland Chinese literature because it provides a critical genealogy of the Evenki ethnic minority instead of typical Han majority experiences. First, I examine how Chi Zijian employs the shaman as an interface—an enchanting Thirdspace—between the spiritual and physical worlds to broach the interplay among animism, modernity, and environmentalism. Second, I explore how the Evenki's perception of the world and the cosmos has forged a utopian otherland, which transcends all forms of dualist thinking inherent in the Han-centered political power.

Narrated through the voice of a ninety-year-old Evenki woman, the wife of the last Evenki clan chieftain, the novel shines a light on the clan's struggle for survival against both natural and political adversities in the twentieth century. As noted by Cheng Li, the Evenki's "spiritualization of nature" transformed an antagonistic relationship between humans and nature into "an intimate, interdependent, and intertwined" one as inseparable components of an all-encompassing divine unity.[25] Shamanism is paramount within Evenki spirituality, which recognizes the omnipotence of natural deities that permeate all living creatures. These natural deities inhabit not only lightning, wind, sky, plants, and animals but also human bodies and souls. Despite the allure of modernization and the Han Chinese-built settlements, the ninety-year-old Evenki grandmother chooses to remain in the forest, for she regards herself as an integral part of a cosmos where human and nature coexist and interconnect. "My body was bestowed by the Spirits, and I shall remain in the mountains to return it to the Spirits," she asserts. She also constantly perceives and senses the spirits in various forms of nature: "I gazed at those figurines of deities made of wood and animal hides for a long time. They all originated in the mountain forests where we lived."[26] This comprises the animist axiom that each living being possesses a soul and spirit. The view that all beings are interconnected supports the principle of equal intrinsic value. As the Han Chinese relentlessly exploit natural resources without regard for ecological deterioration, they propagate a hierarchical dualism between humans and nature, as exemplified by the Maoist adage "Men Must Conquer Nature" (*ren ding sheng tian* 人定勝天).[27] In stark contrast, the Evenki hold the natural world in reverential esteem.

By focusing on the borderland where the Evenki roam and dwell, Chi Zijian skillfully crafts a vibrant patchwork that is wrought with an animistic openness. Taking an ecofeminist perspective, Lanlan Du highlights how Evenki women's deep connection with nature not only promotes ecological harmony but also disrupts the dualistic male/female conflict and fosters a harmonious gender relationship.[28] This ecofeminist stance echoes Val Plumwood's call for "a third way" against coercing women into "the choice of uncritical participation in a masculine-biased and dualized construction of culture."[29] Such an "anti-dualist approach" aims to dismantle the patriarchal binarism that divides men and women into two opposing and exclusive categories. Instead of strengthening the patriarchal dichotomies, Evenki men and women mutually honor and uplift each other amid the harsh natural and societal milieu. It is evident that Chi Zijian idealizes purity and freedom of love between Evenki men and women, liberating the gender relationship from the dualist thinking that privileges men over women. Although Evenki men are primarily responsible for hunting and governance, and women are mainly tasked with childbirth and child-rearing, they exhibit mutual respect, care, and support, complementing each other like the sun and moon, yin and yang. However, in the process of modernization, both Evenki women and nature are inevitably ensnared by "the hierarchical thinking that governs all forms of oppressions such as sexism, racism, and imperialist exploitation."[30]

The emblematic representation of Thirdspace is markedly embodied by two images of the shaman in the novel. As the ethnographer F. Georg Heyne elucidates, the Chinese Reindeer-Evenki are "faithful to their animistic worldview in which the shaman plays a most important role as mediator between human society and the world of spirit."[31] Communicating between this world and the other world, a shaman not only has the healing power to cure the wounded but also guides the departed toward their journeys in the afterlife. In opposition to the May Fourth tradition represented by Zhou Zuoren and Xiao Hong 蕭紅 (1911–1942), who denigrated shamanism as a superstition under the banner of modernity and enlightenment, Chi Zijian glorified its mystical and invigorating power. While Xiao Hong, in her famous novel *Tales of Hulan River* (*Hulan he zhuan* 呼蘭河傳), portrays shamanism as a feudal tool that hinders rational science and progress, Chi Zijian resurrects its enchantment to combat the environmental and ethnic detriments of modernity.[32] As a shaman dwells in both the physical and spiritual realms, he/she embodies a unique duality, simultaneously possessing both human and divine characteristics. Chi Zijian especially highlights this duality, which kindles a transcendental view to cross the boundaries of life and death, a worldview that is also pervasive among the Evenki people.

Nidu the Shaman is both the *urireng*'s shaman and the headman. He has not only a source of great power and insight from the other world but also a prestigious social status to lead the tribe. In addition, he is depicted as a nonbinary individual disregarding gender norms when he is involved in religious practice. In the narrator's eyes, "*Egdi'ama* was a man, but since he was a Shaman, he was obliged to dress like a woman. When he performed a Spirit Dance, his chest was padded. He was very stout, and after he donned the weighty Spirit Robe and Spirit Headdress, I thought he wouldn't even be able to turn around. But he whirled about with great agility as he struck the Spirit Drum."[33] During the shamanistic ceremony, Nidu the Shaman, who is biologically male, wears female attire, assuming a transgender or gender nonconforming role. This practice aligns with his "in-between" status as a mediator between the mundane realm and the spiritual world. In addition, the aesthetic of the shaman's ecstatic dance is described in a feminine way, yet his leadership as a headman has shown robust masculine strength with moral fortitude and unwavering integrity.

Nidu the Shaman embodies both human traits and divine traits. Chi Zijian portrays Nidu's human side by describing his unrelenting anguish over his forbidden love for Tamara, his sister-in-law and the narrator's mother. Following the passing of his brother, Nidu the Shaman yearns for Tamara's affection, an act deemed taboo within their tribe despite their mutual, yet secretive, fondness for each other. To embrace his human nature rather than his quasi-deity status, he sheds his feminine garb and dons a more masculine appearance. This transformation in his attire serves as a symbol of his desire to embrace his humanity and distance himself from the shamanic qualities. However, Nidu the Shaman's divine nature resurfaces during a time of crisis when the Evenki are confronted by the Japanese Commander Yoshida. Nidu summons his last reserves of spiritual power to perform a spirit dance despite his deeply aged body. Miraculously, he uses this power to heal Yoshida's wound and vanquish a warhorse. Following his shamanistic performance, Nidu passes away, leaving a lasting impression on Yoshida, who is filled with a profound admiration for the Evenki people. Nidu the Shaman becomes a multifaceted and complex site where human desires intertwine with quasi-divine qualities and where ethnic identity merges with the transcendental vision.

In *The Last Quarter of the Moon*, Nihao, the second shaman of the tribe, is a profoundly vivid and compelling character. Following Nidu's passing, Nihao emerges as an extraordinarily gifted female shaman, remarkably talented at communicating with the transcendental realm. She is happily married to Luni and a devoted mother to five children, yet this maternal quality becomes the price she must pay for her mystical power. Whenever Nihao performs the spirit dance to rescue anyone on the verge of death, she is fated to lose one of her own children. The haunting interplay between life and death enables a captivating vista into the depths of the Evenki culture's profound creativity and power. What is most intriguing is that the sacrifice of Nihao and her children is unbearably heavy and tragic. Chi Zijian's depiction of shamanism juxtaposes human consciousness and divine ability in a paradoxical manner: a mother's unconditional love for her own children is pushed to the brink, where she must love all living beings selflessly. Even in the face of the anguish and terror that come with losing one of her children, Nihao never falters in her spiritual duty, entering the religious trance without hesitation. By deliberately referring to the "others' child" as "her own child,"[34] Nihao dissolves the boundary between self and other, surpassing the conventional understanding of life and death held by Han Chinese.

Most importantly, Nihao's sacrifice embodies a divine quality that recognizes the intrinsic equality of all beings. Her transcendental vision is the most enthralling embodiment of Thirdspace, as she surpasses not only the boundaries of life and death but also the polarized values of good and evil embraced by ordinary individuals. Puffball, an Evenki man, is shunned by his fellow tribesmen due to his alcoholism and mistreatment of his own daughter. However, when he is near death after choking on a bear bone, Nihao performs the spirit dance to save him. Despite foreseeing that this religious performance will come at the cost of her own daughter Juktakan's life, Nihao proceeds. As Puffball is brought back to life, the narrator feels a sense of unease, as she despises the man for his repulsive behavior. Nonetheless, Nihao disregards the tendency toward moral judgment that resides within human nature. Her benevolent and transcendental demeanor extends even to Han Chinese, as evidenced when a man named He Baolin begs her to revive his child. Nihao accedes to the outsider's request, aware that it will cost the lives of her own children. Despite her trepidation, she presses on, ultimately sacrificing her son Grigori's life. As she says, "The Heavens summoned that child. But I kept him here on the earth, so my child had to go in its place."[35] This is seen again during an encounter with a trio of Han hunters pursuing reindeer during the great famine. One of the perpetrators suffers a grievous injury. Nevertheless, Nihao the Shaman conducts the religious ceremony with the aim of resurrecting the injured individual, but at the heartbreaking expense of her own unborn child's life.

Without presetting "the political court" and "moral court" to make any judgment,[36] Nihao's transcendental vision embodies the most precious aspect of literature: a benevolent heart akin to that of a deity, untainted by the polarities of good and evil or the cultural and ethnic divides between the Evenki and the Han Chinese. Nihao's final shamanistic performance is to quell a raging forest fire that modern chemicals from the Han Chinese cannot extinguish. In this final ritual, she sacrifices her own life, which not only testifies to her unwavering commitment to coexisting with the natural world but also reflects an indiscriminatory view of all creatures as equal. Chi Zijian deftly designs the shaman as a symbol of Thirdspace, using the intricate interplay between Evenki religion and environmentalism to question the hierarchical dualism of the Han Chinese center and the peripheral Evenki.

Influenced by shamanism, the Evenki people embrace a transcendental worldview. They maintain a serene disposition toward death and believe that humans merge with nature upon passing and transform into entities such as birds, trees, or lightning. This distinctive perspective challenges the Western anthropocentric outlook, which prioritizes human interests and frequently exploits nature for human benefit.[37] The Evenki's antidualist view must be understood as an integrative entity reconciling their attitude toward the political and moral standards espoused by the Han Chinese. Residing on the periphery, the Evenki have valiantly striven to preserve their cultural heritage while grappling with complex multiethnic and multinational relations.

Throughout the twentieth century, the Evenki had to deal with successive modern imperial powers—Russian, Japanese, and Chinese—each representing distinct historical epochs. During World War II, the Evenki men were compelled to leave the forest to undergo military training under Japanese rule. Following the establishment of the People's Republic of China in 1949, the Han Chinese not only aggressively exploited natural resources but also attempted to assimilate the Evenki into the "civilized" world by reshaping their nomadic lifestyle. Nevertheless, the Evenki hold a different view toward the dualized conception of morality in the face of political turmoil. After the Japanese were defeated, Wang Lu, who served as a translator for the Japanese, was executed by the Han Chinese on the grounds of being a "Japanese collaborator." However, this political judgment left the Evenki people perplexed, as they viewed Wang Lu's crime as simply the ability to speak Japanese. If punishment was deemed necessary, the severing of Wang Lu's tongue would have been sufficient. Even the Japanese officer Yoshida cannot be regarded as an enemy because he was impressed by the Evenki's coexistence with nature and their magical shamanism, consistently providing assistance. The Evenki's divergent perspective on the Japanese and their translator reveals a third way that poignantly defies the moral binary of right and wrong deeply fixed within modern Han Chinese nationalism.

Through both centering and marginalizing Evenki culture, Chi Zijian has constructed a utopian Thirdspace distinguished by its alternative perception of the world and cosmos. This perspective allows for a scathing critique of all the imperial powers that remain mired in endless conflict due to their rigid either/or mindset. Fortunately, the Evenki were spared the tumultuous political struggles that ravaged the Chinese people throughout the twentieth century, including the Land Reform, the Great Famine, and the Cultural Revolution. As a result, within the novel, a Han Chinese film projectionist and university professor who is condemned as a "rightist," lauds the Evenki way of life as the poetic "Peach Blossom Spring," an idyllic and tranquil paradise free from political strife.[38]

However, this ideal paradise was fated to be lost, as the Communist-led Han Chinese government was determined to alter the Evenki's nomadic way of life by relocating them from their mountainous ancestral home, destroying this cherished Thirdspace along with its ecological harmony. The passing of Nihao the Shaman, whose spirit robe, skirt, and headdress are donated to the local folk museum, becomes symbolic of the disappearance of the animistic pathways for the Evenki. The younger generation, exemplified by Irina, a talented painter, is torn between the allure of modernity and the Evenki religious values. Ultimately, plagued by this dichotomy, she chooses to commit suicide. In general, *The Last Quarter of the Moon* beautifully pays homage to the Thirdspace by illustrating an enthralling borderland saturated with a poignant mourning for its impending demise.

Mapping the Heterotopias of Taipei

Chu Tien-hsin is one of the most eminent contemporary female writers in Taiwan. Born into a literary family—her father, Chu Hsi-ning 朱西甯 (1927–1998), and her elder sister, Chu Tien-wen 朱天文 (1956–), are also celebrated writers—she embarked on her literary career in the 1970s. From a young age, she was deeply inspired by the Chinese literary tradition and embraced her father's patriotic passion, which reflected the ideology of the KMT. Before and after the annulment of martial law in 1987, her literary writings transformed to navigate the complex political, cultural, and ethnic identities in Taiwan. Inevitably, Chu Tien-hsin was put in a perilous situation riven by the tense conflicts between the KMT and the DPP. A second-generation mainlander from a military village (*juancun* 眷村), she found herself distant from the nationalistic obsession of her father's generation; at the same time, she was excluded by the prolocal discourse endorsed by the native Taiwanese.

Chu Tien-hsin's response to the politically divided climate is to foster a "heterotopia" of Taipei through her role as a city flâneur.[39] As elucidated by Michel Foucault, the concept of heterotopia not only involves the juxtaposition of one real place and other places but also relates to the societal and personal spaces that have been marginalized by mainstream ideologies. Foucault's heterotopia is deemed by Edward Soja as an open and inclusive Thirdspace contrasting with the confined places controlled by authoritative power.[40] Chu Tien-hsin's literary works, particularly *The Old Capital* (*Gudu* 古都), skillfully capture the essence of heterotopia, existing in the interstices where reality and memory interweave. The novel provides a thought-provoking critique of the competing utopian visions promoted by both the KMT and the DPP. She not only employs literary language to describe the heterotopia but also attempts to realize it through tangible social and political actions. Her engagement in democratic political activities and animal activism exemplifies her endeavors to pioneer a Thirdspace within the sphere of social reality.

Facing the aggressive opposition between the Chinese mainlanders (*waishengren* 外省人) and native Taiwanese (*benshengren* 本省人), Chu Tien-hsin has never faltered in criticizing the political-polarized reality. Her works, including *I Remember* (*Wo jide* 我記得), *In Remembrance of My Brothers in the Military Compound* (*Xiang wo juancun de xiongdimen* 想我眷村的兄弟們), and *A Novelist's Political Journal* (*Xiaoshuojia de zhengzhi zhouji* 小說家的政治周記), reflect a growing concern for the dwindling Thirdspace in post-martial law Taiwan. In the novel *In Remembrance*, depicting life in a military village, the protagonist finds herself trapped between two conflicting roles: daughter to a *waishengren* "father" and wife to a *benshengren* "husband." Compounding this, the "husband" frequently derides her for having "grown up drinking diluted KMT's milk," due to her father's outsider status, completely ignoring the protagonist's nuanced feelings and critical attitude toward the political party.[41] The story mirrors the author's dilemma and intense sense of anxiety that lingers in her later literary works.

Despite repeated accusations of political incorrectness, she was resolute in her refusal to be confined by the narrow definition of "authentic Taiwanese" prescribed by both the KMT and the DPP.[42] Courageously expressing herself and actively participating in political movements, she remained committed to speaking truth to power. In *Thirty-Three Years of Dream* (*Sanshisan nian meng* 三十三年夢), Chu Tien-hsin recalls her past involvement in the democratic process in Taiwan, including her support of the founder of the Chinese Social Democratic Party (*Zhongguo shehui minzhudang* 中華社會民主黨), Chu Kao-cheng 朱高正 (1954–2021), and her candidacy in the 1992 by-election for National Assembly representative. Drawing inspiration from the middle-leaning-left German Social Democratic Party, Chu Kao-cheng was dissatisfied with the political positions of both parties in Taiwan. It was precisely this middle ground that sparked Chu Tien-hsin's enthusiasm for taking part in the social democratic movement. She strongly believed that in the midst of the politically charged binary opposition between the Blue (the KMT) and Green (the DPP) camps, a third force was necessary.[43] After strenuous efforts, the third force ultimately failed after the Chinese Democratic Society joined the New Party; due to internal political struggles, Chu Kao-cheng was expelled from the latter. Nevertheless, for Chu Tien-hsin, what matters most is the fight for "personal freedom liberalism," championing individual freedom, self-discipline, and autonomy, as the foundation for Taiwan's future democratization.[44]

Confronting the prolocal discourse promoted by the DPP Chu Tien-hsin has always believed that pluralism is the way forward for Taiwan. In *The Old Capital*, she endeavored to sustain and expand Thirdspace by exploring pluralism and cultural hybridity within the postcolonial condition. Most impressively, she charts unexplored territories to find intangible connections between collective history and personal memory. David Der-wei Wang argues that, through the narrator's wandering in Taipei/Kyoto, history transforms into a tapestry of geographical landscapes, while memory assumes the role of an archaeological expedition. With this profound and flexible interplay of spatial dynamics, history is no longer a linear and monolithic territory.[45] When we read *The Old Capital*, we are ushered into Chu Tien-hsin's unfolding of the multidimensional space of the virtual and invisible, the past and the present. It is a Thirdspace or "a space of ambivalence" constructed by pastiche, described by Lingchei Letty Chen as a postmodern narrative method to invoke cultural hybridization and pluralism against Taiwan's homogeneity and essentialism.[46] This Thirdspace can also be understood as a heterotopia, a multilayered and overlapping space that synthesizes different structures of power to disturb exclusionist identity politics.[47] Through her embodiment of the roles of an exile at home, a melancholic flâneur, and a heterotopia agent,[48] the female narrator situates herself on the margins of Taiwan's political landscape. Drawing upon a multitude of experiences and fragmented memories associated with an elusive home, she deftly conjures a vivid and evocative portrayal of a postcolonial Taipei in flux. Within this captivating and fertile domain, the narrator explores a plurality of values and identities, reshaping the very fabric of political reality. Thus, her wandering, as well as a perpetually poignant and bittersweet quest for belonging, map out a nonconformist "other space" and surpass the limitations of preconceived political ideologies. It bears indelible imprints of her distinct voice and pathway.

Chu Tien-hsin's idea of carving out a third political space or establishing a third force motivated her involvement in the Ethnic Equality Agreement Alliance (Zuqun pingdeng xingdong lianmeng 族群平等行動聯盟) in 2004, which advocates that citizens should enjoy "freedom from fear, the right to determine one's own way of remembering, living, thinking, and pursuing happiness." These fundamental human rights should be legally protected "to ensure that no resident is threatened or discriminated against based on gender, religion, physical or mental ability, parental place of birth, cultural identity, or any other grounds."[49] This resonates with Yin Haiguang's demand for negative freedom that was inspired by thinkers like John Locke, John Stuart Mill, Friedrich Hayek, and Isaiah Berlin. In opposition to the "polarization of society by the state," Chu Tien-hsin and her friends also agreed to join the Democratic Action Alliance (Minzhu xingdong lianmeng 民主行動聯盟), which later evolved into the Taiwan Democratic School (Taiwan minzhu xuexiao 台灣民主學校),[50] aiming to reconstruct a Thirdspace—civil society—against a hostile environment increasingly characterized by intense binary opposition between the two major political parties. However, the third force has never coalesced into a solid political force in Taiwan and was quickly engulfed within the pan-Blue versus pan-Green political rivalry.

In her political commentaries, Chu Tien-hsin has fearlessly articulated her nuanced perspective, challenging the "bloodline theory" (xuetong lun 血統論) that confines an individual to a fixed political position and identity that he/she can hardly escape.[51] She repeatedly emphasized that even among the second-generation mainlanders from a military village, there were tremendous divergences in values and identities.[52] By deliberately employing the provocative headline "I Do Not Love Taiwan" ("Wo bu'ai Taiwan" 我不愛台灣),[53] she audaciously expressed her views and remained unaffiliated with either of the two opposing camps. Her most striking and controversial proclamation was the concept of "freedom of nonidentification" (bu rentong de ziyou 不認同的自由),[54] which she declared at a time when the issue of cultural and political identity was at the forefront, both locally and globally. She was deeply upset by the way the DPP, ostensibly utilizing a so-called authentic Taiwanese identity, "swiftly and coarsely bifurcates individuals who hold a plurality of cultural values and backgrounds into two distinct factions: those Taiwanese who passionately cherish their homeland, and the seemingly disloyal mainlanders who, without apparent reason, harbor intentions of betraying Taiwan."[55] She was irked by such a simplistic, either/or political mindset. Therefore, she has repeatedly dedicated herself to building a civil society that will accommodate a variety of languages that express different identities, rather than the simplified language designated by those in power as politically correct: "I naïvely hoped to carve out some space for dissent or individual expression amidst a chorus of unified identity on this island."[56] Unsurprisingly, her passionate advocacy for the concept of "freedom of nonidentification" has sparked intense criticism, particularly from proponents of the indigenization movement. Nevertheless, scholars came to her defense, arguing that a tolerant and democratic society should allow the coexistence of disparate perspectives, even those that choose not to align with any particular identity.[57] Despite Chu Tien-hsin's valiant efforts to seek out a Thirdspace, she remains burdened by an unshakeable anxiety and melancholy stemming from the ongoing political struggles of the present reality.

In addition, Chu Tien-hsin placed a particular emphasis on protecting her personal space and freedom, especially her freedom as a writer. She once expressed that she became anxious because she feared being dictated to by others, be it authoritarian rulers or the opposite party, which seemingly utilizes political correctness to advocate for the disadvantaged.[58] She believes that political positions should never override literary and artistic values, even if she also speaks for the disadvantaged such as foreign workers, immigrants, minority groups, and animals. She opposed using the discourse of indigenization (*bentuhua* 本土化) as the sole criterion for evaluating works of art, arguing that "The era of the party, politics, and ideology dominating literature and art should come to an end! Otherwise, in this new era of meaning, wouldn't it mean that the creators who need spiritual freedom the most are being locked up in another cage?"[59] Furthermore, she expressed the idea that writers should possess "freedom not to write" (*bu xiezuo de ziyou* 不寫作的自由), maintaining their spiritual independence and not being driven by market demands, critics' opinions, or literary awards, or being enslaved or controlled by any political power.

Chu Tien-hsin struck out in a novel direction, beginning in 2003, to cultivate a Thirdspace within the realm of interspecies dynamics, the intricate relationship between animals and humans. In her animal writing, the protagonist/narrator is usually another form of the *flâneur* who roams in Taipei but with a special purpose—feeding street cats; the setting is also another distinct form of "heterotopia" on the fringes of society, transcending the conventional boundaries separating the human and the nonhuman. Within this extraordinary heterotopia, a "shared chronotope" (*gongsheng de shikong* 共生的時空) materializes, intertwining the lives of animal protection volunteers and street cats as they navigate the treacherous terrain that stems from a dearth of empathy toward nonhuman entities. In this interspecies Thirdspace, their own temporal and spatial dimensions unfold around animal ethics. These "cat people" usually embark on solitary expeditions, awaiting the cloak of darkness before venturing forth. Their lonely and personal sojourns serve a dual purpose—evading hindrance and humiliation from neighbors who harbor disdain for animals while safeguarding the precious feline sustenance from the encroachment of the "human species." The enigmatic hiding spots of street cats, nestled beneath cars, on street corners, along riverbanks, and within cemeteries, as well as the distinctive feeding routes of each animal protection volunteer, coalesce to form a multiplicity of alternate spaces that diverge from societal norms. However, the nomadic explorations of humans and nonhumans within this "shared chronotope" audaciously challenge the anthropocentric worldview propagated by global capitalism, which prioritizes human progress at the expense of nonhuman welfare.

Chu Tien-hsin, together with her sister Chu Tien-wen and other animal protection volunteers, collaborates closely with the Taiwan Atlas of Adoption Association (Taiwan renyang ditu xiehui 台灣認養地圖協會), actively implementing the TNR (Trap, Neuter, Return) program. This approach, recognized universally as the epitome of effectiveness and compassion in addressing street animal population control, stands in stark contrast to the previous provisions outlined in the Animal Protection Law (1998). Under the former legislation, shelters were authorized to euthanize stray animals that remained unclaimed beyond a mere twelve-day period.[60] Chu Tien-hsin and the animal protection volunteers are "comrades of the Cat Party" with their respective "cat feeding routes," advocating for the rights of street cats and treating them as independent beings who have the freedom to choose their own lifestyles. They form a loosely organized group, implementing the TNR program in their respective neighborhoods and occasionally collaborating through the internet. Although they rarely organize "group battles," they are genuine activists who work diligently every day to feed street cats. They also give lectures at universities, proactively participate in community meetings, and persuade government officials to change policies. In Chu Tian-hsin's words, they are a group of "the humblest people, like Sisyphus in Greek mythology, toiling on the frontline every day."[61]

In *The Hunters* (*Lieren men* 獵人們), Chu Tien-hsin presents an appealing perspective on cats as self-reliant and self-governing creatures. Drawing a parallel between feline and human existence, she asserts that cats, despite their arduous and challenging lives, possess an inherent dignity. Chu Tien-hsin's scattered observations and reflections on cats serve as a compelling means for her to engage with human social reality, constructing a heterotopic space centered around animal ethics.[62] In her thought-provoking book *That Cat, That Person, That City* (*Namao, Naren, Nacheng* 那貓那人那城),

Chu Tien-hsin not only defends cats' right to be free from hunger but also advocates for a universal obligation of humans to respect all living beings.

However, Chu Tien-hsin's involvement in the animal protection movement demonstrates a balanced approach, employing a typical Thirdspace strategy. This approach is consistent with Lee Haiyan's argument that "between the extremes of anthropocentrism and biocentrism there is a third, pragmatist way of bridging the gap between the human and nonhuman."[63] By eschewing anthropomorphism, it avoids wholeheartedly embracing biocentrism and nonhuman perspectives. It upholds the ethical principles of humanism while subjecting the excessive claims of subjectivity and agency made by biocentrism on behalf of the nonhuman to critical scrutiny. In doing so, it strikes a balance that acknowledges the inherent value of all beings while refraining from exaggerating their capacities and rights.[64] The TNR program precisely epitomizes this third, pragmatist alternative. Through Chu Tien-hsin's meticulous practice of TNR, she successfully departs from the inhumane methods of euthanasia previously sanctioned by the Taiwanese government. Furthermore, she maintains a measured distance from the biocentric critique that sterilization infringes upon the fundamental reproductive rights of animals.[65] Her approach actively seeks a middle ground between the two extremes, recognizing the significance of population control while simultaneously honoring the well-being and autonomy of the animal kingdom.

The middle path advocated by Chu Tien-hsin is marked by a discernible compromise, where the preservation of cats' survival rights takes precedence over their right not to be sterilized.[66] She believes that this reconciliation is essential, driven by her acknowledgment of the intertwined existence of humans and animals within this interspecies heterotopia. With tenacious dedication, she tirelessly partakes in negotiations with the human community, aspiring to forge a consensus not only with those who are indifferent to the welfare of animals but also with other animal protection organizations. Rather than succumbing to hostility based upon divergent beliefs, she seeks to foster an atmosphere of collaboration.

When interviewed by the media regarding her Taiwanese identity, Chu Tien-hsin responded by drawing a metaphorical parallel to a diminutive vessel containing water. This water jug assumes a paramount significance for stray cats, representing a vital lifeline for their survival. Furthermore, it serves as a poignant testament to the fundamental essence of humanity.[67] Were Taiwan to forsake such a humble water jug, together with compassion,

Chu Tien-hsin contends that maintaining her connection to her ancestral homeland would prove onerous. From her perspective, a Taiwanese identity must encompass a comprehensive multispecies outlook,[68] wherein not only street cats and dogs are afforded dignified lives but marginalized or minority groups—such as the disabled, refugees, LGBT+ individuals, and aboriginal Taiwanese—can coexist harmoniously. Only within such an alternative reality, characterized as heterotopia, can the existence of multiple spaces and a multispecies perspective be realized, providing a nurturing environment wherein her Taiwanese identity finds its true home.

The pathways traversed in Thirdspace by the three female writers discussed in this chapter showcase distinct trajectories. Xi Xi perceives Hong Kong as a Thirdspace that harbors an inherent paradox: it embodies positive and creative aspects as well as problematic and uncertain qualities. Nevertheless, it is precisely this paradox of openness and uncertainty that invokes an expansive array of meanings. Xi Xi crafts a metaphorical and transmedia narrative wherein Hong Kong's freedom emerges as a predominant factor for its economic prosperity. Even when ensnared between the imperial powers of China and Britain, the denizens of Hong Kong yearn for the autonomy to shape their own destiny. Chi Zijian's approach champions the circulatory time of the Evenki, mirroring the natural rhythm of the four seasons, defying a unilinear, progressive chronology. Moreover, she highlights their religious beliefs which transcend the boundaries of life and death, human and nonhuman. These elements aggregate to create a distinctive Thirdspace that challenges the limitations imposed by the binary perspective of new versus old in modernity. Critically aware of the intrusion of modernization, Chi Zijian vociferously campaigns for the Evenki people's freedom to preserve their nomadic lifestyle and religious customs. In a similar vein, Chu Tien-hsin not only places value on a third way or a third force within the rigid political struggles of opposing parties but also endeavors to cultivate a harmonious space that allows for the coexistence of animals and humans. She ardently emphasizes the notion of "freedom of nonidentification," resolutely upholding individual autonomy and rejecting any party's hegemonic control over Taiwanese identity. Additionally, Chu Tien-hsin steadfastly fights for the rights of animals, respecting the unhindered lives of street cats.

Despite the differences in their approaches, these three female writers converge in their shared aim of conferring a political connotation of freedom upon Thirdspace. Xi Xi, Chi Zijian, and Chu Tien-hsin all strive to imbue

Thirdspace with the significance of liberation. They assert the imperative for freedom in various contexts: Xi Xi accentuates the prosperity of Hong Kong emanating from its unwavering commitment to political freedom and autonomy, Chi Zijian gives voice to the right for the Evenki people to retain the freedom to preserve their unique cultural practices, and Chu Tien-hsin champions the cause of individual freedom alongside the unimpeded coexistence of animals. In essence, freedom emerges as their shared vehicle for dismantling dualistic constructs within disparate political and cultural landscapes.

Epilogue

The conspicuous lacuna of Thirdspace in modern China is a serious problem that persists into the present era. This book has examined how a cohort of modern and contemporary Chinese intellectuals, literati, and artists, in different times and places, strived to explore and develop the alternative perspective, which resists the extremely corrosive and dogmatic either/or political dichotomy. The issues presented by the concept of Thirdspace in this book are closely intertwined with the political survival of Chinese intellectuals. Under authoritarian regimes, dichotomous thinking firmly grips intellectuals' mindsets, leaving them with only two options: aligning themselves as either enemies or allies of the reigning system. This significantly circumscribes individual expression while stifling the flourishing of pluralistic ideas.

Influenced by the logic of dualism, which "has formed the modern political landscape of the West as much as the ancient one,"[1] these oppositional categories are invariably hierarchical, designed to normalize and reinforce dominant power structures in modern and contemporary China. Moreover, this logic has shaped several generations' simplistic mindsets and value judgments, replete with hostility and intolerance of heterodox or heterogenous opinions. The possibility of Thirdspace was almost entirely excluded within an intricate nexus of hazards wherein scholars and writers undertook considerable risks in their pursuit of alternative trajectories from the oppositional political factions. As a matter of fact, both the ruling and resisting sides were reluctant to permit the existence of Thirdspace and utilized various means to criticize and compress it. However, as Liu Zaifu has stated, the broader the Thirdspace, the healthier, more diverse, and freer society becomes.[2]

What kinds of inspiration from the discursive strategy of Thirdspace will continue to be relevant to the social conditions of our time? Will the mentality of Thirdspace retain an active and interconnecting correlation with reality, continuing to shed new light on how to deal with the ever-changing global phenomena of politics and face the chaotic and complex external and internal worlds? Drawing on both traditional Chinese thought and Western political philosophies, can the notion of Thirdspace defined by Chinese intellectuals—imbued with historical particularities yet simultaneously resonant with universal values—speak to the current problems in our society?

To answer these questions, I first revisit some insights from previous chapters, highlighting important concepts such as neutrality, pluralism, liberalism, aestheticism, positive and negative liberty, proper measure, and yin-yang dialectics. Second, I explore how the political stance of Thirdspace reverberates in Chan Koonchung's novel *The Second Year of Jianfeng: A Uchronia of New China*, which represents a spectacular political heterotopia inspired by Michel Foucault. Then, I examine the problems revealed in the use and misuse of cyberspace—another kind of Thirdspace—during the pandemic period when isolation, quarantine, and drawing physical and political boundaries became a normal existence. By examining the controversies over Fang Fang's *Wuhan Diary* and Yan Lianke's acceptance speech for the 2021 Newman Prize, I reflect upon the resurrection of the either/or mentality in the cultural ecology of China at present. As the contemporary sociopolitical landscape is marred by increasingly pervasive factionalism akin to a new Cold War era, the discourse surrounding Thirdspace has emerged as a compelling framework inspiring alternative thinking patterns, ideas, attitudes, methods, and even lifestyles. It embodies a multifaceted understanding of history and reality in both practical and theoretical terms, responding to the diminishing freedoms experienced at present.

The Contested Thirdspace

The arduous pursuit of Thirdspace by Chinese intellectuals has often been subject to criticism and scrutiny. For instance, Lu Xun, the vanguard of the May Fourth Movement, often held a contemptuous view, perceiving these intellectuals as reclusive individuals or escapists who shirked the social responsibilities of confronting the darkness and lacked the courage to engage in direct combat. However, those who actively probed the potential of Thirdspace exhibited a remarkable dedication to addressing social issues and participating in reform. Their endeavors often made them targets of oppression under authoritarian rule, resulting in persecution, exile, or marginalization. Despite significant obstacles in political struggles, they made a great effort to maintain their distinct propositions and convictions, with the aim of fostering a more pluralistic and inclusive political and cultural environment.

First and foremost, these intellectuals displayed unyielding independence, not relying on political parties, factions, or organizations. They adamantly refused to be manipulated or subjugated by any authority or group, insisting on protecting their rights as autonomous beings. Despite their varying political stances, whether as active public intellectuals or self-reliant individuals, they embodied different forms of nonalignment and resisted simplistic ideological categorizations. Secondly, they evinced a strong sense of inclusivity, calling for the harmonious coexistence of diverse perspectives and a multiplicity of epistemological frameworks. Greatly concerned with individuality, community, freedom, and equality, they eschewed absolute exclusivism and distinguished themselves from both orthodox Marxists on the Left- and Right-wing factions that protect vested interest groups. Notably, they displayed an inclination to embrace the power of tolerating contradiction—an essential yet often neglected strategy that enables the proliferation of a myriad of political positions. Thirdly, recognizing the absence of Thirdspace within the politically charged landscape of modern China, at the core of their investigation lies a pivotal critique of the dualistic framework that underlies Chinese modernity. Employing various methodologies, ranging from philosophical approaches to literary inventions, their objective was to transcend the limitations imposed by rigid binary thinking, which perpetuates a sense of opposition and exclusion. They aimed to dismantle the deeply ingrained either/or logic that inevitably consolidates hierarchical relationships of dominance and subordination.

The intermediate zone in a time of political polarization can be broad and diverse. One of the central arguments in this book revolves around the adaptation of traditional Chinese philosophies, such as Buddhism, Daoism, and Confucianism, as lenses through which to examine the possibility of disrupting the dualism that exerts great impact upon Chinese modernity. Prominent intellectuals such as Zhang Dongsun, Li Zehou, and Liu Zaifu have drawn significantly from earlier Chinese philosophical concepts and practices, formulating their own distinct theories. Zhang Dongsun's idea of "correlation logic," Li Zehou's invention of *du*, and Liu Zaifu's advocacy of Thirdspace and "aesthetic transcendence" all drew significantly from traditional Chinese ideas. The impact of Western modernity has led to the disenchantment with traditional religions through enlightenment and rationalization, resulting in an endless cycle of political rivalries. Challenging the dualistic constructs that underpin Chinese modernity, such as the dichotomies of old versus new, China versus the West, and human versus nature, these Chinese intellectuals brought back multiple strands of traditional wisdom and cosmology, laying the foundation for prioritizing harmony and coexistence.

Zhang Dongsun's "correlation logic" and his pluralistic epistemology are rooted in the wisdom of Confucianism, Buddhism, and Daoism in China. He recognized the dialogical relationship between opposing poles and questioned the absolute truths promulgated by both political factions. Consequently, he refused to be bound by the prevalent Marxist thinking in modern China and forged his own philosophy of epistemological pluralism. The political strategy of the "third route" and middle politics that he proposed and practiced, although met with setbacks, still serves as an alternative path contesting the dominant trend inspired by Western modernity. Li Zehou's concept of *du* also draws wisdom from the dialectics of yin and yang in the *Book of Changes*. It emphasizes the complementary nature of conflicting forces, distinguishing itself from Hegelian dialectics. The method of *du* does not seek to eliminate differences and contradictions to achieve unity but rather strives to skillfully coordinate differing parties and find ways for harmonious coexistence. Liu Zaifu's exploration of Thirdspace and aesthetic transcendence derive from the Middle Way wisdom of Buddhism and the nonduality approach of Chan Buddhism, surpassing the distinction between great virtue and great evil and offering a deeper understanding of the complexities of human nature. To a certain extent, their ideas resonate with Prasenjit Duara's proposal of "dialogical transcendence," which "permits coexistence of different levels and expressions of truth." Their goal of reviving ancient Chinese philosophy and religion is similar, which is to differentiate Thirdspace from "the Hegelian idea of the dialectics where one of the two terms negates and supersedes the other."[3] But most importantly, these Chinese intellectuals' primary objective was to combat the ideology of class struggle derived from Marxism, which inevitably led to "violent revolution" that pervaded China in the twentieth century.

However, as they stressed harmony, rationality, balance, and neutrality—all concepts associated with moderate politics—these intellectuals were often thrust into the tumultuous vortex of controversy. One example is Li Zehou's statement that "harmony is higher than justice." Instead of "seeking for an absolute criterion for distinguishing right from wrong or for defining justice," Li Zehou values harmony grounded in "the wisdom of the pragmatic reason" he ardently espouses.[4] His assertion of harmony does not entail an abandonment of justice; rather, it calls into question the authoritarian forces that define the standards of justice and a priori, universally applicable truth. He emphasizes the value of "pragmatic rationality," which refers to a historical product of human empirical existence.[5] Therefore, the specific context within which the art of *du* is deployed, with the aim of achieving the "common good," is invaluable.[6] In the politically polarized environment where one often has no option other than to align with either the extreme Left or the extreme Right, the concept of justice is frequently hijacked by political parties. Instead, the pursuit of harmony, along with the multifarious approaches laid out by the aforementioned intellectuals, embraces diversity and alleviates the perils of radical opposition and exclusion. It offers an alternative paradigm to reevaluate the trajectory of modernity and revolution and their related ideologies.

Another corpus of arguments put forth by these Chinese intellectuals, who have vividly mapped the realm of Thirdspace, pertains to their adaptation and appropriation of Western political theories. Although they are well informed by a variety of Western philosophies, such as those of Immanuel Kant, G. W. F. Hegel, Karl Marx, John Locke, John Stuart Mill, Jeremy Bentham, Hannah Arendt, Friedrich Hayek, Isaiah Berlin, Karl Popper, A. N. Whitehead, Max Weber, Jürgen Habermas, and John Rawls, they lean toward a moderate way to safeguard freedom, the rule of law, equality, and justice. The central value they collectively defend is individual freedom. More specifically, they are among a few modern Chinese intellectuals who are highly aware of what Berlin calls negative freedom, cherishing a noncoercive personal space and pluralism of immeasurable human values. Berlin's concept of positive freedom, in which a self and a social whole (or a bigger self) are interconnected to reach a higher level of freedom, found easy acceptance among Chinese intellectuals due to its alignment with Confucianism's principle of moral self-cultivation. However, Berlin's concept of negative freedom—a certain minimum area of personal freedom uncoerced by others—is less known and accepted in modern China.[7]

Li Zehou indicates that negative freedom usually prompts reform, while positive freedom gravitates toward revolution or other grand goals. The former finds its grounding in tangible empirical experience, while the latter contains more idealistic aspirations.[8] In his delineation of the Western liberal tradition, Zhang Dongsun traces the concept of individualism and natural law back to Stoic philosophy in Greece, Hugo Grotius's contract theory, and John Locke's liberal political theory.[9] He was impressed with how Western philosophers have valiantly defended the rights of individuals against unjust exercises of political authority. In other words, Zhang Dongsun refused to valorize equality at the expense of sacrificing freedom, respecting the idea of inviolable individual rights and private property. He proposes an "equal life philosophy," which grants all individuals equality in terms of personal dignity as well as opportunities to use their talents. Therefore, freedom, in his definition, is not an ism but a condition to ensure all kinds of isms.[10] Democracy, for Zhang, is not simply a political ideology but rather a comprehensive system that includes morality, thought, society, religion, legislation, and economics and should thoroughly permeate people's daily lives. He even considers democracy an ideal, a spirit, or a kind of civilization totally absent in the Chinese cultural tradition.[11] Liu Zaifu and Gao Xingjian expressed skepticism about the subordination of individuals to overarching ideals of society, be they socialist utopias or nationalist dreams. As expressed by Gao Xingjian in his concept of "without isms," an individual who is free of such manipulation would be a more complete human being. "'Without isms' is not nihilism, nor is it eclecticism, egotism, or dogmatism. It is against both totalitarianism and the self-inflation of oneself as a god or superhuman."[12] Gao Xingjian particularly opposes political means that impose upon individuals in the name of the people, nature, or justice. Upholding the values of negative freedom, these Chinese intellectuals of Thirdspace departed from other revolutionaries who claimed to fight for people's freedom but ultimately sacrificed individual liberty.

In addition, these intellectuals place significant emphasis on the establishment of a "public sphere" as conceptualized by Jürgen Habermas, which entails a civil society where citizens can freely engage in rational debates concerning social and political matters, and even express dissent toward the state. Functioning as an intermediary space between individuals and the state, it rejects manipulation by political authorities or market forces. Crucially, these intellectuals underscore the importance of linking the public sphere with rationality to prevent ignorance and one-sidedness. Zhang Dongsun, driven by his aspirations for political reform in the Republic of China, drew inspiration from Mill's assertion that the truth requires "a diversity of opinions" and "a chance of fair play to all sides of the truth,"[13] which include oppositional or heterogeneous opinions. He firmly believed that the truth could only emerge through unrestricted freedom for rational discourse and refutation. Yin Haiguang contends that only a spectrum of thought without bias and color, whether it leans to the right or the left, can offer a constructive path forward for a healthy political ecosystem. To establish a Thirdspace akin to Habermas's public sphere in Hong Kong, Jin Yong established a journalistic empire, *Ming Pao*, founded solely on the principle of neutrality, distancing itself from both the CCP and the KMT. The public sphere is considered a fundamental element of democratic societies in the Western world; however, in the modern political landscape of China, it is not inherently ingrained in the society. Instead, pursuing such a space presents an ongoing challenge, particularly during revolutionary periods when the very existence of the public space is essentially prohibited. Even in the postrevolutionary era, as the public sphere began to emerge, the pervasive either/or mentality continued to exert a significant influence on the national character, often resulting in polarization between "liberalism" and the "new left wing," as seen in the Chinese intellectual debates in the 1990s.

Echoing the pursuits of the "third force" intellectuals such as Zhang Dongsun, Zhang Junmai, Luo Longji 羅隆基 (1896–1965), Chu Anping, Xiao Qian, and Zhu Guangqian, who attempted to forge a middle ground or a nuanced "third way" within the Chinese political landscape, contemporary Chinese thinkers such as Xu Jilin advocate for a similar solution. Taking inspiration from Anthony Giddens's book, *The Third Way: The Renewal of Social Democracy*, Xu urges us to carefully consider the Polish and Czech experiences, wherein a novel market economy was harmoniously combined with political democracy, without necessitating excessive growth. His idea is clearly derived from the "third force" tradition in the 1940s:

> To my mind, it is necessary therefore to develop a moderate middle force between the two extremes of fin de siècle Chinese "liberalism" and the "new left wing," that is, a middle way that incorporates

the freedom and justice of new liberalism and social democracy. . . . Only when a moderate new liberalism and social democracy, interpolated between the extremes, become the mainstreams of the Chinese intellectuals world will a dialogue and mutual permeation of the other's values be possible. Only then will the China of the twenty-first century be able to avoid a repetition of antagonism and extremism of this century. Only then will there be a "third way" that is "neither Left nor Right," that is rational, energetic, and balanced.[14]

According to Geremie R. Barmé's observations, Chu Anping argued that a "third way" held great importance in cultivating a robust public sphere and moving toward a democratic country. However, it was relentlessly extirpated by Mao Zedong after 1949. Even as early as 1948, Mao Zedong declared in his article "Carry the Revolution Through the End" that the pursuit of any middle path was not the correct choice for China's future.[15] Similarly, under Xi Jinping's regime, which has resurrected the philosophy of struggle, Xu Jilin's rearticulation of a "third way" and his optimistic anticipation of a "Giddens era" were also vanquished.

Furthermore, the rapid growth of internet culture in China since the 1990s has cultivated an unprecedented "cyber public space" with diversified political discourses, plural cultural productions, and dynamic interactions between writers and readers, which has significantly deconstructed and transformed the monism of state-controlled politics.[16] Despite "a residual of socialism" continuing to exert great impact on people's mentality and sensibilities, as Michel Hockx elaborated, this "cyber public space" has posed challenges to the state-regulated cultural paradigms.[17] More importantly, this public space encompasses not only the debates of intellectual elites but also the opinions of the masses. However, this incipient manifestation of a public sphere in cyberspace also faced strict censorship following the outbreak of the pandemic.

Chan Koonchung's Uchronia of New China

In *The Second Year of Jianfeng: A Uchronia of New China*, Chan Koonchung offers an alternate history in which the KMT, instead of the CCP, rules China after 1949. In Chan's speculative imagination, Zhang Dongsun becomes a fictional figure who migrated to Hong Kong in the crucial transitional time of 1949.

> At that time, Dongsun's resolute words echoed through the air: "Not until democracy and freedom of speech grace the land of China shall I tread its soil again, even if it means forsaking the delectable chestnuts of the Zhou dynasty."[18] While many people have offended both the CCP and the KMT, only a small handful of renowned figures, like Dongsun, chose the path of exile in a distant colony rather than bowing to the prevailing victor. In the face of an unfolding saga where the KMT triumphed while the CCP faltered, this unwavering resolve set Dongsun apart—a man who has been persistently loyal to his own ideas and thus has turned into a misfit.[19]

In the novel, the fictional Zhang Dongsun's misfit personality emanates from the third route position he previously advocated, which led to his skepticism toward the KMT's rule. In Chan Koonchung's account, after taking over China and expelling the CCP, Chiang Kai-shek practices one-party dictatorship, insisting on one leader, one doctrine, and one political party, objecting to a real democratic system. This outcome precisely aligns with Zhang Dongsun's prophetic foresight. Firm in his conviction that neither the KMT's autocratic rule nor the CCP's unilaterally pro-Soviet policy constituted the optimal choice, Zhang regarded the "middle of the road" as China's most favorable path. His personal choice to reside in colonial Hong Kong reflects Chan Koonchung's intention of highlighting individual liberty—one of the most important traits of Thirdspace. Living an extremely simple life, Zhang successfully distances himself from both the KMT and the CCP, enabling him to sustain his pursuit of philosophical inquiry and the composition of poetry in the classical style. His embrace of individual liberty, or the negative freedom of noninterference, paves the way for his unceasing insistence on the political stance of the third route. In addition, Zhang Dongsun's political position easily blends into Hong Kong's cosmopolitan environment, which embodies a real version of Thirdspace where the hybridity of culture has been continually privileged and consolidated.

Although Chan Koonchung's novel is based on speculative or counterfactual imagination by altering the historical trajectory at a crucial moment, it closely follows an inherent logic contingent on the protagonist's personality, philosophical thought, political stance, and historical experience. As the literary scholar Josephine Chiu-Duke accurately points out, Chan Koonchung's own political position as a "middle-of-the-road" (*zhongdao* 中道) liberal with "left-wing" leanings is akin to that of the third route intellectuals like Zhang Dongsun. Chan and Zhang would agree that "liberal values protected by constitutional democracy are the necessary foundation for social and economic equality."[20] Indeed, Chan purposely accentuates Zhang Dongsun's unwavering character as an independent intellectual whose insistence on the third route or middle politics strikingly echoes Chan's own political positioning. In Chan's reimagining of China, Zhang emerges as a personification of his political aspiration, which is to embrace "tolerating contradiction" as a strategy to harmonize capitalism and socialism, liberalism and equality, and right-wing and left-wing ideologies.

In his article "Utopia, Dystopia, Heterotopia: Theoretical Crossexaminations on Ideal, Reality, and Social Innovation," Chan Koonchung creatively appropriates Foucault's "heterotopia" to carve out a middle space between optimistic utopian thought and pessimistic dystopian thought. According to Edward W. Soja, Foucault's concept of heterotopology has added significant meaning to Thirdspace by entailing all other places that deviate from the norm in society. He nevertheless is critical of its limits, "narrowly focused on peculiar microgeographies, nearsighted and nearsited, deviant and deviously apolitical."[21] In contrast, Chan Koonchung's appropriation of Foucault's heterotopia may be the best case in point of how spatial imagination can be highly political.

The concept of heterotopia refers to a heterogeneous body of visions and articulations in relation to Thirdspace in both metaphorical and political dimensions. It is integral to Chan Koonchung's vision of a plural society encompassing all kinds of differences. In his own words, "The notion of heterotopia implies imagining a society from multiple angles, similar to the compound eyes of a fruit fly or feline night vision, with which humans might see what they are unable to see now." By employing "compound eyes," he is able to uncover the parts of history hidden from our time. Similar to the Thirdspace that Soja describes, Chan's heterotopia is undeniably all-inclusive, nonlinear, dynamic, centrifugal, and polycentric. It comprises a multiplicity of spaces, such as "physical space, private space, public space, virtual space, imaginary space, outer space. Moreover, it also covers naturescape, artificial landscape, technoscape, semioscape, virtualscape, and mindscape. It could also be any alternative space or any banal, everyday field, as a heterotopia is devoid of an essence or clear boundaries."[22] By crossing the boundaries between the physical and the metaphysical, the visible and invisible, the conscious and unconscious, Chan directly challenges the conventional mode of either/or thinking that divides the world into heaven versus hell, absolute good versus absolute evil, optimistic utopian thought versus pessimistic dystopian thought. More importantly, Chan's heterotopia is solidly rooted in reality and closely associated with his political stance of "via media" or "middle liberal,"[23] which has been essential in creating a spatial perspective to fight against the extreme leftists and the extreme rightists. By doing so, he intends to find a middle ground in which a genuinely diverse society is possible. Drawing on the political viewpoints of Max Weber, Antonio Gramsci, Chantal Mouffe, Ernesto Laclau, Etienne Balibar, and Isaiah Berlin, Chan attempts to transform "Schmittian antagonistic politics into political coexistence,"[24] nurturing a plural and diverse society that celebrates differences, competition, and disagreements. By bridging the gap between the theoretical realm and the practical realm, between the center and the periphery, his heterotopia aims to engage directly with current politics and society, pointing to "an alternate reality" that "may open up more doors to movements in disparate social fields."[25] The inclusion of heterotopia largely corresponds to a more practical, tangible, and reasonable road of democratic socialism, the one advocated by Zhang Dongsun and the third route intellectuals in the 1940s.

According to David Der-wei Wang, Chan's uchronia, or alternate history, forges an interesting dialogue with the past instead of the future, questioning the theory of historical determinism by juxtaposing "the factors of necessity, contingency, and chances."[26] The purpose of Chan's speculative writing lies in its uncanny exploration of various possible historical trajectories that did not happen. He not only criticizes social evolution, historical determinism, and a linear view of history but also calls into question the logic that argues power prevails over truth. Most importantly, he wants to rectify the official history written by the winners, who intentionally wipe out or bury constructive and rational ideas expressed by the defeated. Therefore, Chan's engagement in writing the uchronia of New China is a recuperative attempt to show the diversity of historical pathways, which can enlighten us on how to deal with the present epistemological and practical conundrums. Within his speculative writing, Chan designates another "speculation" by Zhang Dongsun, who deliberates on the consequences if the CCP were to take over China. In Zhang's hypothesis, the Chinese Communist Party would not necessarily have to follow a one-party dictatorship and Stalinist totalitarian line but could instead follow another line of all-party consultation proposed by the CCP in 1946 or the new democracy proposed by Mao Zedong in 1940.[27] Although the CCP unfortunately chose Stalinist totalitarianism in the actual historical picture, the fictional Zhang Dongsun's hypothesis at least evokes the fact that the other two paths, though concealed in history, still have significance and relevance to our present.

Apparently for Chan Koonchung, among the plurality and diversity of historical pathways, the middle of the road appears most inspiring. Narrating in the fictional character Zhang Dongsun's voice, Chan wrote: "The fact that the middle of the road did not materialize does not mean that it is wrong. If someone can explain clearly the options and the missed turns in history, the idea of the middle of the road will inspire the people of today and emerge again at the right time to change the reality."[28] Because he regards the middle of the road as the right way (*zhengdao* 正道), Chan Koonchung lays it out as the foundation of Chiang Ching-kuo's rule in the novel. Corresponding to this political strategy, the uchronia of New China in Chan Koonchung's imagination is based on neither optimistic utopian thought nor pessimistic dystopian thought; instead, it embodies Chan's appropriation of Foucault's heterotopia. Chan's sense of heterotopia stems less from the notions of human rights, democracy, egalitarianism, and social justice than from a mixed economic policy similar to what the real Zhang Dongsun advocated in the 1940s. In the novel, when Chiang Ching-kuo reflects on why China's economy grew so rapidly in the 1960s and entered the era of modest prosperity, he concludes that this was the result of a combination of a planned economy and a market economy, proposed and implemented by the genius economist Zhongrong. "It is not communism, nor is it laissez-faire capitalism. It is not a replica of the mercantilist Colbertism of the Great Powers, nor is it exactly post–World War II Keynesian economics, which bolsters the creation of effective demand, including the stimulation of consumption."[29] Therefore, the fictional Chiang Ching-kuo emphasizes practical efficiency and believes that economic development should be divided into stages, examining the overall balance instead of adhering to one school of thought. He takes the strengths of the socialist planning economy and the capitalist free economy, prompting rapid economic development and maintaining a high average wealth at the same time. This is the realization of Zhang Dongson's political and economic ideal, which blends a capitalist method of economic growth with a socialist system of distribution and equality.

However, different from both utopian and dystopian narratives that "depict a self-contained, monolithic future society, and its hierarchal order (or the lack thereof) is stable and complete,"[30] Chan's heterotopia is not established on a totalizing, fixed, and homogenized narrative. Given the absence of democracy, the empire of Jianfeng is far from perfect, yet it has its own strengths. Such a vision avoids the binary opposition between a utopian imagination of a bright future and a dystopian imagination of a hellish world. It precisely reflects Chan Koonchung's own political stance, different from both the neoleftists who uphold the utopian dream of "Sinocentric" *tianxia* (all under heaven) to promote political sovereignty and equality and the liberals who see an inferno and ruins under the tyrannical state that lacks liberty and political reform.[31] More pertinent to Chan's concern is whether it is possible to find a middle ground to solve the problems generated by those polarized ideological bearings.

In the novel, under Chiang Ching-kuo's rule, what is still lacking is Zhang Dongsun's democratic ideal that highlights the constitutional rule of law, multiparty democracy, restraints on political power, and protection of civil rights and freedom of speech. Despite its "economic miracle," it is still an imperfect and flawed society, which is manifested by the government's crackdown on the gathering of many renowned intellectual dissenters in December 1979. However, instead of casting the Jianfeng empire in an optimistic or pessimistic light, Chan considers polemic issues involved with democracy. Although the empire adheres to the Western democratic system, the gentry class is preserved due to the success of land reform. This gentry class represents the "third person" that Zhang Dongsun values, who can mediate between the government and the lower class of people, serving as an antitoxin to resist the contaminated air emitted by tyrannical politics.[32]

Moreover, Chan Koonchung deliberately portrays the literary field after the KMT takes over China as a thriving polyphony, completely detached from the ideological mindset of the binary rivalry between "us and them." It proves to be a literary realization of Thirdspace: "As long as one does not serve the CCP and does not directly attack the rule of the KMT, there are almost no taboos in literature and art in general. Since there are no taboos in culture, literature naturally flourishes."[33] Not only is there rich development of both serious and popular literature, but Chinese writers, such as Lao She 老舍 (1899–1966) and Lin Yutang, are awarded the Nobel Prize in Literature. Shen Congwen, Zhang Ailing, Qian Zhongshu 錢鍾書 (1910–1998), and Shi Zhecun 施蟄存 (1905–2003) also show great potential to win the Nobel Prize. All writers are against the subjection of literature to politics, preferring to return to nonutilitarian literature free from the chokehold of society and the dogma of ideology. This is the sort of literature Liu Zaifu and Gao Xingjian have called for, which is no longer an instrument for social reform and is based on an unwavering individual position unrestricted by any political groups or movements. As a result, the literary world in the Uchronia of New China blossoms with a variety of genres, including realism, naturalism, modernism, root-seeking fiction, magical realism, vernacular fiction, science fiction, satirical fiction, and martial arts fiction. Different and diverse literary schools, styles, and methods coexist and proliferate, resulting in a post-1949 literary heyday. The so-called fat years are actualized in the literary field in which a Thirdspace of heteroglossia has been established.

A calm, reasonable, and reflexive tone pervades Chan Koonchung's narrative language. Suffused with erudite historical knowledge, his clear-sighted, academic-oriented writing is congruent with "the colorless thought" proposed by Taiwan liberal intellectual Yin Haiguang,[34] inclined to cognitive, logical, and rational thinking. Yin was highly critical of the excessive emotive thinking in revolutionary politics and aesthetics. This emotive thinking is comparable to the "affect theory" that underscores the role of emotion underpinning various types of political regulations.[35] The affective intensities of emotionally laden political ideologies have largely impeded rational thinking. However, since Yin Haiguang consciously navigated feelings and emotions, working toward a spectrum of colorless thought, he avoided a clear-cut bifurcation between reason and emotion. In other words, within the scope of colorless thought, there is a gradually developing middle ground between cognitive thinking and emotive thinking. In *The Second Year of Jianfeng*, Chan Koonchung's narrative language moves toward such a middle ground, starting from Zhang Dongsun's personal choice with distinct emotions such as nostalgia and melancholy, then heading toward cognitions, knowledge, and political judgments that significantly shape the heterotopia of Jianfeng.

Chan Koonchung is representative of contemporary intellectuals who advocate Thirdspace because he particularly challenges the extreme binary positions of the Left and the Right, along with either/or logic. In the post-Mao era, Chinese intellectuals once again fell into the trap of "ideological polarizations," as the literary scholar Tu Hang delineated: "Whereas the liberals hoped to advance liberty and the rule of law through capitalism and political reforms, the Left reaffirmed Maoist egalitarianism and the Leninist Party-state to secure equality and political sovereignty; cultural conservatives, by contrast, sought to rejuvenate the values of Chinese antiquity in the post-revolutionary era."[36] Chan Koonchung is more in favor of both/and also logic, not only striving for freedom and equality at the same time but also firmly embracing a cosmopolitan position that crosses various national and cultural boundaries.

Chan once said in an interview that he hoped to advance "a return to a middle ground in political, economic, and social thinking, a return to the position of social democracy and social liberalism."[37] On the one hand, he opposes orthodox Marxist leftists who still believe in class struggle, dictatorship of the proletariat, linear historicism, and the elimination of private property; on the other hand, he disagrees with rightist groups who endorse market fundamentalism. His position also diverges from that of the "New Leftists," who excelled at utilizing the theoretical resources of postcolonialism as well as Confucian values in their arguments but unfortunately went back to the old path of narrow-minded "nationalism."[38] Similar to Zhang Dongsun, Chan believes that socialism and liberalism are not opposed to each other. His middle-of-the-road position enables him to encompass and identify with different opinions from various groups of intellectuals: he agrees not only with the advocacy of social democracy by Zhang Dongsun, Zhang Junmai, Xiao Gongquan 蕭公權 (1897–1981), Luo Longji, and Chu Anping but also with Hu Shi's position as a left-wing liberal before 1949, and even praises some Communist Party members such as Li Shenzhi 李慎之 (1923–2003), who believed in democratic socialism.[39] Nevertheless, unlike these intellectuals, Chan Koonchung has a distinct cosmopolitan stance that combines "an open and mixed localism," typified by his Hong Kong identity. For him, even the so-called people are no longer a homogenous entity but instead have been transformed into a mixture of various ethnic groups who embody multiculturalism.

The Polarized Cyberspace in the Pandemic

The emergence of the internet since the 1990s has significantly broadened "the public space" where individuals can participate in free discussions through venues such as blogs, microblogs, apps like WeChat, and other social media. The digital media age has nurtured Thirdspace with a diversified civil society in spectacular ways, allowing unofficial, independent, and critical voices about state affairs to speak and a variety of individual literary and artistic creations to be published. Nevertheless, state surveillance and control of this new cyber public sphere never fully disappeared but are always intriguingly accompanied by "the residual of socialist mentality," as Michel Hockx argued.[40]

In the era of Xi Jinping's rule, the government's control over the internet has become tighter and tighter, and heretical voices are severely curtailed to ensure a positive narration of China. During the pandemic, this strict control was taken to another level, with narrow-minded nationalism dividing people into two opposing sides, "patriotic" and "unpatriotic," and not allowing disparate voices critical of the government to be heard. Under such circumstances, Thirdspace diminished again. Most importantly, the either/or mentality that Thirdspace strongly opposes is like a ghost hovering over daily life and continues to interfere with and influence individual behavior and speech.

In *Wuhan Diary: Dispatches from a Quarantined City*, a significant individual documentation of the coronavirus outbreak in Wuhan that caused heated debates and controversies in Chinese cyberspace, the renowned Chinese writer Fang Fang wrote the following on February 28, 2020:

> Yesterday I was chatting with my classmate Yi Zhongtian and I told him that I thought, at their core, those ultra-leftists and ultra-rightists were essentially the same. He wholeheartedly agreed with me. The reason I say these two radical groups are the same is simply because neither one of them is capable of accepting anyone with views different than their own. As Yi Zhongtian described it: "They are like two sides of the same coin; neither one is able to embrace a pluralistic environment; both of them want a world that only accepts one type of voice, one type of viewpoint."[41]

This dialogue was triggered by the fanatical and abusive criticisms Fang Fang received in comments on the daily entries of *Wuhan Diary* she uploaded every night on the Chinese social media platform Weibo. According to Michael Berry, a literature and film scholar and the translator of *Wuhan Diary*, "At the height of the diary's popularity, many of her posts were getting between 3 and 10 million hits in just the span of two or three days; those message boards emerged as a virtual biosphere of vibrant social debate—a place for readers to converge, share, sometimes argue, and often cry."[42] As Fang Fang's diary was transformed from "a private literary form" to "a public platform" where she and readers interacted in "a virtual open book,"[43] she was supported and attacked by different groups. Those who vehemently attacked her used malicious, violent, and offensive language, accusing her of being obsessed with the darkness of society and lacking the so-called positive energy to praise the government's efforts in containing the pandemic. The violent language and mode of thinking harkened back to those of the extreme leftists during the Cultural Revolution who completely rejected heterogeneous voices. Seeing this phenomenon as another kind of virus that poisoned the healthy ecology of the cyber public space and language, Fang Fang wrote: "The spread of the coronavirus led to the unprecedented quarantine of millions of people within this city, while the virus infecting my Weibo account clearly unveiled the true shame of this era."[44] Indeed, this phenomenon testified to the fact that the virus embodying the dichotomous logic of "us and them" is deeply rooted in the Chinese mentality. During the Xi Jinping regime that reinforces the socialist ideology and nationalism, it has been resurrected and invaded many aspects of people's political and social lives.

Fang Fang used the first-person narrator to record and reflect on her real personal experience during the coronavirus outbreak in Wuhan, intertwined with the complex world of the internet. However, she avoided indulging in a profusely sentimental and narcissistic way of storytelling, instead presenting daily life during the quarantine in a concise, controlled, and factual style, accompanied by unyielding criticisms of irresponsible local and national officials. She also objectively presented some positive efforts by government organizations. Her stance in *Wuhan Diary* is neutral and rational, conveying neither radical antiparty criticism nor accolades for the government. Although a sense of anxiety, anger, and frustration lurks behind the account, Fang Fang intentionally recorded her daily activities, concerns, readings, analyses, and judgments in a calm and cognitive manner, refusing to take sides. This kind of objective, rational, and pragmatic voice is distinct from both the frantic, agitated, and frenzied voice ubiquitous in the revolutionary era fueled with a hyperbolic utopian dream and the despondent, pessimistic, apocalyptic voice permeating the dystopian novels. In a time of vast disarray and crisis, while state media were promoting and highlighting the positive stories of fighting coronavirus, Fang Fang's diary served as an honest statement with a social purpose: to reveal the truths covered up by bureaucrats.

However, it inevitably incurred severe attacks from ultra-leftist groups, who claimed the diary "was to be 'weaponized' as a tool for the United States to criticize China."[45]

The attacks soon spread to those who supported Fang Fang, "the collateral casualties of public castigation,"[46] prompting polarization among the intelligentsia, mapping diverse voices into two opposing camps of "us versus them," "patriots versus traitors." Apparently, the majority of the visible and invisible attackers were manipulated by the party-state authorities, who strove to mobilize all the dynamic and contesting narratives into one monotonous rhetoric paying homage to the party's victorious achievements.[47] While translating *Wuhan Diary* into English, Michael Berry found his Weibo account flooded with more than six hundred messages with resentful comments and threats against him and his family.[48] Even if his translation is derived from his literary sensitivity as well as his passion for Chinese literature and culture, he was categorized in the enemy camp of American imperialists for resisting the rise of China. Because he voiced support for Fang Fang, the renowned writer Yan Lianke 閻連科 (1958–) also fell victim to the verbal abuse flooding the internet.

In an interview responding to the debates over *Wuhan Diary* in 2021, Yan Lianke said, "I have Fang Fang to thank for picking up the face of writers and literature that fell to the ground."[49] He demanded reflection on the tolerance of dissenting voices that is "the measure of the degree of human civilization over centuries."[50] However, while the diversified space of society was shrinking again under state control and governance, his call for tolerance and freedom of speech was ruthlessly expelled by mass media that collectively told "the good China story" requested by Xi Jinping. He was soon singled out as a traitorous intellectual and accused of deliberately smearing the image of China in order to obtain more international literary awards.

In his acceptance speech for the 2021 Newman Prize for Chinese Literature, Yan Lianke claimed that the village of his homeland is a microcosm of the entire China and even the entire world. Using the village as a trope to discuss and explore all the possibilities of humanity, ranging from evil to love, he had no intention of cultivating any form of Sinocentrism, chauvinism, or nationalist sentiments. Rather, his reference to villagers' complicated human nature, which is "essentially equivalent to human beings everywhere," was meant to cross national and political boundaries in order to discover the universal value of mankind.[51] To justify his argument, Yan

Lianke told two specific stories, one about hatred and the other about love. The former mentioned a relative who asked him why China could not drop an atomic bomb on every country so that the world would only be Chinese; the latter told of a Japanese soldier who gave a seventy-year-old woman candy when he left China and how this candy becomes a tiny token to heal the trauma caused by the war. However, this speech immediately drew ruthless and ferocious attacks from the internet, incriminating him for elevating the Japanese invaders and belittling his own motherland—a typical performance of a traitor. The attacks were based on hatred, attempting to deepen the confrontation and bifurcation between "us and them." Ironically, what Yan Lianke wanted to emphasize in his speech was a universal love that could transcend the polarization stipulated and strengthened by racial, national, and geopolitical conflicts.[52]

In general, the rise of cyberspace in postsocialist China has cultivated a kind of "civil society" that accords with that of the Western tradition, with distinctive characteristics of an "un-utopian," "bottom-up" milieu associated with ordinary citizens and *minjian* intellectuals. It stands in stark contrast to the "tradition-rooted, utopian, 'top-down' framework of 'civil society'" in the Republican period that has a close affinity with elite intellectuals.[53] The ordinary citizens who are regular bloggers and internet users are more interested in solving pragmatic issues than indulging in the kind of political utopian dreams that fascinate elite intellectuals. However, although cyberspace opened a new ground to produce diversified and contesting voices challenging the monolithic discourse of the ruling party, it inevitably encountered a severe backlash under Xi Jinping's regime. The expanding surveillance apparatus has further entrenched an either/or mentality, particularly during the pandemic, redefining all contentious debates within the narrow confines of an us/them dichotomy. In such a rigidly polarized political environment, the necessity for the existence of a Thirdspace becomes increasingly urgent. Thirdspace encompasses not only tolerant political attitudes but also multiple values, methodologies, and historical perspectives. It serves as a counter-discourse to binary logic and contributes to rectifying the imbalances and pathologies of the collective subconscious, which were formulated during the revolutionary period and continue to exert impact in the present. The revival and expansion of Thirdspace have once again become the premise for restoring a healthy political ecology where everyone has a broader space to survive, breathe, and thrive.

Notes

Introduction

1. In his words, the third space "constitutes the discursive conditions of enunciation that ensure that the meaning and symbols of culture have no primordial unity or fixity; that even the same signs can be appropriated, translated, rehistoricized, and read anew." Homi K. Bhabha, *The Location of Culture* (London: Routledge, 1994), 55.
2. Homi K. Bhabha, "The Third Space," in *Identity, Community, Culture, Difference*, ed. J. Rutherford (London: Lawrence and Wishart, 1990), 211.
3. Henri Lefebvre, *The Production of Space*, trans. Donald Nicholson-Smith (Malden, MA: Blackwell, 1974), 38–40. Edward W. Soja, *Thirdspace: Journey to Los Angeles and Other Real-and-Imagined Places* (Malden, MA: Blackwell, 1996), 6–8.
4. Soja, *Thirdspace*, 7.
5. Henri Lefebvre, *La Présence et l'absence* (Paris: Casterman, 1980), 225 and 143.
6. Lefebvre describes "the perceived—conceived—lived triad (in spatial terms: spatial practice, representations of space, representational space)" in *The Production of Space*, 40. Soja uses the term "trialectics of spatiality" to describe Lefebvre's idea in *Production of Space*. Soja, *Thirdspace*, 6–9.
7. Soja, *Thirdspace*, 57.
8. Val Plumwood, *Feminism and the Mastery of Nature* (London: Routledge, 2002), 3, 45, 60, 2.
9. Soja, *Thirdspace*, 153–154.

10. Jürgen Habermas, *The Structural Transformation of the Public Sphere: An Inquiry into a Category of Bourgeois Society*, trans. Thomas Burger (Cambridge, MA: MIT Press, 1989).
11. Isaiah Berlin, *Liberty*, ed. Henry Hardy (Oxford: Oxford University Press, 2013), 169–178.
12. Soja, *Thirdspace*, 56–57.
13. According to Edward W. Soja, "'The Aleph' is an invitation to exuberant adventure as well as a humbling and cautionary tale, an allegory on the infinite complexities of space and time. Attaching its meanings to Lefebvre's conceptualization of the production of space detonates the scope of spatial knowledge and reinforces the radical openness of what I am trying to convey as Thirdspace: the space where all spaces are, capable of being seen from every angle, each standing clear; but also a secret and conjectured object, filled with illusions and allusions, a space that is common to all of us yet never able to be completely seen and understood, an 'unimaginable universe,' or as Lefebvre would put it, 'the most general of products.'" Soja, *Thirdspace*, 56.
14. Soja, *Thirdspace*, 57.
15. Jorge Luis Borges, "The Zahir," in *Jorge Luis Borges: Collected Fictions*, trans. Andrew Hurley (New York: Penguin, 1998), 248.
16. Peter Ping Li, "The Unique Value of Yin-Yang Balancing: A Critical Response," *Management and Organization Review* 10, no. 2 (July 2014): 322.
17. Yü Ying-shih, "Zhongguo xiandai sixiangshi de jijin yu baoshou" 中國現代思想史的激進與保守 [The radicals and conservatives in modern Chinese thought], in Yü Ying-shih, *Qian Mu yu Zhongguo wenhua* 錢穆與中國文化 [Qian Mu and Chinese culture] (Shanghai: Yuandong chubanshe, 1994), 188–295. The English version of this article is Yü Ying-shih, "The Radicalization of China in the Twentieth Century," *Daedalus* 122, no. 2 (Spring 1993): 125–150.
18. Yü Ying-shih, "The Radicals and Conservatives in Modern Chinese Thought," 198. A contrasting view, expressed by the mainland Chinese scholar Jiang Yihua 姜義華 (1939–), was that conservatism was too strenuous and enduring in the Chinese cultural discourse, preventing the radicals from solving social problems. Jiang Yihua 姜義華, "Jijin yu baoshou: Yu Yü Ying-Shih xiansheng shangque" 激進與保守—與余英時先生商榷 [The radicals and the conservatives—Dialogues with Mr. Yü Ying-Shih], *Ershiyi shiji* 二十一世紀 10 (April 1992): 134–142.
19. Thomas A. Metzger, *The Western Concept of the Civil Society in the Context of Chinese History* (Stanford, CA: Hoover Institute on War, Revolution and Peace, Stanford University, 1998).
20. As Yü Ying-shih indicated, from 1949 to the early 1980s, "there no longer existed any civil spontaneous organizations, including traditional clans, stores, guilds, schools, temples, clansmen's associations, poetry and literature societies, etc."

Not even modern civil organizations were spared, as "political parties, chambers of commerce, trade unions, peer associations, religious groups, literary groups, newspapers, publishing houses, reunion societies" had been either annihilated or assimilated into the Communist Party apparatus. Yü Ying-shih, "Zailun Zhongguo sixiang zhong de jijin yu baoshou: Da Jiang Yihua xiansheng" 再論中國思想中的激進與保守——答姜義華先生 [Re-discussing the radicals and the conservatives in modern Chinese thought—Answering Mr. Jiang Yihua], *Ershiyi shiji* 10 (April 1992): 146.

21. Yü Ying-shih used the terms "deposition" and "inclination" to describe the process of radicalization. "The garden of one's own" is like the title of Zhou Zuoren's essay. See Zhou Zuoren, "Ziji de yuandi" 自己的園地 [My own garden], in *My Own Garden*, in *Zhou Zuoren zibian wenji* 周作人自編文集 [Self-edited collection of Zhou Zuoren] (Shijiazhuang: Hebei jiaoyu chubanshe, 2002), 5–7.
22. Chen Duxiu, "Wenxue geming lun" 文學革命論 [On literary revolution], *Xin qingnian* 新青年 [New youth] 2, no. 6 (February 1917).
23. Howard Y. F. Choy and Liu Jianmei, eds., *Liu Zaifu: Selected Critical Essays* (Leiden, Netherlands: Brill, 2021), 176.
24. Lin Yü-Sheng, *The Crisis of Chinese Consciousness: Radical Antitrationalism in the May Fourth Era* (Madison: University of Wisconsin Press, 1979).
25. Hu Shi, "Wenxue gailiang chuyi" 文學改良芻議 [Inceptive discussion on literary reform], in *Zhongguo xinwenxue daxi* 中國新文學大系 [A corpus of Chinese new literature], ed. Zhao Jiabi 趙家璧. (Shanghai: Shanghai wenyi chubanshe, 1980–1987), 1:44–47.
26. Lu Xun, "On the Third Type of Person," in *Lu Xun Quanji* 魯迅全集 [The complete works of Lu Xun] (Beijing: Renmin wenxue chubanshe, 1993), vol. 4, 440. The translation is adapted from Lu Xun, *Lu Xun Selected Works*, trans. Yang Xianyi and Gladys Yang (Beijing: Foreign Language Press, 1959), 3:190.
27. Liang Shiqiu, "Lun disanzhong ren" 論第三種人 [On the third type of person], *Wenyi yuekan* 文藝月刊 3, no. 7 (January 1933).
28. Wang Fansen 王汎森, "Fan zhuyi de sixiang yanlun: Houwusi zhengzhi siwei de fenlie" 反主義的思想言論——後五四政治思維的分裂 [Anti-Doctrinism Discourse: The Split in the Political Thoughts in Post-May Fourth China], *Dongya guannian shi jikan* 東亞觀念史集刊 14 (June 2018): 22.
29. Zhu Guangqian, "Zhongguo sixiang de weiji" 中國思想的危機 [The crisis of Chinese thought], in *Zhu Guangqian quanji* 朱光潛全集 [The complete collection of Zhu Guangqian] (Hefei: Anhui jiaoyu chubanshe, 1991), vol. 8, 514–518.
30. Liu Jianmei, *Zhuangzi and Modern Chinese Literature* (New York: Oxford University Press, 2016), 72–73.
31. Writers of leisure literature are the runners-up of Chinese Thirdspace. Charles A. Laughlin provides a comprehensive discussion of the leisure literature in

Shanghai during the 1930s. Charles A. Laughlin, *The Literature of Leisure and Chinese Modernity* (Honolulu: University of Hawai'i Press, 2008).

32. Please see Leo Ou-fan Lee's insightful discussion of the school of the new sensibility, which includes writers such as Shi Zhecun, Liu Na'ou, Mu Shiying, whose experimental writing showcased a vivid landscape teeming with both realistic and unrealistic elements. Leo Ou-fan Lee, *Shanghai Modern: The Flowering of A New Urban Culture in China, 1930–1945* (Cambridge, MA: Harvard University Press, 1999).

33. Lu Xun, "Xiaopinwen de weiji" 小品文的危機 [The crisis of little essays], in *The Complete Works of Lu Xun*, vol. 4, 576–577. Translation adapted from Lu Xun, *Lu Xun Selected Works*, vol. 3, 343.

34. Shen Congwen, "Yizhong xinde wenyiguan" 一種新的文藝觀 [A new artistic view], *Wenchao yuekan* 文潮月刊 1, no. 5 (September 1, 1946); Zhu Guangqian, "Tan qunzhong peiyang qienuo yu xiongcan" 談群眾培養怯懦與兇殘 [On the mass's cultivation of cowardice and atrocity], *Zhoulun* 周論 1, no. 5 (February 13, 1948); Xiao Qian, "Ni J. Masalike yishu" 擬J. 瑪薩里克遺書 [Imitating the obituary of J. Masaryk], *Guancha* 觀察 4, no. 7 (April 1948).

35. Guo Moruo, *Moruo wenji* 沫若文集 [Collected works of Guo Moruo] (Beijing: Renmin wenxue chubanshe, 1961) 13:528–534.

36. Xiao Qian, "Imitating the Obituary of J. Masaryk."

37. Wu Lichang 吳立昌, ed., *Wenxue de xiaojie he fanxiaojie: Zhongguo xiandai wenxue paibie lunzhengshi lun* 文學的消解和反消解——中國現代文學派別論爭史論 [The dissolution and antidissolution of literature: On the debates of modern Chinese literary schools] (Shanghai: Fudan daxue chubanshe, 2004), 304.

38. Choy and Liu Jianmei, *Liu Zaifu*, 100.

39. Li Zehou, *The Chinese Aesthetic Tradition*, trans. Maija Bell Samei (Honolulu: University of Hawai'i Press, 2010), x.

40. Choy and Liu Jianmei, *Liu Zaifu*, 103–115.

41. Pierre Bourdieu, "Intellectual Field and Creative Project," *Social Science Information* 8 (April 1969): 89–119.

42. Sebastian Veg, *Minjian: The Rise of China's Grassroots Intellectuals* (New York: Columbia University Press, 2019).

43. Xu Jilin, Liu Qing, Luo Gang, and Xue Yi, "In Search of a 'Third Way': A Conversation Regarding 'Liberalism' and the 'New Left Wing'," in *Voicing Concerns: Contemporary Chinese Critical Inquiry*, ed. Gloria Davies (Lanham, MD: Rowman & Littlefield, 2001), 224.

44. Tu Hang, *Sentimental Republic: Chinese Intellectuals and the Maoist Past* (Cambridge, MA: Harvard University Asian Center), forthcoming in 2025.

45. Plumwood, *Feminism and the Mastery of Nature*, 49.

46. Soja, *Thirdspace*, 65.

47. Recent scholarship in management and psychology has paid attention to indigenous Chinese philosophical approaches that differ from the Western conceptualization of exclusive opposites. See Tony Fang, "From Onion to Ocean: Paradox and Change in National Cultures," *International Studies of Management & Organization* 35, no. 4 (2005–2006): 71–90; Tony Fang, "Yin Yang: A New Perspective on Culture," *Management and Organization Review* 8, no. 1 (2011): 25–50; Ming-Jer Chen, "Transcending Paradox: The Chinese 'Middle Way' Perspective," *Asia Pacific Journal of Management* 19 (2002): 179–199; Peter Ping Li, "Toward a Geocentric Framework of Trust: An Application to Organizational Trust," *Management and Organization Review* 4, no. 3 (2008): 413–439; Peter Ping Li, "Toward an Integrative Framework of Indigenous Research: The Geocentric Implication of Yin-Yang Balance," *Asia Pacific Journal of Management* 29 (2012): 849–872; Peter Ping Li, "The Unique Value of Yin-Yang Balancing: A Critical Response," *Management and Organizational Review* 10, no. 2 (2014): 321–332; Peter Ping Li, "Global Implications of the Indigenous Epistemological System from the East," *Cross Cultural and Strategic Management* 23, no. 1 (February 2016): 42–77; Kaiping Peng and Richard E. Nisbett, "Culture, Dialectics, and Reasoning about Contradiction," *The American Psychologist* 54, no. 9 (1999): 741–754; Peng Kaiping and Richard E. Nisbett, "Dialectical Response to Questions about Dialectical Thinking," *American Psychologist* 55, no. 9 (2000): 1067–1068.
48. Marianne W. Lewis, "Exploring Paradox: Toward a More Comprehensive Guide," *Academy of Management Review* 25 (2000): 762, 760–776.
49. Peter Ping Li, "Global Implications," 46–47.
50. Peter Ping Li, "Global Implications," 47. Peter Ping Li, "Toward an Integrative Framework of Indigenous Research," 849–872. Please also see J. G. Hibben, *Hegel's Logic: An Essay in Interpretation* (Charles Scribner's Sons, 1902; repr., Kitchener, ON: Batoche, 1902/2000).
51. Peter Ping Li, "Global Implications," 58.
52. Kaiping Peng and Nisbett, "Culture, Dialectics, and Reasoning," 741–754.
53. Ming-Jer Chen, "Transcending Paradox," 179–199.
54. Zhang Dongsun, *Zhishi yu wenhua* 知識與文化 [Knowledge and culture] (Changsha: Yuelu shushe, 2010), 212, 215.
55. Jana Rošker, "The Abolishment of Substance and Ontology: A New Interpretation of Zhang Dongsun's Pluralistic Epistemology," *Synthesis Philosophica* 47, no. 1 (2009): 156.
56. Jana Rošker, *Following His Own Path: Li Zehou and Contemporary Chinese Philosophy* (Albany: State University of New York Press, 2019), 268.
57. Li Zehou, *Renlei xue lishi benti lun* 人類學歷史本體論 [The anthropo-historical ontology] (Tianjin: Tianjin shehui kexue chuban she, 2008), 62.
58. Li Zehou, *The Anthropo-Historical Ontology*, 62, 62–65, 63, 63.

59. Li Zehou, *The Anthropo-Historical Ontology*, 65. Similar to Li Zehou's *du*, Peter Ping Li also esteems the yin-yang balancing: "The interface between partial integration and partial separation can be delineated by a threshold (適度 in Chinese) as a range of proper points of balancing between the overlapping and non-overlapping parts in a single domain or across two domains in an entire system." Peter Ping Li, "Global Implications," 54.
60. Rošker, *Following His Own Path*, 270.
61. Jana Rošker, *Becoming Human: Li Zehou's Ethics* (Leiden, Netherlands: Brill, 2020), 30.
62. Li Zehou, "Lishi yanjie he lilun de 'du'" 歷史眼界和理論的 "度" [The historical perspective and the theoretical "proper measure"], *Tianya* 2 (1999): 128–135, 133. Here I am using Jana Rošker's translation in *Becoming Human*, 32.
63. Li Zehou, *The Anthropo-Historical Ontology*, 109.
64. Li Zehou's argument that "harmony is higher than justice" is included in Li Zehou, *Huiying Sangde'er ji qita* 回應桑德爾及其他 [A response to Michael Sandel and other matters] (Beijing: Sanlian shudian, 2014), 46. Also see Rošker, *Becoming Human*, 140.
65. Li Zehou, *A Response to Michael Sandel and Other Matters*, 57.
66. Liu Xiaogan, *Liangji hua yu fencun gan: jindai Zhongguo jingying sichao de bingtai xinli fenxi* 兩極化與分寸感：近代中國精英思潮的病態心理分析 [Polarization and sense of propriety: Analysis of the psychological malaise of modern elite currents of thought] (Taibei: Dongda tushu, 1994), 207–318.
67. Rošker, *Becoming Human*, 30.
68. Liu Xiaogan, *Polarization and Sense of Propriety*, 14–15.
69. Li Zehou and Liu Zaifu, *Gaobie geming* 告別革命 [Farewell to revolution] (Hong Kong: Tiandi tushu, 2015), 124–130.
70. Zhang Taiyan, "Jufen jinhua lun" 俱分進化論 [Dual evolution theory], *Minpao* 民報 [People's newspaper] July 1906, 1–13.
71. Li Zehou, *The Anthropo-Historical Ontology*, 183, 171.
72. According to Thomas A. Metzger's analytical paradigm of "accommodative approach" and "transformative approach," the former prefers a more considerably moderate and conciliatory stance while the latter is inclined to a revolutionary, radical means to change society. Metzger recognized that when China's revolutionary intellectuals aligned with the doctrine of transformation, they clung closely to the radical ideas of Jean-Jacques Rousseau and the French Revolution. In contrast, the Chinese reformists oriented toward the accommodation approach identified with the ideas of John Locke and John Stuart Mill to insist on protecting individual rights from state and public coercion. Thomas A. Metzger, *The International Organization of Ch'ing Bureaucracy: Legal, Normative, and Communication Aspects* (Cambridge, MA: Harvard University Press, 1973); *Escape from Predicament: New-Confucianism and China's Evolving Political Culture* (New York: Columbia University Press, 1977).

73. Leigh K. Jenco, *Making the Political: Founding and Action in the Political Theory of Zhang Shizhao* (Cambridge: Cambridge University Press, 2010), 221–223.
74. James Bryce, *Studies in History and Jurisprudence* (Oxford: Clarendon Press, 1901). See Jenco, *Making the Political*, 198. According to the scholar Guo Huaqing, not only was Zhang Shizhao heavily influenced by the Confucian doctrine of moderation (*zhongyong* 中庸) and the yin-yang dialectics, but he also referenced an extensive Western liberal tradition consisting of thinkers such as John Stuart Mill, Herbert Spencer, Henry Sumner Maine, Edmund Burke, Thomas Huxley, Erskine May, James Bryce, John William Burgess, Francis Lieber, L. T. Hobhouse, Walter Bagehot, A. L. Lowell, Alexis de Tocqueville, and John Morley. See Guo Huaqing 郭華清, *Kuanrong yu tuoxie: Zhang Shizhao de tiaohelun yanjiu* 寬容與妥協——章士釗的調和論研究 [Tolerance and compromise: Research on Zhang Shizhao's theory of accommodation] (Tianjin: Tianjin guji chuban she, 2004).
75. Zhang Shizhao, *Zhang Shizhao quanji* 章士釗全集 [The complete works of Zhang Shizhao] (Shanghai: Wenhui chubanshe, 2000), vol. 3, 253. Here I am borrowing the translation by Leigh K. Jenco. Zhang Shizhao's idea of "active cultivation of opposition," as the political historian Leigh K. Jenco argues, is "a celebration of difference not for its own sake but for its ability to enliven and make available new ways in which the government (and other people) can be challenged." See Jenco, *Making the Political*, 200.
76. Du Yaquan suggested that the stillness-oriented (*jing* 靜) Chinese culture and the mobility-oriented (*dong* 動) Western culture should be supplementing instead of conflicting with each other, an idea that contrasts sharply with that of Chen Duxiu, the editor-in-chief of *New Youth* (Xin qingnian 新青年), who perceived the two cultures as irreconcilable, like ice and fire. Furthermore, Du regarded the conservative faction and the progressive faction as "the two wheels of the cart, the two wings of the bird, both are indispensable to support and help each other." For him, too much progress is dangerous, but too much conservatism retards national growth; therefore, he underscores that the conciliation and balance of both are imperative and axiomatic for the Chinese future. Du Yaquan, "Jing de wenming yu dong de wenming" 靜的文明與動的文明 [The still civilization and the mobile civilization], *Dongfang zazhi* 13, no. 10 (October 1916). Chen Duxiu, "Jinri Zhongguo zhi zhengzhi wenti" 今日中國之政治問題 [The political problem in today's China], *Xin qingnian* 新青年 5, no. 1 (1918): 6–9. Du Yaquan, "Zhengdang lun" 政黨論 [On political parties], *Dongfang zazhi* 8, no. 1 (March 1911).
77. The scholar Gao Like used "harmonious pluralism" to describe Du Yaquan's thought. Gao Like 高立克, *Tiaoshi de zhihui: Du Yaquan sixiang yanjiu* 調適的智慧:杜亞泉思想研究 [The wisdom of accommodation: Research on Du Yaquan's thought] (Hangzhou: Zhejiang renmin chubanshe, 1998), 107–125.

Also see Du Yaquan, "Maodun zhi tiaohe" 矛盾之調和 [The accommodation of contradiction], *Dongfang zazhi* 東方雜誌 15, no. 2 (February 1918).

78. Du Yaquan, "Geren yu guojia zhi jieshuo" 個人與國家之界說 [On the demarcation of the individual and the state], *Dongfang zazhi* 14, no. 3 (March 1917).
79. Zhang Dongsun, "Xianren zhengzhi" 賢人政治 [The elite politics], *Dongfang zazhi* 11 (November 15, 1917).
80. The third-route intellectuals were largely anti-Communist until the 1940s because they could not accept the Communists' violent and authoritarian methods but maintained wariness of the corruption and autocracy of the KMT leadership. Edmund Fung, *In Search of Chinese Democracy* (Cambridge: Cambridge University Press, 2000), 12.
81. John Rawls, *Political Liberalism* (New York: Columbia University Press, 2005), 133.
82. Ian Carter, "Value-Freeness and Value-Neutrality in the Analysis of Political Concepts," in *Oxford Studies in Political Philosophy*, vol. 1, ed. David Sobel, Peter Vallentyne, and Steven Wall (Oxford: Oxford University Press, 2015), 285–286.
83. Yin Haiguang, "Women zou natiao lu" 我們走哪條路？ [Which road should we take?], in *Zhengzhi yu shehui (shang)* 政治與社會（上）[Politics and society (part one)], in *Yin Haiguang quanji* 殷海光全集 [The complete works of Yin Haiguang], edited by Lin Zhenghong 林正弘, vol. 11 (Taipei: Guiguang tushu, 1990): 13–17.
84. Li Zehou, *A Response to Michael Sandel and Other Matters*, 103.
85. Yin Haiguang, *Zhongguo wenhua de zhanwang* 中國文化的展望 [The viewpoints of Chinese culture], in *The Complete Works of Yin Haiguang*, ed. Lin Zhenghong, vol. 7 (Taipei: Guiguang tushu, 1990), 320.
86. David Der-wei Wang, "Standing Alone atop the Mountain, Walking Freely Under the Sea: On Liu Zaifu and Five Autobiographical Accounts," *Prism: Theory and Modern Chinese Literature* 17, no. 1 (2020): 147.
87. Isaiah Berlin, *Liberty*, ed. Henry Hardy (Oxford: Oxford University Press, 2002), 171. According to Tao Jiang, a scholar in philosophy and religion, despite its apolitical position, Zhuangzi's idea of freedom in certain aspects resonates with Isaiah Berlin's negative freedom, because both "cherish the personal space and celebrate the value of pluralism." Tao Jiang, "Isaiah Berlin's Challenge to Zhuangzian Freedom," *Journal of Chinese Philosophy*, supplement to vol. 39 (2012): 69–92.
88. Soja, *Thirdspace*, 5.
89. C. T. Hsia, "Obsession with China: The Moral Burden of Chinese Literature," in *A History of Modern Chinese Fiction*, 3rd ed. (Bloomington: Indiana University Press, 1999), 533–554.
90. Peter Ping Li, "Global Implications," 58.
91. Soja, *Thirdspace*, 60.

92. Walter Benjamin, *The Origin of German Tragic Drama*, trans. John Osbourne (London: Verso, 1985), 34.
93. Liu Zaifu specifically points out that Gao Xingjian "discovered that between two opposite poles there was a third broad space, which could be called a 'third zone.'" See Liu Zaifu, "Gao Xingjian: Exemplifying a Renaissance in Today's World," in *Gao Xingjian and Transmedia Aesthetics*, ed. Mabel Lee and Liu Jianmei (Amherst, NY: Cambria Press, 2018), 50.
94. Gao Xingjian's thirding is mainly derived from intermedia or transmedia practices. In his own words, "The medium between the two is impregnated with mechanisms for producing the myriad things." Gao Xingjian, "Freedom and Literature," in *Gao Xingjian: Aesthetics and Creation*, trans. Mabel Lee (Amherst, NY: Cambria Press, 2012), 233.
95. Mary Mazzilli, "Gao Xingjian's Search for a Scenic Dramaturgy and Cinematic Language in *Song of the Night*," in *Gao Xingjian and Transmedia Aesthetics*, 119. Please also see Izabella Labędzka, *Gao Xingjian's Idea of Theatre: From the Word to the Image* (Leiden, Netherlands: Brill, 2008), 20.
96. Werner Wolf, "Intermedialilty," in *Routledge Encyclopedia of Narrative Theory*, ed. David Herman, Manfred Jahn, and Marie-Laure Ryan (London: Routledge, 2005), 254. Please also see Wu Shengqing, *Photo Poetics: Chinese Lyricism and Modern Media Culture* (New York: Columbia University Press, 2020), 5.
97. Gilbert Fong and Shelby Chan, "Nonattachment and Gao Xingjian's Neutral Actor," in *Gao Xingjian and Transmedia Aesthetics*, ed. Mabel Lee and Liu Jianmei (Amherst, NY: Cambria Press, 2018), 111.
98. Gao Xingjian, *Aesthetics and Creation*, trans. Mabel Lee (Amherst, NY: Cambria Press, 2012), 16.
99. Maurice Merleau-Ponty, "Eye and Mind," in *The Merleau-Ponty Reader* (Evanston, IL: Northwestern University Press, 2007), 351–378.
100. Fong and Chan, "Nonattachment and Gao Xingjian's Neutral Actor," 110–111.
101. Inspired by Merleau-Ponty's "the third eye," Wu Shengqing proposes "the lyrical eye and mind" to emphasize a subjective position that enables "vibrant exchanges between the body and the external object" while observing. Wu Shengqing, *Photo Poetics*, 22.
102. Gao Xingjian, *Aesthetics and Creation*, 166.
103. Lisa Lipinski, *René Magritte and the Art of Thinking* (New York: Routledge, 2019), 2.
104. Yu Zhansui, *Questioning the Chinese Model: Oppositional Political Novels in Early Twenty-First Century China* (Toronto, ON: University of Toronto Press, 2022), 1.
105. As Liu Zaifu expounds, "The most important reason literature has the greatest freedom, besides the fact that the psychological activities of writers do not adhere to the norms of the real world, is that literature has the fundamental characteristic of transcending utilitarian reality." Liu Zaifu, *Shenme shi wenxue:*

Wenxue changshi ershi'er jiang 什麼是文學：文學常識二十二講 [What is literature: Twenty-two lectures on the general knowledge of literature] (Hong Kong: Sanlian shudian, 2018), 58–59, 62–67.
106. Liu Zaifu, *What Is Literature*, 63–64.
107. Borges, "The Zahir," 283.

1. Zhang Dongsun: The Predicament of Thirdspace

1. Zhang Dongsun, "Qin yuan chun: yuzuo mingnian bashi zishouci" 沁園春：預作明年八十自壽詞 [Spring soaks into the garden, the prewritten *ci* for my eightieth birthday], in Zuo Yuhe, *Zhang Dongsun zhuan* 張東蓀傳 [A biography of Zhang Dongsun] (Jinan: Shandong renmin chuban she, 1998), 444–445.
2. Zuo Yuhe, *Zhang Dongsun zhuan*," 444–445.
3. Guo Zhanbo 郭湛波, *Zhongguo jin wushinian sixiang shi* 中國近五十年思想史 [History of Chinese thought in the past fifty years] (Shanghai: Shanghai guji chubanshe, 2005), 132.
4. Zhang Rulun 張汝倫, ed., *Lixing yu liangzhi: Zhang Dongsun wenxuan* 理性與良知：張東蓀文選 [Rationality and conscience: The selection of Zhang Dongsun's essays] (Shanghai: Shanghai Yuandong chuban she, 1995), 636–637.
5. Zhang Yaonan 張耀南, "Zhang Dongsun de 'zhishixue' ji 'xinzixue shidai'" 張東蓀的"知識學"和"新子學時代" [Zhang Dongsun's epistemology and the new era of studying traditional philosophers], in Zhang Dongsun, *Renshi lun* 認識論 [Epistemology] (Shanghai: Shangwu yinshu guan, 2017), 117–118.
6. Zhang Dongsun, "Xianren zhengzhi" 賢人政治 [The elite politics], *Dongfang zazhi* 東方雜誌 [The Eastern miscellany], November 15, 1917.
7. Drawing from Jürgen Habermas's definition of "the public sphere," Nuan Gao points out that Zhang Dongsun and the editors of *Xuedeng* 學燈 [Learning light] represented moderate intellectuals' principles of rationality, openness, tolerance, and pragmatism. See Nuan Gao, "Building Fukan as a Chinese Public Sphere: Zhang Dongsun and Learning Light," *Journal of the Indiana Academy of the Social Sciences* 20, no. 1 (2018): 34–49.
8. Zuo Yuhe, *A Biography of Zhang Dongsun*, 118–165.
9. According to Zuo Yuhe, the article was drafted by Zhang Dongsun. See Zuo Yuhe, *A Biography of Zhang Dongsun*, 293–311. According to Edmund Fung, "It is difficult to determine which of the ideas expressed in that article were Zhang Dongsun's and which were Zhang Junmai's. However, given Zhang Dongsun's long-held view that all political doctrines were capable of continuous improvement through revision, it would appear that he strongly influenced the conception of 'revisionist democracy' with which Zhang Junmai is often credited." See Edmund S. K. Fung, "Socialism, Capitalism, and Democracy in Republican

China: The Political Thought of Zhang Dongsun," *Modern China* 28, no. 4 (October 2002): 414.
10. Edmund Fung, *In Search of Chinese Democracy* (Cambridge: Cambridge University Press, 2000), 260, 143.
11. Zuo Yuhe, *A Biography of Zhang Dongsun*, 336–342.
12. Fung, *In Search of Chinese Democracy*, 260.
13. Zuo Yuhe, *A Biography of Zhang Dongsun*, 293–390.
14. Fung, "Socialism, Capitalism, and Democracy in Republican China," 424.
15. Zuo Yuhe, *A Biography of Zhang Dongsun*, 387.
16. Fung, *In Search of Chinese Democracy*, 298–306.
17. Zuo Yuhe, *A Biography of Zhang Dongsun*, 409–421.
18. Dai Qing 戴晴, *Zai Rulaifo zhang zhong—Zhang Dongsun he tade shidai* 在如來佛掌中—張東蓀和他的時代 [In the palm of Tathāgata: Zhang Dongsun and his time] (Hong Kong: The Chinese University Press, 2008).
19. Zuo Yuhe, *A Biography of Zhang Dongsun*, 432–448.
20. Zhang Dongsun, *Zhishi yu wenhua* 知識與文化 [Knowledge and culture] (Shangsha: Yuelu sheshe, 2010), 276, 275.
21. Zhang Dongsun, "Sixiang ziyou wenti" 思想自由問題 [The problem of freedom of thought], in *Zhang Dongsun juan* 張東蓀卷 [The volume of Zhang Dongsun], ed. Zuo Yuhe (Beijing: Zhongguo renmin chubanshe, 2015), 441.
22. Zhang Dongsun, "Duikang lun zhi jiazhi" 對抗論之價值 [The value of the antagonist theory], *Yongyan* 1, no. 24 (November 16, 1913). Also see Gao Bo 高波, *Zhuixun xin gonghe: Zhang Dongsun zaoqi sixiang yu huodong yanjiu (1886–1932)* 追尋新共和：張東蓀早期思想與活動研究 1886–1932 [Search for a new republic: A study of the thought and activities of Zhang Dongsun in his early years（1886–1932）] (Beijing: Sanlian shudian, 2018), 91.
23. Leigh K. Jenco, *Making the Political: Founding and Action in the Political Theory of Zhang Shizao* (Cambridge: Cambridge University Press, 2010), 198–199. James Bryce, *Studies in History and Jurisprudence*, vol. 1 (New York: Oxford University Press, 1901), 216–262.
24. Qiutong [Zhang Dongsun's pen name], "Zhengli xiangbei lun" 政力向背論 [Theory of political power], *Jiayin zazhi* (July 10, 1914); also see Morikawa Hiroki, *Zhengzhijia de jinchi: Zhang Shizhao he Zhang Dongsun zhengzhi sixiang yanjiu* 政治家的矜持：章士釗和張東蓀政治思想研究 [*The reservedness of politicians: A study of the political thought of Zhang Shizhao and Zhang Dongsun*], trans. Yuan Guangquan (Beijing: Shehui wenxian chubanshe, 2012), 120–123.
25. Zhang Dongsun used the terms "social solidarity" (*shehui de tuanjie yaoqiu* 社會的團結要求) and "social antagonism" (*shehui de lihai chongtu* 社會的利害衝突) in *Lixing yu minzhu* 理性與民主 [Rationality and democracy] (Changsha: Yuelu shushe, 2010), 206. He used the terms "social integrity" (*shehui zhengti* 社

會整體) and "social antagonism" (*shehui duikang* 社會對抗) in Zhang Dongsun, *Knowledge and Culture*, 92.
26. Zhang Dongsun, "The Elite Politics," 91.
27. Zhang Dongsun, *Knowledge and Culture*, 240.
28. Zhang Dongsun, *Rationality and Democracy*, 210–212.
29. Zhang Dongsun, *Knowledge and Culture*, 99.
30. Zhang Dongsun, *Rationality and Democracy*, 129.
31. Zhang Dongsun, *Rationality and Democracy*, 161–162.
32. Zhang Dongsun, "Nidi yu disanzhe zhi zeren" 暱敵與第三者之責任 [The responsibility of the intimate enemy and the third person], *Zhonghua zazhi* 中華雜誌 [China journal], August 1, 1914, 5–6. Also see Morikawa Hiroki, *The Reservedness of Politicians*, 130.
33. Zhang Dongsun, "The Responsibility of the Intimate Enemy and the Third Person," 5–6.
34. Zhang Dongsun, "The Elite Politics," 90–125.
35. Gao Bo, *Search for a New Republic*, 128–130.
36. Zhang Dongsun, *Knowledge and Culture*, 251.
37. Zhang Dongsun, *Rationality and Democracy*, 266.
38. Zhang Dongsun, "Shi de shiming he lixue" 士的使命和理學 [The mission of *shi* and the study of rationality], Zuo Yuhe, *The Volume of Zhang Dongsun*, 496–500.
39. Zhang Dongsun, "Shui neng jiu Zhongguo" 誰能救中國 [Who can save China?], in Zuo Yuhe, *The Volume of Zhang Dongsun*, 183–185.
40. Zhang Dongsun, *Sixiang yu shehui* 思想與社會 [Thought and society] (Changsha: Yuelu shushe, 2010), 278–279.
41. Zhang Dongsun, "The Mission of *Shi* and the Study of Rationality," 500–501.
42. Li Zehou and Liu Zaifu, *Gaobie geming* 告別革命 [Farewell to revolution] (Hong Kong: Tiandi, 2015), 54–57.
43. Zhang Dongsun, *Xin zhexue luncong* 新哲學論叢 [The collection of new philosophy] (Shanghai: Shanghai shangwu yinshuguan, 1929).
44. Zhang Dongsun, *Renshi lun* 認識論 [Epistemology] (Shanghai: Shangwu yinshu guan, 2017).
45. Zhang Dongsun, *Epistemology*, 92.
46. Jiang Xinjang, *Knowledge, Culture, and Chinese Philosophy: A Study and Translation of Zhang Dongsun's Works* (New York: Global Scholarly Publications, 2014), 14–18. Also See Zhang Yaonan, "Zhang Dongsun's Epistemology and the New Era of Studying Traditional Philosophers," 113–135.
47. Zhang Dongsun, *Knowledge and Culture*, 137.
48. Zhang Dongsun, *Knowledge and Culture*, 116.
49. Zhang Dongsun, *Knowledge and Culture*, 137.
50. As Derk Bodde comments, "In the Chinese mind, there is no real distinction between the world of the supernatural, the world of nature, and the world of

man. They are all bound up in one all-embracing unity. 'All things are complete within me,' proclaims the Confucian, Mencius (371–279? BC), thus echoing the sentiment of the Taoist, Chuang Tzu (ca. 369–ca. 286 BC), who says: 'Heaven and Earth came into Being with me together, and with me, all things are one." See Bodde, *Essays on Chinese Civilization* (Princeton, NJ: Princeton University Press, 1981), 138.
51. Zhang Dongsun, "Renshi de duoyuan lun" 認識的多元論 [Theory of epistemological pluralism], in Zhang Rulun, *Rationality and Conscience*, 210.
52. Zhang Dongsun, *Knowledge and Culture*, 110–111.
53. Jiang, *Knowledge, Culture, and Chinese Philosophy*, 20.
54. Jiang, *Knowledge, Culture, and Chinese Philosophy*, 20–21; Also see Zhang Rulun, *Rationality and Conscience*, 232–233.
55. Zhang Rulun, ed., *Rationality and Conscience*, 34–36; Both Jiang Xinyang and Zhang Yaonan discuss how Zhang's cosmology is in accordance with Buddhist cosmology, which has no substance and regards the universe as only a set of functional relations. Please see Jiang, *Knowledge, Culture, and Chinese Philosophy*, 20; also see Zhang Yaonan, *Zhang Dongsun zhishilun yanjiu* 張東蓀知識論研究 [Studies of Zhang Dongsun's epistemology] (Taipei: Hongye wenhua, 1995), 248–266.
56. Yap Key-chong, "Western Wisdom in the Mind's Eye of a Westernized Chinese Lay Buddhist: The Thought of Chang Tung-sun (1886–1962)" (PhD. diss., Hilary Term, University of Oxford, 1991), 555–556.
57. Ye Qing 葉青, *Zhang Dongsun zhexue pipan* 張東蓀哲學批判 [The criticism of Zhang Dongsun's philosophy] (Shanghai: Xinken shudian, 1934).
58. Zhang Dongsun, *Weiwu bianzhengfa lunzhan* 唯物辯證法論戰 [Debates on Marxist materialistic dialectics], 2 vols (Beijing: Beiping minyou shudian, 1934).
59. Yap Key-chong, "Western Wisdom in the Mind's Eye," 550.
60. Jana Rošker, "The Abolishment of Substance and Ontology and Ontology: A New Interpretation of Zhang Dongsun's Pluralistic Epistemology," *Synthesis Philosophica* 47, no. 1 (2009), 156.
61. Zhang Dongsun, *Knowledge and Culture*, 172, 189, 204; also see Zhang Dongsun, *Epistemology*, 38–42.
62. Zhang Dongsun, *Knowledge and Culture*, 212, 215.
63. Lao Tzu, *Tao Teh Ching*, trans. John C. H. Wu (Boston: Shambhala, 1961), 5. Zhang Dongsun, *Knowledge and Culture*, 72–73.
64. Lao Tzu, *Tao Teh Ching*, 119; Zhang Dongsun, *Knowledge and Culture*, 212.
65. Julia Kristeva, "Word, Dialogue and Novel," *The Kristeva Reader*, ed. Toril Moi (New York: Columbia University Press, 1986). 41, 43. Thanks to Cheung Likkwan's discovery, we see how Zhang Dongsun's philosophy had an impact on Western theorists such as Julia Kristeva even if he was not allowed to freely express himself after the 1950s. Kristeva mentioned Zhang Dongsun's correlation

logic in her early article introducing Bakhtin's theory. See Cheung Lik-kwan, "Wenben hushe yu xiangguan lü mingxue: Lun Kristeva dui Zhang Dongsun zhishilun de jieshuo" 文本互涉與相關律名學：論克裡斯蒂娃對張東蓀知識論的接受 [On Kristeva's acceptance of Zhang Dongsun's *Epistemology*], *Fangyuan: Wenxue ji wenhua zhuankan*, no. 2 (2019): 159–176.

66. Charles A. Moore, ed., *The Chinese Mind: Essentials of Chinese Philosophy and Culture* (Honolulu: University of Hawai'i Press, 1967), 6.
67. Edward W. Soja, *Thirdspace: Journeys to Los Angeles and Other Real-and-Imagined Places* (Malden, MA: Blackwell, 1996), 7.
68. Zhang Dongsun, *Knowledge and Culture*, 224.
69. Homi K. Bhabha, *The Location of Culture* (London: Routledge Classics, 2004), 27.
70. Zhang Dongsun, *Rationality and Democracy*, 135, 145.
71. Zhang Dongsun, *Epistemology*, 84. Here, I adopt the translation provided in Rošker, "The Abolishment of Substance and Ontology," 162.
72. Rošker, "The Abolishment of Substance and Ontology," 162.
73. Zhang Rulun, *Rationality and Conscience*, 95.
74. Moore, *The Chinese Mind*, 6.
75. Zhang Dongsun, *Epistemology*, 86–90.
76. Zhang Dongsun, *Knowledge and Culture*, 104–105.
77. Zhang Dongsun, *Knowledge and Culture*, 110.
78. Zhang Dongsun, *Knowledge and Culture*, 260–261.
79. Zhang Dongsun, *Knowledge and Culture*, 109–110.
80. Zhang Dongsun, *Knowledge and Culture*, 111–112.
81. According to Zuo Yuhe, Zhang Dongsun disagreed with Zhang Shizhao's theory of mediation between the old and the new in 1919 but then he made a dramatic transformation by accepting the idea of compromise between Western and Chinese cultures in the 1940s. See Zuo Yuhe, *Zhang Dongsun wenhua sixiang yanjiu* 張東蓀文化思想研究 [A study of Zhang Dongsun's cultural thought] (Beijing: Zhongguo shehui kexue chubanshe, 1997), 70–73.
82. Zhang Rulun, "Zhongguo xiandai zhexueshi shangde Zhang Dongsun" 中國現代哲學史上的張東蓀 [Zhang Dongsun in the history of modern Chinese philosophy], in Zhang Rulun, *Rationality and Conscience*, 15.
83. Zhang Rulun, "Zhang Dongsun in the History of Modern Chinese Philosophy," 16.
84. Zhang Rulun, "Zhang Dongsun in the History of Modern Chinese Philosophy," 23; also see Zhang Dongsun's self-description in Zhang Dongsun, *Knowledge and Culture*, 195.
85. Soja, *Thirdspace*, 60.
86. Bhabha, *The Location of Culture*, 38–39.
87. Zhang Dongsun, *Knowledge and Culture*, 110.

88. Li Zehou, *The Chinese Aesthetic Tradition*, trans. Maija Bell Samei (Honolulu: University of Hawai'i Press, 2010), x–xi.
89. Zhang Dongsun, *Thought and Society*, 82.
90. Zhang Dongsun, *Thought and Society*, 283.
91. Zhang Dongsun, *Thought and Society*, 82.
92. Li Zehou and Liu Zaifu, *Farewell to Revolution*, 46–71.
93. Zhang Dongsun, *Thought and Society*, 286.
94. Zhang Dongsun, *Thought and Society*, 286–299.
95. Zhang Dongsun, *Minzhu zhuyi yu shehui zhuyi* 民主主義與社會主義 [Democracy and socialism] (Shanghai: Shanghai guansha she, 1948), 33.
96. Zhang Dongsun, *Democracy and Socialism*, 35–36; see also Zuo Yuhe, *A Study of Zhang Dongsun's Cultural Thought*, 255–269.
97. Zhang Dongsun, *Thought and Society*, 287–289.
98. Zhang Dongsun, *Rationality and Democracy*, 94.
99. Zhang Dongsun, *Rationality and Democracy*, 94.
100. Zhang Dongsun, *Rationality and Democracy*, 170.
101. Zhang Dongsun, *Rationality and Democracy*, 171.
102. Zhang Dongsun, *Knowledge and Culture*, 284.
103. Zhang Dongsun, *Thought and Society*, 221.
104. Zhang Dongsun, *Thought and Society*, 93–95, 242.
105. Zhang Dongsun mentioned that he started to learn classical Chinese poetry at the age of sixty-seven in the afterword to *Caojian renyu* 草間人語 [Words from a man among grasses]. See Zuo Yuhe, *A Biography of Zhang Dongsun*, 441.
106. According to Zuo Yuhe, most of the poems collected in *Words from a Man Among Grasses* were burned during the Cultural Revolution. Only seventy poems survived the political catastrophe. See Zuo Yuhe, *Zhang Dongsun nianpu* 張東蓀年譜 [A chronicle of Zhang Dongsun's life] (Beijing: Qunyan Press, 2014), 489.
107. Zhang Dongsun, "Ziti" 自題 [Self-titled], *Words from a Man Among Grasses*. See Zuo Yuhe, *A Chronicle of Zhang Dongsun's Life*, 488.
108. Zhang Dongsun, "Shu Liang Rengong lianhou" 書梁任公聯後 [Writing about Liang Qichao], *Words from a Man Among Grasses*. See Zuo Yuhe, *A Biography of Zhang Dongsun*, 441.
109. Zhang Dongsun, "Zhui tiwen ru Weicheng sizhang shi hou" 追題文如圍城四章詩後 [Titled after four-chapter poems of article parallel to besieged city], *Words from a Man Among Grasses*. See Zuo Yuhe, *A Biography of Zhang Dongsun*," 441.
110. Zhang Dongsun, "Ziti" 自題 [Self-titled], *Words from a Man Among Grasses*. See Zuo Yuhe, *A Chronicle of Zhang Dongsun's Life*, 488.
111. Zuo Yuhe, *A Biography of Zhang Dongsun*, 442.
112. Zuo Yuhe, *A Biography of Zhang Dongsun*, 442.

113. Zhang Dongsun, "Zhui tiwen ru Weicheng sizhang shi hou" 追題文如圍城四章詩後 [Titled after four-chapter poems of article parallel to besieged city], *Words from a Man Among Grasses*. See Zuo Yuhe, *A Biography of Zhang Dongsun*, 441, 442.
114. Zhang Rulun, *Shi de zhexue shi* 詩的哲學史 [Poetry of philosophical history] (Guilin: Guangxi shifan daxue chubanshe, 2002), 5.
115. Zhang Dongsun, "Yinzi" 引子 [Preface] to Zhang Rulun, *Poetry of Philosophical History*, 1–2.
116. Zhang Rulun, *Poetry of Philosophical History*, 1.
117. Zhang Dongsun, "Zhongpian" 終篇 [Epilogue]. See Zhang Rulun, *Poetry of Philosophical History*, 219.
118. Please also see David Der-wei Wang, *The Lyrical in Epic Time: Modern Chinese Intellectuals and Artists Through the 1949 Crisis* (New York: Columbia University Press, 2015), 8.
119. David Der-wei Wang, *The Lyrical in Epic Time*, x–xv, 77.
120. Zhu Ziqing 朱自清, *Shiyanzhi bian* 詩言志辨 [Classification of poetry that expresses intent] (Shanghai: Kaiming shudian, 1947), 2.
121. Wu Shengqing translated *yinpi lianlei* as "linking categorical correspondences and making comparisons." Please see Wu Shengqing, *Modern Archaics: Continuity and Innovation in the Chinese Lyric Tradition, 1900–1937* (Cambridge, MA: Harvard University Asia Center, 2013), 33–34. Here, I am using David Der-wei Wang's translation of *yinpi lianlei*. According to him, "By evoking analogues and categorical associations (*yinpi lanlei*), *shuqing* incorporates sensory vibration, metaphorical figures, and intellectual ruminations into a taxonomy of naming the world, thereby giving rise to knowledge." *The Lyrical in Epic Time*, 11.
122. Zhang Dongsun, "Aristotle (Part one)." See Zhang Rulun, *Poetry of Philosophical History*, 47.
123. Bertrand Russell, *History of Western Philosophy* (New York: Simon & Schuster, 1945), 176.
124. Russell, *History of Western Philosophy*, 176, 178.
125. Zhang Dongsun, "Kant." See Zhang Rulun, *Poetry of Philosophical History*, 118.
126. Zhang Dongsun tried to juxtapose empiricism and rationalism, but according to Zhang Yaonan, such a middle way is not very successful. See Zhang Yaonan, *Zhang Dongsun* 張東蓀 (Taipei: Dongda tushu, 1998), 178.
127. Zhang Dongsun, "James." See Zhang Rulun, *Poetry of Philosophical History*, 160.
128. According to Zhang Yaonan, some confused scholars think Samuel Alexander and Conwy Lloyd Morgen are the same person. See Zhang Yaonan, *Zhang Dongsun*, 232.
129. Zhang Dongsun, "Alexander and Morgen." See Zhang Rulun, *Poetry of Philosophical History*, 187.
130. Zhang Yaonan, *Zhang Dongsun*, 232.

131. Zhang Dongsun, *Knowledge and Culture*, 284.
132. Zhang Dongsun, "Whitehead." See Zhang Rulun, *Poetry of Philosophical History*, 192.
133. Zhang Dongsun, "Plato." See Zhang Rulun, *Poetry of Philosophical History*, 42.
134. Zhang Rulun, *Poetry of Philosophical History*, 44.
135. Zhang Dongsun, "Hobbes." See Zhang Rulun, *Poetry of Philosophical History*, 87.
136. Zhang Dongsun, "Hobbes." See Zhang Rulun, *Poetry of Philosophical History*, 87.
137. Russell, *History of Western Philosophy*, 503.
138. Zhang Dongsun, "Locke." See Zhang Rulun, *Poetry of Philosophical History*, 104.
139. Zhang Dongsun, "Hegel." See Zhang Rulun, *Poetry of Philosophical History*, 130.
140. Zhang Rulun, *Poetry of Philosophical History*, 134.
141. Zhang Dongsun, "Bianzhengfa de gezhong wenti" 辯證法的各種問題 [Various kinds of problems of dialectics], in Zuo Yuhe, *Zhang Dongsun juan*, 331–337.
142. Zhang Dongsun, *Knowledge and Culture*, 212, 215.
143. Zhang Dongsun, "Various Kinds of Problems of Dialectics," 337.
144. Zuo Yuhe, *A Biography of Zhang Dongsun*, 445–446.
145. Zhang Dongsun wrote this poem before he planned to write his autobiography, which was unfortunately damaged and lost during the Cultural Revolution. See Dai Qing, *In the Palm of Tathāgata: Zhang Dongsun and His Time*, 476, 492–493.

2. Yin Haiguang: Colorless Thought as Thirdspace

1. Yin Haiguang, "Zhi Hu Yue" 致胡越 [To Hu Yue] (January 3, 1967), in *Yin Haiguang quanji* 殷海光全集 [Complete works of Yin Haiguang], ed. Lin Zhenghong 林正弘, vol. 10, *Yin Haiguang shuxin ji* 殷海光書信集 [The correspondence of Yin Haiguang] (Taipei: Guiguang tushu, 1990), 26–31.
2. Edmund S. K. Fung, *In Search of Chinese Democracy: Civil Opposition in Nationalist China, 1929–1949* (Cambridge: Cambridge University Press, 2000), 10.
3. Yin Haiguang, "Women zou natiao lu" 我們走哪條路 [Which road should we take?], in *Complete Works of Yin Haiguang*, ed. Lin Zhenghong, vol. 11, *Zhengzhi yu shehui (shang)* 政治與社會 （上） [Politics and society (part one)] (Taipei: Guiguang tushu, 1990), 13–17.
4. Yin Haiguang, "Zhi Zhang Hao" 致張灝 [To Zhang Hao] (March 8, 1967), in Lin Zhenghong, *Complete Works of Yin Haiguang*, 10:164–165.
5. Yin Haiguang, "Cong youyanse de sixiang dao wuyanse de sixiang" 從有顏色的思想到無顏色的思想 [From the colorful thought to the colorless thought], in *Yin Haiguang quanji* 殷海光全集 [Complete works of Yin Haiguang], ed. Lin Zhenghong, vol 14, *Xueshu yu sixiang (er)* 學術與思想 （二） [Scholarship and thought (part two)] (Taipei: Guiguang tushu, 1990), 957–994.

6. Yin Haiguang, "Wo weishenme fangong" 我為什麼反共 [Why do I oppose the CCP?], in Lin Zhenghong, *Complete Works of Yin Haiguang*, 11:247.
7. Zhang Zhongdong 張忠棟, *Hu Shi, Lei Zhen, Yin Haiguang: Ziyou zhuyi renwu huaxiang* 胡適、雷震、殷海光—自由主義人物畫像 [Hu Shi, Lei Zhen, Yin Haiguang—The portraits of liberal figures] (Taipei: Zili baoxi chuban, 1990), 214.
8. Yin Haiguang, "Why Do I Oppose the CCP?" 248.
9. Jin Yuelin, "Wo dui Sulian de kanfa de zhuanbian" 我對蘇聯的看法的轉變 [The transformation of my view toward the Soviet Union], in *Jin Yuelin quanji* 金岳霖全集 [Complete works of Jin Yuelin], vol. 4 (Beijing: Renmin chubanshe, 2013), 773–778.
10. Yin Haiguang, "Why Do I Oppose the CCP?" 252, 254–255.
11. Yin Haiguang, *Zhongguo gongchandang zhi guancha* 中國共產黨之觀察 [Observations on the CCP], in *Yin Haiguang quanji* 殷海光全集 [Complete works of Yin Haiguang], ed. Lin Zhenghong, vol. 1 (Taipei: Guiguang tushu, 1990), 187.
12. Yin Haiguang, *Observations on the CCP*, 47.
13. Yin Haiguang, *Observations on the CCP*, 53.
14. Yin Haiguang, *Observations on the CCP*, 53.
15. Yin Haiguang, *Observations on the CCP*, 63.
16. Yin Haiguang, *Observations on the CCP*, 69.
17. Yin Haiguang, *Observations on the CCP*, 160.
18. Yin Haiguang, *Observations on the CCP*, 55.
19. Yin Haiguang, *Observations on the CCP*, 47–48.
20. "Manifesto of the Communist Party," Marxists.org, accessed August 31, 2024, https://www.marxists.org/archive/marx/works/1848/communist-manifesto/ch01.htm.
21. Yin Haiguang said, "Democracy and violence cannot coexist." In Yin Haiguang, *Observations on the CCP*, 66.
22. Yin Haiguang, *Observations on the CCP*, 187.
23. Yin Haiguang, *Observations on the CCP*, 48–49.
24. Yin Haiguang, *Observations on the CCP*, 176.
25. Yin Haiguang, "Why Do I Oppose the CCP?" 255.
26. Yin Haiguang, "Ganjin shoushi renxin" 趕緊收拾人心 [Quickly collect people's hearts], in Lin Zhenghong, *Complete Works of Yin Haiguang*, 11:31–34.
27. Yin Haiguang, "Which Road Should We Take?" 5–24.
28. Yin Haiguang, "Which Road Should We Take?" 19.
29. Yin Haiguang, "Wo dui guogong de kanfa" 我對國共的看法 [My opinions toward the KMT and the CCP], in Lin Zhenghong, *Complete Works of Yin Haiguang*, 11:26.
30. Yin Haiguang, "My Opinions Toward the KMT and the CCP," 27.
31. Yin Haiguang, "Why Do I Oppose the CCP?," 257, 258.

32. Yin Haiguang, "Why Do I Oppose the CCP?" 259.
33. Hannah Arendt, *The Origins of Totalitarianism* (San Diego: Harcourt Brace Jovanovich, 1973), xxxi, 460.
34. Arendt, *The Origins of Totalitarianism*, 460.
35. Yin Haiguang, "Why Do I Oppose the CCP?" 261–262.
36. Arendt, *The Origins of Totalitarianism*, 474–475.
37. John S. Reshetar Jr., *Problems of Analyzing and Predicting Soviet Behavior* (Garden City, NJ: Doubleday, 1955). Yin Haiguang changed the book's title to *Zenyang yanjiu Su'e* 怎樣研究蘇俄 [How to research Soviet Russia] in his translation in *Yin Haiguang quanji* 殷海光全集 [Complete works of Yin Haiguang], ed. Lin Zhenghong, vol. 5 (Taipei: Guiguang tushu, 1990), 80–81, 87, 144.
38. Reshetar, *Problems of Analyzing and Predicting Soviet Behavior*, 144.
39. Reshetar, *Problems of Analyzing and Predicting Soviet Behavior*, 171–172.
40. Yin Haiguang, "Why Do I Oppose the CCP?" 265–266, 264, 263–264.
41. Yin Haiguang wrote several articles criticizing the Red Guard during 1966–1967: "Zheyang de hongweibing" 這樣的紅衛兵 [This kind of Red Guard], "Hongweibing shi yihetuan ma" 紅衛兵是義和團嗎? [Is the Red Guard the Boxer Rebellion?], "Zidongde ba nongbao chuopo le" 自動的把膿包戳破了 [Automatically popped a pustule], "Kuangtu de baotiao" 狂徒的暴跳 [The violent jump of the crazy ones], "Wenhua de zisha" 文化的自殺 [The suicidal culture], "Xiang fenmu jinjun" 向墳墓進軍 [Marching toward the cemetery], "Yaodong xinli de fenxi" 窯洞心理的分析 [The analysis of cave psychology], in *Yin Haiguang quanji* 殷海光全集 [Complete works of Yin Haiguang], ed. Lin Zhenghong, vol 12, *Zhengzhi yu shehui (xia)* 政治與社會（下）[Politics and society (part two)] (Taipei: Guiguang tushu, 1990), 999–1080.
42. Yin Haiguang, "Which Road Should We Take?" 5–24.
43. Yin Haiguang, "Quickly Collect People's Heart," 31–34.
44. Yin Haiguang, "Fan bu'er xiweike zhuyi" 反布爾希維克主義 [Against Bolshevism], in Lin Zhenghong, *Complete Works of Yin Haiguang*, 11:148.
45. Yin Haiguang, "Why Do I Oppose the CCP?" 266–267.
46. Yin Haiguang, "Zheshi Guomindang fanxing de shihou" 這是國民黨反省的時候 [It is time that the KMT should reflect], in Lin Zhenghong, *Complete Works of Yin Haiguang*, 11:350.
47. Yin Haiguang, "It Is Time That the KMT Should Reflect," 354.
48. Yin Haiguang, "Shi shenme, jiu shuo shenme" 是什麼，就說什麼 [To say what it is], in Lin Zhenghong, *Complete Works of Yin Haiguang*, 11:501–502.
49. Yin Haiguang, "Jiaoyubu zhang Zhang Qiyun de minzhuguan: Junzhu de minzhu" 教育部長張其昀的民主觀——君主的民主 [The democratic view of the Minister of Education Zhang Qiyun—The democracy of a monarch], in Lin Zhenghong, *Complete Works of Yin Haiguang*, 11:412.
50. Yin Haiguang, "The Democratic View of the Minister of Education," 413.

51. Yin Haiguang, "To Say What It Is," 506. Please also see Zhang Qing 章清, *Yin Haiguang* 殷海光 (Taipei: Dongda tushu gongsi, 1996), 43.
52. Yin Haiguang, "Xueshu jiaoyu ying duli yu zhengzhi" 學術教育應獨立於政治 [Academic education should be independent from politics], in Lin Zhenghong, *Complete Works of Yin Haiguang*, 12:579–580.
53. Yin Haiguang, "Fangong dalu wenti" 反攻大陸問題 [The problem of counterattacking the mainland], in Lin Zhenghong, *The Complete Works of Yin Haiguang*, 11:519.
54. Yin Haiguang, "Guanyu 'fangong dalu wenti' de wenti" 關於"反攻大陸問題"的問題 [Regarding the problem of "the problem of counterattacking the mainland"], in Lin Zhenghong, *Complete Works of Yin Haiguang*, 11:524.
55. Hu Shi, "Cong zhengqu yanlun ziyou tandao fandui dang" 從爭取言論自由談到反對黨 [From striving for freedom of speech to the opposition party], in Lin Zhenghong, *Complete Works of Yin Haiguang*, 12:623.
56. Chang Hao 張灝, "Yitiao meiyou zouwan de lu" 一條沒有走完的路 [An unfinished road], in *Yin Haiguang quanji* 殷海光全集 [Complete works of Yin Haiguang], ed. Lin Zhenghong, vol. 18, *Yin Haiguang jinian ji* 殷海光紀念集 [The memorial anthology of Yin Haiguang] (Taipei: Guiguang tushu, 1990), 162.
57. Yin Haiguang, "Pouxi Guomindang" 剖析國民黨 [An anatomy of the KMT], in Lin Zhenghong, *Complete Works of Yin Haiguang*, 12:1119.
58. Yin Haiguang, "An Anatomy of the KMT," 1119.
59. Yin Haiguang, "An Anatomy of the KMT," 1119–1120, 1120–1122.
60. Yin Haiguang, "An Anatomy of the KMT," 1126–1128, 1128–1130.
61. Yin Haiguang, "An Anatomy of the KMT," 1128.
62. Yin Haiguang, *The Correspondences of Yin Haiguang*, in Lin Zhenghong, *Complete Works of Yin Haiguang*, 10:27.
63. Yin Haiguang, *The Correspondences of Yin Haiguang*, 38.
64. Yin Haiguang, *The Correspondences of Yin Haiguang*, 28–29.
65. Yin Haiguang, "Lun erfen fa" 論二分法 [On dichotomy], in Lin Zhenghong, *Complete Works of Yin Haiguang*, 12:684–686.
66. Yin Haiguang, "An Anatomy of the KMT," 1121.
67. Yin Haiguang, "On Dichotomy," 688.
68. Yin Haiguang, "An Anatomy of the KMT," 1122.
69. Yin Haiguang, "On Dichotomy," 688–689.
70. Yin Haiguang, "On Dichotomy," 694.
71. Yin Haiguang, "Which Road Should We Take?" 13–17.
72. Yin Haiguang, "Lun ziyou zhuyi zhe jiqi renwu" 論自由主義者及其任務 [On liberals and their duties], in Lin Zhenghong, *Complete Works of Yin Haiguang*, 12:767.
73. Yin Haiguang, *The Correspondences of Yin Haiguang*, 38–39.

74. In 1960, Yin Haiguang published two articles: "Lun meiyou yanse de sixiang" 論沒有顏色的思想 [On colorless thought], in *Yin Haiguang quanji* 殷海光全集 [Complete works of Yin Haiguang], ed. Lin Zhenghong, vol. 13, *Xueshu yu sixiang (yi)* 學術與思想 （一） [Scholarship and thought (part one)] (Taipei: Guiguang tushu, 1990), 23–36; and "From the Colorful Thought to the Colorless Thought," 957–994.
75. Yin Haiguang, "From the Colorful Thought to the Colorless Thought," 959–985.
76. Yin Haiguang, "From the Colorful Thought to the Colorless Thought," 986–988.
77. Yin Haiguang, "To Say What It Is," 499–508, 504.
78. Yin Haiguang, "From the Colorful Thought to the Colorless Thought," 990.
79. Rueylin Chen, "Morality Versus Science: The Two Cultures Discourse in 1950s Taiwan," *East Asian Science, Technology and Society: an International Journal* 4 (2010): 102.
80. Yin Haiguang, "From the Colorful Thought to the Colorless Thought," 990, 992, 994.
81. Yin Haiguang, "Zenyang panbie shifei" 怎樣判別是非 [How to distinguish right and wrong], in Lin Zhenghong, *Complete Works of Yin Haiguang*, 14:761–836.
82. Yin Haiguang, "On Colorless Thought," 35–36.
83. Yin Haiguang, "Ziran sixiang yu renwen sixiang" 自然思想與人文思想 [Natural thought and humanistic thought], in Lin Zhenghong, *Complete Works of Yin Haiguang*, 13:332.
84. Max Weber, "The Meaning of 'Ethical Neutrality' in Sociology and Economics," in *The Methodology of the Social Sciences*, trans. and ed. Edward Shills and Henry Finch (Glencoe, IL: The Free Press of Glencoe, 1949), 1–47. Also see Max Weber, "'Objectivity' in Social Science and Social Policy," in *The Methodology of the Social Sciences*, 50–112.
85. Jay A. Ciaffa, *Max Weber and the Problems of Value-Free Social Science: A Critical Examination of the Werturteilsstreit* (London: Associated University Presses, 1998), 18.
86. Wang Zhongjiang and Kuang Zhao, "Ultimate Concern, Reflection of Civilization, and the Idea of 'Man' in Yin Haiguang," *Frontiers of Philosophy in China* 6, no. 4 (December 2011): 565–584.
87. Yin Haiguang, "'Haiguang wenxuan' zixu" 《海光文選》自敘 [The self-preface of the selection of Yin Haiguang], in *Yin Haiguang jinzuo xuan* 殷海光近作選 [The select recent works of Yin Haiguang] (Hong Kong: The Committee of Haiguang Selective Collections, 1969), 2. Here, I am using Wang Zhongjiang and Kuang Zhao's translation in "Ultimate Concern, Reflection of Civilization, and the Idea of 'Man' in Yin Haiguang," 569.

88. Chen Guying 陳鼓應, ed., *Chuncan tusi: Yin Haiguang zuihou de huayu* 春蠶吐絲：殷海光最後的話語 [Silk from silkworm: The last words of Yin Haiguang] (Taipei: Shijie wenwu gongying she, 1969), 33.
89. Zhang Zhongdong, "Similarities and Differences Between Hu Shi and Yin Haiguang During the Initial Stage of Anti-Communism," *Chinese Studies in History* 38, no. 1 (2004): 77–93.
90. Yin Haiguang, "Ziyou de lunli jichu" 自由的倫理基礎 [The ethical foundation of freedom], in *Yin Haiguang quanji* 殷海光全集 [Complete works of Yin Haiguang], ed. Lin Zhenghong, vol. 15, *Xueshu yu sixiang (san)* 學術與思想（三）[Scholarship and thought (part three)] (Taipei: Guiguang tushu, 1990), 1156.
91. Lydia He Liu, *Translingual Practice: Literature, National Culture, and Translated Modernity—China, 1900–1937* (Stanford, CA: Stanford University Press, 1995), 95.
92. Yin Haiguang, "Minzhu de shijin shi" 民主的試金石 [The touchstone of democracy], in Lin Zhenghong, *Complete Works of Yin Haiguang*, 11:364.
93. Yin Haiguang, "The Touchstone of Democracy," 355–373.
94. Qian Yongxiang 錢永祥, "Yin Haiguang xiansheng de minzhuguan yu minzhu de liangge gainian" 殷海光先生的民主觀與民主的兩個概念 [Mr. Yin Haiguang's democratic viewpoints and two concepts of democracy], in Wei Zhengtong et al., *The Free and Democratic Thought and Culture* (Taipei: Zili wanbao she wenhua chuban bu, 1980), 117–118.
95. Xie Xiaodong 謝曉東, *Xiandai xinrujia yu ziyouzhuyi: Xu Fuguan Yin Haiguang zhengzhi zhexue bijiao yanjiu* 現代新儒家與自由主義：徐復觀殷海光政治哲學比較研究 [Modern New Confucianism and freedom: The comparative research on Xu Fuguan's and Yin Haiguang's political philosophy] (Beijing: Dongfang chubanshe, 2008), 131.
96. Friedrich A. Hayek, *Individualism and Economic Order* (Chicago: University of Chicago Press, 1948), 3–5.
97. Hayek, *Individualism and Economic Order*, 4.
98. Hayek, *Individualism and Economic Order*, 10–11.
99. Yin Haiguang, "The Ethical Foundation of Freedom," 1148.
100. Yin Haiguang, "The Ethical Foundation of Freedom," 1149.
101. Yin Haiguang, "The Ethical Foundation of Freedom," 1149–1150.
102. Yin Haiguang, "The Ethical Foundation of Freedom," 1156.
103. Friedrich A. Hayek, *The Road to Serfdom* (London: Routledge, 1944), 83.
104. Yin Haiguang, "The Ethical Foundation of Freedom," 1174–1175.
105. Yin Haiguang, "The Ethical Foundation of Freedom," 1180.
106. Friedrich A. Hayek, *The Constitution of Liberty* (Chicago: University of Chicago Press, 1960), 133.
107. Yin Haiguang, "The Ethical Foundation of Freedom," 1188, 1189.
108. Yin Haiguang, "The Ethical Foundation of Freedom," 1176.

109. Liu Jianmei, *Zhuangzi and Modern Chinese Literature* (New York: Oxford University Press, 2016), 215.
110. Isaiah Berlin, *Liberty*, ed. Henry Hardy (Oxford: Oxford University Press, 2002), 181–187.
111. Yin Haiguang, *Zhongguo wenhua de zhanwang* (Shang) 中國文化的展望 (上) [The viewpoints of Chinese culture (part one)], in *Yin Haiguang quanji* 殷海光全集 [Complete works of Yin Haiguang], ed. Lin Zhenghong, vol. 7 (Taipei: Guiguang tushu, 1990), 320, 321.
112. Chen Guying, *Silk from Silkworm*, 54.
113. Yin Haiguang, *The Viewpoints of Chinese Culture*, 320.
114. Karl Popper, *The Open Society and Its Enemies*, vol. 1 (London: George Routledge and Sons, 1945), 226.
115. Hu Shi, "Rongren yu ziyou" 容忍與自由 [Tolerance and freedom], in Lin Zhenghong, *Complete works of Yin Haiguang*, 12: 790–797. Yin Haiguang, "Hu Shih lun 'rongren yu ziyou' duhou" 胡適論《容忍與自由》讀後 [After reading Hu Shi's "Tolerance and Freedom"], in Lin Zhenghong, *Complete Works of Yin Haiguang*, 12:790–797, 781–789.

3. Jin Yong: Thirdspace as a Political Stance and Fictional Transgression

1. Liu Zaifu, *Wode sixiang shi* 我的思想史 [History of my thought] (Hong Kong, Sanlian shudian, 2019), 89–90.
2. Isaiah Berlin, *Liberty*, ed. Henry Hardy (Oxford: Oxford University Press, 2002), 165–217.
3. In regard to Jin Yong's revision and canonization of his novels, see John Christopher Hamm, *Paper Swordsmen: Jin Yong and the Modern Chinese Martial Arts Novel* (Honolulu: University of Hawaii Press, 2005), 168–197. Li Yijian, "'Rewriting' Jin Yong's Novels into the Canon: A Consideration of Jin Yong's Novels as Serialized Fiction," in *The Jin Yong Phenomenon: Chinese Martial Arts Fiction and Modern Chinese Literary History*, ed. Ann Huss and Liu Jianmei (Youngstown, NY: Cambria Press, 2007), 73–96.
4. Hamm, *Paper Swordsmen*, 244.
5. Song Weijie, *Cong yule xingwei dao wutuobang chongdong: Jin Yong xiaoshuo zai jiedu* 從娛樂行為到烏托邦衝動——金庸小說再解讀 [From entertainment to the utopian impulse: Rereading Jin Yong's novels] (Nanjing: Jiangsu renmin chubanshe, 1999), 139–158.
6. Chen Pingyuan, "Transcending 'High' and 'Low' Distinctions in Literature: The Success of Jin Yong and the Future of Martial Arts Novels," in Ann Huss and Liu Jianmei, *The Jin Yong Phenomenon*, 58.

7. Liu Xiaomei 劉曉梅. "Wenren lun wu" 文人論武 [Scholars discussing martial arts]. In *Zhuzi baijia kan Jin Yong* 諸子百家看金庸 [An examination of Jin Yong through the lens of the hundred schools of thought]. vol. 3., San Mao et al, 237–245. (Beijing: Zhongguo youyi chubanshe, 1998).
8. Hamm, *Paper Swordsmen*, 125–126. Kwai-Yeung Cheung 張圭陽, *Jin Yong yu baoye* 金庸與報業 [Jin Yong and the press] (Hong Kong: Ming Pao chubanshe, 2000), 53, 373.
9. Jiang Di 江堤 and Yang Hui 楊暉, *Zhongguo lishi dashi* 中國歷史大勢 [The big tendency of Chinese history] (Changsha: Human daxue chubanshe, 2001), 56–57.
10. Jiang Di and Yang Hui, *The Big Tendency of Chinese History*, 57.
11. When Jin Yong visited Japan to meet with reporters of *The Asahi Shimbun* in 1964, he was astonished that the social status of the first-rank journalists in Japan was higher than that of the first-rank politicians. It prompted him to realize the power of journalism: "In a truly democratic society, the government can never influence the newspapers, but the newspapers can influence the government. Politicians can come and go, cabinets can be reshuffled and replaced, but newspapers must be consistent in their statements and positions." Fu Guoyong 傅國涌, *Jin Yong zhuan* 金庸傳 [The biography of Jin Yong] (Beijing: Beijing shiyue wenyi chubanshe, 2003), 195.
12. Hamm, *Paper Swordsmen*, 127.
13. Leng Xia 冷夏, *Wentan xiasheng—Jin Yong zhuan* 文壇俠聖——金庸傳 [The sage of Xia in the literary field—The biography of Jin Yong] (Guangzhou: Guangdong renmin chubanshe, 1995), 107.
14. Leng Xia, *The Sage of Xia in the Literary Field*, 107
15. Kwai-Yeung Cheung, *Jin Yong and the Press*, 184.
16. Hamm, *Paper Swordsmen*, 128.
17. Huang Aihua 黃愛華, *Lun zuguo wenti* 論祖國問題 [On the problem of the home country] (Hong Kong: Ming Pao chubanshe, 1964).
18. Huang Aihua, *On the Problem of the Home Country*, 167.
19. Huang Aihua, *On the Problem of the Home Country*, 163–170.
20. Mill explains, "Utility, or the Greatest Happiness Principle, holds that actions are right in proportion as they tend to promote happiness, wrong as they tend to produce the reverse of happiness." See John Stuart Mill, *Utilitarianism, Liberty and Representative Government* (London: Everyman, 1910), 6.
21. Julia Driver, *Consequentialism* (New York: Routledge, 2012), 2.
22. As Jin Yong wrote: "There is no denying that most members of the Communist Party of China are able to work diligently. They are cultivated, ambitious, and altruistic, striving for the welfare of the people." Huang Aihua, *On the Problem of the Home Country*, 10.
23. Huang Aihua, *On the Problem of the Home Country*, 169.

24. Hans Albert, *Treatise on Critical Reason* (Princeton, NJ: Princeton University Press, 1985), 82.
25. Yang Lige 楊莉歌, *Jin Yong chuanshuo* 金庸傳說 [The legend of Jin Yong] (Hong Kong: Ciwenhua youxian gongsi, 1997), 160–163.
26. Kwai-Yeung Cheung, *Jin Yong and the Press*, 203.
27. Jin Yong, *Zaitai suojian, suowen, suosi* 在台所見所聞所思 [What I saw, heard, and thought in Taiwan] (Hong Kong: Ming Pao youxian gongsi, 1973), 2, 2, 3.
28. Jin Yong, "What I Saw, Heard, and Thought in Taiwan," 18.
29. Driver, *Consequentialism*, 7.
30. Jin Yong, "What I Saw, Heard, and Thought in Taiwan," 18.
31. Jin Yong, "What I Saw, Heard, and Thought in Taiwan," 19.
32. Jin Yong, "What I Saw, Heard, and Thought in Taiwan," 57.
33. Louis Cha, *On Hong Kong's Future: A Collection of Ming Pao Daily News Editorials*, trans. Stephen Wang (Hong Kong: Ming Pao Daily News Ltd., 1984), 17.
34. Jin Yong and Ikeda Daisaku, *Tanqiu yige canlan de shiji* 探求一個燦爛的世紀 [Exploring a splendid century] (Hong Kong: Mingheshe chuban youxian gongsi, 1998), 105–107.
35. Cha, *On Hong Kong's Future*, 162.
36. Cha, *On Hong Kong's Future*, 105.
37. As Jin Yong stresses, "All consideration of Hong Kong's future must be practicable. Talks on theories, ideas, and doctrines may be permitted among people who have their heads buried among books. Such talks are certainly not applicable to the pragmatic people of Hong Kong." Cha, *On Hong Kong's Future*, 88.
38. Cha, *On Hong Kong's Future*, 254.
39. Cha, *On Hong Kong's Future*, 180–182.
40. John Rawls, *Political Liberalism*, expanded edition (New York: Columbia University Press, 2005), 150.
41. Cha, *On Hong Kong's Future*, 307.
42. Cha, *On Hong Kong's Future*, 307.
43. According to Jin Yong, self-rule means basically following the current prevailing model, "featuring stable government and stable policy, devoid of political struggle and factional strife in the assembly and among the community, an independent judiciary, power not being concentrated in the chief executive alone, the administration being fully systemized, all to be done in accordance with the law, a system of consultation and enough regard given to public opinions." Cha, *On Hong Kong's Future*, 328.
44. Michael Yahuda explains: "The Basic Law in the end opted for a gradual approach so that the 60-member legislature would begin with 20 members directly elected, rising to 24 and then to 30 (or half), leaving it open for further changes from the year 2007." Michael Yahuda, *Hong Kong: China's Challenge* (London: Routledge, 1996), 114.

45. Jin Yong and Ikeda Daisaku, *Exploring a Splendid Century*, 250–251.
46. Leng Xia, *The Biography of Jin Yong* (Hong Kong: Ming Pao chubanshe, 1994), 396–397.
47. Yang Lige, *The Legend of Jin Yong*, 224.
48. Kwai-Yeung Cheung, *Jin Yong and the Press*, 179.
49. Song Weijie, "Space, Swordsman, and Utopia: The Dualistic Imagination in Jin Yong's Narratives," in Ann Huss and Liu Jianmei, *The Jin Yong Phenomenon*, 167.
50. Song Weijie, "Space, Swordsman, and Utopia," 156–157.
51. See Song Weijie, "Space, Swordsman, and Utopia," 168.
52. Tao Jiang, "Isaiah Berlin's Challenge to Zhuangzian Freedom," *Journal of Chinese Philosophy*, supplement to volume 39 (2012): 69–92.
53. Charles Taylor, "What's Wrong with Negative Freedom?" in *The Liberty Reader*, ed. David Miller (London and New York: Routledge, 2016), 145.
54. Taylor, "What's Wrong with Negative Freedom?" 142.
55. Tian Xiaofei, "The Ship in a Bottle: The Construction of an Imaginary China in Jin Yong's Fiction," in Ann Huss and Liu Jianmei, *The Jin Yong Phenomenon*, 239.
56. According to the literary scholar Petrus Liu, "*The Smiling, Proud Wanderer* of 1967 has no specified time frame, which gives the novels an explicitly allegorical, even fable-like, feel that draws attention to the connection between the text and the immediate context of the Cultural Revolution." See Petrus Liu, "Jin Yong Publishes *The Smiling, Proud Wanderer* in *Ming Pao*," in *A New Literary History of Modern China*, ed. David Der-wei Wang (Cambridge, MA: The Belknap Press of Harvard University Press, 2017), 687.
57. Jin Yong, *Xiao'ao Jianghu* 笑傲江湖 [The smiling, proud wanderer] (Guangzhou: Guangzhou chubanshe, 2013), vol. 4, 1591. Here I borrow the translation from Hamm, *Paper Swordsmen*, 164.
58. Jin Yong, *The Smiling, Proud Wanderer*, 1:212.
59. "Yinshi" 隱士 [Hermits], in *The Complete Works of Lu Xun*, vol. 6 (Beijing: Renmin wenxue chubanshe, 1993), 223–226.
60. Liu Zaifu, "Xunzhao shengcun de 'disan kongjian'" 尋找生存的"第三空間" [Searching for the survival of Thirdspace], *Yazhou zhoukan* (September 3–9, 2001).
61. Hamm, *Paper Swordsmen*, 150–151. In Hamm's interpretation: "Qu Yang and Liu Zhengfeng propose and Ling Huchong and Ren Yingying confirm, that the value of music and by extension of the artistic and cultural heritage as a whole, lies precisely in its capacity to create an alternative to the Rivers and Lakes and the martial arts that are this area's defining practice." Hamm, *Paper Swordsmen*, 156.
62. Chen Pingyuan, "Transcending 'High' and 'Low' Distinctions in Literature," 60.
63. Jin Yong, *The Smiling, Proud Wanderer*, 4:1451.
64. Jin Yong, *The Smiling, Proud Wanderer*, 4:1453.

65. Gao Xingjian, *Cold Literature: Selected Works by Gao Xingjian*, trans. Gilbert C. F. Fong and Mabel Lee (Hong Kong: The Chinese University Press, 2005), 15.
66. Jin Yong, *The Smiling, Proud Wanderer*, 4:1453.
67. Jin Yong, *The Smiling, Proud Wanderer*, 2:733.
68. Petrus Liu, *Stateless Subjects: Chinese Martial Arts Literature and Postcolonial History* (Ithaca, NY: Cornell University East Asia Program, 2011), 177.
69. Jin Yong and Ikeda Daisaku, *Exploring a Splendid Century*, 197.
70. Liu Zaifu, *Reflections on Dream of the Red Chamber*, trans. Shu Yunzhong (Amherst, NY: Cambria Press, 2008), 269.
71. Liu Zaifu, *Reflections on Dream of the Red Chamber*, 169.
72. Lu Xun, *Lu Xun quanji* 魯迅全集 [The complete works of Lu Xun] (Beijing: Renmin wenxue chubanshe, 1993), vol. 9, 338.
73. Homi Bhabha, "The Third Space: Interview with Homi Bhabha," in *Identity, Community, Culture, Difference*, ed. Jonathan Rutherford (London: Lawrence and Wishart, 1990), 211.
74. Chen Mo 陳墨, "Bu shi zhanglang shi zhanglang: Zhang Wuji xingxiang sanlun" 不識張郎是張郎—張無忌形象散論 [Not recognizing Zhang Lang is Zhang Lang—On the image of Zhang Wuji], in *Jin Yong xiaoshuo guoji yantaohui lunwenji* 金庸小說國際研討會論文集 [The collected articles of the International Conference on Jin Yong Novels], ed. Wu Xiaodong 吳曉東 and Ji Birui 計璧瑞 (Beijing: Beijing daxue chubanshe, 2002), 571–587.
75. Jin Yong, "Afterword," in *Yitian tulong ji* 倚天屠龍記 [The heaven sword and the dragon saber] (Guangzhou: Guangzhou chubanshe, 2013), vol. 4, 1433.
76. Zhao Qi 趙崎, *Mengzi zhushu* 孟子注疏 [Commentary on Mencius] (Shanghai: Shanghai guji chubanshe, 1990), 66.
77. According to Carlos Rojas, "At the time, 'China' was a highly contested conceptual entity, with a number of ethno-political powers asserting varying degrees of sovereignty over territory to the north, west, and south of that controlled by the (Chinese) Song dynasty." Carlos Rojas, *The Naked Gaze: Reflections on Chinese Modernity* (Cambridge, MA: Harvard University Asian Center, 2008), 139.
78. Chen Shixiang's letter to Jin Yong; see Jin Yong, *Tianlong babu* 天龍八部 [The semi-Gods and the semi-devils] (Guangzhou: Guangzhou chubanshe, 2013), 1817.
79. Petrus Liu writes: "In Mahayana Buddhism, *devas* and *nāga* are the two highest categories of the eight entities that protect the Dharma. In his preface to the novel, Jin Yong states that the phrase is commonly found in Buddhist scriptures and commentaries such as *The Lotus Sutra* (Fahua jing)." See Petrus Liu, *Stateless Subjects*, 124.
80. Rojas, *The Naked Gaze*, 140.
81. As Song Weijie points out, "The burden of double identity—of being both Han and Khitan, neither Han nor Khitan—as an inevitable predicament, insures that

Xiao Feng will never attain loyalty and filial piety to the Beggar Gangs in the Song court and to the Liao Kingdom, or to his own Khitan father and to his Han supporting parents." See Song Weijie, "Nation-State, Individual Identity, and Historical Memory: Conflicts Between Han and Non-Han Peoples in Jin Yong's Novels," in Ann Huss and Liu Jianmei, *The Jin Yong Phenomenon*, 136.

82. Jin Yong, *The Semi-Gods and the Semi-Devils*, 756.
83. Zhou Zuoren, "Wode zaxue" 我的雜學 [My miscellaneous studies], in *Zhitang huixiang lu* 知堂回想錄 [The memoir of Zhitang], in *Zhou Zuoren zibian wenji* 周作人自編文集 [Self-edited collection of Zhou Zuoren] (Shijiazhuang: Hebei jiaoyu chubanshe, 2002), 794.
84. Jin Yong, *The Semi-Gods and the Semi-Devils*, 1543.
85. Using the phrase "the dissolution of irony," Tian Xiaofei illustrates that "Xiaobao's utilitarian, pragmatic, and yet often effective way of dealing with the world casts an ironic perspective on his master, the conventional knight-errant hero, *daxia*, who fought for a political ideal." See Tian Xiaofei, "The Ship in a Bottle," 239.
86. As John Christopher Hamm argues, "Concrete or literal manifestations of the *xia*'s oppositional spirit are nonetheless unsuited to modern societies, in which the interests or the rulers and those of the people are (in theory) in accord; the lying and scheming to which Wei Xiaobao's 'adaptability' leads him should be understood as revealing the weaknesses of the Qing society in which he lived, and would properly disappear under more enlightened social conditions, indeed, the prevalence of 'Wei Xiaobao style' (Wei Xiaobao fengdu) of cronyism, self-interest, and disregard of the law has a great deal to do with the Chinese government's continued failure to get on the right track." Hamm, *Paper Swordsmen*, 202.
87. Song Weijie, "Nation-State, Individual Identity, and Historical Memory," 139.
88. Benjamin I. Schwartz, *The World of Thought in Ancient China* (Cambridge, MA: The Belknap Press of Harvard University Press, 1985), 390, 393, 396.
89. Liu Xinwu, "Shifu: yizhong shengcun kunjing" 失父：一種生存困境 [Losing father: A survival dilemma], in *Jin Yong xiaoshuo yu ershishiji Zhongguo wenxue* 金庸小說與二十世紀中國文學 [Jin Yong's fiction and twentieth-century Chinese literature], ed. Lin Lijun (Hong Kong: Minghe she, 2000), 391.
90. Jin Yong, *Luding ji* 鹿鼎記 [The deer and the cauldron] (Guangzhou: Guangzhou chubanshe, 2013), 1823.

4. Liu Zaifu: Envisioning Variations of Thirdspace

1. Liu Zaifu, *Piaobo zhuan—Liu Zaifu haiwai sanwen xuan* 漂泊傳—劉再復海外散文選 [Autobiography of drifting—Selective collection of Liu Zaifu's overseas essays] (Hong Kong: Tiandi tushu, 2009), 14.

2. Liu Zaifu, *Autobiography of Drifting*, 14.
3. Liu Zaifu, *Tianya wuyu* 天涯悟語 [The enlightened words at the edge of the world] (Beijing: Sanlian, 2013), 49–50.
4. Liu Zaifu, "Zailun disan huayu kongjian" 再論第三話語空間 [Rethinking the third discursive space], *Mingpao Monthly*, April 2006.
5. Liu Zaifu, *Xingge zuhe lun* 性格組合論 [A treatise of character composition] (Hefei: Anhui wenhui chubanshe, 1999), 70.
6. Liu Zaifu, *A Treatise of Character Composition*, 151.
7. Yang Shuiyuan 楊水遠, "Zuowei siwei fangshi he lunzheng fangfa de Heige'er: Liu Zaifu zhuti xing wenlun sixiang laiyuan zai kaocha" 作為思維方式和論證方法的黑格爾：劉再復主體性文論思想來源再考察 [Hegel as a way of thought and method of argument: Reexamination of the origin of thought of Liu Zaifu's subjectivity], *Huawen wenxue* 華文文學 [Sinophone literature], no. 4 (2018): 5–13.
8. Based on his research on subjectivity and cultural theory in the 1980s, Liu Kang also draws the following conclusion: "Liu Zaifu acknowledges his indebtedness to Li Zehou on many occasions. However, the difference between their philosophical and methodological points of view is quite remarkable. If Li Zehou's propositions on subjectivity are resonant with Kantian presuppositions, Liu Zaifu's theoretical framework has a much stronger Hegelian bent. Liu Zaifu is most explicit about his objectives of dialectical recovery or return: a recovery of creative subjectivity and a recovery of literature itself ('return to the subject and return to the text,' so to speak)." See Liu Kang 劉康, "Subjectivity, Marxism, and Cultural Theory in China," in *Politics, Ideology, and Literary Discourse in Modern China*, ed. Liu Kang and Xiaobing Tang 唐小兵 (Durham, NC: Duke University Press, 1993), 44.
9. Peter Ping Li, "Global Implications of the Indigenous Epistemological System from the East," *Cross Cultural and Strategic Management* (February 2016): 47. Please also see J. G. Hibben, *Hegel's Logic: An Essay in Interpretation* (Charles Scribner's Sons, 1902; repr., Kitchener, ON: Batoche Books, 2000).
10. Liu Zaifu, *A Treatise of Character Composition*, 518. It is in the postscript Liu Zaifu wrote for the new edition published by Anhui wenyi chubanshe in 1999.
11. Liu Zaifu, "From the Monologic Era to the Polyphonic Era: An Outline of Forty Years of Literary Development in Mainland China," in *Liu Zaifu: Selected Critical Essays*, ed. Howard Y. F. Choy and Liu Jianmei (Leiden, Netherlands: Brill, 2021), 95–96, 103–115.
12. Liu Zaifu, "Lun Bingzai" 論丙崽 [On Bingzai], in *Han Shaogong yanjiu ziliao* 韓少功研究資料 [The research materials of Han Shaogong], ed. Li Li and Hu Jianling (Jinan: Shandong wenyi chubanshe, 2006), 134.
13. Liu Zaifu, "On Bingzai," 135. Here I use Joseph Lau's translation of Liu Zaifu's words. See Joseph S. M. Lau, "Visitation of the Past in Han Shaogong's Post 1985

Fiction," in *From May Fourth to June Fourth: Fiction and Film in Twentieth-Century China*, ed. Ellen Widmer and David Der-wei Wang (Cambridge, MA: Harvard University Asian Center, 1993), 32. Please also see Liu Jianmei, *Zhuangzi and Modern Chinese Literature* (New York: Oxford University Press, 2016), 170–171.
14. Liu Zaifu, "On Bingzai," 136.
15. Li Zehou and Liu Zaifu, *Gaobie geming* 告別革命 [Farewell to revolution] (Hong Kong: Tiandi, 2015), 34. The first edition of this book was published in 1995 by Hong Kong Tiandi.
16. Li Zehou and Liu Zaifu, *Farewell to Revolution*, 34.
17. Tsou Tang 鄒讜, "Geming yu gaobie geming—gei Gaobie geming zuozhe de yifeng xin" 革命與告別革命——給《告別革命》作者的一封信 [Revolution and farewell to revolution—A letter to the authors of *Farewell to Revolution*], in Li Zehou and Liu Zaifu, *Farewell to Revolution*, 18.
18. Li Zehou, *Pipan zhexue de pipan: Kangde shuping* 批判哲學的批判：康德述評 [The criticism of critical philosophy: On Kant] (Beijing: Sanlian shudian, 2015), 241.
19. As Liu Zaifu wrote, "One of the most important meanings of the multiple currents of thought is to respect every element's independent value and right to exist independently." Li Zehou and Liu Zaifu, *Farewell to Revolution*, 39, 60.
20. Li Zehou and Liu Zaifu, *Farewell to Revolution*, 42.
21. Li Zehou and Liu Zaifu, *Farewell to Revolution*, 124–130.
22. Zhang Taiyan, "Jufen jinhua lun" 俱分進化論 [Dual evolution theory], *Minpao* 民報 [People's newspaper] 7 (1906): 1–13.
23. Li Zehou and Liu Zaifu, *Farewell to Revolution*, 223–233. Liu Zaifu, "Literary History as a Paradox," in *Liu Zaifu: Selected Critical Essays*, ed. Howard Y. F. Choy and Liu Jianmei (Leiden, Netherlands: Brill, 2021), 27–29.
24. Li Zehou and Liu Zaifu, *Farewell to Revolution*, 437–450; 452–481.
25. Li Zehou and Liu Zaifu, *Farewell to Revolution*, 59.
26. Dai Qing, *Tian'anmen Follies: Prison Memoirs and Other Writings*, trans. Nancy Yang Liu, Peter Rand, and Lawrence R. Sullivan (Norwald, CT: Eastbridge Books, 2005), 88.
27. Li Zehou and Liu Zaifu, *Farewell to Revolution*, 360.
28. Before he went into exile, Liu Zaifu learned only Russian at Xiamen University and had no opportunity to learn English. When he was a Luce visiting scholar at the University of Chicago during 1989–1991, he started to study it. Although his English capability enables him to handle basic daily life skills in the United States, it is not sophisticated enough for him to read and write English academic books. When he was conceiving of "the third space" in the 1990s, he did not have access to Chinese translations of Western literary and cultural theories.
29. Liu Zaifu, "Xunzhao shengcun de 'disan kongjian'" 尋找生存的第三空間 [Searching for the survival of Thirdspace], *Yazhou zhoukan*, September 3–9, 2001.

30. Liu Zaifu, "Searching for the Survival of Thirdspace."
31. Liu Zaifu, "Searching for the Survival of Thirdspace."
32. Isaiah Berlin, *Liberty*, ed. Henry Hardy (Oxford: Oxford University Press, 2002), 171.
33. Berlin, *Liberty*, 181.
34. Liu Zaifu and Lin Gang 林崗, *Chuantong yu zhongguoren* 傳統與中國人 [Tradition and Chinese] (Beijing: Sanlian shudian, 1988), 178–185.
35. Liu Zaifu wrote: "Lu Xun's 魯迅 criticism of Zhu Guangqian 朱光潛 and Lin Yutang in the 1930s was in fact chastisement of the reclusive spirit. Essays by Lu Xun such as 'Hermits' ('Yinshi' 隱士) and 'Miscellaneous Talk after Illness' ('Binghou zatan' 病後雜談) even directly mocked the reclusive spirit. Of course, his criticism was a rejection of negative freedom and did not imply identification with the state. He himself was also exiling the state, seeking critical and positive freedom, and always opposing the omnipotent center of power through spiritual marginalization. But he lacked tolerance of the reclusive spirit as a form of negative freedom and in practice blocked up writers' free spiritual space." Liu Zaifu, "Literature Exiling the State," in *Liu Zaifu: Selected Critical Essays*, ed. Howard Y. F. Choy and Liu Jianmei (Leiden, Netherlands: Brill, 2021), 193–194.
36. Liu Zaifu, "Searching for the Survival of Thirdspace."
37. Liu Zaifu mentioned Max Weber's value neutrality as well as its connection with responsibility ethics in his article "Rethinking the Third Discursive Space." Zhang Jinghe pays attention to the connection between Weber's value neutrality and Liu Zaifu's concept of Thirdspace in Zhang Jinghe, *Liu Zaifu wenxue xinxing benti lun* 劉再復文學心性本體論 [Liu Zaifu's literary ontology of heart/mind] (Hong Kong: Sanlian, 2020).
38. Wilhelm Hennis, Ulrike Brisson, and Roger Brisson, "The Meaning of 'Wertfreiheit' on the Background and Motives of Max Weber's 'Postulate,'" *Sociological Theory* 12, no. 2 (July 1994): 115.
39. Liu Zaifu, *Huigui gudian, huigui wode liuijng* 回歸古典，回歸我的六經 [Return to the classics, return to my six scriptures] (Beijing: Renmin ribao chuban she, 2011), 155–160.
40. Liu Zaifu, "Searching for the Survival of Thirdspace."
41. Liu Zaifu, *Daguan xinde* 大觀心得 [The comprehension notes on the grand vision] (Hong Kong: Tiandi tushu, 2010), 130.
42. Liu Zaifu, "Literature Exiling the State," 181–182.
43. Liu Zaifu, "Shuangxiang siwei yu da shidai jidiao" 雙向思維與大時代基調 [Bilateral way of thinking and the basic tone of the big era], in Liu Zaifu, *Cangsang baigan* 滄桑百感 [Hundreds of comprehensions in the vicissitudes of life] (Hong Kong: Tiandi, 2004), 34, 35.
44. Li Zehou and Liu Zaifu, *Farewell to Revolution*, 54–57.

45. Edward Said, *Representation of the Intellectual* (New York: Pantheon, 1994), 47–85.
46. Leo Ou-fan Lee, "On the Margins of the Chinese Discourse: Some Personal Thoughts on the Cultural Meaning of the Periphery," *Daedalus* 120, no. 2 (Spring 1991): 207–226.
47. Liu Zaifu, *Wode sixiang shi* 我的思想史 [History of my thought] (Hong Kong: Sanlian, 2020), 148–149.
48. Liu Zaifu, *History of My Thought*, 154–160.
49. Liu Zaifu, *Wode xiezuo shi* 我的寫作史 [History of my writing] (Hong Kong: Sanlian shudian, 2017), 222–223.
50. In his own words, "Materialism and idealism can complement and enhance each other. Neither is absolutely good (correct) nor absolutely bad (wrong)." In Liu Zaifu, *History of My Thought*, 378.
51. Liu Zaifu, *History of My Thought*, 160. Gu Dayong 古大勇, "Li Zehou, Liu Zaifu bijiao lungang" 李泽厚 劉再復比較論綱 [The comparison between Li Zehou and Liu Zaifu], *Huawen wenxue* 1 (2018): 8–19.
52. Liu Zaifu and Liu Jianmei, "Honglou zhensu erdi de hubu jiegou—Guanyu Hongloumeng de zuixin duihua" 紅樓真俗二諦的互補結構——關於紅樓夢的最新對話 [The complementary structure between the truth of the transcendental world and the truth of the mundane world—The most recent dialogue about *Dream of the Red Chamber*], *Huawen wenxue* 5 (2010): 105–112. Please also see Liu Jianmei, *Zhuangzi and Modern Chinese Literature* (New York: Oxford University Press, 2016), 90–91.
53. For Liu Zaifu, these two kinds of "home" also means two kinds of destiny, and two kinds of "state of clarity" (*chengming zhijing* 澄明之境). See Liu Zaifu, *Hongloumeng zhexue biji* 紅樓夢哲學筆記 [Philosophical notes on *Dream of the Red Chamber*] (Beijing: Sanlian shudian, 2009), 201–231.
54. Liu Zaifu, *Reflections on Dream of the Red Chamber*, trans. Shu Yunzhong (Amherst, NY: Cambria Press, 2008), 269, 271.
55. Liu Zaifu wrote: "Hu Feng emphasizes 'embracement,' but I focus on 'transcendence.' Both aim to stimulate writers' subjective initiative, avoiding jumping into the trap of 'objectivism.'" In Liu Zaifu, *The History of My Thought*, 114–115.
56. Liu Zaifu and Lin Gang, *Zui yu wenxue* 罪與文學 [Sin and literature] (Beijing: Zhongxin chubanshe, 2011), 242–296.
57. Tu Hang, "Pleasure and Sin: Li Zehou, Liu Zaifu, and the Political-Theological Motif in Post-Mao Cultural Reflections," *Prism* 17, no. 1 (2020): 165.
58. Liu Zaifu, *Zenyang du wenxue—wenxue huiwu shiba dian* 怎樣讀文學—文學慧悟十八點 [How to read literature—Eighteen points of literary comprehension] (Hong Kong: Sanlian shudian, 2018), 62–64.
59. Immanuel Kant, *Critique of Judgment*, trans. Werner S. Pluhar (Indianapolis, IN: Hackett, 1987), 65, 92.
60. Liu Zaifu, *How to Read Literature*, 62–64.

61. Liu Zaifu, *Philosophical notes on Dream of the Red Chamber*, 205.
62. Liu Zaifu, *Philosophical Notes on Dream of the Red Chamber*, 206.
63. Liu Zaifu, *The History of My Thought*, 147.
64. Liu Zaifu, *Philosophical Notes on Dream of the Red Chamber*, 205.
65. Liu Zaifu, *Reflections on Dream of the Red Chamber*, 264–265.
66. Liu Zaifu, *How to Read Literature*, 211.
67. Liu Zaifu, *Wode xinling shi* 我的心靈史 [History of my heart] (Hong Kong: Sanlian shudian, 2019), 164.
68. Tu Hang, "Pleasure and Sin," 160.
69. Liu Zaifu, *Jiao Baoyu lun* 賈寶玉論 [On Jia Baoyu] (Beijing: Sanlian shudian, 2014), 4. Please also see David Der-wei Wang, "Standing Alone atop the Mountain, Walking Freely Under the Sea: On Liu Zaifu and Five Autobiographical Accounts," *Prism* 17, no. 1 (2020): 153.
70. In Liu Zaifu's own language, "It is where one's heart is, not where one's body is, that matters more. . . . If we take the concept of 'solidifying one's destiny' (*liming* 立命), I would say it is based first on 'solidifying the heart' (*lixin* 立心). Lu Xun once said the prerequisite for 'solidifying the nation' (*liguo* 立國) is 'solidifying the human' (*liren* 立人). Following this logic, I contend that 'solidifying one's destiny' presupposes 'solidifying one's heart.' I harbour no vanity to 'solidify the heart for the universe,' but I have the self-awareness to 'solidify my own heart.'" Here I am using David Der-wei Wang's translation in his article "Standing Alone atop the Mountain," 153.
71. Liu Zaifu, *History of My Heart*, 86–102.
72. Lu Xun, "Wenhua pianzhi lun" 文化偏執論 [On the one-sidedness of cultural development]," in *Luxun quanji* 魯迅全集 [The complete works of Lu Xun] (Beijing: Renmin wenxue chubanshe, 1981), 1:56.
73. Liu Zaifu, *Shenme shi wenxue—wenxue changshi ershier jiang* 什麼是文學—文學常識二十二講 [What is literature? Twenty-two lectures on literary common knowledge] (Hong Kong: Sanlian shudian, 2015), 30.
74. Liu Zaifu, *A Study of Two Classics*, trans. Shu Yunzhong (Amherst, NY: Cambria Press, 2012), 1–27.
75. David Der-wei Wang, "Standing Alone atop the Mountain," 151.
76. David Der-wei Wang, "Standing Alone atop the Mountain," 154.
77. David Der-wei Wang, "Standing Alone atop the Mountain," 151–152.
78. Nick Admussen, *Recite and Refuse: Contemporary Chinese Prose Poetry* (Honolulu: University of Hawai'i Press, 2016), 107.
79. Walter Benjamin, *The Origin of German Tragic Drama* (London: Verso, 2009), 34, 37.
80. Graeme Gilloch, *Walter Benjamin: Critical Constellations* (Cambridge: Polity Press, 2002), 71.
81. Siegfried Giedion, *Mechanization Takes Command: A Contribution to Anonymous History* (New York: Oxford University Press, 1948), 2–3.

82. Marshall McLuhan, *The Gutenberg Galaxy: The Making of Typographic Man* (Toronto, ON: University of Toronto Press, 1962), n.p.
83. Residing overseas, he has written 2,500 pieces of fragmentary writing, including 1,001 pieces in *Solitary Recitations at the Edge of the World* (Duyu tianya 獨語天涯), four hundred pieces in *Record of Meditation Facing a Wall* (Mianbi chensi lu 面壁沈思錄), six hundred reflective pieces on *Dream of the Red Chamber*, three hundred reflective pieces on *Journey to the West*, one hundred reflective pieces on *Water Margin* and *Romance of the Three Kingdoms*, and another one hundred pieces of rumination on life.
84. Liu Zaifu, *Duyu tianya* 獨語天涯 [Solitary recitations at the edge of the world] (Beijing: Sanlian shudian, 2013), 404–405.
85. Liu Zaifu, *Philosophical Notes on Dream of the Red Chamber*, 168.
86. Xiao Tie, *Revolutionary Waves: The Crowd in Modern China* (Cambridge, MA: Harvard University Asian Center, 2017).
87. Liu Zaifu, *Solitary Recitations at the Edge of the World*, 76.
88. Liu Zaifu and Liu Jianmei, *Gongwu honglou* 共悟紅樓 [Comprehending *Dream of the Red Chamber* together] (Beijing: Sanlian shudian, 2009), 4.
89. Liu Zaifu, "Farewell to the Gods: Contemporary Chinese Literary Theory's Fin-de-Siècle Struggle," in *Liu Zaifu: Selected Critical Essays*, ed. Howard Y. F. Choy and Liu Jianmei (Leiden, Netherlands: Brill, 2021), 169–184.
90. Horace Engdahl, *Stilen och lyckan: essäer om litteratur*, in Chinese version *Fengge yu xingfu* 風格與幸福 [Style and pleasure], trans. Wanzhi 萬之 (Shanghai: Fudan daxue chubanshe, 2017), 76–77.
91. Qiao Min, "A Spirit of Internal Exile: On Liu Zaifu's Prose and Criticism after 1989" (MPhil thesis, Hong Kong University of Science and Technology, 2018). See also Qiao Min, "Liu Zaifu 'pianduan xiezuo' shixue lunlüe" 劉再復"片段寫作"詩學論略 [A brief discussion of Liu Zaifu's "Fragmentary Writing"], *Huawen wenxue* 華文文學 6 (2018): 36–41.
92. Qiao Min points out that his wandering is congruent with his fragmentary writing, which is a way to defy a type of limitation and definition. See Qiao Min, "A Brief Discussion," 36–41.
93. Liu Zaifu, *Philosophical Notes on "Dream of the Red Chamber,"* 78.
94. Liu Zaifu, *Mianbi chensi lu* 面壁沈思錄 [Meditation while facing the wall] (Hong Kong: Tiandi tushu, 2004), 16, 305.
95. Liu Zaifu, *Reflections on "Dream of the Red Chamber,"* 3.
96. Liu Zaifu, *Reflections on "Dream of the Red Chamber,"* 1.
97. Gao Xingjian, "Foreword," in Liu Zaifu, *Reflections on Dream of the Red Chamber*. Trans. Shu Yunzhong (Amherst, NY: Cambria Press, 2008), xi.
98. Liu Zaifu points out there are basically three approaches in Redology: comments, disputations, and reflections. His way of reading and exploring *Dream of*

the Red Chamber belongs to reflections. Liu Zaifu, "Preface 2," in *Reflections on Dream of the Red Chamber*, xxi.

99. Liu Zaifu, *Reflections on Dream of the Red Chamber*, xvi.
100. Liu Zaifu, *Shenme shi rensheng—Guanyu rensheng lunli de shitangke* 什麼是人生——關於人生倫理的十堂課 [What is life?—Ten lessons regarding life ethics] (Hong Kong: Sanlian shudian, 2017), 106.
101. Fredric Jameson, *The Prison-House of Language: A Critical Account of Structuralism and Russian Formalism* (Princeton, NJ: Princeton University Press, 1972).
102. Here I am using Arthur Waley's translation. Arthur Waley, *The Way and Its Power: Lao Tzu's Tao Te Ching and Its Place in Chinese Thought* (New York: Grove, 1934), 193.
103. Liu Zaifu, *Solitary Recitation at the Edge of the World*, 352.
104. Liu Zaifu, *Piaoliu shouji* 漂流手記 [Drifting notes] (Taipei: Fengyun shidai, 1994), 300. Qiao Min, "A Spirit of Internal Exile," 2018.
105. Liu Zaifu, "Di'er rensheng sanbuqu" 第二人生三部曲 [Trilogy of the second life], in *Yuedu meiguo* 閱讀美國 [Reading America] (Hong Kong: Xianggang mingbao chubanshe, 2002), 6–20.

5. Gao Xingjian: Transmedia Aesthetics of Thirdspace

1. Gao Xingjian, *Wandering Mind and Metaphysical Thoughts*, trans. Gilbert C. Fong (Hong Kong: The Chinese University Press, 2018), 52.
2. Gao Xingjian, "Freedom and Literature," in *Aesthetics and Creation*, trans. Mabel Lee (Amherst, NY: Cambria Press, 2012), 231.
3. Letizia Fusini, *Dionysus on the Other Shore: Gao Xingjian's Theatre of the Tragic* (Leiden, Netherlands: Brill, 2020), 10–17, 219–222.
4. Fusini, *Dionysus on the Other Shore*, 16–17.
5. Fusini, *Dionysus on the Other Shore*, 220–222.
6. Sau Ching Janet Shum, "Diasporic Aesthetics of Gao Xingjian's Exilic Discourse" (PhD diss., Hong Kong University of Science and Technology, 2010), 11–19, 20–22.
7. Werner Wolf, "Intermediality," in *Routledge Encyclopaedia of Narrative Theory*, ed. David Herman, Manfred Jahn, and Marie-Laure Ryan (London: Routledge, 2005), 252–256. See also Henk Oosterling and Ewa Plonowska Ziarek, eds., *Intermedialities: Philosophy, Arts, Politics* (Lanham, MD: Lexington Books, 2011), 1–14. Wu Shengqing points out that the Chinese poetry-paintings analogy "presents the two close mediums as mutually influenced and cross-fertilized, gives both art forms the advantage of being able to conjointly conjure rich mental images, sentiments, and meanings while at the same time speaking to

shared aesthetic ideals." See Wu Shengqing, *Photo Poetics: Chinese Lyricism and Modern Media Culture* (New York: Columbia University Press, 2020), 3.

8. Scholars such as W. J. T. Mitchell and Gabriele Rippl emphasis the characteristics of "self-reflexive" in their study of "intermediality." Gabriele Rippl, "English Literature and Its Other: Toward a Poetics of Intermediality," in *ImageScapes: Studies in Intermediality*, ed. Christian J. Emden and Gabriele Rippl (Bern, Switzerland: Peter Lang, 2010), 39–66. See also W. J. T. Mitchell, *Picture Theory: Essays on Verbal and Visual Representation* (Chicago: University of Chicago Press, 1944), 154–180.

9. Walter Benjamin, *Illumination: Essays and Reflections*, ed. Hannah Arendt (New York: Schocken, 1985), 221.

10. Gao Xingjian, "Freedom and Literature," 233.

11. Edward W. Soja, *Thirdspace: Journey to Los Angeles and Other Real-and-Imagined Places* (Malden, MA: Blackwell, 1996), 65.

12. Liu Zaifu, "Gao Xingjian's Notion of Freedom," in *Freedom and Fate in Gao Xingjian's Writings*, ed. Michael Lackner and Nikola Chardonnens (Berlin: Walter de Gruyter GmbH, 2014), 77.

13. Liu Zaifu, "Gao Xingjian: Exemplifying a Renaissance in Today's World," in *Gao Xingjian and Transmedia Aesthetics*, ed. Mabel Lee and Liu Jianmei (Amherst, NY: Cambria Press, 2018), 50.

14. Gao Xingjian, *Lun chuangzuo* 論創作 [On creation] (Hong Kong: Mingbao yuekan chubanshe, 2008), 260–261.

15. Gao Xingjian, "Freedom and Literature," 233.

16. Gao Xingjian, "Another Kind of Aesthetics," in *Aesthetics and Creation*, trans. Mabel Lee (Amherst, NY: Cambria Press, 2012), 92.

17. Jean-Pierre Zarader relates Gao Xingjian's criticism of the negation of negation to Hegel's notion of "sublation"; Zarader, "Gao Xingjian and Philosophy," in Lee and Liu Jianmei, *Gao Xingjian and Transmedia Aesthetics*, 36.

18. Lu Xun, "Xiao zagan" 小雜感 [Small miscellaneous thought], in Lu Xun, *The Complete Works of Lu Xun*, vol. 3 (Beijing: Renmin wenxue chubanshe, 1993), 532.

19. Gao Xingjian, "Freedom and Literature," 232.

20. Jean-Pierre Zazader wrote: "Gao, in his recurring critique of 'the negation of negation'—that is, of what is known as 'sublation' (after Derrida, and as a way of translating Hegel's term Aufhebung)—line up on the side of contemporary philosophy, which has never stopped battling a form of thinking about identity and about totality that is suspects of being totalitarian." Zarader, "Gao Xingjian and Philosophy," 36.

21. As Henk Oosterling and Ewa Plonowska Ziarek point out, "In the last thirty-five years different approaches to the notions of difference and alterity, proposed for instance by thinkers like Derrida, Deleuze, Irigaray, Levinas, Kristeva,

Lyotard, and Nancy, elaborated the idea of the 'in-between' as a crucial topic of philosophical, political and ethical investigations." Oosterling and Plonowska Ziarek, *Intermedialities: Philosophy, Arts, Politics*, 2.
22. Gao Xingjian, "Freedom and Literature," 233.
23. Gao Xingjian, "The Art of Fiction," in *Aesthetics and Creation*, trans. Mabel Lee (Amherst, NY: Cambria Press, 2012), 38.
24. Gao Xingjian, "Another Kind of Aesthetics," 126.
25. Gao Xingjian, "The Art of Fiction," 38.
26. Gao Xingjian, *Soul Mountain*, trans. Mabel Lee (Sydney: HarperCollins, 2004), 348.
27. Izabella Labedzka, *Gao Xingjian's Idea of Theatre: From the Word to the Image* (Leiden, Netherlands: Brill, 2008), 32.
28. Gao Xingjian, "Another Kind of Aesthetics," 123.
29. Gao Xingjian, "The Art of Fiction," 25.
30. Jessica Yeung, *Ink Dances in Limbo: Gao Xingjian's Writing as Cultural Translation* (Hong Kong: Hong Kong University Press, 2008), 84–85.
31. Liu Zaifu, "Lun wenxue de zhuti xing" 論文學的主體性 [On the literary subjectivity], in *Wenxue de fansi* 文學的反思 [The retrospection on literature] (Fuzhou: Fujian renmin chubanshe, 2010), 56.
32. Gao Xingjian, *Wandering Mind and Metaphysical Thoughts*, 78–79.
33. Gao Xingjian, *Wandering Mind and Metaphysical Thoughts*, 86–87.
34. Gao Xingjian, *Wandering Mind and Metaphysical Thoughts*, 90–91.
35. Gao Xingjian, *Wandering Mind and Metaphysical Thoughts*, 88–89.
36. Daniel Bergez, *Gao Xingjian: Painter of the Soul* (London: Asia Ink, 2013), 9.
37. Gao Xingjian, "Another Kind of Aesthetics," 134.
38. Gao Xingjian, "Another Kind of Aesthetics," 126.
39. Jason Guo, *The Inner Landscape: The Paintings of Gao Xingjian* (Washington, DC: New Academia Publishing, 2013), 1–24.
40. Gao Xingjian stated that his artwork is more inclined to traditional Chinese art's multiple scattered perspectives. Please see Gao Xingjian, "My Thoughts on Painting," in *Meiyou zhuyi* 沒有主義 [Without isms] (Hong Kong: Cosmos Books, 1996), 292. Please also see Kwok-kan Tam, "The Mind's Eye: Subjectivity in Gao Xingjian's Paintings," in Lee and Liu Jianmei, *Gao Xingjian and Transmedia Aesthetics*, 141–142.
41. Sy Ren Quah, *Gao Xingjian and Transcultural Chinese Theater* (Honolulu: University of Hawai'i Press, 2004), 105–106.
42. Gao Xingjian, "The Potential of Theatre," in *Aesthetics and Creation*, trans. Mabel Lee (Amherst, NY: Cambria Press, 2012), 55.
43. Gao Xingjian, "Dramaturgical Method and the Neutral Actor," in *Aesthetics and Creation*, trans. Mabel Lee (Amherst, NY: Cambria Press, 2012), 166.
44. Gilbert Fong and Shelby Chan, "Nonattachment and Gao Xingjian's Neutral Actor," in Lee and Liu Jianmei, *Gao Xingjian and Transmedia Aesthetics*, 111.

45. Gao Xingjian explains: "Once *you* detaches itself from the self, both the subject and the object are targeted for observation and scrutiny, and this forces the uncontrollable outpourings and expressions of the artist's blind narcissism to yield to concentrated observation, searching, capturing, or pursuing. While *you* and *I* are eyeing one another, that dark and chaotic self begins to reveal itself through a third pair of eyes belonging to *he*." Gao Xingjian, "Another Kind of Aesthetics," 121.
46. Maurice Merleau-Ponty, "Eye and Mind," in *The Merleau-Ponty Reader*, ed. Ted Toadvine and Leonard Lawlor (Evanston, IL: Northwestern University Press, 2007), 356.
47. Lucia Angelino, "Merleau-Ponty's Thinking Eye," *Philosophy Today* 58, no. 2 (Spring 2018): 256–278.
48. When the scholar Jenny Hung interprets the Zhuangzian way to deal with desire, she proposes a Daoist sage can be an observer at a certain time and a performer at other times, and through observation, a practitioner can transform desires into high spirituality. See Jenny Hung, "Is Zhuangzi a Wanton? Observation and Transformation of Desire in the *Zhuangzi*," *Dao: A Journal of Comparative Philosophy* 2, no. 19 (2020): 1–17.
49. Gao Xingjian, "The Art of Fiction," 38.
50. Wu Shengqing, *Photo Poetics*, 18–24.
51. David Der-wei Wang, *The Lyrical in Epic Time: Modern Chinese Intellectuals and Artists Through the 1949 Crisis* (New York: Columbia University Press, 2015), 10.
52. According to Zong Baihua, *kongling* forms an aesthetic state that is akin to how "an antelope dangles horns [on the tree] which leave no traces to be found (*Lingyang guajiao, wuji kexun* 羚羊掛角，無跡可尋)." As a result, it not only transcends images (*chaoyu xiangwai* 超於象外) but also points directly to the Buddhist concept of emptiness. Zong Baihua also explicates that "the emptiness in the vista of art is not the real emptiness" but rather means that "one can acquire fullness (*chongshi* 充實) through emptiness, from the 'remoteness of heart' (*xinyuan* 心遠) to get close to 'genuine meanings' (*zhenyi* 真意)." Zong Baihua 宗白華, *Yijing* 藝境 [The vista of art] (Beijing: Shangwu yinshu guan, 2015), 215.
53. As Tian Xiaofei points out, *guanxiang* (觀想) is to "visualize the object of contemplation in one's mind": "The importance of *guanxiang* lies in the belief that visualization itself is realization. In other words, the Buddha himself is no more than a product of one's mind, a figment of imagination. The mind is so powerful in its highly focused state that it can literally bring Buddha and his kingdom to realization; and yet, this realization itself is empty, unreal, just as dharma and 'dharma-body' (the true nature of Buddhahood) are fundamentally empty. This ingenious formulation—that visualization is realization, and realization is unreal—testifies to the reality and the unreality of the Buddha, an essential

teaching of Mahāyāna Buddhism." Tian Xiaofei, "Seeing with the Mind's Eye: The Eastern Jin Discourse of Visualization and Imagination," *Asia Major* 18, no. 2 (2005): 67–102.
54. Zong Baihua, *The Vista of Art*, 262–263.
55. Gao Xingjian, "The Position of the Writer" in Gao Xingjian, *Aesthetics and Creation*, trans. Mabel Lee (Amherst, NY: Cambria Press, 2012), 16.
56. Gao Xingjian, "Another Kind of Aesthetics," 126.
57. Gao Xingjian, *On Creation*, 211–212.
58. C. T. Hsia, *A History of Modern Chinese Fiction*, 3rd ed. (Bloomington: Indiana University Press, 1999), 533–534.
59. Gao Xingjian, *Cold Literature*, trans. Gilbert C. F. Fong and Mabel Lee (Hong Kong: The Chinese University Press, 2005), 5.
60. Gao Xinjian, *Cold Literature*, 43–57.
61. Zong Baihua uses the notion of "spiritual space" (*lingde kongjian* 靈的空間) to describe the special vista of Chinese calligraphy. See Zong Baihua, *The Vista of Art*, 128.
62. Gao Xingjian, "Concerning *Silhouette/Shadow*," in Gao Xingjian, *Aesthetics and Creation*, trans. Mabel Lee (Amherst, NY: Cambria Press, 2012), 180–181.
63. While talking about the difference between soul and mind, Gaston Bachelard explains: "A consciousness associated with the soul is more relaxed, less intentionalized than a consciousness associated with the phenomena of the mind." Gaston Bachelard, *The Poetics of Space*, trans. Maria Jolas (Boston: Beacon Press, 1994), xxi.
64. Gao Xingjian, "Concerning *Silhouette/Shadow*," 184.
65. Rajewsky elaborates, "And yet it is precisely this illusion that potentially solicits in the recipient of a literary text, say, a sense of filmic, painterly, or musical qualities, or—more generally speaking—a sense of a visual or acoustic presence. Tellingly, it is this sensing by the recipient of another medium's special qualities that has led to the coining of such metaphor." Irina O. Rajewsky, "Intermediality, Intertextuality, and Remediation: A Literary Perspective on Intermediality," *Intermédialitiés* 6 (2005): 55.
66. Rajewsky, "Intermediality, Intertextuality, and Remediation," 57.
67. Leo Braudy, *The World in a Frame: What We See in Films* (Chicago: University of Chicago Press, 1976).
68. Gao Xingjian, "Concerning *Silhouette/Shadow*," 184–185.
69. Rajewsky, "Intermediality, Intertextuality, and Remediation," 44.
70. Gao Xingjian, "Concerning *Silhouette/Shadow*," 185.
71. Kwok-kan Tam, "The Mind's Eye," 157.
72. Gao Xingjian, *Cold Literature*, 3, 11, 39.
73. Gao Xingjian, "Freedom and Literature," 231.
74. Gao Xingjian, "Concerning *Silhouette/Shadow*," 186.

75. Rosalind Silvester, "Intermediality and Film Consciousness in Gao Xingjian's *La Silhouette Sinon L'ombre*," *Forum for Modern Language Studies* 55, no. 1 (January 2019): 53–74.
76. Bergez, *Gao Xingjian*, 29.
77. Gao Xingjian, *Wandering Mind and Metaphysical Thoughts*, 36–37.
78. Tian Xiaofei, "Seeing with the Mind's Eye," 73.
79. Li Zehou, *The Chinese Aesthetic Tradition*, trans. Maija Bell Samei (Honolulu: University of Hawai'i Press, 2010), 163.
80. Gao Xingjian, *Wandering Mind and Metaphysical Thoughts*, 36–37.
81. Gao Xingjian, *Wandering Mind and Metaphysical Thoughts*, 36–37.
82. Zong Baihua, *The Vista of Art*, 263.
83. Gao Xingjian, "After the Flood," in *Aesthetics and Creation*, trans. Mabel Lee (Amherst, NY: Cambria Press, 2012), 222.
84. Frank Kermode, *The Sense of an Ending: Studies in the Theory of Fiction* (London: Oxford University Press, 1967), 25.
85. James Berger, *After the End, Representations of Post-Apocalypse* (Minneapolis: University of Minnesota Press, 1999), xiii.
86. Berger, *After the End*, xiii.
87. Gao Xingjian, "After the Flood," 222.
88. Walter Benjamin, "Theses on the Philosophy of History," in *Illumination*, ed. Hannah Arendt, trans. Harry Zohn (New York: Schocken, 1968), 261.
89. Michael Barkun, "Racist Apocalypse: Millennialism on the Far Right," in *The Year 2000: Essays on the End*, ed. Charles B. Strozier and Michael Flynn (New York: New York University Press, 1997), 201.
90. Megan Evans, "Floods and Forests: Gao Xingjian's Transcultural Aesthetic of Catastrophe," in Lee and Liu Jianmei, *Gao Xingjian and Transmedia Aesthetics*, 183.
91. Gao Xingjian, "After the Flood," 222.
92. Evans, "Floods and Forests," 188.
93. Zong Baihua, *The Vista of Art*, 191, 192.
94. Fiona Sze-Lorrain, "Bodies and Paintings: Gao Xingjian's *After the Flood*," in Lee and Liu Jianmei, *Gao Xingjian and Transmedia Aesthetics*, 198.
95. Gao Xingjian, "Another Kind of Aesthetics," 154.
96. Gao Xingjian, "The Potential of Theatre," 60.
97. Gao Xingjian, "Dramaturgical Method and the Neutral Actor," 166.
98. Benjamin, "Theses on the Philosophy of History," 258.
99. Gao Xingjian, "After the Flood," 223.
100. Gao Xingjian, "After the Flood," 225.
101. Gao Xingjian, introduction to *Requiem for Beauty* (Taipei: National Taiwan Normal University, 2016), 27.
102. Gao Xingjian, *Wandering Mind and Metaphysical Thoughts*, 152–155.
103. Gao Xingjian, *Wandering Mind and Metaphysical Thoughts*, 116–117.

104. Gao Xingjian, "The Aesthetics of the Artist," 65–87.
105. Daniel Bergez, "Gao Xingjian or Requiem's Splendour," in Gao Xingjian, *Requiem for Beauty*, 32.
106. Nathalie Bittinger, "*Requiem for Beauty*: A Contemporary Kaleidoscope," in Gao Xingjian, *Requiem for Beauty*, 47.
107. André Malraux, "Museum without Walls," in *The Voices of Silence*, trans. Stuart Gilbert (Princeton, NJ: Princeton University Press, 1978), 16. Jean-Pierre Zarader mentions that *Requiem for Beauty* is Gao Xingjian's homage to Malraux's Imaginary Museum. See Zarader, "Requiem for Beauty," in Gao Xingjian, *Requiem for Beauty*, 37. Yue Huanyu also points out that, "As a 'museum without walls,' Gao's *Requiem for Beauty* brings artworks from different epochs and various cultural backgrounds into the shared imaginary space of all humanity." Yue Huanyu, "Inlaying Images and Seeing Poetry," in Lee and Liu Jianmei, *Gao Xingjian and Transmedia Aesthetics*, 219.
108. André Malraux, "Museum without Walls," 16.
109. Gao Xingjian, introduction to *Requiem for Beauty*, 29.
110. Zarader, "Requiem for Beauty," 37.
111. Wah Guan Lim, "From Theater to Cine-Poetry: Gao Xingjian's Performance Theories," in Lee and Liu Jianmei, *Gao Xingjian and Transmedia Aesthetics*, 207.
112. Wah Guan Lim, "From Theater to Cine-Poetry," 208.
113. Zong Baihua, *The Vista of Art*, 251.
114. Zong Baihua, *The Vista of Art*, 256.
115. Zong Baihua, *The Vista of Art*, 332–333.
116. Here I use Susan Bush and Hsio-yen Shih's translation of Guo Xi's text. See Susan Bush and Hsio-yen Shih, *Early Chinese Texts on Painting* (Hong Kong: Hong Kong University Press, 2012), 168–169.
117. See Chen Shixiang, *Chen Shixiang wencun* 陳世驤文存 [The collection of Chen Shixiang's essays] (Shenyang: Liaoning jiaoyu chubanshe, 1998), 25–46. See Cheng Yuyu's interpretation of Chen Shixiang's "principle of gesture" in Cheng Yuyu, *Zi yu yan* 姿與言 [Gesture and language] (Taipei: Maitian, 2017), 180.
118. Łabędzka, *Gao Xingjian's Idea of Theatre*, 187.
119. According to Nathalie Bittinger, "The mask, omnipresent in the film, evocative of the *Commedia dell'Arte* and millennial Chinese opera and theatre, can be interpreted in different ways: the mask may symbolize social roles that annihilate individualism; the mask may also represent a reversal of values, of what is beautiful or ugly, what is kitsch or authentic; an aesthetic and dialectic inversion designates what is game, imagination, creation, to create a distance from society or the norms of artistic production." Bittinger, "*Requiem for Beauty*," 48.
120. Thierry Dufrêne, "Notes on *Requiem for Beauty*: A Cinematic Poem by Gao Xingjian (2013)," in Gao Xingjian, *Requiem for Beauty*, 52. Yue Huanyu interprets the Janus masks as two faces of a cine-poem: "film images and the language of

poetry, which complementing each other." See Yue Huanyu, "Inlaying Images and Seeing Poetry," 219.
121. Gao Xingjian, *Wandering Mind and Metaphysical Thoughts*, 162–163.
122. Zarader, "Requiem for Beauty," 38.
123. Bergez, "Gao Xingjian or Requiem's Splendour," 35.
124. Gao Xingjian, *Wandering Mind and Metaphysical Thoughts*, 118–119.
125. Gao Xingjian, *Wandering Mind and Metaphysical Thoughts*, 108–109.
126. Gao Xingjian, *Wandering Mind and Metaphysical Thoughts*, 114–117.
127. Gao Xingjian, *Wandering Mind and Metaphysical Thoughts*, 120–121.
128. Sigmund Freud, "Mourning and Melancholia," in *The Standard Edition of the Complete Psychological Works of Sigmund Freud*, vol. 14 (1914–1916), *On the History of the Psycho-Analytic Movement, Papers on Metapsychology and Other Works* (London: Hogarth Press and the Institute of Psycho-Analysis, 1957), 237–258.
129. Ilit Ferber, *Philosophy and Melancholy: Benjamin's Early Reflections on Theater and Language* (Stanford, CA: Stanford University Press, 2013), 66.
130. Ferber, *Philosophy and Melancholoy*, 13.
131. Zarader, "Requiem for Beauty," 38.
132. Bergez, "Gao Xingjian or Requiem's Splendour," 32.
133. Ronnie Bai, "Dances with Brecht: Huang Zuolin and His 'Xieyi' Theatre," *Comparative Drama* 33, no. 3 (Fall 1999): 345. See also Mary Mazzilli, "Gao Xingjian's Search for a Scenic Dramaturgy and Cinematic Language in Song of the Night," in Lee and Liu Jianmei, *Gao Xingjian and Transmedia Aesthetics*, 122.

6. Chinese Female Writers' Construction of Thirdspace

1. Val Plumwood, *Feminism and the Mastery of Nature* (London: Routledge, 1994), 2.
2. Plumwood, *Feminism and the Mastery of Nature*, 49.
3. Plumwood, *Feminism and the Mastery of Nature*, 52–55.
4. Tan Tianli 譚天麗, "Xi Xi bixia de shengnü" 西西筆下的剩女 [The leftover women under Xi Xi's pen], *Cultural Studies MCS* 34 (April 2013): 49–61.
5. Chi Zijian 遲子建, "Wenxue de qiujing zhilu" 文學的求經之路 [The literary journey of acquiring scripts], The Paper (website), accessed September 2, 2023, https://m.thepaper.cn/baijiahao_10831279. Chi Zijian 遲子建, "Wode nüxing guan" 我的女性觀 [My view on women], in Chi Zijian, *Yuanlai chazi yanhong kaibian* 原來姹紫嫣紅開遍 [Various shades of purple and vibrant red are blooming everywhere] (Hangzhou: Zhejiang wenyi chuban she, 2016), 215–216.
6. Plumwood, *Feminism and the Mastery of Nature*, 30.
7. Xi Xi, *Marvels of a Floating City and Other Stories*, ed. Eva Hung (Hong Kong: Research Center for Translation, the Chinese University of Hong Kong, 1997), 3

8. Wei Yang Menkus, "Unravelling the Urban Myth: History, City, and Literature in Xi Xi's Fiction," *Chinese Literature Today* 8, no. 1 (2019): 58–67.
9. Ilit Ferber, *Philosophy and Melancholy: Benjamin's Early Reflections on Theater and Language* (Stanford, CA: Stanford University Press, 2013), 86.
10. Lisa Lipinski, *René Magritte and the Art of Thinking* (New York: Routledge, 2019), 2.
11. Ho Fuk Yan 何福仁, *Fucheng 1.2.3—Xi Xi xiaoshuo xinxi* 浮城1.2.3: 西西小說新析 [Marvels of a floating city 1.2.3—Interpretations of Xi Xi's novels] (Hong Kong: Sanlian shudian, 2008), 98–100; Wei Yang Menkus, "Unravelling the Urban Myth."
12. Xi Xi, *Marvels of a Floating City*, 5.
13. Xi Xi, *My City: A Hong Kong Story*, trans. Eva Hung (Hong Kong: Research Center for Translation, the Chinese University of Hong Kong, 1993), 119.
14. David Sylvester, *Magritte: The Silence of the World* (New York: The Menil Foundation Inc., 1992), 296.
15. Xi Xi, *Marvels of a Floating City*, 7.
16. Gerrit L. Lansing, "'The False Mirror': Image Versus Reality," *Notes in the History of Art* 4, nos. 2/3 (Winter/Spring 1985): 83–84.
17. Xi Xi, *Marvels of a Floating City*, 11.
18. Xi Xi, *Marvels of a Floating City*, 13.
19. Xi Xi, *Marvels of a Floating City*, 15.
20. Xi Xi, *Marvels of a Floating City*, 21.
21. Lipinski, *René Magritte and the Art of Thinking*, 2–3.
22. Marcel Paquet, *René Magritte 1898–1967: Thought Rendered Visible* (Köln: Taschen, 2000), 85.
23. Edward Soja, *Thirdspace: Journeys to Los Angeles and Other Real-and-Imagined Places* (Malden, MA: Blackwell, 1996), 96–105.
24. David Der-wei Wang, "Introduction: Chinese Literature Across the Borderlands," *Prism: Theory and Modern Chinese Literature* 18, no. 2 (October 2021): 316.
25. Cheng Li, "The Dim Religious Reverence: Spiritualizing Nature and Ethnic Resilience in Chi Zijian's *The Last Quarter of the Moon*," *ISLE: Interdisciplinary Studies in Literature and Environment* 31, no. 2 (Summer 2024): 374–394.
26. Chi Zijian, *The Last Quarter of the Moon*, trans. Bruce Holmes (London: Vintage, 2014), 4.
27. Judith Shapiro, *Mao's War Against Nature: Politics and the Environment in Revolutionary China* (Cambridge: Cambridge University Press, 2001), 67–68.
28. Du Lanlan, "Nature and Ethnic Women: An Ecofeminist Reading of Chi Zijian's *The Last Quarter of the Moon* and Linda Hogan's *Solar Storms*," *Comparative Literature Studies* 55, no. 4 (2018): 787–798.
29. Val Plumwood, *Feminism and the Mastery of Nature*, 792.
30. Lanlan Du, "Nature and Ethnic Women," 793.

31. F. Georg Heyne, "The Social Significance of the Shaman Among the Chinese Reindeer-Evenki," *Asian Folklore Studies* (1999): 377–395.
32. Pan Shuyang, "Religious Imagination of Nature: On Chi Zijian's Writing of Shamanism" (MPhil Thesis, Hong Kong University of Science and Technology, 2016).
33. Chi Zijian, *The Last Quarter of the Moon*, 7.
34. Chi Zijian, *The Last Quarter of the Moon*, 169.
35. Chi Zijian, *The Last Quarter of the Moon*, 169.
36. Liu Zaifu regards the transcendental vision as the most precious quality of literature, for it encompasses a benevolent heart and empathetic understanding toward the intricate nature of humanity. He firmly opposes any imposition of a preconceived "political court" or "moral court," instead advocating for the cultivation of a transcendental perspective. See Liu Zaifu, *Shenme shi wenxue: wenxue changshi ershi'er jiang* 什麼是文學：文學常識二十二講 [What is literature: Twenty-two lessons of literary common knowledge] (Hong Kong: Sanlian shudian, 2015), 17–18.
37. Du Lanlan, "Nature and Ethnic Women," 791–792.
38. Chi Zijian, *The Last Quarter of the Moon*, 280.
39. As Chien-Hsin Tsai argues, *The Old Capital* is "a literary heterotopia that elaborates on the multilayered ways of understanding Taipei." Tsai also points out that de Certeau's theorization of the rhetoric of walking is related to Foucault's concept of heterotopia. Chien-Hsin Tsai, "The Heterotopia Agent in Chu T'ien-hsin's 'The Old Capital,'" *Concentric: Literary and Cultural Studies* 38, no. 2 (September 2012): 139–160. Michel de Certeau, *The Practice of Everyday Life*, trans. Steven Rendall (Berkeley: University of California Press, 1984). Michel Foucault, "Of Other Space," in *Heterotopia and the City: Public Space in a Postcivil Society*, ed. Michiel Dehaene and Lieven De Cauter (London: Routledge, 2008): 13–30.
40. Soja, *Thirdspace*, 162.
41. Chu Tian-hsin, *Xiang wo juancun de xiongdimen* 想我眷村的兄弟們 [In remembrance of my brothers in the military compound] (Taipei: Maitian chuban youxian gongsi, 1992), 92–93.
42. Chu Tian-hsin, *Sanshisan nian meng* 三十三年夢 [Thirty-three years of dream] (Taipei: INK Yinke wenxue, 2015), 148–149.
43. Chu Tian-hsin, *Thirty-Three Years of Dream*, 357.
44. Chu Tian-hsin recorded her participation in supporting Chu Kao-cheng's Chinese Social Democratic Party in detail. See Chu Tian-hsin, *Thirty-Three Years of Dream*, 188–198.
45. David Der-wei Wang, "Xulun: Laolinghun qianshi jinsheng—Zhu Tianxin de Xiaoshuo" 序論：老靈魂前世今生—朱天心的小說 [Prefatory remarks: Old souls reincarnated—The novels of Zhu Tianxin], in Chu Tian-hsin, *Gudu* 古都 [The old capital] (Taipei: Ink Publishing, 2002), 5–27.

46. Lingchei Letty Chen, "Mapping Identity in a Postcolonial City: Intertextuality and Cultural Hybridity in Zhu Tianxin's *Ancient Capital*," in *Writing Taiwan—A New Literary History*, ed. C. Rojas and David Der-wei Wang (Durham, NC: Duke University Press, 2007), 301–323.
47. Chien-Hsin Tsai, "The Heterotopia Agent in Chu T'ien-hsin's 'The Old Capital.'"
48. Chien-Hsin Tsai describes the narrator in *The Old Capital* as "a heterotopia agent." See Chien-Hsin Tsai, "The Heterotopia Agent in Chu T'ien-hsin's 'The Old Capital,'" 139. Rosemary Haddon defines Zhu Hsi-ning as "exile-at-home." See Rosemary Haddon, "Being/Not Being at Home in the Writing of Zhu Tianxin," in *Cultural, Ethnic, and Political Nationalism in Contemporary Taiwan: Bentuhua*, ed. John Makeham and A-chin Hsiau (New York: Palgrave Macmillan, 2005), 103–123.
49. Chu Tian-hsin explains her involvement in the Ethnic Equality Agreement Alliance in the book. The quotes are from "The Declamation of the Ethnic Equality Agreement Alliance." See Chu Tian-hsin, *Thirty-Three Years of Dream*, 344–350.
50. On July 19, 2004, the Taiwan Democratic School claimed to be established. The famous director Hou Xiaoxian 侯孝賢 acted as its the president, Zheng Liwen 鄭麗文 as vice-president, and Yang Guoshu 楊國樞, Xu Zhuoyun 許倬雲, Hu Fo 胡佛, and David Der-wei Wang 王德威 as its honorary advisors. See Chu Tian-hsin, *Thirty-Three Years of Dream*, 352–354.
51. Chu Tian-hsin, *Thirty-Three Years of Dream*, 373.
52. In an interview with Si Fangwei 司方維. See Si Fangwei, *Rentong yu jiegou: Taiwan waisheng dierdai nü zuojia yanjiu* 認同與解構：台灣外省第二代女作家研究 [Identification and deconstruction: A study on female writers of the second-generation mainlanders in Taiwan] (Beijing: Zhongguo shehui kexue chubanshe), 2017.
53. Chu Tian-hsin, "Wo bu ai Taiwan, kebu keyi zheyang shuo?" 我不愛台灣，可不可以這樣說? [Can I say that I do not love Taiwan?], Pititi shiyefang 批踢踏實業坊 [The workshop for solid criticism], accessed February 6, 2024, https://www.ptt.cc/bbs/politics/M.1082634868.A.BBC.html.
54. Wu Xinyi 吳忻怡, "Chengwei rentong guanzhao de tazhe—Zhu Tianxin jiqi xiangguan yanjiu de shehuixue kaocha" 成為認同關照的他者—朱天心及其相關研究的社會學考察 [Becoming "the other" of identification: A sociological examination of Chu Tien-hsin and her related research], *Taiwan Shehui Xuekang* 41 (December 2008): 1–58.
55. Chu Tian-hsin, *Xiaoshuojia de zhengzhi zhouji* 小說家的政治周記 [A novelist's political journal] (Taipei: Shibao wenhua, 1994), 76.
56. Chu Tian-hsin, *The Old Capital*, 43–45.
57. Wu Xinyi, "Becoming 'the Other' of Identification," 42.

58. Chu Tian-hsin, *A Novelist's Political Journal*, 224–225.
59. Chu Tian-hsin, *A Novelist's Political Journal*, 170.
60. Chu Tien-hsin, *Namao, Naren, Nacheng* 那貓那人那城 [That cat, that person, that city] (Zhengzhou: Henan wenyi chubanshe, 2021), 129–133.
61. Chu Tien-hsin, *That Cat, That Person, That City*, 120.
62. Sun Ge 孫歌, "Goulian qi shengming zhong de jiyi" 勾連起生命中的記憶 [Recalling the memories in life], in Chu Tien-Hsin, *Lieren men* 獵人們 [The hunters] (Beijing: Sanlian shudian, 2006), 19.
63. Lee Haiyan, "Through Thick and Thin: The Romance of the Species in the Anthropocene," *International Communication of Chinese Culture* 2 (May 2018): 152.
64. Lee Haiyan, "Through Thick and Thin," 152.
65. Chu Tien-Hsin, *That Cat, That Person, That City*, 261.
66. Chu Tien-Hsin, *That Cat, That Person, That City*, 185–187, 261–262.
67. Chu Tien-Hsin, *That Cat, That Person, That City*, 198–199.
68. Lee Haiyan, "Taiwanimals: Street Dogs and Cats as Remaindered Life," in *A Literary History of Taiwan in the New Millennium*, ed. Pei-yin lin, Wen-chi Li, and Carlos Rojas (Amherst, NY: Cambria Press, forthcoming 2025).

Epilogue

1. Val Plumwood, *Feminism and the Mastery of Nature* (London: Routledge, 2002), 3.
2. Liu Zaifu, "Zailun disan huayu kongjian" 再論第三話語空間 [Rethinking the third discursive space], *Mingpao Monthly*, April 2006.
3. Prasenjit Duara, *The Crisis of Global Modernity* (Cambridge: Cambridge University Press, 2015), 6.
4. Jana S. Rošker, *Becoming Human: Li Zehou's Ethics* (Leiden, Netherlands: Brill, 2020), 137–140.
5. Li Zehou, *Renleixue lishi bentilun* 人類學歷史本體論 [The anthropo-historical ontology] (Tianjin: Tianjin shehui kexueyuan chubanshe, 2008), 90.
6. Li Zehou, *The Anthropo-Historical Ontology*, 107.
7. Isaiah Berlin, *Liberty*, ed. Henry Hardy (Oxford: Oxford University Press, 2013), 169–181.
8. Li Zehou, *The Anthropo-Historical Ontology*, 107.
9. Zhang Dongsun, *Lixing yu minzhu* 理性與民主 [Rationality and democracy] (Changsha: Yuelu shushe, 2010), 66–118.
10. Zhang Dongsun, *Zhishi yu wenhua* 知識與文化 [Knowledge and culture] (Changsha: Yuelu shushe, 2010), 272.
11. Zhang Dongsun, *Rationality and Democracy*, 212.
12. Gao Xingjian, *Meiyou zhuyi* 沒有主義 [Without isms] (Hong Kong: Tiandi dushu, 1996), 4.

13. John Stuart Mill, *On Liberty* (Mineola, NY: Dover, 2002), 39.
14. Xu Jilin, Liu Qing, Luo Gang, and Xue Yi, "In Search of a 'Third Way': A Conversation Regarding 'Liberalism' and the 'New Left Wing,'" in *Voicing Concerns: Contemporary Chinese Critical Inquiry*, ed. Gloria Davies (Lanham, MD: Rowman & Littlefield, 2001), 224.
15. Geremie R. Barmé, "Time's Arrows: Imaginative Pasts and Nostalgic Futures," in Davies, *Voicing Concerns*, 249.
16. Kong Shuyu, *Consuming Literature: Best Sellers and the Commercialization of Literary Production in Contemporary China* (Stanford, CA: Stanford University Press, 2005), 1–2.
17. Michel Hockx, *Internet Literature in China* (New York: Columbia University Press, 2015), 2.
18. This is a reference to the story of the brothers Boyi and Shuqi, loyalists to the Shang dynasty who refused to accept the authority of the Zhou dynasty to the point of starving to death.
19. Chan Koonchung, *Jianfeng ernian: Xin Zhongguo wuyoushi* 建豐二年：新中國烏有史 [The second year of Jianfeng: A uchronia of new China] (Hong Kong: Oxford University Press, 2015), 12.
20. Josephine Chiu-Duke, "The May Fourth Liberal Legacy in Chan Koonchung's *Jianfeng ernian*," in *Remembering May Fourth: The Movement and Its Centennial Legacy*, ed. Carlos Yu-Kai Lin and Victor H. Mair (Leiden, Netherlands: Brill, 2020), 57–58.
21. Edward W. Soja, *Thirdspace: Journeys to Los Angeles and Other Real-and Imagined Places* (Malden, MA: Blackwell, 1996), 162.
22. Chan Koonchung, "Utopia, Dystopia, Heterotopia: Theoretical Cross-examinations on Ideal, Reality, and Social Innovation," in *Utopia and Utopianism in the Contemporary Chinese Context: Texts, Ideas, Spaces*, ed. David Der-wei Wang, Angela Ki Che Leung, and Zhang Yinde (Hong Kong: Hong Kong University Press, 2020), 216.
23. Chan Koonchung, *Wutuobang, etuobang, yituobang: Chen Guanzhong de shidai wenpingji* 烏托邦, 惡托邦, 異托邦: 陳冠中的時代文評集 [Utopia, dystopia, and heterotopia: Chen Guanzhong's selected essays] (Taipei: Maitian, 2018), 161.
24. Chan Koonchung, "Utopia, Dystopia, Heterotopia," 215–216.
25. Chan Koonchung, "Utopia, Dystopia, Heterotopia," 220.
26. David Der-wei Wang, "Shitong san, xiaoshuo xing" 史統散,小說興 [The tradition of historical writing is disappearing and fiction is emerging], preface to Chan Koonchung's *The Second Year of Jianfeng: A Uchronia of New China*, 4–19.
27. Chan Koonchung, *The Second Year of Jianfeng*, 25.
28. Chan Koonchung, *The Second Year of Jianfeng*, 22–23.
29. Chan Koonchung, *The Second Year of Jianfeng*, 87.
30. Chan Koonchung, "Utopia, Dystopia, Heterotopia," 217.

31. Ge Zhaoguang, "Imagining 'All Under Heaven': The Political, Intellectual, and Academic Background of a New Utopia," in *Utopia and Utopianism in the Contemporary Chinese Context: Texts, Ideas, Spaces*, ed. David Der-wei Wang, Angela Ki Che Leung, and Zhang Yinde (Hong Kong: Hong Kong University Press, 2020), 215–216.
32. Zhang Dongsun, *Knowledge and Culture*, 251.
33. Chan Koonchung, *The Second Year of Jianfeng*, 160.
34. Yin Haiguang, "Cong youyanse de sixiang dao wuyanse de sixiang" 從有顏色的思想到無顏色的思想 [From the colorful thought to the colorless thought] in *Yin Haiguang quanji* 殷海光全集 [Complete works of Yin Haiguang], ed. Lin Zhenghong, vol. 14, *Xueshu yu sixiang (er)* 學術與思想 (二) [Scholarship and thought, part two] (Taipei: Guiguan tushu youxian gongsi, 1990), 957–994.
35. Brian Massumi, *Parables for the Virtual: Movement, Affect, Sensation* (Durham, NC: Duke University Press, 2002).
36. Tu Hang, "Sentimental Republic: Chinese Intellectuals and the Maoist Past" (Cambridge, MA: The Harvard Asia Center Publications Program, forthcoming 2025).
37. Chan Koonchung, *Utopia, Dystopia, and Heterotopia*, 400.
38. Chan Koonchung, *Utopia, Dystopia, and Heterotopia*, 408.
39. Chan Koonchung, *Utopia, Dystopia, and Heterotopia*, 414.
40. Hockx, *Internet Literature in China*, 2–3.
41. Fang Fang, *Wuhan Dairy: Dispatches from a Quarantined City*, trans. Michael Berry (New York: HarperCollins, 2020), 179.
42. Michael Berry, "Translator's Afterword," in Fang Fang, *Wuhan Dairy*, 362.
43. Michael Berry's terms in "Translator's Afterword," in Fang Fang, *Wuhan Dairy*, 361.
44. Fang Fang, *Wuhan Dairy*, 290.
45. Michael Berry, "Translator's Afterword," in Fang Fang, *Wuhan Dairy*, 364.
46. Yuan Zeng, "Beyond Control and Resistance: The Dual Narrative of the Coronavirus Outbreak in Digital China," in *Political Communication in the Time of Coronavirus*, ed. Peter Van Aelst and Jay G. Blumler (New York: Routledge, 2022), 41, 33–47.
47. As Yuan Zeng states, "The contesting narrative—Fang Fang and her supporters—thereby becomes the 'traitor,' and is made into part of the symbolic resources the party-state mobilizes into framing the nationalistic narrative which serves to legitimize and reinforce the party rule amidst the public crisis." See Yuan Zeng, "Beyond Control and Resistance," 44.
48. Michael Berry, "Translator's Afterword," in Fang Fang, *Wuhan Dairy*, 369.
49. "Rip: Twenty-Five Scholars Debates on Wuhan Diary," Weixin gongzhong pingtai 微信公眾平台 [The public platform of wechat], accessed December 10, 2021, https://mp.weixin.qq.com/s/3mzEDSgyT8XmjF1gwRBpsQ.
50. Yan Lianke, unpublished interview with a reporter from *Caijing*, provided by Yan Lianke.

51. Yan Lianke, "A Village Greater than the World: Acceptance Speech for the 2021 Newman Prize for Chinese Literature," trans. Eric Abrahamsen, *Chinese Literature Today* 10, no. 1 (2021): 12–15.
52. In Yan Lianke's words, "Nothing that belongs to humanity can surpass love in value. We see a villager hoping that China will use atomic weapons to destroy the rest of the human race, but we also see the village's most tender, expansive heart, full of love for humanity and the world, wishing that every corner of the world were filled with love." See Yan Lianke, "A Village Greater than the World," 15.
53. Thomas A. Metzger, *The Western Concept of the Civil Society in the Context of Chinese History* (Stanford, CA: Hoover Institute on War, Revolution and Peace, Stanford University, 1998). Sebastian Veg, *Minjian: The Rise of China's Grassroots Intellectuals* (New York: Columbia University Press, 2019), 3.

Bibliography

Admussen, Nick. *Recite and Refuse: Contemporary Chinese Prose Poetry*. Honolulu: University of Hawaiʻi Press, 2016.

Albert, Hans. *Treatise on Critical Reason*. Princeton, NJ: Princeton University Press, 1985.

Angelino, Lucia. "Merleau-Ponty's Thinking Eye." *Philosophy Today* 58, no. 2 (Spring 2018): 265–278.

Arendt, Hannah. *The Origins of Totalitarianism*. San Diego: Harcourt Brace Jovanovich, 1973.

Bachelard, Gaston. *The Poetics of Space*. Trans. Maria Jolas. Boston: Beacon Press, 1994.

Bai, Ronnie. "Dances with Brecht: Huang Xuolin and His 'Xieyi' Theatre." *Comparative Drama* 33, no. 3 (Fall 1999): 339–364.

Barkun, Michael. "Racist Apocalypse: Millennialism on the Far Right." In *The Year 2000: Essays on the End*, ed. Charles B. Strozier and Michael Flynn, 190–205. New York: New York University Press, 1997.

Barmé, Geremie R. "Time's Arrows: Imaginative Pasts and Nostalgic Futures." In *Voicing Concerns: Contemporary Chinese Critical Inquiry*, ed. Gloria Davies, 227–258. Lanham, MD: Rowman & Littlefield, 2001.

Benjamin, Walter. *Illumination: Essays and Reflections*. Ed. Hannah Arendt. New York: Schocken, 1985.

———. *The Origin of German Tragic Drama*. London: Verso, 2009.

———. *The Origin of German Tragic Drama*. Ed. Hannah Arendt. Trans. John Osbourne. London: Verso, 1985.

———. "Theses on the Philosophy of History." In *Illumination*. Ed. Hannah Arendt. Trans. Harry Zohn. New York: Schocken, 1968.

Berger, James. *After the End: Representations of Post-Apocalypse*. Minneapolis: University of Minnesota Press, 1999.

Bergez, Daniel. "Gao Xingjian or Requiem's Splendour." In *Mei de zangli* 美的葬禮 [Requiem for beauty], ed. Gao Xingjian, 32–35. Taipei: National Taiwan Normal University, 2016.

———. *Gao Xingjian: Painter of the Soul*. London: Asia Ink, 2013.

Berlin, Isaiah. *Liberty*. Ed. Henry Hardy. Oxford: Oxford University Press, 2002.

Bhabha, Homi K. "The Third Space: Interview with Homi Bhabha." In *Identity, Community, Culture, Difference*, ed. J. Rutherford, 207–221. London: Lawrence and Wishart, 1990.

———. *The Location of Culture*. London: Routledge Classics, 2004.

Bittinger, Nathalie. "*Requiem for Beauty*: A Contemporary Kaleidoscope." In *Mei de zangli* 美的葬禮. [Requiem for beauty], ed. Gao Xingjian, 47–49. Taipei: National Taiwan Normal University, 2016.

Bodde, Derk. *Essays on Chinese Civilization*. Princeton, NJ: Princeton University Press, 1981.

Borges, Jorge Luis. *Jorge Luis Borges: Collected Fictions*. Trans. Andrew Hurley. New York: Penguin, 1998.

Bourdieu, Pierre. "Intellectual Field and Creative Project," *Social Science Information* 8 (April 1969): 89–119.

Braudy, Leo. *The World in a Frame: What We See in Films*. Chicago: University of Chicago Press, 1976.

Bryce, James. *Studies in History and Jurisprudence*. Vol. 1. New York: Oxford University Press, 1901.

Bush, Susan, and Hsio-yen Shih. *Early Chinese Texts on Painting*. Hong Kong: Hong Kong University Press, 2012.

Carter, Ian. "Value-Freeness and Value-Neutrality in the Analysis of Political Concepts." In *Oxford Studies in Political Philosophy*. Volume 1, ed. David Sobel, Peter Vallentyne, and Steven Wall, 279–306. Oxford: Oxford University Press, 2015.

Cha, Louis. *On Hong Kong's Future: A Collection of Ming Pao Daily News Editorials*, trans. Stephen Wang. Hong Kong: Ming Pao Daily News Ltd., 1984.

Chan Koonchung 陳冠中. *Jianfeng ernian: Xin Zhongguo wuyoushi* 建豐二年：新中國烏有史 [The second year of Jianfeng: A uchronia of new China]. Hong Kong: Oxford University Press, 2015.

———. "Utopia, Dystopia, Heterotopia: Theoretical Cross-examinations on Ideal, Reality, and Social Innovation." In *Utopia and Utopianism in the Contemporary Chinese Context: Texts, Ideas, Spaces*, ed. David Der-wei Wang, Angela Ki Che Leung, and Zhang Yinde, 211–221. Hong Kong: Hong Kong University Press, 2020.

———. *Wutuobang, etuobang, yituobang: Chen Guanzhong de shidai wenpingji* 烏托邦, 惡托邦, 異托邦: 陳冠中的時代文評集 [Utopia, dystopia, and heterotopia: Chen Guanzhong's selected essays]. Taipei: Maitian, 2018.

Chang Hao 張灝. "Yitiao meiyou zouwan de lu" 一條沒有走完的路 [An unfinished road]. In *Yin Haiguang jinian ji* 殷海光紀念集 [The memorial anthology of Yin Haiguang], vol. 18 of *Yin Haiguang quanji* 殷海光全集 [Complete works of Yin Haiguang], ed. Lin Zhenghong, 161–170. Taipei: Guiguang tushu, 1990.

Chen Duxiu 陳獨秀. "Jinri Zhongguo zhi zhengzhi wenti" 今日中國之政治問題 [The political problem in today's China]. *Xin qingnian* 新青年 5, no. 1 (1918): 6–9.

———. "Wenxue geming lun" 文學革命論 [On literary revolution]. *Xin qingnian* 新青年 [New youth] 2, no. 6 (February 1917).

Chen Guying 陳鼓應, ed. *Chuncan tusi: Yin Haiguang zuihou de huayu* 春蠶吐絲：殷海光最後的話語 [Silk from silkworm: The last words of Yin Haiguang]. Taipei: Shijie wenwu gongying she, 1969.

Chen, Lingchei Letty. "Mapping Identity in a Postcolonial City: Intertextuality and Cultural Hybridity in Zhu Tianxin's *Ancient Capital*." In *Writing Taiwan—A New Literary History*, ed. C. Rojas and David Der-Wei Wang, 301–323. Durham, NC: Duke University Press, 2007.

Chen, Ming-Jer. "Transcending Paradox: The Chinese 'Middle Way' Perspective." *Asia Pacific Journal of Management* 19 (2002): 179–199.

Chen Mo 陳墨. "Bu shi zhanglang shi zhanglang: Zhang Wuji xingxiang sanlun" 不識張郎是張郎—張無忌形象散論 [Not recognizing Zhang Lang is Zhang Lang—On the image of Zhang Wuji]. In *Jin Yong xiaoshuo guoji yantaohui lunwenji* 金庸小說國際研討會論文集 [The collected articles of the International Conference on Jin Yong Novels], ed. Wu Xiaodong 吳曉東 and Ji Birui 計壁瑞, 571–587. Beijing: Beijing daxue chubanshe, 2002.

Chen Pingyuan. "Transcending 'High' and 'Low' Distinctions in Literature: The Success of Jin Yong and the Future of Martial Arts Novels." In *The Jin Yong Phenomenon*, ed. Ann Huss and Liu Jianmei, 55–72. Youngstown, NY: Cambria Press, 2007.

Chen, Rueylin. "Morality Versus Science: The Two Cultures Discourse in 1950s Taiwan." *East Asian Science, Technology and Society: An International Journal* 4 (2010): 99–121.

Chen Shixiang 陳世驤. *Chen Shixiang wencun* 陳世驤文存 [The collection of Chen Shixiang's essays]. Shenyang: Liaoning jiaoyu chubanshe, 1998.

Cheng Yuyu 鄭毓瑜. *Zi yu yan* 姿與言 [Gesture and language]. Taipei: Maitian, 2017.

Cheng Li. "The Dim Religious Reverence: Spiritualizing Nature and Ethnic Resilience in Chi Zijian's *The Last Quarter of the Moon*." *ISLE: Interdisciplinary Studies in Literature and Environment* 31, no. 2 (Summer 2024): 374–394.

Cheung Lik-kwan 張歷君. "Wenben hushe yu xiangguan lü mingxue: Lun Kristeva dui Zhang Dongsun zhishilun de jieshou" 文本互涉與相關律名學：論克裡斯蒂娃對張東蓀知識論的接受 [On Kristeva's acceptance of Zhang Dongsun's Epistemology]. In *Fangyuan: Wenxue ji wenhua zhuankan*, no. 2 (2019): 159–176.

Cheung Kwai-Yeung 張圭陽. *Jin Yong yu baoye* 金庸與報業 [Jin Yong and the press]. Hong Kong: Ming Pao chubanshe, 2000.

Chi Zijian 遲子建. *The Last Quarter of the Moon*. Trans. Bruce Holmes. London: Vintage Books, 2014.

——. "Wenxue de qiujing zhilu" 文學的求經之路 [The literary journey of acquiring scripts]. The Paper. Accessed on September 2, 2023. https://m.thepaper.cn/baijiahao_10831279.

——. "Wode nüxing guan" 我的女性觀 [My view on women]. In Chi Zijian. *Yuanlai chazi yanhong kaibian* 原來姹紫嫣紅開遍 Various shades of purple and vibrant red are blooming everywhere], 215–216. Hangzhou: Zhejiang wenyi chuban she, 2016.

Chiu-Duke, Josephine. "The May Fourth Liberal Legacy in Chan Koonchung's *Jianfeng ernian*." In *Remembering May Fourth: The Movement and Its Centennial Legacy*, ed. Yu-Kai Lin and Victor H. Mair, 53–74. Leiden, Netherlands: Brill, 2020.

Choy, Howard Y. F., and Liu Jianmei, eds. *Liu Zaifu: Selected Critical Essays*. Leiden, Netherlands: Brill, 2021.

Chu Tien-hsin 朱天心. *Gudu* 古都 [The old capital]. Taipei: Ink Publishing, 2002.

——. *Namao, Naren, Nacheng* 那貓那人那城 [That cat, that person, that city]. Zhengzhou: Henan wenyi chubanshe, 2021.

——. *Sanshisan nian meng* 三十三年夢 [Thirty-three years of dream]. Taipei: INK Yinke wenxue, 2015.

——. *Wo bu ai Taiwan, kebu keyi zheyang shuo?* 我不愛台灣，可不可以這樣說? [Can I say that I do not love Taiwan?]. Pititi shiyefang 批踢踏實業坊 [The workshop for solid criticism]. Accessed February 6, 2024. https://www.ptt.cc/bbs/politics/M.1082634868.A.BBC.html.

——. *Xiang wo juancun de xiongdimen* 想我眷村的兄弟們 [In remembrance of my brothers in military compound]. Taipei: Maitian chuban youxian gongsi, 1992.

——. *Xiaoshuojia de zhengzhi zhouji* 小說家的政治周記 [A novelist political journal]. Taipei: Shibao wenhua, 1994.

Ciaffa, Jay A. *Max Weber and the Problems of Value-Free Social Science: A Critical Examination of the Werturteilsstreit*. London: Associated University Presses, 1998.

Dai Qing 戴晴. *Tian'anmen Follies: Prison Memoirs and Other Writings*. Trans. Nancy Yang Liu, Peter Rand, and Lawrence R. Sullivan. Norwald, CT: Eastbridge Books, 2005.

——. *Zai rulai fozhang zhong: Zhang Dongsun he tade shidai* 在如來佛掌中：張東蓀和他的時代 [In the palm of Tathāgata: Zhang Dongsun and his time]. Hong Kong: Chinese University of Hong Kong Press, 2008.

Davies, Gloria. *Voicing Concerns: Contemporary Chinese Critical Inquiry*. Lanham, MD: Rowman & Littlefield, 2001.

de Certeau, Michel. *The Practice of Everyday Life*. Trans. Steven Rendall. Berkeley, CA: University of California Press, 1984.

Driver, Julia. *Consequentialism*. New York: Routledge, 2012.

Duara, Prasenjit. *The Crisis of Global Modernity*. Cambridge: Cambridge University Press, 2015.

Dufrêne, Thierry. "Notes on *Requiem for Beauty*: A Cinematic Poem by Gao Xingjian (2013)." In Gao Xingjian. *Mei de zangli* 美的葬禮 [Requiem for beauty], 50–53. Taipei: National Taiwan Normal University, 2016.

Du Lanlan. "Nature and Ethnic Women: An Ecofeminist Reading of Chi Zijian's *The Last Quarter of the Moon* and Linda Hogan's *Solar Storms*." *Comparative Literature Studies* 55, no. 4 (2018): 787–798.

Du Yaquan 杜亞泉. "Geren yu guojia zhi jieshuo" 個人與國家之界說 [On the demarcation of the individual and the state]. *Dongfang zazhi* 14, no. 3 (March 1917).

———. "Jing de wenming yu dong de wenming" 靜的文明與動的文明 [The still civilization and the mobile civilization]. *Dongfang zazhi* 13, no. 10 (October 1916).

———. "Maodun zhi tiaohe" 矛盾之調和 [The accommodation of contradiction]. *Dongfang zazhi* 東方雜誌 15, no. 2 (February 1918).

———. "Zhengdang lun" 政黨論 [On political parties]. *Dongfang zazhi* 8, no. 1 (March 1911).

Engdahl, Horace. "Stilen Och Lyckan: Essäer om Litteratur." In *Fengge yu xingfu* 風格與幸福 [Style and pleasure], trans. Wangzhi 萬之. Shanghai: Fudan daxue chubanshe, 2017.

Evans, Megan. "Floods and Forests: Gao Xingjian's Transcultural Aesthetic of Catastrophe." In *Gao Xingjian and Transmedia Aesthetics*, ed. Mabel Lee and Liu Jianmei, 181–194. Amherst, NY: Cambria Press, 2018.

Fang Fang. *Wuhan Dairy: Dispatches from a Quarantined City*. Trans. Michael Berry. New York: HarperCollins, 2020.

Fang, Tony. "From Onion to Ocean: Paradox and Change in National Cultures." *International Studies of Management & Organization* 35, no. 4 (2005–2006): 71–90.

———. "Yin Yang: A New Perspective on Culture." *Management and Organization Review* 8, no. 1 (2011): 25–50.

Ferber, Ilit. *Philosophy and Melancholy: Benjamin's Early Reflections on Theater and Language*. Stanford, CA: Stanford University Press, 2013.

Fong, Gilbert, and Shelby Chan. "Nonattachment and Gao Xingjian's Neutral Actor." In *Gao Xingjian and Transmedia Aesthetics*, ed. Mabel Lee and Liu Jianmei, 99–114. Amherst, NY: Cambria Press, 2018.

Foucault, Michel. "Of Other Space." In *Heterotopia and the City: Public Space in a Postcivil Society*, ed. Michiel Dehaene and Lieven De Caute, 13–30. London: Routledge, 2008.

Freud, Sigmund. "Mourning and Melancholia." In *The Standard Edition of the Complete Psychological Works of Sigmund Freud*. Vol. 14 (1914–1916), *On the History of the Psycho-Analytic Movement, Papers on Metapsychology and Other Works*, ed. James Strachey, 237–258. London: The Hogarth Press and the Institute of Psycho-Analysis, 1957.

Fu Guoyong 傅國涌. *Jin Yong zhuan* 金庸傳 [The biography of Jin Yong]. Beijing: Beijing shiyue wenyi chubanshe, 2003.

Fung, Edmund. *In Search of Chinese Democracy.* Cambridge: Cambridge University Press, 2000.

———. *The Intellectual Foundations of Chinese Modernity: Cultural and Political Thought in the Republican Era.* Cambridge: Cambridge University Press, 2010.

———. "Socialism, Capitalism, and Democracy in Republican China: The Political Thought of Zhang Dongsun." *Modern China* 28, no. 4 (October 2002): 399–431.

Fusini, Letizia. *Dionysus on the Other Shore: Gao Xingjian's Theatre of the Tragic.* Leiden, Netherlands: Brill, 2020.

Gao Bo 高波. *Zhuixun xin gonghe: Zhang Dongsun zaoqi sixiang yu huodong 1886–1932* 追尋新共和：張東蓀早期思想與活動1886–1932 [Search for a new republic: A study of the thought and activities of Zhang Dongsun in his early years 1886–1932]. Beijing: Sanlian shudian, 2018.

Gao Like 高力克. *Tiaoshi de zhihui: Du Yaquan sixiang yanjiu* 調適的智慧：杜亞泉思想研究[The wisdom of accommodation: Research on Du Yaquan's thought]. Hangzhou: Zhejiang renmin chubanshe, 1998.

Gao, Nuan. "Building Fukan as a Chinese Public Sphere: Zhang Dongsun and Learning Light." *Journal of the Indiana Academy of the Social Sciences* 20, no. 1 (2018): 34–49.

Gao Xingjian 高行健. "After the Flood." In *Aesthetics and Creation*, trans. Mabel Lee, 221–226. Amherst, NY: Cambria Press, 2012.

———. "Another Kind of Aesthetics." In *Aesthetics and Creation*, trans. Mabel Lee, 89–158. Amherst, NY: Cambria Press, 2012.

———. "The Art of Fiction." In *Aesthetics and Creation*, trans. Mabel Lee, 21–40. Amherst, NY: Cambria Press, 2012.

———. *Cold Literature: Selected Works by Gao Xingjian.* Trans. Gilbert C. F. Fong and Mabel Lee. Hong Kong: The Chinese University Press, 2005.

———. "Concerning *Silhouette/Shadow*." In *Aesthetics and Creation*, trans. Mabel Lee, 179–188. Amherst, NY: Cambria Press, 2012.

———. "Dramaturgical Method and the Neutral Actor." In *Aesthetics and Creation*, trans. Mabel Lee, 159–178. Amherst, NY: Cambria Press, 2012.

———. "Foreword." In Liu Zaifu, *Reflections on Dream of the Red Chamber.* Trans. Shu Yunzhong, xi-xiii. Amherst, NY: Cambria Press, 2008.

———. "Freedom and Literature." In *Aesthetics and Creation*, trans. Mabel Lee, 227–236. Amherst, NY: Cambria Press, 2012.

———. *Gao Xingjian: Aesthetics and Creation.* Trans. Mabel Lee. Amherst, NY: Cambria Press, 2012.

———. "Ideology and Literature." In *Aesthetics and Creation*, trans. Mabel Lee, 207–220. Amherst, NY: Cambria Press, 2012.

———. Introduction to *Mei de zangli* 美的葬礼 [Requiem for beauty], 6–9. Taipei: National Taiwan Normal University, 2016.

———. *Lun chuangzuo* 論創作 [On creation]. Hong Kong: Mingbao yuekan chubanshe, 2008.

———. *Mei de zangli* 美的葬礼 [Requiem for beauty]. Taipei: National Taiwan Normal University, 2016.

———. *Meiyou zhuyi* 沒有主義 [Without isms]. Hong Kong: Cosmos Books, 1996.

———. "My Thoughts on Painting." In *Meiyou zhuyi* 沒有主義 [Without isms], 290–295. Hong Kong: Cosmos Books, 1996.

———. "The Potential of Theatre." In *Aesthetics and Creation*, trans. Mabel Lee, 41–64. Amherst, NY: Cambria Press, 2012.

———. *Soul Mountain*. Trans. Mabel Lee. Sydney: HarperCollins, 2004.

———. *Wandering Mind and Metaphysical Thoughts*. Trans. Gilbert C. Fong. Hong Kong: The Chinese University Press, 2018.

Ge Zhaoguang 葛兆光. "Imagining 'All Under Heaven': The Political, Intellectual, and Academic Background of a New Utopia." Trans. Michael Duke and Josephine Chiu-Duke. In *Utopia and Utopianism in the Contemporary Chinese Context: Texts, Ideas, Spaces*, ed. David Der-wei Wang, Angela Ki Che Leung, Zhang Yinde, 15–35. Hong Kong: Hong Kong University Press, 2020.

Giedion, Siegfried. *Mechanization Takes Command: A Contribution to Anonymous History*. New York: Oxford University Press, 1948.

Gilloch, Graeme. *Walter Benjamin: Critical Constellations*. Cambridge: Polity Press, 2002.

Gu Dayong 古大勇, "Li Zehou, Liu Zaifu bijiao lungang" 李泽厚 劉再復比較論綱 [The comparison between Li Zehou and Liu Zaifu]. *Huawen wenxue* 華文文學 1 (2018): 8–19.

Gu Dayong 古大勇 and Liu Zaifu 劉再復. "Zhongxi daguan shiyexia de wenxue piping he wenhua pipan—Liu Zaifu xiansheng fangtan lu" 中西〈大觀〉視野下的文學批評和文化批判—劉再復先生訪談錄 [Chinese literary criticism and cultural criticism under the grand vision—The interview of Mr. Liu Zaifu]. *Gansu shehui kexue* 甘肅社會科學 6 (2015): 95–100.

Guo Huaqing 郭華清. *Kuanrong yu tuoxie: Zhang Shizhao de tiaohelun yanjiu* 寬容與妥協—章士釗的調和論研究 [Tolerance and compromise: Research on Zhang Shizhao's theory of accommodation]. Tianjin: Tianjin guji chuban she, 2004.

Guo, Jason. *The Inner Landscape: The Paintings of Gao Xingjian*. Washington, DC: New Academia Publishing, 2013.

Guo Moruo 郭沫若. *Moruo wenji* 沫若文集 [Collected works of Guo Moruo]. Beijing: Renmin wenxue chubanshe, 1961.

Guo Zhanbo 郭湛波. *Zhongguo Jin wushi nian Zhongguo sixiang shi* 中國近五十年思想史 [The most recent fifty years of Chinese thought]. Shanghai: Shanghai guji chubanshe, 2005.

Habermas, Jürgen. *The Structural Transformation of the Public Sphere: An Inquiry into a Category of Bourgeois Society*. Trans. Thomas Burger. Cambridge, MA: MIT Press, 1989.

Haddon, Rosemary. "Being/Not Being at Home in the Writing of Zhu Tianxin." In *Cultural, Ethnic, and Political Nationalism in Contemporary Taiwan: Bentuhua*, ed. John Makeham and A-chin Hsiau, 103–123. New York: Palgrave Macmillan, 2005.

Hamm, John Christopher. *Paper Swordsmen: Jin Yong and the Modern Chinese Martial Arts Novel*. Honolulu: University of Hawai'i Press, 2005.

Hayek, Friedrich A. *The Constitution of Liberty*. Chicago: University of Chicago Press, 1960.

——. *Individualism and Economic Order*. Chicago: University of Chicago Press, 1948.

——. *The Road to Selfdom*. London: Routledge, 1944.

Hennis, Wilhelm, Ulrike Brisson, and Roger Brisson. "The Meaning of 'Wertfreiheit' on the Background and Motives of Max Weber's 'Postulate.'" *Sociological Theory* 12, no. 2 (July 1994): 113–125.

Heyne, F. Georg. "The Social Significance of the Shaman Among the Chinese Reindeer-Evenki." *Asian Folklore Studies* (1999): 377–395.

Hibben, J. G. *Hegel's Logic: An Essay in Interpretation*. Charles Scribner's Sons, 1902. Reprint, Kitchener, ON: Batoche Books, 2000.

Hockx, Michel. *Internet Literature in China*. New York: Columbia University Press, 2015.

Ho Fuk Yan 何福仁. *Fucheng 1.2.3—Xi Xi xiaoshuo xinxi* 浮城1.2.3: 西西小說新析 [Marvels of a floating city 1.2.3—Interpretations of Xi Xi's novels]. Hong Kong: Sanlian shudian, 2008.

Hsia, C. T. *A History of Modern Chinese Fiction*. 3rd ed. Bloomington: Indiana University Press, 1999.

——. "Obsession with China: The Moral Burden of Chinese Literature." In *A History of Modern Chinese Fiction*, 3rd ed, 563–586. Bloomington: Indiana University Press, 1999.

Huang Aihua 黃愛華. *Lun zuguo wenti* 論祖國問題 [On the problem of the home country]. Hong Kong: Ming Pao chubanshe, 1964.

Hung, Jenny. "Is Zhuangzi a Wanton? Observation and Transformation of Desire in the *Zhuangzi*." *Dao: A Journal of Comparative Philosophy* 2, no. 19 (2020): 1–17.

Hu Shi 胡適. Cong zhengqu yanlun ziyou tandao fandui dang" 從爭取言論自由談到反對黨 [From striving for freedom of speech to the opposition party]. In *Zhengzhi yu shehui (xia)* 政治與社會 （下） [Politics and society (part 2)], vol. 12: 619–626. *Yin Haiguang quanji* 殷海光全集 [Complete works of Yin Haiguang], ed. Lin Zhenghong. Taipei: Guiguang tushu, 1990.

——. "Rongren yu ziyou" 容忍與自由 [Tolerance and freedom]. In *Zhengzhi yu shehui (xia)* 政治與社會 （下） [Politics and society (part 2)], vol. 12: 790–797. *Yin Haiguang quanji* 殷海光全集 [Complete works of Yin Haiguang], ed. Lin Zhenghong. Taipei: Guiguang tushu, 1990.

——. "Wenxue gailiang chuyi" 文學改良芻議 [Inceptive discussion on literary reform]. In *Zhongguo xinwenxue daxi* 中國新文學大系 [A corpus of Chinese new literature], ed. Zhao Jiabi 趙家璧, 1:44–47. Shanghai: Shanghai wenyi chubanshe, 1980–1987.

Huss, Ann, and Liu Jianmei, eds. *The Jin Yong Phenomenon: Chinese Martial Arts Fiction and Modern Chinese Literary History*. Youngstown, NY: Cambria, 2007.

Jameson, Fredric. *The Prison-House of Language: A Critical Account of Structuralism and Russian Formalism*. Princeton, NJ: Princeton University Press, 1972.

Jenco, Leigh K. *Making the Political: Founding and Action in the Political Theory of Zhang Shizhao*. Cambridge: Cambridge University Press, 2010.

Jiang Di 江堤 and Yang Hui 楊暉. *Zhongguo lishi dashi* 中國歷史大勢 [The big tendency of Chinese history]. Changsha: Human daxue chubanshe, 2001.

Jiang Xinyang. *Knowledge, Culture, and Chinese Philosophy: A Study and Translation of Zhang Dongsun's Works*. New York: Global Scholarly Publications, 2014.

Jiang Yihua 姜義華. "Jijin yu baoshou: Yu Yü Ying-Shih xiansheng shangque" 激進與保守—與余英時先生商榷. [The radicals and the conservatives—Dialogues with Mr. Yü Ying-Shih]. *Ershiyi shiji* 二十一世紀 10 (April 1992): 134–142.

Jin Yong 金庸. "Afterword." In *Yitian tulong ji* 倚天屠龍記 [The heaven sword and the dragon saber]. Vol. 4. Guangzhou: Guangzhou chubanshe, 2013.

——. *Luding ji* 鹿鼎記 [The deer and the cauldron]. Guangzhou: Guangzhou chubanshe, 2013.

——. *Tianlong babu* 天龍八部 [The semi-gods and the semi-devils]. Guangzhou: Guangzhou chubanshe, 2013.

——. *Xiao'ao Jianghu* 笑傲江湖 [The smiling, proud wanderer]. Guangzhou: Guangzhou chubanshe, 2013.

——. *Yitian tulong ji* 倚天屠龍記 [The heaven sword and the dragon saber]. Guangzhou: Guangzhou chubanshe, 2013.

——. *Zaitai suojian, suowen, suosi* 在台所見所聞所思 [What I saw, heard and thought in Taiwan]. Hong Kong: Ming Pao youxian gongsi, 1973.

Jin Yong and Ikeda Daisaku. *Tanqiu yige canlan de shiji* 探求一個燦爛的世紀 [Exploring a splendid century]. Hong Kong: Mingheshe chuban youxian gongsi, 1998.

Jin Yuelin 金岳霖. "Wo dui sulian de kanfa de zhuanbian" 我對蘇聯的看法的轉變 [The transformation of my view toward the Soviet Union]. In vol. 4 (first half) of *Jin Yuelin quanji* 金岳霖全集 [Complete works of Jin Yuelin], 773–778. Beijing: Renmin chubanshe, 2013.

Kant, Immanuel. *Critique of Judgment*. Trans. Werner S. Pluhar. Indianapolis, IN: Hackett, 1987.

Kermode, Frank. *The Sense of an Ending: Studies in the Theory of Fiction*. London: Oxford University Press, 1967.

Kristeva, Julia. *The Kristeva Reader*. Ed. Toril Moi. New York: Columbia University Press, 1986.

Kong Shuyu. *Consuming Literature: Best Sellers and the Commercialization of Literary Production in Contemporary China*. Stanford, CA: Stanford University Press, 2005.

Labędzka, Izabella. *Gao Xingjian's Idea of Theatre: From the Word to the Image.* Leiden, Netherlands: Brill, 2008.

Lansing, Gerrit L. "'The False Mirror': Image Versus Reality." *Notes in the History of Art* 4, nos. 2/3 (Winter/Spring 1985).

Lao Tzu. *Tao Teh Ching.* Trans. John C. H. Wu. Boston: Shambhala, 1961.

Lau, Joseph S. M. "Visitation of the Past in Han Shaogong's Post 1985 Fiction." In *From May Fourth to June Fourth: Fiction and Film in Twentieth-Century China*, ed. Ellen Widmer and David Der-wei Wang, 19–42. Cambridge, MA: Harvard University Asia Center, 1993.

Laughlin, Charles A. *The Literature of Leisure and Chinese Modernity.* Honolulu: University of Hawai'i Press, 2008.

Lee Haiyan. "Taiwanimals: Stree Dogs and Cats as Remaindered Life." In *A Literary History of Taiwan in the New Millennium*, ed. Lin Pei-yin, Li Wen-chi, and Carlos Rojas. Forthcoming from Amherst, NY: Cambria Press, 2025.

———. "Through Thick and Thin: The Romance of the Species in the Anthropocene." *International Communication of Chinese Culture*, no. 2 (May 2018): 145–172.

Lee, Leo Ou-fan. "On the Margins of the Chinese Discourse: Some Personal Thoughts on the Cultural Meaning of the Periphery." *Daedalus* 120, no. 2 (Spring 1991): 207–226.

———. *Shanghai Modern: The Flowering of A New Urban Culture in China, 1930–1945.* Cambridge, MA: Harvard University Press, 1999.

Lee, Mabel, and Liu Jianmei, eds. *Gao Xingjian and Transmedia Aesthetics.* Amherst, NY: Cambria Press, 2018.

Lefebvre, Henri. *La Présence et l'absence.* Paris: Casterman, 1980.

———. *The Production of Space.* Translated by Donald Nicholson-Smith. Malden, MA: Blackwell, 1974.

Leng Xia 冷夏. *Jin Yong zhuan* 金庸傳 [The biography of Jin Yong]. Hong Kong: Ming Pao chubanshe, 1994.

———. *Wentan xiasheng—Jin Yong zhuan* 文壇俠聖—金庸傳 [The sage of xia in the literary field—The biography of Jin Yong]. Guangzhou: Guangdong renmin chubanshe, 1995.

Lewis, Marianne W. "Exploring Paradox: Toward a More Comprehensive Guide." *Academy of Management Review* 25 (2000): 760–776.

Li, Peter Ping. "Global Implications of the Indigenous Epistemological System from the East." *Cross Cultural and Strategic Management* 23, no. 1 (February 2016): 42–77.

———. "Toward a Geocentric Framework of Trust: An Application to Organizational Trust." *Management and Organization Review* 4, no. 3 (2008): 413–439.

———. "Toward an Integrative Framework of Indigenous Research: The Geocentric Implication of Yin-Yang Balance." *Asia Pacific Journal of Management* 29 (2012): 849–872.

———. "The Unique Value of Yin-Yang Balancing: A Critical Response." *Management and Organizational Review* 10, no. 2 (2014): 321–332.

Li Yijian 李以建, ed. *Jin Yong juan* 金庸卷 [The volume of Jin Yong]. Hong Kong: Tiandi tushu, 2016.

———. "'Rewriting' Jin Yong's Novels into the Canon: A Consideration of Jin Yong's Novels as Serialized Fiction." In *The Jin Yong Phenomenon: Chinese Martial Arts Fiction and Modern Chinese Literary History*, ed. Ann Huss and Liu Jianmei, 73–96. Youngstown, NY: Cambria Press, 2007.

Li Zehou 李澤厚. *The Chinese Aesthetic Tradition*. Trans. Maija Bell Samei. Honolulu: University of Hawai'i Press, 2010.

———. *Huiying Sangde'er ji qita* 回應桑德爾及其他 [A response to Michael Sandel and other matters]. Beijing: Sanlian, 2014.

———. "Lishi yanjie he lilun de 'du'" 歷史眼界和理論的"度" [The historical perspective and the theoretical "proper measure"]. *Tianya* 2 (1999): 128–135.

———. *Pipan zhexue de pipan: Kangde shuping* 批判哲學的批判：康德述評 [The criticism of critical philosophy: On Kant]. Beijing: Sanlian shudian, 2015.

———. *Renlei xue lishi benti lun* 人類學歷史本體論 [The Anthropo-historical ontology]. Tianjin: Tianjin shehui kexue chuban she, 2008.

———. *Shiyong lixing yu legan wenhua* 實用理性與樂感文化 [Pragmatic reason and a culture of pleasure]. Beijing: Sanlian shudian, 2008.

Li Zehou 李澤厚 and Liu Zaifu 劉再復. *Gaobie geming* 告別革命 [Farewell to revolution]. Hong Kong: Tiandi tushu youxian gongsi, 2015.

Liang Shiqiu 梁實秋. "Lun disanzhong ren" 論第三種人 [On the third type of person]. *Wenyi yuekan* 文藝月刊 3, no. 7 (January 1933).

Lim, Wah Guan. "From Theater to Cine-Poetry: Gao Xingjian's Performance Theories." In *Gao Xingjian and Transmedia Aesthetics*, ed. Mabel Lee and Liu Jianmei, 201–216. Amherst, NY: Cambria Press, 2018.

Lin Yü-Sheng. *The Crisis of Chinese Consciousness: Radical Antitrationalism in the May Fourth Era*. Madison: University of Wisconsin Press, 1979.

Lipinski, Lisa. *René Magritte and the Art of Thinking*. New York: Routledge, 2019.

Liu Jianmei. "Liu Zaifu's Three Voyages of Life." *Prism: Theory and Modern Chinese Literature* 17, no. 1 (2020): 193–198.

———. *Zhuangzi and Modern Chinese Literature*. New York: Oxford University Press, 2016.

Liu, Kang 劉康. *Politics, Ideology, and Literary Discourse in Modern China: Theoretical Interventions and Cultural Critique*, ed. Liu Kang and Tang Xiaobing 唐小兵. Durham, NC and London: Duke University Press, 1993.

Liu, Lydia He. *Translingual Practice: Literature, National Culture, and Translated Modernity—China, 1900–1937*. Stanford, CA: Stanford University Press, 1995.

Liu, Petrus. "Jin Yong Publishes 'The Smiling, Proud Wanderer' in *Ming Pao*." In *A New Literary History of Modern China*, ed. David Der-wei Wang, 685–691. Cambridge, MA: The Belknap Press of Harvard University Press, 2017.

——. *Stateless Subjects: Chinese Martial Arts Literature and Postcolonial History*. Ithaca, NY: Cornell University East Asia Program, 2011.

Liu Xiaogan 劉笑敢, *Liangji hua yu fencun gan: jindai zhongguo jingying sichao de bingtai xinli fenxi* 兩極化與分寸感：近代中國精英思潮的病態心理分析 [Polarization and sense of propriety: Analysis of the psychological malaise of modern elite currents of thought]. Taibei: Dongda tushu, 1994.

Liu Xiaomei 劉曉梅. "Wenren lun wu" 文人論武 [Scholars discussing martial arts]. In *Zhuzi baijia kan Jin Yong* 諸子百家看金庸 [An examination of Jin Yong through the lens of the hundred schools of thought]. vol. 3., San Mao et al, 237–245. Beijing: Zhongguo youyi chubanshe, 1998.

Liu Xinwu 劉心武. "Shifu: yizhong shengcun kunjing" 失父：一種生存困境 [Losing father: A survival dilemma]. In *Jin Yong xiaoshuo yu ershishiji Zhongguo wenxue* 金庸小說與二十世紀中國文學 [Jin Yong's fiction and twentieth-century Chinese literature], ed. Lin Lijun 林麗君, 383–400. Hong Kong: Minghe she, 2000.

Liu Zaifu. *A Study of Two Classics: A Cultural Critique of Romance of the Three Kingdoms and Water Margin*. Trans. by Yunzhong Shu. Amherst, NY: Cambria, 2012. "Bilateral Way of Thinking and the Basic Tone of the Big Era." In *Cangsang baigan* 滄桑百感 [Hundreds of comprehensions in the vicissitudes of life]. Hong Kong: Tiandi, 2004.

——. *Cangsang baigan* 滄桑百感 [Hundreds of comprehensions in the vicissitudes of life]. Hong Kong: Tiandi, 2004.

——. *Daguan xinde* 大觀心得 [The comprehension notes on the grand vision]. Hong Kong: Tiandi tushu, 2010.

——. "Di'er rensheng sanbuqu" 第二人生三部曲 [Trilogy of the second life]. In *Yuedu meiguo* 閱讀美國 [Reading America]. Hong Kong: Xianggang mingbao chubanshe, 2002.

——. *Duyu tianya* 獨語天涯 [Solitary recitations at the edge of the world]. Hong Kong: Tiandi tushu, 1999.

——. "Farewell to the Gods: Contemporary Chinese Literary Theory's Fin-de-Siècle Struggle." In *Liu Zaifu: Selected Critical Essays*, ed. Howard Y. F. Choy and Liu Jianmei. Leiden, Netherlands: Brill, 2021.

——. "The Failure of the May Fourth Movement and My Two Struggles." Trans. Guo Yijiao. *Prism: Theory and Moden Chinese Literature* 17, no. 1 (March 2020): 127–142.

——. "From the Monologic Era to the Polyphonic Era: An Outline of Forty Years of Literary Development in Mainland China." In *Liu Zaifu: Selective Critical Essays*, ed. Howard Choy and Liu Jianmei. Leiden, Netherlands: Brill, 2021.

——. "Gao Xingjian: Exemplifying a Renaissance in Today's World." In *Gao Xingjian and Transmedia Aesthetics*, ed. Mabel Lee and Liu Jianmei. Amherst, NY: Cambria Press, 2018.

——. "Gao Xingjian's Notion of Freedom." In *Freedom and Fate in Gao Xingjian's Writings*, ed. Michael Lackner and Nikola Chardonnens, 73–78. Berlin: Walter de Gruyter GmbH, 2014.

——. *Hongloumeng zhexue biji* 紅樓夢哲學筆記 [Philosophical notes on *Dream of the Red Chamber*]. Beijing: Sanlian shudian, 2009.

——. *Huigui gudian, huigui wode liuijng* 回歸古典，回歸我的六經 [Return to the classics, return to my six scriptures]. Beijing: Renmin ribao chuban she, 2011.

——. *Jia Baoyu lun* 賈寶玉論 [On Jia Baoyu]. Beijing: Sanlian shudian, 2014.

——. "Literary History as a Paradox." In *Liu Zaifu: Selected Critical Essays*, ed. Howard Y. F. Choy and Liu Jianmei. Leiden, Netherlands: Brill, 2021.

——. "Literature Exiling the State." In *Liu Zaifu: Selected Critical Essays*, ed. Howard Y. F. Choy and Liu Jianmei. Leiden, Netherlands: Brill, 2021.

——. "Lun Bingzai" 論丙崽 [On Bingzai]. In *Han Shaogong yanjiu ziliao* 韓少功研究資料 [The reseach materials of Han Shaogong], ed. Li Li 李莉 and Hu Jianling 胡建玲, 134–140. Jinan: Shandong wenyi chubanshe, 2006.

——. "Lun wenxue de zhuti xing" 論文學的主體性 [On the literary subjectivity]. In *Wenxue de fansi* 文學的反思 [The retrospection on literature]. Fuzhou: Fujian renmin chubanshe, 2010.

——. *Mianbi chensi lu* 面壁沈思錄 [Meditation while facing the wall]. Hong Kong: Tiandi tushu, 2004.

——. *Piaobo zhuan—Liu Zaifu haiwai sanwen xuan* 漂泊傳—劉再復海外散文選 [Autobiography of drifting—Selective collection of Liu Zaifu's overseas essays]. Hong Kong: Tiandi tushu, 2009.

——. *Piaoliu shouji* 漂流手記 [Drifting notes]. Taibei: Fengyun shidai, 1994.

——. *Reflections on Dream of the Red Chamber*. Trans. Shu Yunzhong. Amherst, NY: Cambria Press, 2008.

——. *Shenme shi rensheng—Guanyu rensheng lunli de shitangke* 什麼是人生——關於人生倫理的十堂課 [What is life?—Ten lessons regarding life ethics]. Hong Kong: Sanlian shudian, 2017.

——. *Shenme shi wenxue: wenxue changshi ershi'er jiang* 什麼是文學：文學常識二十二講 [What is literature? Twenty-two lectures on literary common knowledge]. Hong Kong: Sanlian shudian, 2018.

——. "Shuangxiang siwei yu da shidai jidiao" 雙向思維與大時代基調 [Bilateral way of thinking and the basic tone of the big era]. In *Liu Zaifu, Cangsang baigan* 滄桑百感 [Hundreds of comprehensions in the vicissitudes of life]. Hong Kong: Tiandi, 2004.

——. *A Study of Two Classics: A Cultural Critique of The Romance of the Three Kingdoms and The Water Margin*. Trans. Yunzhong Shu. Amherst, NY: Cambria, 2012.

——. *Suixinji* 隨心集 [Collection of heart following]. Beijing: Sanlian shudian, 2012.

——. *Tianya wuyu* 天涯悟語 [The enlightened words at the edge of the world]. Beijing: Sanlian, 2013.

——. *Wode sixiang shi* 我的思想史 [History of my thought]. Hong Kong: Sanlian shudian, 2019.

——. *Wode xinling shi* 我的心靈史 [History of my heart]. Hong Kong: Sanlian shudian, 2019.

——. *Wode xiezuo shi* 我的寫作史 [History of my writing]. Hong Kong, Sanlian shudian, 2020.

——. *Xingge zuhe lun* 性格組合論 [A treatise of character composition]. Hefei: Anhui wenhui chubanshe, 1999.

——. "Xunzhao shengcun de 'disan kongjian'" 尋找生存的第三空間 [Searching for the survival of Thirdspace]. *Yazhou zhoukan* 亞洲周刊, September 3–9, 2001.

——. "Zailun disan huayu kongjian" 再論第三話語空間 [Rethinking the third discursive space]. *Mingpao Monthly*, April 2006.

——. *Zenyang du wenxue: wenxue huiwu shiba dian* 怎樣讀文學：文學慧悟十八點 [How to read literature: Eighteen points of literary comprehension]. Hong Kong: Sanlian shudian, 2018.

——. *Zouxiang rensheng shenchu* 走向人生深處 [Going to the depth of life]. Interview by Wu Xiaopan 吳小攀. Beijing: Zhongxin chubanshe, 2011.

Liu Zaifu and Lin Gang 林崗. *Chuantong yu zhongguoren* 傳統與中國人 [Tradition and Chinese]. Beijing: Sanlian shudian, 1988.

——. *Zui yu wenxue* 罪與文學 [Sin and literature]. Beijing: Zhongxin chubanshe, 2011.

Liu Zaifu and Liu Jianmei. *Gongwu honglou* 共悟紅樓 [Comprehending *Dream of the Red Chamber* together]. Beijing: Sanlian shudian, 2009.

——. "Honglou zhensu erdi de hubu jiegou—Guanyu Hongloumeng de zuixin duihua" 紅樓真俗二諦的互補結構——關於紅樓夢的最新對話 [The complementary structure between the truth of the transcendental world and the truth of the mundane world—The most recent dialogue about *Dream of the Red Chamber*]. *Huawen wenxue* 華文文學 5 (2010): 105–112.

Lu Xun 魯迅. *Lu Xun quanji* 魯迅全集 [The complete works of Lu Xun]. Beijing: Renmin wenxue chubanshe, 1993.

——. *Lu Xun Selected Works*. Trans. Yang Xianyi 楊憲益 and Gladys Yang. Beijing: Foreign Languages Press, 1959.

——. "Lun disanzhong ren" 論第三種人 [On the third type of person]. In *Lu Xun quanji* 魯迅全集 [The complete works of Lu Xun], vol. 4, 438–444. Beijing: Renmin wenxue chubanshe, 1993.

——. "Yinshi" 隱士 [Hermits]. In Lu Xun quanji 魯迅全集 [The complete works of Lu Xun], vol. 6, 223–226. Beijing: Renmin wenxue chubanshe, 1993.

——. "Wenhua pianzhi lun" 文化偏執論 [On the one-sidedness of cultural development]. In *Lu Xun quanji* 魯迅全集 [The complete works of Lu Xun], vol. 1, 44–62. Beijing: Renmin wenxue chubanshe, 1981.

——. "Xiaopinwen de weiji" 小品文的危機 [The crisis of little essays]. In *Lu Xun quanji* 魯迅全集 [*The complete works of Lu Xun*], vol. 4. 574–577. Beijing: Renmin wenxue chubanshe, 1993.

——. "Xiao zagan" 小雜感 [Small miscellaneous thought]. In *Lu Xun quanji* 魯迅全集 [The complete works of Lu Xun], vol. 3, 530–534. Beijing: Renmin wenxue chubanshe, 1993.

Mair, Victor H. *Wandering on the Way: Early Taoist Tales and Parables of Chuang Tzu*. Honolulu: University of Hawai'i Press, 1994.

Malraux, André. "Museum without Walls." In *The Voices of Silence*, trans. Stuart Gilbert. Princeton, NJ: Princeton University Press, 1978.

Massumi, Brian. *Parables for the Virtual: Movement, Affect, Sensation*. Durham, NC: Duke University Press, 2002.

Mazzilli, Mary. "Gao Xingjian's Search for a Scenic Dramaturgy and Cinematic Language in Song of the Night." In *Gao Xingjian and Transmedia Aesthetics*, ed. Mabel Lee and Liu Jianmei, 115–130. Amherst, NY: Cambria Press, 2018.

McLuhan, Marshall. *The Gutenberg Galaxy: The Making of Typographic Man*. Toronto, Canada: University of Toronto Press, 1962.

Menkus, Wei Yang. "Unravelling the Urban Myth: History, City, and Literature in Xi Xi's Fiction." *Chinese Literature Today* 8, no.1 (2019): 58–67.

Merleau-Ponty, Maurice. "Eye and Mind." In *The Merleau-Ponty Reader*, ed. Ted Toadvine and Leonard Lawlor, 351–378. Evanston, IL: Northwestern University Press, 2007.

Metzger, Thomas. *Escape from Predicament: New-Confucianism and China's Evolving Political Culture*. New York: Columbia University Press, 1977.

——. *The International Organization of Ch'ing Bureaucracy: Legal, Normative, and Communication Aspects*. Cambridge, MA: Harvard University Press, 1973.

——. *The Western Concept of the Civil Society in the Context of Chinese History*. Stanford, CA: Stanford University Press, 1998.

Mill, John Stuart. *On Liberty*. Mineola, NY: Dover, 2002.

——. *Utilitarianism, Liberty and Representative Government*. London: Everyman, 1910.

Mitchell, W. J. T. *Picture Theory: Essays on Verbal and Visual Representation*. Chicago: University of Chicago Press, 1944.

Moore, Charles A., ed. *The Chinese Mind: Essentials of Chinese Philosophy and Culture*. Honolulu: University of Hawai'i Press, 1967.

Morikawa Hiroki 森川裕貫. *Zhengzhijia de jinchi: Zhang Shizhao Zhang Dongsun zhengzhi sixiang yanjiu* 政治家的矜持：章士釗張東蓀政治思想研究 [The reservedness of politicians: A study of the political thought of Zhang Shizhao and Zhang Dongsun], trans. from the Japanese by Yuan Guangquan 袁廣泉. Beijing: Shehui wenxian chubanshe, 2012.

Oosterling, Henk, and Ewa Plonowska Ziarek, eds. *Intermedialities: Philosophy, Arts, Politics*. Lanham, MD: Lexington Books, 2011.

Pan Shuyang. "Religious Imagination of Nature: On Chi Zijian's Writing of Shamanism." MPhil Thesis, Hong Kong University of Science and Technology, 2016.

Paquet, Marcel. *René Magritte 1898–1967: Thought Rendered Visible*. Köln: Taschen, 2000.
Peng, Kaiping, and Richard E. Nisbett. "Culture, Dialectics, and Reasoning About Contradiction." *The American Psychologist* 54, no. 9 (1999): 741–754.
——. "Dialectical Response to Questions about Dialectical Thinking." *American Psychologist* 55, no. 9 (2000): 1067–1068.
Plumwood, Val. *Feminism and the Mastery of Nature*. London: Routledge, 2002.
Popper, Karl. *The Open Society and Its Enemies*. Vol. 1. London: George Routledge and Sons, 1945.
Qian Yongxiang 錢永祥. "Yin Haiguang xiansheng de minzhuguan yu minzhu de liangge gainian" 殷海光先生的民主觀與民主的兩個概念 [Mr. Yin Haiguang's democratic viewpoints and two concepts of democracy]. In *The Free and Democratic Thought and Culture*, ed. Wei Zhengtong 韋政通 et al., 107–124. Taipei: Zili wanbao she wenhua chuban bu, 1980.
Qiao Min 喬敏. "Liu Zaifu 'pianduan xiezuo' shixue lunlüe" 劉再復"片段寫作"詩學論略 [A brief discussion of Liu Zaifu's "fragmentary writing"]. *Huawen wenxue* 華文文學 6 (2018): 36–41.
——. "Rethinking 'Subjectivity' in Literature: Liu Zaifu's Theoretical Construction and Cultural Reflection." *Prism: Theory and Modern Chinese Literature* 17, no. 1 (2020): 172–182.
——. "A Spirit of Internal Exile: On Liu Zaifu's Prose and Criticism after 1989." MPhil Thesis, Hong Kong University of Science and Technology, 2018.
Quah, Sy Ren. *Gao Xingjian and Transcultural Chinese Theater*. Honolulu: University of Hawai'i Press, 2004.
Rajewsky, Irina O. "Intermediality, Intertextuality, and Remediation: A Literary Perspective on Intermediality." *Intermédialitiés* 6 (2005): 43–64.
Rawls, John. *Political Liberalism*, expanded edition. New York: Columbia University Press, 2005.
Reshetar, John Stephen. *Problems of Analyzing and Predicting Soviet Behavior*. Garden City, NJ: Doubleday, 1955.
Rippl, Gabriele. "English Literature and Its Other: Toward a Poetics of Intermediality." In *ImageScapes: Studies in Intermediality*, ed. Christian J. Emden and Gabriele Rippl, 39–65. Bern, Switzerland: Peter Lang, 2010.
Rojas, Carlos. *The Naked Gaze: Reflections on Chinese Modernity*. Cambridge, MA: Harvard University Asia Center, 2008.
Rošker, Jana. "The Abolishment of Substance and Ontology: A New Interpretation of Zhang Dongsun's Pluralistic Epistemology." *Synthesis Philosophica* 47, no. 1 (2009): 153–165.
——. *Becoming Human: Li Zehou's Ethics*. Leiden, Netherlands: Brill, 2020.
——. *Following His Own Path: Li Zehou and Contemporary Chinese Philosophy*. Albany: State University of New York Press, 2019.

Rutherford, J., ed. *Identity, Community, Culture, Difference*. London: Lawrence and Wishart, 1990.
Russell, Bertrand. *History of Western Philosophy*. New York: Simon & Schuster, 1945.
Said, Edward. *Representation of the Intellectual*. New York: Pantheon, 1994.
Sandel, Michael J. *Justice: What Is the Right Thing To Do?* New York: Farrar, Straus, and Giroux, 2010.
Schwartz, Benjamin I. *The World of Thought in Ancient China*. Cambridge, MA: The Belknap Press of Harvard University Press, 1985.
Shapiro, Judith. *Mao's War Against Nature: Politics and the Environment in Revolutionary China*. Cambridge: Cambridge University Press, 2001.
Shen Congwen 沈從文. "Yizhong xinde wenyiguan" 一種新的文藝觀 [A new artistic view]. *Wenchao yuekan* 文潮月刊 1, no. 5 (September 1, 1946).
Shum, Sau Ching Janet. "Diasporic Aesthetics of Gao Xingjian's Exilic Discourse." PhD diss., Hong Kong University of Science and Technology, 2010.
Si Fangwei 司方維. *Rentong yu jiegou: Taiwan waisheng di'erdai nü zuojia yanjiu* 認同與解構：台灣外省第二代女作家研究 [Identification and deconstruction: A study on female writers of the second-generation mainlanders in Taiwan]. Beijing: Zhongguo shehui kexue chubanshe, 2017.
Silvester, Rosalind. "Intermediality and Film Consciousness in Gao Xingjian's *La Silhouette Sinon L'ombre*." *Forum for Modern Language Studies* 55, no. 1 (2019): 53–74.
Soja, Edward W. *Thirdspace: Journeys to Los Angeles and Other Real-and-Imagined Places*. Malden, MA: Blackwell, 1996.
Song Weijie 宋偉傑. *Cong yule xingwei dao wutuobang chongdong: Jin Yong xiaoshuo zai jiedu* 從娛樂行為到烏托邦衝動—金庸小說再解讀 [From entertainment to the utopian impulse: Rereading Jin Yong's novels]. Nanjing: Jiangsu renmin chuban she, 1999.
——. "Nation-State, Individual Identity, and Historical Memory: Conflicts Between Han and Non-Han Peoples in Jin Yong's Novels." In *The Jin Yong Phenomenon*, ed. Ann Huss and Liu Jianmei, 121–154. Youngstown, NY: Cambria Press, 2007.
——. "Space, Swordsman, and Utopia: The Dualistic Imagination in Jin Yong's Narratives." In *The Jin Yong Phenomenon*, ed. Ann Huss and Liu Jianmei, 155–178. Youngstown, NY: Cambria Press, 2007.
Sun Ge 孫歌. "Goulian qi shengming zhong de jiyi" 勾連起生命中的記憶 [Recalling the memories in life]. In Chu Tien-Hsin. *Lieren men* 獵人們 [The hunters], 14–21. Beijing: Sanlian shudian, 2006.
Sylvester, David. *Magritte, The Silence of the World*. New York: The Menil Foundation Inc., 1992.
Sze-Lorrain, Fiona. "Bodies and Paintings: Gao Xingjian's *After the Flood*." In *Gao Xingjian and Transmedia Aesthetics*, ed. Mabel Lee and Liu Jianmei, 195–200. Amherst, NY: Cambria Press, 2018.

———, ed. *Silhouette/Shadow: The Cinematic Art of Gao Xingjian*. Paris: Contours, 2007.

Tam, Kwok-kan. "The Mind's Eye: Subjectivity in Gao Xingjian's Paintings." In *Gao Xingjian and Transmedia Aesthetics*, ed. Mabel Lee and Liu Jianmei, 141–168. Amherst, NY: Cambria Press, 2018.

Tan Tianli 譚天麗. "Xi Xi bixia de shengnü" 西西筆下的剩女 [The leftover women under Xi Xi's pen]. *Cultural Studies MCS* 34 (April 2013): 49–61.

Tao Jiang. "Isaiah Berlin's Challenge to Zhuangzian Freedom." *Journal of Chinese Philosophy*. Supplement to vol. 39 (2012): 69–92.

Taylor, Charles. "What's Wrong with Negative Freedom?" In *The Liberty Reader*, ed. David Miller. London: Routledge, 2016.

Tian Xiaofei. "Seeing with the Mind's Eye: The Eastern Jin Discourse of Visualization and Imagination." *Asia Major* 18, no. 2 (2005): 67–102.

———. "The Ship in a Bottle: The Construction of an Imaginary China in Jin Yong's Fiction." In *The Jin Yong Phenomenon*, ed. Ann Huss and Liu Jianmei, 219–240. Youngstown, NY: Cambria Press, 2007.

Tsai, Chien-Hsin. "The Heterotopia Agent in Chu T'ien-hsin's 'The Old Capital.'" *Concentric: Literary and Cultural Studies* 38, no. 2 (September 2012): 139–160.

Tsou Tang 鄒讜, "Geming yu gaobie geming—gei Gaobie geming zuozhe de yifeng xin" 革命與告別革命——給《告別革命》作者的一封信 [Revolution and farewell to revolution—A letter to the authors of *Farewell to Revolution*]. In Li Zehou and Liu Zaifu, *Gaobie geming* 告別革命 [Farewell to revolution], 7–24. Hong Kong: Tiandi, 2015.

Tu Hang. "Pleasure and Sin: Li Zehou, Liu Zaifu, and the Political-Theological Motif in Post-Mao Cultural Reflections." *Prism: Theory and Modern Chinese Literature* 17, no. 1 (2020): 157–171.

———. *Sentimental Republic: Chinese Intellectuals and the Maoist Past*. Cambridge, MA: Forthcoming from Harvard University Asia Center Publications Program, 2025.

Veg, Sebastian. *Minjian: The Rise of China's Grassroots Intellectuals*. New York: Columbia University Press, 2019.

Waley, Arthur. *The Way and Its Power: Lao Tzu's Tao Te Ching and Its Place in Chinese Thought*. New York: Grove, 1934.

Wang, David Der-wei. *Fin-de-Siècle Splendor: Repressed Modernities of Late Qing Fiction, 1848–1911*. Stanford, CA: Stanford University Press, 1997.

———. "Introduction: Chinese Literature Across the Borderlands." *Prism: Theory and Modern Chinese Literature* 18, no. 2 (October 2021): 315–320.

———. *The Lyrical in Epic Time: Modern Chinese Intellectuals and Artists Through the 1949 Crisis*. New York: Columbia University Press, 2015.

———, ed. *A New Literary History of Modern China*. Cambridge, MA: The Belknap Press of Harvard University Press, 2017.

———. "Shitong san, xiaoshuo xing" 史統散, 小說興 [The tradition of historical writing is disappearing and fiction is emerging]. Preface to the Taiwan edition of

Chan Koonchung, *Jianfeng ernian: Xin Zhongguo wuyoushi*, 4–19. Taibei: Maitian, 2015.

———. "Standing Alone atop the Mountain, Walking Freely Under the Sea: On Liu Zaifu and Five Autobiographical Accounts." *Prism: Theory and Modern Chinese Literature* 17, no. 1 (2020): 143–156.

———. "Xulun: Laolinghun qianshi jinsheng—Zhu Tianxin de xiaoshuo" 序論：老靈魂前世今生—朱天心的小說 [Prefatory remarks: Old souls reincarnated—The novels of Zhu Tianxin]. In Chu Tien-hsin. *Gudu* 古都 [The old capital], 5–27. Taipei: Ink Publishing, 2002.

Wang Fansen 王汎森. "Fan zhuyi de sixiang yanlun: Hou Wusi zhengzhi siwei de fenlie" 反主義的思想言論—後五四政治思維的分裂 [Anti-Doctrinism Discourse: The Split in the Political Thoughts in Post–May Fourth China]. *Dongya guannian shi jikan* 東亞觀念史集刊 14 (June 2018): 3–32.

Wang Zhongjiang and Kuang Zhao. "Ultimate Concern, Reflection of Civilization, and the Idea of 'Man' in Yin Haiguang." *Frontiers of Philosophy in China* 6, no. 4 (December 2011): 565–584.

Weber, Max. "The Meaning of 'Ethical Neutrality' in Sociology and Economics." In *The Methodology of the Social Sciences*, trans. and ed. Edward Shills and Henry Finch, 50–112. Glencoe, IL: The Free Press of Glencoe, 1949.

———. *The Methodology of the Social Sciences*. Trans. and ed. Edward Shills and Henry Finch. Glencoe, IL: The Free Press of Glencoe, 1949.

———. "'Objectivity' in Social Science and Social Policy." In *The Methodology of the Social Sciences*, transl. and ed. Edward Shills and Henry Finch, 1–47. Glencoe, IL: The Free Press of Glencoe, 1949.

Wolf, Werner. "Intermediality." In *Routledge Encyclopaedia of Narrative Theory*, ed. David Herman, Manfred Jahn, and Marie-Laure Ryan, 252–256. London: Routledge, 2005.

Wu Lichang 吳立昌, ed. *Wenxue de xiaojie he fanxiaojie: Zhongguo xiandai wenxue paibie lunzhengshi lun* 文學的消解和反消解—中國現代文學派別論爭史論 [The dissolution and antidissolution of literature: On the debates of modern Chinese literary schools]. Shanghai: Fudan daxue chubanshe, 2004.

Wu Shengqing. *Modern Archaics: Continuity and Innovation in the Chinese Lyric Tradition, 1900–1937*. Cambridge, MA: Harvard University Asia Center, 2013.

———. *Photo Poetics: Chinese Lyricism and Modern Media Culture*. New York: Columbia University Press, 2020.

Wu Xinyi 吳忻怡, "Chengwei rentong guanzhao de tazhe—Zhu Tianxin jiqi xiangguan yanjiu de shehuixue kaocha" 成為認同關照的他者—朱天心及其相關研究的社會學考察 [Becoming "the other" of identification: A sociological examination of Chu Tien-hsin and her related research]. *Taiwan Shehui Xuekang* 41 (December 2008): 1–58.

Xi Xi 西西. *Marvels of a Floating City and Other Stories*. Ed. Eva Hung. Hong Kong: Research Center for Translation, the Chinese University of Hong Kong, 1997.

——. *My City: A Hong Kong Story*. Trans. Eva Hung. Hong Kong: Research Center for Translation, the Chinese University of Hong Kong, 1993.

Xiao Qian 蕭乾. "Ni J. Masaryk yishu 擬 J. 瑪薩里克遺書" [Imitating the obituary of J. Masaryk] *Guancha* 觀察 4, no. 7 (April 1948).

Xiao Tie. *Revolutionary Waves: The Crowd in Modern China*. Cambridge, MA: Harvard University Asia Center, 2017.

Xie Xiaodong 謝曉東. *Xiandai xinrujia yu ziyou zhuyi: Xu Fuguan Yin Haiguang zhengzhi zhexue bijiao yanjiu* 現代新儒家與自由主義：徐復觀殷海光政治哲學比較研究 [Modern new Confucianism and freedom: The comparative research on Xu Fuguan's and Yin Haiguang's political philosophy]. Beijing: Dongfang chubanshe, 2008.

Xu Jilin, Liu Qing, Luo Gang, and Xue Yi. "In Search of a 'Third Way': A Conversation Regarding 'Liberalism' and the 'New Left Wing'." In *Voicing Concerns: Contemporary Chinese Critical Inquiry*, ed. Gloria Davies, 199–226. Lanham: Rowman & Littlefield, 2001.

Yahuda, Michael. *Hong Kong: China's Challenge*. London: Routledge, 1996.

Yan Lianke 閻連科. "A Village Greater than the World: Acceptance Speech for the 2021 Newman Prize for Chinese Literature," trans. Eric Abrahamsen. *Chinese Literature Today* 10, no. 1 (2021): 12–15.

Yang Lige 楊莉歌. *Jin Yong chuanshuo* 金庸傳說 [The legend of Jin Yong]. Hong Kong: Ciwenhua youxian gongsi, 1997.

Yang Shuiyuan 楊水遠. "Zuowei siwei fangshi he lunzheng fangfa de Heige'er: Liu Zaifu zhuti xing wenlun sixiang laiyuan zai kaocha" 作為思維方式和論證方法的黑格爾：劉再復主體性文論思想來源再考察. [Hegel as a way of thought and method of argument: Reexamination of the origin of thought of Liu Zaifu's subjectivity]. *Huawen wenxue* 華文文學 [Sinophone literature] 4 (2018): 5–13.

Yap Key-chong. "Western Wisdom in the Mind's Eye of a Westernized Chinese Lay Buddhist: The Thought of Chang Tung-sun (1886–1962)." PhD diss., Hilary Term, University of Oxford, 1991.

Ye Qing 叶青. *Zhang Dongsun zhexue pipan* 張東蓀哲學批判 [The criticism of Zhang Dongsun's philosophy]. Shanghai: Xinken shudian, 1934.

Yeung, Jessica. *Ink Dances in Limbo: Gao Xingjian's Writing as Cultural Translation*. Hong Kong: Hong Kong University Press, 2008.

Yin Haiguang 殷海光. "Cong youyanse de sixiang dao wuyanse de sixiang" 從有顏色的思想到無顏色的思想 [From the colorful thought to the colorless thought]. In *Xueshu yu sixiang (er)* 學術與思想 (二) [Scholarship and thought, part two], vol. 14: 957–994. *Yin Haiguang quanji* 殷海光全集 [Complete works of Yin Haiguang], ed. Lin Zhenghong 林正弘. Taipei: Guiguang tushu, 1990.

——. "Fan bu'er xiweike zhuyi" 反布爾希維克主義 [Against Bolshevism]. In *Zhengzhi yu shehui (shang)* 政治與社會 （上） [Politics and society (part 1)], vol. 11:141–149. *Yin Haiguang quanji* 殷海光全集 [Complete works of Yin Haiguang], ed. Lin Zhenghong. Taipei: Guiguang tushu, 1990.

——. "Fangong dalu wenti" 反攻大陸問題 [The problem of counterattacking the mainland]. In *Zhengzhi yu shehui (shang)* 政治與社會 （上） [Politics and society (part 1)], vol. 11: 509–521. *Yin Haiguang quanji* 殷海光全集 [Complete works of Yin Haiguang], ed. Lin Zhenghong. Taipei: Guiguang tushu, 1990.

——. "Ganjin shoushi renxin" 趕緊收拾人心 [Quickly collect people's hearts]. In *Zhengzhi yu shehui (shang)* 政治與社會 （上） [Politics and society (part 1)], vol. 11: 31–34. *Yin Haiguang quanji* 殷海光全集 [Complete works of Yin Haiguang], ed. Lin Zhenghong. Taipei: Guiguang tushu, 1990.

——. "Guanyu 'fangong dalu wenti' de wenti" 關於"反攻大陸問題"的問題 [Regarding the problem of "the problem of counterattacking the mainland"]. In *Zhengzhi yu shehui (shang)* 政治與社會 （上） [Politics and society (part 1)], vol. 11: 523–534. *Yin Haiguang quanji* 殷海光全集 [Complete works of Yin Haiguang], ed. Lin Zhenghong. Taipei: Guiguang tushu, 1990.

——. "Hongweibing shi yihetuan ma" 紅衛兵是義和團嗎? [Is the Red Guard the Boxer Rebellion?]. In *Zhengzhi yu shehui (xia)* 政治與社會 （下）, [Politics and society (part 2)], vol. 12: 1011–1021. *Yin Haiguang quanji* 殷海光全集 [Complete works of Yin Haiguang], ed. Lin Zhenghong. Taipei: Guiguang tushu, 1990.

——. "Hu Shih lun 'rongren yu ziyou' duhou" 胡適論《容忍與自由》讀後 [After reading Hu Shih's "Tolerance and Freedom"]. In *Zhengzhi yu shehui (xia)* 政治與社會 （下）, [Politics and society (part 2)], vol. 12: 781–789. *Yin Haiguang quanji* 殷海光全集 [Complete works of Yin Haiguang], ed. Lin Zhenghong. Taipei: Guiguang tushu, 1990.

——. "Jiaoyubu zhang Zhang Qiyun de minzhuguan: Junzhu de minzhu" 教育部長張其昀的民主觀——君主的民主 [The democratic view of the Minister of Education Zhang Qiyun—The democracy of a monarch]. In *Zhengzhi yu shehui (shang)* 政治與社會 （上） [Politics and society (part 1)], vol. 11: 405–413. *Yin Haiguang quanji* 殷海光全集 [Complete works of Yin Haiguang], ed. Lin Zhenghong. Taipei: Guiguang tushu, 1990.

——. "Kuangtu de baotiao" 狂徒的暴跳 [The violent jump of the crazy ones]. In *Zhengzhi yu shehui (xia)* 政治與社會 （下）, [Politics and society (part 2)], vol. 12: 1033–1043. *Yin Haiguang quanji* 殷海光全集 [Complete works of Yin Haiguang], ed. Lin Zhenghong. Taipei: Guiguang tushu, 1990.

——. "Lun erfen fa" 論二分法 [On dichotomy]. In *Zhengzhi yu shehui (xia)* 政治與社會 （下）, [Politics and society (part 2)], vol. 12: 685–695. *Yin Haiguang quanji* 殷海光全集 [Complete works of Yin Haiguang], ed. Lin Zhenghong. Taipei: Guiguang tushu, 1990.

——. "Lun meiyou yanse de sixiang" 論沒有顏色的思想 [On colorless thought]. In *Xueshu yu sixiang (yi)* 學術與思想 （一） [Scholarship and thought (part 1)], vol.

13: 23–36. *Yin Haiguang quanji* 殷海光全集 [Complete works of Yin Haiguang], ed. Lin Zhenghong. Taipei: Guiguang tushu, 1990.

——. "Lun ziyou zhuyi zhe jiqi renwu" 論自由主義者及其任務 [On liberals and their duties]. In *Zhengzhi yu shehui (xia)* 政治與社會 （下） [Politics and society (part 2)], vol. 12: 763–770. *Yin Haiguang quanji* 殷海光全集 [Complete works of Yin Haiguang], ed. Lin Zhenghong. Taipei: Guiguang tushu, 1990.

——. "Minzhu di shijin shi" 民主底試金石 [The touchstone of democracy]. In *Zhengzhi yu shehui (shang)* 政治與社會 （上） [Politics and society (part 1)], vol. 11: 355–373. *Yin Haiguang quanji* 殷海光全集 [Complete works of Yin Haiguang], ed. Lin Zhenghong. Taipei: Guiguang tushu, 1990.

——. "Pouxi Guomindang" 剖析國民黨 [An anatomy of the KMT]. In *Zhengzhi yu shehui (xia)* 政治與社會 （下）, [Politics and society (part 2)], vol. 12: 1117–1156. *Yin Haiguang quanji* 殷海光全集 [Complete works of Yin Haiguang], ed. Lin Zhenghong. Taipei: Guiguang tushu, 1990.

——. "The Self-Preface of the Selection of Yin Haiguang." In *Yin Haiguang jinzuo xuan* 殷海光近作選 [The select recent works of Yin Haiguang], 1–2. Hong Kong: The Committee of Haiguang Selective Collections, 1969.

——. "Shi shenme, jiu shuo shenme" 是什麼，就說什麼 [To say what it is]. In *Zhengzhi yu shehui (shang)* 政治與社會 （上） [Politics and society (part 1)], vol. 11: 499–507. *Complete works of Yin Haiguang*, ed. Lin Zhenghong. Taipei: Guiguang tushu, 1990.

——. "Wenhua de zisha" 文化的自殺 [The suicidal culture]. In *Zhengzhi yu shehui (xia)* 政治與社會 （下）, [Politics and society (part 2)], vol. 12: 1045–1055. *Yin Haiguang quanji* 殷海光全集 [Complete works of Yin Haiguang], ed. Lin Zhenghong. Taipei: Guiguang tushu, 1990.

——. "Wo dui guogong de kanfa" 我對國共的看法 [My opinions toward the KMT and the CCP]. In *Zhengzhi yu shehui (shang)* 政治與社會 （上） [Politics and society (part one)], vol. 11: 25–29. *Yin Haiguang quanji* 殷海光全集 [Complete works of Yin Haiguang], ed. Lin Zhenghong. Taipei: Guiguang tushu, 1990.

——. "Women zou natiao lu" 我們走哪條路？ [Which road should we take?]. In *Zhengzhi yu shehui (shang)* 政治與社會 （上） [Politics and society (part 1)], vol. 11: 5–23. *Yin Haiguang quanji* 殷海光全集 [Complete works of Yin Haiguang], ed. Lin Zhenghong. Taipei: Guiguang tushu, 1990.

——. "Wo weishenme fangong" 我為什麼反共 [Why do I oppose the CCP?]. In *Zhengzhi yu shehui (shang)* 政治與社會 （上） [Politics and society (part 1)], vol. 11: 247–267. *Yin Haiguang quanji* 殷海光全集 [Complete works of Yin Haiguang], ed. Lin Zhenghong. Taipei: Guiguang tushu, 1990.

——. "Xiang fenmu jinjun" 向墳墓進軍 [Marching toward the cemetery]. In *Zhengzhi yu shehui (xia)* 政治與社會 （下）, [Politics and society (part 2)], vol. 12: 1057–1068. *Yin Haiguang quanji* 殷海光全集 [Complete works of Yin Haiguang], ed. Lin Zhenghong. Taipei: Guiguang tushu, 1990.

———. "Xueshu jiaoyu ying duli yu zhengzhi" 學術教育應獨立於政治 [Academic education should be independent from politics]. In *Zhengzhi yu shehui (xia)* 政治與社會 （下）, [Politics and society (part 2)], vol. 12: 579–586. *Yin Haiguang quanji* 殷海光全集 [Complete works of Yin Haiguang], ed. Lin Zhenghong. Taipei: Guiguang tushu, 1990.

———. "Yaodong xinli de fenxi" 窯洞心理的分析 [The analysis of cave psychology]. In *Zhengzhi yu shehui (xia)* 政治與社會 （下）, [Politics and society (part 2)], vol. 12: 1069–1080. *Yin Haiguang quanji* 殷海光全集 [Complete works of Yin Haiguang], ed. Lin Zhenghong. Taipei: Guiguang tushu, 1990.

———. "Zenyang panbie shifei" 怎樣判別是非 [How to distinguish right and wrong]. In *Xueshu yu sixiang (er)* 學術與思想(二) [Scholarship and thought, part 2], vol. 14: 761–836. *Yin Haiguang quanji* 殷海光全集 [Complete works of Yin Haiguang], ed. Lin Zhenghong. Taipei: Guiguang tushu, 1990.

———. "Zheshi Guomindang fanxing de shihou" 這是國民黨反省的時候 [It is time that the KMT should reflect]. In *Zhengzhi yu shehui (shang)* 政治與社會 （上） [Politics and society (part 1)], vol. 11: 347–354. *The Yin Haiguang quanji* 殷海光全集 [Complete works of Yin Haiguang], ed. Lin Zhenghong. Taipei: Guiguang tushu, 1990.

———. "Zheyang de hongweibing" 這樣的紅衛兵 [This kind of red guard]. In *Zhengzhi yu shehui (xia)* 政治與社會 （下） [Politics and society (part 2)], vol 12: 999–1010. *Yin Haiguang quanji* 殷海光全集 [Complete works of Yin Haiguang], ed. Lin Zhenghong. Taipei: Guiguang tushu, 1990.

———. "Zhi Hu Yue" 致胡越 [To Hu Yue] (January 3, 1967). In *Yin Haiguang shuxin ji* 殷海光書信集 [The correspondence of Yin Haiguang], vol. 10: 26–31. *Yin Haiguang quanji* 殷海光全集 [Complete works of Yin Haiguang], ed. Lin Zhenghong. Taipei: Guiguang tushu, 1990.

———. "Zhi Zhang Hao 致張灝 [To Zhang Hao] (March 8, 1967)." In *Yin Haiguang shuxin ji* 殷海光書信集 [The Correspondences of Yin Haiguang], vol. 10: 164–175. *Yin Haiguang quanji* 殷海光全集 [Complete works of Yin Haiguang], ed. Lin Zhenghong. Taipei: Guiguang tushu, 1990.

———. "Zhongguo gongchandang zhi guancha" 中國共產黨之觀察 [Observations on the CCP]. In vol. 1 of *Yin Haiguang quanji* 殷海光全集 [Complete works of Yin Haiguang], ed. Lin Zhenghong. Taipei: Guiguang tushu, 1990.

———. *Zhongguo wenhua de zhanwang* 中國文化的展望 [The viewpoints of Chinese culture]. In vol. 7 of *Yin Haiguang quanji* 殷海光全集 [Complete works of Yin Haiguang], ed. Lin Zhenghong. Taipei: Guiguang tushu, 1990.

———. "Zidong de ba nongbao chuopo le" 自動的把膿包戳破了 [Automatically popped a pustule]. In *Zhengzhi yu shehui (xia)* 政治與社會 （下） [Politics and society (part 2)], vol. 12: 1023–1032. *Yin Haiguang quanji* 殷海光全集 [Complete works of Yin Haiguang], ed. Lin Zhenghong. Taipei: Guiguang tushu, 1990.

———. "Ziran sixiang yu renwen sixiang" 自然思想與人文思想 [Natural thought and humanistic thought]. In *Xueshu yu sixiang (yi)* 學術與思想(一) [*Scholarship and thought (part one)*], vol. 13: 321–351. *Yin Haiguang quanji* 殷海光全集 [Complete works of Yin Haiguang], ed. Lin Zhenghong. Taipei: Guiguang tushu, 1990.

———. "Ziyou de lunli jichu" 自由的倫理基礎 [The ethical foundation of freedom]. In *Xueshu yu sixiang (san)* 學術與思想(三) [*Scholarship and thought (part three)*], vol. 15: 1139–1199. *Yin Haiguang quanji* 殷海光全集 [Complete works of Yin Haiguang], ed. Lin Zhenghong. Taipei: Guiguang tushu, 1990.

Yü Ying-shih 余英時. *Qian Mu yu zhongguo wenhua* 錢穆與中國文化 [Qian Mu and Chinese culture]. Shanghai: Yuandong chubanshe, 1994.

———. "The Radicalization of China in the Twentieth Century." *Daedalus* 122, no. 2 (Spring 1993): 125–150.

———. "Zailun Zhongguo sixiang zhong de jijin yu baoshou: Da Jiang Yihua xiansheng" 再論中國思想中的激進與保守—答姜義華先生 [Re-discussing the radicals and the conservatives in modern Chinese thought—Answering Mr. Jiang Yihua]. *Ershiyi shiji* 二十一世紀 10 (April 1992): 143–149.

———. "Zhongguo xiandai sixiangshi de jijin yu baoshou" 中國現代思想史的激進與保守 [The radicals and conservatives in the history of modern Chinese thought]. In Yü Ying-shih, *Qian Mu yu Zhongguo wenhua* 錢穆與中國文化 [Qian Mu and Chinese culture], 188–222. Shanghai: Yuandong chubanshe, 1994.

Yu Zhansui. *Questioning the Chinese Model: Oppositional Political Novels in Early Twenty-First Century China*. Toronto, ON: University of Toronto Press, 2022.

Yuan Zeng. "Beyond Control and Resistance: The Dual Narrative of the Coronavirus Outbreak in Digital China." In *Political Communication in the Time of Coronavirus*, ed. Peter Van Aelst and Jay G. Blumler, 33–47. New York: Routledge, 2022.

Yue Huanyu. "Inlaying Images and Seeing Poetry." In *Gao Xingjian and Transmedia Aesthetics*, ed. Mabel Lee and Liu Jianmei, 217–228. Amherst, NY: Cambria Press, 2018.

Zarader, Jean-Pierre. "Gao Xingjian and Philosophy." In *Gao Xingjian and Transmedia Aesthetics*, ed. Mabel Lee and Liu Jianmei, 23–42. Amherst, NY: Cambria Press, 2018.

———. "Requiem for Beauty." In Gao Xingjian. *Mei de zangli* 美的葬禮. [Requiem for beauty], 36–46. Taipei: National Taiwan Normal University, 2016.

Zhang Dongsun 張東蓀. "Bianzhengfa de gezhong wenti" 辯證法的各種問題 [Various kinds of problems of dialectics]. In *Zhang Dongsun juan* 張東蓀卷 [The volume of Zhang Dongsun], ed. Zuo Yuhe 左玉河, 331–337. Beijing: Zhongguo renmin chubanshe, 2015.

———. "Duikang lun zhi jiazhi" 對抗論之價值 [The value of the antagonist theory]. *Yongyan* 1, no. 24 (November 16, 1913).

———. "Duoyuan lun renshi chongshu" 多元論認識重述 [The reiteration of epistemological pluralism]. *Dongfang zazhi* 東方雜誌 [The eastern miscellany] 33, no. 19 (1936).

———. "Guomin wuzui" 國民無罪 [The citizen does not have a crime]. *Zaisheng* 再生 [The national renaissance] 1, no. 8 (December 20, 1932).

——. *Lixing yu minzhu* 理性與民主 [Rationality and democracy]. Changsha: Yuelu shushe, 2010.

——. *Minzhu zhuyi yu shehui zhuyi* 民主主義與社會主義 [Democracy and socialism]. Shanghai: Shanghai guanchashe, 1948.

——. "Minzhu zhuyi yu shehui zhuyi buyi" 民主主義與社會主義補遺 [The supplements of *Democracy and Socialism*]. *Guancha* 觀察 [Observations] 5, nos. 1, 2, 3 (August 28, September 4, September 11, 1948).

——. "Nidi yu disanzhe zhi zeren" 昵敵與第三者之責任 [The responsibility of the intimate enemy and the third person]. *Zhonghua zazhi* 中華雜誌 [China journal] 1, no. 8 (August 1, 1914): 5–6.

——. "Renshi de duoyuan lun" 認識的多元論 [Theory of epistemological pluralism]. In *Lixing yu liangzhi: Zhang Dongsun wenxuan* 理性與良知：張東蓀文選 [Rationality and conscience: The selection of Zhang Dongsun essays], ed. Zhang Rulun 張汝倫, 58–109. Shanghai: Shanghai yuandong chubanshe, 1995.

——. *Renshi lun* 認識論 [Epistemology]. Shanghai: Shangwu yinshu guan, 2017.

——. "Renshi lun de duoyuanlun" 認識論的多元論 [Theory of epistemological pluralism]. *Dalu zazhi* 大陸雜誌 [Continental magazine] 1, nos. 3, 4, 5 (1932).

——. "Shi de shiming he lixue" 士的使命和理學 [The mission of shi and the study of rationality]. In *Zhang Dongsun juan* 張東蓀卷 [The volume of Zhang Dongsun], ed. Zuo Yuhe 左玉河, 496–500. Beijing: Zhongguo renmin chubanshe, 2015.

——. "Shui neng jiu Zhongguo" 誰能救中國 [Who can save China?]. In *Zhang Dongsun juan* 張東蓀卷 [The volume of Zhang Dongsun], ed. Zuo Yuhe 左玉河, 183–185. Beijing: Zhongguo renmin chubanshe, 2015.

——. *Sixiang yu shehui* 思想與社會 [Thought and society]. Changsha: Yuelu shushe, 2010.

——. "Sixiang ziyou wenti" 思想自由問題 [The problem of freedom of thought]. In *Zhang Dongsun juan* 張東蓀卷 [The volume of Zhang Dongsun], ed. Zuo Yuhe 左玉河, 429–444. Beijing: Zhongguo renmin chubanshe, 2015.

——. "Weiwu bianzhengfa lunzhan" 唯物辯證法論戰 [Debates on Marxist materialistic dialectics]. 2 vols. Beijing: Beiping minyou shudian, 1934.

——. "Xianren zhengzhi" 賢人政治 [The elite politics]. *Dongfang zazhi* 東方雜誌 [The Eastern Miscellany] 11, November 15, 1917.

——. *Xin zhexue luncong* 新哲學論叢 [The collection of new philosophy]. Shanghai: Shanghai shangwu yinshuguan, 1929.

——（under the pen name Qiutong）. "Zhengli xiangbei lun" 政力向背論 [Theory of the political reverse]. In *Jiayin zazhi* 甲寅雜誌 [Tiger Magazine], July 10, 1914.

——. *Zhishi yu wenhua* 知識與文化 [Knowledge and culture]. Changsha: Yuelu sheshe, 2010.

——. "Zhongxi sixiang zhi genben yidian" 中西思想之根本異點 [The fundamental differences between Chinese and Western thoughts]. In *Lixing yu liangzhi:*

Zhang Dongsun wenxuan 理性與良知：張東蓀文選 [Rationality and conscience: The selection of Zhang Dongsun essays], ed. Zhang Rulun 張汝倫, 283–293. Shanghai: Shanghai yuandong chubanshe, 1995.

——. "Zhuishu women nuli jianli 'lianhe zhengfu' de yongyi" 追述我們努力建設"聯合政府"的用意 [Tracing our intention of establishing a United Government]. In *Zhang Dongsun juan* 張東蓀卷 [The volume of Zhang Dongsun], ed. Zuo Yuhe 左玉河, 502–505. Beijing: Zhongguo renmin chubanshe, 2015.

Zhang Jinghe. *Liu Zaifu wenxue xinxing benti lun* 劉再復文學心性本體論 [Liu Zaifu's literary ontology of heart/mind]. Hong Kong: Sanlian, 2020.

Zhang Qing 章清. *Yin Haiguang* 殷海光 [Yin Haiguang]. Taipei: Dongda tushu gongsi, 1996.

Zhang Rulun 張汝倫., ed. *Lixing yu liangzhi: Zhang Dongsun wenxuan* 理性與良知：張東蓀文選 [Rationality and conscience: The selection of Zhang Dongsun essays]. Shanghai: Shanghai yuandong chubanshe, 1995.

——. *Shi de zhexue shi* 詩的哲學史 [Poetry of philosophical history]. Guilin: Guangxi shifan daxue chubanshe, 2002.

——. "Zhongguo xiandai zhexueshi shangde Zhang Dongsun" 中國現代哲學史上的張東蓀 [Zhang Dongsun in the history of modern Chinese philosophy]. In *Lixing yu liangzhi: Zhang Dongsun wenxuan* 理性與良知：張東蓀文選 [Rationality and conscience: The selection of Zhang Dongsun essays], ed. Zhang Rulun, 1–29. Shanghai: Shanghai yuandong chubanshe, 1995.

Zhang Shizhao 章士釗. *Zhang Shizhao quanji* 章士釗全集 [The complete works of Zhang Shizhao]. Shanghai: Wenhui chubanshe, 2000.

Zhang Taiyan 章太炎, "Jufen jinhua lun" 俱分進化論 [Dual evolution theory]. *Minpao* 民報 [People's newspaper], July 1906, 1–13.

Zhang Yaonan 張耀南. *Zhang Dongsun* 張東蓀. Taipei: Dongda tushu gongsi, 1998.

——. "Zhang Dongsun de 'zhishixue' ji 'xinzixue shidai' " 張東蓀的"知識學"及"新子學時代" [Zhang Dongsun's epistemology and the new era of studying traditional philosophers]. In Zhang Dongsun *Renshi lun* 認識論 [Epistemology], 141–179. Shanghai: Shangwu yinshu guan, 2017.

——. *Zhang Dongsun zhishilun yanjiu* 張東蓀知識論研究 [Studies of epistemology]. Taipei: Hongye wenhua, 1995.

Zhang Zhongdong 張忠棟. *Hu Shi, Lei Zhen, Yin Haiguang: Ziyou zhuyi renwu huaxiang* 胡適、雷震、殷海光—自由主義人物畫像 [Hu Shi, Lei Zhen, Yin Haiguang—The portraits of liberal figures]. Taipei: Zili baoxi chuban, 1990.

——. "Similarities and Differences Between Hu Shi and Yin Haiguang During the Initial Stage of Anti-Communism." *Chinese Studies in History* 38, no. 1 (2004): 77–93.

Zhao Qi 趙崎. *Mengzi zhushu* 孟子注疏 [Commentary on Mencius]. Shanghai: Shanghai guji chubanshe, 1990.

Zhou Zuoren 周作人. "Wode zaxue" 我的雜學 [My miscellaneous studies]. In *Zhitang huixiang lu* 知堂回想錄 [The memoir of Zhitang]. In *Zhou Zuoren zibian wenji* 周作人自編文集 [The self-edited collection of Zhou Zuoren], 746–799. Shijiazhuang: Hebei jiaoyu chubanshe, 2002.

———. "Ziji de yuandi" 自己的園地 [My own garden]. In *Ziji de yuandi* 自己的園地 [My own garden]. *Zhou Zuoren zibian wenji* 周作人自編文集 [Self-edited collection of Zhou Zuoren], 5–7. Shijiazhuang: Hebei jiaoyu chubanshe, 2002.

Zhu Guangqian 朱光潛. "Tan qunzhong peiyang qienuo yu xiongcan" 談群眾培養怯懦與兇殘 [On the mass's cultivation of cowardness and atrocity]. *Zhoulun* 周論 1, no. 5, February 13, 1948.

———. "Zhongguo sixiang de weiji" 中國思想的危機 [The crisis of Chinese thought]. In *Zhu Guangqian quanji* 朱光潛全集 [The complete collection of Zhu Guangqian], vol. 8, 514–518. Hefei: Anhui jiaoyu chubanshe, 1991.

Zhu Ziqing 朱自清. *Shiyanzhi bian* 詩言志辨 [Classification of poetry that expresses intent]. Shanghai: Kaiming shudian, 1947.

Zong Baihua 宗白華. *Yijing* 藝境 [The vista of art]. Beijing: Shangwu yinshu guan, 2015.

Zuo Yuhe. 左玉河., ed. *Zhang Dongsun juan* 張東蓀卷 [The volume of Zhang Dongsun]. Beijing: Zhongguo renmin chubanshe, 2015.

———. *Zhang Dongsun nianpu* 張東蓀年譜 [A chronicle of Zhang Dongsun's life]. Beijing: Qunyan Press, 2014.

———. *Zhang Dongsun wenhua sixiang yanjiu* 張東蓀文化思想研究 [A study of Zhang Dongsun's cultural thought]. Beijing: Zhongguo shehui kexue chubanshe, 1997.

———, ed. *Zhang Dongsun zhuan* 張東蓀傳 [A biography of Zhang Dongsun]. Jinan: Shandong renmin chuban she, 1998.

Index

absurdist plays, 196
accommodation, 21–22, 47; relativism and, 23–24; yin-yang relation to, 26
"accommodative approach," 270n72
actors, 192, 209, 213
aesthetics, 25–26, 192–193, 212; alternative, 186; freedom of, 161; ontology of, 170; politics relation to, 34; *Requiem for Beauty* and, 220
"Aesthetics of the Artist, The" (Gao Xingjian), 212
aesthetic transcendence, 5, 26–27, 168–169, 170, 248
After the End (Berger), 205
After the Flood (Gao Xingjian), 205–207, 209–211, 212, 214
"Against Bolshevism" (Yin), 91
"Against Liberalism" (Mao), 85
Ah Q, 152, 159–160
Albert, Hans, 101, 119
Aleph, 6, 33, 52, 170, 266n13
Alexander, Samuel, 63, 72
allegorical form, 223–224

alternative aesthetics (*lingyizhong meixue*), 186
Analects (Confucius), 133
"Anatomy of the KMT, An" (Yin), 94
Angelus Novus (painting), 210
animal ethics, heterotopias and, 240–241
Animal Protection Act (1998), 240
animism, 230–231, 235
"Another Kind of Aesthetics" (Gao Xingjian), 192
antagonism (*duikang lun*), 46
antagonistic binaries, 10
anthropocentrism, 241
anti-British colonial movement, Cultural Revolution and, 116–117
Anti-Extradition Law Amendment Bill Movement, 228
antinomy (*erlü beifan*), 153–155, 165–166
antipodal rivalry, 141
Arendt, Hannah, 88
Aristotelian logic, 55
Aristotle, 15, 70, 99, 151

art: freedom in, 27; mechanical techniques and, 183; politics relation to, 25; society relation to, 213; total, 196–197
art revolution, 211
Asahi Shimbun, The (newspaper), 288n11
atomic weapons, 313n52
authoritarianism, 76, 245, 247
authority, freedom *versus*, 47
"awakening" (*jue*), 175

Bachelard, Gaston, 303n63
Bakhtin, Mikhail, 55, 151, 216
balance, competition relation to, 21
Barmé, Geremie R., 252
Baroque aesthetic, 212
Basic Law, 125, 289n44
Basic Law Drafting Committee, 124–125
Bay, Christian, 104
beauty, 17, 211–212, 218–219
benevolent despotism, 92
"benevolent heart" (*buren zhixin*), 137
Benjamin, Walter, 29, 174–175, 177, 183, 206, 218; allegorical form and, 223–224; on *Angelus Novus*, 210
Bentham, Jeremy, 103, 118, 120–121
bentuhua (indigenization), 239
Berger, James, 205
Bergez, Daniel, 191, 202, 212, 217
Berlin, Isaiah, 26, 104, 105; negative freedom and, 128, 159, 249–250, 272n87
Berry, Michael, 260–262
Bertomeu, Thierry, 206
Bhabha, Homi K., 2–3, 56, 136, 157, 173–174, 265n1; on cultural hybridity, 60; on hybrid identity, 143
binarism, 45, 230
binary logic, 96, 97, 131, 155, 157, 263; in society, 130, 158–159; totalitarianism relation to, 14

Bingzai (fictional character), 152
biocentrism, 241
Blackmur, R. P., 215
"bloodline theory" (*xuetong lun*), 238
blue literature, 12
Bodde, Derk, 276n50
Bolshevik mentality, 82
Book of Changes, 144, 165, 248
"Book of South Qi," 68
Borges, Jorge Luis, 6, 52, 170
"both/and" logic, 3, 56, 137, 225–226; of Chan Koonchung, 258–259; either/or mindset relation to, 60
Botticelli, 226
Braudy, Leo, 197
Bryce, James, 21, 46
Buddhism, 53, 66, 72, 140–141, 145, 204; *Dream of the Red Chamber* relation to, 179; emptiness and, 302n52; Mahayana, 291n79, 302n53; *Semigods and the Semidevils, The* relation to, 138–141. *See also* Chan Buddhism
bu rentong de ziyou ("freedom of nonidentification"), 238–239
buren zhixin ("benevolent heart"), 137

Cai Yuanpei, 170, 210
"Can Democracy Be Practiced?" (Jin Yong), 124
Caojian renyu (Zhang Dongsun), 279n105
Cao Xueqin, 135, 166–167, 170, 178
capitalism, 38–39, 42, 177, 258–259; democracy and, 43–44; individualism relation to, 60–61
"Carefree as a Bird" (Gao Xingjian), 198, 202–204
"Carry the Revolution Through the End" (Mao), 252
Castle in the Pyrenees, The (painting), *xii*, 1, 21, 223

causality, 187–188
CCP. *See* Chinese Communist Party
Celestial Eye, The (painting), *31*
Central Daily, The (newspaper), 83, 87, 90
Cha, Louis. *See* Jin Yong
Chan, Shelby, 192
Chan Buddhism, 30, 160, 189–191, 193, 194; death relation to, 200; *Dream of the Red Chamber* relation to, 179; Gao Xingjian relation to, 186–187, 202; middle way in, 7, 14, 165–166; nonduality and, 163–164, 169, 248; "sudden enlightenment" and, 29, 176, 178, 189
Chang Hao, 94
Chan Koonchung, 23, 259; heterotopias relation to, 33, 254–255, 256–257; *Second Year of Jianfeng, The* of, 36, 246, 252–258
Chan state, 29, 186–189, 191, 193–194, 204; Christianity relation to, 202; fragmentary writing relation to, 180; in *Soul Mountain*, 200; third eye relation to, 31
character composition, 150, 151
Chen Duxiu, 10, 41–42, 271n76
Chen Lingchei Letty, 237
Cheng Li, 229
Chen, Ming-Jer, 15
Chen Mo, 137
Chen Pingyuan, 112, 132
Chen Shixiang, 138, 215
Chen Yi, 116
Chen Yizi, 148
Cheung Lik-kwan, 277n65
Chiang Ching-kuo, 120, 256
Chiang Kai-shek, 24, 93, 94, 95, 253, 257; Yin relation to, 80, 82, 83, 90, 91
chifan zhexue ("philosophy of eating"), 165

"child prodigies," 227–228
China Journal, 41
China Times, The (newspaper), 41
Chinese Communist Party (CCP), 9–10, 22, 43, 107, 159, 266n20; heart relation to, 171; Jin Yong relation to, 116, 117–118, 119, 288n22; KMT relation to, 39, 94; in *Second Year of Jianfeng, The*, 252–253, 255–256; Taiwan relation to, 121; Yin relation to, 79–80, 82, 83–87, 89, 95, 102; Zhang Dongsun relation to, 12, 44
Chinese Democratic League, 44
Chinese Mind, The (Moore), 55
Chinese modernity, 4, 51, 61; Zhang Dongsun relation to, 40
Chinese Nationalist Party (KMT), 12–13, 22, 42, 43–44, 95, 107; binary logic relation to, 97; CCP relation to, 39, 94; Chu Tien-hsin relation to, 235, 236; Jin Yong relation to, 119; in *Second Year of Jianfeng, The*, 252–253, 257; Yin relation to, 79–80, 82–84, 86, 90–95, 102
Chiu-Duke, Josephine, 254
Chi Zijian, 228, 242–243; *Last Quarter of the Moon, The* of, 32, 35–36, 222, 229–235
Christianity, 202, 210
Chuang Tzu, 276n50
Chu Anping, 44, 252
Chu Hsi-ning, 235, 309n48
Chu Kao-cheng, 236
Chu Tien-hsin, 23, 222, 236, 243; Ethnic Equality Agreement Alliance and, 237–238, 309n49; heterotopias and, 32, 36, 222, 235; street cats and, 239–242
Chu Tien-wen, 235, 240
ci, 37

cine-poems, 183, 188, 195, 196–197. *See also* Gao Xingjian
civil society, 9, 238; cyberspace relation to, 259–260, 263. *See also* society
civil spontaneous organizations, 266n20
class stratifications, 47
class struggle, 13, 63, 76, 85–86, 150; either/or mindset relation to, 12, 22, 152; Marxism and, 42, 248–249; Zhang Dongsun relation to, 44, 47, 86
close form, 207
Colbertism, 256
cold literature, 194
Cold War mentality, 8, 45, 113–114, 115, 126
Collection of Drizzles (Liu Zaifu), 175
collective unconscious, 58, 60
collective will, 73
collectivism, 18, 148–149; individualism relation to, 104; state-led, 108
Collingwood, R. G., 63
colorful thought, 99, 102
colorless thought, 19, 80–81, 98–99, 100–101, 108, 160; in *Second Year of Jianfeng, The*, 258
Commedia dell'Arte, 305n119
communism, 91, 96–97. *See also* Chinese Communist Party; Marxism
Communist Manifesto, The (Marx), 85
compassion, freedom and, 172
competition, balance relation to, 21
complementary paradox, 19–20
complete drama, 30
"Concerning *Silhouette/Shadow*" (Gao Xingjian), 197
concrescence, 63, 72
Confucianism, 7, 14, 125, 140–141, 159; *du* relation to, 123, 170; liberalism relation to, 107; Lu Jiuyuan and, 170–171; moderation relation to, 100, 165, 271n74; morality and, 28, 102; self-cultivation relation to, 249–250; Xiao Feng relation to, 145; in Yellow River region, 189
Confucius, 133
consciousness, 303n63
consequentialism, 121, 122
conservatism, 266n18
constellation, 29, 174–175
Constitution of Liberty, The (Hayek), 24, 107
contradiction, 15, 247
co-presence, 63
correlation logic (*xiangguanlü mingxue*), 5, 54, 76, 248
correlative duality, 15–16
cosmology, 19, 191; epistemology and, 52–53; of yin-yang, 144; of Zhang Dongsun, 276n55
COVID-19 pandemic, 34, 205
"Crisis of Chinese Thought, The" (Zhu), 11
Criticism on Dream of the Red Chamber (Wang Guowei), 178
Critique of Judgment (Kant), 168–169
Critique of Pure Reason (Kant), 71
cultural hybridity, 60, 63
cultural interactionism, 45, 58, 77
"cultural-psychological formation" (*wenhua xinli jiegou*), 13, 60
Cultural Revolution, 12–13, 28, 89–90, 91–92, 129–130, 148; anti-British colonial movement and, 116–117; either/or mindset in, 184; Jin Yong relation to, 117, 119, 145; radicalization relation to, 9; "school of wandering" and, 157; *Smiling, Proud Wanderer, The* relation to, 132, 134, 290n56; third persons relation to, 51; Zhang Dongsun relation to, 38, 45, 66, 281n145

"cultural satisfaction" (*wenhua manzu gan*), 58
cultural sedimentation (*wenhua jidian*), 60
culture fever, 148, 149–150
cyberspace, 246; civil society relation to, 259–260, 263; monism relation to, 252

Dad, Dad, Dad (Han), 152
Dagong pao (newspaper), 116
Dai Qing, 156
dance, 207, 208–209, 214; in *Requiem for Beauty*, 213
Daoism, 19, 159–160, 208, 302n48; freedom relation to, 28; music relation to, 132
daxia, 292n85
"dead literature" (*si wenxue*), 10
death: of beauty, 211–212; Chan Buddhism relation to, 200; Evenki people relation to, 232
Debates on Marxist Materialistic Dialectics (Zhang Dongsun), 54
"deep ecology," 221
Deer and the Cauldron, The (Jin Yong), 129, 142–145, 161
democracy, 2, 250, 251–252, 257; capitalism and, 43–44; CCP relation to, 84–85; Chinese culture relation to, 101; communism relation to, 91; *Free China* relation to, 87; individualism relation to, 62–63; Jin Yong relation to, 123–125; journalism relation to, 288n11; liberalism and, 259; monarchical, 92; revolution relation to, 85; Taiwan and, 236–237; Zhang Dongsun relation to, 45–46
Democracy and Socialism (Zhang Dongsun), 62

Democratic Action Alliance, 238
Democratic Association, 84–85
Democratic Progressive Party (DPP), 32; Chu Tien-hsin relation to, 235, 236–237; either/or mindset and, 238
democratic socialism, 255, 259
Deng Xiaoping, 78, 109, 116; Jin Yong relation to, 122
"Denouncing Reactionary Literature and Art" (Guo), 12
devas, 291n79
dialectical logic, 15, 225
dialogical transcendence, 248
Diamond Sutra, The, 170–171, 176–177, 178
diaspora, 149
dichotomies, 95, 97, 99; authoritarianism and, 245; in Chinese modernity, 51; gender, 222; Marxism relation to, 56; Zhang Dongsun on, 53–54
Dionysus on the Other Shore (Fusini), 182
disan zhe (third persons), 48, 50–51
dogmatism, 140; dualism and, 136; either/or mindset and, 33; literature and, 151–152
Dostoyevsky, Fyodor, 151
DPP. *See* Democratic Progressive Party
Dream of the Red Chamber (Cao Xueqin), 135–136, 137, 162, 164, 178–179, 298n83; aesthetic transcendence and, 169; heart in, 172; middle way and, 166
Drifting Notes (Liu Zaifu), 174
Driver, Julia, 118
du, 18–19, 48, 248, 249; Confucianism relation to, 123, 170; middle way relation to, 16–17
Du Lanlan, 230
"dual evolution theory" (*jufen jinhua lun*), 19, 155

INDEX [347]

dualism, 5, 11, 35, 158, 221, 245;
dogmatism and, 136; hierarchical
relationships and, 3; modernity and,
247–248; struggle relation to, 14
duality, 15–16, 231
Duara, Prasenjit, 248
duikang lun (antagonism), 46
dunwu ("sudden enlightenment"), 29,
176, 178, 189
Du Yaquan, 21–22, 271n76;
accommodation relation to, 47

Eastern Journal, 21
eclecticism, 54
ecofeminist theory, 3, 230; "third
position" in, 221
ecology, 221, 230
economic development, 61, 120
economic equality, 88
either/or mindset, 13, 15, 48, 130, 263;
Aristotle relation to, 151; "both/and"
logic relation to, 60; class struggle
relation to, 12, 22, 152; communism
relation to, 96–97; cosmology
relation to, 19; in Cultural
Revolution, 184; cyberspace relation
to, 260; dogmatism and, 33; DPP
and, 238; *du* relation to, 16; in
fiction, 150; in *Heaven Sword and the
Dragon Sabre, The*, 137; hierarchical
relationships relation to, 247;
iconoclasm relation to, 10; monism
relation to, 167; polarization relation
to, 251; revolution relation to, 153;
in Xi Jinping regime, 8; Yin relation
to, 102
elite politics (*xianren zhengzhi*), 41,
48–49
"Elite Politics" (Zhang Dongsun), 47
emptiness, 194–195, 199, 200, 204,
302n52

End of the World, The (painting), 207
Engdahl, Horace, 177
"enlightening verification" (*wuzheng*),
176
Enlightenment, 9, 78
epistemological pluralism, 28, 42, 45,
52–53, 56–57
epistemology, 28, 52–53
equal intrinsic value, 230, 233
erlü beifan (antinomy), 153–155, 165–166
Essay on Philosophical Method, An
(Zhang Dongsun), 63–64
ethereal emptiness (*kongling*), 194–195,
199, 200, 204, 302n52
ethicalism, 19
ethical neutrality, 101
Ethics (Aristotle), 70
Ethnic Equality Agreement Alliance,
237–238, 309n49
Evans, Megan, 206, 207
Evenki people, 32, 36, 222, 230–231;
death relation to, 232; Han Chinese
relation to, 233, 234; modernity and,
229, 235, 242
exile: freedom in, 13–14; Gao Xingjian
in, 182, 197; Liu Zaifu in, 149–150,
151, 158, 177–178; Tiananmen Square
movement relation to, 156
expatriate democratic community,
148–149
"Eye and Mind" (Merleau-Ponty), 193

False Mirror, The (painting), 225
Fang Fang, 34, 246, 260–262, 312n47
Farewell to Revolution (Li Zehou and
Liu Zaifu), 61, 153–156; *shi* and,
162–163
Feminism and the Mastery of Nature
(Plumwood), 221
fencun gan (propriety), 18–19
Feng Youlan, 144

Ferber, Ilit, 218, 223–224
Fertile Soil Town tales, 224
Fichte, Johann Gottlieb, 76
fiction, 127–129, 152, 188; either/or mindset in, 150; political reality relation to, 130
flâneur, 177, 239
Flying Carpet (Xi Xi), 223
Fong, Gilbert, 192
Foucault, Michel, 2, 33, 235, 246
fragmentary writing (*pianduan xiezuo*): of Liu Zaifu, 29, 174–178, 180, 298n83; society relation to, 179
Free China (journal), 80, 81–82, 87, 90–91; KMT relation to, 93; "Recent Issues" of, 92
freedom, 5, 21, 106–107, 132, 243; of aesthetics, 161; in art, 27; authority *versus*, 47; Chinese culture relation to, 61; compassion and, 172; Daoism relation to, 28; in exile, 13–14; *Free China* relation to, 87; Hong Kong relation to, 122–123; literature relation to, 27, 33, 173, 273n105; Liu Zaifu relation to, 149, 246; Mao relation to, 75; "Marvels of a Floating City" relation to, 226–227; personal space relation to, 158; of silence, 7, 88, 104, 162; of speech, 84–85, 92, 115, 121, 185; spiritual, 177–178, 181–182, 189–190; of street cats, 240–242; totalitarianism relation to, 90–91; value, 101, 160–161; Yin relation to, 82. See also negative freedom; positive freedom
"Freedom and Literature" (Gao Xingjian), 183
"freedom of nonidentification" (*bu rentong de ziyou*), 238–239
French Revolution, 270n72
Freud, Sigmund, 218

Fu Lei, 44
Fundamental Verses on the Middle Way (Nāgārjuna), 166
Fung, Edmund, 43, 274n9
Fusini, Letizia, 182

Gao Like, 271n77
Gao Nuan, 41, 274n7
Gao Xingjian, 13–14, 29, 35, 106–107, 173, 178; aesthetics and, 25–26, 192–193; artistic creativity and, 183; "Carefree as a Bird" of, 198, 202–204; on causality, 187–188; Chan Buddhism relation to, 186–187, 202; dance relation to, 208–209; on emptiness, 194–195; *After the Flood* of, 205–207, 209–211, 212, 214; Huineng relation to, 199; on individualism, 250; Liu Zaifu compared to, 183–185; on Mao, 133; "negation of negation" and, 300n20; "omniscient Chan" and, 191; *Requiem for Beauty* of, 211–217, 218–219, *219*, 220, 305n107; *Silhouette/Shadow* of, 195, 197, 200, 204–206, 214; spiritual freedom and, 181–182, 189–190; third eye and, 30, 31, 192–194, 302n45; "third zone" and, 273n93; "total art" of, 196–197
"gap man" (*xifeng ren*), 29
Gautama, Siddhartha, 169
gender, 222, 230–232
gender dichotomies, 222
gender neutrality, 222
German Social Democratic Party, 236
Giddens, Anthony, 13, 251
Gide, Andre, 177
Giedion, Siegfried, 174–175
God, 202; paradox relation to, 165–166
Golconda (painting), 224–225
golden mean, 70

gongsheng de shikong ("shared chronotope"), 239–240
governance, 169
Greatest Happiness Principle, 288n20
Great Leap Forward, 115, 117
Grotius, Hugo, 250
guan (observation), 193, 194
guanxiang, 302n53
guild socialism, 42, 45
guild system, 124
Guo Huaqing, 271n74
Guo Moruo, 12
Guo Xi, 215

Habermas, Jürgen, 4, 250–251
Hamm, John Christopher, 115, 292n86
Han Chinese, 229, 230, 233, 234
Han Shaogong, 152
harmonious pluralism, 22, 271n77
harmony, 19–20, 47–48; justice relation to, 7, 18, 24, 249
Hayek, Friedrich, 24, 87, 102, 103–104, 105–106, 107
Healer, The (painting), 226–227
"heart of nondistinction" (*wu fenbie xin*), 169
Heaven Sword and the Dragon Sabre, The (Jin Yong), 135, 136–137
Hegel, G. W. F., 2, 75–76, 78, 150–151, 185; dialectical logic of, 225
Hegel's Holiday (Magritte), 225–226
hermits, 10, 131–132, 133–134, 145
heterogeneous writings, 152
heterotopias, 33, 237, 241, 246, 308n39; Chan Koonchung relation to, 33, 254–255, 256–257; Chu Tien-hsin and, 32, 36, 222, 235; interspecies dynamics and, 239–240
heterotopology, 2, 254
Heyne, F. Georg, 230–231
hierarchical relationships, 3, 230, 247

historical determinism, 186, 255
historical materialism, 2, 76
historical nihilism, 155
History of My Heart, The (Liu Zaifu), 171
History of My Thought, The (Liu Zaifu), 111
Hitler, Adolf, 95, 106
Hobbes, Thomas, 74–75, 92
Hockx, Michel, 252, 260
Hong Kong, 1, 32, 111, 112, 114, 242; *Farewell to Revolution* relation to, 153; Jin Yong on, 122–123, 289n37; "Marvels of a Floating City" relation to, 35, 223, 224, 226; New Confucianism in, 81, 95, 100; protests in, 8, 125; refugee crisis in, 115–116; value neutrality in, 23; "Wings" relation to, 227; Xi Jinping relation to, 228
hooks, bell, 229
Huang Zuolin, 192
Hu Feng, 167
Huineng, 176, 184, 199
human dignity, 210
humanism, 61, 220, 241
Hung, Jenny, 302n48
Hunters, The (Chu Tien-hsin), 240
huo wenxue ("living literature"), 10
Hu Ping, 155
Hu Qiuyuan, 11
Hu Shi, 10, 24, 87, 93, 97, 108; liberalism and, 80; Yin compared to, 102–103
Hu Yue, 79
hybrid identity, 143

iconoclasm, 10, 25, 41–42, 55–56
idealism, 165
imperialism, 61
inclusiveness, 1, 247
indigenization (*bentuhua*), 239

individualism, 24–25, 26–27, 108–109, 250; capitalism relation to, 60–61; collectivism relation to, 104; democracy relation to, 62–63; liberalism relation to, 102–103, 105; masks relation to, 305n119; totalitarianism relation to, 34–35, 103
individual property, 105
industrialization, 42, 62
infinite inclusiveness, 6
inner universe, 189
In Remembrance (Chu Tien-hsin), 236
intangible imaginary space, 8
intermediality, 28, 204, 210; cine-poems and, 183, 196–197
"intermedial reference," 196
interspecies dynamics, 239–240
intuitive reflection, 178–179
irrationalism, 63
"It Is Time That the KMT Should Reflect" (Yin), 91

James, William, 71
Janus, 216
Jenco, Leigh K., 271n75
Jia Baoyu, 164, 169
jiagou lun (structure), 72
Jiang Yihua, 266n18
Jin Yong, 13, 28–29, 100, 112, 127–128, 288n22; *Asahi Shimbun, The*, and, 288n11; Cultural Revolution relation to, 117, 119, 145; *Deer and the Cauldron, The*, of, 129, 142–145, 161; democracy relation to, 123–125; *Heaven Sword and the Dragon Sabre, The*, of, 135, 136–137; Hong Kong relation to, 122–123, 289n37; Liu Zaifu relation to, 110–111; neutrality of, 118–119, 126; refugee crisis relation to, 115–116; on self-rule, 289n43; *Semigods and the Semidevils, The*, of, 138–141; *Smiling, Proud Wanderer, The* of, 110, 129–134, 162, 290n56; utilitarianism of, 120–121; valorization and, 160; value neutrality relation to, 23, 26, 113–114; Yin relation to, 98
Jin Yuelin, 81, 82, 88
journalism, 114–115, 288n11
Journey to the West (novel), 172, 173, 298n83
jue ("awakening"), 175
jufen jinhua lun ("dual evolution theory"), 19, 155
Jung, C. G., 58, 60
justice, 22, 73; harmony relation to, 7, 18, 24, 249

Kang Youwei, 154
Kant, Immanuel, 52, 77–78, 151, 153–155, 165–166; *Critique of Judgment* of, 168–169; *Critique of Pure Reason* of, 71
Kermode, Frank, 205
Kirsteva, Julia, 39
KMT. *See* Chinese Nationalist Party
kongjian yishi (spatial consciousness), 214–215
kongling (ethereal emptiness), 194–195, 199, 302n52; in *Silhouette/Shadow*, 200, 204
Kristeva, Julia, 55, 277n65

Łabędzka, Izabella, 216
land reforms, 13
Laozi, 54, 134, 169, 180, 183–184; *Tao Te Ching* of, 6, 7, 14, 164, 176
Last Quarter of the Moon, The (Chi), 32, 35–36, 222, 229–235
Laughlin, Charles A., 267n31
Learning Light (newspaper supplement), 41

Lee Haiyan, 241
Lee, Leo Ou-fan, 148, 164
Lefebvre, Henri, 2–3, 14, 55, 265n6, 266n13; Soja relation to, 59–60, 184
leisure literature, 267n31
Lei Zhen, 87, 89, 93
Leviathan (Hobbes), 74–75, 92
Li, Peter, 15, 270n59
Liang Qichao, 25, 42, 46, 66, 154
Liang Shiqiu, 11
Liang Shuming, 59, 65–66
liberalism, 20, 98, 107, 121, 251–252; democracy and, 259; Hu Shi and, 80; individualism relation to, 102–103, 105; Jin Yong relation to, 124; Marxism relation to, 85; in Taiwan, 91, 93, 97, 102; Zhang Dongsun relation to, 41, 45–46
Li Dazhao, 42
Lim, Wah Guan, 213
liming ("solidifying one's destiny"), 297n70
Lin Daiyu (fictional character), 166, 179
Lin Gang, 167
Linghu Chong (fictional character), 133–134, 145, 162
lingyizhong meixue (alternative aesthetics), 186
Lin Yutang, 11
Lipinski, Lisa, 228
liren ("solidifying the human"), 297n70
literati (*shi*), 49–50, 62, 156, 162–163
literature, 25, 150, 167, 196, 303n65, 308n36; aesthetic transcendence and, 168–169; cold, 194; dogmatism and, 151–152; freedom relation to, 27, 33, 173, 273n105; heart relation to, 172; leisure, 267n31; native soil, 228–229; revolutionary, 10–11, 12; in *Second Year of Jianfeng, The*, 257–258
Liu Bingyan, 148, 155, 156

Liu Kang, 293n8
Liu Xiaogang, 18, 19
Liu Xinwu, 144
Liu Zaifu, 5, 13–14, 164, 167, 173, 273n93; aesthetics and, 25–26; aesthetic transcendence and, 26–27, 168–169, 248; character composition relation to, 150, 151; collectivism relation to, 148–149; dualism relation to, 35; *Farewell to Revolution* of, 61; fragmentary writing of, 29, 174–178, 180, 298n83; on freedom, 149, 246; Gao Xingjian compared to, 183–185; *History of My Heart* of, 171; on individualism, 250; intuitive reflection and, 178–179; Jin Yong relation to, 110–111; on literature, 273n105; Li Zehou and, 153–157, 293n8; Lu Xun relation to, 160; on materialism, 172; on nonduality, 170; on personal space, 132, 158; on positive freedom, 159; on reclusive spirit, 295n35; on Redology, 298n98; on rights, 162; "Searching for the Survival of Thirdspace" of, 110, 157; on *shi*, 162–163; on "solidifying one's destiny," 297n70; spiritual freedom of, 177–178; Tiananmen Square movement relation to, 29, 147; on transcendental vision, 308n36; *Treatise of Character Compositions, A*, of, 135, 148, 150; value-freedom and, 161
Liu Zhengfeng (fictional character), 131–132, 133
"living literature" (*huo wenxue*), 10
lixin ("solidifying one's heart"), 297n70
Li Zehou, 5, 13, 16–18, 48, 248; on accommodation, 24; aesthetic transcendence and, 170; on Buddhism, 204; on complementary paradox, 19–20; on cultural

sedimentation, 60; *Farewell to Revolution* of, 61; on harmony, 249; Jin Yong compared to, 123; Liu Zaifu and, 153–157, 293n8; middle way and, 164–165, 166–167; on negative freedom, 250

Li Zicheng, 143

Location of Culture, The (Bhabha), 2, 56

Locke, John, 74–75, 99, 250

logical analysis, 108

Lu Jiuyuan, 170–171

Lu Junyi (fictional character), 157–158

Lu Xun, 26, 103, 106, 131, 144, 157; Ah Q and, 152; on hermits, 10; on literature, 25, 33; literature relation to, 11; Liu Zaifu relation to, 160; May Fourth movement relation to, 95, 246–247; on "negation of negation," 186; "On the One-Sidedness of Cultural Development" of, 171–172; "Resurrecting the Dead" of, 29, 146; on "solidifying the nation," 297n70

Magritte, René, 1, 21, 31–32, 223, 224, 225, 226

Mahayana Buddhism, 291n79, 302n53

Malraux, André, 213, 305n107

Manchester Guardian (newspaper), 120

Manichean dichotomy, 95, 97

Mannheim, Karl, 46, 57

Man Who Questions Death, The (Gao Xingjian), 186, 197, 198, 211

Mao Zedong, 12, 75, 89, 131, 133; "Against Liberalism" of, 85; "Carry the Revolution Through the End" of, 252; Chiang Kai-shek compared to, 95; recluse culture relation to, 159; third persons relation to, 51; totalitarianism and, 88; Zhang Dongsun relation to, 44–45, 64

"Marvels of a Floating City" (Xi Xi), 1, 31–32, 35, 222, 223–224, 227–228; "both/and" logic in, 225–226

Marx, Karl, 2, 78; class struggle relation to, 76, 85–86

Marxism, 44, 47, 75, 121, 259; CCP relation to, 117–118; class struggle and, 42, 248–249; dichotomies relation to, 56; historical determinism of, 186; liberalism relation to, 85; material determinism relation to, 188; middle ground relation to, 64

Marxist materialism, 165

masks, 216, 305n119

masses, 48–49, 51

material determinism, Marxism relation to, 188

materialism, 2, 76, 226; Marxist, 165; modernity and, 171–172

materialist dialecticism, 78, 84

May Fourth movement, 10, 24, 95; iconoclasm in, 25, 55–56; Lu Xun relation to, 246–247; shamanism relation to, 231; Yin on, 79, 80

mechanical techniques, art and, 183

"medium," 150–151

meiyou zhuyi ("no-ism"), 194

melancholy, 218–219, 220

Mencius, 276n50

Merleau-Ponty, Maurice, 30, 193, 200; third eye and, 273n101

meta-language, 119

Metzger, Thomas A., 9, 270n72

Miaoyu (fictional character), 169

Michel, Robert, 49

middle action (*zhongwei*), 19

middle attitude (*zhongjian taidu*), 39

middle ground, 56–57; actors and, 192; Marxism relation to, 64

middle medium (*zhongjian meijie wu*), 62

middle politics, 34, 46, 47
middle way, 7, 14, 63, 135; in Chan Buddhism, 7, 14, 165–166; contradiction relation to, 15; *du* relation to, 16–17; Liu Zaifu relation to, 149; Li Zehou and, 164–165, 166–167; third force movement and, 241–252
"Middle Way as a Political Route, The" (Zhang Dongsun), 44
Mill, James, 103, 105
Mill, John Stuart, 24, 107; on Greatest Happiness Principle, 288n20; Jin Yong relation to, 118
Mind's Gaze, The (painting), 224
Ming Pao (newspaper), 35, 111, 112, 119, 122; *Deer and the Cauldron, The* in, 142; democracy and, 125; *Heaven Sword and the Dragon Sabre, The*, in, 135; neutrality of, 114–115, 126, 251; refugee crisis relation to, 115–116; *Semigods and the Semidevils, The*, in, 138; *Smiling, Proud Wanderer, The* in, 129; "What I Saw, Heard, and Thought in Taiwan" in, 120. See also Jin Yong
moderation, 42, 45, 47, 56; class struggle relation to, 63; Confucianism relation to, 100, 165, 271n74; *du* relation to, 16–17; harmony and, 48
modernity: crisis and, 205; dualism and, 247–248; Evenki people and, 229, 235, 242; materialism and, 171–172; shamanism relation to, 231
monarchical democracy, 92
monism, 84, 97, 128, 163; cyberspace relation to, 252; either/or mindset relation to, 167
Month of the Grape Harvest, The (painting), 228
Moore, Charles A., 55, 57

morality, 24, 28, 102
Morgen, Conwy Lloyd, 72
mourning, 218
Mou Zongsan, 81–82
Mozart, 216
multicultural interactionism, 59
multiplicity, oneness relation to, 7
music, Daoism relation to, 132
My City (Xi Xi), 223, 224
mystic integralism, 52–53, 58

nāga, 291n79
Nāgārjuna, 135, 166
National Renaissance, The, 42
National Socialist Party, 42
National Southwestern Associated University, 82
native soil literature, 228–229
Natural Graces (Magritte), 227
negation, paradox relation to, 151
"negation of negation," 185–186, 300n20
negative freedom, 17–18, 103, 106, 108–109, 129, 295n35; Berlin and, 128, 159, 249–250, 272n87; pluralism relation to, 5, 26; positive freedom compared to, 140; society relation to, 133; Yin Haiguang and, 104, 238
neutral actor, 209
neutrality, 97–98, 115, 251; ethical, 101; gender, 222; of Jin Yong, 118–119, 126; in public sphere, 158; value, 23–24, 26, 113–114, 160, 162
neutralization (*zhezhong*), 46, 57
New Confucianism, 81, 83, 100; Yin relation to, 95, 101–102
new literary era, 148
New Party, 93
New Youth (magazine), 271n76
nexūs, 72–73
Nidu (fictional character), 231–232

Nihao (fictional character), 232–233, 234–235
nihilism, 250; historical, 155; relativism and, 129, 146
1984 (Orwell), 87
Nisbett, Richard E., 15
Nixon, Richard, 45
noh theater, 196
"no-ism" (*meiyou zhuyi*), 194
nonaction (*wuwei*), 19
nonattachment, 30, 192, 199
nonduality, 14, 163–164, 169, 170, 248
Nostalgia (film), 202
Not to Be Reproduced (painting), 226

objective analysis, 18
object-language, 119
observation (*guan*), 193, 194
Old Capital, The (Chu Tien-hsin), 32, 235, 237, 308n39
oligarchy, 49, 90
"omniscient Chan," 191
"On Bingzai" (Liu Zaifu), 152
oneness, multiplicity relation to, 7
one-party dictatorships, 88; KMT and, 90–91, 93, 107; in *Second Year of Jianfeng, The*, 253, 255–256
One Universe, 14
On Liberty (Mill, J. S.), 24, 107
"On Literary Revolution" (Chen), 10
On Literary Subjectivity (Liu Zaifu), 148
"On the One-Sidedness of Cultural Development" (Lu Xun), 171–172
"On the Problem of the Home Country" (Jin Yong), 117, 119
ontology, 171; of aesthetics, 170; of monism, 167
Oosterling, Henk, 300n21
open form, 207
organismic philosophy (*youji zhexue*), 52

Origin of German Tragic Drama (Benjamin), 174
Origins of Totalitarianism, The (Arendt), 88
Orwell, George, 87
ostracization, societal, 21
outer universe, 189

panmoralization, 88, 92; colorless thought relation to, 101
panpoliticization, 88–89, 92; colorless thought relation to, 101
panstructuralism, 51–52, 73
paradox, 14–15, 129, 228, 242; complementary, 19–20; God relation to, 165–166; negation relation to, 151; of tolerance, 108
paradoxical integration, 15
"Paradox of Tolerance," 108
Past Charities no.1, 2000 (painting), 200, 201, 202
patriarchal binarism, 230
Peng Kaiping, 15
personal space, 132, 158
Perspectives on Chinese Culture (Yin), 94
Philosophical Criticism of Zhang Dongsun, The (Ye), 54
philosophical poetry, 34, 40–41, 66–76; intermediality in, 28. See also Zhang Dongsun
"philosophy of eating" (*chifan zhexue*), 165
pianduan xiezuo (fragmentary writing), 29, 174–178, 179–180
pink literature, 12
Platform Sutra of the Sixth Patriarch, The (Huineng), 170–171, 175, 176–177, 180
Plato, 73
Plumwood, Val, 3, 221, 230

pluralism, 128; epistemological, 18, 42, 45, 52–53, 56–57; harmonious, 22, 271n77; negative freedom relation to, 5, 26; value, 20, 27
plurimediality, 196; cine-poems and, 183
Poetry of Philosophical History (Zhang Dongsun), 66
polarity, 216; politics of, 2
polarization, 8; CCP relation to, 10; either/or mindset relation to, 251; in *Last Quarter of the Moon, The*, 229; radicalization and, 27
political compulsion, 106
political correctness, 239
political factions, accommodation and, 21–22
political reality, 126, 130
politics, 3; aesthetics relation to, 34; art relation to, 25; elite, 41, 48–49; middle, 34, 46, 47; of polarity, 2; society relation to, 46
Politics and I (Zhang Dongsun), 77
Popper, Karl, 101, 108
"Position of Writer, The" (Gao Xingjian), 194
positive freedom, 103, 104–105, 159, 173, 249; Jin Yong relation to, 128–129; negative freedom compared to, 140; Xiao Feng and, 141
postapocalypse, 205, 210
postcolonial theory, 39–40
postmodern theory, 39–40
"pragmatic rationality" (*shiyong lixing*), 16, 145, 249
pragmatism, 126; in *Deer and the Cauldron, The*, 142
Primavera, The (painting), 226
Problems of Analyzing and Predicting Soviet Behavior (Reshetar), 88

propaganda, 13, 95; of CCP, 85, 118; of KMT, 84, 93
proper measure, 5
propriety (*fencun gan*), 18–19
protests, in Hong Kong, 8, 125
"psychological field," 182
public sphere, 4, 250–251, 274n7; civil society compared to, 9; in cyberspace, 252; neutrality in, 158
Puël, Gaston, 224
"pure-hearted person" (*suxin ren*), 193–194

Qian Yongxiang, 103
Qiaojie (fictional character), 166
Qiao Min, 177
Quantum Theory, 54
"Quickly Collect People's Hearts" (Yin), 86, 90
Qu Yang (fictional character), 132

radical empiricism, 71–72
radical exclusion, 14, 221
radicalization, 20, 267n21; accommodation relation to, 22; Cultural Revolution relation to, 9; polarization and, 27; in U.S.-China relations, 8
radical openness, 6
Rajewsky, Irina O., 196, 303n65
Rawls, John, 22, 123
Ready-Made Banquet, The (painting), 226
"Recent Issues" of *Free China*, 92
recluse culture, 159–160
reclusive spirit, 295n35
Record of Meditation Facing a Wall (Liu Zaifu), 298n83
Record of Practical Living (Wang Yangming), 175
Red Guard, 89–90, 283n41
Redology, 178, 298n98

Reflections on Dream of the Red Chamber (Liu Zaifu), 135–136, 137, 178
reflective words (*wuyu xiezuo*), 175
reform, 13, 251; revolution compared to, 10, 17, 20, 154
refugee crisis, in Hong Kong, 115–116
"relatedness" (*yinyuan*), 53
relativism: accommodation and, 23–24; Jin Yong relation to, 115; nihilism and, 129, 146
repentance, 167–168
Republic (Plato), 73
Requiem (Mozart), 216
Requiem for Beauty (Gao Xingjian), 211–214, *219*, 305n107; gesture in, 215–217; melancholy and, 218–219, 220
Reshetar, John S., Jr., 88
"Resurrecting the Dead" (Lu), 29, 146
revolution, 270n72; democracy relation to, 85; either/or mindset relation to, 153; "negation of negation" and, 185–186; reform compared to, 10, 17, 20, 154; violence in, 132, 156. *See also* Cultural Revolution
revolutionary literature, 10–11, 12
revolutionary mentality, struggle relation to, 7
rhythm, 215–216
"rhythm of life" (*shengming de jiezhou*), 207, 208
Righteousness (magazine), 41
righteous rhetoric, 143
Road to Serfdom, The (Hayek), 87, 102
Romance of the Three Kingdoms, The (novel), 172, 298n83
Rošker, Jana S., 17, 54
Rousseau, Jean-Jacques, 177, 270n72
rule, of law, freedom relation to, 106, 122–123

Russell, Bertrand, 70, 74
Russia, 88, 89

Said, Edward, 164
"school of wandering," 157
Schwartz, Benjamin I., 144
Scott, C. P., 120
"Searching for the Survival of Thirdspace" (Liu Zaifu), 110, 157
seclusion, 128, 133
Second Sino-Japanese War, 43, 80
Second Year of Jianfeng, The (Chan Koonchung), 36, 246, 252–258
self-censorship, 168
self-consciousness, 188–189
"Self-Criticism" (Jin Yuelin), 81
self-cultivation, 145, 249–250
self-determination, 140
self-enlightenment, 198
self-realization, 140, 145
self-reflection, 179, 199
self-rule, 289n43
Semigods and the Semidevils, The (Jin Yong), 138–141
Seven Sages, 104
shamanism, 32, 36, 229–230; equal intrinsic value relation to, 233; gender relation to, 231–232
"shared chronotope" (*gongsheng de shikong*), 239–240
shehui duikang (social antagonism), 47
shehui zhengti (social integrity), 47
Shen Baoxin, 114
Shen Congwen, 12, 228–229
shengming de jiezhou ("rhythm of life"), 207, 208
shi (literati), 49–50, 62, 156; *Farewell to Revolution* and, 162–163
Shi Fuliang, 44
Shum, Sau Ching Janet, 182

shiyong lixing ("pragmatic rationality"), 16, 145, 249
silence, freedom of, 7, 88, 104, 162
Silhouette/Shadow (Gao Xingjian), 195, 197; *After the Flood* compared to, 205, 206; *kongling* in, 200, 204; *Requiem for Beauty* contrasted with, 214
Silvester, Rosalind, 200
Sin and Literature (Lin Gang and Liu Zaifu), 167–168
Sino-British Joint Declaration, 124
Sinophone world, 4
si wenxue ("dead literature"), 10
skeptical mindset, 108
Smiling, Proud Wanderer, The (Jin Yong), 110, 129–131, 162; Cultural Revolution relation to, 132, 134, 290n56; hermits in, 133–134
Snow in August (Gao Xingjian), 197, 198, 199
social antagonism *(shehui duikang)*, 47
"social ecology," 221
social integrity *(shehui zhengti)*, 47
socialism, 38–39; democratic, 255, 259; economic development relation to, 61; guild, 42, 45; industrialization and, 62
socialist realism, 13
societal ostracization, 21
society, 213; binary logic in, 130, 158–159; fragmentary writing relation to, 179; negative freedom relation to, 133; politics relation to, 46; public sphere relation to, 250–251; *shi* relation to, 50, 162–163
Soja, Edward W., 2–3, 4, 55, 59–60, 170, 235; on Aleph, 266n13; on heterotopology, 254; Lefebvre relation to, 184; Liu Zaifu compared to, 173–174; on radical openness, 6;

"thirding-as-Othering" and, 229; on "trialectics of spatiality," 265n6
"solidifying one's destiny" *(liming)*, 297n70
"solidifying one's heart" *(lixin)*, 297n70
"solidifying the human" *(liren)*, 297n70
Solitary Recitations at the Edge of the World (Liu Zaifu), 298n83
Song Weijie, 127–128, 143, 291n81
Soul Mountain (Gao Xingjian), 106–107, 187, 188, 189, 196, 198–199; Chan state in, 200; masks in, 216
sovereignty, of Hong Kong, 1, 122–123
spatial consciousness *(kongjian yishi)*, 214–215
speech, freedom of, 84–85, 92, 115, 121, 185
Spirit of Geometry, The (painting), 227
spiritual freedom, 177–178, 181–182, 189–190
spirituality, 193, 220
"spiritual warrior" mentality, 156
Stalin, Josef, 95, 106
Stalinist Russia, 88
state-led collectivism, 108
"state of being," 208
Storm, William, 182
street cats, 239–242
structure *(jiagou lun)*, 72
struggle, 7, 14, 100–101, 210; CCP relation to, 87; harmony relation to, 47–48; Xi Jinping relation to, 252. *See also* class struggle
Studies in History and Jurisprudence (Bryce), 46
sublation, 300n20
"sudden enlightenment" *(dunwu)*, 29, 176, 178, 189
Sun Wukong (fictional character), 173
Sun Yat-sen, 41, 91, 94
surveillance, 263

Su Shi, 204
Su Wen, 11
suxin ren ("pure-hearted person"), 193–194
Sword of Loyalty, The (Jin Yong), 143
Sze-Lorrian, Fiona, 208

tabula rasa, 99
Taiwan, 32, 87, 90, 94, 242; CCP relation to, 121; civil society in, 238; democracy and, 236–237; heterotopias in, 36; Jin Yong relation to, 120; KMT in, 12–13; liberalism in, 91, 93, 97, 102; TNR in, 240–241; totalitarianism in, 95; Yin in, 24, 81, 87
Taiwan Atlas of Adoption Association, 240
Taiwan Democratic School, 238
Tales of Hulan River (Xiao Hong), 231
"Talks at the Yan'an Forum on Literature and Art" (Mao), 12
Tao Jiang, 272n87
Tao Te Ching (Laozi), 6, 7, 14, 164, 176
Tao Yuanming, 193–194
Tarkovsky, Andrei, 202
Taylor, Charles, 128
teleology, 168
tetraspatiality, 197
That Cat, That Person, That City (Chu Tien-hsin), 240–241
Thatcher, Margaret, 122
Theory of Poetry (Zhu Guangqian), 215
Theory of Relativity, 54
thesis-antithesis-synthesis, 75–76, 151
third eye, 198, 213–214, 273n101; Gao Xingjian and, 30, 31, 192–194, 302n45
third force movement, 43, 241–252
"thirding-as-Othering," 229
third persons (*disan zhe*), 48, 50–51

"third position," in ecofeminist theory, 221
"Third-Side-of-the-Straits Complex," 225
thirdspace. *See specific topics*
Thirdspace (Soja), 55
Third Way, The (Giddens), 13, 251
"third zone," 273n93
Thirty-Three Years of Dream (Chu Tien-hsin), 236
This Is Not an Apple (painting), 225
"Three Principles of the People," 120–121
Tiananmen Square movement, 25, 109, 125, 155–156; Liu Zaifu relation to, 29, 147
Tian Xiaofei, 292n85, 302n53
time disparity, 61
TNR. *See* trap, neuter, return
tolerance, 108, 162, 164
"total art," 196–197
totalitarianism, 14, 61, 87–89, 92, 102, 106; freedom relation to, 90–91; individualism relation to, 34–35, 103; negative freedom relation to, 104; in Taiwan, 95
"total theater," 30, 196
transcendental vision, 308n36
"transformative approach," 270n72
transmediality, 197
trap, neuter, return (TNR), 240–241
Treatise of Character Compositions, A (Liu Zaifu), 135, 148, 150
"trialectics of spatiality," 2, 265n6
tripartite film theory, 195, 206, 211
tripronouns, 188, 192
trispatiality, 197
Tsai, Chien-Hsin, 308n39
Tsou Tang, 153–154
Tu Hang, 168, 258–259
"turtle intestine," 68

uchronia, 255, 256, 258. *See also Second Year of Jianfeng, The*
us-and-them mentality, 263; in class struggle, 13; Xi Jinping relation to, 14
U.S.-China relations, 8
utilitarianism, 105, 118, 144, 168; in *Deer and the Cauldron, The*, 142; of Jin Yong, 120–121
utopia, 73; harmony relation to, 19–20
"Utopia, Dystopia, Heterotopia" (Chan Koonchung), 254

valorization, 160
value-freedom (Wertfrei), 101, 160–161
value neutrality, 24, 160, 162; Jin Yong relation to, 23, 26, 113–114
value pluralism, 20, 27
"Various Kinds of Problems of Dialectic" (Zhang Dongsun), 75–76
Veg, Sebastian, 13
"village worthies" (*xiangyuan*), 98
violence, in revolution, 132, 156
Voice of Silence, The (Malraux), 213

"Wandering Mind and Metaphysical Thoughts" (Gao Xingjian), 181, 189
Wang, David Der-wei, 69, 172, 237, 255
Wang Guowei, 178
Wang Lu, 234
Wang Yangming, 72, 171, 175
Water Margin (novel), 157, 172, 298n83
Weber, Max, 101, 160–161
Weibo, 260–262
Wei Xiaobao (fictional character), 28–29, 142–146, 161, 292n86
wenhua jidian (cultural sedimentation), 60
wenhua manzu gan ("cultural satisfaction"), 58
wenhua xinli jiegou ("cultural-psychological formation"), 13, 60

Wertfrei (value-freedom), 101, 160–161
Western art history, 185
Westernization, 109
Western middle class, 50
Western philosophy, 55, 66–68; *Dream of the Red Chamber* relation to, 179; Zhang Dongsun and, 38, 39–41, 51
Western political theories, 249
"What I Saw, Heard, and Thought in Taiwan" (Jin Yong), 120
"What's Wrong with Negative Liberty?" (Taylor), 128
"Which Road Should We Take?" (Yin), 90
Whig party, 105
Whitehead, Alfred North, 15, 54, 55, 56, 63; on nexūs, 72–73
white literature, 12
White Terror, 95
"Why Do I Oppose the CCP" (Yin), 82
"Wings" (Xi Xi), 226–227
Wolf, Werner, 30
"Word, Dialogue and Novel" (Kristeva), 55
Words From A Man Among Grasses (Zhang Dongsun), 64
"Words We Want to Say, The" (Zhang Dongdun and Zhang Junmai), 42
wu fenbie xin ("heart of nondistinction"), 169
Wuhan Diary (Fang), 34, 246, 260–262
Wu Shengqing, 193, 273n101, 299n7
wuwei (nonaction), 19
wuyu (reflective words), 175
wuzheng ("enlightening verification"), 176

xiangguanlü mingxue (correlation logic), 5, 54, 76, 248
xiangyuan ("village worthies"), 98

xianren zhengzhi (elite politics), 41, 48–49
Xiao Feng (fictional character), 140–141, 145, 291n81
Xiao Hong, 231
Xiao Qian, 12
xieshi drama, 192
xieyi drama, 192
xifeng ren ("gap man"), 29
Xi Jinping, 109, 162, 185, 261; cyberspace relation to, 260; either/or mindset and, 8; Hong Kong relation to, 228; struggle relation to, 252; us-and-them mentality relation to, 14
Xi Xi, 227, 242–243; "Marvels of a Floating City," 1, 31–32, 35, 222, 223–226, 228
"X-space," 111
Xuedeng, 274n7
xuetong lun ("bloodline theory"), 238
Xu Fuguan, 83
Xu Jilin, 13, 251–252

Yahuda, Michael, 289n44
Yan'an, 13, 84–85
Yangtze region, 188, 189
Yan Lianke, 246, 262–263, 313n52
Yap Key-chong, 53, 54
yellow literature, 12
Yellow River region, 189
Yenching Society, at Harvard University, 94
Ye Qing, 54
Yeung, Jessica, 188
Yin Haiguang, 12–13, 79, 94–96, 109, 251; Chiang Kai-shek relation to, 80, 82, 83, 90, 91; colorless thought of, 19, 80–81, 98–99, 100–101, 108, 160, 258; either/or mindset relation to, 102; on freedom, 84–85, 106–107;

Hu Yue relation to, 79; individualism relation to, 24–25, 26, 34–35, 102–104; individual property relation to, 105; Lei relation to, 93; at National Taiwan University, 87, 90; negative freedom and, 104, 238; neutrality relation to, 97–98; "Quickly Collect People's Hearts" of, 86, 90; Red Guard relation to, 283n41; on totalitarianism, 88–89; Zhang Qiyun relation to, 92
yin-yang, 7, 14, 21, 270n59; accommodation relation to, 26; cosmology of, 144; du relation to, 17; in Semigods and the Semidevils, The, 141; Zhang Dongsun and, 55
yinyuan ("relatedness"), 53
Yoshida (fictional character), 232, 234
youji zhexue (organismic philosophy), 52
Yuan Shikai, 41
Yuan Zeng, 312n47
Yue Huanyu, 305n107
Yü Ying-shih, 9, 266nn20–21

Zahir, 19
"Zahir, The" (Borges), 6–7
Zarader, Jean-Pierre, 186, 213, 218, 300n20
Zen, 177, 178
Zha Liangyong. See Jin Yong
Zhang Dongsun, 5, 21, 37, 65, 67–71; on accommodation, 22, 26; "both/and" logic and, 56; Caojian renyu of, 279n105; CCP relation to, 12, 44; Chan Koonchung relation to, 254, 255, 259; class struggle relation to, 44, 47, 86; correlation logic and, 248; correlative duality and, 15–16; cosmology of, 276n55; on cultural interactionism, 58; Cultural

Zhang Dongsun (*continued*)
Revolution relation to, 38, 45, 66, 281n145; on dichotomies, 53–54; Enlightenment relation to, 78; on epistemological pluralism, 52–53, 56–57; on Hegel, 185; on imperialism, 61; on individualism, 250; on irrationalism, 63; Kristeva relation to, 277n65; Liang Qichao relation to, 42, 46; Liu Zaifu compared to, 149, 163; on Locke, 74–75; Mao relation to, 44–45, 64; on middle medium, 62; on panstructuralism, 51–52; philosophical poetry of, 28, 34, 40–41; *Poetics of Philosophical History* of, 66; *Politics and I* of, 77; postmodern theory and, 39–40; reform relation to, 251; in *Second Year of Jianfeng, The*, 36, 252–253, 255–257, 258; on *shi*, 49–50; Taiwan relation to, 32; on third persons, 48; on Western culture, 59; Western philosophy and, 38, 39–41, 51; on Whitehead, 72–73; *Xuedeng* and, 274n7; Yin compared to, 100; yin-yang and, 55; Zhang Junmai relation to, 42–43, 44, 274n9; Zhang Shizhao relation to, 278n81

Zhang Ertian, 41

Zhang Junmai, 22; Zhang Dongsun relation to, 42–43, 44, 274n9

Zhang Qiyun, 92

Zhang Rulun, 59

Zhang Shizhao, 21, 46, 271nn74–75, 278n81; accommodation relation to, 47

Zhang Taiyan, 19–20, 155

Zhang Wuji (fictional character), 136–138, 145

Zhang Yaonan, 72

zhezhong (neutralization), 46, 57

zhongjian meijie wu (middle medium), 62

zhongjian taidu (middle attitude), 39

zhongwei (middle action), 19

Zhou Zuoren, 10, 11, 140–141, 231

Zhuangzi, 25–26, 33, 128, 159–160, 170

Zhu Guangqian, 11, 12, 215

Zhu Yuanzhang, 137

Ziarek, Ewa Płonowska, 300n21

Zong Baihua, 208, 214; on *kongling*, 302n52

Zuo Yuhe, 274n9, 278n81

GPSR Authorized Representative: Easy Access System Europe, Mustamäe tee
50, 10621 Tallinn, Estonia, gpsr.requests@easproject.com

www.ingramcontent.com/pod-product-compliance
Lightning Source LLC
Chambersburg PA
CBHW022027290426
44109CB00014B/774